张伯香《英美文学选读》教材详解与自考辅导

姚绍德　姚　远◎著

北京工业大学出版社

内 容 提 要

本书以英美文学选读全国高等教育自学考试大纲为准则,针对张伯香主编的《英美文学选读》进行教材详解和自考辅导,着重加强学生对大纲要求掌握的基础知识和基础理论的理解和运用,提供详细的讲解分析和实例示范,帮助学生解决实际应用中的困难,同时对英语诗歌的格律和韵律进行适当介绍,增强学生对英语诗歌的分析和理解能力。

图书在版编目(CIP)数据

张伯香《英美文学选读》教材详解与自考辅导/姚绍德,姚远著. —北京:北京工业大学出版社,2015.9
ISBN 978 - 7 - 5639 - 4372 - 2

Ⅰ.①张… Ⅱ.①姚… ②姚… Ⅲ.①英语—阅读教学—高等教育—自学考试—自学参考资料 ②英国文学—文学欣赏 ③文学欣赏—美国 Ⅳ.①H319.4:Ⅰ

中国版本图书馆 CIP 数据核字(2015)第 175106 号

张伯香《英美文学选读》教材详解与自考辅导

著　　者:姚绍德　姚　远
责任编辑:钱子亮
封面设计:何　强
出版发行:北京工业大学出版社
　　　　　(北京市朝阳区平乐园 100 号　100124)
　　　　　010 - 67391722(传真)bgdcbs@ sina. com
出 版 人:郝　勇
经销单位:全国各地新华书店
承印单位:徐水宏远印刷有限公司
开　　本:787 毫米×1092 毫米　1/16
印　　张:36.75
字　　数:1012 千字
版　　次:2015 年 10 月第 1 版
印　　次:2015 年 10 月第 1 次印刷
标准书号:ISBN 978 - 7 - 5639 - 4372 - 2
定　　价:68.00 元

前言

PREFACE

    本书的编写以英美文学选读全国高等教育自学考试大纲的要求为准则，以辅导和帮助考生更好地掌握教材和抓住大纲要求的重点，事半功倍地复习并顺利通过考试为目的。对大纲要求"标记""领会""应用"的基础知识和理论，本书提纲挈领地进行归纳和总结，同时伴以大量同步练习和一定量的模拟试卷来巩固学生对这些知识和理论的理解与运用，从而帮助学生在考试中获得优异成绩。

    但这些并不是本书的独特之处！

    因为几乎所有的自学考试辅导书都是这样编写的。据笔者所见，目前学生常用的《英美文学选读》自考辅导书基本都不注意强化学生对教材语言的理解，只给出文学选段的中文译文而没有对原文的解析。这种设计没有考虑到许多英语专业的自考生课上完了，却根本没读过教材，也读不懂教材，甚至连一些考试过关的学生也没读过教材，只是努力钻研了几本同步练习和模拟试题集罢了。事实上他们对英语文学作品没有多少学习体会。至于其中的诗歌，别说学生，就连目前不少年轻的任课教师自己也不甚了然，学生就更搞不明白辅导书中的译文是怎么得出来的，而诗歌的语言分析和格律欣赏在目前的辅导书里更是从未提及。这些都是缺憾！

    本书的独特之处正在于竭力弥补这些缺憾，目的是帮助学生在真正理解教材原文的基础上做好考试准备。我们同时也希望本书能成为任课教师手中一本真正有用的教学参考书。

    以下是本书的特点：

    从古代和中世纪英国文学简介开始，对教材中各章节的英语原文，按顺序进行详细的词语解释和难句分析，尽量减少学生阅读原文中的困难。针对目前自考学生中普遍存在的语法理解、翻译和写作上的困难，重点进行这些方面的讲解分析和实例示范。

    对英语原文的内容、思想进行归纳整理，提纲挈领；对新的概念、术语、文学流派以及不常见的说法等都给予尽可能准确的解释；对文中有可能成为考点却又容易被一眼带过的信息句子，列出提示。这样一来，自考大纲中要求的重点自然更加突出。

对教材中的诗歌，逐句进行句法分析，使学生明白译文的意义从何而来，从而提高学生独立理解、翻译诗歌的能力。我们给出的参考译文和个别名家译文示范，都尽量贴近原文，便于学生理解和模仿。

结合对教材中所选诗歌的学习，对英语诗歌的格律和韵律概念做适当介绍，使学生能对英语诗歌的格律和韵律进行正确的判断和划分，并特别附上英语诗歌格律划分、韵律判断方面的练习题。

为加强学生对英语文学作品的理解和进行翻译训练，特编辑了诗歌和小说、散文中的大量选段作为翻译练习题。

每一章后面都附有同步练习题，内容涵盖全章内容。书后选编了两份模拟试卷，供学生检验学习效果。

上述所有同步练习、翻译练习和格律划分、韵律判断习题都附有答案。为使学生更好地理解，许多答案还附有分析解释。

附录部分收录文学术语简释一百三十余条，对一些重要的或生僻的术语结合作品实例进行有针对性的解释，使抽象的意义变得具体形象。

本书的解释部分以中文为主，并适当地辅以英文表达，使自学英美文学的学生和读者感到亲切易懂，不会觉得生疏和"高不可攀"，有阅读的兴趣。由于分析解释时绝大多数原文都对应地列在旁边，即使没买教材的校外读者和一般文学爱好者，阅读此书也会有所受益，对《英美文学选读》原著的内容有所了解和体会，不会感到解释部分不知对谁而发。

作为此书的作者，我们的愿望是：学生和其他读者一书在手，就好比有了一本查阅自如的工具书，就可以使对《英美文学选读》这门课程的学习顺利进行下去，并取得好成绩，真正做到学有体会，考有自信，而且越来越喜欢英美文学。

目录

CONTENTS

第一部分
英国文学 ENGLISH LITERATURE

古代和中世纪英国文学简介
An Introduction to Old and Medieval English Literature

词语解释和难句分析

1. be conquered by   被……所征服

   be not much affected by   没有受到……太多的影响

   to feel the full weight of (the other two conquests)   充分感受到(另外两个征服者)的巨大影响/威力

2. to extend from. . .to. . .   从……延伸到……

3. be both bold and strong, mournful and elegiac in spirit   精神气概上既粗犷豪勇又悲情哀婉,集粗犷勇烈与哀婉悲情于一体

4. biblical themes   有关《圣经》的主题

5. the religious group and the secular one   宗教类和世俗类

6. to stride to embrace death and victory   勇往直前,拥抱死亡和胜利

   * stride   v. 阔步行进,大踏步走过,跨过

7. be portrayed as   被描写为

   * describe, depict, picture 和 represent 等词皆可作"描写"用。

8. *Genesis A/B*《创世纪》甲/乙本;*Exodus*《出埃及记》;*The Dream of the Rood*《十字架之梦》

9. to take on the burden of his suffering   (十字架本身)承担起基督的苦难

   * to take on   承担,承当,呈现

10. religious compositions 宗教作品;national epic poem 民族史诗;more or less lyrical poems of shorter length 多少带点带抒情意味的短篇诗歌

11. . . . , which do not contain specific religious doctrines but evoke the Anglo-Saxon sense of the harshness of circumstance and the sadness of the human lot.   这些世俗诗歌(譬如史诗《贝奥武夫》*Beowulf*)不含有具体的宗教教义,但却唤起了盎格鲁-撒克逊人对环境之恶劣和人类命运之不幸的感知。

    * 注意句中 specific, evoke, sense 和 human lot 的译法。

12. the tone or mood of the poets   诗人在诗歌中透露出来的语气和情绪基调

13. The life is sorrowful, and the speakers are fatalistic, . . .   生活忧愁凄苦,诗人笔下流露出宿命论的思想……

* 句中讲话人 speakers 指的是诗人。

14. *The Wanderer*《流浪者》；*Deor*《狄奥尔》；*The Seafarer*《航海者》；*The Wife's Complaint*《妻子的抱怨》；*Beowulf*《贝奥武夫》

15. to have nothing/a great deal/a little/little to do with　与……毫无/有很大/有一点儿/几乎没有关系

16. bards/minstrels/scops　古代盎格鲁－撒克逊的行吟诗人或吟游诗人

17. be composed against a background of impending disaster ...　是以迫在眉睫的灾难为背景而创作/写作的……

    * 注意句中的 impending 是正在逼近、即将发生的意思。

18. exploits of a Scandinavian hero 一个斯堪的纳维亚英雄的业绩/功勋；in fighting /to fight against 与……做斗争；revengeful mother 一心想复仇的母亲；fire-breathing dragon 喷火的巨龙

19. In these sequences Beowulf is shown not only as a glorious hero but also as a protector of the people.　依此一连串的英雄事迹,贝奥武夫逐步被描写/展示为既是光辉的英雄又是人民的保护神。

    * in these sequences 本为按照这样的顺序之意,这里是指上句中列举的与妖怪格兰德尔(Grendel)及其母亲以及火龙进行战斗等种种英雄业绩。

20. to present a vivid picture of　展现了一幅……的栩栩如生的画面

21. to wage heroic struggles against the hostile forces of the natural world under a wise and mighty leader 在大智大勇的领袖率领下与大自然的重重险恶(敌对力量)做英勇的斗争(战天斗地)

    * 注意 to wage struggle against 的用法；mighty 意为 strong and powerful,强有力的。

22. the mingling of nature myths and heroic legends　自然神话与英雄传奇的结合

    * 注意动词 mingle 是混合、结合的意思。

23. For instance, the battle between ... symbolically represents that phase of Winter and Summer myth in which the Summer God, here embodied by Beowulf, fights his last battle against the Winter Dragon in order to rescue the treasures of earth, that is, the golden corn and ruddy fruits.　例如,贝奥武夫与火龙的战斗就象征性地表现了有关冬神与夏神时期的神话,由贝奥武夫体现的夏神,为了抢救、保住大地的财富——金黄的玉米和鲜红的水果——(不被严寒戕害)而与冬龙展开了最后的战斗。

24. Having given them back to men, Beowulf himself dies of the Winter's breath.　当贝奥武夫把这些大地的财富(粮食、水果)归还给人民后,他自己却死在了冬神喷出的毒气(气息)中。

    * 句中现在分词短语完成时 having given them back to men 表明 give 的动作早于主句中谓语动词 die 的动作,相当于 after/when he gave them back to men。

25. The Norman Conquest brought England more than a change of rulers.　诺曼征服者给英格兰带来的不只是统治者的更替。

    * more than = not only/merely　不只是,不仅是

26. the Rome-backed Catholic Church　受到罗马教廷支持的天主教会

27. to have a (much) strong(er) control over the country　对该国实施(更)强大(得多)的控制,大大加强了对这个国家的(宗教)控制

28. the principal tongue of church affairs　宗教事务/教会的主要语言

29. be opened up to　向……敞开了大门

30. barren period in literary creation　文学创作上的荒漠期

31. to start to flourish with the appearance of　随着……的出现开始繁荣起来

32. in comparison with　与……相比

33. Middle English literature deals with a wider range of subjects, is uttered by more voices and in a greater diversity of styles, tones and genres.　中世纪英语文学主题/取材更加广泛,叙述、风格、基调和体裁更加丰富多彩。

* be uttered by more voices　用更多的表达方法来表达/表现

* a greater diversity of styles, tones and genres　更为多种多样的风格(文体)、基调和体裁、样式

34. popular folk literature　通俗民间文学

35. to occupy an important place in　在……方面占有/拥有重要地位

36. ..., though the originality of thought is often absent in the literary works of this period.　虽然这个时期的文学作品缺乏思想创见和新颖性,……

* originality　原创性,独创性,新颖别致,即有创见之意

* be absent in　在……方面缺乏

37. to reflect the principles of the medieval Christian doctrine　反映了中世纪基督教教义的原则

38. be primarily concerned with the issue of personal salvation　主要涉及个人自救/人类自救的主题

* be primarily concerned with　主要与……有关系

39. Romance which uses narrative verse or prose to sing knightly adventures or other heroic deeds is a popular literary form in the medieval period.　用叙述性的韵文或散文歌颂骑士的冒险经历或其他英雄业绩的骑士传奇是中世纪一种流行的通俗文学形式。

* which ... heroic deeds 是一个修饰 romance 的定语从句,可以作接近英文的如上翻译,也可按汉语的习惯句式把定语从句单列出来译为:骑士传奇是中世纪一种流行的文学形式,它以叙述性韵文或散文歌颂骑士的冒险经历或其他英雄业绩。对定语从句的理解和翻译是自考生的一大难关。

40. It has developed ... the beautiful beloved.　这种文学形式(骑士传奇)发展了具有中世纪特点的主题——探寻并遭遇妖魔鬼怪、救出心爱的美人。

* 句中的 the characteristic medieval motifs of the quest, the test, the meeting with the evil giant and the encounter with the beautiful beloved 可直译为:具有中世纪特点的关于探险、经受考验、遭逢邪恶巨人以及邂逅美女情人的主题故事。注意其中的 encounter with, 此处 encounter 作名词,也常作动词。

41. to set out on the journey to accomplish some missions　出发踏上征程/旅程去完成一系列任务

42. to attack infidelity 抨击/讨伐宗教叛逆/无宗教信仰的人;to rescue a maiden 救出美人/美少女;to meet a challenge 迎接挑战;to obey a knightly command 服从骑士的指令,遵守骑士式的风范

43. a liberal use of the improbable, sometimes even supernatural, things in romance　骑士传奇里大量运用/随意出现许多荒谬不真、有时甚至是超自然的事物

* mysteries and fantasies　神秘事物和离奇空想

44. characterization is standardized 人物塑造标准化、模式化,千人一面;wicked stewards 邪恶管家、邪恶仆从

45. While the structure is loose and episodic, the language is simple and straightforward.　(骑士传奇诗)结构是松散的、片段式的,语言是简练直白的。

46. The importance of the romance... of the world.　骑士传奇诗的重要意义就在于它表现了理想化世界观里的贵族男女的生活。

* can be seen as 可以被看成/当作……;in relation to 与……有关系;one's idealized view of the world 某人的理想化世界观

47. heroic age 英雄时代;chivalric age 骑士(精神的)时代

48. *Sir Gawain and the Green Knight*《高文爵士和绿衣骑士》;*The Vision of Piers Plowman*《农夫皮尔斯的梦幻》;*The Canterbury Tales*《坎特伯雷故事集》

49. However, it is Chaucer alone who,... in his masterpiece *The Canterbury Tales*.　然而,唯有乔叟,在英国文学史上第一次向我们展现了他那个时代英国社会全面的现实主义画卷,在他的代表作《坎特伯雷故事集》中栩栩如生地塑造了一个完整的涵盖社会各阶层人生百态的人物画卷。

* 注意这是一个强调句型,it is Chaucer alone who,... 强调的是主语 Chaucer;alone ＝ only,只有、唯有的意思。

* a whole gallery of vivid characters 一个完整的栩栩如生的人物画廊/画卷

* all walks of life 各社会阶层的人生活百态,各方面的生活状况

* to present to us a comprehensive realistic picture of 向我们展现了一个全面/综合的……现实主义画卷(其中 to us 是状语)

50. Although he was born a commoner, he did not live as a commoner. 虽然他生而为平民/出生于一个平民家庭,但他从未过过平民生活。

51. Although he was accepted... , he must always have... a true member. 尽管他被贵族所接受,但他必须时时提醒自己他并不真正属于那个只凭出身决定身份/地位的社会。

* 在 must always have been conscious of the fact that... 中,完成时态表示从过去到现在一直要时时提醒自己……; be conscious of the fact that...,意识到这个事实,事实是……;that 引导的是 fact 的同位语从句,等于 fact。

* ... that society of which birth alone could make one a true member. 关键的语言点在于认识 of which 引导了一个定语从句修饰 that society;关系代词 which 就是指 that society;of which birth ＝ birth of which ＝ birth of the society; alone,副词,only 的意思;make one a true member, 其中 one 是宾语, a true member (of the society) 是宾语补足语,意为使人成为(某个特定社会阶级的)一分子,即决定人的特定社会地位。

52. Chaucer characteristically regarded... as a purely practical matter. 乔叟一方面用贵族阶级独特的理想眼光看待生活,但另一方面对生活又不失现实的态度。

* in terms of 根据,以 …… 的方式/态度;to regard/regarding life as a purely practical matter 把现实生活看成纯粹/完全/非常实际的事情; never lost ability of doing sth. 从未丧失做……的能力,从来就没有放弃做 ……

53. The art of being at once involved in and detached from a given situation is peculiarly Chaucer's. 乔叟文学艺术的独到特点便是根据特定情景随时入世或出世。

* 译时已将句中较短的表语部分译成了主语,较长的主语部分译成了表语; peculiarly Chaucer's ＝ Chaucer's peculiar art。

* be involved in a given situation 投入/进入一个特定情景

* be detached from a given situation 与特定情境分离/分开,脱出特定情景

* at once 立刻,随时

* 此句也可按原文的顺序译为:随时进入和脱出特定情景的艺术特点便是乔叟的独到之处。

54. 乔万尼·薄伽丘 (Giovanni Boccaccio,1313 ~ 1375),意大利文艺复兴时期杰出的人文主义作家,反贵族、拥共和,代表作为《十日谈》(Decameron)。

彼特拉克(Petrarch,1304 ~ 1374),意大利人文主义代表作家、学者、诗人,著有《爱情诗集》,以及描写第二次布匿战争的史诗《非洲》。

55. Chaucer affirmed man's right to pursue earthly happiness and opposed asceticism. 乔叟肯定人类追求尘世幸福的权利,反对禁欲主义。

to pursue earthly happiness and oppose asceticism 追求尘世快乐/幸福的权利,反对禁欲主义/苦行僧的生活方式

* 注意不定式短语是修饰 man's right 的定语短语。

56. man's energy, intellect, quick wit and love of life 人类的能力、智慧、机敏和对生活/生命的热爱

to expose and satirize the social vices, including religious abuses 揭露和嘲讽社会邪恶(道德沦丧),

包括宗教迫害

to bear marks of humanism and anticipate a new era to come　打上/印有/带有人文主义的痕迹/印记,预示一个新时代即将到来

　　* to come 是修饰 new era 的定语,直译为预示一个即将到来的新时代。

57. ... and his <u>observant mind</u> made the most of this <u>ever-present opportunity</u>.　他敏锐的思维和洞察力使他对这种随时都存在的机遇能够加以充分利用。

58. wide range of reading　博览群书,广泛阅读

　　to give him plots and ideas　给他提供了故事情节和构思的想法

　　models of characters　人物原型,人物范本

　　to explore the theme of individual's relation to the society in which he lives　对个人与社会的关系这个主题进行探讨,而他本人正生活在这个社会中间

　　* 句中 in which he lives 是修饰 the society 的定语从句,意即他生活(在其中)的社会。in which he lives = he lives in which = he lives in the society,关系代词 which 就是指 the society。

59. clashes of characters' temperaments　人性格气质上的不协调/摩擦

　　conflicts over material interests　物质利益上的冲突

60. He also shows the comic and ironic effects obtainable from the class distinctions felt by the newly emerged bourgeoisie as <u>in the case of</u> the Wife of Bath who <u>is depicted as</u> the new bourgeois wife asserting her independence.　他以幽默讽刺的笔触描写了新兴城市资产阶级所反感的阶级差别问题,比如其中的一个角色"巴斯夫人",就被描写成一位新兴资产阶级主妇,她维护着自己的独立与权利。

　　* obtainable from the class distinction　由阶级差别所产生/引发的(喜剧讽刺效果);

　　* ... felt by the newly bourgeoisie　新兴资产阶级所感受/体会到的……

　　* as in the case of the Wife of Bath　就像"巴斯夫人"的例子/故事一样

　　* be depicted as　被描写为……

　　* asserting her independence　主张和维护自己的独立与权利(此为现在分词短语,作 bourgeois wife 的定语)

61. to develop his characterization to a higher artistic level by doing...　通过做……,他把人物形象的塑造提到更高的艺术水平

　　to present characters with both typical qualities and individual dispositions　从典型性和个性两方面来表现人物的性格

62. to introduce from France the rhymed stanzas of various types to English poetry　把各种各样的押尾韵诗章从法国引入英语诗歌

　　to replace the Old English alliterative verse　代替古英语诗押头韵的做法

63. *The Romaunt of the Rose*　《玫瑰传奇》

　　octosyllabic couplet　八音节对句/偶句

64. In *The Legend of Good Women*, he used for the first time in English the rhymed couplet of iambic pentameter which is to be called later the heroic couplet.　在《好女人传奇》中,他第一次把后来称作英雄偶句体的五步抑扬格押韵对偶句引入英语。

　　* 在 to use in English the rhymed couplet of iambic pentameter 中 in English 是状语,在宾语较短时,多放在最后。

　　* which is ... couplet 是修饰 pentameter 的定语从句。

65. to employ the heroic couplet with true ease and charm　轻松自如/悠闲潇洒地运用/采用英雄偶句体

66. In addition to his contribution to... any other medieval literature.　除了他对英语诗体学/韵律学的贡献之外,他对文学艺术本身的发展也超过了任何其他中世纪文学中所能见到的。

* English prosody 英语诗体学/韵律学

* to be found in any medieval literature 是修饰 anything 的定语。

67. In *Troilus and Criseyde*, he gave the world what is virtually the first modern novel. 在《特洛伊勒斯与克瑞西达》中,他实质上是向世界展示/奉献了第一部现代小说。

* what...novel 是一个名词性从句,作 gave 的直接宾语从句。

68. He developed his art of poetry still further towards drama and the art of the novel. 他更进一步向戏剧和小说艺术的方向发展诗歌艺术。

69. be entirely rooted in the soil of 完全植根于……的土壤中

His art is so fully realized as to carry him beyond his time. 他的艺术得到如此充分的表现,以致超越了他的时代。

70. to modernize several of *The Canterbury Tales* 把《坎特伯雷故事集》中的几个故事改写成现代英语(诗歌)

to call Chaucer the father of English poetry 称乔叟为英语诗歌之父

* 其中 Chaucer 为宾语,the father of English poetry 为宾补。

71. Chaucer dominated the works of... followers and ... Chaucerians. 乔叟对 15 世纪英国后来的诗人和所谓的"苏格兰乔叟专家/崇拜者们"的诗歌作品产生了决定性的影响。

* dominate 意为"对……产生决定性影响",而不是"主宰、垄断"的意思。followers 为"后继者、追随者、信徒"之意。

72. 荷马(Homer),古希腊时期的行吟诗人。公元前 800 年左右,他创作了伟大史诗《奥德赛》(*Odyssey*)和《伊利亚特》(*Iliad*),使特洛伊木马的故事以及木马屠城以后发生的种种传奇流传至今,对后世产生了巨大影响。

73. to pay tribute to sb. as 把某人尊称为……

* tribute 敬意,赞颂

74. to show thorough assimilation of Chaucer's comic spirit 表明完全吸收了乔叟的喜剧精神

* thorough assimilation 完全/彻底的吸收/同化

75. Today, Chaucer's reputation has been securely established as one of the best English poets for his wisdom, humor, and humanity. 今天,乔叟凭借他的智慧、幽默和人文精神,盛名不衰,被公认为英国最卓越的诗人之一。

* be securely established as 被确认为,被肯定无疑地认为

主要内容归纳和总结

1. 英国的早期居民(early inhabitants)凯尔特人(Celts)曾先后被罗马人(the Romans)、盎格鲁 - 撒克逊人(the Anglo-Saxons)和诺曼人(the Normans)征服。罗马人统治时间较短,无大影响;盎格鲁 - 撒克逊人带来了日耳曼(Germanic)语言、文化和特殊的诗歌传统;而诺曼人则给英格兰带来了地中海文明(Mediterranean civilization),希腊文化(Greek culture),罗马法律(Roman law)以及基督教信仰(Christian religion)。

2. 古英语文学时期(450 ~ 1066),实际上是古英语诗歌时期。古英语诗歌分两类,一为宗教类(religious group),一为世俗类(secular group)。

a. 宗教类作品

《创世纪》甲/乙本 *Genesis A/ B*;《出埃及记》*Exodus*;《但以理》*Daniel*;《犹滴》*Judith*;《基督与撒旦》*Christ and Satan*;《安德列》*Andreas*;《使徒的命运》*The Fates of the Apostles*;《埃琳娜》*Elene*;

《朱莉安娜》*Juliana*（以上均出自旧约全书 the Old Testament）

《十字架之梦》*The Dream of the Rood*（出自新约全书 the New Testament）

b. 世俗类作品

《贝奥武夫》*Beowulf*；《流浪者》*The Wanderer*；《狄奥尔》*Deor*；《航海者》*The Seafarer*；《妻子的抱怨》*The Wife's Complaint*；《莫尔登战役》*The Battle of Malden*

3. 中世纪时期的英国文学分两个阶段

a. 文学创作的荒漠时期（barren period,1066～14 世纪中期），300 年间无作品。

b. 文学创作开始繁荣时期（14 世纪下半叶～1510），杰弗瑞·乔叟（Geoffrey Chaucer）、威廉·朗格兰（William Langland）和约翰·高厄（John Gower）等文学巨星出现。

c. 乔叟的作品

1360s～1372：初学时期

《玫瑰传奇》*The Romaunt of the Rose* 译自法国纪尧姆·德·洛里和让·德·默恩的同名诗作

《公爵夫人书》*The Book of Duchess*

1372～1398：受意大利影响时期

《百鸟之会》*The Parliament of Fowls*

《特洛伊勒斯与克瑞西达》*Troilus and Criseyde*

《好女人的传说》*The Legend of Good Women*

《声誉之宫》*The House of Fame*

* 此一时期乔叟受但丁（Dante）、彼特拉克（Petrarch）、薄伽丘（Boccaccio）的影响,从浪漫主义向现实主义转变。

1387～1400：创作成熟期

《坎特伯雷故事集》*The Canterbury Tales* 英国历史上第一部现实主义典范之作

d. 约翰·高厄的作品

《沉思者之镜》*Mirour de l' Omme*（1376～1378）法语

《呼号者的声音》*Vox Clamantis*（1379～1381）拉丁语

《恋人的忏悔》*Confessio Amantis*（1390）

e. 威廉·朗格兰的作品

《农夫皮尔斯的梦幻》*The Vision of Piers Plowman*

f. 骑士传奇和高文诗人作品

《高文爵士和绿衣骑士》*Sir Gawain and the Green Knight*

* 中世纪骑士传奇类诗歌多种多样,但技巧和故事结构没有超过《高文爵士和绿衣骑士》的。所谓高文诗人乃得名于不列颠图书馆一部手抄本里的四首诗,其中三首是《玉净》（*Cleanness*）《耐心》（*Patience*）和《珍珠》（*Pearl*）,《高文爵士和绿衣骑士》是第四首,也是最长最好的一首,作者无名,即以"高文诗人"名之。

4. 诺曼征服者给英格兰带来三大变化

a. 政治上,建立了封建制度。（Politically, feudalism was established in England.）

b. 得到罗马教廷支持的天主教会施行更强大的控制。（Religiously, the Rome-backed Catholic Church had a stronger control over the country.）

c. 语言发生了很大变化。（Great changes took place in language.）

诺曼征服后,英格兰三种语言并存（co-existed）：

法语——官方语言（official language）,用于王室、朝廷和诺曼贵族；

拉丁语——宗教事务和大学通用语言；

旧式英语——普通百姓使用的语言。

重要信息句子

1. The period of Old English literature extends from about 450 to 1066.

2. The Anglo-Saxon language is the basis of Modern English.

3. However, the hero and the setting of *Beowulf* have nothing to do with England, for the story took place in Scandinavia.

4. *Beowulf* was originally in an oral form, sung by the bards at the 6th century. The present script was written down in the 10th century. 《贝奥武夫》(原本)在公元 6 世纪时就由行吟诗人以口头形式流传,现在的版本是公元 10 世纪的手写本。

5. The Norman Conquest starts the medieval period in English literature, which covers about four centuries.

6. Geoffrey Chaucer is the greatest writer of the Medieval Age.

7. John Dryden, who modernized several of *The Canterbury Tales*, called Chaucer the father of English poetry.

8. Edmund Spenser paid tribute to Chaucer as his master.

9. Many of Shakespeare's plays show thorough assimilation of Chaucer's comic spirit.

古代和中世纪英国文学简介同步练习与答案

1. Historically, the early inhabitants _____ in England have been conquered three times. They were conquered by the _____ , _____ and Normans.
   - a. British/Ancient Greeks/French
   - b. Scots/English/Germans
   - c. Welsh/Romans/Trojans
   - d. Celts/Romans /Anglo-Saxons

2. The Anglo-Saxons brought to England _____ and _____.
   - a. the Germanic language/the Viking tradition
   - b. the Norwegian culture/Scandinavian language
   - c. the Germanic language/culture
   - d. the Christian religion/Greek culture

3. The _____ brought a fresh wave of Mediterranean culture, which includes Greek culture, _____ and the Christian religion.
   - a. Germans/Byzantium laws
   - b. Romans/Latin language
   - c. Normans/Roman laws
   - d. French language/Egyptian culture

4. It is _____ that provided the source for the rise and growth of English literature.
   - a. the Normans
   - b. the Romans
   - c. Anglo-Saxons
   - d. a and c

5. The period of Old English literature extends from _____ to 1066, the year of the _____ conquest of England.
   - a. 450/Romans
   - b. 450/Normans
   - c. the 7th century/Greeks
   - d. 450/Germans

6. Germanic tribes brought with England not only _____ language, but also a specific _____ tradition.

a. Anglo-Saxon/poetic   b. German/philosophy

    c. Scandinavian/Viking   d. Norwegian/badminton

7. _____ is the basis of Modern English.

    a. French   b. German

    c. Latin   d. Anglo-Saxon language

8. The Germanic specific poetic tradition in _____ language is characteristic of being _____, mournful and elegiac.

    a. English/soft and weak   b. Anglo-Saxon/bold and strong

    c. Greek/sad and sorrowful   d. French/clear and beautiful

9. Generally speaking, the Old English poetry that has survived can be divided into two groups: the religious group and the _____ one. The former is mainly on _____ themes.

    a. secular/catholic   b. pagan/Islamic

    c. popular/Christian   d. secular/biblical

10. *The Dream of the Rood* belongs to the group of _____, based on _____.

    a. religion/the Old Testament   b. religion/the New Testament

    c. secular theme/the national legends   d. earthly theme/common people

11. *Beowulf*, a typical example of Old English poetry, the hero and setting of which has nothing to do with _____, for the story took place in _____.

    a. France/England   b. Germany/Sweden

    c. England/Denmark   d. England/Scandinavia

12. The present script of *Beowulf* was written down in _____.

    a. the 6th century   b. the 8th century BC

    c. the 10th century   d. the 12th century BC

13. *Beowulf* is an example of the mingling of _____ myths and heroic legends. For instance, the battle between Beowulf and the Dragon symbolically represents that phase of _____ and Summer myth in which the Summer God is embodied by _____.

    a. primitive/Autumn/nature   b. nature/Winter/Beowulf

    c. English/Spring/Summer God   d. Scandinavian/Winter /Grendel

14. The Norman Conquest brought England three changes: a. establishment of _____ in England; a much stronger control over the country by the Rome-backed _____ and the co-existence of three languages.

    a. Catholic Church/Queen   b. feudalism/Pope

    c. churches/king   d. feudalism/Catholic Church

15. The co-existence of three languages means respectively French as the _____ used by the king and the Norman lords; _____, the principal tongue of church affairs and in universities; and _____ spoken only by the common people.

    a. official language/Latin/Old English   b. popular language/French/Old English

    c. formal language/Greek/Old English   d. communicational language/Latin/Norwegian

16. From 1066 to the mid-14th century, the medieval English literature is called a _____ in creation. There is _____ to say.

    a. potential period/little   b. developing period/something

    c. barren period/nothing   d. flourishing period/much

17. English literature started to flourish with the appearance of writers like _____, _____

and _____.

   a. Ben Johnson/Edmund Spenser/William Shakespeare

   b. Daniel Defoe/Jonathan Swift/Henry Fielding

   c. William Bake/William Wordsworth/John Keats

   d. Geoffrey Chaucer/William Langland/John Gower

18. Middle English literature strongly reflects the principles of the _____ , which were primarily concerned with the issue of _____.

   a. humanism/human right

   b. medieval Christian doctrine/personal salvation

   c. naturalism/natural selection

   d. feudalist society/the supreme king's authority

19. Romance which uses narrative verse or prose to sing _____ or other _____ is a popular literary form in the medieval period.

   a. warrior's adventures/religious affairs   b. knightly adventures/heroic deeds

   c. military action/brave soldiers   d. the exciting battle/courageous fighters

20. If the epic reflects a heroic age, the romance reflects a _____ one.

   a. romantic   b. comic

   c. chivalric   d. full-of-love

21. Among three great Middle English poets, the author of *Sir Gawain and the Green Knight* produced _____ of the period; William Langland dealt with a more realistic _____ issues of his day in *Piers Plowman*; and Chaucer presented to us a _____ of the English society of his time in his masterpiece *The Canterbury Tales*.

   a. the best narrative poem/agricultural/colorful picture

   b. the most interesting story/social/whole gallery of vivid characters

   c. the best epic/religious/great many very real stories

   d. the best romance/religious and social/comprehensive realistic picture

22. _____ is the greatest English writer of the medieval period.

   a. William Langland   b. Geoffrey Chaucer

   c. John Gower   d. Sir Gawain

23. It is _____ who introduced from France the rhymed stanzas of various types to English poetry to replace _____.

   a. Chaucer/alliterative verse   b. Langland/rhymed tail

   c. John Gower/narrative story   d. Edmund Spenser/octosyllabic couplet

24. In _____, Chaucer used for the first time in English the rhymed couplet of iambic pentameter which is to be called later the _____.

   a. *The Romaunt of the Rose*/octosyllabic couplet

   b. *The Canterbury Tales*/heroic couplet

   c. *The Vision of Piers Plowman*/rhymed stanza

   d. *The Legend of Good Women*/heroic couplet

25. In _____, Chaucer employed the _____ with true ease and charm for the first time in the history of English literature.

   a. *Sir Gawain and the Green Knight*/alliterative verse

   b. *The Romaunt of the Rose*/rhymed stanza

c. *The Canterbury Tales*/heroic couplet

    d. *The Legend of Good Women*/heroic couplet

26. _____ called Chaucer the father of English poetry.

    a. John Gower   b. John Dryden

    c. William Shakespeare   d. Ben Johnson

Keys：dccdb/adbdb/dcbda/cdbbc/dbadc/b

第一章　文艺复兴时期 The Renaissance Period

词语解释和难句分析

1. to mark a transition from...to... 　标志着从……到……的过度/跨越

2. to refer to + *n*.　指的是……

3. with the flowering of painting, sculpture and literature　随着绘画、雕塑和文学的繁荣/兴旺

4. The Renaissance, which means..., is ... the economic expansion.　文艺复兴,本意是再生和复活,实际是一系列历史事件刺激下产生的运动,例如古罗马、古希腊文化的重新发现、地理和天文方面的新发现、宗教改革以及经济的大发展。

　　* which means rebirth and revival 是非限制性定语从句,其本意是再生和复活。

　　* (be) stimulated by 意为受到……的刺激、激励, 句中为过去分词短语,作 movement 的定语。

5. humanist thinkers and scholars　人文主义的思想家和学者

   to make attempt to do　企图/想要做

   to get rid of...　清除……

   to introduce new ideas that...　引进……的新思想

   to recover the purity of　恢复……的纯洁性

6. domestic unrest　国内的动荡不安

   volcanic period of English history　英国历史上的激烈动荡时期

   frightful reign of Richard III　理查三世国王的恐怖统治

7. The Wars of Rose　玫瑰战争(1455～1485)。战争发生在金雀花王朝(The Plantagenet Dynasty)——也叫安茹王朝(The Angevin Dynasty)时期,双方都是英国王室、金雀花家族的成员,都是爱德华三世的子孙,战争的目的是争夺王位。事情发生在亨利六世(属于兰开斯特家族)时期,玛格丽特王后婚后8年无所出,使得王室成员冈特的约克(York)家族和兰开斯特(Lancaster)家族都产生了争夺王位的妄想,尽管不久之后,王后产下了一个小王子,但已燃起的欲火无法熄灭。他们的夺位战争持续了30年,最后约克家族获胜,爱德华四世(Edward IV)建立了约克王朝。由于在战争中,约克家族以白玫瑰为家徽,兰开斯特家族以红玫瑰为家徽,所以19世纪的历史小说家沃尔特·斯科特爵士(Sir Walter Scott)杜撰了"玫瑰战争"这个词语,得到了普遍接受。又由于战争后来演变为王后一党与约克家族的战争,王后与国王亨利六世一派自然代表前朝——兰开斯特王朝,所以玫瑰战争又被说成是前后两个王朝的战争。

　　然而,战争并没到此结束。爱德华四世于1483年逝世,他12岁的王子爱德华五世和王子的弟

弟临时住在伦敦塔里,等待加冕典礼,却神秘失踪,结果由爱德华四世的弟弟,摄政王格洛斯特公爵(Duke of Gloucester)取而代之,隆重加冕,是为理查三世(Richard III)。人们一直认为理查三世杀侄篡位,莎士比亚为此还创作了历史剧《理查三世》揭露他的阴谋丑态。两年后,兰开斯特家族的一个子孙亨利·都铎(Henry Tudor)反叛,理查三世战死,亨利·多铎登上王位,为亨利七世(Henry VII),王权又回到兰开斯特家族手中。为求平衡、稳定,亨利七世娶了爱德华四世(属约克家族)的女儿做王后,两个家族才算统一起来,玫瑰战争才真正结束。

　　自此,金雀花王朝结束,都铎王朝开始。至于历史上理查三世是否真的杀侄篡位,一直没有确切证据,史学家们至今仍有争论。

8. be revitalized　重获生机,得到再生、复兴

　　be much read　得到广泛阅读

9. to have no sharp break with the past　没有与过去发生明显的决裂

10. Attitudes and feelings which had been characteristic of the 14th and 15th centuries persisted well down into the era of Humanism and reformation.　具有 14 和 15 世纪特征的创作态度和情感一直贯穿到人文主义和宗教改革时期。

　　＊ be characteristic of　为……(时代)特点的,具有……特点的

　　＊ to persist well down into...　坚持到……,贯穿到……

11. It (humanism) sprang from... of all things.　人文主义产生于恢复中世纪就开始的尊崇古希腊、古罗马文明的努力,人文主义也常常在意识和理智上被看作是文艺复兴的开始,因为古希腊、古罗马文明的根本思想观念就是:人是万物之灵/之本。

　　＊ to spring from　产生于……,由……而发生

　　＊ to restore a medieval reverence for　恢复中世纪(开始的)对……的尊重

　　＊ antique authors　古代作者/作家,即古希腊、古罗马时期的作家

　　＊ on the conscious and intellectual side　从意识和理智的角度

　　＊ be based on such a conception that...　基于……的观念(that 引导一个同位语从句)

12. to see the arts of splendor and enlightenment... in the works　看到古典作品中灿烂的艺术和启蒙的精神

13. be subordinated to...　从属于/隶属于/附属于……

14. ... and in medieval theology, people's relations to ... for a future life.　在中世纪的神学中,人与周围环境之间最多只是消极适应或消极遁世的关系(不可积极追求幸福快乐),人们竭力为死后灵魂超脱认真修行。

　　＊ be largely reduced to + n.　大多/主要归结为……

　　＊ adapting or avoiding the circumstances of earthly life　适应或回避尘世/世俗的生活环境

　　＊ in an effort to prepare their souls for a future life　竭力为来世的生活做好灵魂上的准备(即为死后灵魂超脱潜心修行)

15. to find a justification to exalt human nature　发现了歌颂人性的充分理由

　　glorious creature capable of individual development in the direction of perfection　能够自我发展、自我完善的崇高的生物

　　＊ in the direction of　沿着……的方向

16. The world they inhabited was theirs not to despise but to question, explore, and enjoy.　他们居住的世界是属于他们自己的,不可鄙视,但可以怀疑、探索和享受。

　　＊ they inhabited (vt.)　是 world 的定语从句,前面省略了在从句中作宾语的关系代词 which。

17. to voice their beliefs that...　喊出/表达/发表他们的信仰……

　　to have the ability to perfect himself and to perform wonders　有能力完善自己、创造奇迹

* to perfect himself and to perform wonders 是 ability 的定语。

18. Humanism began <u>to take hold in</u> England when... 　当……的时候,人文主义开始在英国生根/扎根/确立/固定下来。

　　to teach the classical learning 　教授古典学术(古希腊、古罗马学术)

19. <u>be marked by</u> the steady increase of the national power 　标志着国力的不断增强

　　<u>be entitled to</u> interpret the Bible for himself 　有权自己诠释《圣经》

　　<u>be encouraged by</u> Luther's preaching 　受到马丁·路德布道教义的鼓舞

　　to recover the purity of the early church from the corruption and superstition of the Middle Ages 恢复早期教会的纯洁性,去除中世纪的腐败和迷信

　　to simplify the colorful and dramatic ritual of the Catholic Church 　简化天主教繁复夸张的仪规/仪式

20. Indulgences, pilgrimages, and other practices were condemned. 　天主教的豁免、朝圣以及其他活动都被禁止。

21. legitimate male heir 　合法男性继承人

　　to <u>cut ties with</u> Rome 　割断与罗马的联系

　　to be <u>dissatisfied with</u> 　对……不满意

　　to <u>break away from</u> Rome 　与罗马断绝关系

　　to declare himself through the approval of parliament as 　通过议会的批准宣布自己为

　　<u>in its full swing</u> 　处于轰轰烈烈、全面展开的全盛时期

22. ... and services were held in English instead of Latin so that people could understand. 　……宗教活动都是用英语而不是用拉丁语进行的,使得人们都能听懂。

23. But after Mary ascended the throne, there was <u>a violent swing to</u> Catholicism. 　但是玛丽女王执政之后,宗教上又出现了倒退回天主教的大复辟。

　　* to ascend the throne 　升上/登上王位,上台执政

　　* a violent swing to 　猛烈倒向,向……摆去/倒退

24. ..., with a certain extent of compromise between Catholicism and Protestantism. 　……天主教和新教达成了一定程度的妥协/折中。

25. the class struggle <u>waged by</u> the rising bourgeoisie against the feudalist class and its ideology 　新兴资产阶级反抗封建阶级及其思想观念而发动的一场阶级斗争

26. in the time of the Tudors 　都铎王朝时期

　　to <u>give a incentive to</u> the cultural development 　激励/刺激了文化发展

　　<u>in place of</u> the old monasteries 　代替原先/古老的修道院

27. *Malory's Morte Darthur* by Chaucer 　乔叟的《马洛利的默特·达瑟》

28. to come into being 　产生,出现,形成

　　Plutarch's *Lives of the Noble Grecians and Romans* translated by Thomas North 　托马斯·诺斯翻译的普鲁塔克的《古希腊古罗马名人列传》

　　Ovid's *Metamorphoses* by Golding 　古尔丁译奥维德的《变形记》

　　Homer's *The Iliad* by Chapman 　查普曼译荷马的《伊利亚特》

　　Montaigne's *Essays* by Florio 　弗洛里奥译蒙田的《随笔集》

29. imitation and assimilation 　模仿和消化/同化

　　academies after the Italian type 　意大利式的各种学院

　　* after = modeled after 　模仿,仿照

　　be regarded as the fountainhead of literature 　被当作文学的源泉

30. For it was Petrarch and his successors who established the language of love and sharply distinguished the

love poetry of the Renaissance from its counterparts in the ancient world. 因为正是彼特拉克及其后继者描述爱情的语言,把文艺复兴时期爱情诗歌与以往的爱情诗区别开来。

* to distinguish. . . from. . . 把……与……区别开来

* counterpart n. 对应物,句中的对应物即指 love poetry 爱情诗。

31. Wyatt and Surrey began. . . native stock. 怀亚特和萨里把意大利诗歌的形式和优美韵味、风格(通过自己的作品)烙印到/融进本国诗人的作品中。

* to engrave. . . upon. . . 把……刻进/烙进……,给……以深刻印象

* native stock 本土的家族世系,此处指当时英国本土的诗人/诗歌

32. the Petrarchan sonnet introduced by Wyatt 怀亚特引进的彼特拉克的十四行诗

blank verse, i. e. the unrhymed iambic pentameter line by Surrey 萨里引入了无韵诗,即无韵的五步抑扬格诗行

the sestina and terza rima and with various experiments in classic meters by Sidney 西德尼引入了六节六行诗和隔句押韵的三行诗节,以及尝试各种古典诗歌格律的创作

33. to give new vigor to the blank verse with his "mighty lines" 他以气魄宏大的诗句给无韵体诗注入了勃勃生机

34. From Wyatt and Surrey onwards. . . into high belief. 从怀亚特和萨里往后,人文主义诗歌的目标是:熟练运用传统习俗和驾驭语言的力量,而且,最为重要的是发展修辞模式,即将格律、韵律、组织结构和议论结合在一起,以勾画出情感主题并将其充分表现出来。

* to throw it into high relief 将其(it = emotional theme 情感主题) 充分表现/高度释放/出来

35. a concentrated exercise of the mind, of craftsmanship, and of learning 集思想、技艺和学术于一体的最凝练的表达

36. Spenser's *The Shepheardes Calendar* 斯宾塞的《牧人日记》

be adopted to a variety of subjects, moral or heroic 被应用于各种各样的主题,不论是道义的还是英雄主义的

* moral and heroic 是 subjects 的后置定语。

37. . . . and how the rules of decorum, or fitness of style to subject, could be applied through variations in the diction and metrical scheme. ……如何通过措辞和格律的变化来应用合乎经典的规则或者切合主题的风格。

* 注意由 to fit . . . to. . . 演变到fitness of style to subject 的用法。

38. In "The Passionate Shepherd to His Love", Marlowe spoke with a voice so innocent that it would be very difficult for us to connect it with the voice in his tragedies. 在《深情的牧羊人致恋人》中,马洛的诗歌语气非常纯真,以致我们很难把它与他悲剧中的语气联系在一起。

39. be carried on by 被……所继承

be labeled as the metaphysical poets 被贴上玄学派诗人的标签

to represent a sharp break from the poetry by their predecessors and most of their contemporaries 表现出一种与他们的先辈和大多数同时代人明显的决裂/完全的不同

40. the Elizabethan drama 伊丽莎白时代的戏剧

in its totality 总体上讲

the mainstream of the English Renaissance 英国文艺复兴的主流

be dated back to + *n.* 追溯到……

interludes and morality plays thriving in the medieval period 中世纪兴盛起来的幕间剧和道德剧

be popular down to Shakespeare's time 直到莎士比亚时代还受欢迎

sophisticated art form 成熟/精致的艺术形式

41. Lively, vivid native English material was put into the regular form of ...　将活泼生动的英国本土素材用……的正规形式来表现。

42. the fusion of classical form with English content　经典形式与英国本土内容的融合

    to <u>bring about</u> the possibility of a mature and artistic drama　可能产生成熟的有很高艺术性的戏剧

    to write plays with such universal qualities of greatness　写出了举世称颂的伟大戏剧

    by imitating the romances of Italy and Spain　通过模仿意大利和西班牙的骑士抒情诗

    to embrace the mysteries of German legend　采用/吸取德意志传奇的神秘性

    to combine the fiction of poetic fancy with the fact of daily life　把诗歌想象的虚构与日常生活的事实结合起来

    to make a depiction of the sharp conflicts between ... and ...　描写了……与……的尖锐冲突

    with Shakespeare as the master　以莎士比亚为导师/旗帜/榜样

    to leave a monument of the Renaissance <u>unrivaled</u> for pure creative power <u>by</u> any other product of that epoch　单就创作能力而言，留下了同时代代任何其他艺术形式无可匹敌的文艺复兴的丰碑

    ＊unrivaled by...　是 monument of Renaissance 的后置定语。

43. to pave the way for　为……铺平道路

    be undoubtedly one of the representatives of　无疑是……的代表之一

主要内容归纳和总结

1. 人的价值在中世纪和文艺复兴时期的不同

    在中世纪，人作为个人从属于(subordinate to)封建主义统治(the feudalist rule)，没有任何自由和独立性。人只能适应和回避尘世的环境(adapt to or avoid the circumstances of earthly life)，为死后的灵魂超脱而苦苦修行(to prepare their souls for a future life)。

    文艺复兴阶段的人文主义者从古希腊、古罗马的经典著作中发现了赞颂人性的雄辩论据(a justification to exalt human nature)，认为人是能够自我发展、自我完善的光荣的生物(glorious creatures capable of individual development in the direction of perfection)，有权享受生活，有能力完善自己并创造奇迹(to perfect himself and perform wonders)。周围的世界固然不可鄙视(despise)，但却可以怀疑、探索、和享受。总之人的尊严(dignity)应当受到尊重。

2. 文艺复兴发生的原因

    a. 古罗马、古希腊文化的重新发现(the rediscovery of ancient Roman and Greek culture)；

    b. 地理和天文方面的新发现(the new discoveries in geography and astrology)；

    c. 宗教改革(the religious reformation)；

    d. 经济大发展(the economic expansion)。

3. 文艺复兴在英国两个阶段

    a. 早期阶段：对意大利人文主义诗人和学者的模仿和同化(imitation and assimilation)阶段。例如怀亚特和萨里(Wyatt and Surrey)引进了彼特拉克(Petrarch)的十四行诗(sonnet)、无韵诗(unrhymed blank verse)，即不押韵的五步抑扬格诗行(unrhymed iambic pentameter line)。在早期阶段，诗与诗剧(poetic drama)是最杰出的文学形式(literature forms)。

    b. 成熟阶段：伊丽莎白一世女王(Queen Elizabeth I)时期。此时戏剧是英国文艺复兴的主流(mainstream)。

    生动鲜活的英国本土素材(native material)加上古希腊、古罗马的经典形式(classic /regular form)创造出了成熟、精致(sophisticated)的戏剧艺术。例如喜剧学习了古罗马剧作家普劳图斯

（Plautus）和特伦斯（Terence）的形式，悲剧用的是塞内加（Seneca）的形式。

重要信息句子

1. The Renaissance was slow in reaching England not only because of England's separation from the Continent but also because of its domestic unrest (The War of the Rose).　文艺复兴较晚才传入英国不仅因为英国作为岛国疏离于欧洲大陆，也因为英国国内的动荡不安（30 年的玫瑰战争）。
2. Humanism is the essence of the Renaissance.
3. Man is the measure of all things.
4. One of the men who made a great contribution in this respect (the English Renaissance) was William Caxton, for he was the first person who introduced printing into England.
5. Only his need for a legitimate male heir, and hence a new wife, led him (Henry VIII) to cut ties with Rome.　亨利八世因为想要一个合法的男性继承人，因而想换一个（能生王子的）新王后（未得到罗马教皇的批准），导致他切断与罗马教廷的一切联系。

I. 埃德蒙·斯宾塞 Edmund Spenser（1552～1599）

词语解释和难句分析

1. to record his laments over the loss of Rosalind in *The Shepheardes Calender*　在《牧人日记》中表达了他对罗莎琳早逝的沉痛哀悼
   be made secretary to Lord Grey of Wilton, the queen's deputy in Ireland　担任女王的驻爱尔兰代理、威尔顿的格雷伯爵的秘书
2. *Epithalamion*《新婚喜歌》；wedding hymn 婚礼赞美诗
3. to abandon Kilcolman Castle　放弃吉尔卡尔曼城堡
4. He returned to England heartbroken. 他痛苦得碎心断肠地回到了英格兰。
   ＊heartbroken 是主语补语。该句等于 He returned to England and was heartbroken.
5. He died "for want of bread."　他死于贫困和饥饿。
6. He speaks of 12 virtues of the private gentleman, and plans 12 books, each one with a different hero distinguished for one of the private virtues.　他讲到绅士个人的 12 种美德，（全诗）设计成 12 卷本，每一卷都有一个不同的英雄，具备其中的一种美德。
   ＊注意 speaks of 和 plans 是同一主语的两个并列谓语动词；distinguished for 引导一个过去分词短语作 hero 的定语。
7. to possess all of these virtues　拥有所有这些美德
   to play a role in each of the 12 major adventures　在 12 种主要冒险经历的每一种中都发挥作用
   the recurring appearances of Arthur　亚瑟形象的重复出现
   to serve as a unifying element for the poem as a whole　起着统一全诗整体的作用
   to contribute to the unity of the work　起着贯穿/统一整部著作的作用

8. at one's bidding 听从/遵循某人的旨意/命令/召唤

   to set out on his particular adventure 踏上他特定的冒险历程

9. Arthur's great mission 亚瑟的伟大任务

   to <u>fall in love</u> through a love vision 通过一个爱情幻象坠入爱河/情网

10. be full of adventures and marvels, dragons, witches, enchanted trees, giants, jousting knights, and castles 历经各种冒险和奇迹,见到龙、女巫、施了魔法的树、巨人、角斗的骑士以及各种城堡

11. The Red crosse Knight <u>stands for</u> St. George, the patron saint of England 红十字骑士代表英格兰护教圣徒圣乔治

12. Holiness 名为"神圣"的美德;Temperance 名为"节制欲望"的美德

    be <u>in a way</u> an epitome of the whole poem 某种程度上是全诗的象征/缩影/梗概

    the purpose of sb.'s quest 某人追求的目标

    to <u>free</u> original mankind – the parents of Una – <u>from</u> the power of the Devil 从恶魔的手中解救人类始祖——尤娜的父母

    in the opening canto 在开篇的诗章中

    to easily rout the dragon of Error in the Wandering Wood 在"彷徨"森林中轻易打垮/大败名叫"谬误"的恶龙

    the fallen world of man 堕落的人类世界

    be full of delusion 充满谬误和错觉

13. Overconfident knight soon <u>falls into</u> the snares (= traps) of Archimago. 过分自信的骑士 很快落入了大巫师阿奇梅戈的圈套。

14. be parted in the dark world of deceit 在"欺骗"的黑暗中被分开

    to fall for the illusory charms of Duessa 为杜伊沙迷人的魅力而堕落

15. The <u>quest against</u> outer evil becomes an experience of inner sin. 对外部邪恶的探险和挑战变成了对内心邪恶/心魔的体验。

16. to fall further into error 进一步滑向错误的深渊

    to <u>pose</u> a great threat <u>to</u> sb. 对某人造成极大的威胁

17. misled by his purely worldly chivalry 受纯粹的尘世骑士精神的误导

    be taken by... to the House of Pride 被……带到/引入"傲慢"公主的宫殿

    to witness the pageant of the seven deadly sins 目睹了七个致命罪恶的欢乐庆典

18. to contrive to escape 谋划/设法逃跑

    to fall prey to Orgoglio 为奥嘎格里欧所捕获/捕食

    to triumph over 胜过,战胜

    to despair at his error 对他的错误感到绝望

    to mark the beginning of his struggle back to truth 标志着他转而为真理而斗争/努力追回真理的开始

    be comforted by Una 受到尤娜的抚慰

19. The process of his moral rebirth is concluded. 他的道德新生的过程结束了。

20. be ready to fight with 准备与……做斗争

    be ravishing the Eden of Una's parents 正在强夺尤娜父母的伊甸园

    fierce fighting 激烈/猛烈的战斗

    to rescue Una's parents 拯救尤娜的父母

    to end with a happy wedding between... with... 以……与……的婚礼结尾

    arms and the man 战争与男人

    fierce warres(= wars) and faithful loves 激烈的战争与忠贞的爱情

plains and forests and caves and castles and magic trees and springs　平原、森林、洞窟、城堡、魔树和泉水

dwarfs and giants and lions and pilgrims and magicians　侏儒、巨人、狮子、朝圣者和魔术师

21. The good people are subjects of the Faerie Queene and are called Faeries, who undergo the trials and tribulations men undergo in the ordinary world.　善良的人们都是仙后的臣民,被称为仙子,他们经受普通人在凡人世界所承受的煎熬和苦难。

　　＊ 句中 men undergo in the ordinary world 是 trials and tribulations 的定语从句,省略了在从句中作宾语的关系代词 which。

22. be told in a romantic, fantastic way in order to arouse wonder　以一种浪漫、幻想的方式进行讲述,旨在激起一种奇异/神秘之感

23. be often revealed to the reader by their names or by the short verse summaries at the beginning of each canto but not revealed to the hero until he has conquered them　（邪恶的东西)常常在每篇诗章的开头直接用名字或总结性的短诗向读者揭示,而对书中的主人公/英雄,则要等到他征服了这些邪恶之后才能将他揭示

24. to stand for abstract virtues or vices　代表抽象的美德或邪恶

25. The five main qualities of Spenser's poetry are :1) a perfect melody; 2) a rare sense of beauty; 3) a splendid imagination; 4) a lofty moral purity and seriousness; and 5) a dedicated idealism.　斯宾塞诗歌的五大特质是:1)完美的韵律;2)罕见的美感;3)瑰丽恢宏的想象;4)崇高的道德纯洁性和严肃性;5)忠诚的理想主义。

26. strange forms of speech　怪异的讲话方式

obsolete words　过时的老式词语

to increase the rustic effect　增强乡土/乡村气息

exquisite melody　精美的韵律

to make him known as "the poets' poet"　使他成为著名的"诗人中的诗人"

英语诗歌的格律、韵律与诗歌的理解和翻译

　　有人认为用普通英语的主、谓、宾、定、状、补及三类非谓语动词引导的短语那一套基本语法来解释英语诗歌,似乎有点不灵了。产生这种认识实际上是因为对诗歌结构变化的特点不太了解,了解了这些特点就会发现用基本语法解释英语诗歌还是管用的。

　　诗歌的创作是受格律和韵律限制的,为了表意和满足特定格律、韵律的需要,常常享有诗论中所说的诗歌特许权(poetic licence),即可以适当"忽视"语言规律。下面就是这种"忽视"的几种常见情况。

1. 为了符合节奏和格律而调整词序

She 'found/me' roots/of 're/lish 'sweet,　　　她为我找来美味的草根,

And 'ho/ney 'wild,/and 'man/na 'dew,　　　天赐的甘露和野地的蜂蜜。

And 'sure/in 'lang/uage 'strange/she 'said —　　她用奇异的语言说话——

"I 'love/thee 'true."　　　"想必我真的爱你!"

(约翰·济慈 John Keats《妖女无情》*La Bale Dame Sans Merci*)

第一行中的 sweet,第二行中的 wild 以及第三行中 strange 都是后置形容词,本应在三个被修饰的名词 relish, honey, language 前面,即 sweet relish, wild honey 和 strange language,现在放在三个名词后面是为了让第一行的第四音步,第二行的第二音步以及第三行的第三音步形成抑扬格,而与全诗的格律一致。明白了这一点,就不会因词序颠倒而理解不了诗句的含义。再如:

With ˈfingers/ˈweary and ˈworn,	手指磨破,疲惫不堪,
With ˈeyelids/ˈheavy and ˈred,	眼皮又红肿,抬不起来,
A ˈwoman ˈsat,/in unˈwomanly ˈrags,	女人穿着男式的破衣服,
ˈPlying her/ˈneedle and ˈthread —	坐在那里走线飞针——
ˈStitch! Stitch! ˈStitch!	忙着缝呀,缝呀,缝!

(托马斯・胡德 Thomas Hood《衬衫之歌》*The Song of The Shirt*)

这节诗没有采用固定格律,为了有节奏感,就把修饰 fingers 和 eyelids 的 weary and worn 和 heavy and red 放到诗行末尾,使得与三、四行的(un)womanly rags 和 needle and thread 节奏一致,都是扬抑抑扬格,产生和谐的感觉。

2. 为了符合节奏而增、减单词的音节数

例如雪莱在《致云雀》(*To a Skylark*)中写出了 Things more true/and deep,而不是 Things truer and deeper 这样更合语法的句子,就是因为 Things more ˈtrue 与上句第一音步的 Thou of ˈdeath 和下句第一音步的 Than we ˈmor/(tals)的扬抑抑扬格一致,而 Things ˈtruer 则是扬扬抑抑格,与它们不一致。原诗是:

ˈWaking ˈor/aˈsleep,	你无论醒时睡时,
ˈThou of ˈdeath/must ˈdeem	对于死的面目,
ˈThings more ˈtrue/and ˈdeep	一定比我们凡夫俗子,
ˈThan we ˈmor/tals ˈdream,	看得更深更透,
…	

3. 为了押韵而调整词序

a. 为押韵把动词不定式或动词从句移至行尾,下面是动词不定式移至行尾的例子,选自布莱克的《老虎》(*The Tyger*)第五节第三、四行:

ˈDid he/ˈsmile to/ˈsee his /ˈwork to ˈsee?	他可曾对自己的作品微笑?
Did he/who made the/ˈLamb make ˈthee?	莫不是他,羔羊的作者把你造?

前一句阴影部分的不定式短语移到句尾,就是为了使 see 与下句的 thee 押韵,同时又不违背原句 ˈDid he/ˈsmile to/ˈsee his ˈwork? 的格律,因为移动前后的句子都是三个音步,都是扬抑、扬抑、扬抑扬格。请看移动后的句子:ˈDid he/ˈsmile his/ˈwork to ˈsee?

b. 为押韵把祈使句中的动词或主谓语结构移至行尾,例如罗勃特・彭斯(Robert Burns)的《玛丽・莫里森》(*Mary Morison*)第一节开头三句:

O ˈMa/ry,be ˈat/thy ˈwin/dow ˈ be, [iː]	啊,玛丽,守候在窗口吧,
It is the wish'd, the trysted hour!	现在是我们祈盼的幽会良辰!
Let me see Those ˈsmiles/and ˈglan/ces ˈ let/me ˈsee, [iː]	让我看看你的笑容和眼神,

他把阴影部分的词语 be 和主谓语结构 let me see 移动到画线位置,移动的目的就是为了使一、三句押尾韵[iː]。如果不移动,window 与 glances 是不押韵的。

c. 为押韵把含情态动词的主谓语结构或现在分词移至行尾,例如:

I would fly ˈup to/ˈthee would/I ˈfly [ai]	现在我就飞到你的身旁

移动的目的是与本节最后两行的 high 和 sky 押尾韵,最后两行是:

ˈLift me,/ˈguide me,/ˈhigh and ˈhigh [ai]	激励我,指引我向上再向上,
To ˈthy/ˈbanquet/ting-place/in the ˈsky [ai]	直到你云天设宴的地方!

(威廉・华兹华斯 William Wordsworth《致云雀》*To a Skylark*,第二节)

再如:

I ˈsaw/her ˈsin/ging ˈat/her ˈwork,	我看她一边唱一边干活,
And ˈ bending ˈo'/er/the ˈsi/ckle ˈbending [endiŋ]	看她弯着腰挥动镰刀;

移动的目的是为了与本节第二行的 ending 押尾韵。本节共四行,前两行为:

What ·e'/er the ·theme/, the ·mai/den ·sang　　　　　不管这少女唱的是什么,

As ·if/her ·song/could ·have/no ·ending [endiŋ]　　　她的歌就像永远唱不完;

(华兹华斯《孤独的收割者》*The Solitary Reaper*)

d. 为押韵把前置的副词、形容词或句子的主语移至行尾,例如:

·Merrily,/·merrily/they ·mingle ·they [ei]

·Waken,/·lords and/·ladies ·gay [ei]

主语 they 移到行尾是为了与下句末尾的 gay 押韵。

e. 为押韵故意避开常见的规范用语,选择不常用的词或者常用词的不常见用法(在下文的诗歌解析中会有很多例子)。

4. 为押韵而调整发音

Should auld acquaintance be forgot,　　　　怎能忘记旧日朋友,

And never brought to min'? [ain]　　　　　心中能不怀想?

Should auld acquaintance be forgot,　　　　旧日朋友岂能相忘,

And auld lang syne? [ain]　　　　　　　　　友谊地久天长?

第二行末尾本来是 mind,为了与第四行 syne 押韵,略去了辅音[d],把 mind 变成了 min'。

　　上述这种种变通会给诗歌翻译者带来困难,不过在了解了这些之后,就可以把弄乱了的头绪理顺,进入基本语法的系统,就容易理解了。上面所述仅仅是部分例子。

埃德蒙·斯宾塞作品选读

《仙后》*The Faerie Queene* 第一卷第一章节选

词语解释和难句分析

1. 《仙后》是文艺复兴时期一部伟大的史诗,作者的主要创作意图是塑造一位完美的绅士典型,即具备了 12 种美德的绅士或贵族。全书分 12 卷,每一卷塑造一位英雄,代表一种美德。而贯穿全诗、代表全部 12 种美德的大英雄是亚瑟(Arthur),他的任务就是寻找仙后——贯穿全诗的另一位主人翁格劳丽安娜(Gloriana),他们已在梦境中坠入情网,最后也确实好梦成真。人们认为格劳丽安娜就是伊丽莎白一世女王的象征。12 位英雄就是从格劳丽安娜的宫殿中出发,奉旨踏上冒险的路程的。第一卷中的英雄是红十字骑士,历险的目的是从恶魔手中解救人类的祖先——尤娜的父母,尤娜是本卷的女主人公。第一卷故事的结尾是红十字骑士杀死恶龙,救出尤娜的父母,与尤娜举行婚礼。选段是红十字骑士出发踏上危险历程,战胜邪恶的一段经历。

1

2. 头四行实为一个完整的诗句:A Gentle knight was pricking on the plaine (= plain),/Ycladd (= clad = clothed) in mightie (= mighty) armes (= arms) and silver shielde (= shield),/Wherein old dints of deepe (= deep) wounds did remaine (= remain),/The cruell markes (= cruel marks) of many a bloudy fielde (= bloody field);意为:高贵的骑士正策马驰在平原上,他全身披挂,手持银盾,盾上仍留着深深的旧伤痕,那是多少次血腥残酷战斗的标志/标志着多少次血腥残酷的战斗;

* ycladd 引导一过去分词短语,作主语 a gentle knight 的后置定语;第三句是关系副词 wherein 引导的定语从句,修饰 silver shielde。第四句 The cruell markes of <u>many a</u> bloudy fielde,为 old dints 的同位

语,即 old dints = the cruell markes。

3. 第五句实际上可改写为：Yet till that time he did never wield（=used）the armes（=arms）. 意为：但这些武器他至今还未用过。

4. 第六句中 angry steede（=steed）意为愤怒的战马；chide his foming（=foaming）bitt 意为战马愤怒得直喷白沫（foaming with anger），疯狂地咬着马嚼子（grinding mouthpiece of the brittle），不可理解为责骂冒白沫的系缆桩。

5. 第七句是第六句的方式状语。As much disdayning（=disdaining，鄙视）to the curbe（=curb=mouthpiece）to yield. 可改写为：As if（the horse was）too proud to yield to the curb. 意为就仿佛这马太桀骜不驯而不受马勒的拘束,即不愿受主人的束缚。

6. 第八、第九句的结构类似第六、第七句,可改写为：He seemed fully jolly knight, and did sitt faire（=sit fairly）,/As if he was one for knightly giusts（=jousts,马背上的长矛格斗）and fitt fierce encounters. 意思很明白,可译为：他似乎是一个十分快乐的骑士,端坐在马上,好像一个要比武的骑士,迎战凶猛的对手。

2

7. 第一、二句诗可整理为：But on his brest（=breast）he bore a bloudie（=bloody）Crosse（=Cross）,/The deare（=dear）remembrance of his dying Lord（=Jesus）. 意为：然而,他胸前佩戴血十字徽章/这是他对濒临死亡的耶稣的珍贵记忆。第二句是前一句中 bloudie Crosse 的同位语。

8. 第三、第四句可改写为：For whose sweete（=sweet=Lord）sake, he wore that glorious badge,/And adored（=worshiped）him dead as living ever. 意为：为了亲爱的人（耶稣）,他戴着光荣的徽章/他崇敬着耶稣死亦永生。

9. 第五句可改写为：the like（=bloudie Crosse）was also scored upon his shield. 意为：他的盾牌上也留有同样的刻痕（前文中的血十字）。

10. 第六句中 which 指的是上句中的 the like,即 bloudie Cross。in his helpe（=help）意为在基督耶稣（Christ Jesus）的帮助下。此句可改写为：With the help of Christ, he had the bloudie Crosse for sovereign hope. 意为：他是在耶稣基督的帮助下才获得这标志最崇高希望的血十字的。

11. 第七、第八句是同一主语（he）、并列两谓语动词（was and did seeme）的一个分为两行的简单句,可改写为：He was right faithful true in deede（=deed）and word,/But he did seeme（=really seemed）too solemne and sad of his cheere（=cheer=countenance/expression）. 意为：他言行忠诚正直,但表情/面容却似乎过于庄严忧郁。

12. 第九句相对直白,可改写为：Yet he did dread nothing, but（=only/merely）was ever ydrad（=dreaded）. 意为：但他的确一无所惧,只是让别人胆寒。

3

13. 开头五行实为一个大复合句。第一行为主要句架,等于：He was bond upon a great adventure. 意为：他承担着一个冒险的壮举。两个 that 引导两个定语从句修饰 adventure。
That greatest Gloriana to him gave（=gave to him）,/That greatest Glorious Queene of Faerie Lond（=Land）,/To winne（=win）him worship, and her grace to have（=to have her grace）,/Which of all earthly things he most did crave（=he did crave most her grace of all earthly things）; 这是伟大的格劳丽安娜（伊丽莎白一世 Elizabeth I 的昵称）赋予的使命,也是仙国最伟大的光荣天后赢得他的崇敬、给予他恩宠的使命,是尘世万物中他最大的渴求。
＊注意,第四行的两个不定式短语可理解为第二个定语从句的谓语,这样就多出了两个 to,可理解为诗歌中常有的语法宽容；另外,这两个不定式的逻辑主语是不一致的,前者是仙后,后者是红十字骑士。第五行 which 引导的定语从句修饰 her grace,表示在尘世中她的恩宠就是他最大的渴求。

14. 第六句到第八句是一个完整的大句：And ever as he rode, his heart did earne（=earn=yearn）/ To

prove his puissance (= braveness/prowess) in battell (= battle) brave/Upon (in brave fight against) his foe (= enemy), and his new force to learne (= learn). 意为:当他骑马前行,他的心渴望在抗击敌人的战斗中证明自己的勇敢、无畏,证明他学习的潜力。

15. 第九句中 upon his foe = in battle upon his foe, foe 的同位语就是 a Dragon horrible and stearne(= stern). 可译为:抗击他的敌人———一个可怕而凶猛的恶龙。

4

16. A lovely lady rode him faire (= fair) beside,/Upon a lowly Asse (= Ass) more white then (= than) snow, 可改写为:A lovely Lady rode beside him faire/Upon a lowly Asse more white then snow. 可直译为:一位可爱的女士骑着一头比雪还白的温驯的白驴,彬彬有礼地伴他同行。

17. Yet she much whiter = Yet she was much whiter (than the Asse), 意为:而她本人更白。后面的 but the same did hide /Under a vele = the same white face did hide under a veil,意为:同样白的脸藏在面纱后面。that wimpled was full low = that was plaited in folds and falling to cover her face, 是 vele 的定语从句,意为:面纱带着褶皱低垂着覆盖了她的脸。

18. And over all a blacke (= black) stole she did throw,/As one that inly mourned: so was she sad,/And heavie sat upon her palfrey slow (= a saddle horse); = And she did throw a blacke stole over all,/As one who was sorrowful at heart, indeed she was,/And sat upon her slow palfrey; 她又用一条黑披巾蒙住全身,/就像一个心怀哀思的人,的确非常忧伤,/她坐在缓慢的坐骑上,神思沉郁。

19. Seemed in heart some hidden care she had,/And by her in a line a milke (= milky) white lambe (= lamb) she lad (= led). = It seemed that she had some hidden care in heart,/And by her she lad a milke white lambe in a line. 似乎她内心隐藏着某种关切,身边还用绳子牵着一只乳白色的小羊羔。

5

20. So pure an innocent, as that same lambe,/She was in life and every virtuous lore,... = She was so pure an innocent, as that same lambe (= lamb = the Lamb of God = Jesus Christ),/in life and every virtuous (= virtuous) lore,... 在生活里和每一个关于美德的传说中,她都像那只上帝的羔羊,纯洁无瑕。

21. 第三、四两句与第二句是同一主语,即 she。
And by descent from Royall (= Royal) lynage (= lineage)came/Of ancient Kings and Queenes (= Queens), that had of yore (= in the old days)/Their scepters stretcht from East to Westerne shore,/And all the world in their subjection held; = By descent she came from Royall lynage /of ancient Kings and Queenes, that had of yore/their scepters stretch from East to Westerne shore,/and held all the world in their subjection; 血缘上她为王室后裔,是国王与王后的后代,他们往日的权势横跨东西海岸,全世界都在他们的统治之下。

* 句中 that 引导的是非限制性定语从句,修饰 Kings and Queenes。

22. Till that infernall (= infernal) feend (= fiend) with foule(= foul) uprore (= uproar)/Forwasted all their land, and them expeld (= expelled):/Whom to avenge, she had this knight from far compeld (= compelled). = Till that infernal fiend with foul uproar/Forwasted all their land, and expelled them:/Whom to avenge, she had this knight compelled from far. 直到那可怕的恶魔肆虐喧器,践踏蹂躏他们的全部国土,并将他们赶走。为了给他们报仇,她执意请来了这位远方的骑士。

* infernal fiend 可怕的恶魔;foul uproar 邪恶下流的喧器/骚动;forwaste = devastate 摧毁、蹂躏;to avenge sb. 为了给某人报仇;whom to avenge = to avenge Kings and Queenes 为了给国王和王后报仇;to have sb. compelled 执意/坚持请来/招来某人

6

23. 从第一行的 Behind 到第四行的 at his back 是一个完整的复合句:Behind her farre (= far) away a

Dwarfe（=Dwarf）did lag,/That lasie（=lazy）seemed in being ever last,/Or wearied（=tired）with bearing of her bag/Of needments（=necessities）at his backe（=back）. = A Dwarf did lag far away behind her/That seemed lazy in being ever last,/Or wearied with bearing of her bag/Of necessities（生活必需品）at his back. 其中 that 引导的定语从句修饰 Dwarf。此句可直译为：一个侏儒远远地落在她身后，似乎因总在后面而索性懒洋洋的，或者因背上背着个衣物袋而疲惫不堪。

24. 从第四行后半部的 Thus as they past 到最后一行结束,实际上是一个大复合句,其中有一连串隐藏的短语,语序颠倒了。例如：be overcast with 被……所遮盖/笼罩；to pour an hideous storme of raine into... 把可怕的暴风雨倾注到……之中；to constrain to shrowd 被迫躲避/隐藏；so fast that... 如此迅疾以致……；be eke fain to shroud 也很高兴地躲避之中, 等等。此句可整理成正常语序: Thus as they past,/The day was suddeine（=sudden）overcast with cloudes（=clouds）,/And angry Jove（=Jupiter）did poure（=pour）an hideous storme of raine（=storm of rain）/Into his Lamans（=sweetheart's）lap so fast/That every wight did constrain to shrowd（=shroud）it,/And this faire（=fair）couple were eke（=also）fain（=glad）to shroud themselves. 可直译为：当他们这样行进时,白昼突然被乌云笼罩,愤怒的朱庇特把可怕的暴风雨倾注到他爱人的怀中,如此迅猛,以致每一个生灵都被迫隐藏躲起来避(它),这一对美丽人儿也乐意顺天应势,躲避起来。

7

25. 前三句可以改写为：Enforst（v. = go into a forest）to seeke（=seek）some covert nigh（ad. = nearby）at hand,/They spide（= spied, spy 的过去式）a shadie grove not far away,/That promist（= promised）ayde（= aid）to withstand the tempest. 这样就比较容易理解,可直译为：他们走进树林欲就近寻一个隐蔽之处,结果发现不远处的一片树荫(可提供帮助),助他们抵御风雨。
    * 注意 that 是关系代词,指代 shadie grove,引导一非限制性定语从句。

26. 第四、五、六句总体上是个非限制性定语从句,修饰 shadie grove。
    Whose loftie trees yclad（= clad = clothed）with sommers pride,/Did spred（= spread）so broad, that heavens light did hide,/Not perceable（= unperceable）with power of any starre（= star）. 其中,yclad with... 为过去分词短语作定语,修饰 loftie trees,spred 是 loftie trees 的谓语动词；另外,形容词性短语 not perceable with 不可被穿透,是 loftie trees 的定语短语。此句可直译为：林中高大的树木披着夏日的骄傲,树荫广被,致使天光被挡,连星星也没有能力穿透。

27. And all within were pathes and alleies（= alleys）wide,/With footing worne（= worn）, and leading inward farre（= far）:/Faire（= fair）harbour that them seemes; so in they entered arre（= there）. = And within all were wide pathes and alleies,/With footing worne, and leading inward farre:/That seems to them to be faire harbour; and so they entered arre. 第七行是个倒装句,all within... 实际上是 wide pathes and alleies were within all,意为在浓密树荫下有……；第八句中 with 结构与 leading 分词短语都是 wide paths and alleies 的定语；That seems ... 从句是个定语从句,that 指的是 all, 即"树荫",faire harbour = fair shelter。整体可译为：浓荫下,有宽宽的路径和小道,行旅不断走过,远远通向树荫深处;树荫对他们而言似乎是宁静港湾,于是他们走了进去。

参考译文——姚绍德

仙后(节选)

1

一位高贵的骑士正策马在平原上驱驰,
他全副武装,手持银盾,
银盾上残留着许多凹陷的旧伤痕,
标志着往日许多血腥残酷的战斗,
但这些武器他至今还未曾用过;
他愤怒的战马猛咬马勒直喷白沫,
太桀骜、太傲慢,不服马勒的管束;
他似乎是十分快乐的骑士,端坐马上,
像一个要比武的骑士,迎战凶猛的对手。

2

然而,他胸前佩戴着一个血十字,
这是他对将死的耶稣的珍贵记忆,
就为了耶稣——亲爱的人,他戴上那光荣的徽章,
崇敬耶稣虽死犹生:
他盾牌上也同样有血十字刻痕,
耶稣的帮助使他得到这代表最高希望的标记:
他忠诚正直,言行一致,
但他的表情却太过严肃和忧郁;
他无所畏惧,却令人畏惧。

3

他承担着一个冒险的壮举,
这是最伟大的格劳丽安娜赋予他的使命,
这是仙国最伟大的光荣之后
赢得他的崇拜、给予他恩典的使命,
这恩典是他在尘世万物中的最大渴望;
当他纵马疾驰时,他内心希望
在抗击敌人的战斗中
证明他的勇敢、无畏和学习的潜力;
他将去抗击他的敌人——一头可怕而凶猛的恶龙。

4

一位可爱的女士彬彬有礼地伴他同行,
骑着一头比雪还白的温驯的白驴,
而她本人更白,但她雪白的脸却藏在
面纱之后,而面纱带着折皱垂下盖住她的脸,
她又用一条黑披肩蒙住全身,

像一个心怀哀思的人,的确十分忧伤,
稳坐在温驯的白驴上缓缓前行;
她内心似乎隐藏着关切,
身边还牵着一头乳白色的小羊羔。

5

在生活里和每一个关于美德的传说中,
她都是那样纯洁无瑕,就像那只上帝的羊羔;
血缘上她为皇室的后裔,
是老国王与王后的子孙;
他们往昔的权势曾横贯东西海岸,
把整个世界都纳入他们的治下;
直到那可怕的恶魔邪恶地喧嚣,
肆意践踏他们的全部国土,将他们赶走,
为了给他们报仇,她执意请来这远方的骑士。

6

一个侏儒远远地落在她身后,
似乎因为总是落后,他索性懒洋洋的,
或是因为背上背着一袋衣物,
已经十分疲惫。当他们这样走过,
白昼突然被乌云笼罩,
愤怒的朱庇特将一场可怕的暴风雨
迅猛地倾注到他大地爱人的怀中,
每个人都被迫找地方躲避,
这漂亮的一对人儿也很高兴地隐蔽他们自己。

7

他们走进森林,想就近找个隐蔽之处,
发现不远处的一片树林有浓密树荫,
可以让他们藏身,帮他们抵挡暴风雨;
那些高高的大树披着夏日的骄傲,
绿荫广被,可挡天上日光,
连星星也都没有能力穿透;
浓荫下有宽宽的路径,
曾被行人踩踏,通向远远的深处;
那里对他们而言似乎是平静的港湾,于是他们向深处走去。

主要内容归纳和总结

1. 埃德蒙·斯宾塞出生在英国伦敦,少年时先受教于泰勒商人学校(Merchant Taylor's School),后就读于剑桥彭布罗克(Pembroke)学院。离校后他去了英格兰北部,结识了恋人罗莎琳(Rosalind),罗莎琳的早逝所加之于他的深节哀痛,在他的《牧人日记》(*The Shepheardes Calender*)中得到体现。他曾经为女王在爱尔兰的代理威尔顿(Wilton)的格莱勋爵做私人秘书十多年,获得了巨大财富,且拥吉尔卡尔曼(Kilcolman)城堡。1598年的一次爱尔兰叛乱使他肝胆俱裂,逃回英格兰,死于伦敦威斯特敏斯特的一个小酒馆里。据本·约翰所说,最终他死于饥饿(for want of bread),后来葬于威斯特敏斯特教堂他的导师乔叟(Chaucer)的墓旁。

斯宾塞的诗歌有五大特质:1)完美的韵律(a perfect melody);2)罕见的美感(a rare sense of beauty);3)恢宏的想象(a splendid imagination);4)崇高的道德纯洁性和严肃性(a lofty moral purity and seriousness);5)一种为之献身的理想主义(a dedicated idealism)。精美优雅的诗文韵律使他成为诗人中的诗人(the poets' poet)。

2. 埃德蒙·斯宾塞的主要作品:

《牧人日记》*The Shepheardes Calendar* (1579)

《情诗集》*Amoretti* (1595)包含89首诗

《婚礼喜歌》*Epithalamion*

《仙后》*The Faerie Queene*

重要信息句子

1. It is Spenser's idealism, his love of beauty, and his exquisite melody that make him known as "the poet's poet".

2. Spenser's masterpiece is *The Faerie Queene*, a great poem of its age.

诗歌艺术欣赏

1. 格律和韵律的基本知识

诗歌的美是因为它有乐感。诗人是通过节奏(rhythm)和韵律(尤其是尾韵规律)来体现诗歌的乐感的。节奏,又叫格律,通过音节数以及重读音节和非重读音节的巧妙安排来实现;韵律则通过同一声音的规律性重复来实现。

语言不同,诗歌的乐感也不同。中文诗歌的乐感主要由单词的声调(平仄)来体现,希腊诗歌和拉丁诗歌的乐感主要由单词声音的长短来体现,英语诗歌的乐感则主要由单词声音的强弱来体现。就英语诗而言,所谓格律就是指重读音节和非重读音节合理有序地按一定的音节数目出现的规律。轻重音节出现的次序搭配合理,就会产生节奏,就有乐感。由两个或多个音节组成一个轻重音节的搭配,就叫一个"格"或者"音步"(meter/foot/measure)。通常,一首英语诗歌中有多个诗节(stanza),一个诗节有若干诗行,而每一诗行又分多个格或音步。格就是轻重节奏。

格的类型很多,但最常用的只四种,叫基调格。1)抑扬格(iambus)包含两个音节,前轻后重,例如 de'cay, at 'night;2)扬抑格(trochaics)包含两个音节,前重后轻,例如 'tiger, 'driver, 'perfect;3)抑抑扬格(anapest)包含三个音节,轻轻重搭配,例如 at the 'foot, volun'teer, in the 'field;4)扬抑抑格(dactylic)包含三个音节,重轻轻搭配,例如 'circumstance, 'desperate, 'think of it。另外还有难得一见的非基调格,就不多做介绍了。

每一诗行都会有几个这样的轻重节奏,即有几个"格"、几个"音步"。格的类型和诗行的格数或音步数,就决定了诗歌的格律,如三(音)步抑扬格(iambic trimeter),五(音)步抑扬格(iambic pentameter),四(音)步扬抑格(trochaic tetrameter)等。下面是一首罗勃特·赫里克(Robert Herrick)的三步抑扬格的诗《致伊莱克特拉》(*To Electra*):

I 'dare/not 'ask/a 'kiss,　　　　　　我不敢奢望你一吻,

I 'dare/not 'beg/a 'smile,　　　　　　我不敢乞求你一笑,

Lest ·hav/ing ·that,/or ·this,	生怕得到你一吻或一笑,
I ·might/grow ·proud/the ·while.	我就会变得骄傲。

·No, ·no,/the ·ut/most ·share	不,不,最可能实现的
Of my/de·sire/shall ·be	我的愿望——
·Only/to ·kiss/that ·air	只是亲吻那空气,
That ·late/ly ·kiss/ēd ·thee.	那空气定会吻到你。

诗中标注"·"的为重音节,未标注的为轻音节,可以看出除第二节头三行的第一音步分别为扬扬格、抑抑格和扬抑格,其余的所有音步都是抑扬格,所以总体上,这首诗为抑扬格。又每诗行都含三个音步,故此诗为三步抑扬格。值得注意的是最后一行中的 kissed,本来是不应当用过去式的,而现在不仅加了 ed 而且还加了上划线,就是要在这里补一个轻音节。ed 本来不发音,加个上划线要求 e 发[i]音,从而增加一个音节,使这个音步有了轻重两个音节,形成一个完整的抑扬格。<u>为了符合格律而增加或减少音节,甚至违背语法常规都是常有的事</u>。

再谈英语诗歌的韵,也就是英语格律诗的韵——自由诗是没有严格的格律和韵律的。英语诗歌的韵在学术专著上是非常全面、颇为复杂的。我们只介绍两种,即行内韵(internal rhyme)和尾韵(end rhyme),其中尾韵是运用最广的韵。

a. 行内韵指押韵的单词出现在同一诗行内,分为头韵(alliteration)和里奥韵(Leo rhyme)。

古英语史诗《贝奥武夫》(Beowulf)用的就是头韵。请看英语国家训练儿童发音的顺口溜中展示的头韵:

Betty Botter brought some butter,	贝蒂·巴特带来一些黄油,
But, she said, the butter's bitter;	但她说黄油是苦的;
If I put it in my batter,	假如放在我的蛋奶糊里,
It will make my batter bitter,	它会使我的蛋奶糊变苦
But a bit of better butter,	但是加一点好黄油,
That would make my batter better.	就会使我的蛋奶糊不苦。

同一诗行内两个或多个同一辅音字母开头的单词所押的韵,称为头韵。在这首诗中,画线单词都是以辅音字母 b 开头、发[b]音的单词,押的即是头韵。

里奥韵是由 12 世纪巴黎圣维多克大教堂的神职人员里奥(Leo)在拉丁文诗作中首创的。其诗行内都有两个意群,意群之间不留空白,前一意群末尾的词与后一意群末尾的词押韵,这种语言共鸣现象,即是里奥韵。下面是雪莱的诗作《云》(The Cloud)的第三节,单数行以里奥韵入诗,双数行以尾韵入诗。诗句中画线部分押里奥韵,阴影部分押尾韵。

I bring fresh showers for the thirsting flowers,	我为干渴的花朵送去甘霖,
From the seas and streams;	从海洋与河流;
I bear light shade for the leaves when laid	我给绿叶带来凉爽的庇荫,
In their noonday dreams.	当它们做午梦的时候。

From my wings are shaken the dews that waken	我的翅膀摇落滴滴水珠,
The sweet buds every one,	洒醒每一颗蓓蕾,
When rocked to rest on their mother's breast,	当它们的母亲向着太阳跳舞,
As she dances about the sun.	它们在她怀里安睡。

I wield the flail of the lashing hail,	我挥动猛烈冰雹的打禾棒,
And whiten the green plains under,	给底下的绿野涂上白粉;

And then <u>again</u> I dissolve it in <u>rain</u>,　　　　　　　然后再用雨水把它洗光，

And laugh as I pass in <u>thunder</u>.　　　　　　　　　　我还一路响着轰雷般的笑声。

b. 尾韵是英语格律诗中最普遍采用的押韵方式（韵式，rhymed pattern），也是学习的重点。尾韵种类很多，但我们只需抓住一点，即所谓尾韵就是诗行末尾押的韵，即诗行末尾单词倒数第一、第二或第三个元音（vowel sound）相同，元音后的发音也相同，而各自前面的辅音（含三种情况）不同，如 pot/not（只含一个元音节，押阳韵）；bacon/taken，sodium/podium（两、三个元音节，押阴韵），这就是完美韵（perfect rhyme），或满韵（full rhyme）、真韵（true rhyme）。这方面涵盖的内容很多，我们只需知道这种元音鉴定法就可以解决问题了。

格律诗的押韵方式通常用 abcd…来标示。尾韵相同的诗行，用相同的字母表示，不押韵的用不同的字母表示；或者标示在行尾，右侧竖排，或者标示在诗的末行下方，排成横列。以威廉·布莱克（William Blake）的名作《老虎》（*The Tyger*）的第二节为例：

In what distant deeps or sk<u>ies</u>［aiz］　　　　　a

Burnt the fire of thine <u>eyes</u>?［aiz］　　　　　a

On what wings dare he asp<u>ire</u>?［aiə］　　　　b

What the hand, dare seize the f<u>ire</u>?［aiə］　　　b

（韵式为 aabb）

现在结合实际，来判断一下刚刚学习的《仙后》选段用的是什么韵式。虽然它有 7 个诗节，但各节的韵式基本相同，我们只取第一节每个诗行的最后一个单词来标示即可代表：plaine/shielde/remaine/fielde/wield/bitt/yield/sitt/fitt，根据前述的元间鉴定法，韵式为：ababbcbcc。这是斯宾塞诗体的规定韵式。

所谓诗体（style of a poem）即诗人在长期创作中形成的具有固定格式的诗歌形式，对诗行、音节、格律和韵律都有固定的要求。如斯宾塞诗体（Spenserian style）的要求是：九行诗节，前八句为五步抑扬格（iambic pentameter），第九句为六步抑扬格（iambic hexameter），韵式为前述的 ababbcbcc；另外还有乔叟（Geoffrey Chaucer）的七行诗体（septet），采用五步抑扬格，韵式为 ababbcc。他在《由怨生悔》（*Complaint unto Pity*）一诗中第一次中运用此诗体。

诗体中特别著名的有英雄偶句体（heroic couplet），其特点是：1）诗行数为偶数；2）两行为一个单元；3）奇数行与偶数行押韵；4）韵式为 aabbcc…。只要符合这几个条件，行数是不限的。所谓英雄体，即史诗体，这种押韵双行诗体或者说对句体，常被史诗用来描写英雄、骑士，故而又称英雄押韵双行诗体或英雄偶句体。在英语诗歌的创作中首先采用这种诗体的是乔叟，他的《坎特伯雷故事集》（*The Canterbury Tales*），用的就是英雄偶句体。该书是一群朝圣者在骑马去坎特伯雷大教堂朝圣的路上，互相讲的故事的汇编，所以这种诗体又叫骑马韵体（riding rhyme）。后来拜伦（Byron）、济慈（Keats）、雪莱（Shelley）和莎士比亚（Shakespeare）都常用这种诗体形式。济慈的《恩底弥翁》（*Endymion*）竟长达 4040 行。十四行诗（sonnet）也是英诗中著名的诗体。莎士比亚、怀亚特（Wyatt）、斯宾塞（Spenser）以及意大利彼特拉克（Petrarch）都有自己独特形式的十四行诗。人们常常只想到莎翁是伟大的剧作家，殊不知他还是个创作了 154 首十四行诗的大诗人。

2. 格律分析

格律分析（scansion）即音步分析、节奏分析，也即轻重音节的类型和数量分析。在学术专著中，这一部分会讲得很详细，这里只概括地讲几条实用的大原则。

a. 确定一首诗有多少音节，多少音步（多少重音和非重音组合），哪一种格律类型占多数，是主要类型（基调格是什么）。譬如，是抑扬格还是扬抑格？占多数的格再加上诗行的音步数就是这首诗的格律类型。如莎翁的诗多用五步抑扬格（iambic pentameter），即每一行诗由 5 个音步、5 个轻重音节组合，每个音步或多数音步都是前轻后重两个音节。

b. 格律诗的格律虽有规则，但并非一成不变，有时，会因表意、押韵等的需要，做一些变格。进行节奏分析时，切勿机械教条。例如，兰德（Landor）的这首诗的第一节：

·Mother, /I ·can/not ·mind/my ·wheel;	母亲,我已意识不到我的生命之轮;
My ·fin/gers ·ach, /my ·lips/are ·dry;	我的手指疼呀,我的唇又干;
O, ·if/you ·felt/the ·pain/I ·feel!	啊,你可感受到我的痛苦!
But ·O,/who e/ver ·felt/as ·I?	但是啊,谁又会与我同感?

可以看出,除第一行第一音步为扬抑格外,其他所有的音步都是抑扬格。第一行第一音步的变格不影响整首诗为四步抑扬格。

又如威廉·布莱克的《老虎》,全诗共6节,每节4行,每行3个音步,共72个音步,其中33个音步是扬抑格,占多数,是基调格;39个音步是多种不同的其他格。分析该诗的第一节,也可看出同样的道理:

·Tyger! /·Tyger! /·burning ·bright	七音节三音步
·In the/·forests/of the ·night,	七音节三音步
·What im/·mortal/·hand or eye	七音节三音步
Could ·frame/thy ·fearful/·symmetry?	八音节三音步

第一节共12个音步,6个非阴影的音步为扬抑格音步,其余为扬抑扬格2个,抑抑扬格1个,扬抑抑格1个,抑扬抑格1个,抑扬格1个,那么这个诗节的格律为扬抑格。按严格的格律规则,抑扬格或扬抑格诗歌,三音步应为6音节,而现在出现了3个七音节,1个八音节,这都是表意的需要,不影响按多数原则确定基调格为扬抑格。

另外还有缺音节而硬加个音节,甚至不惜违背语法规则的情况,前面举例过的罗勃特·赫里克的三步抑扬格诗《致伊莱克特拉》的最后两句中就有这种情况:

·Only/to ·kiss/that ·air

That ·late/ly ·kiss/ed ·thee.

其中 ed 就是硬加上的一个非重读音节,好与 thee 构成一个抑扬格,从语法上看是错误的。因为"只是想吻吻空气,那空气定会亲吻到你",想象中的"将来亲吻"怎么可能用过去式呢?

c. 格律分析的基本单元是音节的划分,大多情况下单词的重读音节就是诗行中的重读音节,因此节奏分析中音节划分是非常重要的。

所有的元音都是成节音,无论是单元音还是双元音(如[ai],[ei],[ou])都按一个音节算,三元音(如[aiə],[auə])在以往的诗歌中,有时当作一个音节,有时当作两个音节。

复合辅音也是成节音,例如 [vn],[sn],[bl],[dl],[gl],[kl],[pl],[tl] 等在单词中都可算一个音节,但在英语诗歌格律中也与三元音的情况一样,有不同的算法。

3.《仙后》(*The Faerie Queene*)选段的格律分析

以第一、第二诗节为例进行行律分析(重音符号"·";非重音符号"ˆ"):

1

A ·Gen/tle ·Knight/was ·prick/ing on/the ·plaine,	ˆ/ˆ·/ˆ·/ˆ·/ˆˆ/ˆ
Y·cladd/in ·migh/tie ·armes/and ·sil/ver ·shielde,	ˆ/ˆ·/ˆ·/ˆ·/ˆ·/ˆ
·Wherein /old ·dints /of ·deepe/wounds ·did/re·maine,	·ˆ/ˆ·/ˆ·/ˆˆ/ˆ·/ˆ
The ·cru/ell ·markes/of ·many a/·blou/dy ·fielde;	ˆ·/ˆ·/ˆˆ/ˆ·/ˆ·/ˆ
Yet ·armes/till ·that/time ·did/he ·ne/ver ·wield:	ˆ·/ˆ·/ˆ·/ˆ·/ˆ·/ˆ
His ·ang/ry ·steede/did ·chide/his ·fo/ming ·bitt,	ˆ·/ˆ·/ˆ·/ˆ·/ˆ·/ˆ
As ·much/dis·dain/ing to/the ·curbe/to ·yield;	ˆ·/ˆ·/ˆˆ/ˆ·/ˆ·/ˆ
·Full ·jol/ly ·knight/he ·seemed/, and ·faire/did ·sitt,	··/ˆ·/ˆ·/ˆ·/ˆ·/ˆ
As ·one/for ·knight/ly ·giusts/and ·fierce/en·coun/ters ·fitt.	ˆ·/ˆ·/ˆ·/ˆ·/ˆ·/ˆ·/ˆ

2

·But on/his ·brest/a ·blou/die ·Crosse/he ·bore,	ˆ·/ˆ·/ˆ·/ˆ·/ˆ·/ˆ

The ·deare/re·mem/brance of/his ·dy/ing ·Lord,	^·/^·/^^/^·/^·
For ·whose/sweete ·sake/that ·glor/ious ·badge/he ·wore,	^·/^·/^·/^·/^·
And ·dead/as ·li/ving ·e/ver him/a·dored:	^·/^·/^·/^·/^·
U·pon/his ·shield/the ·like/was ·al/so ·scored,	^·/^·/^·/^·/^^
For ·sove/raine ·hope,/ which in/his ·helpe/he ·had:	^·/^·/·^/^·/^·
Right ·faith/ful ·true/he ·was/in ·deede/and ·word,	^·/^·/^·/^·/^·
·But of/his ·cheere/did ·seeme/too ·so/lemne ·sad;	·^/^·/^·/^·/^·
Yet ·no/thing ·did/he ·dread/, but ·e/ver ·was/y·drad.	^·/^·/^·/^·/^·/^·.

诗行中的阴影部分是变格(抑抑格和扬扬格,不符合基调格抑扬格,故称为变格),但绝大多数的音步都是抑扬格,而且,前8行为五步抑扬格,第九行为六步抑扬格。它的韵律前面已分析过,为ababbcbcc。这正是斯宾塞九行诗体所要求的。

Ⅱ. 克里斯托弗·马洛 Christopher Marlowe (1564~1593)

词语解释和难句分析

1. King's School   王室学校
   during one's stay at Cambridge   在剑桥大学就读期间

2. one's career as a man of letters got started   某人做文学家的生涯开始了
   to turn out to be a sweeping success on the stage   结果在舞台上取得全面成功/大获成功
   be surging with the ideals of the Renaissance   为文艺复兴的理想而思潮激荡,受到文艺复兴思想的极大影响

3. to find expression in   体现在……中,在……中得到了体现/表现

4. Marlowe had also the unbridled passion and the conceit of a young man who had just entered the realms of knowledge.   马洛还具有放荡不羁的激情和刚进入知识王国的青年常有的自负。
   * who had just entered the realms of knowledge 是 young man 的定语从句。

5. to lead a tempestuous life   经历/过着疾风骤雨般的生活
   be killed in a quarrel over a tavern bill   在一次小酒馆付账问题引发的口角中械斗被杀

6. the most gifted of the "University Wits"   "大学才子"中最有才华的佼佼者
   * 所谓"大学才子",是对莎士比亚之前英国人文主义剧作家的总称。

7. an ambitious and pitiless Tartar conqueror who rose from a shepherd to an overpowering king   一个从牧羊人成长为权势熏天的国王的野心勃勃、残暴无情的鞑靼征服者
   to flout the given order   藐视既定的规则、秩序
   to trample on despairing princes   践踏蹂躏/粗暴对待陷入绝境的王公贵族

8. Tamburlaine displayed a high-aspiring mind that was... moral existence.   帖木儿展示了抱负很大的野心,这野心是自发产生、带有不受道德约束的放纵的情欲和梦想。
   * 注意句中短语 high-aspiring mind, self-created and carried by love and dream 和 beyond the limits of moral existence 的含义和用法。

9. a triumph of immense natural energy and of ruthlessness over equally cruel but weak and decadent brutal force   巨大的自然力和残暴手段对同样残暴但软弱颓废的野蛮力量的胜利

to depict a great hero with high ambition and sheer brutal force   描述了一个雄心勃勃、绝对野蛮暴力的大枭雄

to voice the supreme desire of the man of the Renaissance for infinite power and authority   表达了文艺复兴时期人们对无穷力量和无限权力的至高欲望

10. In fact, Tamburlaine is a product of Marlowe's characteristically Renaissance imagination, fascinated by the earthly magnificence available to men of imaginative power who have the energy of their convictions. 事实上，帖木儿为那具有坚定信仰和丰富想象力的人才会获得的尘世辉煌所吸引和迷惑，是马洛典型的文艺复兴时期想象力产生的人物形象。

　　* 注意画线词语的译法。

11. the German legend of a magician aspiring for knowledge   关于一个魔法师渴求知识的德国传奇故事
    to meet his tragic end   落得个悲剧下场

12. The play's dominant moral is human rather than religious.   该剧的主导精神是人文的而不是宗教的。

13. to celebrate the human passion for knowledge, power and happiness.   赞颂人对知识、力量和快乐的欲望
    to reveal man's frustration in realizing the high aspirations in a hostile moral order   揭示人在严酷的不利道德秩序中实现高远志向所遭遇的挫折/付出的代价

14. The confinement to time is the cruelest fact of man's conditions.   人生/时光有限是人类面临的最严酷的事实。

15. to lie in   在于
    to perfect the blank verse   完善无韵诗
    to make the blank verse the principal medium of English drama   使无韵诗成为英国戏剧的主要媒介
    be rather inflexible and can produce merely exotic effects   比较僵化死板，只能产生舶来品/异国情调的效果
    to bring vitality and grandeur into the blank verse with his "mighty lines", which carry strong emotions 用激情澎湃的豪迈诗句把勃勃生机和雄浑壮阔注入无韵诗中
    to employ hyperbole as his major figure of speech   采用夸张作为主要修辞手段
    instead of referring to the exaggeration of the language   不是指语言的夸张
    the poetic energy and intensity conveyed through the verse   用诗韵所表达/传达的诗的活力和强度

16. individualistic and full of ambition   利己主义和野心勃勃的
    to face bravely the challenge from both gods and men   勇敢面对来自神和人两方面的挑战
    to embody Marlowe's humanistic ideal of human dignity and capacity   体现了马洛肯定人的尊严、人的能力的人文主义理想
    to seek the way to heaven through salvation and God's will   通过灵魂救赎/超脱和上帝意志而寻求升入天堂之路
    be against conventional morality   反对传统道德
    to contrive to obtain heaven on earth through his own efforts   通过自身努力设法获得尘世的天堂
    the endless aspiration for power, knowledge, and glory   对力量、知识和荣耀的无限渴求
    to interpret the true Renaissance spirit   诠释/体现真正的人文精神
    to find consummate happiness in subduing other kingdoms   在征服其他王国的过程中找到完美无缺的快乐
    to admit his limitations of achievements, and even his limitations as a human being   承认他成就的有限性，甚至承认他作为一个人的局限性

17. In portraying Faustus, ... and trust in Devil.   在描写浮士德的时候，作为一个更善于反思的、更富

于哲理性的人,马洛在赞颂他高涨的求知欲的同时,也告诫人们不要犯傲慢的过错,因为浮士德的堕落正是由他对上帝的绝望和对魔鬼的信任引起的

＊ a more introspective and philosophical figure = as a more introspective and philosophical figure,是主句主语 Marlowe 的同位语,不是浮士德的同位语。

his soaring aspiration for knowledge   他高昂的求知欲

to <u>warn against</u> the sin of pride   告诫人们不要犯傲慢的过错

be caused by his despair in God and trust in Devil   ……是由他对上帝的绝望和对魔鬼的信任引起的

18. be <u>masterful in</u> handling blank verse and creation dramatic effects   技巧娴熟地处理无韵诗和创造戏剧效果

to raise him to an eminence as the pioneer of English drama   把他提升到英国戏剧先驱/开拓者的崇高地位

克里斯托弗·马洛作品选读

1.《浮士德博士的悲剧》*Dr. Faustus* 第一幕第三场

词语解释和难句分析

1. 本来这是一个古老的日耳曼传奇故事,马洛将它重新架构而成为英国文艺复兴时期的戏剧名著。学者浮士德渴望得到各种知识,最后结交非人,与魔鬼的仆人梅菲斯特(Mephistophilis)签下协议,将灵魂卖给魔鬼,换来魔鬼的魔法使用权 24 年。结果魔法虽成,他自己却经历了激烈的灵魂煎熬。下面的选段为第一幕第三场,即他与魔鬼签协议的场景。

2. to have a strong desire to acquire all kinds of knowledge   对获得各种知识有着强烈的欲望

   be <u>bored of</u> his present study on the academic curriculum   对他目前学术研究的课题感到厌烦

   to turn to <u>black magic</u>   转而研究魔法/巫术

3. By conjuration he calls up Mephistophilis, the Devil's servant.   他用咒语招来了魔鬼的仆人梅菲斯特。

4. Faustus makes a bond to sell his soul to the Devil <u>in return for</u> twenty-four years of life in which he may have the services of Mephistophilis to give him everything he desires.   浮士德签下协议,把灵魂出卖给魔鬼,以换得在 24 年的时间里梅菲斯特必须服务于他,满足他的各种欲望。

   ＊ 此句中的关键在于定语从句 in which he may have... 是修饰 twenty-four years of life 的。其中 in return for 意为以……作为回报,换回……。

5. to <u>bring</u> his magical art <u>into full play</u>   使他的魔法得到充分发挥,把他的魔法施展得淋漓尽致

6. Meanwhile Faustus has experienced much internal conflict, symbolized in the appearance of both Good Angel and Bad Angel.   同时,浮士德经历了许多内心的思想冲突,这是通过善天使与恶天使同时出场的方式来表现/体现的。

   ＊ symbolized 引导的过去分词短语是修饰前面整个句子的定语,相当于 which is symbolized in...。

7. In the final scene, there remains only the terrifying soliloquy(=monologue) in which the anguish of the hero's mind is poignantly expressed.   在最后一幕中,只剩下可怕的自言自语式独白,把主人公痛苦的思想透彻地表达出来。

   ＊ in which = in the soliloquy,注意它引导的定语从句用来修饰 soliloquy。

8. Enter Faustus to conjure.   浮士德上场作法。

9. Now that the gloomy shadow of the night,/Longing to view Orion's drizzling look,/Leaps from the

Antarctic world unto the sky/And dims the welkin with her pitchy breath,...　独白的开头四句实是一个大句，一个完整的意群。主语为 that the gloomy shadow of the night（那黑夜朦胧的阴影）；并列谓语动词为 leaps 和 dims；longing to view...为分词短语作原因状语。句意为：那黑夜朦胧的阴影，渴望观看猎户座烟雨蒙蒙的样子，从南极地区跃上天空，她漆黑的气息遮蔽了苍穹。

10. Faustus, begin thine incantations/And try if devils will obey thy hest,...　第五、第六句是一个完整的祈使句：浮士德，你开始作法吧，看魔鬼是否服从你的命令。注意 thine incantations 和 thy hest 的区别。thine 后跟的是元音开头的名词，thy 后跟的是辅音开头的名词。另外，thine 还可以做名词性物主代词，而 thy 不可，只能做形容词性物主代词。

11. Seeing thou has prayed and <u>sacrificed to</u> them./Within this circle is Jehovah's name/Forward and backward anagrammatized,/The breviated names of holy saints,/Figures of every <u>adjunct to</u> the heavens/And characters of signs and erring stars,...　第七句中的 seeing thou... = seeing that thou has prayed...，一直到第十二行的 and erring stars 全可看作是 seeing 宾语从句里的内容。因为是浮士德的内心独白，seeing that... 实际上就是 I have seen that...；自言自语的 thou 实际上就是他自己，他在自说自话。他说"看到了你已经……"实际上就是他知道自己做了什么。因此可以直接把看到的内容写出来。另外 thou has... = you have...，这是那个时代的英语。这一段可译为：你已经祈祷并向他们献过祭品，在这圆圈里有耶和华的名字，这名字是字母前后颠倒拼成的（forward and backward anagrammatized = which is... 修饰上行 Jehovah's name），还有众圣徒的名字缩写，有附属于天的各种天体形象，还有种种天宫和在歧路上飞驰的流星的形象……

＊ 注意 Within this circle is <u>Jehovah's name</u> 是个倒装句，主语摆在后面一是为了好加 forward and backward anagrammatized 这个后置过去分词定语，二是为了与另三个主语并列，它们是：the ... names of <u>holy saints</u>,figures of... the heavens 和 characters of ... <u>erring stars</u>。

12. 第十三句 By which the spirits are enforced（= forced）to rise 是前述各项的定语从句，其中的 by which = by all the above,意为：凭上述这些，就可迫使鬼魂出现。

13. Then fear not, Faustus, but be resolute/And try the uttermost magic can perform. = Faustus, don't fear, but be resolute,/And try the uttermost（= utmost）(which) magic can perform.　可译为：浮士德，别害怕，要坚定，试试魔法所能创造的最大奇迹。

＊ magic can perform 是修饰 the uttermost 的定语从句。

14. in the shape of a dragon　以魔鬼的形象

15. to charge thee（= you）to return and change thy（= your）shape　命令你回去，改变你的形象
to attend on sb.　侍奉/照料某人
to return an old Franciscan friar　变成一个圣方济各会的老修士回来
to become a devil best（ad.）　最适合变成一个魔鬼

16. be s virtue in my heavenly words　我的咒语有功效

17. be proficient in this art　精通这项法术/这门艺术

18. How pliant is this Mephistophilis,/Full of obedience and humility!　可改写为：How pliant is this Mephistophilis/And he is full of obedience and humility!　意为：梅菲斯特是多么顺从！十分服从，十分恭顺！

19. the force of magic and my spells　我的魔法和符咒的法力
thou art conjurer laureate = you are ...　你是桂冠魔术师
That canst command great Mephistophilis. = Who can order ...　这是上一句中桂冠魔术师的定语从句，意为：你可以命令神通广大的梅菲斯特。其中 that 为关系代词。

20. *Quin redis, ...fratris imagine*!　= Return, ... in the likeness of a friar!　回来，梅菲斯特，像一个托钵修士的样子！

21. to charge thee (to) <u>wait upon</u> me whilst I live　命令你终身侍候我

　　Be it be make the moon drop from her sphere/ Or the ocean to overwhelm the world.　不论是让月亮脱离轨道,还是让海洋吞没/席卷大地。

22. a servant to great Lucifer　法力通天的鲁西弗的一个仆人

　　not follow thee without his leave　未经他的允许,不能跟着你

　　No more than he commands must we perform. = We must perform no more than he commands.　我们绝不可超越他的命令擅自行动。

　　* no more than = only　只能,不超越

23. to charge thee to appear to me　命令你在我面前出现/到我跟前来

　　to come hither (=here) <u>of my own accord</u>　出于我自己的意愿到这儿来

24. Did not my conjuring speeches raise thee?　不是我的咒语把你召唤来的吗?

25. *per accidens* = incidentally　偶然,碰巧

　　to rack(= torment) the name of God　侮辱/戏弄上帝的名字

　　to abjure the Scripture and his Saviour Christ　放弃《圣经》和救世主基督

　　in hope to get his glorious soul　想要攫取他好虚荣吹嘘的灵魂

26. in danger to be damned　有被罚入地狱的危险

　　the shortest cut for conjuring　念咒召唤鬼魂的捷径/快捷方法

　　to abjure the Trinity　放弃基督教的三位一体,即圣父、圣子、圣灵

　　to pray devoutly to the prince of hell　虔诚地向地狱之王祈祷

27. So I have done, and hold this principle. = I have done so, ...　我已这样做了,并且坚守这一原则/信念。

28. There is no chief but only Belzebub/To whom Faustus doth dedicate himself.　这两句是一个复合句,to whom 引导的是 Belzebub 的定语从句。意为:除了贝尔扎博,再无任何领袖,浮士德的确效忠于他。

　　* to dedicate himself to　献身于……,把它全部身心都奉献给……

29. to confound hell in Elysium = do not distinguish hell from Elysium (= heaven for kind people to stay after death)　对地狱和天堂混淆不清/不能区分

30. My ghost be (= would be) with the old philosophers!　我的鬼魂将去和古代的哲学家做伴!

　　But leaving these vain trifles of men's souls　但是且不谈那些人类灵魂的无用的废话

31. What is that Lucifer thy lord (= your god /master, Lucifer 的同位语)?　你的那位主宰/主人鲁西弗是个什么人物呢?

　　(He is the) Arch-regent and commander of all spirits.　他是一切鬼怪精灵的最高统帅和司令。

　　* arch-regent　最高统治者

32. most dearly loved of God = He is most dearly loved of God.　他最受上帝的宠爱。

　　How comes it, then, that he is <u>prince of devils</u>?　那么,他是怎么变成魔鬼之王的呢?

　　* How comes it? = How it comes? 其中 it = that he is... 相当于一个同位语从句。

33. by aspiring pride and insolence　由于追求骄狂傲慢

　　to throw sb. from <u>the face of heaven</u>　把某人从天堂扔下来

34. What are you that live with Lucifer?　你们这些与鲁西弗在一起的是什么角色?

　　* that 从句是 you 的定语从句。

　　(We are) Unhappy spirits that <u>fell</u> with Lucifer, / <u>Conspired against</u> our God with Lucifer, /And <u>are forever damned</u> with Lucifer.　我们是不幸的精灵,过去与鲁西弗一起堕落,一起共谋反叛上帝,现在又与他一起永受炼狱煎熬。

　　* that 从句是 spirits 的定语从句,三组画线动词是从句中并列的谓语动词,时态各不相同,翻译时要体现出来。

35. How comes it, then, that thou art (= you are) out of hell?　那么,你又是怎么出的地狱?

36. to see the face of God　见到上帝的面容

to taste the eternal joys of heaven　尝过天堂的永恒之乐

be tormented with ten thousand hells　经受成千上万种地狱的折磨

be deprived of everlasting bliss　被剥夺了永恒的天堂极乐

Thinkst thou that I who... bliss? = Do you think that ... bliss?　你认为在我见过上帝的面容、尝过天堂的永恒之乐而又被剥夺之后,会不受千百种炼狱的折磨吗?

　＊ who tasted the eternal joys of heaven 是修饰 I 的定语从句;in being deprived of... 介词短语是修饰主句谓语 am not tormented with... 的状语。

37. ... leave these frivolous demands/Which strike a terror to my fainting soul!　抛开这些无价值的琐细问题,它们只能给我虚弱的灵魂注入/增添恐怖!

38. What, is great Mephistophilis so passionate/For being deprived of the joys of heaven?　这是个一般疑问句,what 只是个感叹词,for being deprived of the joys of heaven 是原因状语。整个句子可译为:啊,伟大的梅菲斯特会因被剥夺天堂的快乐而如此激愤吗?

39. Learn thou of Faustus manly fortitude(= Thou should learn manly fortitude of Faustus)/And scorn those joys thou never shalt (= shall) possess.　你要学学浮士德男子汉的刚毅(manly fortitude),藐视/别在意你永远得不到的快乐。

40. to bear these tidings to sb.　把消息带给/传达给某人

Seeing (that) Faustus.... by　亲眼看到浮士德因为……而遭到/招致……

to incur eternal death　招致/引起永久死亡的后果

by desperate thoughts against Jove's deity　因违抗神明朱庇特/上帝意旨的无法无天的狂妄思想而被……

to surrender up to him his soul = to surrender up his soul to him　把自己的灵魂奉献/出让给他

to spare him four and twenty years　再赦/让/宽容他多活 24 年

to live in all voluptuousness　生活纵情享乐/极尽奢华

to have thee (= you) ever to attend on me　让你永远侍候我

to slay mine (= kill my) enemies and aid (= help) my friends　杀死我的敌人,帮助我的朋友

be obedient to my will　服从我的意志

41. to resolve me of thy (= your) master's mind　告诉我你主人的意愿是什么

42. Had I as many ... as ... stars/I'd give ... Mephistophilis!　可改写为:If I had as many souls as there be stars I'd give them all for Mephistophilis! 意为:如果我的灵魂有天上的星星那么多,我就全部都奉献给梅菲斯特!

43. By him I'll be great emperor... = Depending upon him I'll be ...　依靠他,我要做世上伟大的帝王。

to make a bridge thorough (*prep.* = through) the moving air　在翔动变化的空中建一座贯通的大桥

to pass the ocean with a band of men　带一队人马跨越海洋

44. to join the hills that bind the Afric (= Africa) shore　把横亘在非洲海岸的山岳连成一片

to make that country continent to Spain　使那一方土地一直延伸到西班牙

both (are) contributory to my crown　双方都向我(的王冠/王权)称臣纳贡

45. The emperor shall not live but by my leave,/Nor any potentate of Germany.　帝王不服从我的命令就不能活,哪一个德国君主也不例外。

46. Now that I have obtained what I desire (宾语从句)/I'll live in speculation of this art/Till...　既然我已获得想要的一切,就要对这门技艺进一步研究思考,直到……

名家译文——戴骝龄

浮士德（书选）

[浮士德上场,作法]

浮:大地阴沉沉的黑影,

因贪瞧猎户星的带雨的面容,

正从世界的南极奔向中天,

用它漆黑的气息蒙蔽太空,

浮士德,开始念你的咒文吧,

试一试魔鬼们是否听从,

你既向他们祈祷过,并献过牺牲。

这符圈里是耶和华的名字,

[他在地上画了一个圈]

正着倒着把名字拆开乱排,

还有圣徒们的简名,

天上每颗恒星的图形,

以及十二宫和行星的记号,

这一切就一定能招来精灵,

别害怕,浮士德,下定决心,

把魔术能做到的一切尽量试演。[雷声]

   * * * * *

[梅菲斯特走进来,形象似魔鬼]

我令你回转去换个形状,

你这般丑陋怎配跟我?

去扮成个修道老僧再来,

那副圣容对魔鬼才最相宜。

[梅菲斯特下]

我的神咒功用真不小,

这种道术谁不愿精通?

梅菲斯特是多么柔顺,

他非常听话,非常谦逊!

魔法和符咒竟有这般力量,

浮士德,你是头号魔术家,

你能呼唤那伟大的梅菲斯特,

"真的,你指挥着装扮成修道士的梅菲斯特!"

[梅菲斯特又上,像个修道士]

梅:现在,浮士德,你要让我干什么?

浮:要你伺候我一辈子;

浮士德命令你干的事你都得干,

不管是要月亮从天空掉下，

或是要海水淹没世界。

梅：我是伟大的鬼王的一个仆人，

未经他许可就不便对你遵从：

他不曾命令的，我碍难执行。

浮：他没吩咐你在我面前出现吗？

梅：没有，我自动到来的。

浮：你说说，是不是我的咒词将你招来？

梅：那虽是一个原因，但也出自偶然。

因为当我听见有人踩躏天帝的名字，

并且誓绝《圣经》和救世主耶稣，

我们就飞来想摄取他的灵魂，

当然也还有一个条件，

那就是他用的法术，

已使他自己遭到打入地狱的危险；

因此学到魔术最简洁的法门，

便是干脆誓绝三位一体的圣灵，

虔诚地转向魔王祈祷。

浮：浮士德已经这样做了，他已坚信一条原则：

除掉恶魔就再没有别的主子。

浮士德已决定把自己奉献给他。

"打下地狱"吓唬不了浮士德，

天堂与地狱于他毫无分别；

让我的幽灵追随过去的方术大师吧！

但是，这些关于灵魂的废话且不必谈它，

你只说说你的主子那个魔王究竟是什么？

梅：他是一切幽灵的头目和统帅。

浮：他过去不也是一个天使吗？

梅：而且天帝还极其宠爱他。

浮：如今他怎么变成了魔王？

梅：哦，因为他骄傲与狂妄，

天帝把他逐出了天堂。

浮：你们那些人是谁——与魔王生活在一起？

梅：与他一起遭谴的伤心的幽灵，

因和他同谋反抗天帝，

也就如他一样永受天罚。

浮：你们被罚在何处？

梅：被罚在地狱。

浮：怎么你现在走出了地狱？

梅：并未走出来呀，这里就是地狱啊。

你想想，我曾瞻仰天帝的圣颜，

也曾分享过天国中永恒的欢乐，

如今永恒的幸福既已被剥夺，

我怎能不在无穷尽的地狱里受熬煎?
莫再提那些无聊的问题,
那叫我沮伤的心更感惊惶。
浮:啊,伟大的梅菲斯特竟如此悲伤
只因天堂的快乐被剥夺,
学学浮士德大丈夫的坚韧吧,
不能再得的幸福就莫再留恋。
去,把这消息转告给伟大的鲁西弗:
浮士德已被注定遭受永历万劫的死亡;
由于肆无忌惮地反抗了天帝,
他甘愿向魔王献上灵魂,
只要魔王偿他再活二十四整年,
由他尽情去享受一切,
并有你时刻相随在身边:
要什么就给我什么,
问什么就答我什么,
杀死我的仇敌,帮助我的朋友,
永远服从我的意愿。
回去见那伟大的魔王,
半夜里到我书房来再相见,
回复我你主子的心意。
梅:我遵命就去,浮士德。
浮:纵令我的灵魂像星星那么多
也愿意全部拿来把梅菲斯特交换。
有他相随我就是全世界的主宰,
我要造一座大桥穿过长空,
同一大伙人跨过海洋;
我要接连起环绕非洲海岸的群山,
使非洲和西班牙连成一片,
并使他们都拜倒在我的王座前。
德意志大地和任何国家的君主,
不经我许可就坐不稳江山。
既然我已如愿以偿,
且把这法门揣摩揣摩,
直到梅菲斯特回到面前。

2. 深情的牧羊人致恋人 *The Passionate Shepherd to His Love*

词语解释和难句分析

1. 这首诗被认为是英国文学中最优美的抒情诗(lyrics)之一,源自田园诗(pastoral)传统。诗中的牧羊人享受着理想的乡村生活,珍惜(cherish)一种牧歌式(pastoral)的、纯洁的恋情。诗歌描写了恋人陶醉在大自然的美景中,不受世俗的干扰,表达出他们真挚热烈的情感。

2. to derive from　由……而来,源出于……,由……导出

to cherish a pastoral and pure affection for his love　珍惜一种牧歌式的、纯洁的恋情

3. Come live with me and be my love,/And we will all the pleasures prove(＝And we will prove all the pleasures).　来与我同住吧,做我的爱人/我们将共享这一切欢乐。第二句谓语与宾语位置的调换是为了 prove 与 love 的押韵, prove 意为 experience,enjoy,体验、享受的意思。后边第三、第四行的 that 从句是一个定语从句,修饰前面的 pleasures, 从句谓语是 yields,产生、赋予的意思。意即我们将共享一切欢乐,而这欢乐又是大自然的恩赐,是从河谷、树丛、田野、森林中产生的。

4. to feed their flocks　喂羊吃草,放牧羊群

By shallow rivers to whose falls/Melodious birds sing madrigals.　身旁是清浅的小河流淌,/悦耳的鸟鸣伴着飞瀑歌唱。

　＊ sing . . . to whose falls＝sing madrigals to rivers' falls, 小鸟唱歌与小河流瀑形成呼应。

5. to make thee beds of roses＝to make beds of roses for thee (＝you)　用玫瑰花为你做床

6. 第三节的第三、第四行可改为:I will make thee a cap of flowers, and a kirtle/Embroidered all with leaves of myrtle. 意为:(还要为你做)一顶花冠,一件长裙,长裙上绣满桃金娘。

　＊第四行的过去分词短语是 kirtle 的后置定语。

7. 第四节的第一、第二行可改写为:A gown is made of the finest wool /Which we pull from our pretty lambs. 意为:用最精细的羊毛织成一件长袍,羊毛尽出自美丽的羊羔。

第三、第四行写成普通英语句子是:Fair lined slippers are made to you for the cold,/With buckles of the purest gold. 意为:衬里精美的软鞋为你御寒,上面还饰有纯金的搭扣。

8. a belt of straw and ivy buds　用麦草和常青藤芽蕾(为你)编织的腰带

with coral clasps and amber studs　再配上珊瑚带扣和琥珀饰钉

if these pleasures may thee move (＝may move you)　如果这些快乐能使你动心

9. The shepherds' swains shall dance and sing/For thy delight each May morning;　求婚的牧羊人为讨你的欢心,每个五月的早晨都来唱歌跳舞。

If these delights thy mind may move, . . . ＝If these delights may move thy mind, . . .　如果这些快乐能使你动心……

参考译文——姚绍德

深情的牧羊致恋人

来吧,与我同住,做我的爱人,
我们将共享这一切的欢乐,
那是河谷、树丛、山峦、田野所赋予的,
那是荞林或峻岭所恩赐的。

我们会悠闲地坐在岩石上,
看牧羊人放牧羊群的景象,
身旁是清浅的小河流瀑,

还有那小鸟儿伴唱着情歌。

我要用玫瑰花为你做床，
还有那上千捧花束，
我要为你编织一项花冠，
给你的长裙上绣满桃金娘。

用最精细的羊毛给你织一条长袍，
这羊毛尽出自我们可爱的羊羔，
精美的衬绒软鞋为你御寒，
鞋面上还有纯金的带扣。

用麦草和常青藤芽蕾为你做腰带，
再配上珊瑚别针和琥珀带扣，
假如这欢乐能使你动心，
来吧，与我同住，做我的爱人。

求婚的牧羊人将唱歌跳舞，
为讨你欢心，五月清晨，日日歌舞，
假如这欢乐能打动你芳心，
那就来做我的爱人吧，与我同住！

格律和韵律分析

下面对《深情的牧羊人致恋人》开头三节进行分析：

ˈCome ˈlive/with ˈme/and ˈbe/my ˈlove,	˘ˊ/˘ˊ/˘ˊ/˘ˊ
And ˈwe/will ˈall/the ˈplea/sures ˈprove	ˊ/˘ˊ/˘ˊ/˘ˊ
That ˈval/leys, ˈgroves,/ˈhills, and ˈfields,	ˊ/˘ˊ/˘ˊ/˘ˊ
ˈWoods, or ˈstee/py ˈmoun/tain ˈyields.	˘ˊ/˘ˊ/˘ˊ
And ˈwe/will ˈsit/uˈpon/the ˈrocks,	˘ˊ/˘ˊ/˘ˊ/˘ˊ
ˈSeeing/the ˈshe/pherds ˈfeed/their ˈflocks,	˘ˊ/˘ˊ/˘ˊ/˘ˊ
By ˈshal/low ˈri/vers to/whose ˈfalls	ˊ/˘ˊ/˘ˊ/˘˘ˊ
ˈMelo/dious ˈbirds/sing ˈma/dri/gals.	˘ˊ/˘ˊ/˘ˊ/˘ˊ
And ˈI/will ˈmake/thee ˈbeds/of ˈroses	˘ˊ/˘ˊ/˘ˊ/˘ˊ
And a/ˈthousand/ˈfragrant/ˈposies,	˘˘ˊ/˘ˊ/˘ˊ/˘ˊ
A ˈcap/of ˈflo/wers, and/a ˈkirtle	˘ˊ/˘ˊ/˘ˊ/˘˘ˊ
Emˈbroi/dered ˈall/with ˈleaves/of ˈmyrtle;	˘ˊ/˘ˊ/˘ˊ/˘ˊ

根据上述格律分析可知，除了阴影部分外，大多数音步为抑扬格(36个)。除了第一节的第三、四行为三音步外，其余诗行都为四音步，因此可以断定此诗格律为四步抑扬格。抑扬格为基调格，

非基调格有几种,共 10 个:第一节的第一行第一音步为扬扬格,第三行的第三音步和第四行的第一音步均为扬抑扬格;第二节第二、四两行的第一音步为扬抑格,第三行的第三音步为抑抑格;第三节第二行的第一音步为抑抑格,第二、三、四音步为扬抑格。根据诗行末尾单词的发音,可以断定其韵律为 aabb.…。

主要内容归纳和总结

1. 克里斯托弗·马洛出生于坎特伯雷一个鞋商家庭,靠奖学金先在王室学校(King's School)上学,后就读于剑桥大学,学生时代就开始了文学生涯,创作了《帖木儿大帝》(Tamburlaine),并一炮走红,有"大学才子"(University Wits)之谓。他是个激情如脱缰野马(unbridled)的人,过着暴风骤雨般(tempestuous)的生活。他在短短的一生,完成 6 部诗剧,最后这位青年才俊竟死于酒吧斗殴。他一生的艺术成就都表现在诗歌和诗剧创作方面,其突出的贡献有两点:

   a. 完善了无韵体诗(blank verse)。此前,虽也有萨科威尔和诺顿(Sackville and Norton)在合作的诗剧《戈尔伯德克的悲剧》中采用了无韵体诗,但过于死板。而马洛以"雄伟的诗句和澎湃的激情"为无韵体诗注入生机,使无韵体诗表现出旺盛的生命力。

   b. 塑造了文艺复兴时期的英雄形象。这种英雄有着独立的精神和雄心,渴求知识、权力和荣耀,反对传统道德,强调自我的奋斗,不把目标的实现寄托在上帝身上。这些特点是与传统文学作品中的英雄形象截然不同的。

2. 克里斯托弗·马洛的主要作品:

   a. 诗剧

   《帖木儿大帝》*Tamburlaine*(*Part I &II*)(1587～1588)

   《浮士德博士的悲剧》*The Tragical History of Dr. Faustus*(1589 完成,1604 出版)

   《爱德华二世》*Edward II*(1592～1593)

   《马耳他的犹太人》*The Jew of Malta*(1592 上演,1633 出版)

   b. 诗歌

   《深情的牧羊人致恋人》*The Passionate Shepherd to His Love*

   《海洛与勒安德耳》*Hero and Leander*(818 行,1598 出版)后四章由乔治·查普曼续写完成

   c. 译诗

   奥维德《爱的艺术》Ovid's *Amores*

   《卢肯著作第一卷》*Lucan's First Book*

重要信息句子

1. Marlowe's greatest achievement lies in that he perfected the blank verse and made it the principal medium of English drama.

2. Marlowe's second achievement is his creation of the Renaissance hero for English drama. Such a hero is always individualistic and full of ambition, facing bravely the challenge from both gods and men.

Ⅲ. 威廉·莎士比亚 William Shakespeare（1564~1616）

词语解释和难句分析

1. playwright = dramatist　剧作家

   the world over = all over the world　全世界

   books and essays on Shakespeare and his works　论述莎士比亚和他的著作的书籍和论文

   to have kept coming out in large quantities　一直不断地大量涌现

2. be born into a merchant's family in Stratford-on-Avon　出生/诞生于埃文河畔斯特拉福德一个商人家庭。

   ＊英国叫斯特拉福德的小镇不少，但只有埃文河边的斯特拉福德小镇才是莎士比亚的故乡。

   be described as glover, wool-dealer, farmer, and butcher　被描述为手套商、羊毛经销商、农场主和肉贩

   a member of the town council　是镇委员会的委员

   be a man of some importance in the town　是个在镇上有点身份的人

   to give birth to three children　生下三个孩子

3. to go to London which afforded a wonderful environment for the development of drama　去到能为戏剧发展提供绝佳环境的伦敦

   to act with and write for the Lord Chamberlain's Men　为宫廷内侍编剧，并与他们共演

   be renamed the King's Men　被更名为国王侍从

   resentfully declared him to be "an upstart crow"　不无怨言/带着妒意地宣布他为一个"骤起/暴发的星座"

   in the prime of his dramatic career　在他戏剧创作生涯的旺盛/主要时期

   to come out one after another　（作品）一本接一本地被创作出来

   to confine his genius to the theater　把他的天才局限在剧院里

   be dedicated to sb.　被奉献给某人

   be so prosperous that he bought the largest house in Stratford, known as New Place　处于（创作的）繁荣/旺盛时期以致在斯特拉福德购买了这座以"新宅"闻名的大房子

4. narrative poems　叙事诗

   to hold different views to the division of his dramatic career　对他戏剧生涯的划分持有不同的观点

   be divided into four periods　被划分成四个阶段

5. highly individualized period in style and approach　风格和艺术手法高度个性化的阶段

   third period of his greatest tragedies and dark comedies　大悲剧和黑色幽默的第三阶段

   his last period of principal romantic tragicomedies　写作主要浪漫悲喜剧的第四阶段

6. authentic non-dramatic poetry　真正的非戏剧诗

   his sequence of 154 sonnets　他的154首同主题组诗

   the only direct expression of the poet's own feelings　仅仅是诗人自己直抒胸臆

   be addressed to a young man... of superior beauty and rank but of ... constancy　是写给/寄给一个诗人挚爱的年轻人的，他外表俊美、地位显赫，但在道德和忠贞方面却有点问题

to form a less coherent group　形成前后不太连贯的组诗

be sensual, promiscuous, and irresistible　性感、淫乱却又魅力不可抗拒

translations and adaptations of some version of Greek epigram　某个版本的希腊讽喻短诗的译文和改编本

evidently refer to the hot springs at Bath　明显指的是巴斯温泉

with three exceptions　有三个例外

popular English form　流行的英语诗歌形式

three quatrains and a couplet　三个四行诗节和一对偶句

The rhetorical organization also follows this structure.　修辞手法也因循结构的要求。

to tie the sonnet to one of the general themes of the series　把十四行诗与组诗的一个总主题联系起来

to leave the quatrains free to develop the poetic intensity　使四行诗节自由发挥强烈的诗意

to make the separate sonnets memorable　使十四行诗各具特点,引人注意

7. national unity under a mighty and just sovereign　强大而英明的君主统领下的国家统一

　　to reveal a troubled reign in the 15th century　揭示 15 世纪动荡不安的政局

　　to present the patriotic spirit　表现出爱国精神

　　to mourn over the loss of English territories in France　凭吊/哀悼在法国的英国领土的丧失

　　to condemn the War of the Roses waged by the feudal barons　谴责封建贵族发动的玫瑰战争

　　to liberate himself from any imitations of the contemporary example　摆脱了/不局限于同时代剧作家盛行的模仿

8. to take an optimistic attitude toward love and youth　对爱情和青春持乐观的态度

　　be brought into full play　……得到充分发挥

　　to create tension, ambiguity, a self-conscious and self-delighting artifice　创造紧张悬念、语义双关以及一种自我意识、自我心喜的机巧聪明的计谋

　　be intellectually exciting and emotionally engaging　智慧上受到激发,情感上很吸引人

9. The sophistication derives in part from the play between high, outgoing romance and dark forces of negativity and hate.　情节的精密复杂部分是源于张扬外露的高度浪漫气息和否定、憎恨产生的隐秘力量的协调运用。

10. to idealize Portia as a heroine of great beauty, wit and loyalty　把鲍西亚理想化为美艳、聪慧和忠实的女英雄

　　to expose the insatiable greed and brutality of the Jew　揭露那个犹太人永不满足的贪婪和残忍

　　After centuries' abusing of the Jews, especially the holocaust (= massacre = slaughter) committed by the Nazi Germany...　经过了几个世纪的对犹太人的毁谤、虐待之后,尤其是德国纳粹对犹太人进行大屠杀之后……

11. And many people today tend to regard the play as a satire of the Christians' hypocrisy and their false standards of friendship and love, their cunning ways of pursuing worldliness and their unreasoning prejudice against Jews.　今天,许多人往往把这部剧看成是对基督徒伪善、虚伪的友谊和爱情标准, 追逐名利的狡诈手段以及对犹太人毫无道理的偏见的讽刺。

12. to take a step forward in its realistic presentation of human nature and human conflict　在表现人性和人性冲突方面又向现实主义前进了一步

13. the part of characters restrained by their limitations　具有局限性的人物角色

　　in contrast to/with　与……相比, 与…… 不同

　　medieval emphasis on future life in the next world　中世纪对来世生活的强调/重视

　　Though there is a ridiculous touch on the part ... in the next world.　虽然在塑造有一定局限性的人

物角色上有荒唐的败笔(笔触/描写),但是莎士比亚充满青春活力的欢乐的文艺复兴精神却到处可见,与中世纪强调来世生活的倾向截然不同。

14. to eulogize the faithfulness of love and the spirit of pursuing happiness. 歌颂、赞美对爱情的忠贞和追求快乐的精神

    be permeated with optimistic spirit 充满乐观主义精神

15. to have some characteristics in common 有某些共同的特点

    to portray some noble hero 描写一些贵族出身的主人公

    to face injustice of human life 面对人类生活中践踏公平正义的方面

    be caught in a difficult situation 陷入困境

    be closely connected with the fate of the whole nation 与整个国家的命运紧密联系在一起

16. the melancholic scholar prince 忧郁型的学者王子

    to face the dilemma between action and mind 面临采取行动还是深思熟虑的两难境地

    to suffer from treachery and infidelity 遭逢变节和背叛

17. Macbeth's lust for power stirs up his ambition and leads him to incessant crimes. 麦克白的权力欲激荡起他的野心,使他接连不断地犯下罪行。

18. With the concentration on the tragic hero, Shakespeare dramatizes the whole world around the hero. 在集中笔墨刻画悲剧人物的同时,莎士比亚也对他周围的世界做了戏剧化的处理/表现。

19. be a great realist in the true sense 究其实质/实质上某人是一个伟大的现实主义者

20. most popular play on the stage 最受欢迎/最负盛名的舞台剧

    to have the qualities of a "blood-and-thunder" thriller and a philosophical exploration of life and death 具有血腥暴力、惊险刺激剧的氛围和对生死进行哲理性探讨的性质

    be based on a widespread legend in northern Europe 以北欧广泛流传的传奇为基础

21. to take the bare outlines of Revenge Tragedy 采用明显的复仇悲剧的轮廓/框架

    the timeless appeal of this mighty drama 这部巨作的永恒魅力

    combination of intrigue, emotional conflict and searching philosophic melancholy 把阴谋伎俩、情感冲突和对忧郁的哲理性探讨结合在一起

    to appear in a mood of world-weariness 带着悲观厌世的情绪出场/出现

    be occasioned by his father's recent death and by his mother's hasty remarriage with Claudius, his father's brother 是由他父亲最近的死亡以及他母亲与克劳迪斯——他的叔叔的匆忙再婚引起的

22. be informed that... (某人)得知/获悉/被告知……

    to take both his father's throne and widow 既占有了他父亲的王位,也占有了他父亲的遗孀

    be urged by the ghost to seek revenge for his father's "foul and most unnatural murder" 被鬼魂催促,为父亲受到邪恶的最无人性的谋杀报仇

    to have none of the single-minded blood lust of the earlier revengers 一点也不具备早期复仇者头脑简单、嗜血成性的素质

23. The cast of his mind is so speculative, so questioning, and so contemplative that action, when it finally comes, seems ... the stature of the hero. 他的思想气质、类型太过思虑、太多疑、太沉思默想,到最终采取行动的时候,好像几乎都失败,结果总削弱了他的英雄形象,而不是增光添彩。

24. Trapped in ..., and apparently bearing ... language and action. 哈姆雷特陷入一个不断试探、考量和谋划的噩梦般的世界,明显承担着他承受不了的为父报仇的责任/重担,被迫居住在阴影笼罩的世界里,生活在分不清事实与虚构/幻想、语言与行动的悬疑之中。

    * trapped 和 bearing 各引导一个分词短语作状语,主句是 Hamlet is obliged to inhabit...。注意下列短语:

bé trapped in nightmare world 陷入一个噩梦般的世界

bearing the intolerable burden of the duty 承担着承受不了的责任/重担

be obliged to inhabit a shadow world 被迫居住在阴影笼罩的世界里

25. His life is one of constant role-playing, examining the nature of action only to deny its possibility, for he is too sophisticated to degrade his nature to the conventional role of a stage revenger. 他的生活就是不断地变换角色,探察行动的性质,而最终只是否定其可能性,因为他过于精密复杂,不可能把自己降格到通常的/老一套的舞台复仇者的样子。

  * 注意下面两个短语的用法:

  only to deny its possibility 最终否定其可能性

  to degrade his nature to 降低他的形象

26. a necessary release of anguish 必要的痛苦释放

  to possess surpassing power and insight (内心独白)具有非凡的力度和洞察力

  to have survived centuries of being torn from their context 作为脱离上下文而独立出来的经典(独白)台词已经流传了几百年

  the most detailed exposé of a corrupted court — "an unweeded garden" 最详尽地暴露了一个腐朽的宫廷——"杂草丛生的花园"

27. there is nothing but "a foul and pestilent congregation of vapours" 只有腐朽肮脏的痴心妄想的大杂烩(汇聚)

28. to reveal the power-seeking, the jostling for place, the hidden motives, the courteous superficialities that veil lust and guilt 揭露追逐权力、争夺地盘、暗藏的动机以及掩盖着欲望和罪恶的谦恭有礼的面纱

  to condemn the hypocrisy and treachery and general corruption at the royal court 谴责宫廷里的伪善、背叛和普遍的腐败

29. a prevalent Christian teaching of atonement (= redemption) 盛行的基督教关于赎罪的教义

  an imagined pastoral world 幻想的田园世界

  to right the wrongs and to realize his ideals 纠正错误,实现理想

  an elaborate and fantastic story 精致离奇的幻想故事

30. The characters are rather allegorical and the subject full of suggestion. 塑造的人物极富寓言意义,主题充满暗示/暗含的寓意。

31. the humanly impossible events 人力不可违的事件

  to resort to + n. 借助于,诉诸

  be no more than (= only) a dream 只不过/仅仅是一个梦

  his pessimistic view towards human life and society 对人生和社会的悲观主义态度

32. be shocked by feudal tyranny and disunity and internal struggle for power at the court 对封建暴政、国家分裂和宫廷内部的权力斗争感到震惊

  to describe the cruelty and anti-natural character of the civil wars 描述了内战的残忍暴虐和违背天理(的性质)

  to uphold social order 维护社会秩序

  be carried on 被贯彻、继续、坚持/保持下去

33. be against religious persecution and radical discrimination, social inequality and the corrupting influence of gold and money 反对宗教迫害、种族歧视、社会不平等和拜金主义的腐败影响

  the two-fold effects, exerted by the feudalist corruption and the bourgeois egoism 封建主义腐败和资产阶级自我中心主义所施加的双重影响

to corrode the ordered society　腐蚀/腐化有序的社会

to fear anarchy, hate rebellion and despise democracy　害怕无政府主义,憎恨造反和鄙视民主

to find no way to solve the social problems　找不到解决社会问题的办法

to escape from the reality to seek comfort in his dream　逃离现实,在梦幻中寻求安慰

34. There is also a limit to his sympathy for the downtrodden.　对被压迫、被蹂躏的下层人民的同情也是有限的/不彻底的。

35. to claim through the mouth of Hamlet that the "end" of dramatic creation is to give faithful reflection of the social realities of the time　通过哈姆雷特的嘴说出戏剧创作的目的就是忠实地反映当时的社会现实

to reflect nature and reality　反映自然和现实

to reach immortality　达到不朽

to sing the immortality of poetry　讴歌诗歌的不朽与永恒

36. neither merely individuals nor type ones　既不完全是个性化的,也不完全是类型化的

individuals representing certain types　代表一定类型人物的个性化形象,即既有典型性又有个性的人物形象

to share features with others　与别人有共同特性

to apply a psycho-analytical approach　采用心理分析的方法

to succeed in exploring the characters' inner mind　成功地探讨人物的内心世界

to portray his characters in pairs　通过两个人物的参照对比,更鲜明地塑造人物

to bring vividness to his characters　使人物形象更加栩栩如生

37. be well-known for their adroit plot construction　以奇妙的情节设计著称

to make the play more lively and compact　使得剧情更加生动紧凑

to shorten the time and intensify the story　缩短时间强化情节

38. There are usually several threads running through the play, thus providing the story with suspense and apprehension.　通常有好几个线索贯穿全剧,给故事提供悬念和焦虑。

39. Irony is a good means of dramatic presentation.　冷嘲热讽是很好的喜剧表现手法。

40. be ignorant of the truth　不知事实,不明真相

to do ridiculous things　做出许多愚蠢可笑的事情

41. Disguise is also an important device to create dramatic irony, usually with woman disguised as man.　乔装改扮也是创造喜剧讽刺的重要手段,通常是女扮男装。

42. to study the subtlest of his instruments the — language　研究他的巧妙的工具——他的创作语言

beautiful and mighty blank verse　雄浑壮美的无韵诗

to have an amazing wealth of vocabulary and idiom　拥有丰富得惊人的词汇量和成语量

43. His coinage of new words and distortion of the meaning of the old ones also creates striking effects on the reader.　他杜撰的新词和老词的转义也对读者产生了惊人的影响。

be above all writers in the past and in the present time　古往今来的作家都无出其右/不可与之媲美

the immeasurable influence on later writers　他对后来作家产生了无可估量的影响

44. to have a profound meditation on　对……进行深刻思考

the eternal beauty brought forth by poetry to the one he loves　献给爱人的情诗所产生的永恒之美

to last for ever　永久地持续下去,永恒

莎士比亚作品选读

1. 十四行诗 18 *Sonnet* 18

词语解释和难句分析

1. 这是莎翁最美的一首十四行诗,诗中对时光的破坏力和献给情人的诗所带来的美进行了深刻的思考。夏天虽美却很短暂,而诗歌之美却能永恒。对此他确信无疑。

2. to compare A to B   拿 A 与 B 做比较

   Thou art... = you are...

   summer's lease   夏季持续的时间;hath = has

   too short a date = very short a period of time   很短的一个时期

3. Rough winds do shake the darling buds of May,/And summer's lease hath all too short a date;   劲疾的风的确可摇落五月娇嫩的蓓蕾,夏季持续的时间又是多么的短促。

   * date = the period of a lease,延续的时间。

4. 第五行和第六行可改写为:Sometimes the eye of heaven (= the sun) shines too hot /And his gold complexion is often dimmed;   有时太阳(天上的眼睛)照得太热,他金色的面庞又常暗淡无光。

5. 第七、八行可改写为:Every fair sometimes declines from fair,/And is untrimmed (= stripped of gay apparel) by chance or nature's changing course;哪一种美都会褪色、减弱,而且随着机遇或者自然的变化也会被剥去欢乐的盛装/外衣。

6. 第九、十行主语是 thy eternal summer,有两个并列谓语动词 fade 和 lose, lose 的宾语是 possession of that fair, thou ow'st = thou ownest = you own, 是 that fair 的定语从句,即你所拥有的那种美。

7. 第十一、十二行可改写为:Death shall not either (= Nor shall death) brag that thou wonder'st (= you wander) in his shade/When thou grow'st (= you grow) to time in eternal lines.   当你在不朽的诗行中与时光共存的时候,死神也不能吹嘘你会在它的阴影下徘徊。

   * grow to time   与世长存

8. 第十四行中,this 是指 my poems, 复数作为整体,当单数看。So long lives this = This lives so long,即我的诗将永远存在/永远流传。

参考译文——姚绍德

十四行诗 18

我能否把你比作夏天?
你比夏天更温婉、娇媚:
五月的蓓蕾经不起急风摇曳,
而夏天又是多么短促的季节。
有时天上的眼睛酷热难当,
但金色面庞也时常暗淡无光。

任何一种美都有褪色的时候——
时机或自然进程会剥去它的盛装。
可你的夏日永恒,不会衰退,
永享美丽的姿容,不会凋败;
当你在不朽的诗行中与时光同在,
死神安敢吹嘘,你在它的阴影下徘徊?
只要还有人呼吸,眼睛还能看,
我的诗就会永远流传,并给你生命。

格律和韵律分析

Shall ·I/com·pare/thee to/a ·sum/mer's ·day?	a
Thou ·art/more ·love/ly and/more ·tem/pe·rate:	b
Rough ·winds/do ·shake/the ·dar/ling ·buds/of ·May,	a
And ·sum/mer's ·lease/hath ·all/too ·short/a ·date:	b
·Sometime/·too ·hot/the ·eye ·of ·hea/ven ·shines	c
And ·of/ten is/his ·gold/com·ple/xion ·dimmed;	d
And ·eve/ry ·fair/from ·fair/some·times/dec·lines,	c
By ·chance/or ·na/ture's ·chan/ging ·course/un·trimmed;	d
·But ·thy/e·ter/nal ·sum/mer shall/not ·fade,	e
·Nor ·lose/po·sse/ssion of/that ·fair/thou ·ow'st;	f
·Nor ·shall/death ·brag/thou ·wan/der'st in/his ·shade,	e
When in/e·ter/nal ·lines/to ·time/thou ·grow'st:	f
·So long/as ·men/can ·breathe,/ or ·eyes/can ·see,	g
·So ·long/lives ·this,/ and ·this/gives ·life/to ·thee.	g

上述分析中,带"·"号的为强音节,未标注者为弱音节,基本上是根据人们朗读时自然发出的强弱音标注的(大多与单词的自然重音相同)。全诗共70个音步,56个音步为抑扬格,占绝大多数,故这首诗为抑扬格;每行诗有5个音步,故这首诗为五步抑扬格。其他的非基调格有14个,可以分类数一数,就知道有哪几种,每种几个音步。但非基调格不影响诗的主格律判断。另外,根据前面讲的尾韵知识进行判断,同韵者用同一个字母表示(见行尾标注),连起来即成韵律:ababcdcdefefgg。

2.《威尼斯商人》*The Merchant of Venice* 第四幕第一场

词语解释和难句分析

1. 故事有两大情节:1)一贫如洗的威尼斯青年巴萨尼奥(Bassanio)为了迎娶贝尔蒙(Belmont)家族的美貌且富有的女继承人鲍西亚(Portia),向他的好友安东尼奥(Antonio)借贷,安东尼奥又向犹太人威尼斯的夏洛克(Shylock)转借,等商船回来归还。巴萨尼奥与鲍西亚初逢之时,就坠入爱河。但在准备嫁娶时,根据鲍西亚亡父的遗命,巴萨尼奥还得通过金、银、铅三种不同的小盒的正确选择的考验,拿到一个盒子里的鲍西亚肖像,最后巴萨尼奥凭真爱击败了摩洛哥王子、阿拉贡亲王等权贵,选择了装有肖像的铅盒。但风波突起,借款给巴萨尼奥的安东尼奥的远洋商船遭风暴袭击,货物尽失,无钱还贷;2)犹太人夏洛克当初与安东尼奥订协议时,有个奇特的规定:如逾期不还,安东尼奥必须让夏洛克割一磅肉。事情交由法庭判决,鲍西亚女扮男装被推荐当了法官,她先劝夏洛克向善不成,继而严责夏洛克割肉必须刚好一磅,不可多一点,不可少一点,更不可流一滴血,否则罚没他全部的财产,而且还要他背离犹太教,皈依基督教,这彻底打垮了夏洛克,使一对爱侣得成连理。后来众人得知安东尼奥的商船脱险,顺利归来,一时间皆大欢喜。选段为法庭审案一场。

2. an impoverished (= penniless) young Venetian　一个家财耗尽/一贫如洗的威尼斯青年

to ask sb. for a loan so that...　向某人借贷/借款以便……

to gain the hand of Portia in marriage　向鲍西亚求婚

to fall in love at first sight　一见钟情

to surrender herself　(女性)出嫁,答应求婚

to pass the test of caskets, ordained by her dead father　通过她已故父亲遗命的小盒考验

be invested in mercantile expeditions　投资远洋商船贸易

the Jewish usurer　犹太高利贷者

to surrender a pound of his flesh　交出一磅肉

to fail to repay him within a certain period of time　一定时间内不能归还

sb's letter now releases that...　某人的信透露……

to have to pay the pound of flesh　必须换还一磅肉

3. The two plots join in the trial scene of Act IV.　两个情节在第四幕的法庭上合二而一。

4. to appear disguised as a young lawyer instructed to judge the case　女扮男妆成青年律师出场,她被指定审理此案

to appeal to Shylock to have mercy　请求/吁请夏洛克要有同情心

to insist on the letter of the law　坚持按法律条文办案

to take his pound of flesh　从他身上取一磅肉

5. to shed a single drop of a Christian's blood　淌一滴基督徒的血

be confiscated by the state　被国家没收

to undergo certain severe penalties　受到严厉的惩罚

compulsory conversion to Christianity　强制皈依/转信基督教

jubilant celebrations of the happy union of several pairs of lovers　好几对恋人愉快结合的喜气洋洋的庆祝活动

to form the climax of the play　形成该剧的高潮

Magnificoes　(威尼斯的)贵族,权贵,要人

His/Her/Your Grace　(对公爵、公爵夫人或主教的尊称)大人/殿下

Ready, so please your Grace. = Yes, please, Your Grace　是/我在,您请吩咐,大人/殿下!

6. I am sorry for thee (= you, thou 的宾格)　我为你难过/惋惜/不安

to answer (= have dealings with) a stony adversary, an inhuman wretch　与铁石心肠的对手——一个没有人性的恶棍法庭对质/对簿公堂

* 两处画线部分为同位语。

uncapable of pity　没有同情心,不知怜悯的

void and empty from any dram of mercy　空无一点儿/没一点儿善心和仁慈

* 上述两个形容词性短语都是 a stone adversary 和 an inhuman wretch 这一对同位语的后置定语。所以 thou art come (= you are here) to answer ... any dram of mercy. 可直译为:你到这儿来是要和一个铁石心肠、没有怜悯、毫无人性的恶徒对簿公堂。

7. Your Grace hath (= has) ta'en (= taken) great pain to qualify (= limit)/His rigorous course;　大人您已经费了很大劲儿(has taken great effort)想劝阻他实施那苛刻残忍的处罚,……

to stand obdurate (*adj.*)　坚执,顽固不化

no lawful means can carry me out of his envy reach　没有合法的手段解救我逃脱他的毒手

to oppose my patience to his fury　以沉默/隐忍应对他的凶狂暴怒

be arm'd (= armed) to suffer … the very tyranny and rage of his　做好准备(be prepared to do…)忍受他的暴虐疯狂

with a quietness of spirit　平心静气,镇定平静

8. go one　去个人

to make room (for sb.)　(为某人)让位,让路

Shylock, the world thinks, and I think so too,/That…　夏洛克,大家都认为,我也这么认为……

* that 引导的是 thinks 的宾语从句。

Thou but leadest this fashion of thy malice/To the last hour of act; = You only lead this fashion of your malice/ To the last hour of act.　你不过是要把这种蓄意害人的恶毒样子装到/拖延到最后一刻。

9. and then, 'tis (= it is) thought (that),/Thou'lt (= thou shalt/wilt = you shall/will) show thy mercy and remorse, more strange/Than is thy strange apparent cruelty (*is*).　然后,大家都认为你会大发慈悲、悔恨自责,比你表露的奇特残暴来得更加奇特,出人意料。

* than 后面是一个倒装语序, is 应在句末斜体字 is 的位置上。

10. And where (= in your cruelty) thou now exacts the penalty,/Which is a pound of this poor merchant's flesh, …　你的残暴使你现在要施加惩罚——那只是这可怜商人身上的一磅肉。

* where 和 which 都引导一个定语从句,where 从句修饰上句中的 cruelty,which 从句修饰本句中的 penalty。

11. Thou wilt = You will

be touch'd (= touched) with by human gentleness and love　为人类的温良和爱心所感动

not only loose (= abandon/give up) the forfeiture, but forgive a moiety of the principal.　不仅放弃惩罚/赔偿,而且还要豁免部分本金

12. to glance an eye of pity on his losses　怀着同情之心看一看他接连的损失

of late = recently　近来

to huddle on one's back　聚成一团,堆压在某人背上

Enow (= enough) to press a royal merchant down/And pluck commiseration of his state/From…　足以压垮一个钦定的皇商,从……引发出对他这种处境/状态的同情。

From brassy bosoms and rough hearts of flint,/From stubborn Turks and Tartars, never train'd (= trained) to offices of tender courtesy.　从顽劣的突厥人和鞑靼人的钢铁胸膛和铁石心肠中(引发出同情),尽管他们从未受过温情礼貌方面的训练。

* 第二个 from 引导的介词短语是 brassy bosoms and rough hearts of flint 的定语,而 never train'd of tender courtesy to offices 又是 Turks and Tartars 的后置定语。其中 be trained of … to offices 意为在……方面受过专门教育或训练。

13. to possess oneself of …　得到,获得,把……拥为己有

to possess sb. of what I purpose　使/让某人知道了我的意图/想法

by our holy Sabbath have I sworn　凭我们神圣的安息日起誓

to have the due and forfeit of my bond　获得按借约规定应得的罚款/赔偿

14. let the danger light/Upon your charter and your city's freedom　让您的豁免特权和贵市的自由有丧失的危险

rather choose to have/A weight of carrion flesh than to receive/Three thousand ducats　宁愿要一块腐肉而不要 3000 达科特金币

15. I'll not answer that, But say it is my humour.　我就不回答你这个问题了,不过可以告诉你这是我的喜好/兴趣。

16. What if my house be troubled with a rat,/And I be pleas'd（=pleased）to give ten thousand ducats/To have it ban'd（=banned）?　假如我家里闹老鼠,我乐意花 1 万块钱来灭鼠,那又怎么样呢?/谁管得着?

17. Some men there are love not a gaping pig;/ Some that... and others, ... contain their urine;　本句可改写为:There are some men love not a gaping pig;/Some that are mad if they behold（=see）a cat;/And others, when the bagpipe sings i'th'（=in the）nose,/Cannot contain（=control）their urine.
　本句讲了三种类型的人,some...;some...;and others.... 整个句子可译为:有些人不喜欢张开大嘴的猪;有些人则是见猫就发狂;而另一些人,一听到风笛呜呜的响声,就憋不住会尿裤子。

18. to sway it to...　使倒向/陷入……的境地,使不由自主地显出……
　...for affection,/Mistress of passion, sways it（=passion）to the mood/Of what it likes or loathes. 因为人的癖好,是激情的主宰,它会使激情不由自主地显出喜好什么和憎厌什么的情绪。
　* 本句是上句的原因状语从句,主谓结构是 affection sways it to...;mistress of passion 是 affection 的同位语。

19. Now, for your answer:　现在,就给您如下的/这样的回答——
　As there is no firm reason to be rend'red（=rendered=given=provided）/Why... but of force...;/So can I give no reason, nor I will...　因为根本说不出任何可靠的理由,为什么……,为什么……,所以我说不出什么理由,我也不愿说什么理由……

20. to abide a gaping pig　忍受得了张开大嘴巴的猪
　to dislike a harmless necessary cat　厌恶有益无害的猫
　Why he, a woollen bagpipe, but of force（=unavoidably=certainly）/Must yield to such inevitable shame/ As to offend, himself being offended;　为什么他听不得咿咿呜呜的风笛,而抑制不住出乖露丑,以致失礼于他人,也为他人所不齿。

21. So can I give no reason, nor I will not,/ More than a lodg'd（=lodged）hate and a certain loathing/I bear Antonio, that I follow thus/A losing suit against him.　所以,除了我对安东尼奥怀有的根深蒂固的仇恨和厌恶,我不能也不愿给出任何理由,使我愿意打这一场于他有害于己无益的官司。
　* more than...短语作句子的状语,句中 I bear Antonio 是 a lodg'd hate and a certain loathing 的定语从句;give no reason that...意为给不出(打这场官司)的理由, that 从句可认为是关系副词引导的定语从句,修饰 reason。

22. This is no answer, thou unfeeling man,/To excuse the current of thy cruelty.　可改写为:Thou unfeeling man, this is no answer/To excuse the current of thy cruelty. 你这冷酷无情的家伙,这种回答不能为你的残忍开脱罪责。

23. Hates any man the things he would not kill?　= Does any man hate the thing he would not kill? 不愿杀死的东西还有人恨吗?

24. Every offence is not a hate at first.　不要冒犯一次就立刻当成仇恨。

25. What,wouldst thou（=would you）have a serpent sting thee twice?　什么! 你愿意毒蛇咬你两次么?

26. I pray you,（please）think（that）you question with the Jew.　我恳求你,请想一想你是在与犹太人讲道理/谈问题。

27. You may as well go stand upon the beach/And bid the main flood bate his usual height;　你就像站在

海滩上命令海涛降低平日的潮头。

　　* 注意画线部分是 bid 带了一个不带 to 的不定式短语作 main flood 的宾补。

28. to use question with the wolf,/why he hath (= has) made ewe bleat for the lamb;　向狼提出质问:为什么它使得母羊为它的小羊羔咩咩地惨叫。

29. You may as well forbid the mountain pines/To wag their high tops and to make no noise/When they are fretten (= disturbed) with the gusts of heaven;　你还可以在高天的罡风吹过时禁止山上的松树摇动树冠和发出喧嚣

30. You may as well do any thing most hard/As seek to soften that — than which what's harder? /His Jewish heart.　你还可以像在做着最困难的事情一样来软化他这颗犹太人的心——世上还有什么比它更坚硬?

　　* 注意句中破折号的解释,that = which = his Jewish heart。

31. I do beseech you, /Make no offers, use no farther means,/But with all brief and plain conveniency (= convenience)/Let me have judgment, and the Jew his will.　我恳求你们,不要再做任何努力/提任何提议,不要再想什么方法,让我简单爽快地接受审判,得遂这个犹太人的心愿。

　　* the Jew his will = let the Jew have his will

32. I would not draw (= accept = take) them; I would have my bond.　我也不会要,我要按借约索赔。

33. How shalt thou hope for mercy, rend'ring none? = How shall/will you hope for mercy, giving none (= giving no mercy to others)?　你对别人毫无慈悲之心,又怎么能指望将来别人对你慈悲呢?

34. What judgment shall I dread, doing no wrong?　没做错事,我怕什么审判?

35. You have among you many a (= many) purchas'd (= purchased) slave, /Which (= whom), like your asses and your dogs and mules,/You use in abject (= wretched, miserable) and in slavish parts,/Because you bought them.　你们家里使唤着买来的奴隶,把他们当作驴、狗和骡子一样看待,用他们干凄苦低贱的活计,原因就是他们是你们买来的。

　　* which you use... 是 slave 的定语从句,which 在从句中做宾语。

36. Let them be free, marry them to your heirs;　让他们自由吧,让他们跟你们的子女通婚吧。

　　Let their beds/Be made as soft as yours　让他们的床也跟你们的一样柔软吧。

　　Let their palates/Be season'd (= seasoned) with such viands;　让他们的嘴巴也(因)吃遍美味佳肴(而锻炼得坚强有力)吧。

　　Why sweat they under burdens? = Why do they sweat under burdens?　为什么他们要背负重担流血流汗呢?

37. The pound of flesh which I demand of him/Is dearly bought;　我向他要的这一磅肉是重金买来的。

　　* which...him 是 flesh 的定语从句。

　　If you deny me, fie upon your law! /There is no force in the decrees of Venice.　你们要是不给我,那么呸! 让你们的法律见鬼去吧! 威尼斯的法令就毫无权威!

38. Upon my power I may dismiss this court,/Unless Bellario, a learned doctor, /Whom I have sent for to determine this,/Come here to-day.　我已派人去请一个有学问的博士来断案,他叫贝拉里奥,要是他今天来不了,我就有权终止这场法庭审判。

　　* whom I have sent for to determine this, 是 doctor, 即 Bellario 的非限制性定语从句。

39. My lord, here stays...from Padua. = My lord, A messenger stays here without (*ad.* = outside the door) with letters from the doctor, new (= just) come from Padua.　殿下,正有一个信使待在门外呢,刚从帕杜亚来,带来了那个博士的信。

40. good cheer!　放宽心! /情绪好点儿!

　　The Jew shall have my flesh, blood, bones, and all,/Ere thou shalt (= shall) lose for me one drop of blood. 宁可让这个犹太人拿走我的血肉、骨头和一切,也不能让你为我流一滴血。

41. I am a tainted wether (= sick sheep) of the flock,/Meetest for (= most suitable to) death; 我是羊群中的一只病羊,要死也是最先轮到我。

    You cannot better be employ'd (= employed),Bassanio,/Than to live still,and write mine (= my + n. , with e or h as the first letter) epitaph. 说到你(的用处),巴萨尼奥,最好不过的就是继续活着,我死了,由你为我写墓志铭吧。

42. lawyer's clerk 律师书记

    to greet your Grace 问候大人/殿下您

    Why dost thou(= do you)whet thy knife so earnestly? 你为什么那么使劲儿地磨刀?

    to cut the forfeiture from that bankrupt there 从那个破产者身上割下抵偿品

43. Not on thy sole, but on thy soul, harsh Jew/Thou mak'st (= makest = make) thy knife keen; 你不是在鞋底上磨刀,而是在你的灵魂上磨刀,狠心的犹太人,你是把刀磨快了!

44. but no metal can,/No, not the hangman's axe, bear half the keenness/Of thy sharp envy. = But no metal can/Bear half the keenness of thy sharp/Envy, even the hangman's axe cannot either. 但是没有任何铁器,甚至连刽子手行刑的巨斧都没有你尖刻的嫉恨一半锋利。

    Can no prayers piece thee? 难道任何的恳求都不能打动你的铁石心肠吗?

45. No, none that thou hast wit enough to make. 不,你费尽心思想出的恳求/劝告都不能打动我。

    * 句中 that 引导的定语从句修饰 none, none 是 make 的宾语。Thou hast... = You have... 为第二人称单数的古用法。

46. O, be thou damn'd (= damned), inexecrable dog ! /And for thy life let justice be accus'd (= accused). 句子开头就是一个感叹句,相当于 O, what a damn'd, inexecrable dog thou art! 意为:啊,你这该死的、杀千刀的狗才! 画线部分为介词短语作原因状语,意为:因为你活着,让正义蒙羞(受到指责/不得伸张)。

47. Thou almost mak'st me waver in my faith,/To hold opinion with Pythagoras/That souls of animals infuse themselves/Into the trunks of men. 你几乎弄得我动摇了信仰,转而相信毕达哥拉斯的轮回观点:动物的灵魂竟注入了人的躯干。

48. Thy currish spirit/Govern'd (= governed) a wolf who, hang'd (= hanged) for human slaughter,/Even from the gallows did his fell soul fleet,/And, whilst thou layest (= lay) in thy unhallowed dam, /Infus'd (= infused) itself in thee. 你恶狗的灵魂支配了一只因吃人被吊死的恶狼,狼的凶恶的灵魂甚至从绞架上逃跑了,当时你正躺在亵渎神圣的罪恶的母狗胎里,于是,它的灵魂就钻进了你体内。

    * 注意 who, hang'd for human slaughter = who was hanged for human slaughter,是 a wolf 的定语从句;后面的三行诗句可改写为较好理解的普通句式:Even his fell soul did fleet from the gallows and infus'd itself in thee whilst thou layest in thy unhallowed dam. 句中 layest = lay, 为 lie 的过去式。

49. for thy desires/Are wolfish, bloody, starv'd (= starved), and ravenous. 因为你像豺狼一般凶残、血腥和贪婪。

50. Till thou canst (= can) rail the seal from off my bond,/Thou but offend'st (= offendest = offend) thy lungs to speak so loud; (骂吧,骂吧!)就是你把契约上的印记骂掉了,这么使劲地嚷也只能伤了你的肺。

51. Repair thy wit, good youth, or it will fall/To cureless ruin. I stand here for law. 修补修补你的才智吧,小伙子,要不就会落下不可救药的病根。我就站在这儿等候法律的审判。

52. He attendeth (= attends) here hard by (= nearby)/To know your answer, whether you'll admit him. 他就在这附近候着听你的回话呢! 你让他进来吗?

53. With all my heart. Some three or four of you/Go give him courteous conduct to this place.　　衷心欢迎。你们去三四个人礼迎他来此。

54. Your Grace shall understand that at the receipt of you(r) letter I am very sick.　　公爵大人明鉴,收到贵函之时,我正重病在身。

But in the instant that your messenger came, in loving visitation was with me a young doctor of Rome — his name is Balthazar.　　然信使至时,恰逢罗马青年博士鲍尔萨泽登门问候。

* 注意 in loving visitation was with me a young doctor of Rome = a young doctor of Rome was in loving visitation with me。

55. I acquainted him with (= make him acquainted with) the cause in controversy between the Jew and Antonio the merchant;　　我让他熟知了/我与他详谈了那位犹太人和商人安东尼奥之间的民事纠纷案的前因后果。

56. We turn'd o'ver (= turned over) many books together; he is furnished with my opinion which, bettered with his own learning — the greatness whereof I cannot enough commend — comes with him at my importunity to fill up your Grace's request in my stead.　　我们一起遍查各种法律典籍,我的审案意见,他尽皆知晓,并以我难以尽言的高才卓识使其更臻完善,经我执意相求,促成他应殿下之请,为我代庖。

* 注意 which comes with him ... in my stead 是 my opinion 的定语从句。大意为:我的意见随他而来(他把我的意见带来),应公爵大人之请,他代我执法。Whereof I cannot enough commend 是由关系副词 whereof 引导的定语从句,修饰 the greatness,而 the greatness 就等于前面的 his own learning,是其同位语。从句可译为:关于他的高才卓识,我怎么高评/赞美都不过分。

* 另外,掌握下列各种短语也很重要:

to turn over　　翻阅

be furnished with　　洞悉,了解

be bettered with　　因⋯⋯而变得更好/更臻于完善

at one's importunity　　在某人的强求/执意相求之下

to fill up your Grace's request　　响应/满足公爵大人的要求

in my stead　　代替/代表我,为我代庖

57. I beseech you let his lack of years be no impediment (n.) to let him lack a reverend estimation;　　直译为:我恳请您别让他因年少而有在接待礼节上受到忽视怠慢之障碍。即不要在接待礼节上因他是黄口小儿而瞧不起他。

* 不定式短语 to let him lack a reverend estimation 是 impediment 的定语。

for I never knew so young a body with so old a head.　　因为如此少年老成之士,我从无所知/闻所未闻/见所未见。

58. I leave him to your gracious acceptance, whose trial shall better publish his commendation.　　我推荐/委托他前来,希望您礼貌相待,他的断案如神必定会更好地说明我对他的赞誉并非虚言。

59. You hear the learn'd (= learned) Bellario, what he writes;/And here, I take it, is the doctor come (= I think, here is the doctor come).　　贝拉里奥的来函,你们都听到了。我想,是(他推荐的)那位博士来了。

60. Come you from old Bellario? = Do you come from old Bellario?　　您是从贝拉里奥老先生那儿来的吗?

61. Are you acquainted with the difference/That holds this present question in the court?　　今天我们法庭上要审理的案件争辩的焦点,你都清楚了吗?

I am informed thoroughly of the cause.　　这个案件我已完全清楚了。

62. to stand forth 站到前面来,往前站

    to follow suit 进行诉讼,打官司

    as you do proceed 当你确实进行办理时(真的进入诉讼程序时)

    to stand within his danger 命运操纵在他手里/受到他的威胁

    鲍西亚的四行话:Of a strange nature is the suit you follow (= the suit you follow is of a strange nature); /Yet in such rule that the Venetian law/Cannot impugn you as you do proceed. /[*turns to Antonio*] You stand within his danger, do you not ? 你打的官司很奇怪(具有古怪的性质);但根据诉讼程序,你若真的进行诉讼,威尼斯法律不能反驳你。[转对安东尼奥]你现在可要任他宰割了,是吧?

63. Do you confess the bond? 你承认这个借据/契约吗?

64. On what compulsion must I (be merciful)? 根据什么强制性义务/凭什么我非得要仁慈一点?

65. The quality of mercy is not strain'd (= strained); 慈悲(的品质)不是逼出来的(强求的、压出来的、勉强的)。

    It droppeth(= drops) as the gentle rain from heaven/Upon the place beneath. 慈悲像甘霖从天而降,落下凡尘。

    It is twice blest (= blessed): 慈悲享有/带来天国双重的护佑和福祉。

    It blesseth (= blesses) him that gives and him that takes. 慈悲既赐福给施予者也赐福给被施予者/获取者。

    ＊ that gives 和 that takes 都是 him 的定语从句。

    'Tis (= It is) mightiest in the mightiest; 慈悲是最强大的威力中之至高至强者/他的威力高于一切。

    It becomes/The throned monarch better than his crown。 慈悲成了比皇冠更有威权的在位之君王。

66. His sceptre shows the force of temporal power, /The attribute to awe and majesty, 君王的权杖显示的(只)是俗世/人世威权的力量,是君王尊严的标志

    ＊ the attribute to awe and majesty 是 shows 的宾语同位语,等于 the force of temporal power;下句是宾语也是宾语同位语的定语从句,由关系副词 wherein 引导。

    Wherein doth sit the dread and fear of kings; = Wherein the dread and fear of kings doth (= does) sit; 君王之令人敬畏,缘由正在于此。

67. But mercy is above this sceptred sway, 但慈悲高于这种授予的王权统治,

    It is enthroned in the hearts of kings, 它(慈悲)为国王所敬仰/占据他的心,

    It is an attribute to God himself; 它就是上帝本身的象征/标志;

    And earthly power doth then show likest (*adj.* = most like) God's/When mercy seasons (= moderate, reconcile) justice. 当在执法公正中调剂进仁慈的考虑,尘世的权力就最类似于上帝的神权。

68. Though justice be thy plea, consider this —/That in the course of justice none of us /Should see salvation; 虽然你要求的是正义公平,但请想一想真要这么做了(坚持公平正义,即按借约定割安东尼奥一磅肉),我们当中就没有人死后会获得上帝的拯救。

    ＊ that 引导的是 this 的同位语,等同于 consider 的宾语从句。in the course of justice 可直译为:在这样实施公正的过程中,但如下译法更好:这样实施公正的最后结果,就是……

    We do pray for mercy, /And that same prayer doth (= does) teach us all to render/The deeds of mercy. 我们祈祷着(获得上帝的)慈悲,而这同样的祈祷词也确实在训诫我们自己去做悲天悯人之事。

69. I have spoke thus much/To mitigate the justice of thy plea, /Which if thou follow, this strict court of

Venice/Must needs give sentence 'gainst (= against) the merchant there. 我说了这么多,就是希望能缓和一下,请你不要太过坚持司法审判的要求,假如你一定要坚持,那么,严格执法/执法如山的威尼斯法庭必定对眼前的这个商人(安东尼奥)依法惩处。

＊ which 引导的是 the justice of thy plea 的非限制性定语从句。

70. My deeds (will be) upon my head! = I shall be responsible for whatever I'll do. 我的事情,我自己负责。

I crave the law,/The penalty and forfeit of my bond. 我希望法律按借约进行惩罚和赔偿。

71. Is he not able to discharge the money? 他不能偿还/清偿这笔债款吗?

72. Yes; here I tender (= pay off) it for him in the court; 不,我愿当堂为他还清债款,

Yea(= yes), twice the sum; if that will not suffice (= make sb. satisfied), 对,还愿加倍还他;假如那还不能使他满意,

I will be bound to pay it ten times o'er (= over) 我定会再加 10 倍,

On forfeit of my hands, my head, my heart; 甚而以我的手、我的头和我的心作为赔偿。

If this will not suffice, it must appear/That malice bears down truth. 假如这还不能使他满意,那明显是仇恨压倒了天理。

＊ to bear down 压倒,击败,把……压下去

And, I beseech you,/Wrest once the law to your authority; 我恳请您利用您的权威变通一次法律。

To do a great right do a little wrong,/And curb this cruel devil of his will. = I beseech you to do a little wrong to do a great right/And curb . . . of . . . 我恳请您为做大善而犯一次小过,阻止这个残忍的魔鬼得逞恶愿。

＊ I beseech you 后面跟着三个不定式短语 to wrest. . . and (to) do a little wrong and (to) curb this cruel devil of . . . ,作谓语动词 beseech 的宾语补语。

73. It must not be. 这样的事绝不能发生/存在。

to alter a decree established 改变一条定律

'Twill (= It will) be recorded for a precedent,/And many a errors, by the same example,/Will rush into the state; 改变既定法律那样的事会被记载为先例,由于有先例可援,以后会发生许多类似的错误。

74. A Daniel come to judgment! 丹尼尔来审案了!

＊ 丹尼尔是《圣经》中真实性可疑的旁经(Apocrypha)曾提到过的一位公正的青年法官。

How I do honour thee! 我是多么敬佩您! /我对您真是五体投地!

＊ do honour 中的 do 是强化语气的助动词,比较常见,相当于 really。

75. Shylock, there's thrice (= triple) thy money off'red (= offered) thee. 夏洛克,他们愿赔你三倍的钱呢!

I have an oath in heaven. 我已经对天发过誓。

Shall I lay perjury upon my soul? 难道让我的灵魂负上背誓的大罪吗?

No, not for Venice. = No, I shall not lay perjury upon my soul for getting a Venice (= if you give me a Venice). 不,即使给我一个威尼斯,我也不违背誓言。

76. Why, this bond is forfeit ;/And lawfully by this the Jew may claim/A pound of flesh, to be cut off/Nearest the merchant's heart. 那好吧,就按契约赔偿。从法律上讲,犹太人按借约有权得到一磅肉,要从这位商人离心脏最近的地方割下。

＊最后的不定式短语 to be cut off. . .可以看作是 a pound of flesh 的定语。

77. (Please) bid me tear the bond. = Please allow/tell/let me to tear the bond. 请让我撕了这借约。

78. When it is paid according to the tenour (= term). 照约赔偿之后就可以让你撕掉。

It doth（＝does）appear you are a worthy judge.　看起来你是个值得敬重的法官。

Your exposition hath（＝has）been most sound（＝reasonable, intelligent）.　你的解释也非常有道理。

I charge you by the law,/Whereof（＝of the law）you are a well-deserving pillar,/Proceed to judgment. 现在我依法要求你——你是这法律界的中流砥柱——立即进行审判。

　＊Whereof you are...pillar, ＝You are a well-deserving pillar of the law, 是 the law 的非限制性定语从句。proceed（*vi.*）to judgment 直译为：进行到审判程序了。

79. By my soul I swear/There is no power in the tongue of man/To alter me. I stay here on my bond.　我凭灵魂起誓，人的嘴巴改变不了我。我等着执行借约。

80. You must prepare your bosom for his knife.　你得准备好让他的尖刀插进你的胸膛。

For the intent and purpose of the law/Hath（＝has）full relation to the penalty,/Which here appeareth（＝appears）due upon the bond.　因为法律的本意和主旨与借约上规定的应得惩罚并不矛盾/完全兼容。

　＊to have full relation to ＝ be totally proper or suitable to, 与……完全适合/兼容，没有抵触/矛盾。which 引导的从句是修饰 the penalty 的非限制性定语从句。

81. How much more elder art（＝are）thou than thy looks!　你（的见识）比你的相貌真是要老成得太多了!

82. lay bare your bosom.　袒露你的胸脯。

Ay, his breast —　对,是他的胸口——

So says the bond; doth it not, noble judge?　契约上是这么写的,不是吗,尊敬的法官?

"Nearest his heart", those are the very words.　"离心脏最近的地方",借约上就是这么写的。

83. Have by some surgeon, Shylock, on your charge,/To stop his wounds, lest he do bleed to death. ＝ Have to stop his wounds by some surgeon, lest he（should）do bleed to death. Shylock, on your charge.　得找个外科大夫给他堵住伤口,免得他流血过多致死。夏洛克,由你付费。

84. Is it so nominated in the bond?　契约中是这样规定的吗?

It is not so express'd（＝expressed）, but what of that（＝what's matter of that）? /'Twere（＝It were）good you do so much for charity.　契约上没这样规定,但那有什么关系? 你多做善事会有好报。

85. But little（＝I have only little to say）: I am arm'd（＝armed）and well prepar'd（＝prepared）...fare you well.　我只说几句话:我已经准备好了。把手给我,巴萨尼奥,再会了。

Grieve not（＝Don't grieve）that I am fall'n（＝fallen）to this for you,/For herein Fortune shows herself more kind/Than is her custom（＝than her custom is）.　别因我为你落到如此地步而悲伤,因为在这件事情上,命运之神已经比平时表现得仁慈了。

　＊I am fall'n to this. 应看成是系表结构,而不要当作被动语态,因为按后者,fall 是及物动词,"我被杀死/击倒",意思不当。

86. It is still her use（＝habit）/To let the wretched man outlive his wealth,/To view with hollow eye and wrinkled brow/An age of poverty; from which ling'ring（＝lingering）penance/Of such misery doth（＝does）she cut me off.　她的习惯依然是让不幸的可怜人财产丧尽还气息奄奄地活着,漠然地看着一个满脸（额头）皱纹眼窝空洞的穷困潦倒的老人。但这种拖延时日、缠绵不绝的受苦遭罪,她却给我赦免了。

　＊It 是形式主语,两个不定式短语 to let...和 to view an age of poverty with...是真正主语。from which ling'ring penance... ＝ she does cut me off from which ling'ring...misery. 其中 which 是形容词性的关系代词,相当于"这样的",指代前面两个主语不定式短语所表达的那

种在穷困潦倒中苦熬晚年的生活状态。因此 from which 引导的是修饰不定式动词宾语的非限制性定语从句。

＊to outlive his wealth 意为：人的生命超过了拥有财产的时间,可译为：财产耗尽,人还在苟延残喘。

87. Commend me to (＝remember me to) your honourable wife;/Tell her the process of Antonio's end;/Say how I lov'd (＝loved) you; speak me fair in death; 请代我问候你可敬的妻子,告诉她我安东尼奥走向结局的过程,就说我是多么爱你,证明我在死亡面前的慷慨坦然。

And, when the tale is told, bid her be judge/Whether Bassanio had not once a love (＝a bosom friend). 等故事讲完之后,要请她做个判断:巴萨尼奥是否曾有过一个肝胆相照的朋友?

88. Repent but you (＝Only you repent) that you shall lose your friend, /And he repents not (＝does not repent) that he pays your debt; 只要你为失去朋友而感到痛悔,那么你的朋友为你还债就会死而无怨。

For if the Jew do cut but deep enough,/I'll pay it instantly with all my heart. 因为只要这犹太人的刀子扎得深一点,我就会一下子把全部债务还清。

89. be married to sb. 嫁给某人, 娶某人

be as dear to me as life itself 对我来说,……就像生命本身一样宝贵

be not with me esteem'd (＝esteemed) above thy life 对我来说,（这一切）都不如你的生命宝贵

I would lose all, ay, sacrifice them all/Here to this devil, to deliver you. 为了解救你,我愿失去一切,全都(作为牺牲)奉献给这个魔鬼。

＊to deliver you 是作目的状语的不定式短语。

90. Your wife would give you little thanks for that,/If she were by (＝be present ＝be here) to hear you make the offer. 假如你的妻子在这儿听到了你讲的话,她不见得会感激你。

91. I would she were in heaven, so she could /Entreat some power to change this currish Jew. 我宁愿她马上升天,好去 求告某个天神,来改变这恶狗似的犹太人。

92. 'Tis (＝It is) well you offer it behind her back;/The wish would make else an unquiet house. 你躲在她背后这么说说是可以的, 否则你这心愿会使你家里闹翻天/不得安宁。

93. [Aside] These (would) be the Christian husband! I have a daughter —/(I) Would any of the stock of Barrabas/Had been her husband, rather than a Christian! —/We trifle time; I pray thee pursue sentence. [旁白] 这些就是基督教徒的丈夫! 我有一个女儿——我宁愿把她嫁给巴拉巴斯强盗的子孙也不愿把她嫁给一个基督教徒! ——我们浪费时间了,请你快进行判决吧。

＊would . . . rather than. . . ＝would rather . . . than . . . "宁愿…… 而不愿……"之意,句子要用虚拟语态,这里该用现在完成时态的(当时他的女儿已经与青年绅士洛伦佐 Lorenzo 私奔),用了过去完成时态。

the stock of Barrabas 耶稣时代犹太人匪徒的头子巴拉巴斯的家族/世系/后裔

to trifle time (away) 浪费时间

to pursue sentence 赶快进行/实施宣判

94. The court awards it and the law doth give it. 法庭判给你,法律也确实执行/确实给你。

The law allows it and the court awards it. 法律许可你,法庭判给你。

95. Most learned judge! A sentence! (＝What a sentence!) Come, prepare. 最博学的法官! 判得真好! 来,准备执行吧。

96. Tarry a little. 等一等。/耽搁一会儿。

＊to tarry for 等候……

This bond doth give thee here no jot of blood；/The words expressly are "a pound of flesh". 这借约没允许给你一滴血，条款很明确，是给你"一磅肉"。

If thou dost shed/One drop of Christian blood, thy lands and goods/Are, by the law of Venice, confiscate/Upon the state of Venice. 如果让基督教徒滴一滴血，按威尼斯法律，你的土地和商品就得没收充公，归威尼斯政府。

＊ be confiscate upon 被没收充公，归……所有

97. Mark, Jew. O learned judge! 听着！注意！犹太人！啊，博学的法官！

98. Thyself shalt（＝shall）see the act; 你自己可以去查查法律条文。

For, as thou urgest justice, be assur'd（＝assured)/Thou shalt have justice, more than thou desir'st（＝desirest＝desire). 因为你急切要求公道，那就保证你会得到公道，比你想要的还要公道。

＊ be assur'd...＝It will be assured that thou shalt have more justice than thou desir'st. 请放心/我保证你会得到比你想要的还要公道。 其中 it 是形式主语，that 引导的名词性从句是真正的主语。

99. I take this offer then: pay the bond thrice（ad.)/And let the Christian go. 我接受这个提议！按借约数目的三倍赔给我，让这个基督徒走吧。

100. Soft!（＝just a moment) 别忙！且慢！[古]从容不迫一点！

The Jew shall have all justice. Soft! No haste. 这犹太人要求完全的法律公道。等等，别忙。

He shall have nothing but the penalty. 除了规定的违约处罚外，他什么也得不到。

101. Therefore, prepare thee（＝thyself）to cut off the flesh. 因此，你准备割肉吧。

Shed thou（＝thou shed）no blood, nor cut thou less nor more/but just a pound of flesh.（＝neither you cut less nor more but just a pound of flesh.) 你不能让他淌一滴血，割肉既不能多一点也不能少一点，只能刚好一磅。

102. If thou tak'st more/Or less than a just pound — be it but so much/As makes it light or heavy in the substance, /Or the division of the twentieth part/of one poor scruple; nay, if the scale do turn/But in the estimation of a hair — Thou diest, and all thy goods are confiscate. 假如你割下的不是刚好一磅，不是多，就是少——哪怕只是多一点儿或少一点儿，只差一个斯克鲁普尔的二十分之一，不，不仅如此，即使只差影响天平平衡/会使天平倾斜的一根头发丝儿——你就要抵命，你所有的商品货物都要被没收充公。

＊ be it so/that... 即使……

be it but（＝only）so much as makes it（＝it makes）light or heavy in the substance. 即使割的肉只是轻一点儿或是重一点儿（it＝the flesh cut by Shylock)。最后的 in the substance 意为在物质上，无须译出来，意思也已有了。scruple 为古罗马时代的钱币，等于二十四分之一盎司

103. A second Daniel,...Jew! 丹尼尔再世，犹太人！

Now, infidel（＝pagan), I have you on the hip. 哈，你这异教徒，这回我可镇住你了。

104. Take thy forfeiture. 拿你的抵偿品啊！

Give me my principal; 把本金给我吧。

He hath refus'd（＝has refused）it in the open court. 他已经当庭公开拒绝了。

A Daniel still say I（＝I still say "a Daniel"),.../I thank thee, Jew, for teaching me that word. 我还是要说"他是丹尼尔再世"，我谢谢你，犹太人，你教会了我这个词（丹尼尔）。

105. Shall I not have barely（＝only）my principal? 我只拿本金也不可以么？

Thou shalt have nothing but the forfeiture/To be so taken at thy peril（＝at your risk), Jew. 犹太人，你只能冒生命危险割那一磅肉（作为违约抵偿品）。

Why, then the devil give him good of it! /I'll stay no longer question. 嘿，那就让恶魔给他这个便

宜占吧！我无话可说了。

106. The law hath yet another hold on you.　法律对你还另有处置/约束。

It is enacted in the laws of Venice,　这在威尼斯法律中有明文规定，

If it be prov'd (＝proved) against an alien/That by direct or indirect attempts/He seek the life of any citizen,　假如是一个外国人，他被证明用直接或间接的方法剥夺任何公民的生命，

The party 'gainst (＝against) the which he doth contrive /Shall seize one half his goods; the other half/Comes to the privy coffer of the state.　那么，他所谋害的公民(受害者)应获得/依法占有他一半的财产，另一半则被罚没充入国(家秘密金)库。

　＊ to contrive against sb.　谋划/设计陷害某人

　＊ against the which he doth contrive 是定语从句，修饰 the party (＝the victim)。

107. And the offender's life lies in the mercy/Of the Duke only, 'gainst (＝against) all other voice.　犯法者的生命只取决于公爵大人的仁慈，别人说了不算/其他人的意见不管用。

108. In which predicament, I say, thou stand'st (＝standest＝stand). ＝I say, thou stand'st in which predicament.　我看你现在正陷入这生死攸关的危险处境。

For it appears by manifest proceeding/That indirectly, and directly too,/Thou hast contrived against the very life/Of the dependent; and thou hast incurr'd (＝incurred)/The danger formerly by me rehears'd (＝rehearsed).　因为事实的进展表明：你已经直接并间接地谋害被告人的生命，并且你已经招致了我前面讲到的性命之危。

Down (＝Knee down), therefore, and beg mercy of the Duke.　快快跪下，求公爵发善心吧！

109. Beg that thou mayst have leave to hang thyself；求公爵准许你上吊自杀，

And yet, thy wealth being forfeit to the state,　不过，你的财富都已被罚没充公/作为没收充公的罚款。

　＊ thy wealth being … 是独立分词短语作状语，下一行为主句。

Thou has not left the value of a cord；　连买一根上吊绳的钱都没留下；

Thou must be hang'd (＝hanged) at the state's charge.　所以你上吊还得公家付费。

110. That thou shalt see the difference of our spirit,/I pardon thee thy life before thou ask it. ＝I pardon thee thy life before thou ask it (so) that thou shalt see the difference of our spirit.　为了让你看看我们基督徒与你不同的精神，不用你恳求，我先免了你的死罪。

For half thy wealth, it is Antonio's;　作为代替，你的一半财产罚归受害者安东尼奥所有，

The other half comes to the general state,　另一半则没收充入国库，

Which humbleness may drive unto a fine.　不过假如你态度谦恭，没收充公可从轻改为一定的罚款。

　＊ which … fine 为非限制性定语从句，修饰被罚没充公的那一半财产，关系代词 which 指代 the other half，在从句中作 drive 的宾语。

111. You take my house when you do take the prop/That doth sustain my house; you take my life/When you do take the means whereby I live.　你抽掉了我支撑房屋的顶梁柱，就等于拿走了我的房子；你取走我赖以生存的工具，就等于要了我的命。

112. What mercy can you render (＝give＝provide) him, Antonio?　安东尼奥，你能给他点儿什么慈悲？

A halter gratis (＝free); nothing else, for God's sake!　免费/白白送他上吊绳一根儿；上帝呀，再不能给别的了！

113. So please my lord the Duke and all the court,/To quit the fine for one half of his goods, ＝If my lord the Duke and all the court so please to quit the fine for one half of his goods,　要是公爵殿下和各位法官/法庭方面愿意免除代替充公的一半财产的罚款。

I am content, so he will let me have/The other half in use, to <u>render it</u>/Upon his death <u>unto</u> the gentleman/That lately stole his daughter —— 我也会很满意。不过他得让我接管另一半财产,好在他死后把这些财产移交给最近刚偷了他女儿的心/刚与他女儿私奔的那位绅士。

114. Two things provided more: that, for this favour,/He presently become a Christian; 还要加两个条件:一是因给他这个帮助/恩典,他得立刻皈依基督教,成为基督徒。

  ＊注意句子的总体格式是 one is that ...；the other is that ...。

  The other, that he do record a gift,/Here in the court, of all he dies possess'd (= possessed)/Unto his son Lorenzo and his daughter. 二是他得当庭立下文契,死后把所有财产授予女婿和女儿。

  ＊句子的主干是 He do record a gift of all he dies possessed unto... 即他得立下一个死后把所有财产授予……的赠予文契,he dies possessed 是 all 的定语从句,即他死后所拥有的一切财产,possessed (all) 在从句中作伴随状语,起补充说明的作用。

115. He shall do this, or else I do recant (= cancel = withdraw)/The pardon that I late (= lately) pronounced here. 他必须这么做,否则,我就撤销刚才宣布的赦免。

116. to draw a deed of gift 起草/写一张财产赠予的文书/契约

  give me a leave to go <u>from hence</u> 请允许我离开这里

  send the deed after me and I will sign it. 文书随后带给我,我签字就是。

  Get thee gone, but do it. 可以让你走,但要签字哟。

117. In christ'ning (= christening) shalt thou have two god-fathers; = Thou shalt have two god-fathers in christening; 洗礼时,你会有两个教父。

  Had I been judge, thou shouldst have had ten more,/To bring thee to the gallows, not to the font. 假如我是法官,你就应当还有十个教父,是送你去绞刑架,而不是去洗礼盆。

  ＊此句是个与过去事实相反的虚拟条件句,两个不定式短语是目的状语。

118. Sir, I entreat you home with me to dinner. 先生,我恳请你光临寒舍与我共进晚餐。

  I humbly do <u>desire your Grace of</u> pardon; 我恭请大人原谅,

  I must (be) away this night toward Padua, 今晚我得赶往帕度亚,

  And it is meet(= appropriate) I presently <u>set forth</u>. 最好现在立即出发。

119. I am sorry that your leisure serves you not. 真遗憾你贵人事忙,使我不得尽心。

  Antonio, gratify this gentleman, 安东尼奥,你应当谢谢这位先生,

  For in my mind you <u>are much bound to</u> him. (因为)我觉得你俩应当多亲近亲近。

120. [*Exeunt* Duke, Magnificoes, *and* Train]. 公爵、权贵和侍从退场。

名家译文——朱生豪

威尼斯商人(节选)

第四幕 第一场 威尼斯 法庭

[公爵,众绅士,安东尼奥,巴萨尼奥,葛莱西安诺,撒拉林诺及余人同上]

公爵 安东尼奥有没有来?

安东尼奥 有,殿下。

公爵 我很替你不快乐;你是来跟一个心如铁石的对手当庭质对,一个不懂得怜悯,没有一丝慈悲心的不近人情的恶汉。

安东尼奥　听说殿下曾经用尽力量劝他不要过为已甚,可是他一味坚执,不肯略作让步,既然没有合法的手段可以使我脱离他的怨毒的掌握,我只有用默忍迎受他的愤怒,安心等待着他的残暴的处置。

公爵　来人,传那犹太人到庭。

撒拉林诺　他在门口等着;他来了,殿下。

[夏洛克上]

公爵　大家让开些,让他站在我的面前。夏洛克,人家都以为你不过故意装出这一副凶恶的姿态,到了最后关头,就会显出你的仁慈恻隐来,比你现在这种表面上的残暴更加出人意料,现在你虽然坚持着照约处罚,一定要从这不幸的商人身上割下一磅肉来,到了那时候,你不但愿意放弃这一种处罚,而且因为受到良心上的感动,说不定还会豁免他一部分的欠款。人家都是这样说,我也是这样猜想着。你看,他最近接连遭逢的巨大损失,足以使无论怎样富有的商人倾家荡产,即使铁石一样的心肠,从来不知道人类同情心的野蛮人,也不能不对他的境遇发生怜悯。犹太人,我们都在等候你一句温和的回答。

夏洛克　我的意思已经向殿下告禀过了;我也已经指着我们的圣安息日起誓,一定要照约执行处罚;要是殿下不准许我的请求,那就是蔑视宪章,我要到京城里上告去,要求撤销贵邦的特权。您要是问我为什么不接受3000块钱,宁愿拿一块腐烂的臭肉,那我可没有什么理由回答您,我只能说我喜欢这样,这是不是一个回答? 要是我的屋子里有了耗子,我高兴出1万块钱叫人把它们赶掉,谁管得了我? 这不是回答了您吗? 有的人不爱看张开嘴的猪,有的人受不住一头有益无害的猫,还有的人受不住咿咿呜呜的风笛的声音,这些都是毫无充分的理由的,只是因为天生的癖性,使他们一受到感触,就会情不自禁地显出丑相来;所以我不能举什么理由,除了因为我对安东尼奥抱着久积的仇恨和深刻的反感,所以才会向他进行着一场对于我自己并没有好处的诉讼。现在您不是已经得到我的回答了吗?

巴萨尼奥　你这冷酷无情的家伙,这样的回答可不能作为你的残忍的辩解。

夏洛克　我的回答本来不是要讨你的喜欢。

巴萨尼奥　难道人们对于他们所不喜欢的东西,都一定要置之死地吗?

夏洛克　哪一个人会恨他所不愿意杀死的东西?

巴萨尼奥　初次的冒犯,不应该就引为仇恨。

夏洛克　什么! 你愿意给毒蛇咬两次吗?

安东尼奥　请你想一想,你现在跟这个犹太人讲理,就像站在海滩上,叫那大海的怒涛减低它奔腾的威力,责问豺狼为什么害母羊为了失去它的羔羊而哀啼,或是叫那山上的松柏,在受到天风吹拂的时候,不要摇头摆脑,发出欷歔的声音。要是你能够叫这犹太人的心变软——世上还有什么东西比它更硬呢? ——那么还有什么难事不可以做到? 所以我请你不用再跟他商量什么条件,也不用替我想什么办法,让我爽爽快快受到判决,满足这犹太人的心愿吧。

巴萨尼奥　借了你3000块钱,现在拿6000块钱还你好不好?

夏洛克　即使这6000块钱中间的每一块都可以分作六份,每一份都可以变成一块钱,我也不要它们,我只要照约处罚。

公爵　你这样一点没有慈悲之心,将来怎么能希望人家对你慈悲呢?

夏洛克　我又不干错事,怕什么刑罚? 你们买了许多奴隶,把他们当作驴狗骡马一样看待,叫他们做种种卑贱的工作,因为他们是你们出钱买来的。我可不可以对你们说,让他们自由,叫他们跟你们的子女结婚吧;为什么他们要在重担之下流着血汗呢? 让他们的床跟你们的床铺得同样柔软,让他们的舌头也尝尝你们所吃的东西吧,你们会回答说:"这些奴隶是我们所买的。"所以我也可以回答你们:我向他所要求的这一磅肉,是我出了很大的代价买来的;它是我的所有,我一定要把它拿到手里。您要是拒绝了我,那么你们的法律根本就是骗人的东西! 我现在等候着判决,请快些回答我,我可不可以拿到这一磅肉?

公爵　我已经差人去请裴拉里奥,一位有学问的博士,来替我们审判这件案子了;要是他今天不来，我可以有权宣布延期判决。

撒拉林诺　殿下，外面有一个使者刚从帕度亚来，带着这位博士的书信，等候着殿下的召唤。

公爵　把信拿来给我，叫那使者进来。

巴萨尼奥　高兴起来吧，安东尼奥！喂，老兄，不要灰心！这犹太人可以把我的肉，我的血，我的骨头，我的一切都拿去，可是我决不让你为了我的缘故流一滴血。

安东尼奥　我是羊群里一头不中用的病羊，死是我的应分，最软弱的果子最先落到地上，让我就这样结束了我的一生吧。你应当继续活下去，巴萨尼奥；我的墓志铭除了你以外，是没有人写得好的。

[聂莉莎扮律师书记上]

公爵　你是从帕度亚裴拉里奥那里来的吗？

聂莉莎　是，殿下。裴拉里奥叫我向殿下致意。

[呈上一信]

巴萨尼奥　你这样使劲儿磨刀干么？

夏洛克　从那破产的家伙身上割下那磅肉来。

葛莱茜安诺　狠心的犹太人，你的刀不应该放在你的靴底下磨，应该放在你的灵魂里磨，才可以磨得锐利；就是刽子手的钢刀，也赶不上你的刻毒的心肠厉害。难道什么恳请都不能打动你吗？

夏洛克　不能，无论你说得多么婉转动听，都没有用。

葛莱茜安诺　万恶不赦的狗，看你死后不下地狱！让你这种东西活在世上，真是公道不生眼睛。你简直使我的信仰发生摇动，相信起毕达哥拉斯所说的畜生的灵魂可以转生人体的议论来了；你的前生一定是豺狼，因为吃了人给人捉住吊死，它那凶恶的灵魂就从绞架上逃了出来，钻进了你那老娘的胎里，因为你的性情正像豺狼一样贪婪。

夏洛克　除非你能把我这一张契约上的印章骂掉，否则像你这样拉开了喉咙直嚷，不过白白伤了你的肺，何苦来呢？好兄弟，我劝你还是修养修养你的聪明吧，免得它将来一起毁坏得不可收拾。我在这儿要求法律的裁判。

公爵　裴拉里奥在这封信上介绍一位年青的有学问的博士出席我们的法庭，他在什么地方？

聂莉莎　他就在这儿附近等着您的答复，不知道殿下准不准许他进来？

公爵　非常欢迎。来，你们去三四个人，恭恭敬敬领他到这儿来，现在让我们把裴拉里奥的来信当庭宣读。

书记　"尊函到时，鄙人抱疾方剧；适有一青年博士鲍尔萨泽君自罗马来此，致其慰问，因与详讨安东尼奥与犹太人一案，遍稽群籍，折中是非，遂恳其为鄙人庖代，以应殿下之召，凡鄙人对此案所具意见，此君已深悉无遗；其学问才识，虽穷极赞词，亦不足道其万一，务希勿以其年少而忽之，盖如此少年老成之士，实鄙人生平所仅见也。倘蒙延纳，必能不辱使命。敬祈钧裁。"

公爵　你们已经听到了博学的裴拉里奥的来信，这儿来的大概就是那位博士了。

[鲍西霞扮律师上]

公爵　把您的手给我。足下是从裴拉里奥老前辈那里来的吗？

鲍西霞　正是，殿下。

公爵　欢迎欢迎；请上坐，您有没有明了今天我们在这儿审理的这件案子的两方面的观点？

鲍西霞　我对于这件案子的详细情形已经完全知道了。这儿哪一个是那商人，哪一个是犹太人？

公爵　安东尼奥，夏洛克，你们两人都上来。

鲍西霞　你的名字就叫夏洛克吗？

夏洛克　夏洛克是我的名字。

鲍西霞　你这场官司打得倒也奇怪，可是照威尼斯的法律，你的控诉是可以成立的。[向安东尼奥]你的生死现在操在他的手里，是不是？

安东尼奥　他是这样说的。

鲍西霞　　你承认这借约吗？

安东尼奥　　我承认。

鲍西霞　　那么犹太人应该慈悲一点。

夏洛克　　为什么我该慈悲一点？把您的理由告诉我。

鲍西霞　　慈悲不是出于勉强，它像甘霖一样从天上降下尘世，它不但给幸福于受施的人，也同样给幸福于施予的人；它有超乎一切的无上威力，比皇冠更足以显出一个帝王的高贵：御杖不过象征着俗世的威权，使人民对君上的尊严凛然生畏；慈悲的力量却高出于权力之上，它深藏在帝王的内心，是一种属于上帝的德性，执法的人倘能把慈悲调剂着公道，人间的权力就和上帝的神力没有差别。所以，犹太人，虽然你所要求的是公道，可是请你想一想，要是真的按照公道执行起赏罚来，谁也没有死后得救的希望；我们既然祈祷着上帝的慈悲，就应该自己做一些慈悲的事。我说了这一番话，为的是希望你能够从你的法律的立场上做几分让步；可是如果你坚持着原来的要求，那么威尼斯的法庭是执法无私的，只好把那商人宣判定罪了。

夏洛克　　我只要求法律允许我照约执行处罚。

鲍西霞　　他是不是不能清还你的债款？

巴萨尼奥　　不，我愿意替他当庭还清；照原数加倍也可以；要是这样他还不满足，那么我愿意签署契约，还他十倍的数目，倘然不能如愿，他可以割我的手，砍我的头，挖我的心；要是这样还不能使他满足，那就是存心害人，不顾天理了。请堂上运用权力，把法律稍微变通一下，犯一次小小的错误，干一件大大的功德，别让这个残忍的恶魔逞他杀人的兽欲。

鲍西霞　　那可不行，在威尼斯谁也没有权力变通既成的法律；要是开了这个恶例，以后谁都可以借口有例可援，什么坏事情都可以干了。这是不行的。

夏洛克　　一个但尼尔来做法官了！真的是但尼尔再世！聪明的青年法官啊，我真佩服您！

鲍西霞　　请你让我瞧一瞧那借约。

夏洛克　　在这儿，可尊敬的博士；请看吧。

鲍西霞　　夏洛克，他们愿意出三倍的钱还你呢。

夏洛克　　不行，不行，我已经对天发过誓啦，难道我可以让我的灵魂背上毁誓的罪名吗？不，把整个儿的威尼斯给我，我都不能答应。

鲍西霞　　好，那么就应该照约处罚；根据法律，这犹太人有权要求从这商人的胸口割下一磅肉来。还是慈悲一点，把三倍原数的钱拿去，让我撕了这张约吧。

夏洛克　　等他按照约中所载条款受罚以后，再撕不迟。您瞧上去像是个很好的法官；您懂得法律，您讲的话也很有道理，不愧是法律界的中流砥柱，所以现在我就用法律的名义，请您立刻进行宣判，凭着我的灵魂起誓，谁也不能用他的口舌改变我的决心。我现在单等着执行原约。

安东尼奥　　我也请求堂上从速宣判。

鲍西霞　　好，那么就是这样；你必须准备让他的刀子刺进你的胸膛。

夏洛克　　啊，尊贵的法官！好一位优秀的青年！

鲍西霞　　因为这约上所订定的惩罚，对于法律条文的含义并无抵触。

夏洛克　　很对很对！啊，聪明正直的法官！想不到您瞧上去这么年青，见识却这么老练！

鲍西霞　　所以你应该把你的胸膛袒露出来。

夏洛克　　对了，"他的胸膛"，约上这么说的——不是吧，尊贵的法官？——"靠近心口的所在"，约上写得明明白白的。

鲍西霞　　不错，称肉的天平有没有准备好？

夏洛克　　我已经带来了。

鲍西霞　　夏洛克，你应该自己拿出钱来，请一位外科医生替他堵住伤口，免得他流血而死。

夏洛克　　约上有这样的规定吗？

鲍西霞　约上并没有这样的规定，可是那又有什么相干呢？为了人道起见，你应该这样做的。

夏洛克　我找不到，约上没有这一条。

鲍西霞　商人，你还有什么话说吗？

安东尼奥　我没有多少话要说；我已经准备好了，把你的手给我，巴萨尼奥，再会吧！不要因为我为了你的缘故遭到这种结局而悲伤。因为命运对我已经特别照顾了：他往往让一个不幸的人在家产荡尽以后继续活下去，用他凹陷的眼睛和满是皱纹的额头去挨受贫困的暮年；这一种拖延时日的刑罚，她已经把我豁免了。替我向尊夫人致意，告诉她安东尼奥的结局。对她说我怎样爱你，替我在死后说几句好话；等到你把这一段故事讲完之后，再请她判断一句，巴萨尼奥是不是曾经有过一个真心爱他的朋友。不要因为你将要失去一个朋友而懊恨，替你还债的人是死而无怨的；只要那犹太人的刀刺得深一点，我就可以在一刹那的时间把那笔债完全还清。

巴萨尼奥　安东尼奥，我爱我的妻子，就像我的生命一样；可是我的生命，我的妻子，以及整个的世界，在我的眼中都不比你的生命更为贵重；我愿意丧失一切，把他们献给恶魔做牺牲，来救出你的生命。

鲍西霞　尊夫人要是就在这儿听见你说这话，恐怕不见得会感谢您吧。

葛莱西安诺　我有一个妻子，我可以发誓我是爱她的；可是我希望她马上归天，好去求告上帝改变这恶狗一样的犹太人的心。

聂莉莎　幸亏尊驾在她的背后说这样的话，否则府上一定要吵得鸡犬不宁的。

夏洛克　这些便是相信基督教的丈夫！我有一个女儿，我宁愿她嫁给强盗的子孙，不愿她嫁给一个基督徒，别再浪费光阴了；请快些儿宣判吧。

鲍西霞　那商人身上的一磅肉是你的；法庭判给你，法律许可你。

夏洛克　公平正直的法官！

鲍西霞　你必须从他的胸前割下这肉来；法律许可你，法庭判给你。

夏洛克　博学多才的法官！判得好！来，预备！

鲍西霞　且慢，还有别的话哩。这约上并没有允许你取他的一滴血，只是写明着"一磅肉"，所以你可以照约拿一磅肉去，可是在割肉的时候，要是流下一滴基督徒的血，你的土地财产，按照威尼斯的法律，就要全部充公。

葛莱西安诺　啊，公平正直的法官！听着，犹太人；好一个博学多才的法官！

夏洛克　法律上是这样说吧？

鲍西霞　你自己可以去查查明白，既然你要求公道，我就给你公道，不管这公道是不是你所想要的。

葛莱西安诺　啊，博学多才的法官！听着，犹太人；啊，博学多才的法官！

夏洛克　那么我愿意接受还款；照约上的数目三倍还我，放了那基督徒吧。

巴萨尼奥　钱在这儿。

鲍西霞　别忙！这犹太人必须得到绝对的公道，别忙！他除了照约处罚以外，不能接受其他的赔偿。

葛莱西安诺　啊，犹太人！一个公平正直的法官，一个博学多才的法官！

鲍西霞　所以你准备着动手割肉吧。不准流一滴血，也不准割得超过或是不足一磅的重量。要是你割下来的肉，比一磅略轻一点或是略重一点，即使相差只有一丝一毫，或者仅仅一根汗毛之微，就要把你抵命，你的财产全部充公。

葛莱西安诺　一个再世的但尼尔，犹太人！现在你可掉在我的手里了，你这异教徒！

鲍西霞　那犹太人为什么还不动手？

夏洛克　把我的本钱还我，放我去吧。

巴萨尼奥　钱我已经预备好在这儿，你拿去吧。

鲍西霞　他已经当庭拒绝过了；我们现在只能给他公道，让他履行原约吧。

葛莱西安诺　好一个但尼尔！一个再世的但尼尔！谢谢你，犹太人，你教会我说这句话。

夏洛克　难道我不能单单拿回我的本钱吗？

鲍西霞　犹太人,除了冒着你自己生命的危险,割下那一磅肉以外,你不能拿一个钱。

夏洛克　好,那让魔鬼保佑他去享用吧!我不打这场官司了。

鲍西霞　等一等,犹太人,法律上还有一点牵涉你。威尼斯的法律规定凡是一个异邦人企图用直接或间接手段,谋害任何公民,查明确有实据者,他的财产的半数应当归被企图谋害一方所有,其余的半数没入公库,犯罪者的生命悉听公爵处置,他人不得过问。你现在刚巧陷入这一法网,因为根据事实的发展,已经足以证明你确有运用直接或间接手段,危害被告生命的企图,所以你已经遭逢着我刚才说起的那种危险了。快快跪下来,请公爵开恩吧。

葛莱西安诺　求公爵开恩,让你自己去寻死,可是你的财产现在充了公,一根绳子也买不起啦,所以还得要公家破费把你吊死。

公爵　让你瞧瞧我们基督徒的精神,你虽然没有向我开口,我自动饶恕了你的死罪,你的财产一半划归安东尼奥,还有一半没入公库;要是你能够诚心悔过,也许还可以减处你一笔较轻的罚款。

鲍西霞　这是说没入公库的一部分,不是说划归安东尼奥的一部分。

夏洛克　不,把我的生命连同财产一起拿了去吧,我不要你们的宽恕。你们夺去了我的养家活命的根本,就是夺去了我的家,活活地要了我的命。

鲍西霞　安东尼奥,你能不能够给他一点慈悲?

葛莱西安诺　白送给他一根上吊的绳子吧;看在上帝的面上,不要给他别的东西!

安东尼奥　要是殿下和堂上愿意从宽发落,免于没收他的财产的一半,我就十分满足了;只要他能够让我接管他的另外一半的财产,等他死了以后,把它交给最近和他的女儿私奔的那位绅士;可是还要有两个附带的条件:第一,他接受了这样的恩典,必须立刻改信基督教;第二,他必须当庭写下一张文契,声明他死了以后,他的全部财产传给他的女婿罗伦佐和他的女儿。

公爵　他必须履行这两个条件,否则我就撤销刚才所宣布的赦令。

鲍西霞　犹太人,你满意吗?你有什么话说?

夏洛克　我满意。

鲍西霞　书记,写下一张授赠产业的文契。

夏洛克　请你们允许我退庭,我身子不大舒服,文契写好了送到我家里,我在上面签名就是了。

公爵　去吧,可是临时变卦是不成的。

葛莱西安诺　你在受洗礼的时候,可以有两个教父;要是我做了法官,我一定给你请十二个教父,不是领你去受洗,是送你上绞架。

[夏洛克下]

公爵　先生。我想请你到舍间去用餐。

鲍西霞　请殿下多多原谅,我今天晚上要回帕度亚去,必须现在动身,恕不奉陪了。

公爵　您这样匆忙,不能容我略尽寸心,真是抱歉得很。安东尼奥,谢谢这位先生,你这回全亏了他。

[公爵和众士绅及侍从等下]

3.《哈姆雷特》*Hamlet* 第三幕第一场［城堡中一室］

词语解释和难句分析

1. to be, or not to be = to live on in the world or to die　是生存/继续存在下去,还是死亡?其暗含的意思就是 to suffer or to take action? 即面对当前的处境,是继续承受现实的痛苦,还是采取反击的行动?

2. 第二、三、四、五行 Whether 'tis（＝it is）nobler...to suffer...or to take...end them? 是一个选择问句,两个不定式短语代表的两个选项是:

in the mind to suffer/The slings and arrows of outrageous fortune　思想上忍受残暴命运的明枪暗箭

to take arms against a sea of troubles,/And by opposing end them?　拿起武器直面苦海,通过抗争结束苦难

这个句子的"问题"是:采取哪一种做法才是高尚的呢?

3. To die, to sleep —/No more.　死去,睡着了——万事皆休,一切都完了(再不会有烦恼)。

and by a sleep to say（that）we end/The heart-ache and the thousand natural shocks/That flesh is heir to.　（鉴于/因为/考虑到）为了结束心灵的创伤和血肉之躯注定要承受的自然降临的千般苦难而长眠/通过长眠,我们结束了心灵的创伤和……

　＊ to say（that）...（宾语从句）　就……而论,考虑到,鉴于……

4. 'tis（＝it is）a consummation/Devoutly to be wished.　句中的 it 就等于前面说的 to die, to sleep 和 by a sleep to say we end...,所以,整个句子的意思是:死亡解脱正是(被)衷心盼望的最后结局。

5. perchance ＝ maybe ＝ perhaps

6. 从 Ay, there's the rub 到 give us a pause 是一个完整的句子,主句是 there's the rub,但关键在后面的原因状语从句 for...的语法结构,从句的主语是名词性从句 what dreams may come,谓语是 must give us a pause,看出这些关键点,就比较容易地直译如下:唉,这就是障碍,因为当我们摆脱掉这凡夫俗子的肉体羁绊之后,在死亡的长眠中,会有什么样的梦境出现,必定会使我们踌躇顾虑。

7. to shuffle off this mortal coil　摆脱、推开这尘世的喧嚣烦恼/抛却这肉体的羁绊

8. There's the respect/That makes calamity of so long life；　存在/有了这方面的疑虑,就有了漫长一生的灾难/就甘心忍受一生的苦难。

　＊ that 引导的是 respect 的定语从句。

9. 下面 For 引导的许多句子实质上都是原因状语,说明人间多苦难而人们却不愿选择死亡的原因。开头一个反义疑问句是个纲,For who would bear the whips and scorns of time 意为:因为谁愿忍受人间的鞭挞和嘲笑,接着铺开来历数人间的苦难,而最终不肯"一了百了"的原因是对死后世界的"未知"的恐惧。

the oppressor's wrong　压迫者的歧视、虐待

the proud man's contumely（n. ＝ contempt）　横霸者的侮慢

the pangs of despis'd（＝despised）love　被轻蔑的爱情的痛苦

the law's delay　法律的延误

the insolence of office　官府/官吏的骄横

the spurns/That patient merit of th'（＝the）unworthy takes　微贱者忍受苦难屈辱(的美德)所得到的/换来的鄙视

　＊用 th' 代替 the 是为了节约一个音节,使这行诗刚好符合五步抑扬格,要不就多一个音节。

10. to make his quietus with a bare（＝mere）bodkin　仅凭一把短剑就可以了却一切烦恼/清算一切债务

Who would these fardels bear? ＝ Who would bear these burdens?　谁愿承受这些重担?

to grunt and sweat under a weary life　在辛劳疲惫的生命重压下呻吟流汗

11. But that the dread of something after death —/The undiscover'd（＝undiscovered＝unknown）country, from whose bourn（＝boundary）/No traveler returns — puzzles the will/And makes... 句中画线部分为主谓句架,意为:对死后的恐惧迷惑了人们的意志,使得…… the undiscover'd country 是 something after death 的同位语,from whose...是 country 的非限制性定语从句,意为:死亡的冥界——一个神秘未知的国度,从无旅行者能从那里回归。

to make us rather bear those ills we have/Than fly to others that we know not of（＝we don't know of) 使得我们宁愿忍受已有的不幸和苦难而不愿飞到我们所未知的其他地方

* 把上述分开解析的含义连贯起来就是连续五行的这个复合句的完整意思。

11. Thus conscience does make cowards of us all; 这样,内心的思想意识(畏惧和顾虑)使我们全成了懦夫。

12. the native hue of resolution 决心的本色

be sicklied o'er(= over) with the pale cast of thought 显示出思想犹疑低沉(苍白的色调)的病容

13. enterprises of great pitch (= importance) and moment 伟大时刻的雄心勃勃的事业

with this regard 由于这方面的考虑/疑虑

to turn awry and lose the name of action 偏转方向,失去行动的本意/目标

名家译文——朱生豪

哈姆雷特(节选)

[哈姆雷特上]

生存还是毁灭,这是一个值得考虑的问题;

默然忍受命运的暴虐的毒箭,

或是挺身反抗人世无涯的苦难,

在奋斗中结束了一切,这两种行为,

哪一种是更勇敢的? 死了;睡着了;

什么都完了;要是在这一种睡眠之中,

我们心头的创痛,以及其他无数血肉之躯

所不能避免的打击,都可以从此消失,

那是我们求之不得的结局。死了;睡着了;

睡着了也许还会做梦;嗯,阻碍就在这儿:

因为当我们摆脱了这一具朽腐的皮囊之后,

在那死的睡眠里,究竟将要做些什么梦,

那不能不使我们踌躇顾虑。人们甘心

久困于患难之中,也就显了这个缘故;

谁愿意忍受人世的鞭挞和讥嘲,

压迫者的冷眼,傲慢者的侮慢,

被轻蔑的爱情的惨痛,法律的迁延,

官吏的横暴,和微贱者费尽辛劳所换来

的鄙视,要是他只用一柄小小的刀子,

就可以清算他自己的一生?

谁愿意负着这样的重担,

在烦劳的生命的迫压下呻吟流汗,

倘不是因为惧怕不可知的死后,

那从来不曾有一个旅人回来过的

神秘之国,是它迷惑了我们的意志,

使我们宁愿忍受目前的折磨,

不敢向我们所不知道的痛苦飞去?
这样的理智使我们全变成了懦夫,
决心的炽热的光彩,
被审慎的思维盖上了一层灰色,
伟大的事业在这一种考虑之下,
也会逆流而退,
失去了行动的意义。

＊名家译文中的方框部分是笔者根据原文加译的,笔者收藏的朱生豪莎剧译本上无此一句。
＊这段哈姆雷特的戏剧独白基调格律为五步抑扬格。

主要内容归纳和总结

1. 莎士比亚出生于英格兰一个商人家庭,家住埃文河畔斯特拉福德(Stratford-on-Avon),一生写了38部剧本、154首十四行诗和2首长诗。

2. 莎士比亚的戏剧创作可分为四个阶段
   a. 第一阶段:学徒阶段——5部历史剧,4部喜剧
   《亨利四世》(第一、二、三册) *Henry VI* (*book I, II, III*)
   《理查三世》*Richard III*
   《泰特斯·安德洛尼克斯》*Titus Andronicus*
   《错误的喜剧》*The Comedy of Errors*
   《维洛那二绅士》*The Two Gentlemen of Verona*
   《驯悍记》*The Taming of the Shrew*
   《爱的徒劳》*Love's Labour's Lost*
   b. 第二阶段:风格和艺术手法都个性化了的阶段——5部历史剧,6部喜剧,2部悲剧
   《理查四世》*Richard IV*
   《约翰王》*King John*
   《亨利四世》(第一、二部) *Henry IV* (*Parts I, II*)
   《亨利五世》*Henry V*
   《仲夏夜之梦》*A Midsummer Night's Dream*
   《威尼斯商人》*The Merchant of Venice*
   《无事生非》*Much Ado about Nothing*
   《皆大欢喜》*As You Like It*
   《第十二夜》*Twelfth Night*
   《温莎的风流娘儿们》*The Merry Wives of Windsor*
   《罗密欧与朱丽叶》*Romeo and Juliet*
   《尤利乌斯·恺撒》*Julius Caesar*
   c. 第三阶段:创作大悲剧和黑色幽默喜剧阶段——8部悲剧,2部喜剧
   《哈姆雷特》*Hamlet*
   《奥赛罗》*Othello*
   《李尔王》*King Lear*
   《麦克白》*Macbeth*

《安东尼和克里奥帕特拉》*Antony and Cleopatra*

《特洛伊勒斯和克里西达》*Troilus and Cressida*

《克里奥兰纳斯》*Coriolanus*

《雅典的泰门》*Timon of Athens* 与人合著

《终成眷属》*All's Well That Ends Well*

《一报还一报》*Measure for Measure*

d. 第四阶段:主要浪漫主义悲喜剧阶段——4 部悲喜剧,2 部其他剧

《匹力克利斯》*Pericles*

《辛白林》*Cymbeline*

《冬天的故事》*The Winter's Tale*

《暴风雨》*The Tempest*

《亨利八世》(又名《一切都是真的》) *Henry VIII(All Is True)*

《两位贵族亲戚》*The Two Noble Kinsmen*

3. 莎士比亚戏剧按类型可分四类

a. 喜剧(Comedies)12 部

《温莎的风流娘儿们》*The Merry Wives of Windsor*(1579)

《维洛那二绅士》*The Two Gentlemen of Verona*(1587)

《驯悍记》*The Taming of the Shrew*(1588)

《错误的喜剧》*The Comedy of Errors*(1589~1594)

《爱的徒劳》*Love's Labour's Lost*(1593~1594)

《仲夏夜之梦》*A Midsummer Night's Dream*(1595~1596)

《威尼斯商人》*The Merchant of Venice*(1596~1597)

《无事生非》*Much Ado about Nothing*(1598~1599)

《皆大欢喜》*As You Like It*(1599~1600)

《第十二夜》*Twelfth Night*(1601)

《终成眷属》*All's Well That Ends Well*(1603)

《一报还一报》*Measure for Measure*(1604)

b. 悲剧(Tragedies)10 部,标 * 号者为莎士比亚四大悲剧

《罗密欧与朱丽叶》*Romeo and Juliet*(1594~1595)

《尤利乌斯·恺撒》*Julius Caesar*(1599)

* 《哈姆雷特》*Hamlet*(1599~1601)

《特洛伊勒斯和克里西达》*Trodus and Cressida*(1602)

* 《奥赛罗》*Othello*(1604)

《雅典的泰门》*Timon of Athens*(1604)与人合著

* 《李尔王》*King Lear*(完成于 1605,出版于 1606)

* 《麦克白》*Macbeth*(1606)

《安东尼和克里奥帕特拉》*Antony and Cleopatra*(1607)

《克里奥兰纳斯》*Coriolanus*(1608)

c. 历史剧(History Plays)11 部

《泰特斯·安德洛尼克斯》*Titus Andronicus*(完成于 1587,出版于 1594)

《亨利四世》(第一、二、三册) *Henry VI (Parts I, II, III)*(1588~1591)

《理查三世》*Richard III*

《理查四世》*Richard TV*(1595~1597)

《约翰王》*King John*（1595）

《亨利四世》（第一、二部）*Henry IV（Parts I, II）*（1596~1597）

《亨利五世》*Henry V*（1599）

《亨利八世》（又名《一切都是真的》）*Henry VIII（All is True）*（1612~1613）

　　d. 浪漫主义悲喜剧（Romantic Tragicomedies）4 部

《匹力克利斯》*Pericles*（1607~1608）

《辛白林》*Cymbeline*（1610~1611）

《冬天的故事》*The Winter's Tale*（1609~1610）

《暴风雨》*The Tempest*（1610~1611）

　　e. 其他剧（Others）1 部

《两位贵族亲戚》*The Two Noble Kinsmen*

重要信息句子

1. Shakespeare's father：John Shakespeare

   Shakespeare's wife：Anne Hathaway

   Shakespeare's matrimonial time：1582

   Shakespeare's three children：Susana and the twins, Judith and Hammer

2. The most important play among the comedies is *The Merchant of Venice*.

3. The successful romantic tragedy is *Romeo and Juliet*, which, though a tragedy, is permeated with optimistic spirit.

4. *The Tempest*, an elaborate and fantastic story, is known as the best of his final romances. 《暴风雨》，精致的幻想故事，是莎士比亚最后阶段创作的浪漫传奇剧中的最佳作品。

5. *Sonnet* 18 is one of the most beautiful sonnets written by Shakespeare.

IV. 弗朗西斯·培根 Francis Bacon（1561~1626）

词语解释和难句分析

1. to lay the foundation for　为……奠定基础

   the first example of that genre in English literature　英国文学中那种体裁最早的典范

   be recognized as an important landmark　被认/誉为重要的里程碑

2. Elizabeth's first Lord Keeper　伊丽莎白一世女王的首任掌玺大臣/内务总管

   to have a fortunate heritage and background　有着豪富的遗产和门第

   at the highest of his career　达到人生的极盛时期

   Lord Chancellor of England　英国大法官

   be accused of taking bribes in office　被指控以权谋私/涉嫌受贿

   to defend the justice of his act　辩解自己行为正当

a token imprisonment   象征性的监禁

to retire in disgrace to his estate of Gorhambry   不光彩地退出官场回到高翰姆布雷的庄园/宅邸养老

3. to take all knowledge to be his province   涉足一切知识领域

a great tract on education   论述教育的一篇伟大的论文

to refute the objections to learning   驳斥对学习的反对意见

to outline the problems with which his plan is to deal   概述了他计划要解决的问题

* 画线部分为定语从句,to deal with which,which 指 the problems。

the knowledge obtained from the Divine Revelation and the knowledge from the workings of human mind
通过神的启示获得的知识和人类用头脑思考所获得的知识

the orthodox Christian thought   正统的基督教思想

to separate theology from scientific observations and experiments   把神学与科学观察和试验区分开来

to make a great step forward in science   在科学领域向前迈了一大步

a survey of learning   学习概论

history to man's memory   人类回忆的历史学

poetry to man's imagination and creation   基于人类想象力和创造力的诗歌

philosophy to man's reason   基于人类理性的哲学

4. a successful treatise written in Latin on methodology   一篇用拉丁文写作的关于方法论的优秀论文

the impressive display of Bacon's intellect   培根智慧的深刻展示

inductive method of reasoning   归纳推理法

to expound the four great false conceivings   详述了四大错误概念

to beset men's mind and prevent them from seeking the truth   困扰/束缚人类思想、妨碍他们寻找真理

to proceed from the particular to the general   从特殊推理到一般

deductive reasoning   演绎推理法

to proceed from the general to the particular   从一般推理到特殊

as a humanist intellect   作为一个人文主义的智者

to show the new empirical attitudes toward truth about nature   对自然科学真理表现出全新的实验主义的态度

to challenge the medieval scholasticists   挑战中世纪的经院哲学家

5. the economical and flexible way of writing   间接灵活的写作方法

be unlike in temperament, outlook and writing style   具有不同的气质、观念和写作风格

to show a strong personal touch   显示出强烈的个人独特风格

to put stress on the tentative nature of his mind   强调思想的短暂和犹疑不决

informal intimacy   不拘形式的亲密随和的语气

to arouse readers of different types to probe into the true nature under human experience   唤起/激起各类读者去探讨实践中的人类本性

to write for the ambitious Elizabethan and Jacobean youth of his class   为雄心勃勃的伊丽莎白一世到詹姆斯一世时代的本阶级(贵族阶级)青年而写作

to make their way in public life   他们进行社交的方法

to present the mode of thought and interest of the ruling class in his day   表现当时统治阶级的思想方式和情趣

6. Bacon cares more about axioms under the guidance of which man thinks and acts than human nature or morality.   培根更关心人类思想行为的指导原则,而不是人性或道德准则。

* 句中的关系代词 which 指的是 axioms;under the guidance of which ... or morality 是定语从句,可

改写为 man thinks and acts under the guidance of which (= axioms)。

7. to esteem the performance of public duty his highest aim 把承担公众义务当成他最高目标/理想

austere creed 严肃/严酷的信念

8. be charged and crowded with symmetries 充满了对称结构

be composed in a rather affected way （句子)矫揉造作、不自然

to enlarge the range of theme 扩大主题的范围

to bring forth the looser and more persuasive style 采用较为松散、更具说服力的文体

9. The essays are well-arranged and enriched by Biblical allusions, metaphors and cadence. 这些散文结构巧妙,含有很多《圣经》典故、比喻和变化的节奏。

培根作品选读
《论学习》Of Studies

词语解释和难句分析

1. It analyzes what studies chiefly serve for. 本文分析了学习/读书的主要目的/究竟是为了什么。

to exert influence over human character. 对人的性情/品性产生影响

to reveal to us Bacon's mature attitude towards learning 向我们揭示了培根对待学习的成熟、理性的态度

2. Studies serve for delight, for ornament, and for ability. 读书可以作为消遣,作为装饰,也可以增长才干。

3. Their chief use for delight is in privateness and retiring; for ornament, is in discourse; and for ability, is in the judgment and disposition of business. 孤独寂寞时,阅读可以消遣;高谈阔论时,知识可供装饰;处事行事时,正确运用知识意味着才干。

* 注意 their chief use 对应三个介词短语,for delight; for ornament 和 for ability,它们都分别是它的定语。the judgment and disposition of business 意为对事务的判断和处置。

4. For export men can execute, and perhaps judge of particulars, one by one; but the general counsels, and the plots and marshaling of affairs, come best from those that are learned. 因为有实际经验的人虽然能逐一处理、实施或判断具体的事情,但是总体的策划、各种事务的运筹和全局把握,则唯有博学者最能胜任/只能出自博学高才的智者。

* 注意 that are learned 是定语从句,修饰 those,即"那些有学问的人"。

5. To spend too much time in studies is sloth; to use them too much for ornament is affection; to make judgment wholly by their rules is the humor of a scholar. 读书花费太多的时间是拖沓懒散的行为,经常用读书来装饰门面是矫揉造作的做法,而完全依据书中的规定/条文判断事物则是学究气的表现。

* 第二句中的 them 指的是 studies, 读书、学习的意思。the humor of a scholar 意为学究的脾气、脾性,学究气。

6. They perfect nature, and are perfected by experience; for natural abilities are like natural plants, that need pruning by study; and studies themselves do give forth directions too much at large, except they be bounded in by experience. 读书求知可完善人的天性,又通过经验得到改进、丰富而臻于完善。因为天生的才智就像野生的草木,需要通过读书来修剪整理;而读书求知本身所获得的众多指导、教诲,若不通过实践经验确定如何运用,就难免失之过滥和空泛。

* 句中画线部分意为:(书中)无意中/随便地给出了太多的指导和教诲。at large 即不受约束、随便的、充分的意思。be bounded in by experience 意为为实践经验所限定/确定(实用)范围、界限,即如何运用。

7. Crafty men contemn studies, simple men admire them, and wise men use them, for they teach not (= do not teach) their own use; but that is a wisdom without them, and above them, won by observation.　技艺高超者轻视读书,头脑简单者羡慕读书,聪明的人善用书中的学问,读书并不教人如何运用书本知识,如何运用是书外的、超越书本之上的智慧,要通过观察才能获得。

   * 句中的 they, them 均指 studies; that 指 their own use, 即对读书所得知识的运用; won by observation 是过去分词短语, 作 wisdom 的后置定语。

8. Read not to contradict and confute, nor to believe and take for granted, nor to find talk and discourse, but to weigh and consider.　读书不为存心找矛盾,辩驳耍嘴;不可全信书中所言,当作理所当然的真理;也不是为了寻找谈资和话题,而应当仔细掂量和思考。

   * not to contradict and confute 为作目的状语的不定式短语,修饰动词 read,后面的几个排比的不定式短语也是同样的作用。

9. Some books are to be tasted, others to be swallowed, and some few to be chewed and digested; that is, some books are to be read only in parts; others to be read, but not curiously; and some few to be read wholly, and with diligence and attention.　有些书只需浅尝,有些书囫囵吞枣即可,很少的书值得细嚼慢咽,好好消化。也就是说,有些书只需部分选读;有些可以全读,但无须津津有味过细阅读;只有极少的书需要通读,而且要孜孜不倦,全神贯注地读。

   * 这一串句子是一组相同的"主语 + are to be done"结构的排比句,只是后面的句子省略了 are 罢了。

10. Some books also may be read by deputy and extracts made of them by others, but that would be only in the less important arguments and the meaner sort of books; else distilled books are like common distilled waters, flashy things.　有些书也可由代理人或副手代读,由别人代做内容摘要,但那只限于不太重要的论述和价值不太大的那类书籍。否则,经过摘选的书籍就像经过蒸馏的普通水,华而不实,淡而无味。

    * extracts made of them by others = extracts of them made by others, 由别人代做的书籍摘录,them 即 books。

11. Reading maketh (= makes) a full man, conference (maketh) a ready man, and writing (maketh) exact man.　读书使人充实,讨论使人机敏,写作使人精确。

    * 三个句子为同一结构,后两句省略了谓语动词。

12. ... if a man write little, he had need (= had to) have a great memory; if he confer little, he had need have a present wit; and if he read little, he had need have more cunning, to seem to know that he doth not.　如果一个人懒于动笔,他得有极强的记忆力;如果他不大与人交流,他得天生有临场机变的急智;如果他不常读书,他需要有更多的狡黠,能假装懂得自己不懂的东西。

13. Histories makes men wise; poets, witty; the mathematics, subtle; natural philosophy, deep; moral, grave; logic and rhetoric, able to contend.　读史使人睿智,读诗使人聪慧,数学使人精细,自然哲学使人深刻,伦理学使人庄重, 逻辑学和修辞学则使人善辩。

    * 所有句子都是同一结构,第一个句子表示了完整结构后,后面几个句子都省略了与前相同的词语 makes men,因而显得简练。

14. *Abeunt studia in mores.* [拉丁语] = Studies become ways of life.　读书成了人们的生活方式。

15. Nay,there is no stond or impediment in the wit but may be wrought out by fit studies, like as diseases of the body may have appropriate exercises.　不,没有什么智力上的障碍,不可以通过适当的读书学习

而得到贯通解决的,就像身体的疾病可通过适当锻炼而康复一样。

　　* there is no . . . but . . . 没有……不……;be wrought out = be worked out 被解决/贯通;like as . . . 中的 as 等于 when,直译为:就像身有疾病要适当运动锻炼的时候一样(没有不消除障碍、得到康复的)。

16. Bowling is good for the stone and reins (= the bladder and kidneys), shooting for the lungs and breast, gentle walking for the stomach, riding for the head, and the like. 　保龄球运动有益于肾,射击有益于胸肺,慢走有益于胃,骑马有益于脑,等等。

　　* 并列各句谓语部分都是 is good for,故除第一句外,后面各句都省略了相同谓语部分。

17. So if a man's wit be wandering, let him study the mathematics; for in demonstrations, if his wit be called away never so little, he must begin again. 　所以,假如一个人的智力不集中,就让他研究数学(做数学题),因为在演算数学时,如果脑子稍一走神,就必须从头再来。

　　* call away 思想转移,走神,不集中;never so = very 非常

18. If his wit be not apt to distinguish or find differences, let him study the schoolmen (= medieval theologians), for they are *Cumini sectores*. 　如果他不善于区分辨异,就让他研究中世纪神学家的经院哲学,因为他们和他们的这门学问是最吹毛求疵、烦琐辩证的。

　　* be apt to do. . . = be easy to do. . .

19. If he be not apt to beat over matters and to call up one thing to prove and illustrate another, let him study the lawyer's cases. 　假如他不善于全面考察事物,不善于从考察一件事物来证明和阐释另一件事物,那么就让他去研究律师的案卷。

　　* beat over matters = make thorough examinations of things 全面彻底地考察事物;call up = put sth. into consideration 提出……来考虑

20. So every defect of the mind may have a special receipt. 　这样,头脑里的每一个瑕疵都可能获得一个具体的药方。

主要内容归纳和总结

1. 弗朗西斯·培根是英国文艺复兴时期的著名哲学家、文学家和科学家。他反对经院哲学,首倡实验科学,第一个提出"知识就是力量",第一个主张把哲学从神学中分离出来,他的散文是英语文学语言的典范。

　　培根出身于贵族家庭,从小就受到良好的教育。他的父亲是伊丽莎白一世女王的掌玺大臣,他自己在巅峰时期也做到了国王詹姆士的掌玺大臣。后来他因被指控受贿而坐牢,出狱后回到府邸度过了一生最后的五年,而正是这五年,成就了他在文学、哲学和科学上的崇高地位,算是不幸中的大幸。

2. 培根的主要作品:

a. 学术和哲学类

《学术的进展》 *The Advancement of Learning* (1605)英语

《新工具论》 *Novum Organum* (1620)拉丁语,《学术的进展》的拉丁文扩展版

b. 文学作品

《亨利七世统治的历史》 *The History of the Reign of Henry VII* (1622)

《散文全集》 *Essays* (1625)共58篇

《新老格言集》 *Apophthagmes New and Old* (1625)

《新大西岛》 *The New Atlantis* 未完

c. 法学或法律方面的著作

《法律原理》*Maxims of Law*（1642）

《法令使用读本》*The Learned Reading upon the Statute of Uses*（1642）

3. 培根的主要学术思想和贡献

a. 培根把知识分成两种，一是来自神的启示（the Divine Revelation）；另一种来自人类头脑的思维（the workings of human mind）。虽然他没有否定正统的基督教思想（the orthodox of Christian thought），但是这样一个折中（compromise）在当时却有重大意义，因为他把神学（theology）与科学观察和实验（scientific observation and experiments）区别开来（见《学术的进展》）。

b. 他认为人的认识与学问包括三部分：1）基于人类回忆的历史学（history to man's memory）；2）生发于人类想象力和创造力的诗歌（poetry to man's imagination and creation）；3）源于人类理性的哲学（philosophy to man's reason）。

c. 他第一个提出归纳推理法（inductive reasoning），并用它来代替亚里士多德（Aristotle）的演绎推理法（deductive reasoning），即用从特殊到一般的推理方法（proceeding from the particular to the general）代替从一般到特殊的推理方法（from the general to the particular）（见《新工具论》）。

4. 培根散文的特点是简洁（brevity），紧凑（compactness），有力度（powerfulness），早期的版本追求排列的均匀对称（charged and crowded with symmetries），不够自然，后来的版本则改进为结构较为随意松散（looser）、更有说服力（more persuasive）的文风。散文结构巧妙（well-arranged），含有丰富的圣经典故（Biblical allusions）、比喻（metaphors）和活泼多变的节奏（cadence）。

重要信息句子

1. Bacon lays the foundation for modern science with his insistence on scientific way of thinking and fresh observation rather than authority as a basis for obtaining knowledge. 培根坚持用科学的思想方法，注意观察新事物，而不是把权威当作获得知识的依据，从而为现代科学奠定了基础。

2. The *Advancement of Learning* is a great tract（论文，专著）on education.

3. *Novum Organum* is a successful treatise（专题论著）written in Latin on methodology.

4. Montaigne（蒙田，法国作家），the first great modern essayist, is the predecessor of Bacon. The term "essay" was borrowed from Montaigne's *Essais* which appeared from 1580 to 1588.

V. 约翰·邓恩 John Donne（1572～1631）

词语解释和难句分析

1. metaphysical poets 玄学派诗人

the leading figure of the "metaphysical school" 玄学派的领袖人物

to break away from the conventional fashion of the Elizabethan love poetry 打破伊丽莎白时代爱情诗的传统形式

to echo the words and cadences of common speech 反映日常普通语言的词语和节奏

2. the imagery drawn from the actual life 取自实际生活的诗歌意象

The form is frequently that of an argument with the poet's beloved, with God, or with himself. 诗歌常常以与诗人所爱的人、与上帝或与自己争论的形式而存在。

3. to witness a renewed interest in Donne and other metaphysical poets （这段时期）见证了邓恩和其他玄学派诗人的作品重新得到人们的青睐

4. This new recognition has <u>arisen from</u> a realization of the seriousness of their art, an interest in their spirit of revolt, their realism, and other affinities with modern interests, as well as from the fact that they produced some fine poetry. 这种重新承认和肯定产生于人们对他们诗歌艺术严肃性的认识,对他们的反叛精神、现实主义以及现代欣赏情趣的偏爱,同时也因为他们确实写出了不少优秀的诗歌作品。

   * affinity with 与……的亲和/兼容,倾向相同,脾胃相投

5. His poems give a more inherently <u>theatrical impression</u> by exhibiting a seemingly unfocused <u>diversity of</u> experiences and attitudes, and <u>a free range of</u> feelings and moods. 他的诗似乎零散地展示了多种多样的人生经历和人生态度,以及一种漫无边际、信马由缰般的情感世界,因而显示出一种天生的戏剧性。

6. The mode is dynamic rather than static, with ingenuity of speech, vividness of imagery and vitality of rhythms, which <u>show a notable contrast to</u> the other Elizabethan lyric poems which are pure, serene, tuneful, and smooth-running. 诗歌形式是动态的,而不是静态的,语言精巧,意象生动,节奏/韵律充满活力,与伊丽莎白时代纯洁宁静、音调优美、平缓无波地向前推进的抒情诗相比,显示出明显的不同。

   * which 为关系代词,引导一个非限制性定语从句,修饰 the mode。

7. its tang of reality （邓恩诗歌的）现实气息
   in the sense that... 在……的意义上/方面
   to reflect life in a real rather than a poetical world 反映现实的世界而不是诗歌的世界

8. be born into a prosperous merchant family 出生于一个成功的富商家庭
   <u>be attended to</u> by a private tutor （教育）是在家庭教师的指导下完成的
   to leave without <u>taking a degree</u> because of his Catholic background 由于他的天主教家庭背景,没取得任何学位就离开了（学校）
   to begin his <u>legal studies</u> at <u>the Inns of Court</u> in London 开始了他在伦敦法学院的学习

9. the eminent <u>Lord Keeper of the Great Seal</u> 著名的掌玺大臣
   his great prospects of the worldly success 他世俗成功的光辉前程/仕途的锦绣前程
   be ruined by his secret marriage with 被他与……的秘密婚姻毁于一旦

10. Donne's conversion to Anglicanism <u>had no single date</u>, rather it was a gradual process. 邓恩转而皈依国教/新教/圣公会非一日之功,而是一个渐进的过程。
    at secular preferment 在俗世的仕途晋升方面
    to take orders 获得晋升/升职
    to take his new vocation seriously and perform his <u>holy duties</u> exceptionally well 对待新职严肃认真,对神职工作异常敬业
    to acquire a great reputation as an <u>impressive deliver</u> of <u>insightful sermons</u> 作为一个布道见解深刻的著名布道者,他得到了极大声誉
    to <u>devote all his time and efforts to</u> his priestly duties 为牧师的传教工作献出了全部时间和精力
    be appointed the Dean of St. Paul's 被任命为圣保罗教堂的教长

11. *The Elegies and Satires* 《挽诗与讽刺》
    Songs and Sonnets 《歌与短歌》

Holy Sonnets 《圣歌集》

A Hymn to God the Father 《圣父赞美诗》

12. Donne holds that the nature of love is the union of soul and body. The operations of the soul depend on body. The perfection of human lovers will not be made with souls alone. 邓恩认为爱情的真谛/本质是灵魂之爱与肉体之爱的结合。灵魂之爱要依靠肉体之爱来实现。爱情的完美单靠灵魂之爱是不能实现的。

13. This thought is quite contrary to the medieval love idea which merely put stress on spiritual love. 这种思想与中世纪只强调精神恋爱的爱情观截然不同。

14. the change and death confronting human love 与人类爱情相对立的变心和死亡

the futility and instability of love 爱的无用和变化不定

Farewell to Love 《告别爱情》

to eugloize a woman with telling very little about her physical beauty 赞美一个女子,却很少谈到她的肉体美。

to dramatize and illustrate the state of being in love 生动地刻画恋爱中的感觉与状态

15. This is distinctive from the Petrarchan sonneteers who paid so much attention to physical charms. 这不同于彼特拉克时期写作十四行诗的诗人们,他们非常注意描写肉体的魅力。

16. Only in *A Hymn to God the Father* do we find an assured faith; elsewhere there is always an element of conflict or doubt. The best of the *Holy Sonnets* express these struggles with unparalleled force. 只有在《圣父赞美诗》中,我们才能感到邓恩对上帝的笃信和忠诚;而在其他诗中,却总有矛盾或怀疑的成分存在。《圣歌集》中的最佳作品都强有力地表达了这种矛盾斗争。

17. to apply conceits, i. e. extended metaphors involving dramatic contrasts 采用别出心裁甚至牵强附会的手法,例如,带有戏剧性对比的扩展了的暗喻

18. Easy conceits, found in all Elizabethan poetry with images concerning mythology and natural objects, are not a novelty; but the difficult ones rely largely on the choice of imagery. 容易的别出心裁的比喻,可见于伊丽莎白时代的诗歌之中,带有与神话和自然界事物关联的意象,不足为奇;但较难的比喻主要依赖意象的选择。

19. Donne's images are linked with new resources such as law, psychology and philosophy which endow his poetry with learning and wit, and which provide certain intellectual difficulties. 邓恩诗歌的意象与新的源泉相联系,譬如法律、心理学和哲学,这赋予他的诗歌以学识和智慧的灵光,同时也增加了理解的难度。

20. in rigid syllogistic form 以生硬的三段论形式

to raise the topic and try to persuade, convince or upbraid him 提出论题,试图劝说、说服对方接受自己的观点,甚至训斥他

to begin with a certain idea but end in quite a contrary one 开始时是一种观点,结束时却是完全相反的观点

be not only playful but paradoxical; not only witty, but implies different kinds of feelings 不仅滑稽可笑,而且自相矛盾;不仅充满智慧,而且暗含着不同的感受

be interpreted through the rhythms and inflections of the verse 通过诗歌的韵律和语调的抑扬变化来诠释

21. to exhibit the same kind of physical vigor and scholastic complexity as his poetry （他的散文）体现出与他的诗歌同样的生命活力和学术难度

22. As a matter of fact, his weekly sermons are an intellectual exercise supplying food for thought, a purging

of conscience, and a study of rhetoric. 其实,他每周的布道就是一次为他的思考提供精神食粮的智力操练,一次良心的净化,一次修辞学的研究。

23. Some of Donne's sermons <u>are</u> carefully <u>contrived with</u> a dramatic, irregular immediacy to express a concern with personal <u>quest for</u> religious experience rather than <u>settled certainties</u>. 邓恩的一些散文把他突发的、不规则的即兴感受加以精心构思,以表达他对个人宗教经历追求的关切,而不是关心上天既定的不可变之事。

24. And it is the <u>obsession with</u> death that characterizes Donne's mature religious works. 他沉湎于对死亡的探索成为他成熟的宗教作品的特征。

　　* it is...that... 构成了一个强调句式。

约翰·邓恩作品选读
1. 升起的太阳 *The Sun Rising*

词语解释和难句分析

1. unruly　难驾驭的,不安分的,不守规矩的
   Why dost thou thus, = Why do you do so, 为什么你如此做
   call on　拜访,探望

2. Must to thy motions lovers' seasons run? = Must <u>lover's seasons</u> run to thy motions? 情人/恋人的季节必须跟着你的步调运行吗?

3. Saucy pedantic wretch 轻佻、迂腐的家伙
   sour prentices (= apprentices) 拙劣的学徒
   go chide/Late schoolboys and sour prentices = go to chide late schoolboys and sour prentices 去责骂迟到的学生和愚钝的学徒

4. Go (to) tell court huntsmen (= hunters) that the King will ride. 去告诉宫廷猎手,国王就要上马出猎了。
   　* 这里的 King 指詹姆斯一世国王,他是个打猎上瘾的国王。

5. Call country ants to harvest offices; 呼唤乡村蚂蚁快去收集食物。
   　* country ants 取材于一个关于蚂蚁和蚂蚱(grasshopper)的古老寓言故事;to harvest offices = to do harvest offices, 去做收获的活计/杂活。这里 harvest offices = autumn chores,指秋收时节家庭、农庄的杂活,对蚂蚁而言,即搜罗、搬运食物之类的活计。

6. Love, all alike, no seasons knows nor clime, /Nor hours, days, months, which are the rags of time. = Love, all alike, knows no seasons nor clime, ... of time. 爱情,全都一样,不知季节和气候,也不知小时,日子,月份,那都是时光的碎布头。

7. Thy beams, so reverend and strong/Why shouldst thou (= should you) think? = Why shouldst thou think thy beams, so reverend and strong? 你凭什么以为你的光芒如此威严,如此强烈?

8. I could <u>eclipse and cloud</u> (*vt.* 遮蔽,遮盖) them (= beams) <u>with a wink</u>, 我一眨眼就可使光线被遮蔽/变昏暗(眼的开合,使光线忽明忽暗)。
   But that I would not lose her sight so long; 但我不愿长久看不到她的目光、容颜。
   　* 因为阳光一昏暗,就看不见情人了。

9. to blind thine = to blind your eyes 使你(太阳)的光线暗淡/变暗

Look，and tomorrow late，tell me，/Whether both th'（=the）Indias of spice and mine /Be where thou leftst（=left）them，or lie here with me. 那么，去瞧瞧，明天晚些时候告诉我，盛产香料的东印度和盛产金矿的西印度是仍在你离开它们的地方，还是在这里与我在一起。

* whether...or...引导的名词性从句是 tell 的宾语从句。

* 祈使句中的第二人称指太阳。

10. Ask for those kings whom thou saw'st（=saw，与第二人称单数 thou 连用）yesterday，/And thou shalt（=shall）hear，All here in one bed lay（=All lay here in one bed）. 去打听一下你昨天见过的国王何处去了，你就会听说，他们全都在这里躺在一张床上。

11. She（=one bed）is all states，and all princes（am）I， 她是所有的国家，所有的君王就是我。
Nothing else is.=Nothing is else. 别的什么也不是。

12. Princes do but（=only do）play us；compared to this， 君王只是扮演我们玩，与此相比，目睹此情此景……
All honor's mimic，all wealth（is）alchemy. 一切荣誉都是作假、仿冒，一切财富都是欺骗、幻术。

* alchemy n. 炼金术，魔力，神秘变化

13. Thou，sun，art half as happy as we，/ In that（=therefore）the world's contracted thus； 你，太阳，只有我们一半快乐，因此，你眼里世界竟缩小至此。

* 诗的意境中，心理上的主观意象成分很多，这里的我、你、她，我们包括她和我两人，而你——太阳，只有一人，故而你的快乐也只有我们的一半，在你看来，世界也缩小了很多。

14. Thine age asks ease，and since thy duties be /To warm the world，that's done in warming us. 你年事已高需要安逸，既然你的职责是温暖世界，那温暖了我们即已尽责。

* 从 thine age 和 thy duties 两个词组的用法上可看出，thine 和 thy 做形容词性物主代词时，后跟的名词，一为元音开头的 age，另一为辅音开头的 duties，这是它们的区别。当然，thine 还可做名词性物主代词，相当于 yours，而 thy 则不能做名词性物主代词。

15. Shine here to us，and thou art everywhere； 在这里照耀了我们，你就无处不在。
This bed thy center is（=this bed is thy center），these walls（is）thy sphere. 这张床是你的中心，这四壁是你运行的轨迹。

* 根据古代托勒密天文学（Ptolemaic astronomy）的地心说（Geocentric theory），太阳围绕地球转。诗中的床指大地，床周围的四壁则是太阳运行的轨道。

参考译文——姚绍德

升起的太阳

忙碌的老傻瓜，没规矩的太阳，
你怎会如此没个样——
探望我们还要穿帘爬窗？
情人的季节还必得与你同步奔忙？
轻佻而又迂腐的家伙，去呵斥
迟到的学童和笨拙的学徒吧，
去告知宫廷猎手，国王要骑马射猎，
召呼乡下农夫蚂蚁似地去忙碌收获；
爱情，永远一样，不管什么气候、季节，

也不分小时和日月——那些时光的碎布头。

凭什么你傲慢地以为
你的光芒威严而强烈?
我一眨眼便可使你光华暗淡,
只是我不愿长久看不见她的容颜;
假如她的眼睛没有遮蔽你的,
你就去瞧瞧,明天晚时来告诉我——
东印度的香料和西印度的黄金
还在你离开它们的地方,或是与我同在一处?
去打听你昨天见过的君主们今日在何方,
你会听到,他们全都躺在这里的同一张床上。

她就是世界各国,我就是天下君王,
除此以外,什么也没有。
君王也只是扮演我们;感悟此情景,
一切荣誉不过作戏,一切财富只是幻象。
太阳,你只有我们一半快乐,
因而,你眼中的世界都缩小至此;
你年迈需要安逸,既然你的职责
是温暖世界,那么温暖了我们就算完事。
照耀了这里的我们,你就照耀了天下;
这床是你的中心,这四壁,是你的疆界。

格律和韵律分析

这首诗分为 3 个诗节,每个诗节的格律和韵律都是一样的。分析一节,即知全貌。来看第一节:

'Busy/old 'fool,/ un'ru/ly 'sun,	a
'Why dost/thou 'thus,	b
Through 'win/dows and/through 'cur/tains 'call/on 'us?	b
'Must to/thy 'mo/tions 'lo/vers' 'sea/sons 'run?	a
'Saucy/pe'dan/tic 'wretch,/ go 'chide	c
Late 'school/boys and/sour 'pren/ti'ces,	d
Go 'tell/court 'hunts/men that/the 'King/will 'ride,	c
Call 'coun/try 'ants/to 'har/vest 'o/ffices;	d
'Love, 'all/a'like,/ no 'sea/son 'knows/nor 'clime,	e
Nor 'hours,/ 'days, 'months,/ 'which are/the 'rags/of 'time.	e

10 行诗句的音步数分别为 4255445555,根据重音的标注,可以看出,大多数音步为抑扬格,3 个诗节皆是如此。因此可以说这首诗的格律为 4255445555 步抑扬格,显然不规则。根据诗句的尾韵,很容易判断这首诗的韵律为 abbacdcdee。

2. 死神,你别得意 *Death, Be Not Proud*

词语解释和难句分析

1. though some have called thee/Mighty and dreadful, 虽然有人夸你无比强大和可怕……

2. For those whom thou think'st thou dost overthrow/Die not, poor Death, nor yet canst thou kill me. 可改写为:For those whom you think you do overthrow do not Die/Are still living, poor Death, nor yet can you kill me. 意为:你以为你已确实打倒的那些人,并没有死/依然活着,可怜的死神,你也不能杀死我。

   * whom thou … overthrow 是 those 的定语从句,die not 才是 those 的谓语动词;nor can … 是倒装句,相当于 you can not kill me either yet。

3. From rest and sleep, which but thy pictures be, /Much pleasure; then from thee much more must flow. 可改写为:Much pleasure (flows) from rest and sleep, which (should) be but (= only) thy picture; then much more must flow from thee. 意为:休息和睡眠,只是你(死神)的影像,从中流出许多快乐,那么,从你那里必定流出更多。

   * which but … be 是 rest and sleep 的非限制性定语从句;括号中的 flows 是根据下一句中的 must flow from 补上的,前后两句应当都有 flow from 的相似结构。

4. And soonest our best men with thee do go (= do go with you), /Rest of their bones, and soul's (= soul is) delivery. 我们最优秀的人士很快都随你而去,骸骨得以休息,灵魂得到解脱。

   * 古希腊寓言有云:Whom the gods love die young. 意为:为众神所爱的人死得早。

5. Thou art slave to fate, chance, kings, and desperate men, 你是命运、机会、国王和亡命徒的奴隶 And (thou) dost with poison, war, and sickness dwell, = (You) do dwell with poison, war, and sickness, … 你与毒药、战争和疾病同居为伴

6. And poppy or charms can make us sleep as well/And better than thy stroke; why swell'st thou then ? 罂粟或者符咒也可能使我们睡去, 比你的打击还要管用;你还得意什么?

   * why swell'st thou then? = Why do you swell? 你凭什么趾高气扬?

7. One short sleep past, we wake eternally/And death shall be no more; Death, thou shalt die. 短睡过去,醒来即永远,死亡不复存在;死神你却将死亡。

参考译文——姚绍德

死神,你别得意

死神,你别得意,虽有人夸你强大,
其实,你并没有那么可怕;
因为,那些你以为打倒了的人并没死,
可怜的死神,你也同样杀不了我!
休息和睡眠,只是你的影像,竟涌流出
快乐,你本身,不更是快乐的泉源?

我们的英才早早随你而去,

骸骨得休息,灵魂获解脱。

你是命运、机遇、帝王和亡命徒的奴仆,

你与毒药、战争和疾病为伍,

而罂粟和符咒也能使我们安眠,

且比你的功效更强,那你又何以狂傲?

一次短睡过后,我们便醒来而获永生,

死亡将不复存在,死神,你才必将死亡!

格律和韵律分析

'Death, * /be 'not/'proud, 'though/some 'have/called 'thee	a
'Mighty/and 'dread/ful, for/thou 'art/not 'so;	b
For 'those/whom 'thou/'think'st 'thou/dost 'ov/er' throw	b
Die 'not,/ poor 'Death, / 'nor yet/'canst thou/'kill me.	a
From 'rest/and 'sleep,/which 'but/thy 'pic/tures 'be,	a
'Much 'plea/sure; 'then /from 'thee/much 'more/must 'flow,	b
And 'soon/est our/'best 'men/with 'thee/do 'go,	b
'Rest of/their 'bones, / and 'soul's/de'li/very.	a
Thou 'art/'slave to/'fate, 'chance, / 'kings, and/'desper/ate 'men,	c
And 'dost/with 'poi/son, 'war,/ and 'sick/ness 'dwell,	d
And 'poppy/or 'charms /can 'make/us 'sleep/as 'well	d
And 'bet/ter than/thy 'stroke;/ why 'swell'st/thou then?	c
One 'short/'sleep 'past, / we 'wake/e'ter/nally	e
And 'death/shall 'be/'no 'more;/'Death, thou/'shalt 'die.	e

根据上面的格律分析,可以看出这首诗的基调格是五步抑扬格。第一诗行第一音步缺一个音节,用＊号表示,第九诗行为6个音步,其他各诗行均为完整的5个音步。虽有一些音步为扬抑格、扬扬格、抑抑格,但数量相对较少(19个,阴影部分),占多数的仍是抑扬格(51个)。这首诗的韵律明显是 abbaabbacddcee,为典型的彼特拉克十四行诗的格律和韵律形式(Petrarch pattern)。

主要内容归纳和总结

1. 约翰·邓恩,英国诗人,玄学派诗歌(metaphysical poetry)的代表人物。邓恩出身于英国富商家庭,家庭教师(private tutor)的指导帮他完成了早期教育。后来他就读于牛津大学和剑桥大学,因为他信仰罗马天主教,所以未能获得学位;19岁时他到伦敦法学院(the Inns of Court in London)学习法律、语言、文学和神学。毕业后,他有幸成为掌玺大臣(Lord Keeper of the Great Seal)托马斯·埃格顿爵士(Sir Thomas Egerton)的秘书,却又因他秘密迎娶埃格顿夫人的娘家侄女而毁了仕途。生计难求,屡经蹉跎,他只好放弃天主教信仰,皈依国教,殷勤布道,由于学识渊博,积功而被任命为伦敦圣保罗教堂的教长(Dean of St. Paul's),一直任职到去世。

   邓恩一生的创作可分为两个阶段,前半段写诗,后半段写散文。他的诗歌多为爱情诗和宗教诗,散文多为布道文和宗教训诫。他的爱情诗,如《歌与短歌》(*The Songs and Sonnets*),注重刻画恋爱中的感觉和状态,不同于彼特拉克时期的十四行诗诗人(Petrarchan sonneteers)侧重描写体貌之美,他认为爱情的真谛在于灵魂之爱与肉体之爱的结合。他的宗教诗《圣父赞美诗》(*A Hymn to God the Father*)表现了对上帝的笃信与忠诚,《圣歌集》(*Holy Sonnets*)则让人感到他强烈的内心矛盾。

邓恩及其他玄学派诗人具有强烈的反叛精神,他们打破伊丽莎白时代爱情诗和抒情诗的传统,意象取自现实,口语入诗,措辞更加简单,形式表现仿佛在与人或上帝争论。邓恩更常常是别出心裁,不仅把传统的神话和自然物体用作诗中的意象,而且把法律、心理学、哲学作为新的意象源泉,赋予诗以学术和智慧的灵光。诗中比喻有浅显和深奥之别,浅显者可见于伊丽莎白时代的诗,深奥者意象选择的源泉常常出人意料,自相矛盾(paradoxical),甚至艰涩难懂。这就是玄学派诗歌的特点。

2. 约翰·邓恩的主要作品:

《挽诗与讽刺》*The Elegies and Satires*

《歌与短歌》*The Songs and Sonnets*

《圣父赞美诗》*A Hymn to God the Father*

《圣歌集》*Holy Sonnets*

重要信息的句子

1. John Donne is the leading figure of the "metaphysical school."

2. The term "metaphysical poetry" is commonly used to name the work of the 17th-century writers who wrote under the influence of John Donne. "玄学派诗歌"这个术语普遍用来指称17世纪在约翰·邓恩的影响下写作的作家的作品。

3. Donne's great prose works are his sermons, which are both rich and imaginative, exhibiting the same kind of physical vigor and scholastic complexity as his poetry. 邓恩的伟大散文作品都是他的布道文,文采华美,富有想象力,表现了与诗歌同样的生命活力和学术难度。

4. *The Songs and Sonnets*, by which Donne is probably best known, contains most of his early lyrics. Love is the basic theme. 邓恩赖以成名的诗集《歌与短歌》包含了他早期的大多数抒情诗,爱情是基本主题。

5. Donne's chief power as a religious poet is shown in the *Holy Sonnets* and the last hymns. 邓恩作为宗教诗人的主要才华都体现在他的《圣歌集》和赞美诗中。

VI. 约翰·弥尔顿 John Milton(1608～1674)

词语解释和难句分析

1. to greedily drill the treasures over the fields of 如饥似渴地潜心研究……领域的宝藏

   to complete his preparation for his literary career 完成了他文学生涯的准备工作

2. Milton once had an ambition to write an epic which England would "not willingly let die;" 弥尔顿一度雄心勃勃地想写一部流芳千古的不朽史诗。

3. be occupied with the thoughts of fighting for human freedom　充满了为人类自由而斗争的思想

4. to put his pen to the service of the revolutionary cause　用笔为革命事业服务

5. be threatened with stains　受到过度紧张/劳累的威胁/影响

6. to hold steadily to his purpose of using his pen in the service of his country　坚持不懈地用笔为自己的国家服务

7. to dictate his grand epic　口述他的伟大史诗

8. *Paradise Lost*《失乐园》;*Paradise Regained*《复乐园》;*Samson Agonistes*《力士参孙》

9. a collection of elegies dedicated to sb.　献给某人的挽歌集

   a fellow undergraduate of Milton's at Cambridge　弥尔顿在剑桥大学读书时的同学

   be drowned in the Irish sea　溺死于爱尔兰海

10. the sense of irrecoverable loss in the silencing of a young poet　对一个年轻诗人永久的沉默有一种无可挽回的痛失感

    to swell to a passionate questioning, rage, sorrow and acceptance　发展到激情难抑地爆发质问,愤怒,而又不得不接受事实

11. The feelings begin in a low key but move on to the large questions of divine justice and human accountability.　诗中的情感低调开始,但逐步发展,终于激烈起来,以至对神的正义和人的可靠性发出大量的疑问。

12. the blistering attack on the clergy　对牧师的猛烈抨击

    be corrupted by self-interest　因自私而腐败

13. at least not unfavorably　至少毫不逊色,并不相形见绌

    be a great plea for freedom of the press　是一个要求新闻自由的伟大主张

14. the only generally acknowledged epic since *Beowulf*　自《贝奥武夫》之后唯一得到普遍认可的史诗

    the most perfect example of the verse drama after the Greek style in English　最完美的古希腊风格的英文诗剧的典范

15. man's disobedience and the loss of Paradise　人类的反叛和天堂的失去

    the prime cause　主要起因

    to lead a rebellion against God　领导一场对上帝的反叛/造反

    be cast into Hell　被打入地狱

16. to refuse to accept his failure, vowing that "all was not lost"　拒绝失败,发誓说"一切还没完/还可挽回"

    to seek revenge for his downfall　为他的失败而寻机报仇

    to take revenge by tempting Adam and Eve　通过诱惑亚当和夏娃报复(上帝)

17. be driven out of Paradise　被逐出天堂

    be sorry for what they have done and pray to God　他们后悔自己所做的事,乞求上帝原谅

    be given the hope for redemption　获得/被给予拯救的希望

18. to expose the ways of Satan and to "justify the ways of God to men"　揭露撒旦的做法(反叛),为上帝对人类的做法(惩罚)辩护

    the conflict between human love and spiritual duty　人类爱情与精神上的道义责任之间的矛盾、冲突

    the freedom to submit to God's prohibition on eating the apple and the choice of disobedience made for love　屈从于上帝的禁令不吃苹果的自由和为了爱情而进行造反的选择

19. be seduced by Satan's rhetoric and her own confused ambition — as well as the mere prompting of hunger　被撒旦的花言巧语和她自己困惑的潜在欲望——譬如纯粹的食欲刺激——所引诱

    to fall into sin through innocent credulity　因天真轻信而犯下罪孽

be the sequel to another and more stupendous tragedy　是另一个更加惊人的巨大悲剧所带来的结果

20. By <u>lifting</u> his argument <u>to</u> that plane, Milton raises the problem of evil in a more intractable form. 弥尔顿把他的论点上升到更高的层面,以更加放纵/难以驾驭的方式,高屋建瓴地叙述了罪恶的问题。

lust　*n.* a strong sexual desire or a eager desire for possessing of something 肉欲,贪欲

wrath　*n.* revenge, punishment 报复,惩罚,天谴

avarice　*n.* greediness 贪婪,贪得无厌

21. At the exaltation of the Son these forces erupted and <u>were cast forth</u>. But God <u>suffered</u> them <u>to</u> <u>escape</u> <u>from</u> Hell and <u>infect</u> the Earth.　在上帝提升自己儿子的时候,这些罪恶也纷纷出笼/粉墨登场/走上前台了,但上帝听任他们越狱逃窜,流毒人间。

22. be re-enacted　被重新颁布,重新上演

to <u>lay hold of</u> it (grace) by an act of free will　根据自由意志/自主选择,维持(人类的)体面和尊严

be the keystone of Milton's creed　成为弥尔顿信念/信条的基础/基石

23. His poem attempts to convince us that the unquestionable Biblical revelation means that an <u>all-knowing</u> <u>God</u> was just in allowing Adam and Eve to be tempted and, of their free will, to choose sin and its inevitable punishment.　他的诗竭力要说服我们相信:无可怀疑的圣经启示表明洞察天机/一切的上帝,听任亚当和夏娃被诱惑,让他们自主选择罪孽而遭到不可避免的惩罚,都是正确公正的。

24. to <u>open the way for</u> the voluntary sacrifice of Christ　为基督的自愿献身开辟了道路/做好了铺垫

the mercy of God in <u>bringing good out of evil</u>　上帝拯救人类弃恶从善的仁慈

25. <u>in the person of</u> Christ　以基督的身份

in the divine favor　在神的帮助下

to follow the account in the fourth chapter of Matthew's gospel　遵循/根据马太福音第四章的叙述

noble thought and splendid imagery <u>equal to</u> the best of *Paradise Lost*　可以与《失乐园》的宏大构思媲美的神圣思想和恢宏意象

to <u>fall below</u> the level of the first　没有达到第一部著作(《失乐园》)的水平

26. to <u>turn to</u> a more vital and personal theme　转向一个更重要、更贴近自己的主题

<u>be afflicted by</u> thoughtless enemies but preserving a noble ideal <u>to the end</u>　尽管受到那些愚蠢敌人的折磨,但却始终坚持自己崇高的理想

<u>be a fitting close to</u> <u>the life work</u> of the poet himself　非常切合诗人本人的毕生事业

to mark the Old Greek dramas　带有古希腊戏剧的烙印

to <u>bring destruction down upon</u> the enemy <u>at the cost of</u> his own life　不惜牺牲个人的生命来摧毁敌人

27. to <u>make him tower over</u> all the other English writers of his time　使他赫然屹立于/超越他同时代的其他英国作家(之中)

to exert a great influence over later ones　对后来作家产生了巨大影响

弥尔顿作品选读

《失乐园》*Paradise Lost* 第一卷节选

词语解释和难句分析

1. to rebel against　造……的反,反叛……

the furnace of Hell　地狱的熔炉

to fight back 反击

to assume the shape of a snake 假装成蛇的形象

the Garden of Eden 伊甸园

to send the Archangel Raphael to warn Adam and Eve of Satan 派遣天使长拉斐尔告诫亚当和夏娃防备撒旦

to succeed in seducing Eve to eat the fruit from the Tree of Knowledge 成功地引诱夏娃吃了智慧树上的果子

be exiled by God from the paradise and thereafter live a life full of hardship 被上帝从天堂驱逐出去，此后过着充满艰辛的生活

2. If thou beest he — but O how fallen! = If you be/are he — but O how fallen you are! 难道你就是他——啊，你怎么如此落魄！

   * 潜台词是：你与那个英雄盖世的"他"判若两人，颓败至此，以致我一下子没看出来。

3. How changed/(you are) From him who in the happy realms of light/Clothed with transcendent brightness didst outshine/Myriads, though bright (= though they are bright)! 你的变化多么大呀！简直没有原来的样子了。当初，你在快乐的光明王国里，身披万丈霞光，气度非凡，虽群星闪耀，但你比群星更灿烂！

   * 在 who 引导的定语从句中，画线部分为核心句架，介词短语 in the happy realms of light 和过去分词短语 clothed with transcendent brightness 都是谓语动词 didst outshine 的状语。

   * myriads n. 无数，一万，成千上万，这里指"群星"。

4. 从第四行的 If he whom 到第 11 行的 of those dire arms 是一个完整的大句子。

5. If (thou beest) he whom (似应为 who) mutual league,/United thoughts And counsels, equal hope/And hazard in the glorious enterprise,/Joined with me once, ... 如果你是他，曾与我在一起，相互结盟，共同协商，思想一致，在光辉的伟业中希望相同，风险同当……

   * 在定语从句中，句架可认为是 who joined with me once, 其他的短语均可看作 with 的宾语，如 with mutual league, united thoughts ... in the glorious enterprise。

6. now misery hath (= has) joined/In equal ruin; into what pit thou seest/From what height (hath) fallen, ... 现在，饱受煎熬的苦难连同毁灭的危险一起降临到我们的头上，你看是从何等的高度落到何等的深渊。

   * 注意 fallen 前面实际上是有个 hath 省略了，另外 thou seest 是插入语。

7. so much the stronger proved /He with his thunder = He proved so much the stronger (than us) with his thunder. 挟雷霆之威，他的确（表现得）比我们强大得多。
   and till then who knew/The force of those dire (= dreadful) arms? 迄今为止/以前，谁知道那些可怕武器的威力呢？

8. 从第 11 行的 Yet not for those 到第 22 行的 shook his throne 是一个完整的句子。

9. Yet not for those (= those arms), /Nor what the potent Victor in his rage/Can else inflict, do I repent or change,/Though changed in outward luster, that fixed mind /And high distain, from the sense of injured merit, ... 然而那些武器，以及强大的胜利者在狂怒中可能使用的另外的什么武器，都不能使我后悔和改变那坚定的意志和因感受到价值观受到伤害而产生的极度轻蔑，尽管我失去了外表的光辉。

10. That with the Mightiest raised me to contend,/And to the fierce contention brought along/Innumerable force of spirits armed,/That durst (= dared) dislike his rein, and me preferring,/His utmost power with adverse power opposed/In dubious battle on the plains of Heaven,/And shook his throne. 这实际上是 that fixed mind and high distain 的定语从句，调整语序，可改写为：that raised me to contend with the

Mightiest (= God)/And brought along innumerable armed force of spirits/That durst (= dared) dislike his rein and prefer me to the fierce contention /And opposed his utmost power with adverse power/In dubious battle on the plains of Heaven/And shook his throne. 意为：这（坚定意志和高度轻蔑）使我挺身而起与上帝拼搏，率领无数敢于蔑视他的统治而愿意拥戴我的武装的精灵，投入这激烈的斗争中，用叛逆的力量对抗他至高无上的权威，在天国的平原上，打一场胜负未定的生死决战，动摇他的王座。

　　* 句中第二个 that 引导了又一个定语从句，修饰 force of spirits。

11. What though the field be lost? /All is not lost: the unconquerable will,/And study of revenge, immortal hate,/And courage never to submit or yield;/And what is else not to be overcome? 尽管战场失败，可那又有什么？ 并非全都输光：不可征服的意志，复仇的渴望，不灭的仇恨，永不屈服的勇气，依然还在，另外还有什么不可战胜的呢？

　　* 句中画线部分的不定式短语是 courage 的定语。what is else not to be overcome? = what else is not to be overcome?

12. That glory never shall his wrath or might /Extort from me. = His wrath or might shall never extort that glory from me. 任凭他如何狂怒，施展多大威力，都休想夺去我得到的这份荣耀。

13. To bow and sue for grace/With suppliant knee, and deify his power/Who from the terror of this arm so late/Doubted his empire — that were low indeed;/That were an ignominy and shame beneath /This downfall;... 因为他的武装已经对我们最近的造反军产生了恐惧，开始怀疑他对天国的统治，再对他卑躬屈膝，乞求宽恕，神化他的军队确实是太可耻了，甚至是比这次的失败还要大的耻辱。

　　* Who from the terror of this arm so late/Doubted his empire = who doubted his empire from the terror of this arm so late，是 his power 的定语从句，但翻译时把它当成了状语摆在句首。

14. since, by fate, the strength of gods/And this empyreal substance cannot fail; 因为，命中注定，众天使的神力和天堂圣洁的灵质不会朽败。

15. Since, through experience of this great event,/In arms not worse, in foresight much advanced,/We may with more successful hope resolve/To wage by force or guile eternal war,/ Irreconcilable to our grand Foe,/Who now triumphs, and in th' (= the) excess of joy/Sole reigning holds the tyranny of Heaven. 因为，有了这一伟大的（反叛）事件的经验，有了不差的武器，有了更超前的远见，我们满怀成功的希望，决心打一场有勇有谋的持久的战争。我们绝不向强大的敌人妥协让步，他目前陶醉在胜利之中，欣喜若狂，唯我独尊的独裁统治，掌控着天庭的霸权。

16. So spake (= spoke) th' (= the) apostate angel, though in pain,/Vaunting aloud, but racked with deep despair;/And him thus answered soon his bold compeer (= companion): 可改写为：The apostate angel spake so, though in pain,/Vaunting aloud but racked with deep despair;/And his bold compeer soon answered him thus. 意为：叛乱的天使这样说，虽然心里很痛苦，仍大声疾呼，心中却深受绝望的折磨；他那勇敢的伙伴很快回答他说：……

17. O prince, O chief of many throned powers,/That led th' embattled seraphim to war/Under thy conduct, and in dreadful deeds/Fearless, endangered Heaven's perpetual King,/And put to proof his high supremacy,/Whether upheld by strength, or chance, or fate! 啊，大王，许多掌权天使（宝座天使）的首领呵，天使们率领斗志昂扬、跃跃欲试的撒拉弗大军，在你的指挥下，投入战争，在可怕的战斗中，英勇无畏，使天国的永恒之王陷于危境，考验他的无上威权，究竟是靠力量支持，还是靠侥幸，抑或命运！

　　* that 引导定语从句修饰 throned powers。Put to proof his high supremacy = put his high supremacy to proof，意为：考验他至高无上的权威。Whether held by strength... = Whether his supremacy was held by strength...

18. Too well I see and rue the dire event/That with sad overthrow and foul defeat/Hath lost us Heaven, ... = I see and rue too well the dire event/That hath lost us Heaven/With sad overthrow and foul defeat, ...   我目睹这场可怕的灾难而且深感遗憾,它已使我们被可悲地打倒,遭逢可耻的失败,因而失去了天界。

19. and all this mighty host/In horrible destruction laid thus low,/As far as gods and heavenly essences/Can perish: ...   这样强大的军队在可怕的大失败中竟全军沉沦若此,就天使和天上的精灵而言,可谓破灭到了极点

20. for the mind and spirit remains/Invincible, and vigor soon returns,/Though all our glory extinct, and happy state/Here swallowed up in endless misery.   因为我们的思想和灵魂永远不可战胜,我们的精力很快就会恢复,尽管我们的荣耀已全被剥夺,快乐的心境此刻也被无尽的痛苦所吞噬。

21. what if ...   要是……又怎么样? 即使……又有什么关系?
    of force = perforce, necessarily, to have to (do)   必须,必定,不得不,只能
    to suffice his vengeful ire   满足他复仇的怒火
    his thralls by right of war   他的战俘/因战争的权利而获得的奴隶

22. But what if he our Conqueror (Whom I now /Of force believe almighty, since no less /Than such could have o'verpowered such force as ours)/have left us this our spirit and strength entire,/Strongly to suffer and support our pains,/That we may so suffice his vengeful ire,/Or do him mightier service as his thralls/By right of war, whate'er business be,/Here in the heart of Hell to work in fire,/Or do his errands in the gloomy deep?   可是他,我们的征服者,(现在我只能承认他的全能,因为只有这样的人才能打垮我们这样的大军),即使没有摧毁而留存下我们精神和力量的完整性又怎么样呢?不过是使我们能够承受痛苦,以便满足他复仇的怒火,或者做他的战俘奴隶,为他服更大的苦役,不论他要我们干什么,是在这地狱中心的烈火中服刑,还是在阴沉混沌的深渊中受差遣?

23. What can it then avail though yet we feel/Strength undiminished, or eternal being/To undergo eternal punishment?   即使我感觉力量未灭,甚至永生,也只为了承受永久的惩罚,那又有什么益处呢?
    * undiminished 和 eternal being 都是 feel 的宾语补足语。

24. whereto   ad. (关系副词)对此(对刚刚那个跟他造反的天使说的话)
    Th' arch-fiend = Satan   恶魔
    aught good = anything good, all good things   好事
    sole delight   唯一乐事

25. Whereto with speedy words th' arch-fiend replied:/"Fallen cherub, to be weak is miserable,/Doing or suffering: but of this be sure (= but this be sure of),/To do aught good never will be our task,/But ever to do ill (be) our sole delight,/As being the contrary to his high will/Whom we resist. ... "   对此,大魔头立即急促地回答说:"堕落的天使呀,软弱才是悲惨,不论是采取行动还是承受苦难,但这一点是肯定的,行善绝不是我们的使命,作恶才是我们唯一乐事,就像我们一贯做的那样,永远与他的最高意志作对……"

26. providence   n. 天意,天命
    to bring forth... out of ...   从……产生出……
    to pervert that end   破坏/曲解/颠倒那个/原定目标,与原定目标相反

27. If then his providence/Out of our evil seek to bring forth good,/Our labor must be to pervert that end,/And out of good still to find means of evil;   如果他的天意是要从恶中产生出善,我们的事业就得是破坏那个目标,还得要从善中找出作恶的途径。

28. ofttimes = often   ad. 经常
    inmost counsels   内心深处的想法/意图/计划

destined aim 原定/既定目标

29. Which ofttimes may succeed, so as perhaps/Shall grieve him, if I fail not, and disturb/His inmost counsels from their destined aim. 如果我所言非虚/判断不错,这(我们善中生恶的努力)常常会成功,也许会使他伤心,搅乱了他内心的计划,偏离了原定的目标。

30. to recall ... back to the gates of Heaven 把……召回到天界

his ministers of vengeance and pursuit 他的(参加)复仇和追击的天使大臣们

31. the sulphurous hail,/ Shot after us in storm, o'er blown hath laid/The fiery surge that from the precipice/of Heaven received us falling; 硫黄霰弹,曾像暴风雨一样追击过我们,业已风平浪静,使得接待我们从天界的悬崖下来的翻腾火海也趋于平静。

   * 这个句子要仔细分析才能搞清语法关系,否则会理解错误,出现乱猜现象。句子的主架是 the sulphurous hail hath laid the fiery surge. 意为(不再打了的)霰弹使火海平静下来。而 shot after us in storm 和 overblown 为过去分词(短语)作 the sulphurous hail 的定语,相当于定语从句 which once shot after us in storm and has been overblown;overblown 常有(暴风雨)趋于平息的意思,句中指霰弹不打了。that 引导的定语从句修饰 the fiery surge,可改写得更好理解些:That received us falling from the precipice of Heaven.

32. and the thunder,/ Winged with red lightning and impetuous rage,/Perhaps hath spent his shafts, and ceases now/To bellow through the vast and boundless deep. 雷霆挟着红色闪电和暴怒的狂风飞行,也许已放完了利剑,现在停止了响彻广漠无垠的深渊的吼叫。

33. Let us not slip th' occasion, whether scorn/Or satiate fury yield it from our Foe. = Let us not slip th' occasion, whether scorn/Or satiate fury from our Foe yield it (= the occasion). 我们别错过这个机会,不管这机会是产生于敌人的轻蔑还是愤怒的火头已过。

34. yon dreary plain 远处那片阴郁沉闷的平原

   be void of light 完全没有光明

   to cast pale and dreadful 投射青灰色的可怕的光

   * 这里 cast 可看成联系动词。

35. Seest thou yon (= Do you see) dreary plain, forlorn and wild,/The seat of desolation, void of light,/Save what the glimmering of these livid flames/Casts pale and dreadful? 你可看见远处那片沉闷阴郁的平原,荒芜苍凉;你可看到那片渺无人烟的荒原,没有一点光明,除了这灰蓝色光焰的闪烁投射下恐怖的幽光?

   * forlorn and wild 和 void of light 两个形容词短语分别是 dreary plain 和 the seat of desolation 的后置定语。

36. Thither (= there) let us tend /From off the tossing of these fiery waves; = Let us tend thither/From off the tossing of these fiery waves; 让我们去那里,一避火海的冲击/颠簸。

37. There rest, if any rest can harbor there; 如果能在那里驻足休息,那就在那里休息一下;

38. And reassembling our afflicted powers, 召集我们受重创的军队(分词短语作状语),

   Consult how we may henceforth most offend/Our enemy, our own loss how repair (= how we may repair our loss), 商讨今后如何最有效地打击敌人,如何弥补我们自己的损失,

39. How (we may) overcome this dire calamity, 如何克服这惨痛的灾难,

   What reinforcement we may gain from hope, 从希望中获得一些支援,

   If not, what resolution (we may gain) from despair. 要不然,又能从绝望中做出什么决策。

名家译文——朱维之

失乐园(节选)

"是你啊;这是何等的坠落!
何等的变化呀! 你原来住在
光明的乐土,全身披覆着
无比的光辉,胜过群星的灿烂;
你曾和我结成同盟,同心同气,
同一希望,在光荣的大事业中
和我在一起,现在,我们是从
何等高的高天上,沉沦到了
何等深的深渊呀! 他握有雷霆,
确是强大,谁知道这凶恶的
武器竟有那么大的威力呢?
可是,那威力,那强有力的
胜利者的狂暴,都不能
叫我懊丧,或者叫我改变初衷,
虽然外表的光彩改变了,
但坚定的心志和岸然的骄矜
绝不转变;由于真价值的受损,
激动了我,决心和强权决一胜负,
率领无数天军投入剧烈的战斗,
他们都厌恶天神的统治而来拥护我,
拿出全部力量跟至高的权力对抗,
在天界疆场上做一次冒险的战斗,
动摇了他的宝座。我们损失了什么?
并非什么都丢光:不挠的意志,
热切的复仇心,不灭的憎恨,
以及永不屈服、永不退让的勇气,
还有什么比这些更难战胜的呢?
他的暴怒也罢,威力也罢,
绝不能夺去我这份光荣。
经过这一次战争的惨烈,
好容易才使他的政权动摇;
这时还要弯腰屈膝,向他
哀求怜悯,拜倒在他的权力之下,
那才真正是卑鄙,可耻,
比这次的沉沦还要卑贱。
因为我们生而具有神力,

秉有轻清的灵质,不能朽坏,
又因这次大事件的经验,
我们要准备更好的武器,
更远的预见,更有成功的希望,
用暴力或智力向我们的大敌
挑起不可调解的持久战争。
他现在正自夸胜利,得意忘形,
独揽大权,在天上掌握虐政呢。"
背叛的天使这样说了,虽忍痛说出
豪言壮语,心却为深沉的失望所苦。
他那勇敢的伙伴立即回答他说:
"大王,掌权天使的首长啊,
掌权者们率领英勇的撒拉弗天军
在你指挥之下去作战,
大无畏地,投身于惊险的行动,
使天上永生的王陷于危急,
他靠暴力,侥幸,或靠命运,
来支持自己至高无上的权力,
我目睹而哀痛这次可怕的事件,
可悲的覆没,可耻的败绩,
使我们失去天界;这样的大军
竟遭到这么大的失败,
沉沦到这样的阴间里来,
我们原是神灵,气质轻清,
论破灭可说已经到了尽头,
因为我们还留有心志和精神,
不可战胜,很快就会恢复元气。
虽然我们的全部光辉黯淡了,
快乐被无限的悲惨所吞没;
可是他,我们的征服者,(现在,
我只能相信他的全能,否则,
他不可能击破我们这样的大军,)
他使我们还留有这样的精力,
大概是要使我们更能忍受痛苦,
吃足苦头,承受他那报复的怒火;
或者是要我们服更大的苦役,
把我们当作俘虏,当作奴隶,
在地狱猛火的中心来干苦活,
在幽暗的深渊中为他奔走。
这样,我们将永受无穷刑法,
即使是自己觉得力量还没衰退,
甚至是永生的,那又有什么好处?"
大魔王立刻用急激的话语回答他:

"坠落的天使呀,示弱是可悲的,
无论做事或受苦,但这一条是明确的:
行善绝不是我们的任务,
作恶才是我们的唯一乐事,
这样才算是反抗我们敌对者的
高强意志。如果他想要
从我们的恶中寻找善的话,
我们的事业就得颠倒目标,
就要寻求从善到恶的途径。
如果我不失算,定会屡次奏效,
使他烦恼,搅乱他极密的计划,
使它们对不准所预定的目标。
你看,那愤怒的胜利者已经
把复仇和袭击的使者召回天门;
暴风雨一般追击我们的
硫黄霹弹已经静下来了,
迎接我们从天界的悬崖上
坠落下来的火焰的洪波也平静些了,
以赭红的闪电和狂暴的愤怒,
因为带翅膀的轰雷,大概已经
用完了弹头,现在已经不在
这广漠无边的深渊中吼响了。
我们不要放过这机会,
不管这是由于敌人的轻蔑,
或者是由于他气头已过的机会。
你没看见那一片荒凉的原野吗?
寂寞、荒芜、绝无人迹、不见亮光。
只有这么一些铅色的幽焰,
闪着青灰色的,可怕的幽光。
我们往那儿去,一避火浪的冲击,
可以休息的话,就休息一下,
重新集合我们疲惫的队伍,
大家讨论,怎样给敌人更多的损害,
怎样弥补我们自己的损失,
怎样战胜这个可怕的灾祸,
从希望中可以得些怎样的援助,
或从失望中来一个怎样的决策。"

主要内容归纳和总结

1. 约翰·弥尔顿出生于伦敦,父亲既是学者又是商人。他先后就读于圣保罗学校和剑桥大学,毕业后用六年时间在父亲的乡间别墅里潜心研究各种学问。他是激进的革命家、政论家,资产阶级革命的领导人物、议长克伦威尔(Oliver Cromwell)的文胆,同时他又是大诗人。他彻底的革命精神和非凡的诗歌才华对后来者影响深远。

2. 弥尔顿的文学创作分三个阶段

a. 第一阶段为早期阶段,主要是继承伊丽莎白一世时代的优秀文学作品的风格,代表作是《利西达斯》(*Lycidas*),是献给溺死在爱尔兰海中的剑桥大学同学爱德华·金(Edward King)的一部挽诗集。

b. 第二阶段他献身于克伦威尔领导的资产阶级革命,把20年的大好年华贡献给为政治自由、宗教自由和个人自由而斗争的事业,写了无数的战斗檄文,以政治小册子的形式宣传发行,成为当时最伟大的散文家,代表作是《论出版自由》(*Areopagitica*)。

c. 第三阶段是在克伦威尔去世后,英王复辟,弥尔顿遭受打击,眼盲之后,通过口述完成了三大英语史诗:

《失乐园》*Paradise Lost*（1667）

《复乐园》*Paradise Regained*（1671）

《力士参孙》*Samson Agonistes*（1671）

重要信息句子

1. *Paradise Lost* is the greatest, indeed the only generally acknowledged epic in English literature since *Beowulf*.

2. Milton devoted almost 20 years of his best life to the fight for political, religious and personal liberty as a writer. His powerful pamphlets written during this period make him the greatest prose writer of his age.

3. In his life, Milton shows himself a real revolutionary, a master poet and a great prose writer.

4. *Paradise Lost* and *Samson Agonistes* borrow stories from the Bible; *Paradise Regained* shows how mankind, in the person of Christ, withstands the tempter and is established once more in the divine favor.

英国文艺复兴时期文学同步练习与答案

1. The Renaissance, which means _____ or _____, is actually a movement stimulated by a series of historical events, such as _____ and the economic expansion.

a. reformation/revolution; the rediscovery of ancient Roman and Greek culture

b. rebirth/revival; the new discoveries in geography and astrology

c. rebirth/revival; the rediscovery of ancient Roman and Greek culture, the religious reformation

d. b and c

2. The Renaissance, in essence, is a historical period in which the European humanist thinkers and scholars made attempts to _____.

a. get rid of those old feudalist ideas in medieval Europe

b. introduce new ideas that expressed the interests of the rising bourgeoisie

c. recover the purity of the early church from the corruption of the Roman Catholic church

d. all above

3. The Renaissance was slow in reaching England because of _____.

a. England's separation from the Continent　　　b. its domestic unrest

    c. the Wars of Roses   d. a and b

4. England's Golden Age, especially in literature, means the period of _____.

    a. Medieval Age   b. Old English

    c. Enlightenment   d. Renaissance

5. The essence of the Renaissance is _____.

    a. religious reformation   b. ideological emancipation

    c. freedom of speech   d. humanism

6. The Greek and Roman civilization was based on such a conception that _____.

    a. God blesses all creatures   b. democracy has spread over everywhere

    c. man is the measure of all things   d. all men are created equal

7. In medieval theology, people's relations to the world about them were reduced to a problem _____.

    a. in an effort to prepare their souls for a future life

    b. to perfect themselves and perform wonders

    c. to pray for God's bless

    d. to conquer the nature

8. According to Martin Luther, _____.

    a. Pope is the representative of God

    b. only clergymen could interpret the Bible

    c. every true Christian was his own priest and was entitled to interpret the Bible for himself

    d. the colorful and dramatic ritual of the Catholic Church should be kept

9. When _____ declared himself through the approval of the Parliament as _____ in 1534, the Reformation in England was in its full swing.

    a. Charles II/the King of England

    b. Martin Luther/the Roman Pope

    c. John Calvin /a rebel against Roman Catholic Church

    d. Henry VIII/the Supreme Head of the Church of England

10. _____ was the first person who introduced printing into England.

    a. William Caxton   b. Montaigne

    c. Chapman   d. Plutarch

11. The first period of the English Renaissance was one of _____; the real main stream of the English Renaissance, in totality, is _____.

    a. inheriting the tradition of Medieval literature/Elizabethan poetry

    b. imitation and assimilation/Elizabethan drama

    c. introducing the foreign literary form/Victorian novels

    d. rediscovery of the Old Greek and Roman culture/the revival of the Old Greek Roman philosophy

12. By imitating the romances of _____ and _____, embracing the mysteries of _____, and combining the fictions of poetic fancy with the facts of daily life, they made a vivid depiction of the sharp conflicts between feudalism and _____ in a transcend period.

    a. Italy/Spain/German Legend/the rising bourgeoisie

    b. Greece/Roman/Scandinavian Legend/Roman Catholic Church

    c. England/France/Norway stories/north European Viking

    d. Italy/Greece/Trojan war/the Orthodox Eastern Church

13. _____, the founder of modern science in England, is best known for his _____ which greatly influenced the development of this literary form.

a. Shakespeare/drama
b. Plautus and Terence/Latin comedies
c. Francis Bacon/essays
d. Christopher Marlowe/*Dr. Faustus*

14. Edmund Spenser's masterpiece is _____. His principal intention of writing is to present the example of a perfect gentleman possessing of _____ virtues, who is _____, serving as a unifying element for the poem as a whole. Another character contributing to the unity of the work is _____, the Fairy Queen.
    a. *Faerie Queene*/12/Arthur/Gloriana
    b. *Faerie Queene*/12/St. George/Una
    c. *Faerie Queene*/12/Redcrosse/Una
    d. *Dr. Faustus*/12/Dr. Faustus/Duessa

15. It is _____ idealism, his love of beauty, and his exquisite melody that make him _____.
    a. Marlowe's/"the poet's poet"
    b. Bacon's/the founder of the modern science
    c. Spenser's/"the poet's poet"
    d. John Donne's/the leader of Metaphysical poets

16. As the most gifted of the "University Wits," Marlowe composed _____ plays within his short lifetime. Among them the most important are: _____, Part I & II, _____, _____ and *Edward II*.
    a. six/*Tamburlaine*/*Dr. Faustus*/*The Jew of Malta*
    b. six/*Faerie Queene*/*Dr. Faustus*/*Henry VIII*
    c. four/*Essays*/*Novum Organum*/*The Advancement of Learning*
    d. four/*Areopagitica*/*Paradise Lost*/*Paradise Regained*

17. Marlowe's greatest achievement lies in that he perfected _____ and made it the principal medium of English _____.
    a. drama/poetry
    b. English language/drama
    c. blank verse/drama
    d. poetic rhyme/poetry

18. Marlowe's second achievement is his creation of _____ for English drama.
    a. vivid character
    b. interesting stories
    c. the Renaissance hero
    d. a magician

19. *Dr. Faustus* is a play based on _____ of a magician aspiring for _____ and finally meeting his tragic end as a result of selling his soul to the Devil.
    a. the Italian Legend/technology
    b. the German legend/knowledge
    c. the Greek theology/powerful force
    d. the Indian Buddhism/supernatural power

20. William Shakespeare writes _____ plays, _____ sonnets and _____ long poems.
    a. 3/50/3
    b. 54/10/1
    c. 38/154/2
    d. 1/20/1

21. In his prime period of writing career, Shakespeare published two long non-dramatic narrative poems, _____ and _____, both of which were dedicated to the Earl of Southampton.
    a. *Venus and Adonis*/*The Rape of Lucrece*
    b. *Antony and Cleopatra*/*Troilus and Cressida*
    c. *Paradise Lost*/*Paradise Regained*
    d. *Ode to the West Wind*/*The Waste Land*

22. Generally Shakespeare's dramatic career is divided into four periods: 1). the 1st period was one of _____; 2). in the 2nd period, his style and approach became highly _____; 3). his 3rd period includes his _____ and his so-called dark comedies; 4). in the last period his work includes his principal _____ and his two final plays.

a. apprenticeship/typified/greatest tragedies/romantic comedies

b. apprenticeship/individualized/dark comedies/romances

c. apprenticeship/typed/tragedies/tragicomedies

d. apprenticeship/individualized/greatest tragedies/romantic tragicomedies

23. Shakespeare's greatest tragedies are _____, _____, _____, and _____.

a. *Hamlet/Antony and Cleopatra/Othello/Coriolanus*

b. *Cymbeline/King Lear/Macbeth/Troilus and Cressida*

c. *Hamlet/King Lear/Othello/Macbeth*

d. *Romeo and Juliet/Julius Caesar/Hamlet/King Lear*

24. Shakespeare's history plays are mainly written under the principle that _____ under a mighty and just sovereign is a necessary.

a. national unity   b. national war

c. national independence   d. Rose War

25. In his romantic comedies, Shakespeare takes an _____ toward love and youth. The most important one of his comedies is _____.

a. humorous attitude/*A Midsummer Night's Dream*

b. optimistic attitude/*The Merchant of Venice*

c. satiric attitude/*Much Ado About Nothing*

d. ironic attitude/*The Merry Wives of Windsor*

26. The successful romantic tragedy is _____. Though a tragedy, it is permeated with _____.

a. *The Winter's Tale*/interest   b. *The Tempest*/joyousness

c. *Pericles*/celebration   d. *Romeo and Juliet*/optimistic spirit

27. Shakespeare's four greatest tragedies have two characteristics in common, which are _____.

a. 1) Each portrays some noble hero facing the injustice of human life and a difficult situation, whose fate is closely connected with the fate of the whole nation; 2) Each hero has his weakness of nature.

b. Each hero encounters a tragic fate and finally reaches a victorious end.

c. Four tragedies portray about the same kind heroes, who have about the same fortune and the same personalities.

d. All the four tragedies have the similar beginning and the similar end.

28. The main character portrayed in each one of Shakespeare's four greatest tragedies has his weakness. Hamlet is a _____ scholar-prince and always in the dilemma between _____; Othello's _____ is made use of by the outside evil force; the old king Lear is _____, and therefore makes him suffer from treachery and infidelity; Macbeth's _____ starts up his ambition and leads him to incessant crimes.

a. childish/love and sadness/jealousy/preferring to flatterers/lust for power

b. bookish/hesitation and decision/prejudice to white beauty/preference to his wife

c. indecisive/deep thinking and decision making/jealousy/a stubborn old man/cruelty

d. melancholic/action and mind/inner weakness/unwilling to totally give up his power/lust for power

29. _____, the first of the great tragedies, is generally regarded as Shakespeare's most popular play on the stage.

a. *Romeo and Juliet*   b. *Othello*

c. *Antony and Cleopatra*   d. *Hamlet*

30. In his late years, the whole life to Shakespeare is no more than a dream. Thus, _____ is a typical example of his pessimistic view towards human life and society in his late years.

a. King Lear　　　　　　　　　　b. Othello

c. Tempest　　　　　　　　　　　d. Macbeth

31. Shakespeare, after accepting the Renaissance views on literature, holds that literature should be a combination of beauty, kindness and truth, and should reflect _____.

a. nature and reality　　　　　　　b. man and nature

c. human nature and human right　　d. man's personality and similarity

32. Shakespeare's major characters are neither merely individual ones nor type ones; they are _____.

a. certain types representing individuals

b. individuals representing certain types

c. characters in pairs

d. characters sharing feature with others

33. Francis Bacon's works can be divided into three groups: _____, _____, and _____.

a. *Novum Organum/Essays/Maxims of Law*

b. education/literature/*The Learned Reading upon the Statute of Uses*

c. learning and philosophy/literary works/laws

d. reading and learning/literature and history/philosophy and law

34. *Novum Organum* is a successful treatise written in Latin on _____.

a. literature　　　　　　　　　　b. learning

c. how to use tools　　　　　　　d. methodology

35. In *Novum Organum*, Bacon suggests _____ in scientific study in place of the Aristotelian method of _____, i. e, proceeding from the _____ to the _____ , instead of proceeding from the _____ to the _____.

a. the deductive method of reasoning/inductive reasoning/particular/general/general /particular;

b. the inductive method of reasoning/deductive reasoning/general/particular/particular/general;

c. the inductive method of reasoning/deductive reasoning/particular/general/inductive/deductive

d. the inductive method of reasoning/deductive reasoning/particular/general/general/particular

36. The term "metaphysical poetry" is commonly used to name the work of the 17th-century writers who wrote under the influence of _____.

a. T. S. Eliot　　　　　　　　　　b. Allen Tate

c. John Ransom　　　　　　　　　d. John Donne

37. _____, by which Donne is probably best known, contains most of his early lyrics. _____ is the basic theme.

a. *The Elegies and Satires*/lament　　b. *The Songs and the Sonnets*/love

c. *Holy Sonnets*/religious sermons　　d. *A Hymn to God the Father*/theology

38. John Donne's interest lies in dramatizing and illustrating the state of _____ instead of paying much attention to physical charms like Petrarchan sonneteers.

a. being in love　　　　　　　　　b. Plato's love in spirit

c. physical love　　　　　　　　　d. lewdness

39. Donne's images are linked with new resources such as law, psychology and philosophy which endow his poetry with _____ and _____, and of course, certain intellectual difficulties.

a. learning/wit　　　　　　　　　b. music/art

c. intellect/reasoning　　　　　　　d. abstraction/suggestion

40. Donne's poetry involves a certain kind of _____, sometimes in rigid syllogistic form.

    a. logic reasoning   b. unique imagination

    c. strange metaphor   d. argument

41. _____ is a typical example of John Milton's early poetic works, composed for a collection of elegies dedicated to Edward King.

    a. *Areopagitica*   b. *Samson Agonists*

    c. *Paradise Regained*   d. *Lycidas*

42. Milton devoted almost 20 years of his best life to the fight for liberty as a writer. _____ is his most memorable prose work. It is a great plea for _____.

    a. *Lycidas*/freedom of speech

    b. *Areopagitica*/freedom of press

    c. *Novum Organum*/right to advance

    d. *Apophthagmes New and Old*/right to say

43. *Paradise Lost* is a long epic divided into 12 books, which is originated from _____, and of which the theme is the _____.

    a. German legend/fight against evil   b. knight romance/love and chivalry

    c. Genesis 3 of the Bible/"Fall of Man"   d. Chinese theology/origin of man

44. *Paradise Regained* shows how mankind, in the person of _____, withstands the _____ and is established once more in the divine favor.

    a. Christ/tempter   b. God/bless

    c. Satan/instigation   d. Jesus/advice

45. In *Samson Agonistes*, Milton borrows his story from _____. But the picture of Israel's mighty champion is fitting close to the life and work of _____.

    a. Italian epic/Italian poet, Dante   b. the Bible/the poet himself

    c. Scandinavian legend/Beowulf   d. Greek theology/Zeus

46. The real mainstream of the English Renaissance is _____.

    a. the Elizabethan drama   b. the Elizabethan prose

    c. ancient poem   d. romantic novel

47. The most significant intellectual movement of the Renaissance was _____.

    a. the Reformation   b. humanism

    c. the Italian revival   d. geographical explorations

48. Which of the following plays does NOT belong to Shakespeare's great tragedies? _____.

    a. *Romeo and Juliet*   b. *King Lear*

    c. *Hamlet*   d. *Macbeth*

49. Which statement about the Elizabethan age is NOT true? _____

    a. It is the age of translation.

    b. It is the age of bourgeois revolution.

    c. It is the age of exploration.

    d. It is the age of the protestant reformation.

50. In *The Faerie Queene* Spenser impresses us with his skilled _____ blending of religious and historical _____.

    a. symbolism/lyricism   b. allegory/romance

    c. elegy/narrative   d. personification/irony

51. Una in *The Faerie Queene* stands for _____.

    a. chastity   b. holiness

c. truth   d. error

52. _____ first made blank verse the principal instrument of English drama.

    a. Shakespeare   b. Wyatt

    c. Sidney   d. Marlowe

53. The literary form of *The Faerie Queene* is _____.

    a. allegorical poem   b. lyric poem

    c. ironic poem   d. narrative poem

54. "To fashion a gentleman or noble person in virtuous and gentle discipline", best describes _____ principal intention.

    a. Edmund Spenser's   b. Daniel Defoe's

    c. Walt Whitman's   d. William Shakespeare's

55. According to Bacon, man's understanding consists of three parts, which of the following sentences is NOT one of the three parts? _____

    a. The reflection of current situation.

    b. History to man's memory.

    c. Poetry to man's imagination and creation.

    d. Philosophy to man's reason.

56. _____ holds that the nature of love is the union of soul and body.

    a. John Milton   b. John Donne

    c. John Keats   d. John Bunyan

57. Which of the following is NOT true according to Donne? _____

    a. John Donne is the leading figure of the "metaphysical school."

    b. The most striking feature of Donne's poetry is precisely its tang of romance.

    c. Donne is best known by *The Songs and Sonnets*.

    d. Donne's great prose works are his sermons.

58. "All is not lost: the unconquerable will,/And study of revenge, immortal hate,/And courage never to submit or yield:/And what is else not to be overcome?" The above comes from _____.

    a. *Dr. Faustus*   b. *Paradise Lost*

    c. *Paradise Regained*   d. *Tamburlaine*

59. _____ shows how mankind, in the person of Christ, withstands the tempter and is established once more in the divine favor.

    a. *Paradise Lost*   b. *Paradise Regained*

    c. *Samson Agonistes*   d. *Beowulf*

60. Of the following lines from *The Merchant of Venice*, what statement is NOT true? _____

        "For herein Fortune shows herself more kind

        Than in her custom. It is still her use

        To let the wretched man outlive his wealth,

        To view with hollow eye and wrinkled brow

        An age of poverty; from which ling' ring penance

        Of such misery doth she cut me off. "

    a. Lady Fortuna is not always kind towards the fallen man.

    b. It is her usual habit to take away the fallen man's wealth and let him live in poverty.

    c. Antonio thinks she is more kind toward him because she is taking away both his wealth and life.

    d. She is kind to Antonio because she does not take his life away though she destroys his ships.

61. Of the following lines from Milton's *Paradise Lost*, what statement is correct? _____

    "To bow and sue for grace
    With suppliant knee, and deify his power
    . . . —that were low indeed;
    That were an ignominy, and shame beneath
    This downfall;. . . "

    a. To beg God for mercy and worship his power were as low as this downfall.

    b. To beg God for mercy and worship his power were more shameful and disgraceful than this downfall.

    c. To beg God for mercy is more shameful than worship his power.

    d. To fight against God is as low as to worship Satan.

62. In the sonnet "Death, Be Not Proud", Donne says to death: "For those whom thou think'st thou dost overthrow/Die not, poor Death, nor yet canst thou kill me." What does he mean ? _____

    a. Death is very strong.

    b. Death is not death, because after death we wake up to live eternally.

    c. One must face death courageously and defiantly.

    d. Death is not as strong as he thinks he is.

63. "Read not to contradict and confute, nor to believe and take for granted" is one of the epigrams found in

    _____ .

    a. Bacon's *Of Study*   b. Bunyan's *Pilgrim's Progress*

    c. Thomas More's *Utopia*   d. Fielding's *Tom Jones*

64. Which of the following is NOT typical of metaphysical poetry best represented by John Donne's works? _____ .

    a. Common speech   b. Conceit

    c. Argument   d. Elegant language

65. In *Paradise Lost*, Satan says: "We may with more successful hope resolve/To wage by force or guile eternal war, /Irreconcilable to out grand Foe." What is the "eternal war" Satan and his followers were to wage against God? _____

    a. To plant a tree of knowledge in the Garden of Eden.

    b. To turn into poisonous snakes to threaten man's life.

    c. To remove God from his throne.

    d. To corrupt God's creation of man and woman.

66. *Dr. Faustus* is a play based on the German legend of a magician aspiring for _____ And finally meeting his tragic end as a result of selling his soul to the Devil.

    a. money   b. immortality

    c. knowledge   d. political power

Keys: ddddd/cacda/bacac/accbc/adcab/daddc/abcdd/dbaad/dbcab/ababb/cdaaa/bbbbc/bdadd/c

第二章 新古典主义时期 The Neoclassical Period

词语解释和难句分析

1. the return of the Stuarts to the English throne 英国斯图亚特王朝的复辟
   the full assertion of Romanticism 充分主张浪漫主义,浪漫主义盛行
   Lyrical Ballads 《抒情歌谣集》
2. a turbulent society 动荡、骚动的社会
   the Restoration of King Charles II 查理二世国王的复辟
   the Great Plague 大瘟疫、鼠疫(特指英国 17 世纪发生的特大瘟疫)
   the Great London Fire 伦敦大火
   the Glorious Revolution 光荣革命(1689)
3. the Tories and the Whigs 托利党和辉格党,17 世纪英国议会的两大政党,托利党曾反对詹姆斯二世继位,辉格党后来发展为自由党,美国的辉格党曾支持独立战争,后来发展成共和党。
   opposing religious sects 对立的宗教派别
   Roman Catholicism 罗马天主教
   the Anglican Church 英国圣公会,英国国教会
   Dissenters 英国不信国教的新教徒
   full of conflicts and divergence of values 充满价值观的冲突和分歧
   Acts of Enclosure 圈地运动/法案
   wage earners 拿工资的人,雇佣劳动者
   be plundered from the colonies 从殖民地掠夺来的
   be flooding foreign markets far and near 正像潮水一样涌进世界各地的市场
4. This coming together of free labor from the home and free capital gathered or plundered from the colonies was the essence of the Industrial Revolution. 这种来自家庭的自由劳动力和从殖民地聚集或掠夺来的自由资本的大汇聚成了工业革命实实在在的基础。
5. self-restraint 自控,自我约束
   self-reliance 自立,依靠自己,自力更生
   self-contained 自给自足,不受外界影响的,有自制力的
   self-independent 自我独立,独立自主的
6. the Age of Enlightenment or the Age of Reason 启蒙运动时期或理性时期
   a progressive intellectual movement flourished in France 在法国兴起并充分发展的进步智力运动
   a furtherance of the Renaissance 对文艺复兴运动的一次促进/推动
   reason/rationality 理性,理智
   to call for a reference to order, reason and rules 要求有序、理性和规则,要求以秩序、理性和规则为基准、标准
7. They believed that when reason served as the yardstick for the measurement of all human activities and

relations, every superstition, injustice and oppression was <u>to yield place to</u> "eternal truth," "eternal justice" and "natural equality." 他们认为,当理性成为衡量一切人类行为和关系的标尺时,一切迷信、非正义和压迫都要让位于"永久真理","永久正义"和"天然的平等"。

8. literature ... heavily didactic and moralizing 道德说教/道德教化气息浓重的文学

the two pioneers of familiar essays 日用散文创作方面的两位先驱

a revival to interest in the old classical works 对古希腊古罗马经典作品的兴趣复燃

be modeled after 模仿……

9. They believed that the artistic ideals should be order, logic, restrained emotion and accuracy, and that literature should be judged in terms of its service to humanity. 他们认为艺术理想应当是有序、有逻辑的,情感准确、有节制的,而且,文学的价值应当根据它对人文主义所起的作用来判断。

＊ 两个 that 引导两个名词性从句作为 believed 的并列宾语从句。

10. This belief led them to seek proportion, unity, harmony and grace in literary expressions, <u>in an effort to</u> delight, instruct and correct human beings, primarily as social animals. 这种信念使他们在文学创作中追求协调、统一、和谐和典雅,竭力使作为基本社会动物的人感到喜闻乐见、有教益、有指正的作用。

11. a polite, urbane, witty, and intellectual art 一门彬彬有礼,温文尔雅,风趣睿智的艺术

every genre of literature 每一种文学风格/体裁

the three unities of time, space and action 时间、空间和动作三要素统一

be adhered to 坚守,坚持

type characters rather than individual 类型人物而不是个性人物

12. be rebelled against and challenged by the sentimentalists 受到感伤主义者的反叛和挑战

in due time 整个期间,到期满时

classical grace 古典气质,经典艺术的典雅气质

clarity and conciseness 简明凝练

13. to climax with John Drydon 以约翰·德莱顿等作家的出现而达到高潮/极盛期

the last standard-bearer of the school 该流派最后的旗手

<u>be noted for</u> its seriousness and earnestness in tone and constant didacticism 以其语调的严肃性和不断的说教而著称

mock epic, romance, satire and epigram 讽刺/喜剧史诗,骑士抒情诗,讽喻诗和讽刺短诗

the elegant poetic structure and diction 典雅的诗歌结构和措辞

14. <u>be predominated by</u> a newly rising literary form — the modern English novel 被现代英语小说这个新兴的文学形式所主宰

be <u>contrary to</u> the traditional romance of aristocrats 与传统的贵族传奇故事不同

a natural product of the Industrial Revolution 工业革命的自然产物

15. an apparent <u>shift</u> of interest <u>from</u> the classic literary tradition <u>to</u> originality and imagination 读者的阅读兴趣明显从古典文学传统转移到独创和想象方面来

Gothic novels 哥特式小说

to <u>take place</u> in some haunted or dilapidated Middle Age castles 发生在某些鬼魂出没或者破败坍塌的中世纪城堡中

<u>be turned out</u> profusely by male and female writers 被男男女女的作家大量创作出来

eulogizing or lamenting lyrics by nature poets 自然诗人创作的颂扬或哀悼抒情诗

the leading figure among <u>a host of</u> playwrights 一大批剧作家中的领军人物

the best model of satire 最佳讽喻诗的典范

主要内容归纳和总结

1. 新古典主义时期英国的社会动荡和思想状态

   a. 查理二世的复辟(the Restoration of Charles II in 1660)。

   b. 1665 年的大瘟疫(the Great Plague),仅伦敦就因黑死病(black death)死了 7 万。

   c. 伦敦大火(the Great London Fire)烧毁了大部分城市,三分之二的市民无家可归。

   d. 作为天主教徒的詹姆斯二世国王的信奉新教的女儿玛丽(Mary)和女婿荷兰的奥兰治(Orange)公爵于 1689 年进行"光荣革命"(the Glorious Revolution),取代了父王,实行夫妇联合执政,结束了克伦威尔去世后查理二世和詹姆斯二世的君主复辟,之所以叫"光荣革命"是因为在整个革命过程中没有流血。

   e. 君主和议会,议会内两大政党托利党(the Tories)和辉格党(the Whigs),各宗教派别等之间的斗争非常激烈。

   f. 对外在北美、印度、西印度群岛(the West Indies)进行扩张,国内的圈地运动(Acts of Enclosure)迫使千百万农民离开土地去工厂当雇佣工人(wage earners)。

   g. 18 世纪是启蒙运动时期或者理性的时代(the Age of Enlightenment or the Age of Reason),进一步促进了 15 世纪、16 世纪的文艺复兴运动,也为 1789 年的法国大革命和 1776 年的美国独立战争打下理论基础。

2. 启蒙运动的宗旨和思想

   启蒙运动是进步知识分子的运动,发端于法国,其宗旨是用现代哲学与艺术思想的晨光启迪整个世界(to enlighten the whole world with the light of modern philosophical and artistic ideas)。

   启蒙主义者赞颂理性、平等与科学,主张理性是任何人思想、行动的唯一缘由,理性应当成为人类行为和人类关系的衡量尺度,一旦实现理性原则,一切的迷信、不公和压迫都会让位给"永久的真理"(eternal truth)"永久的公正"(eternal justice)和"天然的平等"(natural equality),他们提倡的重点就是秩序(order)、理性(reason)和法律(law)。另外,他们还认为人有局限性(limited)、两面性(dualistic)及不完美性(imperfect),提倡普及教育,使人人臻于完美和理智,则建立民主平等的社会大有希望。

3. 新古典主义文学的原则和要求

   在文学领域,启蒙运动使人们重新对古希腊、古罗马时代的经典著作产生兴趣,这股思潮就是新古典主义。

   新古典主义要求所有的文学作品都效仿古希腊、古罗马时代文学大师(荷马、维吉尔、贺拉斯、奥维德等)以及当时法国文学大师的经典著作,文学作品的评判标准就是看它们是否为人文主义服务,追求的目标就是表达与措辞的协调、统一和描写的和谐与典雅。

   新古典主义者几乎对所有的文学形式都设定了规矩和框框:散文必须简洁、直白、通顺,有灵活性;诗歌必须抒情、壮美,隐含教义、讽喻,有戏剧性;戏剧必须用英雄偶句体,即五步抑扬格押韵双行诗;作品中的人物要代表一类人,而不是个性化的人;时间、地点、时间三要素缺一不可,不可混乱。

   这种状况一直持续到 18 世纪后期,文学形式出现叛逆,感伤主义崛起(首先在法国),受达尔文的进化论和弗洛伊德的精神分析等新思想的影响,新古典主义才逐步被浪漫主义所代替。

4. 新古典主义时期出现的现代小说的先驱

   丹尼尔·迪福(Daniel Defoe):《鲁滨孙漂流记》(*Robinson Crusoe*)

   塞缪尔·理查德森(Samuel Richardson):《帕米拉》(*Pamela*)被称为英国第一部小说

亨利·菲尔丁(Henry Fielding):《汤姆·琼斯》(*Tom Jones*)

劳伦斯·斯特恩(Lawrence Sterne):《项狄传》(*The Life and Opinions of Fristram Shandy, Gentlman*)

奇特,怪诞,被认为是意识流小说之先驱

托比亚斯·斯摩莱特(Tobias George Smollett):《蓝登传》(*The Adventures of Roderick Random*)

奥利弗·哥尔斯密(Oliver Goldsmith):《威克菲尔德的牧师》(*The Vicar of Wakefield*)

重要信息句子

1. The English society of the neoclassical period was a turbulent one. Of the great political and social events there were the Restoration of King Charles II in 1660, the Glorious Plague of 1665 which took 70 000 lives in London alone, the Great London Fire which destroyed a large part of the city, leaving two-thirds of the population homeless, the Glorious Revolution in which King James II was replaced by his Protestant daughter Mary and her Dutch husband William, Duke of Orange, in 1689, and so on.

2. The 18th century saw the fast development of England as a nation.

3. The 18th century England is also known as the Age of Enlightenment or the Age of Reason. The Enlightenment Movement was a progressive intellectual movement which flourished in France and swept through the whole Western Europe at the time.

4. In the field of literature, the Enlightenment Movement brought about a revival of interest in the old classical works. This tendency is known as neoclassicism.

5. According to the neoclassicists, all forms of literature were to be modeled after the classical works of the ancient Greek and Roman writers (Homer, Virgil, Horace, Ovid, etc.) and those of the contemporary French ones.

I. 约翰·班扬 John Bunyan (1628 ~ 1688)

词语解释和难句分析

1. be born into a poor tinker's family 出生于一个穷苦的补锅匠家庭

   to take up his father's trade 继承父亲的事业

   to have the least promise of becoming a writer 丝毫没指望成为一个作家

   to join a Nonconformist church 加入非国教的新教教会

   to begin to preach by the roadside or on the village green 开始在路边或者村中公共绿地传教

   to tell people of his vision and interpretation of God's doctrine 给人们宣讲他对上帝教义的看法和解释

   to take a vow to give up preaching 发誓放弃传教

   be imprisoned in again on charge of the same offence 被指控犯同样罪行而被投入监狱

2. to have a deep hatred for 对……怀有深刻的仇恨

   to accumulate their wealth "by hook and by crook" 通过陷阱和欺骗/煞费苦心地积累财富

   the reader of the least education 几乎没受过教育的读者

   to share the pleasure of reading his novel 分享阅读他的小说的快乐

   to relive the experience of his characters 重新经历他书中人物的生活

约翰·班扬作品选读

《天路历程》*The Pilgrim's Progress*
第一部分"名利场" "The Vanity Fair"

词语解释和难句分析

1. the oncoming disaster　即将来临的大灾难

   in search of salvation　寻找拯救

   to stumble into a pit, the Slough of Despond　跌进一个深坑,叫绝望坑

   to join sb.　加入到某人的队伍中,与某人在一起/一起行动

   to set out later but have made better progress　出发虽晚了一点,但进步却快

   to claim them to be his subjects and refuses to accept their allegiance to God　要求他们臣服于他,并且拒绝接受他们对上帝的忠诚

   alien agitators　外来的煽动者

   be condemned to death　被判死刑

   to get away and reach the Celestial City　逃脱并最终到达了天国

   to enjoy eternal life in the fellowship of the blessed　在上帝保佑的众伙伴中享受长生不老

2. religious allegory　宗教寓言

   to abide by Christian doctrines　遵循基督教教义

   to bear much relevance to the time　与时代紧密相关,紧扣时代脉搏

   predominant metaphor　主要隐喻

   be homely and commonplace　朴实无华和大众寻常

   spiritual significance　精神上的意义

   commonplace details　寻常琐事

3. The strange is combined with the familiar and the trivial joined to the divine　陌生奇特与平常熟悉的事物结合,世俗琐事与神祇教义交融。

4. be lighter than vanity　比名利还要虚浮

   as the saying of the wise　正如智者/哲人所言

   new-erected business　刚兴起的行业/商业

   a thing of ancient standing　一件古已有之的事情

5. Celestial City　天国之城

   to lie through this town of Vanity　贯穿这名利城镇

   be kept all the year long　长年保持,终年不散

   to contrive to set up a fair　计划/策划建立一个集市

   to last all the year long　整年持续进行

   to perceive by the path that the pilgrims made, that...　从朝圣者踏出来的小路就感知到/认识到……

6. ...all such merchandise sold, as ... trades, places, honors, preferments, titles, countries, kingdoms, lusts, pleasures, and delights of all sorts, as whores, bawds, ..., lives, blood, bodies, souls, ..., precious stones, and what not.　诸如……行业、位置、升迁、头衔/爵位、国家、王国、欲望、快乐以及各种各样的娱乐享受,像妓女、老鸨、生命、鲜血、肉体、灵魂……宝石,等等等等诸如此类的商品,应有尽有。

7. And, moreover, at this fair there is <u>at all times</u> to be seen jugglings, cheats, games, plays, fools, apes, knaves, and rogues, <u>and that of every kind</u>.　还有,这集市上随时都可以看到变戏法、行骗、竞技、赌博、小丑、模仿人的人、无赖以及流氓恶棍等一应俱全。

　　* 此举为倒装句,there is 后面的主语较长,故移到 to be seen 后面去了。

8. Here are to be seen, too, and <u>that for nothing</u>, thefts, murders, adulteries, false swearers, and that of a blood-red colour. = thefts, murders, adulteries, false swearers, and that of a blood-red colour are to be seen here, too, and that for nothing.　在这里还可以看到盗窃、谋杀、通奸、信誓旦旦而谎话连篇的人和鲜血淋漓的场景,而且是免费白看。

　　* 这同样是一个倒装句。

9. And as in other fairs <u>of less moment</u>, there are the several rows and streets, under their proper names, where <u>such and such</u> wares are vended; so here likewise you have the proper places, rows, streets (viz., countries and kingdoms), where the wares of this fair are soonest to be found.　就像另外一些不太重要的集市一样,这里有好多的街道,标有专门的名称,出售这样那样与街道名称相符的商品。你也可以在那里看到特定的地点,特定的街道(表示特定的地区、特定的王国),在这些地方可很快找到他们上市销售的货物。

10. be greatly promoted in this fair　(商品)在该集市上特别旺销

　　to take a dislike thereat (= for that)　对此感到讨厌

11. lusty fair　繁华闹市

　　the Prince of princes　王子中的王子,即耶稣基督 Jesus Christ

　　that upon a fair-day = that is upon/on a fair-day = the temptation of Jesus by Satan was on a fair-day　魔鬼引诱耶稣的阴谋就发生在一个开市的日子

　　the chief lord of this fair　这个集市的主人/大老板

　　to do sb. reverence　对某人表示尊重

　　to make sb. lord of the fair　让某人当集市的主人

12. the way to the Celestial City lies just through this town where this lusty fair is kept; and he that will go to the city, and yet not go through this town, <u>must needs</u> "go out of the world".　通往天国之城的路就穿过这拥有繁华集市的城镇,要去天国之城,却又不想经过此城镇的人,必须得"离开这个世界"。

13. and as I think, it was Beelzebub, the chief lord of this fair, that invited him to buy of his vanities; …　我想,正是集市的主人魔王比尔兹布博邀请他去买市上虚华的东西。

14. it was Beelzebub that would have made him <u>lord of the fair</u>, would he but have done him reverence as he went through the town. = If he (= Jesus) but have done him (= Beelzebub) reverence, Beelzebub would have made him lord of the fair.　假如耶稣(经过集市时)对魔王尊重些,魔王会让他当集市主人的。

15. a man of honor　有声望的人

　　to allure the Blessed One (= Jesus Christ) to cheapen (= ask the price of) and buy some of his vanities　诱惑基督询问价格,买一些虚华的商品

　　to have no mind to the merchandise　对商品毫无兴趣

　　to lay so much as one farthing upon these vanities　没花一分钱买这些空名虚利

　　must needs do = have to do　不得不做

16. be moved　(人)骚动起来

　　as it were　仿佛,就像

　　in a hubbub　处于喧嚷/骚动之中

　　be diverse from　不同于

the raiment of any that traded in the fair　集市上销售的任何服装

to make a great gazing upon sb.　注视某人

be bedlams = be insane asylums; be mad men or lunatics from Bethlehem hospital　精神病院,伯利恒医院的精神病人

outlandish men　外国模样的人

17. to <u>wonder at</u> their apparel　对他们的服饰衣着感到奇怪

to speak the language of Canaan　讲的是迦南话/天国话

＊迦南是上帝赐予亚伯拉罕(Abraham)的应许之地(Promised Land),是期望中的乐土,后为以色列人的子孙所征服、居住,所以迦南话即以色列话,即圣经里的话,即天国的话。

be the men of this world　是这个世界的人,即世俗的人

to seem barbarians each to the other　每个人都视对方为野蛮人

18. (do) not a little amuse sb.　使某人感到有趣/觉得好笑(并非只是一点儿)

to set very light by　瞧不起……

to care not so much as to look upon sth.　对某物连看都不看

to call upon sb. to buy...　向某人兜售……

to turn away mine eyes from...　别让我们的眼睛看……

to signify that their <u>trade and traffic</u> was in heaven　表示他们的买卖交易在天国之中

19. to chance mockingly to say unto sb. ...　偶尔(会有人)嘲笑某人说……

the <u>carriages</u> of the men　这些人的姿态/举止/样子

to look gravely upon sb.　严肃地看着某人

20. there was an occasion taken = there was an chance/reason made use of　有了一个可以利用的机会/理由

to smite sb. 惩治/严办/狠打某人

21. One chanced mockingly, beholding the carriages of the men, to say unto them, What will ye buy? = Seeing the carriages of the men, one chanced mockingly to say unto them what you will buy.　有人看了这些人的样子,偶尔会嘲笑他们说,你们要买什么?

22. At that there was an occasion taken to despise the men the more; some (was) mocking, some was taunting, some (was) speaking reproachfully, and some (was) <u>calling upon</u> others to smite them.　这样一来,就有了可以利用的机会来更加鄙视这些人,有人嘲讽,有人耍笑,有人指责,有人呼吁别人揍他们一顿。

23. At last things came to a hubbub and a great stir in the fair, in so much that all order was confounded.　最后事情发展为集市上一片喧嚷骚动,以致秩序全都混乱了。

24. Now was word presently brought to the great one of the fair. = Now word was presently brought to the great one of the fair.　不久话传到了集市的大官耳里。

25. to depute (=entrust) some of his most trusty friends to take these men into examination, about whom the fair was almost overturned　授权/委托几个他最信任的朋友把这些人带去检查,周围的集市几乎乱翻了天

to sit upon sb.　审理/管教/压制某人

be pilgrims and strangers in this world　是朝圣者,是这里的过客(非世俗之人)

the Heavenly Jerusalem　天国的耶路撒冷

to give no occasion to sb. to abuse them　没给某人任何机会伤害他们

to let sb. in his journey　阻碍某人的旅程

except it was for that　除非是为了这样而这样,除非是无事生非、没事找事

26. The men told them that they were pilgrims..., and that they were going to ..., which was the Heavenly

Jerusalem; and that they had given no occasion to . . . , thus to abuse them, and to let . . . , except . . . , when . . . , they said they would buy the truth. 这些人告诉他们(审问他们的人)他们是过路的朝圣者,并非这里的人,他们要回自己的国家,那是天国的耶路撒冷;他们并没做什么事让这镇上的人和集市上的商人来歧视他们,阻碍他们去天国的旅程,除非是没事找事。当有人问他们要买什么的时候,他们说要买真理。

＊ 总的句子结构是 The men told them that . . . , and that . . . ; and that . . . 这样的带多个宾语的结构,三个 that 分别引导三个直接宾语从句,有的宾语从句本身又是复合句,带定语从句,带状语从句,看懂了句架,意思也就容易明白了。

27. they that were appointed to examine them 被任命来审查他们的人

not any other than = nothing other than = nothing but = only 只是/仅仅

not believe them to be any other than bedlams and mad 绝不相信他们不是精神病和疯子,认为他们除了是疯子不可能是别的/只能是疯子、神经病

or else such as came to put all things into a confusion in the fair 否则,就不会像这样把集市上的一切都搞乱

to be smear sb. with dirt 用污物涂某人一身

be made a spectacle to all = be made an object of public shame, disrespect and laugh 被公开示众,当作羞辱嘲笑的对象

主要内容归纳和总结

1. 约翰·班扬出生在英格兰贝福德郡(Bedfordshire)一个修锅匠家庭(a tinker's family),没有受过正规的教育,后因娶了一个信奉基督教的妻子,而进入了贵族阶层。他加入了不信奉国教的新教教会(Nonconformist Church),并积极传教,因而两次入狱。正是在第二次入狱的过程中,他写出了他的代表作《天路历程》。

班扬是一个坚定的清教徒(puritan),深信人一定能通过精神上的奋斗得到拯救。其写作风格与《圣经》异曲同工,情节鲜明逼真,语言通俗生动,受教育不多的人也能感受到阅读他的作品的乐趣。

2. 约翰·班扬的主要作品:

《罪人受恩记》(又名《功德无量》) *Grace Abounding to the Chief of Sinners* (1666)

《天路历程》上卷 *The Pilgrim's Progress I* (1678)

《拜德先生传》*The Life and Death of Mr. Badman* (1680)

《神圣战争》*The Holy War* (1682)

《天路历程》下卷 *The Pilgrim's Progress II* (1684)

重要信息句子

1. *The Pilgrim's Progress* is the most successful religious allegory in the English language.

2. The predominant metaphor of *The Pilgrim's Progress* is life as a journey. 《天路历程》的主要隐喻就是人生如旅。

Ⅱ. 亚历山大 · 蒲伯 Alexander Pope (1688～1744)

词语解释和难句分析

1. be born into a well-to-do merchant family of Roman Catholic faith   出生于一个信奉罗马天主教的富商家庭

   from the cradle to the grave   从襁褓到坟墓，从出生到死亡，一辈子

   to hold public office   保有公职

2. literary men = the men of letters   文学家

   in a scheme to do sth.   计划/打算做某事

   false learning and pedantry in literature   虚假的学识和迂腐的文学

   butt of satire   讽刺的靶子

   to foster a satiric temper   培养出一种讽刺的品性气质

3. to find expression in   在……里得到了表现

   be loved and respected by many honorable, eminent and gifted men of his time   为许多有声望、有天才的名人所热爱所尊敬

   be envied, derided and attacked by some less talented   受到一些天才不足的人的嫉妒、嘲笑和攻击

   physical deformation   身体残疾、畸形

   sensitive man   敏感的人

   to strike back hard   狠狠地回击

   constant verbal battles   不断的笔墨之战

   a style of biting satire   犀利的讽刺文风

4. to uphold the existing social system as an ideal one   维护现有社会制度为理想的制度

   be blind to the rapid moral deterioration   对道德的迅速蜕化视而不见

   money-worship   拜金主义

   to invade all aspects of national life   侵蚀/渗透到国家生活的各个方面

   to assume the role of champion of traditional civilization   担当传统文明捍卫者的角色

   classical learning, sound art, good taste and public virtue   经典学术，完美艺术，高雅品位和公共美德

5. This emphasis on order found expression in all his works.   这种对有序的强调体现在他所有的作品中。

6. to make his name as a great poet with   随着……奠定了他伟大诗人的地位

   mock epic   喜剧讽刺史诗

   an actual episode   一段实际的经历，一个实际发生的事件

   to break up the friendship between the two families   使两个家庭的友谊破裂

   to write something to restore peace   写点儿什么解决矛盾，写一个团圆的结局

   to ridicule the trivial incident   嘲弄这琐碎小事

   to emphasize the pettiness of the quarrel   强调这场争吵的渺小/微不足道

   to satire the foolish, meaningless life of the lords and ladies in the aristocratic bourgeois society   讽刺贵族资产阶级社会里的老爷小姐愚蠢无聊的生活

7. to go deep in meaning and work at many levels   （作品）意义深刻，涵盖面广

be directed at Dullness in general　（讽刺）直指普遍存在的麻木愚蠢

be expertly exposed and satirized　被予以专门的/特别的暴露和讽刺

8. be judged by classical rules of order and decorum　（作品）根据是否符合有序规则和经典规范加以判断

to work painstakingly on his poems　他呕心沥血/煞费苦心地创作诗篇

to bring the heroic couplet to its last perfection　对英雄偶句诗作了最后的完善

亚力山大·蒲伯作品选读

《论批评》*An Essay on Criticism* 第二部分

词语解释和难句分析

1. didactic poem　说教诗

to lament the dearth of true taste in poetic criticism of his day　哀叹当时诗歌批评方面缺乏真正的体验和品味

to call on people to turn to the old Greek and Roman writers for guidance　号召人们转向古希腊古罗马的作家寻求指导

to trace the history of literary criticism from Aristotle down to Boileau and Roscommon　探寻从亚里士多德到伯瓦罗和罗士卡门文学批评的历史

to advocate the classical rules　倡导古典规则

to popularize the neoclassicist tradition　普及新古典主义的文学传统

2. be written in a plain style　用朴素的文风写作

hardly contain any imagery or eloquence　几乎不用任何形象化的比喻或修辞

artificial use of Conceit　过分雕琢/牵强附会的比喻

true wit which is best set in a plain style　蕴含在朴素文风里的真正的智慧

3. Some to conceit alone their taste confine, = Some confine their taste to conceit alone (= only)，有些人将自己的趣味局限于矫揉造作

And glittering thoughts struck out (= devised/invented) at every line; = And there are glittering thoughts struck out at every line; 每一行都有编造出来的闪光的思想，

* struck out 是过去分词短语作 glittering thoughts 的定语，即人为雕琢出来的闪光思想，

4. nothing is just or fit　没一处是适当的、恰如其分的，一无是处，毫无可取之处

chaos and wild heap of wit　混乱和胡乱堆砌的机智

5. Pleased with a work where nothing's just or fit,/One glaring chaos and wild heap of wit.　为一部毫无可取之处的作品沾沾自喜,作品里充斥着混乱和胡乱堆砌的机智。

* where nothing's just or fit 是 a work 的定语从句; glaring chaos and wild heap of wit 是分词短语作 one 的定语,而 one 指的是上一行中 a work,分词短语起补充说明的作用。

6. Poets, like painters, thus unskilled to trace (= portray)/The naked nature and the living grace,　诗人,就像画家,由于没有技巧去追寻(描画)真实的大自然和鲜活的自然美,

* unskilled to trace... 实际上是 because they are unskilled to trace..., 此句真正的谓语动词是下面两行中的 cover 和 hide。

With gold and jewels cover every part,/And hide with ornaments their want of art. = Cover every part with gold and jewels/And hide their want of art with ornaments.　就用金子和珠宝缀满每一块地方,用装饰

掩盖艺术上的不足/无能。

7. True wit is Nature to advantage dressed, = True wit is Nature dressed <u>to advantage</u>, 真正的机智是打扮得当的大自然,

   * to/with advantage 有利的/有效的衬托,使突出优点

   What oft（=often）was thought, but ne'er so well expressed; =（True wit）is what often was thought but never expressed so well; (真正的机智)是人们常常想到、却从未表达得这样好(的东西);

8. Something whose truth convinced at sight we find, = True wit is something whose truth we find convinced at sight, 真正的机智就是一见其真情就信服的东西;

   That gives us back the image of our mind. = that gives us the image of our mind back. 就是再现我们头脑中形象的东西。

   * 注意 whose 和 that 引导两个定语从句修饰 something,而 something 是 true wit 的表语。

9. As shades more sweetly recommend the light, 正如阴影将光明衬托得更美好,

   So modest plainness <u>sets off</u> sprightly wit; 谦逊质朴也把机智衬托得生气勃勃;

   For works may have more wit than does them good, = For works may have more wit than it（=wit）does them（=works）good, 因为超过了恰到好处,作品就成了技巧卖弄,

   As bodies perish through excess of blood. 好比是血液过多人体就会死亡。

10. Others for language all their care express, = Others express all their care for language, 另一些人全部的专注都在诗的语言,

    And value books, as women men, for dress. = and value books as women value men for dress. (他们)评价书籍就像女人评价男人,只看衣着。

11. Their praise is still（=always）— the style is excellent; 他们的赞扬总是——风格十分出色;

    The sense they humbly take upon content. = They humbly <u>take the sense upon</u> <u>content</u>. 而对于思想内容/含义则掉以轻心/轻易满足。

12. Words are like leaves; and where they most abound（vi.）, 辞藻就像树叶,树叶茂密的地方,

    Much fruit of sense beneath is rarely found. 就几乎见不到丰硕的思想之果。

13. False eloquence, like the prismatic glass, 浮华的修辞就像三棱镜,

    Its gaudy colors spreads on every place; 俗艳的色彩射向四方;

14. The face of Nature we no more survey, = We survey no more the face of Nature, 我们再不能看到大自然的本色面貌

    All glares alike, without distinction gay（= without gay distinction）. 所有的光芒全都一样,没有鲜明的特色和区别。

15. But true expression, like the unchanging sun, 但真实的表达,就像不变的太阳,

    Clears and improves whate'er it shines upon; 凡它照耀的万物都变得更清晰美好;

    * 此句中 true expression 是主语,clears and improves 是谓语动词,whatever it shines upon 是宾语从句。

    It gilds all objects, but it alters none. 它给万物洒上金辉/镀上金边,却什么也不改变。

16. Expression is the dress of thought, and still 表达是思想的外衣,而且

    Appears more decent as more suitable. = the more suitable the expression is, the more decent it appears. 表达越恰当,就越显得体面。

17. A vile conceit in pompous words expressed/Is like a clown in regal purple dressed: = A vile conceit expressed in pompous words is like a clown dressed in regal purple: 用华而不实的辞藻表现出来的卑劣的做作,就像一个穿上宫廷紫袍的小丑;

18. For different styles with different subjects sort,/As several garbs with country, town, and count. = For different styles <u>sort with</u> different subjects, as several garbs <u>sort with</u> country, town, and count. 因为不

同的风格适合不同的主题,就像有多种不同的服装适合乡村、城镇和宫廷。

19. Some by old words to fame have made pretense, = Some have <u>made pretense</u> to fame by old words, 有些人竟用古老的词语(作秀/作假)来沽名钓誉,

 Ancients in phrase, mere moderns in their sense. = They are ancients judged by their language, but mere moderns judged by the idea they express. 他们是词语上的古人,思想上的现代人。

20. Such labored nothings, in so strange a style, 如此苦心孤诣的空洞表达,如此怪癖的文风,

Amaze the unlearn'd, and make the learned smile; 令无知者困惑惊愕,令饱学者感到可笑;

21. Unlucky as Fungoso in the play, 像剧中的冯戈索一样倒霉,

＊Fungoso,本·琼森剧本《自寻烦恼的俗人》(*Everyman Out of His Humour*)中的一个角色,他总是赶时髦,学间谍、学弄臣,结果全都学不像,因为"时髦"变换太快了。

These sparks with awkward vanity display 这些赶时髦的人以笨拙的虚荣

What the fine gentleman wore yesterday; 展示高雅绅士昨日穿过的衣衫;

＊what 引导的名词性从句是谓语动词 display 的宾语从句。

And but so mimic ancient wits at best, 而他们如此卖力地模仿古人的机智,

As apes our grandsires in their doublets dressed. = As apes mimic our grandsires dressed in their doublets. 就像猿猴模仿我们的祖先穿上紧身衣。

22. In words as fashion the same rule will hold, = In words the same rule as fashion will hold (*vi.*),用词与穿衣一样也要遵循同样的规则,

Alike fantastic if too new or old: = they are both absurd if words are used too new or too old: 太新潮或太古老都同样荒谬。

23. Be not the first by whom the new are tried, 不做第一个试用新词的人,

＊by whom ... 引导的是修饰 the first 的定语从句。

Nor yet the last <u>to lay the old aside</u>. 也不做最后一个抛弃旧词的人。

＊to lay the old aside 是修饰 the last 的定语不定式。

参考译文——姚绍德

论批评(节选)

有些人将自己的趣味局限于矫揉造作,
每一行都编造出一些闪光的思想;
为一篇一无是处的作品沾沾自喜,
作品中闪耀着一团胡乱堆砌的机智。
诗人,如同画家,没有技巧去追寻
大自然的朴实无华和鲜活的美,
就只有用金子和珠宝到处乱缀,
用装饰掩盖他们低能的艺术。
真正的机智是打扮得体的自然,
人们常想到,却总是可望而不可即;
我们一见其真情就信服,
它把我们的思想再现。

正如阴影将光明衬托得更加美好，
谦逊的质朴衬托出生机勃勃的机智；
因为超过了恰到好处，作品就会弄巧成拙，
好比是血液过多，身体就会死灭。
还有人只专注于语言雕饰，
评价书籍就像女看男，全凭衣着。
他们的赞扬永远是——风格极佳，
对内涵却往往轻易满足。
辞藻像树叶，哪里叶太多，
哪里就难见思想的硕果。
虚假的雄辩，就像三棱镜，
浮华的色彩到处漫射；
再见不到自然的真实和本色，
所有的光华都一样，没有特色和区别。
但真实的表达，像不变的太阳，
使照耀的万物，变得更加完美、清晰；
它给万物镀金，却无一件改变。
表达是思想的外衣，永远是——
越合适的就越显得体面。
用浮夸的辞藻表现出卑劣的做作，
像是穿着宫廷紫袍的弄臣小丑：
因为不同风格适合不同的主题，
就像乡村、城镇和宫廷各有不同的装束。
有人用古词语作秀，沽名钓誉，
以古人的词语表达今人的思想。
如此煞费苦心的空洞，如此古怪的文风，
令无知者困惑惊愕，使饱学者耻笑不已；
倒霉得像戏中的冯戈索，
这些赶时髦的人以笨拙的虚荣，
展示高雅绅士昨日穿过的衣衫；
他们如此卖力地模仿古人的机智，
像猿猴模仿我们的祖先穿上紧身衣。
说话像时装，要遵循同样的原则，
太新潮太守旧同样荒谬：
试用新词不为天下先，
抛弃旧词也不落最后。

格律和韵律分析

'Some to/con·ceit/a·lone/their 'taste/con·fine,   a

And 'glit/tering 'thoughts/'struck out/at 'eve/ry 'line;   a

'Pleased with/a 'work/where 'no/thing's 'just/or 'fit,   b

One ·gla/ring ·cha/·os and/wild ·heap/of ·wit.　　　　　b

Po·ets,/ like ·pain/ters, thus/un·skilled/to ·trace　　　c

The ·na/ked ·na/ture and/the ·li/ving ·grace,　　　　　c

With ·gold/and ·jew/els ·co/ver ·eve/ry ·part,　　　　　d

And ·hide/with ·or/naments/their ·want/of ·art.　　　　d

取诗中一个诗节(8 行)作为分析样本,每行诗句均为 5 个音步,整个诗节 8 行为 40 个音步,除第一行第一音步为扬抑格,第二行第二音步为抑抑扬格、第三音步为扬抑格,第三行第一音步为扬抑格,第四行第三音步为扬抑格,第五、六、八行的第三音步为抑抑格外(以上各处用阴影部分标出),其余 32 个音步均为抑扬格,故可认为该诗的基调格为五步抑扬格,韵律为 aabbccdd....。整首诗中,除两个地方出现三行同韵外,其余绝大多数诗行皆为双行同韵,故诗的格律、韵律为五步抑扬格押韵双行诗体,属典型的英雄偶句体形式。

主要内容归纳和总结

1. 亚历山大·蒲伯出生在伦敦一个信奉罗马天主教的富商家庭。他一辈子疾病缠身,可以说从襁褓到坟墓,始终与疾病为伴。他性好交际,与各派作家保持着深厚的交情,不论他们是辉格党人还是托利党人。

   蒲伯是启蒙主义时期的代表人物,他第一个将理想主义引入英国。虽然他看到了社会的腐败、商业化和严重的拜金主义,但还是将现行制度奉为理想制度。他大力倡导古典主义,理性和秩序在他看来是不可颠覆的信条。1714 年,他创立了文学俱乐部,目的就是要批判文学、哲学、科学以及其他学术界的虚伪迂腐的学风,结果最大成果却是培养了一种讽刺的笔调。这种讽刺笔调在他后来的说教诗(didactic poem)《论批评》(*An Essay on Criticism*)、讽刺史诗(satiric epic)《夺发记》(*The Rape of the Lock*)中都得到了充分体现。

   另外,蒲伯还使德莱顿(Dryton)曾经在戏剧中运用过的英雄偶句体臻于完美。他是那个时代最伟大的诗人。

2. 亚历山大·蒲伯的主要作品:

   《论批评》*An Essay on Criticism* (1711)

   《夺发记》*The Rape of the Lock* (1712)

   《群愚史诗》*The Dunciad* (1728)

   《论人类》*An Essay on Man* (1733 ~ 1734)

   主要译著为荷马史诗的英译本:

   《伊利亚特》*Iiad* (1720)

   《奥德赛》*Odyssey* (1726)

重要信息句子

1. As a representative of the Enlightenment, Pope was one of the first to introduce rationalism to England.

2. Pope made his name as a great poet wit the publication of *An Essay on Criticism* in 1711.

3. *The Dunciad*, generally considered Pope's best satiric work, took him over ten years for final completion.

4. Pope was the greatest poet of his time.

Ⅲ. 丹尼尔·迪福 Daniel Defoe（1660~1731）

词语解释和难句分析

1. Dissenting academies　不信奉国教的新教学院

   to undergo many ups and downs　经历许多起落沉浮

   abundant energy and never-failing enthusiasm　充沛的精力和永不言败的热情

   to bring him back on his feet after a fall　失败了又重新站起来

   to leave sb. fairly well provided　留给某人一笔丰厚的财富/生活费或生活必需品

2. to have a zest for politics　有政治热情

   to go through pubic exposure in the pillory　经历过戴枷示众

   The Shortest Way with the Dissenters　《成为异教徒的捷径》

   The True-born Englishmen　《地道的英国人》

   to win him friendship from the king　为他赢得了国王的友谊

   government agent　政府代表/公务员/官员

   the best informed political and economic pamphleteers of the time　当时最博学的政治论和经济论小册子作者

3. immediate success　立即大获成功

   a pseudo-factual account of the Great Plague　大瘟疫的模拟纪实报道

4. be traced from　由……开始

   through many vicissitudes in life to their final prosperity or repentance　经历许多世事变迁,最后发迹或者悔恨终身

   the all-powerful influence of ... upon ...　……对……的最为强大的影响

   to come into conflict with　与……发生冲突

   bold adventures　大胆的冒险

   to manifest Defoe's deep concern for　表明迪福对……的深刻关心

5. As Flanders says: "Vice came in always at the Door of Necessity, not at the Door of Inclination. "　如弗朗德斯所言:"罪恶总是守在贫困的门口,而与癖好无关。"

6. Roxana says in self-defense: "Honesty is Out of the Question when Starvation is the Case. "　罗克萨那自卫地说:"还吃不饱肚子的时候,诚实就绝无可能。"

7. the lower class people　下层阶级的人民大众

   to enjoy great popularity among the less educated readers　在受教育程度不高的读者中非常受欢迎

   to give his praise to the hard-working, sturdy middle class　赞扬勤劳、坚毅的中产阶级

   to show his sympathy for the downtrodden, unfortunate poor　对遭受蹂躏的穷人表现出同情

8. to have a gift for organizing minute details　具有组织琐碎微小细节的天赋

   be sometimes short, crisp and plain, and sometimes long and rambling　语言时而短小、利落、朴素,时而冗长、散漫、随意

   to leave on the reader an impression of casual narration　给读者一个漫不经心、随意叙述的印象

   colloquial and mostly vernacular　多用口语和方言俗语

   at its best　全盛时期,鼎盛时期

丹尼尔·迪福作品选读

《鲁滨孙漂流记》Robinson Crusoe 第四章

词语解释和难句分析

1. to stay alone on the uninhabited island　一人孤独地待在无人居住的荒岛上

   a work of sheer imagination　一部纯粹想象的著作

   to get shipwrecked and marooned on a lonely island　遭遇海难船毁而孤独无援地待在寂寞的荒岛上

   to get relieved　获救,获得释放

   an experienced teenager and a young man full of bright fancies about the future　一个对前途充满幻想的不谙世事的少年

   to mean a chance to live a chivalrous life　意味着有机会过浪漫的骑士生活

   to make a fortune　发一笔大财

   the call of the sea　大海的召唤

   to embark on another voyage　着手准备又一次航海

   frightful storm　可怕的风暴

   to blow the boat off its course and shipwreck it near an island　把小船刮离了航线,在一个小岛附近翻了船

2. to escape to the shore after strenuous efforts　经过紧张激烈的奋斗之后,逃上了海岸

   to salvage from the wrecked ship some stores of necessities = to salvage some stores of necessities from the wrecked ship　从沉船上打捞出一些储存的生活必需品

   several futile attempts to leave the island　徒劳地进行了几次离开荒岛的努力

   to settle himself down to a hard and lonely life　扎下根来过艰苦孤独的生活

   to domesticate animals　驯养动物

   to take a turn for the better　向好的方面转化,转好

   to save from the hands of savages a young Negro = to save a young Negro from the hands of savages　从野蛮人手里救了一个黑人青年

   an indispensable help to him　对他是不可或缺的助手/帮助

3. to trace the growth of Robinson from a naive artless youth into a shrewd and hardened man, tempered by numerous trials in his eventful life　追寻鲁滨孙从一个天真单纯的青年到一个在坎坷不断的人生中经受了无数磨难锤炼的精明坚韧的人的成长轨迹

4. the struggle of Robinson single-handedly against the hostile nature　鲁滨孙单枪匹马地与恶劣的大自然进行斗争

   inexhaustible energy　永不枯竭/用不完的精力

   be the very prototype of the empire builder, the pioneer colonist　正是帝国建造者的典范,殖民主义者的先锋

   to glorify human labor and the Puritan fortitude　颂扬/赞美人类的劳动和清教徒的坚韧/刚毅

   to toil for the sake of substance　为生活所需的物质而辛苦劳作

5. be cast into the shore of an island　被抛落到一个岛的海岸边

6. My thoughts were now wholly employed about securing myself against either savages . . . or wild

beasts, ... 我所有的思想全部用来/一门心思考虑如何保护自己,防止野人或野兽的伤害……

7. to have many thoughts of the method 对……的方法想了很多

8. In short, I resolved upon both, the manner and description of which it may not be improper to give an account of. 简言之,我对两者都打定了主意,下面不妨对其方法和细节做个描述。

　　* the manner and ... of which ...是 both 的非限制性定语从句,which = both; to give an account of the manner and description,描述一下(两种建房的)方法和细节。

9. be upon a low moorish ground near the sea 处在位于近海的低洼沼泽地上

not be wholesome 无益于健康

no fresh water 没有淡水

10. I consulted several things in my situation which I found would be proper for me: ... 根据我当时的处境,我想了好几种我认为适合我的方案……

11. shelter from the heat of the sun (住地)不受骄阳暴晒

security from ravenous creatures 不受食肉类动物的侵害

to send any ship in sight (上帝)将船送入我的眼帘,让我看到船

12. I might not lose any advantage for my deliverance, of which I was not willing to banish all my expectation yet 我不可能失去获得解救的机会,我不愿放弃一切获得这种机会的希望。

　　* of which ... yet 为非限制性定语从句,关系代词 which 是指 advantage (= chance);to banish all my expectation of any advantage 意为放弃任何获得这种机会的希望。

13. I found a little plain on the side of a rising hill, whose front towards this little plain was steep as a house-side, so that nothing could come down upon me from the top; 我发现一座高高突起的山坡前有一小块平地,朝向这小平地的山坡前面像屋墙一样陡,任何东西也不能从山顶冲下来袭击我。

　　* whose front ... was steep ... , so that ... the top 是非限制性定语从句,修饰 a rising hill,而这定语从句本身又是一个复合句,含有结果状语从句 so that ... 以至于。

14. to pitch my tent 搭起我的帐篷

be not above a hundred yards broad and about twice as long 宽不超过一百码,长约二百码

to descend irregularly every way down into the low-grounds by the seaside 向下随意蔓延直到海边的平地

on the N. N. W side of the hill = on the north by northwest side of the hill 在山坡的北面偏西北

15. to pitch two rows of strong stakes 打下两排结实牢固的木桩

to drive sth. into the ground 把某物打入地下

be out of the ground about five foot and a half 露出地面五英尺半高

to lay cables in rows one upon another 把缆绳一层层堆起来

16. ... placing other stakes in the in-side, leaning against them, ... , like a spur to a post, ... 另外再在里面插入一些木桩,卡住这些缆绳……就像木桩上的刺尖……

17. be completely fenced in 完全围在篱笆里面

be fortify'd (= fortified) from all the world 被堡垒围住,与外界隔绝

to apprehend danger from the enemies 感觉到/担心敌人的威胁

18. There was no need of all this caution from the enemies that I apprehended danger from. 对于我所担心的会有危险的敌人/敌人的危险,完全不必如此谨慎小心。

19. to carry all my riches, all my provisions, ammunition, and stores, of which you have the account above into this fence or fortress 把我所有的财富,所有的给养,弹药,和一切你可从前面的描述中知晓的储存物品搬进篱笆或者说堡垒里

20. I made me a large tent, which, to preserve me from the rains that in one part of the year are very violent there, I made double, viz. one smaller tent within, and one larger tent above it, and covered the uppermost with a large tarpaulin which I had saved among the sails.　我为自己搭了一个大帐篷,这里一年中有一段时间会有暴雨,为保护自己不受雨淋,我搭了两层帐篷,即里面一层小帐篷,上面还有一层大帐篷,最外边又盖了一层大篷帆布,这是我从船上的篷帆中留存下来的。

　　* which I made double, and covered the uppermost with a large tarpaulin... 是修饰 tent 的定语从句的主架,关系代词 which 是 made 的宾语。不定式短语 to preserve me from... 是从句中的目的状语。另外,大从句中还含有两个小从句:一个是修饰 rains 的 that in one part of the year are very violent there,另一个是修饰 tarpaulin 的 which I had saved among the sails。

21. to lie no more for a while in the bed　有一段时间没睡在床上

　　to lie in a hammock　睡在吊床上

　　the mate of the ship　船上的大副

22. everything that would spoil by the wet　一切会受潮损坏的东西

　　to enclose all my goods　把所有物品都围在篱笆内

　　to make up the entrance, which till now I had left open　堵上当时我还留着的入口

　　to pass and repass by a short ladder　靠一架短梯进出篱笆

　　to work my way into the rock　往岩石里挖出洞穴

　　to lay them (the earth and stones) up within my fence in the nature of a terrace　把泥土和石块堆在篱笆内,垒成类似台阶的样子

23. At the same time it happened, after I had laid my scheme for the setting up my tent and making the cave, that a storm of rain falling from a thick dark cloud, a sudden flash of lightning happened, and after that a great clap of thunder, as is naturally the effect of it.　我刚计划支帐篷、挖洞穴,这时浓云密布,暴雨倾盆,闪电过后,必然而至的就是一阵惊雷炸响。

24. be not so surprised with/at... as I was (surprised) with...　我对……的吃惊还没有达到对……(另一件事情)吃惊的程度

　　to dart into my mind as swift as...　某一种想法突然像……一样飞快地掠过脑际

25. I was not so much surprised with the lightning as I was with a thought which darted into my mind as swift as the lightning itself: O my powder!　一个像闪电一样飞快掠过脑际的思想比闪电本身更使我大吃一惊:啊呀,天哪,我的火药!

26. My very heart sunk within me when I thought that at one blast all my powder might be destroyed, on which not my defence only, but the providing me food, as I thought, entirely depended (=not only my defence, but the providing me food entirely depended on which [=powder]);　我的心哪,沉了下去,我知道一次爆炸,弹药就全毁了,我的安全保卫和我的食物供给,可都依赖它呢。

27. I was nothing near (=not in the least, not at all) so anxious about my own danger, tho' (=though) had the powder took fire, I had never known who had hurt me.　我一点儿也不担心自己的危险,尽管要是弹药起火,我连谁伤害了我都不知道。

　　* tho' had the powder...hurt me. = though if the powder had taken fire, I would have never known who had hurt me.

28. such impression did this make upon me that... =this made such impression upon me that...　这给我留下了这样的印象……

　　to apply myself to make bags and boxes to separate the powder　专心致志地分包、分盒以分开弹药

　　in my fancy　以我的设想,在我的想象中

29. as well as to divert myself as to see if I could kill any thing fit for food　一边自己消遣消遣散散心,一

边看看能不能打到点儿可食的动物

be attended with this misfortune to me　对我来说,(此事)处理起来非常不顺

be not discouraged at　并不对……感到泄气

to lay wait in this manner for sth.　以这种方式打埋伏守候某物

to run away as in a terrible fright　仿佛受了极大的惊吓逃跑了

by the position of their optics　在眼睛的位置

to have a fair mark　找到一个容易打中的靶子

to give suck to a little kid　给小羊羔喂奶

to grieve me heartily　使我心里难过

to stand stock still by her　呆呆地站在她旁边

to follow me quite to my enclosure　老老实实地跟着我到围栏外

to lay down the dam upon the enclosure　把母羊放在围墙上

to carry it over my pale　把它抱过栅栏

to have it bred up tame　留着驯养它

30. to make conveniences　建造一些生活设施

to give a full account of these in its place　在适当的地方充分地谈谈这些事情

to give some little account of myself　简单地谈谈自己

31. ... which it may well be supposed were not a few. = It may be supposed which were not a few.　可以说,那些想法(谈自己、谈生活的设想)要谈的还不少。

主要内容归纳和总结

1. 丹尼尔·迪福出生在伦敦一个屠户(butcher)家庭。他未上过大学,但在一家最好的不信国教的学院(Dissenting Academies)受到了良好的教育。他热心政治,写过许多政论小册子,曾因一册《成为异教徒的捷径》(*The Shortest Way with the Dissenters*)而身陷囹圄,也曾因一册《地道的英国人》(*The True-born Englishman*)而成为国王的好友。

他是讲故事的天才,细节的描述栩栩如生,使故事显得又神奇又可信。他用的都是大众化语言,方言俗语自然流畅,文化程度不高的读者非常欢迎他的作品。他的第一部小说《鲁滨孙漂流记》(*Robinson Crusoe*)就大获成功,它歌颂了作者所属的中产阶级坚忍不拔、艰苦奋斗的精神。他后来的作品基本上都是讲普通人甚至是底层人民的生活历程。

他同情社会底层人民的生活遭遇,在他后来的四部小说中表达了对穷苦百姓的关心。他借作品中的人物之口,说出了社会罪恶和人民疾苦的根源。例如他塑造的人物弗朗德斯说:"罪恶总是守在贫困的门口,而与癖好无关。"(Vice came in always at the Door of Necessity, not at the Door of Inclination.)罗克萨那说:"还吃不饱肚子的时候,诚实就绝无可能。"(Honesty is out of the question when Starvation is the Case.)

2. 丹尼尔·迪福的主要作品:

《成为异教徒的捷径》*The Shortest Way with the Dissenters* (1702)

《地道的英国人》*The True-born Englishman* (1701)

《鲁滨孙漂流记》*Robinson Crusoe* (nearly 1720)

《辛利顿船长》*Captain Singleton* (1720)

《莫尔·弗朗德斯》*Moll Flanders* (1722)

《杰克上校》*Colonel Jack* (1722)

《罗克萨那》*Roxana*（1724）

《灾疫之年的日记》*A Journal of the Plague Year*（1722）

重要信息句子

1. It is a real wonder that such a busy man as Defoe would have found time for literary creation. The fact is that, at the age of nearly 60, he started his first novel *Robinson Crusoe*, which was an immediate success.

2. *Robinson Crusoe*, an adventure story very much in the spirit of the time, is universally considered his masterpiece.

3. As a member of the middle class, Defoe's most works gave his praise to the hard-working, sturdy middle class and showed his sympathy for the downtrodden, unfortunate poor.

Ⅳ. 乔纳森·斯威夫特 Jonathan Swift（1667~1745）

词语解释和难句分析

1. posthumous child 遗腹子

   distant kinsman 远亲

   to put his general ideas in order 将笼统的思想整理清楚

   to receive a first-rate education in politics 受到一流的政治教育

   to learn much about the vice, hypocrisy, intrigues, deception and corruption in the political world 了解了很多政界的罪孽、伪善、阴谋、欺骗和腐败

   be at different clerical posts in Ireland 在爱尔兰多处地方任圣职/牧师

   to establish his name as a satirist 确立了讽刺家的名声

   be appointed dean of St. Patrick's Cathedral in Dublin 被任命为都柏林圣帕特里克大教堂主教

   under the pseudonym of Drapier 以德拉皮尔的化名

   the newly-minted English copper coins 新铸造的英格兰铜币

   to further debase the coinage of the already poverty-stricken country 使已经赤贫的国家的货币制度进一步贬值

   to offer 300 pounds for information as to the identity of the Drapier 提供300英镑奖金获取德拉皮尔真实身份的情报

2. a man of great integrity and social charm 一个正直诚实和极具社交魅力的人

   to have a deep hatred/sympathy for 深刻痛恨/深切同情

   to redress human nature 纠正/改造人性，对人性作脱胎换骨的改造

   human institution 由人组成的机构

   an under-or-overtone of helplessness and indignation 一种无助和愤慨的内在含义和弦外之音

3. （his satire）be usually masked by an outward gravity and an apparent earnestness （他的讽刺）通常呈现出一种外在的严肃和表面的真诚

to render his satire <u>all the more</u> powerful   进行了更为有力的讽刺

to make the most devastating <u>protest against</u> the inhuman exploitation and oppression of the Irish people
最强烈地抗议对爱尔兰人民的非人道的剥削压迫

to add force to the bitter irony and biting sarcasm   给作品辛辣的冷嘲和犀利的挖苦讽刺增加了力量

4. be almost unsurpassed in   在······方面几乎无人超越

economy and conciseness of language   语言的惜墨如金和简洁精炼

乔纳森·斯威夫特作品选读

《格列佛游记》 Gulliver's Travels 第一部分第三章

词语解释和难句分析

1. fictional work   小说作品

under the title of   以······为题/书名

Travels into Several Remote Nations of the World, by Samuel Gulliver   《塞缪尔·格列佛偏远国家旅游记》

to meet with shipwreck or piracy or some other misfortune   遭遇沉船、海盗劫掠以及一些其他不幸事件

be simply miniature of what is in the real world   简直就是现实世界的缩微版

to devote all their time and energy to the study of some absurd problem   把他们所有的时间和精力都献给一些以荒诞为题的研究

be endowed with reason   被赋予理性

the governing class   统治阶级,主宰阶级

hairy, wild, low and despicable brutes   长毛、野蛮、卑下而又令人厌恶的兽类

2. Liliput   利立浦国,小人国

Brobdingnag   布罗卜丁奈格国,大人国

Flying Island   飞岛国

Houyhnhnm   智马国

3. at one's best   处于某人的全盛时期

to make an organic whole   形成一个游记的整体

be contrived upon an independent structure   被设计成一个独立的结构

be generally considered the best paired-up work   被普遍认为相互配合最好的著作

exaggerated smallness and exaggerated largeness   夸大的小和夸大的大

4. The similarities between human beings and the Lilliputians and the contrast between the Brobdingnagians and human beings both <u>bear reference to</u> the possibilities of human state.   人类与小人国居民的相似和人类与大人国居民的反差都与现实中可能的人类生存状态有关。

5. Part 3, though seemingly a bit random, furthers the criticism of the western civilization and deals with different malpractices and false illusions about science, philosophy, history and even immortality.   第三部分虽然似乎有点儿随意,但却更进一步促进了对西方文明的批判以及在科学、哲学、历史甚至长生不老领域内种种玩忽职守和虚假幻觉的应对。

6. to <u>allude to</u> the similar ridiculous practices or tricks of the English government　影射了英国政府许多相似的可笑行为或鬼蜮伎俩

　　to <u>hint at</u> the fact　暗示/影射了……的事实

　　be more dexterous and nimble in games　（靠的是）谁比赛中手脚更灵巧、更敏捷机变

7. to <u>gain（up）on</u> the Emperor and his court　博得皇帝和宫廷的好感

　　to conceive hopes of getting my liberty in a short time　感觉到有短期内获得自由的希望

　　to cultivate this favorable disposition　培养/陶冶这种讨人喜欢的性格

　　to come <u>by degrees</u> to be <u>less apprehensive of</u> any danger from me　渐渐地不太担心我有什么危险/不太害怕我

　　to play at <u>hide-and-seek</u> in my hair　在我的头发里玩捉迷藏游戏

　　to <u>entertain me with</u> several of the country shows　用几出该国的表演节目来招待我

　　to exceed all nations I have known both <u>for dexterity and magnificence</u>　其表演的精妙和壮丽超过了我所见过的所有国家

8. I <u>was diverted with</u> none so much as that of the rope-dancers, performed upon a slender white thread, extended about two foot, and twelve inches from the ground.　我从未感到过像看在绳子上跳舞那么快乐，舞者在一根白细绳上表演，绳子拉开有两英尺长，距地面12英尺高。

　　＊ be diverted with 因……而娱乐、消遣；none 和 that 都是指"表演""节目"这类使人消遣的项目。

9. Upon which I shall desire liberty, with the reader's patience, to enlarge a little.　请读者切勿焦躁，容我对此再详细地讲一讲。

　　＊ desire liberty to enlarge a little ＝ I'd like to be allowed to make a more detailed introduction about sth.

10. candidates for <u>great employments, and high favor</u>　候补高官和希望获得国王恩宠的人

　　be of noble birth or liberal education　具有高贵的出身，或受过大学文科教育

　　（great office）be vacant either by death or disgrace　（高官职位）因死亡或失宠而空缺

　　to petition the Emperor to entertain his Majesty and the court with a dance on the rope　向皇帝正式请求在绳子上跳舞以博取陛下和朝廷官员的欢心

　　to succeed in the office　成功就职

　　to <u>cut a caper</u> on the straight rope　在拉直的绳子上蹦跳

　　to do the summerset（＝summersault）several times together upon a trencher fixed on the rope　在固定在绳子上的一个盘子里接连翻了几个跟头

　　be not partial　不偏袒，不偏不倚，公正无私

　　be the second after the Treasurer　仅次于财政大臣

　　be much upon a par　处于同等水平

11. be <u>attended with</u> fatal accidents　伴随着致命的事故

　　to break a limb　断了胳膊腿

　　be commanded to show their dexterity　奉命表演他们的技巧

　　to excel themselves and their fellows　超过过去的自己，也超过同僚

　　to strain so far　太过紧张

12. I was assured, that a year or two before my arrival, Flimnap would have infallibly broke his neck, if one of the king's cushions, that accidentally lay on the ground, had not weakened the force of his fall.　有人确定无误地告诉我，就在我来这儿前一两年，要不是碰巧国王的一个坐垫放在地上减弱了他跌落的力道，弗林奈普就肯定无疑跌断脖子了。

13. These threads <u>are proposed</u> as prizes for those persons whom the Emperor <u>hath a mind to</u> distinguish by a peculiar mark of his favor.　这些丝线被建议作为皇帝的奖品，凭特殊的标志颁给那些他想要挑出

的宠爱之人。

14. his Majesty's great chamber of state　皇帝陛下的皇宫大殿

to undergo a trial of dexterity　经受一次技艺的比试

to perform his part with most agility, and hold out the longest in leaping and creeping　扮演自己的角色最灵敏,蹦跳爬行持续的时间最长

be adorned with one of these girdles　围一条这样的腰带作为装饰

15. royal stables　御马房,皇家马厩

to come up to my very feet without starting　直走到我脚跟前也不会惊跳起来

upon a large courser, took, my foot, shoe and all　骑上一匹大快马,跳过了我的脚、我的鞋,还有穿着鞋的脚

a prodigious leap　不同寻常的惊人一跳

to divert the Emperor　给皇帝消遣,逗皇帝高兴

to command the master of his woods to give directions accordingly　命令掌管森林的官员遵旨下达指示

in a quadrangular figure, two foot and a half square　成两英尺半见方的四边形

to stand erect　垂直竖立

to serve as ledges on each side　做每一边的横挡

to let a troop of his best horse,... come and exercise upon this plain　让他的精锐骑兵上到这平面上进行操练

to get into order　站好队

to perform mock skirmishes　进行模拟战斗表演

to discharge blunt arrows　发射钝箭

to discover the best military discipline I ever beheld　展示出我所见过的最佳军事纪律

close chair　轿子,箱式轿车

to take full view of　充分看到……,有广阔视野看到……

pawing with his hoof struck a hole in my handkerchief　它用蹄子乱刨,在我的手绢上刨出了一个洞

for covering the hole with one hand, I set down the troop with the other, in the same manner as I took them up　我用一只手遮住那个洞,用另一只手以同样的方式,怎么把这支军队拿上去的,又怎么把他们拿下来

be strained in the left shoulder　左肩被扭伤了

to get no hurt　没有受伤

not trust(*vi.*) to the strength of it any more in such dangerous enterprises　不敢相信它(手绢)的强度而再玩这样的危险游戏了

16. be set at liberty = be set free　获得自由,被释放

extending its edges round as wide as his Majesty's bedchamber　周边伸展面积之大如同陛下的寝宫

to get to the top by mounting upon each other's shoulders　用叠罗汉的方式登上顶部

Stamping upon it they found it was hollow within.　他们对着它踹了踹,发现它里面是空的。

17. They humbly conceived it might be something belonging to the Man-Mountain.　他们谦卑地认为/依他们愚见,那可能是属于巨人山的东西。

18. to undertake to bring it with only five horses　负责(着手/开始)仅用五匹马把它运来

be glad at heart to receive this intelligence (= news)　听到这消息心里非常高兴

to stick my hat on all the time I was swimming　在我泅水的全过程中(帽子)一直牢牢地戴在头上

to bore two holes in the brim, within an inch and half of the edge　在离边缘不到1.5英寸的帽檐上

钻了两个孔

be tied by a long cord to the harness 用长绳系到马具上

19. ... the Emperor, having ordered that part of the army which quarters in and about his metropolis to be in a readiness, took a fancy of diverting himself in a very singular manner. 皇上命令驻扎在都城内外的部分军队做好(演练的)准备,原来他又想出了一个奇怪的消遣方式。

* 句子的主架是 the Emperor took a fancy of diverting himself in a ... manner;Having ordered that ... in a readiness 为分词短语作状语,其中 which quarters in and about his metropolis 为定语从句,修饰 that part of the army。

20. with my legs as far as under as I conveniently could. 我尽可能地叉开双腿

to draw up the troops in close order 成密集队形集合部队

the foot by twenty-four in a breast (= in a rank) 步兵 24 个人一排

with drums beating, colors flying, and pikes advanced 战鼓咚咚,军旗飘扬,高举长矛(前进)

upon pain of death = with the punishment of death 以死刑作违令惩戒(威令三军)

to observe the strictest decency with regard to my person 对我遵循最严格的礼仪

to confess the truth 坦白地说

in so ill a condition 情况糟糕得不成话了(裤子破了)

to afford some opportunities for laughter and admiration 提供了让大家哈哈大笑和欣赏的机会/笑料

21. to send many memorials and petitions for my liberty 呈上许多请求恢复我自由的奏章/请愿书

at length 终于

full council 国务会议

be pleased to be my mortal enemy without any provocation 从未对其冒犯却总是喜欢与我为敌/却成了我的死敌

be very much in his master's confidence 深得皇帝的信任

be well versed in affairs 熟悉/精通国家事务

be of a morose and sour complexion 面部表情阴沉刻薄

22. That minister was Galbet, or Admiral of the Realm; very much in his master's confidence, and a person well versed in affairs, but of a morose and sour complexion. 那位大臣是吉尔伯特,就是海军大臣;他深受皇帝(主子)的信任,精通国家事务,但脸上总是一副阴沉刻薄的表情。

23. be at length persuaded to comply 被最终说服,表示服从

be set free upon the articles and conditions 根据这些条件文书而获得自由

to swear to the articles and conditions 宣誓服从/遵守这些条件和文书

be drawn up by sb. ……由某人起草

24. However he was at length persuaded to comply; but prevailed that the articles and conditions upon which I should be set free, and to which I must swear, should be drawn up by himself. 然而,他最终被说服,表示服从;但是却坚持我赖以获得自由、必须宣誓遵守的条件文书应当由他起草。

25. in person 亲自

be attended by two under-secretaries, and several persons of distinction 陪伴/跟随而来的有两位次长和几名显贵

to swear to the performance of them 宣誓遵守那些条件

in the method prescribed by their laws 按照他们法律所规定的方式

be curious to have some idea of the style and manner of expression peculiar to that people 出于好奇想要知道那个国家特有的文风和表达方式

to recover my liberty 恢复我的自由

26. to make a translation of the <u>whole instrument</u>　做了全文翻译

the extremities of the globe　地球的极点

to press down to the centre　脚踏大地中心

to strike against the sun　头顶太阳

at one's nod　某人一点头

to propose sb. the following articles　向某人提出如下条件

to arrive at our celestial dominions　到达我们"天朝"（的疆域）

by a solemn oath　通过庄严宣誓

be obliged to perform...　应该／必须遵守……

our licence under our great seal　加盖我国国玺的许可证

27. He shall not <u>presume to come</u> into our metropolis, without our <u>express order</u>; at which time the inhabitants shall have two hours warning, to keep within their doors.　没有明确的指令,他不可冒昧进入我国首都;即使他获准进入首都,也要提前两小时告诫市民,待在屋里别出来。

28. to <u>confine</u> his walks <u>to</u> our principal high roads　只能在主要大道上行走

the said roads/subjects　上述的道路/臣民

to <u>take the uttermost care</u> not to <u>trample upon</u> the bodies of any of our loving subjects...　要格外小心,避免践踏我国良民

an express to require extraordinary dispatch　需要从速发送的紧急公文

a six days' journey once in every moon（=month）　每月一次六天的行程

to return <u>the said messengers</u> back safe to our <u>Imperial Presence</u>　把前面说到的信使安全地送回皇帝驾前

29. be our ally against our enemies　做我们反对敌人的同盟军

to do utmost to destroy their fleet　尽最大力量摧毁他们的舰队

at his times of leisure　在他休闲的时候

to raise great stones towards covering the wall of the principal park, and other royal buildings　为大公园墙垣和其他皇家宫廷的建筑而搬运巨石

to <u>deliver in</u> an exact survey of the circumference of our dominions by a computation of his own paces round the coast.　他须对海岸步测计算,呈献一份我国疆界的精确测量图/数据

to have a daily allowance of meat and drink <u>sufficient for the support of</u> 1728 of our subjects　享有足以维持1728个我们普通臣民生活的肉食酒类的日常供应

with <u>free access to</u> our <u>Royal Person</u>, and other <u>marks of our favor</u>.　可随时谒见皇帝和享有皇帝其他恩典的条件/凭证

30. Given at our palace at Belfaborac the twelfth day of the ninety-first moon of <u>our reign</u>.　我皇登基/在位第91个月12日于包尔法拉克宫。

31. to <u>subscribe to</u> these articles with great cheerfulness and content　喜气洋洋、心满意足地在这些条约文书上签了名

to proceed wholly from the malice of sb.　事情的进展完全是由于某人的蓄意破坏/动机不良

at full liberty　获得完全的自由

32. The Emperor himself in person <u>did me the honor to be by</u> at the whole ceremony.　皇帝本人特别赏光驾临现场参加了整个仪式。

33. I <u>made my acknowledgement</u> by <u>prostrating myself</u> at his Majesty's feet.　我拜倒/匍匐在皇帝脚下,表示感谢。

34. and after many <u>gracious expressions</u>, which, to avoid <u>the censure of vanity</u>, I shall not repeat, he added,

that he hoped that I should prove a useful servant, and well deserve all the favors he had already conferred upon me, or might do for the future.　他说了许多好话,(那些话我就不重复了,以免别人指责我虚荣。)然后又说,他希望我证明自己是一个有用的仆从,也值得他已经赏给我、也许以后还会赏给我的一切恩典

35. to stipulate to allow me a quantity of meat and drink　(条件文书)规定允许我享有一定量的肉食和酒类

to fix on that determinate number　确定这一定的数量

to take the height of my body by the help of a quadrant　借助四分仪,测出我的高度

in the proportion of twelve to one　比例为 12 比 1

to conceive an idea of the ingenuity of that people, as well as the prudent and exact economy of so great a prince　想象到这个民族的足智多谋,以及一个伟大君主经济头脑的精明和精确

主要内容归纳和总结

1. 乔纳森·斯威夫特是一个英格兰家庭的遗腹子,出生在爱尔兰的都柏林。在叔叔的慷慨帮助下,他就读于都柏林三一学院(Trinity College),后来给一个做外交官的远亲做私人秘书,受到了第一流的政治教育,在与邓波爵士和其他许多政治家交往的过程中,了解了官场的罪恶、虚伪、阴谋、欺骗和腐败。后来他又在爱尔兰做牧师直做到都柏林圣帕特里克大教堂主教。由于他发表了两篇著名的讽刺文章《桶的故事》(A Tale of a Tub)和《书籍的战斗》(The Battle of the Books),奠定了他讽刺大师的地位,被聘为当时执政的托利党的党报《考查者》(The Examiner)的主编。

斯威夫特是爱尔兰广受尊敬的民族英雄,是号召爱尔兰人民反抗英国统治压迫的领袖。他的《一个温和的建议》(A Modest Proposal)是讽刺作品的典范,通过建议爱尔兰父母把一岁的孩子卖给英国贵族当食物,辛辣地嘲讽和抗议了英国统治阶级对爱尔兰人民惨无人道的剥削和压迫。他认为人性永远有瑕疵,应对人性和由人组成的机构进行改良,不过,对此他常感愤懑和绝望。

斯威夫特的文风以简练、朴素、精确为特点,透彻入骨的讽刺为风味,他的小说《格列佛游记》(Gulliver's Travels)想象丰富,直刺现实,故事巧妙,名动世界。

2. 乔纳森·斯威夫特的主要作品:

《书籍的战斗》The Battle of the Books（著于 1679, 出版于 1704）

《桶的故事》A Tale of a Tub（1704）

《德拉皮尔书信》The Drapier's Letters（1724～1725）

《格列佛游记》Gulliver's Travels（首版于 1726）

《一个温和的建议》A Modest Proposal（1729）

重要信息句子

1. Swift is one of the greatest masters of English prose. He is almost unsurpassed in the writing of simple, direct, precise prose.

2. Swift is a master of satirist. His satire is usually masked by an outward gravity and an apparent earnestness which renders his satire all the more powerful.

V. 亨利·菲尔丁 Henry Fielding （1707～1754）

词语解释和难句分析

1. prestigious Eton　声望卓著/闻名遐迩的伊顿公学

   to try his luck at play writing　尝试着写剧本，在戏剧创作方面碰碰运气

   comedies and farces filled with political and social satire　充满政治讽刺和社会讽刺的喜剧和闹剧

   be applauded by the public　受到公众的热烈欢迎

   political censorship of the Licensing Act　许可证法案的政治审查制度

   to come into effect　付诸实施

   to take up law and is admitted to the Bar　从事法律职业，获准开办律师事务所

   be appointed Justice of the Peace for Westminster and then Middlesex　被任命为威斯敏斯特（泰晤士河北岸伦敦西区）然后是米德尔塞克斯郡的治安法官

   a position that brought him little income but much renown　带给他的收入虽少但声望极大的一个职位

   an efficient magistrate　一位有能力的/称职的地方法官

2. witty comedies of manners or intrigues in the Restoration tradition　带有复辟时期文艺传统的具有个人风格或复杂情节的诙谐喜剧

   farces or ballad operas with political implications　带有政治含义的闹剧或民谣歌剧

   burlesques and satires that bear heavily upon the status-quo of England　针对英格兰现状的滑稽讽刺

3. the dubious morality and false sentimentality of Richardson's *Pamela*　理查德森的小说《帕米拉》中模糊不清的道德准则和造作的感伤主义

   in imitation of the manner of Cervantes　模仿塞万提斯的艺术手法

   supposedly the young handsome and chaste brother of Richardson's virtuous heroine Pamela　据称是理查德森小说中那位道德高尚的女主人公帕米拉年轻英俊而又童贞正派的弟弟

   amorous mistress　痴情的/迷人的情妇

   be turned out of doors by sb.　被某人拒之门外

   as exposed in all its variety as Joseph (is exposed)　就像（暴露）约瑟夫一样以各种方式对……进行了揭示

   the amiable quixotic parson journey homeward　和蔼可亲的唐·吉诃德式牧师回家的旅程

   robustness of tone and hilarious, hearty humor　雄健粗犷的笔调和会心的引人发笑的幽默

4. The book quickly turns into a great novel of the open road, a "comic epic in prose," whose subject is "the true ridiculous" in human nature, as exposed in all its variety as Joseph and the amiable quixotic parson journey homeward through the heart of England.　该书迅速转变成思路更为开阔的伟大小说，一部"散文体喜剧史诗"，其主题是对人性的真正的嘲笑，就像对约瑟夫和那位和蔼可亲的唐·吉诃德式的牧师穿越英格兰中心千里归家的历程进行讥嘲一样，也用各种方式对嘲笑人性的主题进行了揭示。

5. satiric bilgraphy　讽刺性传记

   to hark back to　回到……，倾听……

   to take the life of notortious real-life thief as a theme for demonstrating the petty division between a great rogue and a great soldier or a great politician such as Sir Robert Walpole 拿现实生活中臭名昭著的贼的人生作为主题,表现了大流氓、伟大战士以及像首相罗伯特·沃波尔那样的大政治家之间的区别实在微小。

ironical praises for the very qualities of the unscrupulous self-aggrandizement of Wild 对怀尔德先生厚颜无耻的自吹自擂的才艺进行了反语相讥的赞扬

be no better than a great gangster 等同于/无异于伟大的匪徒

a maudlin picture of the social life at the time 当时社会生活的一幅伤感的写照

6. to presenta faithful picture of life 对生活进行真实的描绘

the just copies of human manners with sound teaching <u>woven into</u> their texture 把严肃的说教织进作品的结构,作品成为人生态度的真实拷贝

　* woven into... 是介词宾语 teaching 的宾语补足语。

to teach men to know their spheres and appropriate manners 指导人们认识自己的身份和适宜的人生态度

7. the relating of a story 故事的叙述

either in the epistolary form or the picaresque form 或者以书信体形式,或者以流浪汉历险形式

to retain the grand epical form of the classical works 保留经典著作宏大的史诗形式

to keep faithful to his realistic presentation of common life as it is. 始终忠实于对真实的普通生活做现实主义的表现

ridiculous life of the common people 普通人的荒诞生活

from the middle-class to the underworld 从中产阶级到下层社会

8. His structure carefully planned toward an inevitable ending. 他的作品结构安排仔细精巧,顺理成章、水到渠成地走向结尾。

theatrical devices such as suspense, coincidence and unexpectedness 诸如悬念、巧合和出人意料等喜剧技巧

亨利·菲尔丁作品选读

《汤姆·琼斯》*Tom Jones* 第四册第八章

词语解释和难句分析

1. titular hero of the story 故事/小说的同名主人公

a hypocritical, wicked man 虚伪、邪恶的人

be envious of 妒忌

the well-off squire 富有的乡绅

<u>in rebellion against</u> her father's desire 违背他父亲的愿望

to march out for London 出走伦敦

2. manly virtues 男子汉气概,高尚的美德

high-spirited 百折不挠的精神

impulsive, wanting prudence and full of animal spirits 冲动、莽撞(缺乏谨慎)和洋溢的野性精神

to stand for a wayfaring Everyman 代表普通的旅人

be expelled from the paradise 被逐出天堂

to provide the panoramic view of the 18th century English country and city life　为 18 世纪英国乡村和城市生活提供了一幅全景图

with scores of different places　许多不同的地方

a whole gallery of about 40 characters　约 40 人的人物画廊/群像

a language of clarity and suppleness　明了、灵活的语言

be clearly marked out by the change of scenes　因场景变更而有明显的分界

3. be found pregnant　被发现怀孕了

gamekeeper　猎场看守人

4. to have an estate in this parish　在本教区有一份产业

to come to Divine Service　去做礼拜

be very much pleased with = very much like　非常喜欢

to pity for her simplicity in　同情她在……方面的俭朴

to have occasioned (= aroused) envy among her equals　在她的同类人中引起了嫉妒

to provide for her in the family　留她在家里食宿

5. to place the girl about her own person　把她留在自己身边

be thunderstruck at sth.　被某事物惊得目瞪口呆

be no stranger to the fault in the shape of his daughter　对自己女儿身体的异状并非不知道

(sb.) be too awkward to wait on her ladyship　(女儿)手脚太笨伺候不好您小姐

no matter for that = that doesn't matter　那没关系

be pleased with the girl　喜欢这个女孩儿

be resolved to try her　决定用她试试看

6. to repair (= go) to his wife　去找他老婆

to depend on her prudent counsel to extricate him out of this dilemma　靠她的好主意把自己救出困境(两难之境)/为自己解脱困境

to occasion(= arouse) so great envy that　激起如此大的嫉妒

thither = there

hitherto = so far

to burst into an uproar　爆发为大喊大叫

to vent itself at first in opprobrious words, laughs, hisses, and gestures...　先是轻蔑斥责,嘘声嘲笑,指手画脚……来自我发泄/出气

to betake itself to certain missile weapons　发展到/投身于乱扔武器

to threaten neither the loss of life (n.) or a lamb　既伤不了命也断不了一条胳膊腿

be sufficiently dreadful to a well-dressed lady　足以使衣着讲究的人感到害怕

7. So great envy had this sack occasioned, that when Mr. Allworthy and the other gentry were gone from church, the rage, which had hitherto been confined, burst into an uproar; and, having vented itself at first in opprobrious words, laughs, hisses, and gestures, betook itself at last to certain missile weapons; which, though from their plastic nature they threatened neither the loss of life or a limb, were, however, sufficiently dreadful to a well-dressed lady.　那件长大衣激起如此大的嫉妒,以至于在奥尔华绥先生离开教堂之后,一直憋着的怒气终于爆发了出来,开始是用嗤之以鼻的言辞、嘘声的笑骂、上蹿下跳和指手画脚的动作来自我发泄,到后来就发展到乱扔武器的大战;虽然武器是塑料的,伤不了命,也断不了胳膊腿,但却足以使衣着讲究的人感到害怕。

＊句子的主架是 This sack had occasioned so great envy that the rage burst into an uproar and betook itself at last to certain missile weapons; which were sufficiently dreadful to a well-dressed lady. 在that 引

导的结果状语从句中,又有 when 引导的时间状语从句和 which 引导的定语从句修饰从句主语 rage;状语从句有两个谓语动词 had burst into 和 betook;betook 的宾语 missile weapons 又有一个非限制性定语从句 which were sufficiently dreadful to...;betook 还有一个完成时态的分词短语 having vented itself ... and gestures 作时间状语,相当于"在……之后";另外,在最后的 which 引导的修饰 missile weapons 的定语从句中,还有 though 引导的让步状语从句 though from ... they threatened neither...or...。把这些枝枝蔓蔓的主从关系搞清楚,意思就好理解了。

8. to have much spirit　生性刚烈

　　be diffident of our own abilities　自感能力不足,不自信

　　to invite a superior power to our assistance　请个高手帮助我们

9. whoever ye are, who love to sing battles　不论你是谁,只要歌颂战争……

　　＊ 第二句可认为是 whoever 的定语从句。

10. principally (＝especially) thou who whilom didst recount (＝record/describe) the slaughter in those fields where Hudibras and Trulla fought,...　尤其是你——曾经记录过修底布拉斯和特鲁拉在战场上拼杀的人……

11. wert ＝ were

12. All things are not in the power of all. ＝ Not everybody can do everything.　并非每个人能做每件事/并非人人都能把握所有的事。

13. a vast herd of cows　一大群母牛

　　to lament the robbery which is then committing　因遭受别人抢劫而哀号

　　so roared forth the Somersetshire mob an hallaloo ＝ the Somersetshire so roared forth an hallaloo 萨姆赛特郡的人像母牛似的狂喊乱叫

14. so roared forth the Somersetshire mob an hallaloo, made up of almost as many squalls, screams, and other different sounds as there were persons, or indeed passions among them.　这萨姆赛特郡的人就像母牛一样狂喊乱叫,有多少人,或者说有多少情绪,就有多少喊叫、尖叫,以及其他种种乱七八糟的声音,混杂在一起。

15. some were inspired by rage, others alarmed by fear, and others had nothing in their heads but the love of fun.　有些人受怒火的煽动,有些人受恐惧的刺激,另一些人并没有任何情绪,只喜欢瞎闹腾/瞎起哄

16. to blow up the fury of the women　煽动这些女人的怒火

17. who sooner came up to (＝catch up with) Molly than they pelted her with dirt and rubbish　她们刚一追上莫利,就抓起脏土垃圾,朝她扔去

18. to endeavour in vain to make a handsome retreat　竭力从容撤退,却没有成功

　　to face about　转过身来,改变主意

　　to lay hold of the ragged Bess　抓住穿得破破烂烂的贝丝

　　to fell her to the ground at one blow　只一击就将她打倒在地

　　to give back many paces　向后倒退许多步

　　to pursue her victory　乘胜追击

　　to send forth equally a hollow sound at their meeting　相互一撞发出同样的空空的声音

　　(sb.) to take presently measure of his length on the ground ＝ to fall immediately flat on the ground　立即跌倒、直挺挺躺在地上

　　to take a thigh-bone in her hand, fall in among the flying ranks　手拿一个大腿骨冲进奔逃的人群

　　to deal her blows with great liberality on either side　向左右任意挥舞/乱打

19. to deal a stunning blow to sb.　给某人致命一击

to deal successive blows at the enemy　接连打击敌人

to deal the boy a blow on the ear　打了这男孩一记耳光

to overthrow the carcass of many a mighty hero and heroine　把许多了不起的男男女女的英雄(的躯体)打翻在地

20. Recount the names of those who fell on this fatal day.　记录下那要命的一天被打倒在地的人的名字吧。

to feel on his hinder head the direful bone = to feel the direful bone on his hinder head　感觉到那可怕的大腿骨打在他后脑勺上

the sweetly-winding Stour　曲折蜿蜒的斯陶尔河

to learn the vocal art　学习声乐艺术

to wander up and down at wakes and fairs　来回奔走于各个地方的圣节和庙会

to cheer the rural nymphs and swains　为水村山郭的仙女和情郎们欢呼喝彩

to interweave the sprightly dance upon the green　在绿草地上交织穿梭着翩翩起舞

to stand fiddling and jumping to his own music　他站着拉小提琴,自我忘情地演奏着乐曲

Him the pleasant banks of the sweetly-winding Stour had nourished, = The pleasant banks of the sweetly-winding Stour had nourished him.　曲折蜿蜒的斯陶尔河两岸肥美的土地滋养了他

How little now avails his fiddle! = How little his fiddle avails now!　他的小提琴现在也起不了什么作用了/作用是多么小啊!

to thump the verdant floor with his carcass　他的身体狠砸在青草地上

a swinging fat fellow　一个走路摇摆的胖家伙

to take up his tobacco-box as lawful spoils　把他的香烟盒拿来做合法战利品

to tumble over a tombstone　被墓碑绊倒

to catch hold of her ungartered stocking　挂住了她未系丝带的长筒袜

to invert the order of nature　跌了个倒栽葱

to give her heels the superiority to her head　跌了个四脚朝天

to fall both to the ground　双双跌倒在地

perverse fate　故意作对的命运

21. She salutes the earth, and he the sky. = She fell down on her belly, and he fell down on his back.　她跌了个嘴啃泥(向大地致敬),他跌了个面朝天(向上天致敬)。

the next victim to her rage　她盛怒之下的下一个受打击对象

ingenious workman　巧手工匠

22. The pattern with which he was knocked down was his own workmanship.　把他打倒的木头套鞋正是他自己的手艺。

23. Had he been at the time singing psalms in the church, he would have avoided a broken head. = If he had been ..., he would have ...　如果当时他在教堂唱圣诗,也不会像现在这样被打得头破血流。

24. to keep the sign of the Red Lion　开着红狮招牌的客店

Betty Chambermaid　内室侍女贝蒂

Jack Ostler (= hostler)　马夫杰克

many others of inferior note　许多其他不值得记录的人

to lay rolling among the graves　在墓地中翻滚

25. Not that the strenuous arm of Molly reached all these; for many of them in their flight overthrew each other.　并非全被莫利勇武有力的胳膊打出了这样的局面,因为他们好多人是在奔逃中撞翻的。

26. to act out of character　行为不符身份/有失偏颇

to have inclined too long to the same side　已经偏向一边太过长久

to turn about　转过身来,转回头

27. for now Goody Brown — whom Zekiel Brown caressed in his arms; nor he alone, but half the parish besides.　因为现在布朗大娘挺身而出了,这女人是她丈夫布朗大叔抱在怀里亲吻抚摸的宝贝;还不单是她丈夫,教区里有半数人都抱过她。

　　* nor he alone, but half the parish besides = Nor did he do alone, but half the parish did besides. = Not only did he do, but also half the parish did besides.

28. so famous was she in the fields of Venus, nor indeed less in those of Mars.　她在维纳斯/性爱的战场上是那样闻名,在玛尔斯/打架斗殴的战场上也毫不逊色。

29. to bear about the trophies both these on his head and face　他头上和脸上都戴有这两种战利品(性爱战场和撒泼打架的战场)

to displace the amorous glories by its horns, of a wife　凭借头上的角就可展示他妻子的性爱光荣

30. Nor his well-scratched face less denote her talents (or rather talons) of a different kind.　他抓痕累累的脸也同样昭示出她另一方面(或者不如说魔爪)的才能。

31. No longer bore this Amazon the shameful flight of her party. The shameful fight of her party no longer bore this Amazon.　她的那伙人可耻的溃逃表明她们已不再够格做女神式的战士。

　　* Amazon　希腊神话中居住在黑海沿岸的一个战斗民族被称为亚马孙女战士。

32. to fly from a single woman　被一个单枪匹马的女人打得四散奔逃、落花流水

to have the honour of the victory　抢得这份功劳;赢得胜利的荣誉

to fly at sb.　扑向某人

to wrench the thigh-bone from her hand　从她手里抢过大腿骨

to claw off her cap from her head　抓下她头上的帽子

to lay hold of the hair of Molly　抓住莫利的头发

to attack her so furiously in the face　发疯似的打击她的脸

(blood) to trickle from her nose　(血)一滴滴从她鼻子里淌下来

be not idle this while　这会儿并非无所事事/也不听人摆布

to fasten on her hair with one hand　用一只手抓紧她的头发

33. with the other she caused another bloody stream to issue forth from the nostrils of the enemy.　她用另一只手,使得敌人的鼻孔血流如注

34. to bear off sufficient spoils of hair from the head of antagonist　夺得足够的战利品——从敌手头上抓下的头发

be naked to the middle　腰部以上的衣服全撕光了/上身裸露

35. the seat of fistycuff war　拳击战斗的攻击部位

to seem a little to deviate from sex　似乎有点儿偏离他们的性别

to go forth to battle　出征/上阵参战

36. They never so far forget, as to assail the bosoms of each other. = They never forget so far as to assail the bosoms of each other.　他们从来不会那么严重健忘(不知自己是女人)而互击对方的胸部。

37. This, I know, some derive from their being of a more bloody inclination than the males. = I know that some derive this from their being of a more bloody inclination than the males.　我知道,有人把这种情况(避开胸部打击)说成是因为她们比男人更有嗜血倾向。

38. On which account they apply to the nose, as to the part whence blood may most easily be drawn;由于这个原因,她们拿鼻子做攻击目标,从那里可能最容易打出血来;

39. but this seems a far-fetched as well as ill-natured supposition.　但这么看似乎是一个既牵强附会又怀有恶意的假设

40. to <u>have great advantage of</u> Molly <u>in this particular</u>　在这点上比莫利有很大的优势

　　exactly resembling an ancient piece of parchment　完全像一张古代的羊皮纸

　　to drum a considerable time without doing her great damage　狠打一阵都不会对她有什么大损害

41. be differently formed in those parts（bosoms）　胸部的形状与众不同(异常发达)

　　to put an immediate end to the bloody scene　使得这血腥场面立即结束

42. Molly might have tempted the envy of Brown to give her a fatal blow, had not the lucky arrival of Tom Jones <u>at this instant</u> put an immediate end to the bloody scene（＝if the lucky arrival of Tom Jones at this instant had not put an immediate end to the bloody scene）.　要不是汤姆·琼斯幸运地及时赶到,使一场血腥场景立即结束,那么,莫利可能会引起布朗大娘的嫉妒而给她致命的一击。

43. to mount their horses, <u>after church</u>, to <u>take the air</u>　他们昨晚礼拜完后,骑上马在外面闲逛

　　not idly, but for a reason which we shall unfold as soon as we have leisure　不是随意地(改变思想),而是别有原因,以后有空我们会披露

　　to desire the young gentlemen to ride with him another way than they had at first purposed　要求两位年轻绅士和他一起骑马,不按原来的路走

　　to bring them <u>of necessity</u> back again to the churchyard.　必须把它们带回墓园

　　be compiled with　被遵守/服从

44. This accident was luckily owing to Mr. Square;... at first proposed.　汤姆碰巧到来这个偶然事件得归功于斯夸尔先生,因为他,布里菲尔少爷和琼斯做完礼拜后,就骑马出去溜达,走了约四分之一英里,这时斯夸尔先生改变了主意(并非随意改的,而是另有原因,以后有空会予以披露),他要求另两位绅士与他一起骑马改道,不走原来的路。

45. seeing such a mob assembled and two women in the posture in which we left the combatants,...　看到这样一群人聚在一起,还有两个女人,一副我们前面描写过的斗士的姿态

46. I don't know, master, un't I; an't please your honour, here hath a vight（＝fight）,...＝I don't know, master, I don't know; please don't ask me your honour, there is a vight here,...　我不知道,少爷,我不知道;请别问我,阁下,这里正有一场恶斗。

　　＊ 这是一个没有文化的人急急巴巴地回答少爷的话,语无伦次,不符合语法,大概意思如按意会推测改写的那后面的一行。

47. to discover the features of his Molly through all the discomposure in which they now were.　看到他的莫利脸上的伤痕,也看到了他们周围的一片混乱。

　　...hastily alighted, turned his horse loose,...　匆忙下马,没顾得拴马/散放着马

　　to burst into tears　大哭起来

　　to tell him how barbarously she has been treated.　告诉他她受到了怎样野蛮的虐待。

　　to have no feminine appearance but a petticoat　除了穿一条衬裙,一点女人的样子也没有

　　to give sb. a lash or two with his horsewhip　用马鞭抽了某人一两鞭子

　　to deal his blows so profusely on all sides　他毫不吝啬/疯狂地四面挥鞭乱打

48. Unless I would again invoke the Muse, it would be impossible for me to recount the horsewhipping of that day.　除非我再次劳动/恳求缪斯女神,否则,我就不可能重述那天挥舞马鞭乱打的场景。

49. ... which the good-natured readers may think <u>a little too hard upon</u> her, as she hath so lately been violently sweated.　耐心的读者可能会认为这(劳动缪斯这件事)有点儿太苦累了她了,因为就在不久前她还累得大汗淋漓。

　　＊ which＝to invoke the Muse

50. to scour the whole coast of the enemy　鞭打、惩罚了所有的敌人

　　knight-errant　*n.* 游侠骑士

51. （sb.）in a condition which must give both me and my reader pain, was it to be described here.　某人当时的状态,若是要把它描写出来的话,不仅会使我而且也会使读者感到心痛

52. to rave like madman, beat his breast, ... stamp on the ground, and vow the utmost vengeance on all who have been concerned.　像个疯子样咆哮/叫喊,捶胸……顿足,并发誓对所有相关的人进行最严厉的报复

53. to pull off his coat, and button it round her.　脱下他自己的外衣,裹在她身上,扣好扣子

to call out to the servant to ride as fast as possible for a side-saddle, or a pillion, that he might carry her safe home.　大声吩咐仆人尽快地骑马去拿个偏鞍或者后鞍来,他要把她安全地送回家

54. （sb.）to object to the sending away the servant = to object to the sending the servant away.　反对把仆人打发走

to second the order of Jones　附议/跟着赞成琼斯的命令

be obliged to comply　不得不顺从

55. In which manner she was carried home, Square, Blifil and Jones attending.　就这样她被送回家,由斯夸尔先生、布里菲尔少爷和琼斯三人陪同。

to give her a sly kiss and whisper her that he will return in the evening.　悄悄地吻了她一下,还悄声告诉她晚上他再来

to ride on after his companions　骑马追他的同伴去了

主要内容归纳和总结

1. 亨利·菲尔丁出生于英国一个古老的贵族之家,少时曾在著名的伊顿公学读书,培养了欣赏古希腊古罗马经典文学的品位,后因与父亲不和,过早入世谋生,从剧作入手,九年创作了26部剧,成为红极一时的剧作家,并有了自己的小剧院;后又从事小说创作,为现代小说模式的创立做出很大贡献,从此后,小说不再要么是书信体(epistolary form),要么是流浪汉故事(picaresque stories),不再总用第一人称,而开创了第三人称的叙述方法,作者成了无所不知的"上帝",不仅可以描述人物的外在行为,而且还可以刻画人物的内心活动。因此,他被尊为"英国小说之父"。

他的戏剧创作尝试过许多不同的模式,如诙谐喜剧(witty comedies),政治讽刺剧(political burlesques),民谣歌剧(ballad operas)以及滑稽剧(farces),等等。他嘲讽的对象多为政府官员,尤其是首相沃波尔(Prime Minister Walpole)。同样类型的主题也出现在他的小说中,在《伟大的乔纳森·怀尔德》(*The History of Jonathan Wild the Great*)中,他表述了一个"伟大的"政治家比如首相沃波尔无异于一个大流氓(rogue)、大匪徒(bandit)的思想。

在创作理念上,他坚信文学的教育功能,不仅是为了消遣娱乐;在创作技巧和风格上,他忠于现实主义的表现手法,尽力保留古典作品中的史诗风格。在小说杰作《汤姆·琼斯》(*Tom Jones*)中,他甚至用庄严的史诗口吻描写乡村里打群架的场面,显然带有辛辣的讽刺意味。

2. 亨利·菲尔丁的主要作品:

a. 剧作

《咖啡屋政治家》*The Coffee House Politician* (1730)

《悲剧中的悲剧》*The Tragedy of Tragedies* (1730)

《巴斯昆》*Pasquin* (1736)

《1736年历史年鉴》*The Historical Register for the Year* 1736 (1737)

b. 小说

《约瑟夫·安德鲁和亚伯拉罕·亚当历险记》*The History of the Adventures of Joseph Andrews and of*

His Friend Mr. Abraham Adams (1742)

《伟大的乔纳森·怀尔德》*The History of Jonathan Wild the Great* (1743)

《汤姆·琼斯》*The History of Tom Jones, a Foundling* (1749)

《阿米莉亚》*The History of Amelia* (1751)

重要信息句子

1. During a span of nine years (1729 ~ 1737), he turned out 26 plays and became the most successful living playwright of the time. His plays were mostly comedies and farces (闹剧/滑稽剧) filled with political and social satire, the butt being mainly the government and some government officials, particular the Prime Minister Walpole.

2. Fielding started to write novels when he was preparing himself for the Bar. In 1742 appeared his first novel, *The History of the Adventures of Joseph Andrews and of His Friend Mr. Abraham Adams*. (《约瑟夫·安德鲁和亚伯拉罕·亚当历险记》)

3. *Tom Jones* is a masterpiece on the subject of human nature.

4. Fielding has been regarded by some as "Father of the English Novel." For his contribution to the establishment of the form of the modern novel. He adopted "the third-person narration," in which the author becomes the "all-known God." He "thinks the thought" of all his characters.

5. *Tom Jones* brings its author the name of the "Prose Homer."

VI. 塞缪尔·约翰逊 Samuel Johnson (1709 ~ 1784)

词语解释和难句分析

1. on and off 断断续续

    to quit the university without taking a degree 中途辍学,没获得学位

    to make a futile attempt to set up a school 竭力想建一所学校,但未成功

    to try his fortune(luck) as a literary adventure 在文学创作上闯荡一番,碰碰运气

    to write accounts of parliamentary debates for the book-sellers and edited magazines 为书商和自己编辑的刊物写写议会辩论的报道

    to earn no more than enough to maintain a meager living 所得收入勉强够维持粗茶淡饭的生活/刚够糊口

    to take a turn for the better 开始转好,向好的方向转化

    to give him a special pension which freed him from the burden of "writing for a living" 给他一笔特殊津贴,使他摆脱了卖文度日的重负

    to write as little as he decently can. 只很少地写一点符合他(权威)身份的文字

    sort of as a literary authority 有点儿像文学权威

    literary men = men of letters 文学家

    the elite of the literary circles 文学界的精英

2. to have a hand in all the different branches of literary activities. 涉足各种不同分支的文学活动

lexicographer and publicist   词典编撰家

the vanity of human wishes   人类欲望的虚幻

to distinguish himself as the author of the first English dictionary by an Englishman   作为编撰英文词典的第一个英国人而使自己名动天下

to undertake a gigantic task single-handedly   独自一人承担了一项宏大的任务

3. to try to awaken men to this folly   企图唤醒人们对这种愚昧的认识

to show his dislike for much of the newly rising form of literature   表现出对新文学形式的厌恶

to show his fondness for those writings which carry a lot of moralizing and philosophizing.   对大量说教和哲学思考的作品比较喜欢

to adhere to universal truth and experience i. e. Nature   坚守普遍真理和经验,即自然

not to offend religion or promote immorality   不冒犯宗教或不张扬不道德的行为

be particularly fond of moralizing and didacticism   特别偏爱道德说教

be rather pleased with Richardson's *Pamela* but was contemptuous of Fielding's *Tom Jones*.   宁愿欣赏理查德森的《帕米拉》,却要蔑视菲尔丁的《汤姆·琼斯》

4. be at the opposite extreme from Swift's simplicity or Addison's neatness   与斯威夫特的简洁凝练或爱迪生的工整匀称形成极端的对立

be characteristically general, often Latinate and frequently polysyllabic in language   语言上具有笼统和拉丁语特色,常用多音节词

塞缪尔·约翰逊作品选读

《致尊敬的切斯特菲尔德伯爵》*To the Right Honorable the Earl of Chesterfield*

词语解释和难句分析

1. be addressed to the Earl of Chesterfield   写信寄给切斯特菲尔德伯爵

on the eve of publication of the dictionary   词典出版前夕

highly recommend the dictionary to the public   向公众大肆推荐这部词典

to dedicate the work to him, as was the common practice at the time   按当时的惯例把著作赠送给他一本

be enraged and disgusted by the false, hollow, honeyed words   被其虚伪、空洞的甜言蜜语所激怒,感到恶心

the fame-fishing Chesterfield   沽名钓誉的切斯特菲尔德

2. be written in a refined and very polite language   写作/写信所用语言精心提炼、非常礼貌

with a bitter undertone of defiance and anger   暗含着尖刻的蔑视和愤怒之意

to the best satiric effect   带有最辛辣的讽刺意味

3. The seemingly peaceful retrospection, reasoning and questioning express, to the best satiric effect, the author's strong indignation at the lord's fame-fishing and his firm resolution not to be reconciled to the hypocritical lord.   这看似平和的回顾、说理和质疑,语带机锋地表达了作者对这位贵族爵爷的沽名钓誉的强烈愤慨和不与这伪善的家伙妥协和解的坚定决心。

4. to express explicitly the author's assertion of his independence   明确地表达他的独立主张

to signify the opening of a new era in the development of literature.   象征着开创了文学发展的一个新时代

5. be informed by the proprietor of *The World*, that ...   《人世间》杂志的老板告知(我)说：……

    to be so distinguished is an honor   受到如此青睐/推崇/高看是一种荣耀

    be very little accustomed to favors from the great   很不习惯得到大人物的恩宠

6. be overpowered by the enchantment of your address   为您谈吐的魅力所折服

    (can) not forbear to wish that ...   忍不住希望……，不禁想要……

    to boast myself *Le vainqueur du vainqueur de la terre*   自我标榜大地征服者的征服者

    to suffer me to continue it = to allow me to continue it   允许我把这项工作继续下去

7. I could not forbear to wish that I might obtain that regard for which I saw the world contending; but I found my attendance so little encouraged that neither pride nor modesty would suffer me to continue it.   我不由自主地奢望：也许我能得到那份全世界都为之竞争的关怀；但是我发现我的造访得不到一点鼓励，无论是出于自尊还是出于谦虚，都不容许我把工作继续下去。

8. to exhaust all the art of pleasing which a retired and uncourtly scholar can possess.   穷尽我一个卑微的退休学者所能拥有的全部取悦于人的艺术

9. No man is well pleased to have his all neglected, be it ever so little (= even if it should be so little).   没有人乐意自己所做的一切被人忽视，即使这一切非常渺小。

10. to wait in your outward room   在你的住宅外间等候

    be repulsed from your door   被拒之门外

    to push on my work through difficulties of which it is useless to complain   克服重重困难推进我的工作，抱怨困难是没用的

    to bring it to the verge of publication   这部著作即将出版

    without one act of assistance, one word of encouragement, or one smile of favor   没有一个行动的支持，没有一言的鼓励，也没有一笑的赞许

11. to grow acquainted with Love   最终认识了爱神（指厄洛斯 Eros 或丘比特 Cupid）

    to find him a native of the rocks   发现他是岩石丛中的土著

    to look with unconcern on a man struggling for life in the water   对在水中为求生挣扎的人漠然视之

    to encumber him with help   给他压上受人帮助的负债之累

    the notice which you have been pleased to take of my labors   你对我的辛劳欣然施予的关注

    ＊ to take notice of   注意，关注

    cynical asperity   愤世嫉俗的粗暴

    not to confess obligation where no benefit has been received   不能坦承从未得到好处的恩惠

    to owe that to a patron   （因那样的关注）而亏欠一个恩人的人情

12. The notice which you have been pleased to take of my labors, had it been early, had been kind (= if it had been early, the notice ... had been kind).   对我的辛劳欣然施予的关注要是早一点，本来是出于好心的。

13. but it has been delayed till I am indifferent, and cannot enjoy it; till I am solitary, and cannot impart it; till I am known, and do not want it.   但是这关注却被推迟到我都无所谓了，无法享受了，我孤独一人不能传递了，直到我已为人所知，不再需要它了。

14. I hope it is no cynical asperity not to confess obligation where no benefit has been received, or to be unwilling that the public should consider me as owing that to a patron which Providence has enabled me to do for myself.   我希望不坦承从未得到好处的恩惠，或对于上帝使我能自己完成的事不愿意公众认为我亏欠某个恩人的人情，绝不是愤世嫉俗的粗暴。

15. If less be possible, with less. = If less help be possible, I would like to carry on my work with less help/obligations.   如果没有帮助也可以的话，我就不要任何人的帮助（而完成自己的工作）。

16. Having carried on my work thus （ ＝so） far with so little obligation to any favorer of learning, I shall not be disappointed though I should conclude it, if less be possible, with less.　没有得到任何学术赞助人的恩惠，我已把工作推进到如此地步，虽然没有帮助也应当完成工作，而假如没有帮助我就不要帮助，但对于完成自己的工作我依然充满信心。

17. for I have been long wakened from that dream of hope in which I once boasted myself with so much exultation.　因为很久以前，我就从曾一度欣喜若狂地自我标榜的希望之梦中清醒过来了。

主要内容归纳和总结

1. 塞缪尔·约翰逊出生于英格兰里奇菲尔德(Richfield)，父亲是书商，他先在里奇菲尔德中学学习 8 年，打下了坚实的拉丁文基础，后又就读于牛津大学，还未得到学位，就因父亲病故而中途辍学。后来他与一位富有的老寡妇结婚，经济上略有改善。他虽多才多艺，但文学上的诸多探索成果不大。直到他完成了第一部由英国人编撰的《英文大辞典》，才奠定了他在学术界不可动摇的地位，同时也获得了可观的政府津贴。

　　约翰逊是 18 世纪下半叶最后一位古典主义启蒙文学家。他十分关注人类欲望的虚幻，几乎所有作品都含有这样的主题，希望唤醒人们对这一点的认识。他的创作和评论思想都非常保守，要求作家遵守古典原则，不能冒犯宗教，不能违背传统道德，他像蒲伯(Pope)一样喜欢说教(be fond of moralizing and didacticism)。在文学形式和艺术技巧上，他公开反对任何新兴的模式和探索。他在语言运用上喜欢学者式的长句子，结构严谨，排比、对仗非常工整，尽管复杂，却表达精确，显得博学，也适合教育程度较高的读者群。

2. 塞缪尔·约翰逊的主要作品：
   a. 诗歌
   《伦敦》*London*（1738）
   《人类欲望的虚幻》*The Vanity of Human Wishes*（1749）
   b. 骑士浪漫传奇
   《拉塞拉斯的历史》*The History of Rasselas*（1759）
   《阿比西尼亚王子》*Prince of Abyssinia*（1759）
   c. 剧作
   《艾琳》*Irene*（1749）
   d. 散文
   主要是发表在他编辑的两种期刊《漫谈者》(*The Rambler*)和《悠闲者》(*The Idler*)上的几百篇文章。
   e. 文学编辑和文学评论
   《诗人评传》*Lives of the Poets*（1779~1781）评论了 52 位诗人
   f. 辞典编纂
   《英文大辞典》*A Dictionary of the English Language*（1755）

重要信息句子

1. Samuel Johnson was the last great neoclassicist enlightener in the later 18th century. He was very much concerned with the theme of the vanity of human wishes.

2. Because Johnson tends to use "learned words", reading his works gives the reader the impression that he is talking with a very learned man.

VII. 理查德·布林斯莱·谢立丹
Richard Brinsly Sheridan (1751~1816)

词语解释和难句分析

1. to fight two duels 进行了两次决斗

   to see the appearance of his masterpiece 见证/经历了他杰作的产生

   to bring him quite a fortune 给他带来了一大笔财产,使他发了一大笔财

   to hold various government offices 担任各种政府官职

   Under-secretary of State for Foreign Affairs 外交部次长

   Secretary of the Treasury 财政部部长

   Treasurer of the Navy 海军司库

   be dropped out of the Parliament 被挤出/赶出议会

   to die in neglect and poverty 在贫穷和被人忽视的境况中死去

2. be regarded as important links between the masterpieces of Shakespeare and those of Bernard Shaw 被认为是莎士比亚和萧伯纳的杰作之间的重要纽带

   as true classics in English comedy 作为英国喜剧真正的经典

   to lash harshly at the social vices of the day 猛烈地抨击当时的社会弊病

   to arrange marriages for their children without considering the latter's opinion (父母)为子女包办婚姻而不考虑子女的意见

   (the characters) be exposed scene by scene to their defenseless nakedness (人物的本质)随着一幕一幕的推进,被赤裸裸地暴露出来

3. to inherit from his parents a natural ability and inborn knowledge about the theatre 从他父母那里继承了戏剧天赋和知识才能

   the product of a dramatic genius as well as of a well-versed theatrical man 戏剧天才和精通戏剧之人的作品

   (dramatic techniques) be exploited to the best advantage (戏剧技巧)被开发到了极致

   such devices as disguise, mistaken identity and dramatic irony 诸如化妆假扮、身份的误会和戏剧反语之类的戏剧技巧

   witty dialogues and neat and decent language 幽默诙谐的对话和公正得体的语言

   to make a characteristic of his plays 形成了他剧作的特点

   a burlesque and a satire on sentimental drama 对感伤主义戏剧的嘲弄和讥讽

谢立丹作品选读

《造谣学校》*The School for Scandal* 第三幕第四场

词语解释和难句分析

1. the hypocritical Joseph Surface　虚伪的约瑟夫·塞菲斯

the good-natured, imprudent, spendthrift Charles Surface　本性善良却轻率鲁莽、花钱如流水的查尔斯·塞菲斯

scandal-mongers　制造谣言/散布流言蜚语的人

the busy, mischievous, gossiping upper society　忙忙碌碌、恶作剧不断、流言蜚语满天飞的上流社会

to instigate Joseph to pursue Maria　唆使约瑟夫追求玛丽亚

to make advances to Maria　向玛丽亚发起进攻

to try to seduce Lady Teazle　企图诱奸梯泽尔夫人

be flirting with his young wife　正与他年轻的妻子打情骂俏

on the verge of committing adultery　即将发生通奸的时候

to take cover = to take shelter　躲起来, 寻找躲避处

to hide behind a screen　藏到一个屏风后面

2. to long for his uncle's inheritance　渴望得到他叔叔的遗产

to find out the truth about his nephews for himself　看清他侄子对他的真情实感

to visit Charles in the guise of a usurer　假扮成一个高利贷者来拜访查尔斯

to part with his uncle's portrait　放弃/出卖他叔叔的肖像

on the pretext that...　借口/托词……

3. to end with great disgrace for Joseph and double bliss for Charles　以约瑟夫的羞愧无地和查尔斯的双喜临门作为结束

to win the hand of his beloved and the inheritance of his rich uncle　赢得他爱人的芳心和富豪叔叔的遗产

be reconciled to her husband　与她丈夫言归于好

4. the moral degeneracy of the aristocratic-bourgeois society　贵族资产阶级社会的道德堕落

the vicious scandal-mongering among the idle rich　无所事事、百无聊赖的富人中产生的造谣生事的邪恶风气

the reckless life of extravagance and love intrigues in the high society　上层社会中奢侈浪费、男女通奸的放荡生活

the immorality and hypocrisy behind the mask of honorable living and high-sounding moral principles　隐藏在高贵生活和虚夸的道德准则(的面罩)背后的道德败坏和伪善虚假

to show the playwright at his best　表现出剧作家创作高潮时的状态

Joseph's entanglement with Lady Teazle　约瑟夫与梯泽尔夫人之间的暧昧纠缠/偷情

5. be prevented from coming　不让来, 因受阻碍而来不了

through the scrape I have drawn myself in with the wife.　因我与他妻子的暧昧纠葛

be great points in my favour = be to my great advantage　对我十分有利

to have a particular message for you　有一个给你的特别信息, 特别关照你几句

to leave her chair at the milliner's in the next street   她总是在临街的帽子店门口下车

a maiden lady of so curious a pamper   一位好奇心很重的老处女

6. I have a difficult hand to play in this affair, Lady Teazle has lately suspected my views on Maria — but she must by no means be let into that secret, at least not until I have her more in my power.   在这件事上我很为难,梯泽尔夫人最近总是怀疑我对玛丽亚别有用心——但是绝不能让她知道这个秘密,至少要等到我更能掌控她的时候,才能让她知道。

7. What sentiment in soliloquy! ＝What sentiment you have in soliloquy!   这么多愁善感哪! 还自言自语的。

8. to pretend to look grave   假装严肃(的表情)

9. Punctuality is a species of constancy, a very unfashionable quality in a lady.   守时是一种持之以恒的表现,也是女士的一种品质,尽管不时髦。

10. Upon my word   说实在话,的的确确,我敢保证

be grown so ill-tempered to me of late   最近脾气变得很坏、很暴躁

be grown so jealous of Charles   嫉妒查尔斯

my scandalous friends keep that up (＝spread the scandal)   我的那些专会造谣的朋友把这种谣言(查尔斯与梯泽尔夫人有染)传播开来

her suspicion of my having any design on that silly girl   她怀疑我对那个傻丫头谋不轨

11. be inclined to believe you.   愿意相信你的话

to have the most ill-natured things said to one   对一个人说了许多最恶毒的话

to have circulated I don't know how many scandalous tales of me.   已经散布了不知多少关于我的谣言

without any foundation   毫无根据

to vex me.   使我心烦/恼火

to be sure that is the provoking circumstance   的确那是令人恼火的情况

12. there's the mortification, indeed, — for when a scandalous story is believed against one, there certainly is no comfort like the consciousness of having deserved it.   的确,那是很丢面子的,——因为当一个谣言被人认为是针对某人的时候,没有什么比他认识到这是自作自受更欣慰的了/最大的欣慰莫过于意识到这是自作自受

13. then I'd forgive their malice — but to attack me, who am really so innocent, and who never say an ill-natured thing of anybody — that is, of any friend — and then Sir Peter too — to have him so peevish, and so suspicious...   那么,我就原谅他们的恶意——但是他们攻击我,一个真正非常无辜的、从来不说任何人——也就是任何朋友坏话的人——而彼得爵士——也变得那么乖戾、那么多疑……

    ＊ 可以认为 to attack me, ... 和 to have him so peevish, and so suspicious 是 malice 的定语。

14. when a husband entertains a groundless suspicion of his wife and withdraws his confidence from her, the original compact is broken and she owes it to the honour of her sex to endeavour to outwit him.   当一个丈夫无缘无故地怀疑自己的妻子并以此为乐的时候,当他撤回对妻子的信任的时候,原来的婚约就被撕毁了,妻子努力用智力战胜她的丈夫就属于女性的荣誉

    ＊ owe it to the honour of her sex 中的 it 是形式宾语,真正的宾语是不定式短语 to endeavour to outwit him。

15. Undoubtedly — for your husband should never be deceived in you, and in that case it becomes you to be frail in compliment to his discernment.   毫无疑问——因为你的丈夫绝不应当对你感到怀疑,如果他对你怀疑了,你以不贞来回报他的识人不明,就是理所当然的了。

16. to be sure what you say is very reasonable, and when the consciousness of my own innocence —   你讲

的的确有道理，一想到自己清白无辜——

17. ... there's the great mistake — 'tis this very conscious innocence that <u>is of</u> the greatest prejudice to you. What is it（that）makes you <u>negligent of</u> forms and careless of the world's opinion? Why, the consciousness of your innocence.　大错就在这儿——正是你想到自己的清白无辜，造成了对自己的最大偏见。是什么使得你不注意自己的行为举止，对世人的看法漠不关心？唉，就是想到了自己的清白无辜。

18. What makes you thoughtless in your conduct and apt to run into a thousand little imprudence? Why, the consciousness of your innocence. What makes you impatient of Sir Peter's temper and outrageous at his suspicions? Why, the consciousness of your innocence!　是什么使得你对为人处事的方式不加考虑，轻易地屡屡莽撞行事？唉，就是想到了自己的清白无辜。是什么使你忍受不了彼得爵士乖张的脾气，对他的多疑感到愤愤不平？唉，就是想到了你的清白无辜。

19. If you would but once make a trifling faux pas［slip］（ = false step）, you can't conceive how cautious you would grow — and how ready to humour and agree with your husband.　如果你连一次小小的行为失检都没有，你就不能想象你会变得多么小心谨慎——又是多么容易变得对丈夫曲意迎合和百依百顺。

20. I'm sure on't（ = on it）— and then you would find all scandal would cease at once, for in short, your character at present is like a person in a plethora absolutely <u>dying of</u> too much health.　对此我敢肯定——而且你会发现一切谣言将立即停止，因为简言之，您现在的好名声/好品质就像一个患了多血症的病人，绝对会死于过分的健康。

21. then I perceive your prescription is — that I must sin <u>in my own defence</u> — and <u>part with</u> my virtue to preserve my reputation.　我想你开的处方是——我必须为自卫而犯下罪孽——为维护声誉而抛弃贞节的美德

22. upon my credit　以我的信誉保证

the oddest doctrine　奇怪的教义/主义/理论

the newest receipt for avoiding calumny　避免诽谤的最新处方

an infallible receipt　肯定有效/正确无误的处方

23. Prudence, like experience, must be paid for.　谨慎，就像经验，必须付出代价。

24. — heaven forbid I should persuade you to do anything you thought wrong. No, no, I have too much honour to desire it.　上天不允许我说服你做任何你认为错误的事情。不，不，我的荣誉感太强，不愿做这样的事

25. the ill effects of your country education　你受乡下教育的坏影响

<u>may as well</u> leave honour <u>out of the argument</u>　倒不如把你的荣誉感放到一边不谈

then by this hand which he is unworthy of　就凭这只他不配得到的手；就凭这只手，他就不配得到

26. and I will <u>fairly own to you</u>, that if I could be persuaded to do wrong, it would be by Sir Peter's <u>ill usage</u> <u>sooner than</u>（ = rather than）your honourable logic, after all.　我要向你坦白承认，如果我被你说服去做坏事，那也是彼得爵士对我不好，而绝不是因为你荣誉的逻辑

27. ... but I thought you wouldn't <u>choose</u> Sir Peter to come up without announcing him.　但是我想你不会愿意彼得爵士来到而我不通报吧。

28. O lud! I'm ruined! I'm ruined!　啊！天哪！我完了！我完了！

O I'm undone — what will <u>become me</u> now Mr. Logic?　呵，完了，丢人了——我该怎么办？

Servant pretends to <u>adjust his hair</u>.　仆人假装给他整理头发。

to <u>confide in</u> Joseph that Charles is after his wife Lady Teazle　相信约瑟夫的话：查尔斯正追求他的妻子梯泽尔夫人

to lead the old man to believe the truth of the rumour 引导这位老人相信谣言是真的。

29. What has been the matter? Your fellow would not let me up at first. What, have you had a Jew or a wench with you? 出了什么事了? 你的仆人开始还不让我进来。怎么,有个放高利贷的犹太人还是有个妓女跟你在一起呀?

30. What has made Sir Peter steal off? 什么原因使彼得爵士溜走了?
He was hearing you were coming he did not choose to stay. 他听说你来了,就不愿意待了。

31. ...but I am sorry to find, Charles, that you have lately given that worthy man grounds for great uneasiness. 然而,我很抱歉地发现,查尔斯,你最近使得那位可尊敬的先生感到很不安哪/成了他不安的理由。

32. to endeavour to gain Lady Teazle's affections from him 竭力夺走梯泽尔夫人对他的感情

33. This is no subject to jest on. 这不是开玩笑的(话题)。

34. to charge sb. with... 以……起诉/指控某人
upon my honour 以我的荣誉起誓

35. upon my soul, I never gave her the least encouragement 以灵魂起誓,我从未给她一点念想/鼓励

36. Besides, you know my attachment to Maria. 此外,你知道的,我的爱情归于玛丽亚。

37. to betray (= show/display) the fondest partiality for sb. 表露出对某人极为偏爱
to throw herself in my way 她投怀送抱/主动送上门来
by naming me with Lady Teazle 把我与梯泽尔夫人联系在一起/同日而语
to exchange such significant glances 眉目传情,暗送秋波

38. Why, look'ee (= look ye), Joseph, I hope I shall never deliberately do a dishonourable action—but if a pretty woman were purposely to throw herself in my way — and that pretty woman married to a man old enough to be her father — 嗨,你注意呀,约瑟夫,我希望我永远都不会处心积虑地做一件不光彩的事情——但是如果一个漂亮的女人主动投怀送抱的话——而且那个漂亮女人的丈夫老得足以做她的父亲的话——

39. Why, I believe I should be obliged to borrow a little of your morality, that's all. — But brother, do you know now that you surprise me exceedingly, by naming me with Lady Teazle — for faith, I always thought you were her favourite. 呵,我想我不得不向你借点儿道德,仅此而已。不过哥哥,你可知道你把我和梯泽尔夫人联系在一起使我大为吃惊呢——说实话,我一直认为你才是她喜欢的人。

40. O, for shame, Charles — this retort is foolish. 啊,可耻,查尔斯——你这种反击/反唇相讥是愚蠢的。

41. (I'll say) a word with you! — [aside] Gad (= God), I must stop him. 我跟你说句话! ——[旁白]上帝呀,我得阻止他说下去。

42. — I beg your pardon, but Sir Peter has overheard all we have been saying — I knew you would clear yourself or I should not have consented. 我恳请你原谅,彼得爵士一直在偷听我们的讲话——我知道你要洗刷自己/为自己辩白,否则我是不会同意的。

43. 'fore heaven [poem] = before heaven 天哪!
to come forth 出来
to come into court 公开露面
my old guardian 我的老监护人
to turn inquisitor and take evidence incog (= incognito ad.) 变成了调查员,微服私访

44. But I acquit you. — I promise I don't think near so ill of you as I did. What I have heard has given me great satisfaction. 但我宣告你无罪——我告诉你我认为你不像我过去想的那么坏。我所听到的使我感到十分满意。

45. You would have retorted on him. 你本来可以反击他的。

46. But you might have <u>as well</u> suspected him as me in this matter, <u>for all that</u>. Mightn't he, Joseph? 尽管如此,这件事你本来也可以怀疑他的,就像怀疑我一样,可不可以,约瑟夫?

47. <u>Would</u> they were both out of the room! = I wish they were both out of the room! 但愿他俩都离开房间!

48. I must <u>wait on</u> you downstairs — here's a person come on particular business. 我必须在楼下接待你们——这儿有个人要来谈点儿特别的事。

49. Sir Peter, not a word of the French Milliner. 彼得爵士,法国女帽商的事,一句别提。

50. O not (a word) <u>for the world</u>! — Ah, Charles, if you associated more with your brother, one might indeed hope for your reformation. He is a man of sentiment — well! There is nothing in the world so noble as a <u>man of sentiment</u>! 呵,这方面我不会说一句话!——呵,查尔斯,如果你过去多和你哥哥接触,人们就可以确确实实地指望你洗心革面。你哥哥是个有情有义的人——嗨,这世界上没有什么比有情义的人更高贵的了!

51. Pshaw! He is too moral <u>by half</u>, and so <u>apprehensive of</u> his good name, as he calls it, that I suppose he would <u>as soon</u> let a priest into his house <u>as</u> a girl. 哼!他满嘴仁义道德,也太过分了,那么珍惜他自吹的好名声,我想他让一个神父进入房间,就像让一个姑娘进入他的房间一样迅速。

52. No, no, . . . you <u>wrong</u> him. Joseph is no rake, but he is not such a saint in that respect either — I <u>have a great mind to</u> tell him — we should have a laugh (at him)! 不,不……你冤枉他了。约瑟夫绝不是浪荡子,但他也不是那方面的圣人——我很想告诉他——我们应当好好嘲笑他一番!

53. Oh, hang him! He is a very anchorite, a young hermit. 啊,见鬼!简直是一个离群索居的修道士,一个年轻的隐士。

54. Hark' ee (= listen to me), you must not abuse him. He may <u>chance to hear</u> of it again, I promise you. 听我说,你绝不可责备他。他可能碰巧又听到了,我告诉你。

55. <u>Have you a mind to</u> have a good laugh at Joseph? 你想要好好地嘲笑一下约瑟夫吗?

56. I should like it <u>of all things</u>. 我再喜欢不过了/真想不到,太喜欢了。

57. Then, efaith (= so) we will — I'll <u>quit with</u> him for discovering me. [*aside*] — He had a girl with him when I called. 那么,我们就这么做——[旁白]他揭露了我,我要报复他一下,两不亏欠——我来访的时候,他跟一个姑娘在一起。

58. the best of the jest is—she is in the room now. 最精彩(的笑话)还在后头呢——现在她就在房间里 The devil she is! 她不在才怪呢!

59. Behind the screen — 'slife, let's unveil her! 就在屏风后面——呸,我们来揭露她/揭开屏风,让她露出真相。

60. to have a peep at 窥视
    for the world 不管怎样,无论如何
    to stand by sb. 支持某人,与某人站在一起
    struggling with sb. 与某人拉拉扯扯
    to throw down the screen 撞到了屏风
    <u>by all</u> that's wonderful/horrible 那确实是太精彩/可怕了

61. Not <u>for the world</u>! — Joseph will never forgive me. 无论如何都不行——约瑟夫绝不会原谅我

62. the smartest French milliner 最俊俏的法国女帽商
    to divert yourselves here <u>at hide and seek</u> 你们在这儿东躲西藏地捉迷藏
    in the secret 知道秘密,参与秘密
    out of the secret = in the dark 不知就里,蒙在鼓里
    morality dumb too? = Is morality dumb too? 道德也哑巴了?
    All mute! = All are mute! 所有的人都哑巴了!

63. Well, tho' I can <u>make nothing of</u> the affair I suppose you perfectly understand one another — so I'll <u>leave you to yourselves</u>. 哦,虽然我对此事搞不明白/无能为力,但是我估计你们俩完全可以相互理解——所以我还是离开,让你们自已谈谈吧。

64. Brother, I'm sorry to find you have given that worthy man so much uneasiness! — Sir Peter, there's nothing in the world so noble as a man of sentiment! 哥哥,我很遗憾,看到了你给这位值得敬重的人带来了那么多不安!——彼得爵士,这个世界上没有任何东西比有情意的人更高贵。

65. Sir Peter — <u>notwithstanding</u> I confess that appearances are against me — if you will afford me your patience — I make no doubt but I shall explain everything <u>to your satisfaction</u>. 彼得爵士——尽管我承认表面上看来对我不利——但假如你能耐心听我解释——我肯定能把每一件事情都解释得清清楚楚,让你满意。

66. knowing my pretension to your ward Maria 知悉我对你的被监护人玛丽亚的心意
    <u>being apprehensive of</u> the jealousy of your temper 担心你的嫉妒心理
    to call here = to visit here = to come here 来到这儿,到这里拜访
    to <u>depend on</u> it 相信/依赖它

67. A very clear account <u>upon my word</u>, and I dare swear the lady will <u>vouch for</u> every article of it. 我保证已讲得清清楚楚(是一个清楚明白的陈述),我敢起誓这位夫人会证明我说的每一个细节都是真实的。

68. For not one word of it, = I'll <u>vouch for</u> one word of it. 其中的一句话我也不担保

69. to think <u>it</u> worthwhile <u>to agree in the lie</u> 认为协同撒谎是值得的
    not one syllable of truth in what the gentleman has told you. 这位绅士给你讲的没一句是真的
    to betray sb. 背叛/出卖某人……
    by/with your leave 请原谅,请允许我

70. Let her alone, sir — you'll find she'll make out a better story than you without prompting. 别打搅她,先生——你会发现如果你不催,她会把事情处理得更好。

71. on no matter relating to your ward 没谈论与你的被监护人有关的话题
    be ignorant of this gentleman's pretensions to her 不知道这位绅士对她的意图
    be seduced by his insidious arguments 受了他阴险狡诈的花言巧语的诱惑
    to listen to his pretended passion 听从了他虚伪的热情
    if not to <u>sacrifice</u> your honour <u>to</u> his baseness 假如不是把你的荣誉牺牲给他的卑劣和胆怯

72. She has recovered her senses, and your own arts have <u>furnished her with</u> the means. 她已恢复了理智,你自己的诡计也为她提供了应对的方法和智慧。

73. Sir Peter, I do not expect you to credit me — but the tenderness you expressed for me when I am sure you could not think I was a witness to it, has penetrated to my heart. 彼得爵士,我不指望您相信我——但是,在过去你认为我不可能当场耳闻目睹的时候所表达出来的温情宽厚,已经深深打动了我的心。

74. and had I left(= If I had left) the place without the shame of this discovery, my future life should have spoken the sincerity of my gratitude — 假如我没有这次失检行为败露的蒙羞,本来我是会表现出真诚的感激的——

75. <u>As for</u> that <u>smooth-tongue</u> hypocrite, who would have seduced the wife of his too credulous friend while he affected honourable <u>addresses</u> to his ward — I <u>behold</u> <u>him now in a light</u> so truly despicable, that I should never again respect myself for having listened to him. 至于那个花言巧语的伪君子,在他伪装堂堂正正、气宇轩昂地向一个太过轻信的好朋友的女被监护人侃侃而谈的时候,却差一点儿诱奸了他的妻子——现在我看清了你,如此的卑鄙,因为这次听从了你的话,我永远都会看不起自己。

76. That you are a villain! — and so I leave you to your conscience. 你是一个无赖! ——我让你受良心的谴责。

77. You are too rash, Sir Peter — you shall hear me! the man who shuts out conviction by refusing to — 你太急躁、太草率了,彼得爵士——一个人若是排斥信念,拒绝听取别人的意见——

主要内容归纳和总结

1. 谢立丹,剧作家,爱尔兰都柏林人,出身于戏剧世家,父亲托马斯·谢立丹(Thomas Sheridan)是演员兼剧院经理人。谢立丹少时在哈罗公学(Harrow Public School)受到良好教育,后全家移居巴斯(Bath),在那里他爱上了著名女歌手,经两次决斗,终于与他所深爱的女人结婚。24 岁时,他的剧作《情敌》(*The Rival*)一炮走红,他也拥有了自己的剧院。29 岁时,《造谣学校》(*The School for Scandal*)出版,他财源滚滚,达到戏剧创作的顶峰。遗憾的是后来他当了 32 年议员,只因一场大火烧了他的剧院,使他无钱参加下届竞选,才中断了从政之路。这个议员头衔使一个天才的戏剧艺术家过早地结束了他的创作生涯。他后来因躲债而被捕过,在贫困与孤独中死去。

   谢立丹的戏剧艺术非常保守,道德是他作品永恒的主题。他在艺术技巧上以精致见长,情节结构巧妙,角色性格鲜明,对伪装(disguise)、误会(mistaken identity)、戏剧反语(dramatic irony)等艺术手法驾驭自如,使作品充满灵气。他的代表作《情敌》和《造谣学校》被认为是上承莎士比亚、下启萧伯纳的伟大剧作。

2. 谢立丹的主要作品:
   《情敌》*The Rival* (1775)
   《圣帕特里克日或诡计多端的中尉》*St. Patrick's Day, or the Scheming Lieutenant* (1775)讽刺闹剧
   《杜安纳》*The Duenna* (1775)喜剧歌剧
   《造谣学校》*The School for Scandal* (1777)
   《批评家》*The Critic* (1779)对感伤主义戏剧进行了讽刺
   《皮扎罗》*Pizarro* (1799)改编自德国喜剧的一个悲剧

重要信息句子

1. Richard Brinsley Sheridan was born in Dublin, Ireland, the son of Thomas Sheridan, actor and theater manager.

2. Sheridan was the only important English dramatist of the 18th century. His plays, especially *The Rival* and *The School for Scandal*, are generally regarded as important links between the masterpieces of Shakespeare and Bernard Shaw, and as true classics in English comedy.

VIII. 托马斯·格雷 Thomas Gray（1716～1771）

词语解释和难句分析

1. to befriend Horace Walpole and Richard West　与贺拉斯·沃波尔和理查德·威斯特结交为朋友
   to cause him years of deep grief　使他悲伤了好多年
   to leave Cambridge University without taking a degree　离开剑桥大学而没有取得学位
   to tour the European continent　游历欧洲大陆
   to remain there for the rest of his life except for short intervals　在那里度过了余生，中间只有几次短暂的间隔
   in search of the sublime and the beautiful　寻找高尚和美
   to get his bachelor's degree in law　获得了法学学士学位
   to decline the Poet laureateship　婉辞了桂冠诗人的头衔
   to lead the uneventful life of a scholar all his life　一生都过着一个学者的风平浪静、波澜不兴的生活

2. *Elegy Written in a Country Churchyard*　《写在乡村教堂墓园的挽诗》
   literary output　文学作品的产量
   once and for all　一劳永逸，永远
   sentimental poetry　感伤主义的诗歌
   the Graveyard School　墓园派诗人/诗歌
   to devote to a sentimental lamentation or meditation on life, past and present on life, past and present　（他的诗）着力于对生活、过去和现在的哀悼和沉思

3. The poem once and for all established his fame as the leader of the sentimental poetry of the day, especially "the Graveyard School."　他的诗从一开始就永远确立了他作为当时感伤主义诗歌领军人物的地位/声誉。

4. painstakingly seeking perfection of form and phrase　苦心孤诣地追求形式和语言的完美
   be characterized by an exquisite sense of form　以精美的形式感为其特点
   sophisticated and allusive style　细致精密、长于用典的文风
   be marked with the trait of a highly artificial diction and a distorted word order　鲜明突出的特点是措辞的杜撰和打乱的词序

托马斯·格雷作品选读

写在乡村教堂墓园的挽诗 *Elegy Written in a Country Churchyard*

词语解释和难句分析

1. be the outcome of about eight years' careful composition and polish　历时八年反复推敲、精益求精的结果

be more or less connected with the melancholy event of the death of Richard West　与理查德·威斯特死亡的事件给诗人带来的忧郁多少有关

to reflect on death, the sorrows of life, and the mysteries of human life　对死亡、生命的悲哀和对人生的神秘进行反省沉思

to compare the common folk with the great ones　把普通人与伟人进行对比

to despise the poor and bring havoc on them　鄙视穷人,并给他们带来灾难

2. to abound in images　（诗歌）意象丰富

to arouse sentiment in the bosom of every reader　在每个读者心里激起了伤感

the artistic polish　艺术上的完美高雅

the sure control of language　语言的自如把握

his subtle moderation of style and tone　风格和笔调的中庸平和、细致入微

3. The curfew tolls the knell of parting day,　晚钟为逝去的白昼敲响了丧钟,

The lowing herd wind slowly o'er (= over) the lea,　低鸣的牛群在草原上缓缓绕行,

The plowman homeward plods his weary way,　犁地人累了,吃力地踏上回家之路,

And leaves the world to darkness and me.　把整个世界留给了黑暗和我。

＊ 这一诗节语法平顺如散文,没有任何因格律和韵律需要而进行的顺序调整,比较好理解。

4. Now fades the glimmering landscape on the sight, /And all the air a solemn stillness holds, = Now the glimmering landscape fades on the sight, /And all the air holds a solemn stillness.　现在闪烁的风景渐渐从眼前消逝,/整个天宇笼罩着一片庄严的寂静。

Save where the beetles wheels his droning flight, /And drowsy tinklings lull the distant folds;　只有甲虫嗡嗡地转圈翻飞,/昏沉沉的叮铃声催眠远处的羊栏;

＊ save 为连词,后跟从句,常以 save that... 的形式出现,"只有、只是""要不是"的意思。

5. yonder ivy-mantled tower　远处那青藤披裹的塔楼

to complain of such as (are) doing sth.　抱怨那些做某事的人

＊ as 为关系代词,引导定语从句。

to molest her ancient solitary reign　骚扰她古老幽静的领地

6. Save that from yonder ivy-mantled tower/The moping owl does to the moon complain/Of such, as wondering near her secret bower,/Molest her ancient solitary reign.　只听见远处常青藤披裹着的塔楼上,/抑郁的猫头鹰在对着月亮诉苦,/责怪那漫游人逛进她秘密的家园,/骚扰她古老而幽静的领地。

＊ complain of 与 molest 是 the moping owl 并列的谓语动词。

7. Beneath those rugged elms, that yew tree's shade,　在峥嵘的榆树下,那紫杉的绿荫里,

Where heaves the turf in many a moldering heap, = Where the turf heaves in many a moldering heap,　草皮隆起许多凄凉的荒堆,

＊ heave (vi.) = rise = fall

Each in his narrow cell forever laid, = Each is laid in his narrow cell forever,　各人都永远置身在狭窄的墓穴中,

The rude forefathers of the hamlet (= village) sleep (there).　村里粗俗的乡邻就在那里安睡。

8. The breezy call of incense-breathing Morn (= morning),　清晨飘香的微风的呼唤,

The swallow twittering from the straw-built shed,　茅草棚里传出的燕子的呢喃,

The cock's shrill clarion, or the echoing horn,　不论是雄鸡的高唱,还是猎号的回声/不论是雄鸡尖利的喇叭,还是山鸣谷应的号角,

No more shall rouse them from their lowly bed.　都再不能唤醒他们地下/墓中的长眠。

9. For them no more the blazing hearth shall burn，= The blazing hearth shall no more burn for them， 熊熊的炉火不再为他们燃烧，

Or busy housewife ply her evening care； 忙碌的主妇不再为他们赶做夜活；

No children run to lisp their sire's return， 口齿不清的孩子们不再会跑着说父亲的归来，

Or climb his knees the envied kiss to share. = Or climb his knees to share the envied kiss. 也不会爬上他膝头争抢/分享一个遭人嫉妒的亲吻。

10. Oft did the harvest to their sickle yield，= The harvest oft yielded to their sickle， 以往,他们的镰刀常常带来丰收，

＊ oft = often；yield to 屈从于,产生于

Their furrow oft the stubborn glebe has broke；= Their furrow has oft broken the stubborn glebe（ = soil/turf）； 他们的犁沟常常切开坚实的土地；

How jocund did they drive their team afield（ *ad.* ）！ 他们多么快乐地驱赶牲口下地！

How bowed the woods beneath their sturdy stroke！ 树木多么驯服地在他们的猛砍下低头！

＊ to bow beneath... 在……下低头

11. Let not（ = Don't let）Ambition mock their useful toil，/Their homely joys，and destiny obscure（ = obscure destiny）； 别让胸怀大志者嘲讽这实用的辛劳,/家庭的欢乐,和默默无闻的命运；

Nor（ = Let nor = Don't let either）Grandeur hear with a disdainful smile/The short and simple annuals of the poor. 也别让显赫的要人带着轻蔑的微笑/来倾听穷人们简短而平凡的一生。

12. The boast of heraldry，the pomp of power， 门第的炫耀,权势的显赫，

And all that beauty，all that wealth e'er gave，= All that beauty and wealth ever gave， 美和财富所能赋予的一切，

＊ that beauty/wealth gave 是 all 的定语从句。

Awaits alike the inevitable hour. 都同样等待着那不可避免的时刻。

The paths of glory lead but to the grave. 光荣的道路只能条条通向坟墓。

参考译文——姚绍德

写在乡村教堂墓园的挽诗

晚钟敲响,报道白昼离去,

牛群低鸣,在草原上缓缓绕行,

犁地人疲惫地踏上归途,

天宇下唯有我,独与黄昏相对。

景色光华正慢慢逝去,

四野是一片肃穆宁静,

只听见甲壳虫嗡嗡地绕飞,

昏沉的铃声催眠着远处栏中的羊群。

还有那常春藤披裹的塔楼上,

有只猫头鹰在向月亮发泄怨气,

怪那些游荡者走进了它的秘宅，
搅扰它古老的独家领地。

峥嵘榆树下，紫衫绿荫里，
草皮隆起——荒冢累累，
各自安身在狭小的洞穴中，
粗俗的乡邻父老就在这里长眠。

晨风带香、轻声的呼唤，
草棚茅舍里的呢喃燕语，
雄鸡的高唱，猎号的回声，
再不能把他们从墓穴中唤醒。

熊熊的炉火不再为他们燃烧，
忙碌的主妇也不再为他们赶做夜活；
咬舌的孩子们不再奔告父亲归来，
为一个亲吻爬上爸爸的膝头。

过去他们镰刀起处、庄稼收回，
犁沟切开过多少坚硬的土地；
赶牲口下地是何等欢快！
树木又是如何在他们的砍刀下低头！

雄心大志者别嘲讽他们实用的辛劳，
也别笑他们的家常之乐，不为人知的命运；
显赫的要人别带着轻蔑的冷笑，
来听讲穷人们短促而简单的生平。

高贵的门第，显赫的权势，
美丑贫富赋予的一切，
全都走向那不可避免的时刻：
光荣之路万千条，条条向坟墓。

格律和韵律分析

The ·cur/few ·tolls/the ·knell/of ·par/ting ·day,   a
The ·low/ing ·herd/wind ·slow/ly ·o'er/the ·lea,   b
The ·plow/man ·home/ward ·plods/his ·wear/y ·way,   a
And ·leaves/the ·world/to ·dark/ness and/to ·me.   b

Now ·fades/the ·glim/mering/lands·cape/on the ·sight,   c
And ·all/the ·air/a ·so/lemn ·still/ness ·holds,   d

'Save where/the 'bee/tle 'wheels/his 'dro/ning 'flight,   c
And 'drow/sy 'tink/lings 'lull/the 'dis/tant 'folds;   d

根据两诗节的格律和韵律分析,可以看出,每行诗都为 5 个音步,除了 1 个音节为抑抑格([dark/]ness and),1 个音步为抑抑扬格(on the 'sight),1 个音步为扬抑格('save where)外,其余 37 个音步皆为抑扬格,故可以断定该诗的格律为五步抑扬格。根据尾韵的规律,很容易判断该诗韵律为 ababcdcd。

主要内容归纳和总结

1. 托马斯·格雷出生于伦敦的一个股票经纪人之家,就读于伊顿(Eton)公学,结识了哥特式小说(Gothic novel)《奥特兰托古城堡》(*The Old Castle of Otranto*)的作者贺拉斯·沃波尔(Horace Walpole)等名人,后就读于剑桥大学。1739 年~1741 年,他与沃波尔周游欧洲大陆,后来成了欧洲著名的学者与诗人,1757 年被授予桂冠诗人头衔(婉拒),1768 年被聘为剑桥大学历史学和现代英语教授。

   托马斯·格雷生性淡泊宁静、交游冷落(a quiet man by nature who avoids social activities),作品不多,但代表作《写在乡村教堂墓园的挽诗》(*Elegy Written in a Country Churchyard*)一经发表,就奠定了他墓园派(the Graveyard School)诗歌和感伤主义诗歌(sentimental poetry)创始人的地位。其诗歌意境、结构和语言都十分精美,但用典过多,有些比喻生僻甚至怪诞,自造的词颇多,往往晦涩难懂。

2. 托马斯·格雷的主要作品:
   《写在乡村教堂墓园的挽诗》*Elegy Written in a Country Churchyard*(1751)
   《春之颂》*Ode on the Spring*(1742)
   《伊顿公学展望》*Ode on a Distant Prospect of Eton College*(1747)
   《爱猫之死》*Ode on the Death of a Favourite Cat*(1748)
   《逆境颂歌》*Hymn of Adversity*(1742)
   另有两部译自挪威文学作品的译作:
   《奥丁的血统》*The Descent of Odin*(1761)
   《不幸的姐妹》*The Fatal Sisters*(1761)

重要信息句子

1. Thomas Gray was the son of a London exchange broker.
2. In contrast to those professional writers, Gray's literary output was small. His masterpiece is "Elegy Written in a Country Churchyard".
3. His poems, as a whole, are mostly devoted to a sentimental lamentation or meditation on life, past and present. 从总体上来说,他的诗主要是对生活、过去和现在的感伤主义的哀悼或沉思。

英国新古典主义时期文学同步练习与答案

1. The neoclassical period is the one in English literature between _____ and the publication of *Lyrical*

Ballads by Wordsworth and Coleridge.

a. the Glorious Revolution in which King James II was replaced by his daughter Mary and her Dutch husband William, Duke of Orange, in 1689

b. the Great London Fire

c. the Restoration of King Charles II in 1689

d. the return of the Stuarts to the English throne in 1660

2. In the neoclassical period of England, there was constant strife between the monarch and _____, between the two big parties — the _____ and the _____ over the control of the parliament and government, between opposing religious sects such as the _____, the _____ and the Dissenters.

a. the oppressed people/Labour Party/Conservative Party/Roman Catholicism/Anglican Church

b. parliament/Tories/Whigs/Islam/Christianity

c. parliament/Tories/Whigs/Buddhism/Taoism

d. parliament/Tories/Whigs/Roman Catholicism/Anglican Church

3. The 18th century England is also known as the _____ or the _____.

a. turbulent period/period of the full assertion of Romanticism

b. Renaissance Period/revival of ancient Greek and Roman culture

c. Age of Enlightenment/Age of Reason

d. period of Industrial Revolution/period of rapid industrialization

4. The Enlightenment Movement was flourished in _____ and swept through the whole Western Europe at the time.

a. Italy   b. France

c. Spain   d. Germany

5. When reason served as the yardstick for the measurement of all human activities and relations, the belief provided theory for the _____ of 1789 and the _____ in 1776.

a. French Revolution/American War of Independence

b. Enlightenment Movement/Movement of Rationality

c. French Revolution/American Civil War of the South and the North

d. expansion of colonies/Movement of Enclosure

6. Neoclassicists had some fixed laws and rules for almost every genre of literature. Drama should be written in the _____; the three unities of _____, _____ and _____ should be strictly observed; and _____ rather than individuals should be represented.

a. iambic pentameter/heaven/earth/human/common people

b. iambic pentameter rhymed in two lines/stage/figure/setting/characters of similarity

c. common speech/figure/setting/dialogue/characters of universality

d. Heroic Couplets/time/space/action/type characters

7. In the last few decades of the 18th century, the neoclassical emphasis upon reason, intellect, wit and form was rebelled against and challenged by the _____, and was gradually replaced by _____.

a. sensibility/Victorian novel   b. passion/modernist literature

c. disorder/modernism   d. sentimentalists/Romanticism

8. The mid-18th century was predominated by a newly rising literary form —_____, which, contrary to the traditional romance of aristocrats, gives a realistic presentation of life of the common English people.

a. the modern English novel   b. the Romantic poetry

c. the Renaissance drama   d. Victorian novel

9. From the middle part to the end of the century there was also an apparent shift of interest from the classic literary tradition to _____ and imagination, from society to _____.

    a. originality/individual
    b. imitation/the didactic

    c. disorder/hermit
    d. modernism/solitary

10. Gothic novels — mostly stories of mystery and _____ which take place in some haunted or dilapidated _____ .

    a. excitement/Old Times castles
    b. religion/cathedrals

    c. horror/Middle Age castles
    d. thrilling/bleak houses

11. John Bunyan was thrown into prison in 1660 for _____ without receiving permission from the _____ .

    a. joining a Nonconformist church/government of England

    b. preaching/Established Church

    c. preaching/Roman Catholic Church

    d. preaching/Pope

12. It was during the second term in prison that Bunyan wrote _____ .

    a. *The Holy War*
    b. *Dr. Fostus*

    c. *Robinson Crusoe*
    d. *The Pilgrim's Progress*

13. Bunyan's style was modeled after that of _____ .

    a. epic *Beowulf*
    b. Romance

    c. Gothic novels
    d. the English Bible

14. *The Pilgrim's Progress* is the most successful _____ in the English language. Its purpose is to urge people to abide by Christian doctrines and seek salvation through constant struggles with _____ and all kinds of social evils.

    a. religious stories/tyranny
    b. allegoric stories/injustice

    c. religious allegory/their own weakness
    d. Gothic novel/inhumanity

15. *The Pilgrim's Progress* by Bunyan is often said to be concerned with the search for _____ .

    a. self-fulfillment
    b. spiritual salvation

    c. material wealth
    d. universal truth

16. As a representative of the Enlightenment, _____ was one of the first to introduce rationalism to England.

    a. John Bunyan
    b. Daniel Defoe

    c. Alexander Pope
    d. Samuel Johnson

17. Pope made his name as a great poet with the publication of _____ .

    a. *The Rape of the Lock*
    b. *An Essay on Man*

    c. *The Dunciad*
    d. *An Essay on Criticism*

18. _____ was Pope's finest mock epic.

    a. *The Rape of the Lock*
    b. *Epistle to Dr. Arbuthnot*

    c. *The Dunciad*
    d. *Eloisa to Abelard*

19. _____ was generally considered Pope's best satiric work, its satire directing at the literary men of the age who had made Pope's enemies.

    a. *An Essay on Criticism*
    b. *An Essay on Man*

    c. *The Dunciad*
    d. *The Rape of the Lock*

20. An Essay on Criticism is a _____ written in heroic couplets.

a. lyric ballads   b. mock epic

    c. narrative poem   d. didactic poem

21. Which one of the following is NOT Pope's work? _____.

    a. *An Essay on Criticism*   b. *An Essay on Man*

    c. *Odyssey*   d. *The Dunciad*

22. Pope strongly advocated _____, emphasizing that literary works should be judged by classical rules of order, reason, logic, restrained emotion, good taste and decorum.

    a. idealism   b. neoclassicism

    c. Romanticism   d. sentimentalism

23. Defoe had a zest for _____. His _____ brought him into jail and made him go through public exposure in the pillory, while his _____ won him friendship from the king.

    a. literature/*A Modest Proposal*/*The Coffee House Politician*

    b. politics/*The Shortest Way with the Dissenters*/*The True-born Englishman*

    c. trade/*A Journal of the Plague Year*/*Robinson Crusoe*

    d. adventure/*Moll Flanders*/*Robinson Crusoe*

24. *Robinson Crusoe*, an adventure story very much _____, is universally considered Defoe's masterpiece.

    a. about the personal history of some hero or heroine.

    b. in the spirit of the time

    c. exploration in adventurous circumstance

    d. about the struggles against the evil environment

25. In *Moll Flanders*, Flanders says: "Vice came in always at the Door of Necessity, not at the Door of Inclination." which means _____.

    a. it is easy for people to commit crimes when they are very poor and urgently need something

    b. crimes are not committed because of someone's hobby

    c. Evil Satan is always staying at door of the poor lack of food and clothes but not out of the preference of the rich

    d. a and b

26. In *Roxana*, the titular heroine says in self-defense: "Honesty is out of the question when starvation is the case." which means _____

    a. he who is hungry is honest.

    b. if anyone is not hungry, his honesty is not questionable.

    c. when a starved man is charged to the court, his honesty is out of question.

    d. a man always in hunger can never be honest.

27. The following comments on Daniel Defoe are true EXCEPT _____.

    a. *Robinson Crusoe* is his first novel.

    b. *Robinson Crusoe* is universally considered his masterpiece

    c. he was a member of the upper class

    d. in his novels, his sympathy for the downtrodden, unfortunate poor is shown.

28. Jonathan Swift is a master satirist. The feature of his satire is _____.

    a. that irony is more than satire

    b. that sarcasm is more than ridicule

    c. very bitter but less ridiculous

d. that it is usually masked by an outward gravity and an apparent eagerness which renders his satire all the more powerful

29. Swift is unsurpassed in the writing of simple, direct, precise prose. He defined a good style as "proper words in proper places." which means _____.

a. we should use the words which can accurately express what we want to say

b. we should put the words in the best suitable places which can precisely express meaning

c. we needn't use more words than enough and put the proper words in a wrong place

d. we should use the best words exactly expressing our meaning in the best place, and keep the prose simple at most possible

30. _____ is a typical feature of Swift's writings.

a. Casual narration b. Elegant style

c. Bitter satire d. Complicated sentences

31. The perfect model of Swift's bitter satire under the mask of outward gravity and apparent earnestness is _____.

a. *A Tale of a Tub* b. *A Modest Proposal*

c. *The Battle of the Books* d. *Gulliver's Travels*

32. The most important representative work by Jonathan Swift is _____.

a. *A Tale of Tub* b. *The Battle of the Books*

c. *A Modest Proposal* d. *Gulliver's Travels*

33. As a dramatist, Henry Fielding had attempted a considerable number of forms of plays. Which one is NOT his attempted forms among the following? _____

a. Witty comedies of manners or intrigues.

b. Farces or ballad operas with political implications.

c. Burlesques and satires that bear heavily upon the status-quo of England.

d. comic opera and sentimental drama

34. Which one is NOT the play by Fielding among the following plays? _____

a. *The School for Scandal* b. *The Coffee House Politician*

c. *The Tragedy of Tragedies* d. *Pasquin*

35. Henry Fielding's first novel is _____.

a. *Tom Jones*

b. *The History of Amelia*

c. *The History of the Adventures of Joseph Andrews and of His Friend Mr. Abraham Adams*

d. *The History of Jonathan Wild the Great*

36. Fielding has been regarded as _____ for his contribution to the establishment of the form of the _____.

a. Poets' poet/classical poetry

b. the milestone of drama development/poetic drama

c. Father of the English Novel/modern novel

d. the Pioneer of Romantic Poetry/lyrical poetry

37. Unlike Defoe in *Robinson Crusoe*, Fielding did not tell the story in his works through the mouth of the principal character but adopted " _____," in which the author becomes the " _____".

a. epistolary form/specialist in writing letters

b. the form of storytelling/storyteller

c. the first person narration/hero in the book

  d. the third person narration/all-knowing God

38. In the following writings by Henry Fielding , which one brings him the name of the "Prose Homer"?

  a. *The Coffee House Politician*   b. *The Tragedy of Tragedies*

  c. *The History of Tom Jones, a Foundling*   d. *The History of Amelia*

39. Samuel Johnson wrote several hundred essays which appeared in the two periodicals under his editorship: _____ and _____.

  a. *The Rambler/The Idler*

  b. *The Champion/The True Patriot*

  c. *The Jacobite's Journal/The Convent-Garden Journal*

  d. *The Champion/The Jacobite's Journal*

40. As a lexicographer, Johnson distinguished himself as the author of _____.

  a. the first English dictionary by an Englishman

  b. *Lives of the Poets*

  c. *A Dictionary of the English Language*

  d. a and c

41. Johnson was the _____ great neoclassicist enlightener in the later eighteenth century.

  a. only   b. first

  c. last   d. second to Alexander Pope

42. Johnson was very much concerned with the theme of _____: almost all of his major writings bear this theme.

  a. the cruelty of the oppressors   b. the suffering of the oppressed poor

  c. the violent attack on the feudalist system   d. the vanity of human wishes

43. Johnson's style is typically _____, at the opposite extreme from Swift's simplicity or Addison's neatness, he tends to use _____, _____ "_____." Reading his works gives the reader the impression that he is talking with a very learned man.

  a. neoclassical/simple/clear/daily speech

  b. Renaissance/classical/traditional/refined words and phrases

  c. neoclassical/long/well-structured/learned words

  d. romantic/lyrical/individual/obscure and hard to understand words

44. Richard Brinsley Sheridan was _____ important English dramatist of the 18th century.

  a. the most   b. the first

  c. the last   d. the only

45. Sheridan's plays, especially _____ and _____, are generally considered as important _____ between the masterpieces of Shakespeare and Bernard Shaw.

  a. *The Rivals/Irene*/conflicts   b. *The Rivals/The School for Scandal*/links

  c. *The Critic/Pizarro*/links   d. *Prince of Abyssinia/The Rivals*/ties

46. In the plays by Sheridan, _____ is the constant theme.

  a. morality   b. love

  c. death   d. human dignity

47. Which one of the following groups is really Sheridan's works? _____

  a. *Irene* and *The Rivals*   b. *The Rivals* and *The Critic*

  c. *Pasquin* and *King Lear*   d. *The School for Scandal* and *Dr. Faustus*

48. "Surface", "Sneerwell", "Backbite," and "Gandour" are most likely the names of the characters in _____.
    a. Shaw's *Mrs. Warren's Profession*   b. Sheridan's *The School for Scandal*
    c. Shakespeare's *Love's Labour's Lost*   d. Christopher Marlowe's *Dr. Faustus*

49. Although Thomas Gray is known as one of the most learned men and very successful poet in Europe, he was by nature a _____ man who avoided social activities and even declined _____ in 1757.
    a. shy/gold medal   b. active/an important party
    c. quiet/the Poet laureateship   d. reserved/an honourable certificate

50. In contrary to those professional writers, Gray's literary output was _____.
    a. magnificent   b. large
    c. small   d. extraordinary

51. Gray's masterpiece, "Elegy Written in a Country Churchyard", once and for all established his fame as the leader of the _____ of the day.
    a. sentimental poetry   b. didactic poetry
    c. philosophical poetry   d. pictorial poetry

52. Which one of the following is NOT among "the Graveyard School"? _____.
    a. *Elegy Written in a Country Churchyard*   b. *Ode to the West Wind*
    c. *Ode on the Spring*   d. *Ode on the Death a Favorite Cat*

53. Gray's poems, as a whole, are mostly devoted to a sentimental lamentation or meditation on _____, _____ and _____.
    a. friendship/love/death   b. past/present/future
    c. life/death/nostalgia   d. life, past/present

54. What are those which CANNOT show the features of Gray's poems among the following words or phrases? _____.
    a. Exquisite sense of form.
    b. Sophisticated and allusive style.
    c. Highly artificial diction and distorted word order.
    d. Mock epic, romantic imagination, parallel words and phrases.

55. In *Elegy Written in a Country Churchyard*, Gray reflects on _____, _____, and _____ with a touch of his personal melancholy.
    a. death/the sorrows of life/the mysteries of human life
    b. friendship/death/memory
    c. love/friendship/death
    d. past/present/future

56. In field of literature, the Enlightenment brought about a(n) _____ the old classical works. This tendency is known as neoclassicism.
    a. revived interest in   b. antagonism against
    c. rebellion against   d. rational scrutiny of

57. John Bunyan's *The Pilgrim's Progress* is a(n) _____ .
    a. allegory   b. romance
    c. comedy of manners   d. realistic novel

58. In lines "With gold jewels cover every part,/And hide with ornaments their want of art", Pope rejects _____.

a. the "Follow Nature" fallacy   b. artificiality

c. aesthetic order   d. good taste

59. Which of the following is NOT a typical aspect of Defoe's language? _____.

a. Vernacular   b. Colloquial

c. Elegant   d. Smooth

60. Which of the following is a typical feature of Swift's writing? _____.

a. Great wit   b. Bitter satire

c. Rich mythic allusions   d. Communicated sentence structures

61. In which of the following works can you find the proper names "Lilliput", "Brob-dingnag", "Houyhnhnm" and "Yahoo"? _____.

a. *The Pilgrim's Progress*   b. *The Faerie Queene*

c. *Gulliver's Travels*   d. *The School for Scandal*

62. Who was the first of all the 18th century novelists to set out to write specially a "comic epic in prose", and the first to give the modern novel of its structure and style? _____.

a. Jonathan Swift   b. Daniel Defoe

c. Samuel Richardson   d. Henry Fielding

63. "The novel is structured around the discovery of the hero's origin." This novel is most Probably _____.

a. *David Copperfield*   b. *The History of Tom Jones, a Foundling*

c. *Wuthering Heights*   d. *The Vicar of the Wakefield*

64. "To be so distinguished, is an honor, which, being very little accustomed to favors from the great, I know not well how to receive, or in what terms to acknowledge." This sentence is written in an _____ tune.

a. ironic   b. indifferent

c. delightful   d. jealousy

65. Who was the greatest dramatist in the 18th century? _____.

a. Oliver Goldsmith   b. R. B. Sheridan

c. Laurence Sterne   d. Henry Fielding

66. *The Rape of the Lock* by Alexander Pope is written in the form of a mock _____, which describes the triviality of high society in a grand style.

a. epic   b. elegy

c. sonnet   d. ode

67. Which of the following is NOT a typical feature of Samuel Johnson's language style? _____.

a. His sentences are long and well structured.

b. His sentences are interwoven with parallel phrases.

c. He tends to use informal and colloquial words.

d. His sentences are complicated, but his thoughts are clearly expressed.

68. In his works, Defoe gave his praise to the hard-working, sturdy _____ and showed his sympathy for the downtrodden, unfortunate poor.

a. middle-class people   b. working people

c. Irish farmers   d. aristocrats

69. In *Elegy Written in a Country Churchyard*, Thomas Gray reveals his sympathy for _____, but mocks the great ones who despise them and bring havoc on them.

a. the poor and the unknown   b. the middle class

c. the proletariat   d. the landlords

Key: ddcba/ddbac/bddcb/cbacd/cbbbd/ddddc/bddac/cdcad/cdcdb/abbcc/abdda/aabcb/cdbab/acaa

第三章　浪漫主义时期 The Romantic Period

词语解释和难句分析

1. the passage of the first Reform Bill in the Parliament　第一次改革法案在议会的通过
   current of literature　文学潮流
   a revolt of the English imagination against the neoclassical reason　英国的想象对于新古典主义理性的反叛
   to spring from the confrontation of radicals and conservatives　产生于激进派和保守派的对抗和冲突之中
   at the close/end of the 18th century　在 18 世纪末

2. to publish two books that electrify Europe　出版两本震惊欧洲的书
   implacable resentment against the tyrannical rule　无法平息的/不可调和的对暴政统治的怨恨
   an immense hope for the future　对未来的巨大希望
   the epoch-making French Revolution　划时代的法国大革命
   the storming of Bastille　巴士底风暴
   to arouse great sympathy and enthusiasm in the English liberals and radicals　在英国的自由派和激进派中激起了巨大的同情和热情

3. Liberty, Equality and Fraternity　自由、平等和博爱
   Reflections on the Revolution in France　《法国大革命写照》
   be designed as a crusade against...　旨在开展一场反对……的圣战
   the established privileges enshrined in the church　教会里奉为神圣的既定特权
   the hereditary power of monarchy　君主的世袭特权

4. Burke's pamphlet was designed as a crusade against the spread of such radical innovations and the overthrow of the established privileges he saw enshrined in the church, the hereditary power of the monarchy and the greater landed families.　伯克的政论宣传小册子旨在开展一场圣战,矛头指向不断扩展的激进革命、反对打倒他目睹的教会里奉若神明的既定特权、君主和更大的大地主家族的世袭特权。

5. to pour scorn on the feverish violence of rebellion　对狂热的暴力反叛嗤之以鼻/口诛笔伐
   to prophesy mob-rule and military dictatorship　预言暴民统治和军事独裁
   to raise the most authoritative voice in denouncing the Revolution　发出了痛斥革命的最权威的声音
   to provoke many replies from the radical writers　激起了许多激进派作家的反驳
   to argue for the rights of the people　主张和维护人民的权利
   Thomas Paine's *Declaration of Rights of Man*　托马斯·潘恩的《人权宣言》
   to overthrow any government of oppression　推翻任何压迫的政府

6. By 1789 France was so enmeshed in oppression and misery that nothing short of revolution could set her free.　到 1789 年,法国陷入沉重的压迫和苦难之中,除了革命无法获得解放。

7. *Inquiry Concerning Political Justice* by William Godwin　威廉·戈德温的《有关政治正义的研究》

8. be extolled as "an instinctive defender of masses of the people against the encroachment of the

/161

bourgeoisie." 被颂扬为本能的/天生的人民群众的保卫者和资产阶级侵害的敌对者

9. conventional gender roles 惯常的性别角色/性别歧视

A *Vindication of the Rights of Woman* by Mary Wollstonecraft 玛丽·沃尔斯通克拉夫特的《女权辩护》

to set out the earliest exposition of feminism based on a comprehensive system of ethics 根据综合伦理学体系第一次提出并诠释女权主义

to wage wars against France till... 发动对法国的战争，直至……

10. But later when Jacobeans took over power in France and started to push a policy of violent terror at home and aggressive expansion abroad, most of the English sympathizers dropped their support. 但是后来，雅各宾派攥取了法国的政权，开始对内实行暴力恐怖政策，对外进行侵略扩张，英国的大多数本来同情(法国)大革命的人不再支持革命了。

11. to experience profound economic and social changes 经历深刻的经济和社会变化

the transfer of large masses of population from the countryside to the towns 大量的人口从农村往城镇迁移

the solid base of English society 英国社会的坚实基础

the Enclosures and the agricultural mechanization 圈地运动和农业机械化

to emigrate to the colonies 移民到(海外)殖民地去

to sink to the level of farm laborers 跌落到农村劳动力的地位

to drift to the towns 漂流到城镇

be no better than juggles 不比农村强/与荒野的农村一样差

be herded into factories and overcrowded streets 集聚到/被一起赶进工厂和拥挤的街道

to reduce to the level of commodities 降低/跌落到商品的层次/地位

be valued according to the fluctuating demand for their labor 按波动的需求对他们的劳动力进行论价

12. to come into its full swing 达到高潮/正充分开展

the means of production 生产方式

economic depressions 经济萧条

(price) to rise rocket-high (价格)飞涨

the popular outbreaks of machine-breaking 民众砸毁机器的暴乱

Luddite riots 路德暴乱

the climax of popular agitation and government brutality 民众骚乱和政府暴行的高潮

St. Peter's Field 圣彼得广场

be charged by mounted troops 受到骑兵的冲击

the notorious Peterloo Massacre 臭名昭著的彼得街大屠杀

to die down 减弱，渐渐停止

to fight for its own supremacy in political power against the landed aristocrats 为反对拥有土地的贵族阶级，获得最高政治权力而斗争

to enact the Reform Bill 颁布改革法案

to bring the industrial capitalists into power 使得工业资本家掌握了政权

13. to express a negative attitude toward the existing social and political conditions 表达对现存社会状态和政治状态的否定态度

be deeply immersed in the most violent phase of the transition from a decadent feudal to a capitalist economy 专注于观察从没落的封建经济过渡到资本主义经济的这段最剧烈动荡的时期

to deny people their essential human needs　拒绝接受/承认人的基本需求

to demonstrate a strong reaction against the dominant modes of thinking　表明了对主流思想方式的强烈反抗

to see man as an individual in the solitary state　把人看成是孤立状态下的个体

to emphasize the features that men have in common　强调人的共性

to emphasize the special qualities of each individual's mind　强调每个人思想的独特性质

a change of direction from attention to the outer world of social civilization to the inner world of the human spirit　从注意外部的社会文明到注意人的内心精神世界,发生了方向的变化

to place the individual at the center of art　把个人作为艺术的中心

unique feelings and particular attitudes　独特的情感和特殊的态度

14. to see poetry as a healing energy　把诗歌当作治疗的良药/看到诗歌的治疗功能

to purify both individual souls and the society　既净化个人的灵魂,又净化社会

to call for simple themes drawn from humble life expressed in the language of ordinary people.　要求用老百姓的语言来表达从平凡人生活中提炼出来的平常的主题

to act as a manifesto for the new school　作为新学派的宣言

to set forth one's critical creed　阐明某人的批评纲领

the spontaneous overflow of powerful feelings, which originates in emotion recollected in tranquility.　(诗歌是) 强烈情感的自发流露,这种情感源于平静中积累起来的激情

15. the vital faculty that creates new wholes out of disparate elements　从全无联系的各种元素中创立新型整体的超凡天赋

in communion with the natural universe　与宇宙大自然交流谈心

to exercise this most valuable faculties, the imagination　发挥这最有价值的天赋——想象

the world of Eternity　永恒的世界

the divine bosom　众神的心中(的世界)

our hope of contact with eternal forces　我们与永恒的力量接触联系的希望

to extol the faculty of imagination　歌颂想象的天赋才能

to elevate the concepts of spontaneity and inspiration　强调/高度评价自发性和灵感的概念

16. Where intelligence was fallible, limited, the Imagination was our hope of contact with eternal forces, with the whole spiritual world.　在理智有限、不可靠之处,想象是我们与永恒的力量、与整个的精神世界接触联系的希望。

17. be more something to be seen than something to be known　是给人看的而不是供人研究的

(the nature) to come to the forefront of the poetic imagination　(自然)变成了诗歌想象的首选/首要的素材/对象

the major source of poetic imagery　诗歌意象的主要源泉

the dominant subject matter　主要的主题素材

to conceive nature as "the nurse,/The guide, the guardian of my heart, and soul/Of all my moral being."　把自然想象成"我心灵和全部身心道德的护士、向导和卫士"

the dominant influence in changing people's sensibility　改变人情感的主要支配力量

a source of mental cleanliness and spiritual understanding　心智纯洁和精神融通的源泉

the stepping stone between Man and God　人与上帝联系的阶梯

18. at any rate　无论如何,至少

to articulate an alternative to　明确表达一种与……相关的选择,使……与……相互关联

to turn to other times and places　转到其他的时代和地域

19. To escape from, or at any rate to articulate an alternative to, a world that had become excessively rational, as well as excessively materialistic and ugly, the Romantics would turn to other times and places, where the qualities they valued could be convincingly depicted. 为了逃避一种极端理性、极端物质和极端丑陋的社会，或者至少是明确表达一种与这样的社会相关的选择，浪漫主义作家们常会转入其他的时代和地域,令人信服地描写那里他们所珍惜的社会价值。

20. to escape from the "madding crowd" 逃离"疯狂的人群"
    to reject the entire English society by their self-imposed exile 通过自我放逐否决整个的英国社会

21. Wordsworth, Coleridge and Southey chose to live by the lakeside so as to escape from the "madding crowd," while Byron and Shelley rejected the entire English society by their self-imposed exile. 华兹华斯、科勒律治和骚塞选择在湖滨居住,以逃离"疯狂的人群",而拜伦和雪莱通过自我放逐否决整个的英国社会。

22. to achieve the effect of the individual vision 为了取得个人视角的独特效果/为了表现个人的见解
    to range further afield (视野/笔触)扩大得更远
    to the central Asia fief of Kubla Khan 直至忽必烈汗的中亚领地
    to allow free play to the supernatural — witches, curses, visions and prophesies 放任恣肆、自由发挥,描写许多超自然的故事——女巫、咒语、幻象和预言先知之类。
    without arousing feelings of incongruity 不会引起虚假造作的感觉

23. national heritage 民族传统/遗产
    to glorify Rome and ... as superior to the native traditions 把罗马文化……美化、推崇说成优于自己本民族的传统文化
    to turn to the humble people and the common everyday life for subjects 转而向普通平民和日常生活寻找写作主题
    to seek for the Absolute, the Ideal through the transcendence of the actual 寻求抽象的东西,即寻求超越实际的理想
    to make bold experiments in poetic language, versification and design 在诗歌的语言、诗体韵律和结构方面进行大胆的试验
    to construct a variety of forms on original principles of organization and style 根据谋篇布局和文体风格的创作原则,创新了多种多样的(诗歌)形式
    visionary prophetic poems 充满幻想的预言诗
    mystic ballad 神秘主义的歌谣
    spiritual autobiography 精神自传
    symbolic drama 象征主义戏剧

24. the reading public 好读书的大众群体
    demand for reading materials 对读物的需求(量)
    Edinburgh Review 《爱丁堡新闻综述》
    The Quarterly Review 《新闻综述季刊》
    Blackwood's Magazine 《布莱克伍德杂志》
    London Magazine 《伦敦杂志》
    to make literary comments on writers with high standards 用高标准评论作家的文学创作
    to pave the way for 为……铺平了道路

25. to give strict judgments on the target work 对所评论的作品给予严格的评判
    to point out and validate the author's achievements 指出并论证作者的成就
    with a keen observation and a sharp well-informed mind 观察敏锐,思想机警,见多识广

to develop an eloquent, courageous and arbitrary prose style 形成一种雄辩滔滔、一往无前、随心所欲的文风

Life of Napoleon by William Hazlitt 威廉·赫兹利特的《拿破仑传》

to express a vehement, but qualified, admiration of Napoleon as a man of heroic will and power <u>in the service of</u> the emancipation of mankind. 表达一种强烈但却又恰如其分的对拿破仑的赞赏,说他是一个为解放人类而献身的具有英雄意志和力量的伟人

a mode of intellectual inquiry and moral address 一种知识探讨和道德说教的方式

a medium for a delightful literary treatment of life's small pleasures and reassurances. 对生活中的细小快乐和慰藉做轻快处理的文学体裁/媒介

essential characteristic 本质特征

a strong clear intelligence, commanding in its centrality, its courage, and its vital irony (具有)强烈鲜明的智慧,中心明确的阐述,一往无前的勇气和一针见血的讥讽

Essays of Elia by Charles Lamb 查尔斯·兰姆的《伊利亚散文集》

the keenest intellects of the age 当时最才智非凡的人

wonderful intellect 令人惊叹的才智

<u>be subordinate to</u> his passion for dreaming 隶属于他梦幻的激情/与他激情的梦想联系在一起

Confessions of an English Opium Eater by Thomas De Quincey 托马斯·德·昆西的《英国鸦片吸食者的忏悔》

great literary merit 伟大的文学价值

to <u>lie in</u> his subtle revelation of the potentiality of human dreams 在于他对人类梦想实现的潜在可能性所做的微妙的启示

On the Knocking at the Gate in Macbeth by Quincey 昆西的《论〈麦克白〉中的敲门声》

acute literary insight 敏锐的文学洞察力

His style, sometimes stately, sometimes headlong, now gorgeous, now musical, shows a harmony between the idea and the expression. 他的文风,有时庄严,有时奔放,时而华丽,时而富于乐感,表现出思想内容与表达形式的和谐统一。

26. be of the 18th century in her moral outlook, and in her prose style 她的道德观和散文作风都属于18世纪

be fully aware of the new strains of Romanticism 充分意识到浪漫主义的新笔调

to have no time for emotional excess 没有时间表现过分的激情

to honor the Augustan virtues of moderation, dignity, disciplined emotion and common sense 崇尚新古典主义倡导的谦和、尊严、情感表现有度和通情达理

to <u>hold on</u> a practical idealism 抱有一种实际的理想主义

<u>be justified by</u> reason and disciplined by self-control (爱情)为理性所肯定,用自控来约束

to step beyond the limits of her personal knowledge 超越她个人知识的界限

to choose to stay within the tiny field that she knows best 愿意待在她最熟悉的小天地里

to have in her day a small, select circle of admirers 当时有一批人数不多却很有见识的读者群欣赏她

27. to <u>switch from</u> a writer of romantic historical narrative poetry <u>to</u> novel writing to show a keen sense of 从浪漫主义历史叙事诗的诗人转变为(历史)小说家

28. The rugged grandeur of its scenery, its sturdy, independent peasantry, the bloody yet poignant nature of much of its history all <u>added to</u> its appeal. 它(苏格兰)壮美的景色,坚强、独立的农民,血腥然而壮烈的大部分历史都为它增添了魅力。

29. to <u>establish</u> the historical novel <u>as</u> a viable and worthwhile fictional form 把历史小说确立为一种可独

立发展的、有价值的虚构传奇形式

to <u>set</u> the personal dilemmas of his characters <u>against</u> a background of historical events　把人物个人的两难困境放到具体的历史事件的背景下（去描写）

30. Although his plots are sometimes hastily constructed and his characters sometimes stilted, these works remains valuable for their compelling atmosphere, occasional epic dignity and clear understanding of human nature. 虽然他的小说情节有时结构显得匆忙，人物有时夸张做作，但这些小说因为创造了强烈动人的气氛，偶尔还会有史诗的庄严以及对人性深刻的理解和剖析。

31. to exert a powerful influence on ...　对……施加强大的影响

to predominate in the late 18th century　（哥特式小说）在 18 世纪后期占据主导地位

violence, horror, and the supernatural　暴力、恐怖和鬼神

to <u>appeal</u> to the reader's emotion　吸引了读者的情感

the descriptions of the dark, irrational side of human nature　描写了人性中阴暗的、无理性的一面

to use those fantastic, grotesque, savage and mysterious elements of Gothic fiction in their poetic works　在他们的诗作中运用那些迷幻、怪诞、野蛮和神秘的哥特式故事元素

to <u>try their hand at</u> poetic dramas　尝试诗剧的创作

to renew interest in Shakespeare　对莎翁的戏剧又兴趣复燃

to lead to the rediscovery of his contemporaries　引起他同时代作家（对诗剧）兴趣的回归/的重新关注

主要内容归纳和总结

1. <u>英国浪漫主义时期的历史分野</u>

从 1798 年华兹华斯和科勒律治的《抒情歌谣集》(*Lyrical Ballads*) 正式出版到 1832 年著名历史小说家沃尔特·斯各特去世和议会通过改革法案（选举法修正案，Reform Bill）的这一段历史时期被称为浪漫主义时期。

2. <u>浪漫主义文学时期的历史背景</u>

a. 18 世纪后期一批杰出的思想家，提出了一些发聋振聩的全新的思想，如法国卢梭（Rousseau）的《社会契约论》(*Social Contract*) 和《爱弥尔》(*Emile*, 1762)，托马斯·潘恩的《人权宣言》(*Declaration of Rights of Man*, 1791 ~ 1792)，极大地影响了历史的进程，促进了法国大革命的爆发。

b. 英国发生了工业革命，影响深远。一场圈地运动(Enclosure)把千百万农民赶出了土地，变成了城镇中出卖劳动力的工人阶级。

c. 改革法案实施后，工业资产阶级登上政权宝座，但革命的主体工人阶级却没有得到解放，社会矛盾变成了工人阶级与资产阶级的矛盾。作家们深感社会剥夺了人民的生存权，人权、人本、人情和人性才是艺术家应当关心的主题。

3. <u>浪漫主义与新古典主义的区别</u>

新古典主义强调理性，浪漫主义突出想象；前者强调客观，后者强调主观；前者认为人是社会性的动物，后者认为人是独立自由的个体；前者强调共性，后者强调个性；前者强调客观外部世界，后者强调人的内心和精神；前者强调模仿古典主义的模式或榜样，后者强调个人的创造、个人情感的自然流露以及将平凡生活中的普通语言作为诗歌的语言；前者与后来的现实主义根系相连，后者则对后来的现代主义颇有影响；新古典主义是散文、传奇的时代，浪漫主义是诗歌的时代，是诗人的革命。浪漫主义诗歌打破传统诗歌的格律限制，对诗歌的语言、格律和结构进行了大胆的改革，使诗歌达到一种全新的出神入化的境界。

4. 浪漫主义时期的散文

这一时期的散文主要表现在文学评论方面,代表人物有赫兹利特(William Hazlitt)、兰姆(Charles Lamb)、德·昆西(Thomas De Quincey)和科勒律治(Coleridge)。威廉·赫兹利特是专门评论莎翁和伊丽莎白时代戏剧的伟大评论家,将散文发展成了一种滔滔不绝、鼓舞人心却很随意的文体风格,代表作有《拿破仑传》(*Life of Napoleon*);查尔斯·兰姆的散文轻松愉快,绝不说教,著作有《伊利亚散文集》(*Essays of Elia*),托马斯·德·昆西的《鸦片吸食者的忏悔》(*Confessions of an English Opium Eater*)和《论〈麦克白〉中的敲门声》(*On the Knocking at the Gate in Macbeth*)都非常有文学价值。

5. 浪漫主义时期的小说

a. 基本上还保留着古典现实主义风格的女作家简·奥斯汀(Jane Austen),"一个小村庄,三四户人家……"的背景,爱情和婚姻是主题,爱情受着理智和道德的约束,这就是奥斯汀实际的理想主义。像《傲慢与偏见》(*Pride and Prejudice*)和《理智与情感》(*Sense and Sensibility*)这样的小说,娓娓道来,对乡村小镇的人际关系洞察精微,在她生前不曾引人注意,到了20世纪却读者如云。

b. 当时就非常著名的历史小说家沃尔特·斯各特(Walter Scott),他对苏格兰、英格兰及欧洲大陆从中世纪到18世纪的变迁的描写,表现了对政治与传统的力量和影响的深刻洞察,代表作有《艾凡赫》(*Ivanhoe*)和《威弗利》(*Wavery*)。

c. 盛行于浪漫主义前期的哥特式小说(Gothic novel)主要以恐怖、暴力、超自然力为题材,刺激读者神经,对后来的文坛产生过较大影响。代表作有拉德克利夫(Ann Radcliffe)的《尤道夫之谜》(*The Misteries of Udolpho*),玛丽·雪莱(Mary Shelley)的《弗兰肯斯坦》(*Frankenstein*)。

6. 浪漫主义时期的诗剧

这一时期诗剧的代表作有雪莱(Shelley)的《解放了普罗米修斯》(*Prometheus Unbound*)和《钦契一家》(*The Cenci*),拜伦(Byron)的《曼弗莱德》(*Manfred*)和科勒律治(Coleridge)的《懊悔》(*Remorse*)。

重要信息句子

1. The biggest social change in English history was the transfer of large masses of the population from the countryside to the towns.

2. The Romantic is an age of poetry.

3. The Romantic period is also a great age of prose.

4. William Hazlitt (1778 ~ 1830) is a great critic on Shakespeare, Elizabethan drama, and English poetry.

5. The two major novelists of the Romantic period are Jane Austen and Walter Scott.

6. Gothic novel, a type of romantic fiction that predominated in the late eighteenth century, was one phase of the Romantic Movement.

7. Shelley's *Prometheus Unbound* and *The Cenci* (1819), Byron's *Manfred* (1817), and Coleridge's *Remorse* (1819) are generally regarded as the best verse plays during the period of Romanticism.

Ⅰ. 威廉·布莱克 William Blake（1757～1827）

词语解释和难句分析

1. to carry on a small hosiery business 经营一家小小的制袜企业
   to show a precocious talent for painting as a child 孩提时代就表现出早熟的绘画天才
   be sent to a drawing school 被送到美术学校上学
   be apprenticed to an engraver 给一位雕刻家当学徒
   the Royal Academy of Arts 皇家艺术学院
   to receive commissions from publishers both for book illustrations and for engravings from pictures 接受出版商的委托做书籍插图和雕刻版画
   to live a life of seclusion and poverty 过着贫穷的隐居生活

2. not to try to fit into the world 不想与世俗合流/迎合世俗
   to mix a good deal with the radicals 与激进分子保持密切关系
   to cherish great expectations and enthusiasm for the French Revolution 对法国大革命怀着极大的期望和热情
   to lead to the millennium predicted by the biblical prophets 通往圣经先知们所预测的千年王国
   to show a contempt for the rule of reason 对理性统治表示轻蔑
   to treasure the individual's imagination 珍惜/重视个人的想象

3. prevailing notes 主音符，流行音符
   be derived from 源于……，从……中得出/提取

4. to hint at his later innovative style and themes 在他后来革新的文风和主题中都留下了痕迹

5. For instance, "Holy Thursday" with its vision of charity children lit "with a radiance all their own" reminds us terribly of a world of loss and institutional cruelty. 例如，"神圣星期四"（《天真之歌》中的一首诗）所表现的孤儿院的孩子们点燃圣火照亮自己（以光明照亮自己）的幻觉使我们可怕地联想起失落的世界和宗教慈善机构的残酷。

6. The wretched child described in "The Chimney Sweeper" orphaned, exploited, yet touched by visionary rapture, evokes unbearable poignancy when he finally puts his trust in the order of the universe as he knows it. "扫烟囱的孩子"这首诗所描写的不幸的孩子，被弃为孤儿，遭受剥削，却为幻觉的痴迷（宗教）所惑，最终把自己的一丝信任寄托在他难以深刻认识的社会制度上，这激起人们难以忍受的心酸和痛苦。
   ＊ 这个句子包括一个主句、一个时间状语从句和若干作定语的过去分词和分词短语。主句是 The child evokes poignancy，状语从句是 when he finally puts...，大从句中还包括了一个小方式状语从句 as he knows it。另外，wretched, orphaned, exploited, yet touched by visionary rapture 是作定语的过去分词和分词短语，修饰 child。

7. to quest for 寻求
   to experiment in meter and rhyme 在格律和韵律上进行试验
   to introduce bold metrical innovations 进行大胆的格律创新
   to paint a different world with a melancholy tone 以忧伤的笔调描绘了一个截然不同的世界

the benighted England （不知不觉）陷入黑暗的英格兰

be fed with cold and usurious hand 由冷酷的高利贷者喂养

to sing "notes of woe" 唱起悲伤的音符

the very instruments of repression 就是/正是被人压迫/利用的工具

to become the seat of poverty and despair 贫穷和绝望的所在/世界

to become the seat of man alienated from his true self 成了与真实自我背离的伪君子的世界

to find a counterpart in the *Songs of Experience* 在《经验之歌》中找到了对应篇/相似篇/姐妹篇

be matched with 与……相匹配

be paired with 与……配对,与……一同做某事

to hold the similar subject matter 拥有相似的主题

8. to furnish him with a sharp awareness of the economic exploitation of children 使他在思想上明确地认识/警觉到对儿童的经济剥削

   * to furnish sb. with 给某人装备……/以……的武装

   to provide the context for the opening lines of the "Chimney Sweeper." 为"扫烟囱的孩子"开头第一行提供背景

   to make people compliant to exploitation 使人们屈从于剥削

   to make religion a consolation, a prospect of "illusory happiness" 把宗教作为一种安慰,一种虚幻的幸福希望

   to reveal the true nature of religion 揭露宗教的真实本性

   to help bring misery to the poor children 在给穷孩子们带来悲惨命运上起了推动作用

9. to mark his entry into maturity 标志着他进入成熟期

   to play the double role both as a satire and a revolutionary prophecy 既是讽刺又是革命的预言,发挥双重的作用

   to explore the relationship of the contraries 探讨对立面之间的关系

   a pairing of opposites 一组对立面的统一/配对

   to mean the reconciliation of the contraries, not the subordination of the one to the other 意味着对立面的调和,而不是一方从属于另一方

10. prophetic books 预言性书籍

    to reveal him as the prophet of universal political and spiritual freedom 表明他是普遍的政治自由和精神自由的预言家

    the spokesman of revolt 革命的发言人

11. to feel bound to do sth. 感到有责任去做某事

    be visionary or imaginative 充满幻想或想象的

    to have a strong visual mind 有一个产生强烈视觉形象的头脑

    to vision the ancient kings in Westminster Abbey 看到威斯敏斯特大教堂里安息的古代巨擘们

    to draw "spiritual portraits" of the mighty dead 给这些伟大的死者画过"精神肖像"

12. He believed he saw what Milton saw and all other people could see through the efforts of painting and poetry. 他认为他看到了弥尔顿所看到的东西,对此在诗歌和绘画中所做的表现,别人也都看出来了。

13. to present his view in visual images instead of abstract terms 用视觉形象而不是抽象的术语表现他的观点

    to carry the lyric beauty with immense compression of meaning 诗意深邃,具有抒情美

    to distrust the abstractness and tend to embody his views with visual image 不相信抽象的表现,常用视觉形象来表现他的观点

威廉·布莱克作品选读

1. 扫烟囱的孩子 *The Chimney Sweeper*
选自《天真之歌》*Songs of Innocence*

词语解释和难句分析

1. 'weep = sweep，这是孩子咬舌，口齿不清的发音。

2. So your chimney I sweep, & in soot I sleep. = So I sweep your chimney, & I sleep in soot.　于是，我扫你的烟囱，我在烟灰中睡觉。

3. 第二诗节头两行可简写为：There's little Tom Dacre who cried when his head ... was shav'd（ = shaved）.　有个小汤姆，剃头的时候，伤心得直流泪。

   * Who 引导的定语从句中，还包含着一个 when 引导的时间状语从句。另外，that curld（ = curled）like a lamb's back 是 his head 的定语从句：卷曲得像羊羔背。联系起来这两句可译为：有个小汤姆，头发卷卷像羊羔背，/剃光的时候，伤心得直流泪。

4. never mind it, for when your head's bare, /You know that the soot spoil your white hair.　别在意，（因为）你的头剃光了，/煤灰就不会弄脏你浅色的头发。

   * 注意 that 引导的是一个名词性从句，作 know 的宾语从句。

5. ... he had such a sight! /That ... of black.　他看到这样的景象……

   * 后面 that 引导的从句是 sight 的同位语从句，就是"景象"的内容。句中 thousands of sweepers 与 Dick，Joe，Ned，& Jack 和 all of them 都是主语同位语，意为：千千万万扫烟囱的小孩，狄克、乔、奈德和杰克，全都被锁进黑棺材。

6. And by came an angel who had a bright key, = An angel who had a bright key came by,　后来，来了个天使，拿把金钥匙，

   * 句子之所以用倒装语序，是因为主语有个定语从句，主语在后，加上定语从句，整个句子头轻尾重，比较平衡，而且 key 放在句尾，也符合 aabb 韵律规则的要求。

7. Then down a green plain, leaping, laughing they run = Then they run down a green plain, leaping, laughing　他们跑过绿色的原野，跳啊，笑啊

8. all their bags left behind = all their bags are left behind.　他们的袋子都扔在身后

9. They rise upon clouds, and sport in the wind,　他们升上云端，在云中嬉戏

   * sport *v.* 消遣，娱乐

10. If he'd（ = he should）be a good boy, /He'd（ = he would）have God his father, and never want joy.　如果他做个好孩子，/上帝会做他父亲，他会永远快乐。

    * 这是一个虚拟条件句，与将来事实相反；want 是"缺少"的意思，"绝不缺少快乐"即"永远快乐"。

11. tho' the morning was cold, = though the morning was cold, ...　清晨虽冷……

12. to get with sth.　拿起某物

    to do one's duty　尽自己的责任

参考译文——姚绍德

扫烟囱的孩子

我还很幼小,妈妈就死了,
我话还说不清,爸爸就把我卖了,
几乎还喊不清什么"扫——扫——扫——扫!"
我就给你们扫烟囱,在煤灰里睡觉。

有个小汤姆,哭得好伤心,
头发卷得像羊羔背,全被剃光了,
我说:"汤姆,剃光头发没关系,
煤灰不会弄脏你的白发呢!"

于是,他安静下来,当夜
他做了一个梦,梦境好奇怪,
看见狄克、乔、奈德和杰克,几千个扫烟囱的小孩,
全都被锁进了黑棺材。

有个天使走过来,拿了把闪光的钥匙,
打开了棺材,放他们自由;
他们跳啊,笑啊,跑过绿草地,
到河里洗澡,在阳光下闪耀。

赤裸着身子,白白的,袋子都扔了,
他们升上云端,在风中嬉笑,
天使要汤姆认上帝做父亲,
做个好孩子,说快乐永远都不会少。

汤姆醒了;我们起来,屋子里黑乎乎的,
我们拿起了袋子和扫帚去上工。
清晨虽冷,汤姆却感到快乐温暖;
所以说各尽其责,就不怕灾难。

格律和韵律分析

'When my/'mother/'died I/was 've/ry 'young,　　　　　　a
And my/'father/'sold me/while yet/my 'tongue　　　　　a

Could ˈscarce/ly ˈcry/"ˈˌˈweep! ˈˌˈweep! /ˈˌˈweep! ˈˌˈweep!" b

ˈSo your/ˈchimney/I ˈsweep,/ & in ˈsoot/I ˈsleep. b

There's ˈlit/tle ˈTom/ˈDacre who/ˈcried when/his ˈhead c

That ˈcurl'd/like a ˈlamb's ˈback,/was ˈshav'd,/so I ˈsaid, c

"Hush, ˈTom! / ˈNever/ˈmind it,/for when/your ˈhead's ˈbare, d

You ˈknow that/the ˈsoot/cannot/ˈspoil your/ˈwhite ˈhair." d

And ˈso/he was/ˈquiet,/& that ˈve/ry ˈnight, e

As ˈTom/was a/ˈˌsleeping/he had/ˈsuch a ˈsight! e

That ˈthou/sands of/ˈsweepers,/ˈDick, ˈJoe,/ˈNed, & ˈJack, f

Were ˈall/of them/ˈlock'd up/in ˈcof/fins of ˈblack; f

选前 3 个诗节做格律分析。第一诗节第一、二、四行诗句为 5 个音步,第三行为 4 个音步,共 19 个音步,8 个音步为抑扬格,7 个音步为扬抑格,抑抑格 2 个,扬扬格 2 个。第二诗节每行诗句 5 个音步,共 20 个音步,抑扬格 8 个,扬抑格 5 个,抑抑格 3 个,扬扬格 1 个,抑抑扬格、抑扬扬格和抑抑抑格各 1 个。第三诗节每行诗句 5 个音步,共 20 个音步,抑扬格 8 个,扬抑格 4 个,抑抑格 4 个,扬抑扬格和抑抑扬格各 1 个,扬扬格 2 个。归纳上述分析,三个诗节共 59 个音步,抑扬格占 24 个(阴影部分),扬抑格 16 个,抑抑格 9 个,其他格共 10 个。全诗共 6 节,根据前 3 节的概率分析,可以结论,该诗基本上是五步抑扬格。根据每行诗句的尾韵分析,可得出其韵律为 aabbccddeeff....。需要说明的是第三诗节第一行的 quiet 属于三音节词,在格律分析时,可根据情况既可作 1 个音步也可作 2 个音步处理,这里作 2 个音节看待,成 1 个音步,这一行诗句刚好是 5 个音步,符合总的格律基调。另外符号 & = and,但是用 and 就多了一个音节,而用 & 起到了 and 的作用,却不作为音节看待,影响了音步的划分。

2. 扫烟囱的孩子 *The Chimney Sweeper*
选自《经验之歌》 *Songs of Experience*

词语解释和难句分析

1. crying in notes of woe　用凄惨痛苦的声调哭着

2. They are both gone up to the church to pray. ＝ They have both gone up to the church to pray.　他们都去了教堂做祷告。

　　＊ 两句不同在于前者是系表结构,强调目前所处状态,类似于 They are both in the church to pray. 而后者是动词 go 的完成时态作谓语,表示的是行为动作。

3. 第二、三两诗节都是以小孩回话的方式用直接引语表示的。第二节诗句的谓语动词是过去式 was, smiled, clothed 和 taught,因此翻译时,要注意到时态带来的语境:"我在荒野里曾经很快乐,/还在冬天的雪地里欢笑,/他们就让我穿上黑衣,/叫我唱起悲伤的小调。"

4. 第三节诗句用的都是现在时态,表明"由于我现在依然很快乐,跳舞又唱歌,/所以他们认为没有伤害到我,/没把我伤害够,/于是就去赞美上帝、神父和国王,/正是这些人在我们的痛苦之上建起了天堂"。Who make up a heaven of our misery. 是定语从句,关系代词 who 代表从句所修饰的 God & his Priest & King。

参考译文——姚绍德

扫烟囱的孩子

一个小黑点蠕动在雪地里，
悲伤地哭喊着"扫呀——扫！"
"说呀——你的爸妈哪去了？"
"他们都在教堂做祈祷。"

"因为我在荒原也很快乐，
在冬天大雪里也总能欢笑，
他们就让我穿上这黑丧服，
教我唱这悲伤的曲调。

"我现在还是很快乐，跳舞又唱歌，
他们就以为没把我害够，
又是去赞美上帝、神父和国王——
而他们的天堂就建在我们的苦难上。"

格律和韵律分析

A ·little/black ·thing /a·mong/the ·snow   a
·Crying/"·"·weep！·"weep！"/in ·notes/of ·woe！   b
"·Where are /thy ·fa/ther & ·mo/ther？·Say？"   a
"They ·are/·both ·gone/up to/the ·church/to ·pray.   b

Be·cause/I was/·happy/u·pon/the ·heath,   c
And ·smil'd/a·mong/the ·win/ter's ·snow;   d
They ·cloth'd/me in/the ·clothes/of ·death,   c
And ·taught me/to ·sing/the ·notes/of ·woe.   d

"And be·cause/I am/·happy/& ·dance & ·sing   e
They ·think/they ·have/·done me/no ·in/jury,   f
And ·are/·gone to/praise ·God/& his ·Priest & ·King,   e
Who ·make/up a/·heaven/of ·our/·misery. "   f

3 个诗节中，第一诗节为 4445 音步，第二诗节为 5444 音步，第三诗节为 4545 音步，共有 8 个诗句为 4 音步。全诗共 52 个音步，按朗读时的自然重音来判断，有 30 个音步为抑扬格（阴影部分）。据此基本可认为此诗的格律为四步抑扬格，韵律为 aabbcdcdefef。

3. 老虎 *The Tyger*

词语解释和难句分析

1. 原文的开头两句与教材中略有不同,请注意 Bright, Forests, Night 三个单词的大写字母。Tyger! Tyger! Burning bright/In the Forests of the Night, 强调"燃烧",强调黑夜之多,"黑夜如林",而不是 "黑夜里的林莽"或"夜晚的森林"。故可译为"老虎!老虎!光焰灼灼/燃烧在黑夜之林"。现代 文学批评家沃伦谈论意象、隐喻和象征的时候,说布莱克的老虎是"作者心目中一个幻觉的生物, 既是一件事物,也是一个象征"。它似虎而非虎,但却不能说是比喻,因为说不清在比喻什么。

2. In what distant deeps or skies/Burnt the fire of thine eyes? = In what distant deeps or skies did the fire of thine eyes burn? 在多么遥远的海天深处/有铸造你的神眼之火正燃?

3. On what wings dare he aspire? /What the hand, dare seize the fire = On what the hand dare he seize the fire? 凭什么翅膀他敢飞空? /什么铁掌敢抓住这火焰?

   * aspire (*vi.*)〔古〕上升;aspire for/to/after,渴望、追求、有志于……;根据第二个意思,也有译者 把第一句译成:凭什么翅膀他敢追火?

   * he 即造物主。本诗可想象成造物主在创造一只精神之虎,从虎眼、虎心到脚爪和虎脑,就像个 铁匠在铁砧上打造虎的各个部位一样。

4. And what shoulder, & what art,/Could twist the sinew of thy heart? /And when thy heart began to beat,/ What dread hand? & what dread feet? 什么样的铁臂? 什么样的神工? /能拧成你心脏的肌腱? / 什么样可怕的手? 什么样可怕的脚? /促成你心脏最初的跳动?

   * 据某一文本,最后一句为 What dread hand form'd thy dread feet? 显然,hand 为造物主之手,feet 为 老虎之脚。故后两句也可译成:怎样可怕的手造就了怎样可怕的脚? /又怎样促成了你心脏的初动?

5. What the anvil? What dread grasp/Dare its deadly terrors clasp (= Dare clasp its deadly terrors)? 什么 样的铁砧? 什么样的握力? /敢掐住它致命的恐怖?

6. Did he smile his work to see(= Did he smile to see his work)? /Did he who made the Lamb make thee? 他可曾微笑着看自己的杰作? /可是那造出羔羊(= 耶稣)的也造出了你?

   * 耶稣常被称作上帝的羔羊。

参考译文——姚绍德

老虎

老虎,老虎,火光灼灼的烈焰,
燃烧在如林的黑夜!
何等超凡的神手和神眼
能构造你可怕的美健?

在多么遥远的海天深处,

采得你眼中燃烧的火种？
凭什么神翅他敢飞上高天？
凭什么铁掌他敢捕捉这烈焰？

凭什么样的铁臂、什么样的神工？
能拧成你心脏强大的肌腱？
凭何等可怖的手、何等可怖的脚？
促成你心脏最初的搏动？

用什么样的锤子？什么样的链？
在什么样的炉中把你大脑熔炼？
用什么铁砧？何等的握力？
敢卡住它摄人心魄的神威？

当群星投下长矛，
用泪水洒遍天庭，
看见自己的杰作他可曾微笑？
可是他创造了耶稣又创造了你？

老虎，老虎，火光灼灼的烈焰，
燃烧在如林的黑夜！
何等超凡的神手和神眼
能构成你可怕的美健？

格律和韵律分析

布莱克是个重思想内容、不太受格律和韵律束缚的诗人，有时格律严谨，韵律自由，有时反之。本诗韵律严谨，但是格律就比较自由了。

ˈTyger!／ˈTyger!／ˈBurning ˈbright	a
In the／ˈforests／of the ˈnight,	a
ˈWhat im／ˈmortal／ˈhand or ˈeye?	a
Could ˈframe／thy ˈfear／ful ˈsym／metry?	b
In ˈwhat／ˈdistant／ˈdeeps or ˈskies	c
ˈBurnt the／ˈfire of／ˈthine ˈeyes?	c
On ˈwhat ˈwings／dare ˈhe／as'pire?	d
ˈWhat the ˈhand／, dare ˈseize／the ˈfire?	d
And ˈwhat／ˈshoulder／, & ˈwhat ˈart,	e
Could ˈtwist／the ˈsi／news of／thy ˈheart?	e
And ˈwhen／thy ˈheart／ˈbegan to ˈbeat,	f
ˈWhat ˈdread ˈhand／? & ˈwhat ˈdread ˈfeet?	f

以头 3 个诗节为例进行分析,第一诗节为 3334 音步,共 13 个音步,其中扬抑格 5 个,抑扬格 3 个,抑抑格 2 个,扬抑扬格 2 个,抑抑扬格 1 个。第二诗节为 3333 音步,共 12 个音步,其中扬抑格 3 个,抑扬格 5 个,扬扬格 1 个,扬扬扬格 2 个,抑抑扬格 1 个。第三诗节为 3432 音步,共 12 个音步,其中抑扬格 6 个,抑抑格 1 个,扬扬格 1 个,抑扬格 1 个,扬扬扬格 2 个,扬抑扬格 1 个。3 节 12 行诗,有 9 行为三音步;总共 37 个音步,其中抑扬格 14 个,扬抑格 9 个(阴影部分),其他的格数量很少,因而此诗可算是三步抑扬格,韵律为 aaab/ccdd/eeff。

主要内容归纳和总结

1. 威廉·布莱克出生于伦敦,父亲是爱尔兰人,经营一个小制袜厂。他从小就显示出非凡的绘画才能,曾师从著名雕刻家(engraver)詹姆士·巴塞尔(James Basire)七年,后又进皇家艺术学院(the Royal Academy of Arts)深造,并开始以雕刻谋生。他的一生以诗画雕刻为伴,但他的诗作生前少有人知,死后才被人挖掘出来,一举成名。

布莱克一生激进(radical)、叛逆(rebel),不愿与世俗合流(never try to fit into the world),痛恨资本主义的残酷剥削,赞颂法国大革命,因此他的诗歌猛烈地抨击资本主义制度的残酷和宗教的虚伪。他的互为姐妹篇的两部诗集《天真之歌》和《经验之歌》就是为儿童所遭受的苦难发出的愤怒呼喊。如果说前者对现存制度还保留了一点勉强的希望和乐观的话,那么后者则充满苦难、贫穷、疾病和战争,笔调压抑而忧伤,再没有一点快乐情绪了。

从童年起,布莱克就是个充满想象和幻想的人,他诗中措辞都是令人可视的形象,而并非抽象的词汇。他多用比喻和象征手法,使诗歌意象更加形象鲜明。其诗歌语言直白朴素,既有抒情的美丽,又有深远的内涵。

布莱克的诗从思想内容到创作技巧和形式都彻底背叛了 18 世纪的古典主义。

2. 威廉·布莱克的主要作品:

《诗歌随笔》*Poetical Sketch*(1783)布莱克的第一部诗集

《天真之歌》*Songs of Innocence*(1809)

《经验之歌》*Songs of Experience*(1794)

《天堂与地狱的婚姻》*Marriage of Heaven and Hell*(1790)

他的后期作品多为预言性小册子:

《洛斯之书》*The Book of Los*(1795)

《尤里森之书》*The Book of Urizen*(1794)

《四个左义斯》*The Four Zoas*(1796~1807)

《弥尔顿》*Milton*(1804~1820)

重要信息句子

1. William Blake, an Irishman, was born and brought up in London.
2. Blake began writing poetry at the age of 12, and his first printed work is *Poetical Sketch*.
3. Childhood is central to Blake's concern in the *Songs of Innocence* and *Songs of Experience*.
4. Blake's *Marriage of Heaven and Hell* marks his entry into maturity. The poem was composed during the climax of the French Revolution and it plays the double role both as a satire and a revolutionary prophecy.

II．威廉·华兹华斯 William Wordsworth（1770～1850）

词语解释和难句分析

1. to develop a keen love of nature 对大自然产生热烈的爱恋

   to visit places <u>noted for</u> their scenic beauty 游览那些以风景优美著称的地方/风景优美的名胜之地

   to make a walking tour of the Swiss Alps 徒步游览瑞士的阿尔卑斯山

   to heighten sb.'s exhilarated response to the grandeur of nature 增强了某人对大自然壮美景色兴奋的反应

   to <u>live through</u> the storm and stress of the Revolution 经历大革命的风暴和紧张

   to have a love affair with sb. 与某人相爱

   be disheartened by the outbreak of hostilities between France and England 对英法之间爆发战争感到灰心丧气

   to change into a conservative in politics 转变成一个政治上的保守派

   the formative influence of his early experience of wild nature 早年在大自然荒野中的经历所形成的影响

2. be eased for a time 放松缓解一段时间

   to receive a bequest from a close friend 从密友那里获得一份遗赠

   to collaborate on a book of poems entitled *Lyrical Ballads* 合作完成了一部题为《抒情歌谣集》的诗集

   be portrayed in the charming lyric as "a Phantom of Delight." 在一首迷人的抒情诗中被描写为快乐的化身/幽灵

3. to obtain a sinecure as distributor of stamps with a substantial annual income 获得一份报酬优厚的闲职，做了邮票发行人

   to spend the remainder of his life there, except for periodic travels 在那里度过余生，只是间断性地出去旅游一下

   to receive a government pension 获得政府津贴

   to succeed Southey as Poet Laureate 继骚塞之后成为桂冠诗人

4. be written in the tradition of the 18th-century feeling for natural description 是依据18世纪描写大自然的传统感受来写作的

   to differ <u>in marked ways</u> from his early poetry 与他早期的诗歌有着明显的不同

   the uncompromising simplicity of <u>much of</u> the language 更大程度上坚持语言的简洁凝练

   the strong sympathy not merely with the poor in general but with particular, dramatized examples of them 不仅对一般的穷人而且对其中特殊的、引人注目的典型人物都表现出强烈的同情

   the fusion of natural description with expressions of inward states of mind 把描写自然与表现内心思想状态融合在一起

5. But the *Lyrical Ballads* differs in marked ways... of inward states of mind. 但是，《抒情歌谣集》与他早期的诗作明显不同，令人瞩目的是更大程度上坚持了语言的简洁凝练，不仅对一般穷人而且对

其中特殊的、引人注目的典型人物表现出强烈的同情,同时还把描写自然与表现内心的思想状态融合在一起。

6. after substantial revision 经大量的修正之后

  poetic vision and inspiration 诗歌意象和灵感

  more rhetorical and moralistic poems 更加注意修辞和道德说教的诗作

  be illumined by the spark of his former greatness 受他早期诗歌光芒的照耀/启迪

7. to penetrate to the heart of things and give the reader the very life of nature 洞察事物的实质,向读者展现大自然的真实面貌

  to show the genuine love for the natural beauty 表现了对自然美的真爱

  be the most anthologized poem in English literature 是英国文学中被编选入集次数最多的诗

  to take us to the core of Wordsworth's poetic beliefs 把我们带到华兹华斯诗歌信念依归的核心

  the quiet center of the returning wanderer's thoughts 游子思归的思想静园

  be described with a detail that conveys a sense of natural order at once vivid and eternal 对……进行了详细的描写,传达给读者一种自然规律既栩栩如生又永恒不灭的感觉

8. Beyond the pleasures of the picturesque with their emphasis on the eye and the external aspects of nature, however, lies a deeper moral awareness, a sense of completeness in multiplicity. 在强调目力所及的自然美景和自然永恒所带来的愉悦之外,还表达/存在一种更深层次的道德意识,一种变幻重重中的完美感。

  ＊这是一个倒装句,正常句序应是:However, a deeper moral awareness, a sense of completeness ... lies beyond the pleasures of the ...

9. moral reflections 道德体现/反应

  sublime communion with all things 与万物至高无上的交流/联系

  an inspiring force of rapture 一种令人沉迷的力量

10. As he is aware of his own sublime communion with all things, nature becomes an inspiring force of rapture, a power that reveals the workings of the soul. 当他意识到自己在与万物进行着至高无上的交流的时候,大自然就变成了一种令人沉迷的启迪灵感的力量,一种揭示人内心活动的动力。

11. To Wordsworth, nature acts as a substitute for imaginative and intellectual engagement with the development of human beings in their diverse circumstances. 对华兹华斯来讲,大自然就是在不断变化的环境中影响人类发展的想象和智力的替代物。

12. The "Lucy poems" describe with rare elusive beauty of simple lyricism and haunting rhythm a young country girl living a simple life in a remote village far from the civilized world. 《露西诗草》以简练的抒情风格、难以言表的罕见之美和萦绕于心难以释怀的节奏描写了一个远离文明社会、居住偏远村庄、过着俭朴生活的青年姑娘。

13. They are verses of love and loss which hold within their delicate simplicity a meditation on time and death which rises to universal stature. 这些都是描写爱情和失落的诗歌,以精致简洁的语言对时间和死亡进行沉思,这种思考升华到了具有普遍意义的境界/使作品具有普遍的意义。

14. the irrational mind 没有理性的头脑/人

  the commonsensical 正常心志的人,明白事理的人

  to see deeply into the natural of life 深刻洞察生命的本质

  the grave and tender dignity of Wordsworth's meditations on "man, the heart of man, and human life." 华兹华斯思考"人、人心和生命"时的严肃、温和与庄重

  the timeless mystery of sorrowful humanity and its radiant beauty 忧伤人性永恒的神秘性及其散发出的美

in the eye of nature　在大自然的视线中

be seen as precious for his unique self　因其独特的自我而被视为宝贝

to evoke the benevolence in the small rural community　在小村庄里唤起了恻隐之心

15. The hapless wife of "The Ruined Cottage," <u>dying amid</u> the disintegration of her entire way of life, rouses in the reader the tender, quiet compassion of those who are <u>at one with</u> the timeless truths of existence.　"塌了的茅屋"中那位不幸的妻子,因不适应原来的生活方式完全被毁而死,唤起了广大读者对已经与永恒的事实存在融为一体的人们隐隐的但却敏感的同情之心。

16. In its daring use of subject matter and sense of the authenticity of the experience of the poorest, "Resolution and Independence" is the triumphant conclusion of ideas first developed in the *Lyrical Ballads*.　在大胆使用主题和真实可信地描写穷人生活方面,《抒情歌谣集》第一次表达了成功的思想结论:"决心和独立"。

17. a poet <u>in memory of</u> the past　一个怀念过去的诗人

to open with a literal journey　以文字的旅行开始

to go through the poet's personal history　贯穿诗人个人的历史

to carry the metaphorical meaning of his interior journey　带有隐喻他内心历程的含义

to <u>quest for</u> his lost early self and the proper spiritual home　寻求失落了的早年自我和本身的精神归宿

to chart this growth from infancy to manhood　描绘了从童年到成年的成长

18. We are shown the development of human consciousness under the sway of an imagination united to the grandeur of nature.　这首诗(《序曲》)向我们展示了在想象力和大自然的壮美景色相结合的影响下,人的意识和悟力的发展提升。

19. The concluding description of the ascent of Snowdon becomes a symbol of the poet's climb to the height of his inspired powers and to that state of vision in which, dedicating himself to humanity, he becomes one of the "Prophets of nature."　《序曲》结尾对斯诺顿发展进步的描写标志着他的感悟力和想象力都已达到极致,在这种状态下,他把自己奉献给人文主义,成了一个"大自然的先知"。

＊ to that state ＝ to that height; in which 引导一个定语从句,即"在诗人灵感和想象力都达到很高水平的情况下……"

20. his deliberate simplicity　他刻意追求的简洁

to decorate the truth of existence　粉饰客观存在的事实

<u>in defense of</u> his unconventional theory of poetry　为了捍卫它反传统的诗歌理论

the source of poetic truth　是个真实的来源

the direct experience of the senses　直接的感官体验

to originate from "emotion recollected in tranquility."　起源于平静中的情感回顾

21. Rejecting the contemporary emphasis on form and an intellectual approach that <u>drained</u> poetic writing <u>of</u> strong emotion, he maintained that the scenes and events of everyday life and the speech of ordinary people were the raw material of which poetry could and should be made.　他反对当时强调形式、没有激情(干巴巴)地玩弄智力技巧的诗歌创作方法,坚持主张日常生活中发生的事件和场景、普通人的口语都能够也应当成为诗歌创作的原材料。

22. the leading figure of the Romantic poetry　浪漫主义诗歌主要代表

the focal poetic voice of the period　那个时期主要的诗人代表

the poetry of the growing inner self　表现内心活动的诗歌

to change the course of English poetry　改变英语诗歌的创作路线

using ordinary speech of the language and advocating a return to nature　利用普通的英语口语(入诗)和主张回归自然

23. His is a voice of searchingly comprehensive humanity and one that inspires his audience to see the world freshly, sympathetically and naturally.　他的诗就是一种敏锐、广泛的人文表达,就是一种鼓舞读者以清新、自然和关切的眼光洞察世界的表达。

华兹华斯作品选读

1. 我如行云独自游 I Wandered Lonely as a Cloud

词语解释和难句分析

1. 第一节整个句子的结构是:I wandered lonely as a cloud that floats on high over vales and hills when all at once I saw...意为:我如行云独自游,像云在河谷与群山之上飘飞,这时我突然看到……

   ＊ that 引导的是定语从句,when 引导的是时间状语从句。

2. 第二节描写所见的水仙花:(A host of golden daffodils are) continuous as the stars that shine/And twinkle on the milky way,...意为:连绵不断,像繁星闪亮,闪烁在银河……

   ＊ that 引导的是定语从句修饰 stars,直译是"像银河里闪烁的繁星"。

3. Ten thousand saw I at a glance,/Tossing their heads in sprightly dance. ＝ I saw at a glance ten thousand tossing their heads in sprightly dance.　我一眼便看到成千上万朵(水仙花),摇动花冠,欢快飘舞。

   ＊ tossing...是现在分词短语作定语,修饰 ten thousand。

4. I gazed — and gazed — but little thought/What wealth the show to me had brought:＝ What wealth the show had brought to me. 我凝望——凝望——但却不曾想到/这景色给我带来何等财富:

   ＊ 那么财富是什么呢? 第四节做了回答,就是在一人独处、孤独寂寞之时,一想起这美丽景色就感到的快乐。

   ＊ What 引导的名词性从句做 thought 的宾语。

5. For oft (＝often), when on my couch I lie/In vacant or in pensive mood, ＝ For often, when I lie on my couch in vacant or in pensive mood,　因为在我心境茫然、情怀抑郁/常常躺在卧榻上之时……

   They flash upon that inward eye/Which is the bliss of solitude;　它们会闪现在我心中/这是孤寂中无上的幸福;

   ＊ 关系代词 which 指代的是前面的整个句子,所以它引导的定语从句是修饰前面整个句子的。

参考译文——姚绍德

我如行云独自游

　我如行云独自游,
　在群山峡谷之上高飞,
　蓦然间眼前鲜花展现,
　是一片金色的水仙;

开在树下,开在湖边,
微风中它们舞姿摇曳。

绵绵不断,似繁星闪闪,
像银河晶莹一片;
它们漫无边际地延伸——
沿着湖湾的边缘;
一眼便见千朵万朵,
花冠摇首,欢乐飘舞。

闪光的湖水在近旁波荡,
却比不上水仙花舞得欢畅;
此情此景作旅伴,
诗人怎能不快乐?
我凝望呀我凝望,却不曾想——
这景象给了我什么财富?

多少次我躺在卧榻之上,
或情怀抑郁,或心境迷茫;
脑海中便出现眼前景象,
孤独中给了我幸福的遐想;
那时候我的心涌满快乐,
不由得与水仙共舞翩跹。

格律和韵律分析

I ˈwan/dered ˈlone/ly ˈas/a ˈcloud	a
That ˈfloats/on ˈhigh/o'er ˈvales/and ˈhills,	b
When ˈall/at ˈonce/I ˈsaw/a ˈcrowd,	a
A ˈhost,/ of ˈgol/den ˈdaf/fo·dils;	b
Be·side/the ˈlake,/ be·neath/the ˈtrees,	c
ˈFluttering/and ˈdan/cing in/the ˈbreeze.	c
Con·ti/nuous ˈas/the ˈstars/that ˈshine	d
And ˈtwin/kle on/the ˈmil/ky ˈway,	e
They ˈstretched/in ˈne/ver-ˈen/ding ˈline	d
A·long/the ˈmar/gin of/a ˈbay:	e
Ten ˈthou/sand ˈsaw/I ˈat/a glance,	f
ˈTossing/their ˈheads/in ˈspright/ly ˈdance.	f

通过前两节的格律分析,很容易看出每节6行,每行4音步,总共48个音步中,除了阴影部分的4个音步外,绝大多数音步为抑扬格,所以此诗为四步抑扬格,韵律为 ababcc/dedeff....。

2. 在威斯敏斯特桥上，1802 年 9 月 3 日
Composed upon Westminster Bridge, *September 3*, *1802*

1. Earth has not anything to show more fair：大地从未展示过如此的美丽：

2. Dull would he be of soul who could pass by/A sight so touching in its majesty：= He would be dull of soul who could pass by so touching a sight in its majesty：要是谁竟能漠视如此动人的壮美,他的性灵也真够麻木愚钝：

   * 头三行诗句是总的景色一览和诗人的感慨。下面的景色描写就比较具体了；in its majesty 雄伟,壮丽,例如：They saw the lofty peak in all its majesty. 他们看到了高耸的山峰,气势极其雄伟。

3. This city now doth, like a garment, wear/The beauty of the morning; silent, bare, 这城市此刻披着美丽的晨光,像穿着睡衣,袒露而又安详。

4. Ships, towers, domes, theaters, and temples lie/Open unto the fields, and to the sky; 船,塔,穹顶,剧院和寺庙/敞向田野、敞向天空,一览无余；

5. All (are) bright and glittering in smokeless air. 一切都在明净(烟尘不染)的天空下闪光。

6. Never did sun more beautifully steep/In his first splendor, valley, rock, or hill,/Ne'er saw I, never felt, a calm so deep！= Sun never steep valley, rock, or hill in his first splendor more beautifully, I never saw, never felt so deep a calm！初现的晨曦从未如此绚丽,沐浴着峡谷,磐石和山冈,我从未见过、从未感受如此深邃的静谧！

7. The river glideth (= glides) at his own sweet will：泰晤士河正自由自在/悠闲随意地流淌：

8. Dear God！The very house seem asleep；上帝啊！眼前的房屋似乎还在酣睡；

9. And all that mighty heart is lying still！伦敦,整个儿伟大的心脏仍在静卧休息！

在威斯特敏斯特桥上 ,1802 年 9 月 3 日

大地从未展示过这样的美景：
如此动人,如此壮丽！
性灵愚钝者才会漠然走过；
伦敦城此刻正披着一袭晨衣——
袒露,宁静而清丽,
船、塔、穹顶、剧院和寺庙,
万物都敞向平野、敞向天宇；
一切都在明净的空气中生辉。
第一缕晨曦从未如此绚丽,
山谷、磐石和山峦都沐浴在朝晖里；

我从未见过、从未感受过这深沉的宁静！
泰晤士河自由流淌、随心由意；
上帝啊，眼前的层层屋宇似乎都在酣睡；
伦敦整个宏大的心脏正静卧休息！

格律和韵律分析

·Earth han/·not a/·nything/to ·show/more ·fair:	a
·Dull would/·he be/·of ·soul/who ·could/·pass ·by	b
A ·sight/so ·tou/ching in/its ·ma/jesty:	b
This ·ci/ty ·now/doth, ·like/a ·gar/ment, ·wear	a
The ·beau/ty of/the ·mor/ning; ·si/lent, ·bare,	a
·Ships, ·tow/ers, ·domes,/·theaters,/ and ·tem/ples ·lie	b
·Open/·unto/the ·fields,/ and ·to/the ·sky;	b
All ·bright/and ·glit/tering/in the ·smoke/less ·air.	a
·Never/did ·sun/more ·beau/tiful/ly ·steep	c
In ·his/first ·splen/dor, ·val/ley, ·rock,/ or ·hill;	d
Ne'er ·saw/I, ·ne/ver ·felt,/ a ·calm/so ·deep!	c
The ·ri/ver ·gli/deth at/his ·own/·sweet ·will:	d
Dear ·God! / The ·ve/ry ·hou/ses ·seem/as·leep;	c
And ·all/that ·migh/ty ·heart/is ·ly/ing ·still!	d

根据上述分析可见，这是一首意大利式十四行诗，前8行押搂抱韵，为abbaabba，后6行押交替韵，为cdcdcd。第二行的尾韵为[ai]，第三行的尾韵为[i]，这两行押[i]韵。从格律上说，每行为5音步，总共70个音步中有48个抑扬格（非阴影部分），故此诗为五步抑扬格。第十一行开头的Ne'er舍去v就是为了约音，把两个音节约成一个音节，从而把neer saw划在一个音步，使此行刚好为5个音步。

3. 她住的地方人迹罕至 *She Dwelt among the Untrodden Ways*

词语解释和难句分析

1. A maid whom there were none to praise/And very few to love; 这姑娘生时不曾受人夸赞，/很少人曾把她爱上。

   ＊whom引导的是maid的定语从句，意为姑娘无人赞扬，少有人爱。
2. A violet by a mossy stone/Half hidden from the eye! ＝A violet by a mossy stone is half hidden from the eye! 青苔石旁一株紫罗兰/半遮半掩难看见！
3. — Fair as a star, when only one /Is shining in the sky. ——美得像一颗星星/独一无二地闪烁在天上。

   ＊fair as a star＝She is fair as a star; when引导的是一个状语从句，说明她当时的状态:孤独地闪耀在天上。
4. to cease to be 不再活着,不再存在,死去
5. But she is in her grave, and, oh,/(That is) the difference to me! 但露西现正在坟墓里安眠;/这对

我呀,可真是阴阳相隔,天壤之别!

参考译文——姚绍德

她住的地方人迹罕至

她住的地方人迹罕至,
多夫河畔泉水边的小路间;
姑娘生前无人夸赞,
也很少有人曾把她爱;

她是一朵青苔石旁紫罗兰,
若隐若现难得见!
美得像星星在闪耀,
只是孤独地挂在天上。

露西活着无人知,
死时亦无人晓;
但如今她长眠在墓里,
与我呀,可是天壤之别!

格律和韵律分析

She ˈdwelt/aˈmong/the unˈtrod/den ˈways	a
Beˈside/the ˈsprings/of ˈDove,	b
A ˈmaid/whom ˈthere/were ˈnine/to ˈpraise	a
And ˈve/ry ˈfew/to ˈlove;	b
A ˈvio/let by/a ˈmos/sy ˈstone	c
Half ˈhid/den ˈfrom/the ˈeye!	d
Fair ˈas/a ˈstar,/ when ˈon/ly ˈone	c
Is ˈshi/ning ˈin/the ˈsky.	d
She ˈlived/unˈknown,/ and ˈfew/could ˈknow	e
When ˈLu/cy ˈceased/to ˈbe;	f
But ˈshe/is in/her ˈgrave,/ and, ˈoh,	e
The ˈdif/ference/to ˈme!	f

很明显,3个诗节都是4343音步,大多数音步为抑扬格,所以此诗的格律为四三音步抑扬格,韵律为abab/cdcd/efef。

4. 孤独的收割者 *The Solitary Reaper*

词语解释和难句分析

1. yon〔古〕= yonder　*a. /ad. /pron.* (在)远处(的),那边(的)

2. lass　*n.* (苏格兰)姑娘,少女

3. strain　*n.* 曲调

4. O listen! For the Vale profound/Is overflowing with the sound. = For the profound Vale is overflowing with the sound.　呵,听吧! (因为)那深邃的山谷里/正洋溢着姑娘的歌声。
   * for 是连词,引导一个原因状语从句,说明为什么要你听。

5. chaunt = chant　*v.* 唱;*n.* 歌,曲

6. haunt (*n.*) 常去的地方;shady haunt 有树荫的地方

7. A voice so thrilling ne'er was heard/. . . /Among the farthest Hebrides. = So thrilling a voice was never heard in springtime from the Cuckoo bird, breaking the silence of the seas among the farthest Hebrides.
   在最遥远的赫伯利兹群岛,从未听过春天的布谷鸟有如此动人的歌声,打破了海洋辽阔的沉寂。
   * breaking 引导的分词短语是句子的主语补语。

8. the plaintive numbers　哀伤的曲调,哀婉的音符
   for old, unhappy, far-off things　为了那古老不幸的往事
   some more humble lay = a little more humble lyric poem　更为平常、质朴的(诗)歌
   familiar matter　今日的平凡琐事

9. Some natural sorrow, loss, or pain,/That has been, and may be again? = Is it some natural sorrow, loss, or pain,/That . . . again?　那是自然的悲伤、失望或痛苦,/曾经有过,也可能再次降临?
   * that 是关系代词,指代前面的 sorrow, loss, or pain, 它引导了一个定语从句。

10. I saw her singing at her work,/And o'er the sickle bending; = I saw her singing at her work and bending over the sickle;　我看她一边收割一边唱,/手拿镰刀弯着腰;

11. And, as I mounted up the hill,/The music in my heart I bore,/Long after it was heard no more. = And, as I mounted up the hill, I bore the music in my heart long after it was heard no more.　当我登上小山包,/那歌声早已在耳边消失,/却还久久留在我心上。

参考译文——姚绍德

孤独的收割者

看哪,那孤独的高地姑娘——
在远处的田野里歌唱!
边割边唱,独自繁忙。
你止步听听吧,离去也别声响!
她一个人又割又捆,

唱着一支忧郁的歌；
听啊！幽深的山谷里面，
满是她的歌声荡漾。

从未听过一只夜莺，
唱出如此动听的音符，
对阿拉伯沙漠中的疲旅，
当他们在树荫下休憩的时候；
从未有过一只布谷鸟，
歌声有如此美妙，
打破海洋辽阔的沉寂，
在最遥远的赫伯利兹群岛。

没人会告诉我她在唱什么？
也许这唱不完的凄凉曲
在咏叹过往的不幸——
抑或是历史征战的凭吊；
也许是一首更平常的小曲
唱如今熟悉的琐事？
也许是随时会有的痛苦、失落和悲伤——
过去曾经有，今后还会来？

不管这姑娘唱什么歌，
一唱起来就像没有完；
看见她一边干活一边唱，
弯着腰肢，挥着镰刀——
我一动不动默默倾听……
当我爬上小山包，
她歌声早已听不到，
脑海中却还余音袅袅。

格律和韵律分析

Be·hold/her, ·sin/gle in/the ·field,   a
Yon ·so/lita/ry ·High/land ·lass!   b
·Reaping/and ·sin/ging by/her·self;   c
·Stop here,/ and ·gent/ly ·pass !   b
A·lone/she ·cuts/and ·binds/the ·grain,   d
And ·sings/a ·me/lancho/ly ·strain;   d
O ·li/sten! for/the ·Vale/pro·found   d
Is ·o/ver·flow/ing with/the ·sound.   e

No ·Nigh/tingale/did ·e'ver ·chaunt	e
More ·wel/come ·notes/to ·wea/ry ·bands	a
Of ·tra/velers/in some ·sha/dy ·haunt,	b
A·mong/·Ara/bean ·sands;	a
A ·voice/so ·thrill/ling ·ne'er·was ·heard	b
In ·spring/time from/the ·Cu/ckoo ·bird,	c
·Breaking/the ·si/lence of/the ·seas	c
A·mong/the ·far/thest ·He/bre·des.	c

全诗共 4 节,取前两节进行格律分析,可以看到:所有的诗行都是 4 音步,绝大多数音步都是抑扬格,故该诗格律为四步抑扬格。对全诗进行韵律分析,第一和第三节的韵律为 abcbddee,第二和第四节的韵律为 ababccdd。

主要内容归纳和总结

1. 威廉·华兹华斯出生于英格兰,毕业于剑桥大学圣约翰学院,酷爱自然,经常在英格兰湖滨区居住,与科勒律治、骚塞在此成为密友,并与科勒律治共同完成并出版了《抒情歌谣集》,这本诗集的出版成了浪漫主义时期开始的标志,三位诗人也被共称为"湖滨派诗人"(the Lake Poets)。

他对大自然深沉的迷恋和对法国大革命真诚的拥护、澎湃的热情,都激发起他无穷的想象和对自由、人文、共和的向往。一方面,他歌颂、描写大自然,认为大自然是揭示人内心活动的动力,是人类想象与心智的代替,创造了许多优美而神秘的大自然意境;另一方面,他以普通人的普通生活为诗歌主题,描写普通百姓的喜怒哀乐,寄寓诗人自己的爱恨情仇。在诗人的人生哲学中,生命似轮回的旅程,生命之始也是生命的终结之地,所以他常抒发怀旧之情和对人生的感伤,以及对时间与死亡的沉思。

华兹华斯的诗绝不粉饰真实(refuse to decorate the truth),总给人一种简洁朴素(simplicity)、纯净深远(pure and profound)之美,他的浪漫主义抒情风格给读者展现的总是一幅幅清新(fresh)、自然(natural)、美好的境界(beautiful world),他的诗就是美的象征,是那些了无生趣的学院派诗歌(academic poems of losing any interest of life)无法比拟的。

诗人大半生没有维持生活的职业,43 岁时才获得一份发送邮票的工作,有了年薪。他于 1843 年继骚塞之后成为"桂冠诗人"(Poet Laureate),享受政府的津贴,1850 年去世,葬于格拉斯米尔教堂墓地(Grasmere churchyard)。

2. 华兹华斯的主要作品:

《描写速写——傍晚漫步》*Descriptive Sketches, an Evening Walk* (1793)诗集

《抒情歌谣集》*Lyrical Ballads* (1798)

《序曲》*The Prelude* (1805 完成,1850 作者死后出版)

《双卷诗集》*Poems in Two Volumes* (1807)

《颂歌:永存的暗示》*Ode: Intimations of Immortality* 自传体诗

《决心与独立》*Resolution and Independence* 叙事诗

《远足》*The Excursion*(1814)

3. 根据主题,华兹华斯的短诗可分为两类:

a. 描写大自然的诗

《麻雀巢》*The Sparrow's Nest*

《致云雀》*To a Skylark*

《致杜鹃》To Cuckoo

《致蝴蝶》To a Butterfly

《我如行云独自游》I Wandered Lonely as a Cloud

《傍晚漫步》An Evening Walk

《我心驿动》My Heart Leap up

《丁登教堂》Tintern Abbey

b. 描写生命的诗

《荆棘》The Thorn

《水手的母亲》The Sailor's Mother

《迈克尔》Michael

《玛格丽特所受的折磨》The Affliction of Margaret

《坎伯兰的乞丐》The Old Cumberland Beggar

《白痴男孩》The Idiot Boy

重要信息句子

1. Wordsworth is regarded as a "worshipper of nature."

2. "I Wandered Lonely as a Cloud," "An Evening Walk," "My Heart Leaps up" and "Tintern Abbey," are all masterpieces on nature.

3. "I Wandered Lonely as a Cloud" is the most anthologized（被选收入集次数最多的）poem in English literature.

4. Wordsworth is a poet in memory of the past. To him, life is a cyclical journey. The beginning finally turns out to be its end.

III. 塞缪尔·泰勒·科勒律治
Samuel Taylor Coleridge（1772~1834）

词语解释和难句分析

1. mentally precocious boy　精神上早熟的孩子

   to fall into idleness　无所事事,游手好闲

   to get into debt　负债累累

   to betake himself to London　前往伦敦,决心去伦敦

   to enlist in the 15th Dragoon　应征入第 15 骑兵团

   to join in a utopian plan of establishing an ideal democratic community in America, named "Pantisocracy"　参加一项乌托邦计划,在美洲建立一个理想的民主社会,名曰"大同世界"

2. to fall under sb.'s spell　受到某人的魅力影响下

   the 18th-century idealism of Immanuel Kant　18 世纪康德的唯心主义

   to become addicted to opium　吸食鸦片成瘾

to ease the pain of rheumatism 缓减风湿病的疼痛

to lament over his declining spirit of imagination 哀叹自己想象力的减退

to give his famous series of lectures on literature and philosophy 他做了一系列论文学和哲学的演讲

to estrange from his wife/his family 夫妻分居，与家人分居

to take residence in... 居住在……

some brilliantly perceptive literary criticism 一些才华横溢、洞察力深刻的文学批评

3. He courageously stemmed the tide of the prevailing doctrines derived from Hume and Hartley, advocating a more spiritual and religious interpretation of life, based on what he had learnt from Kant and Schelling. 他勇敢地逆流而上，顶住当时风行的休谟和哈特利的教义，坚持把从康德和谢林那里学到的理论作为基础，主张对人生更多地从精神层面和宗教层面做出解释。

4. the only permanent revelation of the nature of reality. 现实的本质唯一永久的启示

the vague intimations derived from his unconsciousness without sacrificing the vitality of the inspiration. 没有牺牲活跃的思维和灵感，无意中发出的隐约微妙的暗示

a fiery foe of the right of man, of Jacobinism 人权的凶恶敌人，雅各宾主义的敌人

5. He insisted that a government should be based upon the rest of the community from above. 他坚持认为政府应当遵循有产阶级的意志，自上而下地把自己的意志强加给其余的社会阶层。

6. the demonic poems 神祇诗

the conversational poems 对话诗

mysticism and demonism with strong imagination 具有强烈想象的神秘主义和魔鬼信仰

be set in a strange territory of the poet's memory and dream 以诗人的记忆和梦境这一奇特的领域作为创作的背景

be reigned beyond the control of reason 不受理性的羁绊/束缚

7. Unifying the group is a magical quest pattern which intends as its goal to reconcile the poet's self-consciousness with a higher order of being associated with divine forgiveness. 统观神祇类诗，就是一种魔幻的探求方式，其目的就是把诗人的自我意识和与神的宽恕相联系的更高层次和谐地协调起来。

8. to neglect the law of hospitality 忽视友好待客之道

to shoot an albatross 射杀一只信天翁

the hot tropical sun 赤道的炎炎烈日

being tortured all the time with thirst and the horror of death 总是受到口渴和死亡威胁的折磨

9. The story moves on through a world of wonder, from mysterious preface to inevitable close. 故事的演进从神秘的开篇到必然的结束，经历了一个奇妙的世界。

10. to stand out clear and vivid 清晰生动地显示出来

be an ordeal of oppressive weariness 难以忍受的疲惫的折磨和煎熬

to reject a social offering 拒绝一项社会给予的礼物

to represent in a supernatural way the possibility of affection in the world 以超自然的方式表现了世界上可能存在的挚爱情感

11. The mariner's sin was the in killing the albatross he rejected a social offering, he obliterated something that loved him and represented in a supernatural way the possibility of affection in the world. 这水手的罪孽就是他在枪杀信天翁的时候，拒绝了一份社会给予的礼物，消除了深爱自己、并且以超自然的方式表现了这个世界上可能存在的挚爱之情的某种宝贵的东西。

12. From this poem, we can infer that Coleridge believed the universe as the projection not of reasoned beliefs but of irrational fears and guilty feeling. 从这首诗中我们可以推断，科勒律治认为宇宙并非

是理性信仰的设计规划,而是非理性恐惧和负罪情感的反映。

13. He had created the kind of universe which his own inexplicable sins and their consequences might have suggested to him.　他在诗中所创造的宇宙,正是他自己难以言传的罪孽及其后果可能已向他做了暗示的世界。

　　* which 引导的是修饰 universe 的定语从句。

14. His religious conflict enforced him to describe the universe in his work as the Christian universe gone mad.　他在宗教上的矛盾心理迫使他在作品里把宇宙描写成一个疯狂了的基督教世界。

15. to use a freer version of the ballad form to create an atmosphere of the Gothic horror at once delicate and sinister　采用写法更为自由的歌谣形式,创造出一种哥特式恐怖同时又微妙邪恶的气氛

　　to victimize an innocent maiden　陷害/危害天真纯洁的少女

　　the standard trappings of Gothic horror　标准/典型的哥特式恐怖的场景/描写方法

　　the virgin Christabel in peril　处于险境的少女克里斯特贝尔

　　to dramatize a confrontation with evil through disturbing suggestions of the sexual, supernatural and fantastic elements of dream　通过种种性的、超自然力的和梦境中的光怪陆离所形成的令人不安的示意,使得与邪恶力量的冲突更加戏剧化

　　the regular strikes of the clock　规则的钟摆走动声

16. Opposed to the nightmarish are images of religious grace and the spring of love that had gushed from the poet's heart.　与噩梦相对的是诗人心中涌流而出的宗教仁厚和爱之泉源

　　* 这是一个倒装句,可还原为:Images of religious grace and the spring of love that had gushed from the poet's heart are opposed to the nightmarish.

　　* that 引导的是一个定语从句,修饰前面的 images of ...。

17. the images of the river, of the magnificent palace and other marvelous scenes deposited in his unconsciousness.　潜意识中储存/无意中积淀下来的有关河流、辉煌宫殿以及其他奇特美景的意象

　　* deposited 引导的过去分词短语是修饰前面名词 river, palace 和 scenes 的定语短语。

18. intimate record of his personal thoughts　个人思想的忠实/详尽记录

　　an intimate personal piece　一首表达个人私密情感的诗/表达个人感受的诗

　　to utter his innermost thoughts and sentiments　表达出他内心最深处的思想感情

　　to speak more directly of an allied theme　更直接地讲到有关的主题

19. the desire to what Hart Crane beautifully called "improved infancy."　向往哈尔特·克莱恩美称为"进步了的孩童时代"的时期

　　* 哈尔特·克莱恩,20 世纪初的美国诗人,主张诗应当歌颂机器时代,诗作有"白色的建筑物""桥",1932 年因未实现创作目标,于苦闷之中投海自尽。

20. Each of these poems verges upon a kind of vicarious and purgatorial atonement, in which Coleridge must fail or suffer so that someone he loves may succeed or experience joy.　这类诗(对话诗)中的每一首都接近于一种替代别人的炼狱赎罪,在这过程中,科勒律治必须失败、必须遭罪,使得他所爱之人可以获得成功或体验快乐。

21. to give close critical attention to language　对语言要求严格,密切关注语言

　　to sing highly Wordsworth's perfect truth to nature　高度评价华兹华斯对自然完美真实的描写

　　reading more into the subject than the text　更注重解读主题,而不是字面意义

　　going deeper into the inner reality than only caring for the outer form　注重更深层次的内部真实,而不是只关注外部形式

　　be esteemed by some of his contemporaries　受到同时代的诗界同人的尊崇

22. be generally recognized as a lyrical poet and literary critic of the first rank　被普遍认为是第一流的抒

情诗人和文学批评家

to range from the supernatural to the domestic （诗歌主题）范围广阔，从超自然的题材到家庭谈话的内容均有

sb.'s compelling conversational power 某人令人折服的交谈能力

科勒律治作品选读

忽必烈汗 *Kubla Khan*

词语解释和难句分析

1. In Xanadu did Kubla Khan. . . /Down to a sunless sea. = In Xanadu Kubla Khan did (enacted)/A decree (about building) a stately pleasure dome/Where Alph, the sacred river, ran/Through cavens measureless to man/Down to a sunless sea. 忽必烈在上都颁下圣旨:建一座欢乐宫宏伟壮丽,有圣河阿尔夫宫旁流过,层层洞重重穴穿越无数,入大海无阳光沉暗迷蒙。

   * measureless to man = too deep to be measured by man 深不可测,非人力所能测量。该形容词短语是 cavens 的后置定语。

2. So twice five miles of fertile ground/With walls and towers were girdled round: = So twice five miles of fertile ground were girdled round with walls and towers. 大皇宫塔楼耸宫墙环绕,乐逍遥废去了五哩良园。

   And there were gardens bright with sinuous rills 有多少靓丽园曲水流转

   * sinuous rills 许多弯弯曲曲的小溪/小河

   Where blossomed many an incense-bearing tree; = Where <u>many an</u> incense-bearing tree blossomed; 有多少芬芳树花开万朵;

   * where 引导一个定语从句修饰上句的 gardens。

   And here were forests ancient as the hills, = And here forests were ancient as the hills, 花园内参天树山岳同古,

   * here = in the garden

   Enfolding sunny spots of greenery. 林木间环抱着阳光草地。

   * 分词短语可以看作是上一行的伴随状语,做补充说明,其逻辑主语就是 forests。

3. But oh! That deep romantic chasm which slanted/Down the green hill athwart (= across) cedarn cover! 但是那深裂隙惊险斜插,穿青山奔急流雪松如盖。

4. A savage place! <u>as</u> holy and enchanted/ As e'er (= ever) beneath a waning moon was haunted/By (a) woman wailing for her demon lover! 好一个蛮荒地亦神亦魅,恰似那残月夜怨女隐现,哀哀哭切切悲竟为情鬼!

   * A savage place! = What a savage place!; . . . be haunted by (ghosts) . . . (某个地方)常有鬼魂出没,(某个人)常被鬼魂附着在身上

5. And from this chasm, with ceaseless turmoil seething, = And with ceaseless turmoil seething from this chasm, 有激流如汤沸喧腾裂谷,

   As if this earth in fast thick pants were breathing, = As if this earth were breathing in fast thick pants, 仿佛是大地在急促喘息,

   A mighty fountain momently was forced: 时时有大喷泉喷射而出:

6. Amid whose swift half-intermitted burst/Huge fragments vaulted like rebounding hail,/Or chaffy grain beneath

the thresher's flail： 爆发间那飞泉时断时续,巨石块跳跃起如雹反弹,又好比连枷下脱壳谷粒:

* amid whose swift half-intermitted burst 在喷泉急速而有间歇性的喷发过程中……, whose 即指 fountain's 喷泉的。这是个状语短语,后面讲的才是主句。

And (a)mid these dancing rocks at once and ever 一阵阵乱石飞如狂似舞

It flung up momently the sacred river. 这圣河如疯马常跃地面。

* fling up 是不及物动词,"猛冲,急奔,(马)乱跳"的意思,不能把 the sacred river 当成它的宾语;这里 it = the sacred river,之所以重复用,一是为了强化语气,"这圣河……",二是格律和押韵的需要,river 和 ever 押尾韵。

7. Five miles meandering with a mazy motion/Through wood and dale the sacred river ran, = The sacred river ran five miles meandering with a mazy motion through wood and dale, 蜿蜒流五英里如入迷津,穿山林越深谷奔腾起伏,

Then reached the cavens measureless to man,/And sank in tumult to a lifeless ocean: 钻入那不见底连环洞窟,咆哮着跌入海一片死寂:

* ran 和 reached 是主语 the sacred river 的两个并列谓语动词。

8. And 'mid (= amid) this tumult Kubla heard from far/Ancestral voices prophesying war! 喧嚣过忽听得祖先示警,忽必烈知悉了战争将临!

* prophesying war 是分词短语作定语修饰 ancestral voices, 即"祖先预言战争的声音"。

9. The shadow of the dome of pleasure/(was) Floated midway on the waves; 欢乐宫乐逍遥浮华虚影,漂浮在圣河里波峰浪尖;

Where was heard the mingled measure/From the fountain and the caves. = Where the mingled measure was heard/From the fountain and the caves. 在这里可听到美妙音乐,飞泉响洞窟应合奏和鸣。

* mingled measure 合奏和鸣的音乐

10. It was a miracle of rare device,/A sunny pleasure dome with caves of ice! 巧设计夺天工奇迹罕见,欢乐宫冰洞寒阳光灿烂!

* it 指欢乐宫,后面有两个表语短语,一是 a miracle of rare device, 一是 a sunny pleasure dome with caves of ice,后一个实为前一个的诠释,何为罕见奇迹呢? 原来就是"宫里面冰洞寒不惧阳光"。

11. A damsel with a dulcimer/In a vision once I saw: = I once saw in a vision a damsel with a dulcimer: 我曾在幻觉中隐约看见,闺房中一少女怀抱弦琴:

It was an Abyssinian maid, 那是个阿比西尼亚姑娘,

And on her dulcimer she played, = And she played on her dulcimer, 她轻挥指弹奏那怀里弦琴,

Singing of Mount Abora. 边弹拨边吟唱阿波拉山。

* 这是个状语分词短语,作补充说明。

12. Could I revive within me/Her symphony and song, = If I could revive her symphony and song within me, 若是我心里面能够忆起,她的歌她的曲倩影重现,

To such a deep delight 'twould win me, = It would win me to such a delight (= bring me such a deep delight) 必然会激起我身心狂喜。

* 注意上面的句子实际上是虚拟条件句,If I could ...是可以用 Could I ...表示的。

That with music loud and long,/I would build that dome in air, = That I would build that dome in air with music loud and long, 我会用钧天乐悠扬嘹亮,在空中建那座幻境宫殿,

That sunny dome! those caves of ice! 就那座阳光宫! 就那些冰洞重重!

* 这一行诗是两个名词性词组,作 that dome in air 的同位语,强化说明宫殿的特点。

13. And all who heard should see them there,/And all should cry, Beware! Beware! 闻乐者全能见空中宫殿,所有人都会喊:当心! 当心!

His flashing eyes, his floating hair!　他眼如电发飘飞似魔似癫！
Weave a circle round him thrice,　我们要围着他环绕三圈，
And close your eyes with holy dread,　要合双眼避神圣心怀敬畏，
＊Weave .../And close ... dread, 是两个并列的祈使句，是"我们"自己的愿望。
For he on honeydew hath fed, ＝ For he hath <u>fed on</u> honeydew,　因为他已餐食甘露甜蜜，
And drunk the milk of Paradise.　因为他已畅饮天堂乳汁。

参考译文——姚绍德

忽必烈汗

忽必烈在上都颁下圣旨：
建一座欢乐宫宏伟壮丽。
有圣河阿尔夫宫旁流过，
层层洞重重穴穿越无数，
入大海无阳光沉暗迷蒙。
大皇宫塔楼笙宫墙环绕，
乐逍遥废去了五哩良园。
有多少靓丽园曲水流转，
有多少芬芳树花开万朵；
花园内参天树山岳同古，
林木间怀抱着阳光草地。

但是那深裂隙惊险斜插，
穿青山过林莽雪松如盖。
好一个蛮荒地亦神亦魅，
恰似那残月夜怨女隐现，
哀哀哭切切悲竟为情鬼！
有激流如汤沸喧腾裂谷，
仿佛是大地在急促喘息，
时时有大喷泉喷射而出：
爆发间那喷泉时断时续，
巨石块跳跃起如霌反弹，
又好比连枷下脱壳谷粒：
一阵阵乱石飞如狂似舞，
这圣河如疯马常跃地面。
蜿蜒流五英里如入迷津，
穿山林越深谷奔腾起伏，
钻入那不见底连环洞窟，
咆哮着跃入海一片死寂：
喧嚣过忽听得祖先示警，

忽必烈知悉了战争将临！
欢乐宫乐逍遥浮华幻影，
漂浮在圣河里波峰浪尖；
在这里可听到美妙音乐，
飞泉响洞窟应合奏和鸣。
巧设计夺天工奇迹罕见，
欢乐宫冰洞寒阳光灿烂！

我曾在幻觉中隐约看见，
闺房中一少女怀抱弦琴：
那是个阿比西尼亚姑娘，
她轻挥指弹奏那怀里弦琴，
边弹拨边吟唱阿波拉山。
若是我心里面能够忆起，
她的歌她的曲倩影重现，
必然会激起我身心狂喜，
我会用钧天乐悠扬嘹亮，
在空中建那座幻境宫殿，
就那座阳光宫！
就那些冰寒洞！
闻乐者全能见空中宫殿，
所有人都会喊"当心！当心！"
他眼如电发飘飞似魔似癫！
我们要围着他环绕三圈，
合双眼避神圣心怀敬畏，
因为他已餐食甘露甜蜜，
因为他已畅饮天堂乳汁。

格律和韵律分析

本诗共 3 节，第一节 11 行，第二节 25 行，第三节 18 行，共 54 行，格律和韵律都很自由，下面仅就第一节进行分析，可见一斑。

In ˈXa/nadu/did ˈKu/bla ˈKhan	a
A ˈstate/ly ˈplea/sure ˈdome/dec'ree：	b
Where ˈAlph/, the ˈsa/cred ˈri/ver, ˈran	a
Through ˈca/verns ˈmea/sureless/to ˈman	a
ˈDown to/a ˈsun/less ˈsea.	b
So ˈtwice/five ˈmiles/of ˈfer/tile ˈground	c
With ˈwalls/and ˈto/wers ˈwere/ˈgirdled ˈround：	c
And ˈthere/were ˈgar/dens ˈbright/with ˈsi/nuous ˈrills	d
Where ˈblo/ssomed ˈma/ny an ˈin/cense-ˈbea/ring ˈtree；	b
And ˈhere/were ˈfo/rests ˈan/cient as/the ˈhills,	d

En·fol/ding ·sun/ny ·spots/of ·gree/nery.　　　　　　　　　　　　b

此节共 11 行,为 44443445555 音步,共 47 个音步,其中 42 个音步为抑扬格。后面诗节的行数不同,每行也以 4 音步和 5 音步为多。根据第一节分析,绝大多数音步为抑扬格则可以肯定。第一节的韵律是 abaabccdbdb。不过后面两节行数不同,韵律规则自然也不同了。所以,总的来讲,这是一首格律和韵律都不严格,比较自由的诗。

主要内容归纳和总结

1. 科勒律治出身于英格兰德文郡的一个牧师家庭,曾在剑桥大学读过书。他有激进的理想主义,曾想与骚塞一起到美国去建立乌托邦社会,未获成功。他与华兹华斯和骚塞曾居住在英格兰大湖风景区,互唱互和,流连忘返,作品不断,形成了文学史上著名的"湖滨派诗人",与华兹华斯共同完成的《抒情歌谣集》,成了英国文学史上浪漫主义时期开始的里程碑。

   科勒律治认为艺术是唯一能永远揭示现实本质的形式,诗人应当表现无意识中感受到的微妙启示,而不牺牲自己的活跃思维和灵感。他的神祇诗常表现陷入魔法的迷茫、吸食鸦片后的梦魇之类的神秘想象,他的对话诗多表现归家的渴望、对孩儿的思念以及童年的回顾等芸芸众生的情感。诗人精于推敲文字,主张诗歌应通过美给人以愉悦。他对华兹华斯"纯金的语言""深邃的思想"极为赞赏,但不同意他"诗歌语言与普通百姓的生活语言没什么两样"的观点。

2. 柯勒律治的主要作品:

   a. 神祇类诗作,其中有他的三大杰作

   《古舟子咏》*The Rime of the Ancient Mariner*(1798)

   《克里斯特贝尔》*Christabel*(1797~1798)

   《忽必烈汗》*Kubla Khan*(1797~1798)

   b. 对话类诗作

   《子夜霜寒》*Frost at Midnight*(1797~1798)

   《沮丧:一段颂歌》*Dejection:An Ode*

   《这酸橙树荫——我的监狱》*This Lime — Tree Bower My Prison*(1797~1798)

   《夜莺》*The Nightingale*(1797~1798)

   c. 文学批评论著

   《文学传记》*Biographia Literaria*(1817)

   d. 悲剧剧本

   《悔恨》*Remorse*(1813)

重要信息句子

1. Art is the only permanent revelation of the nature of reality.　艺术是现实本质的唯一永恒的启示。

2. The true end of poetry is to give pleasure through the medium of beauty.　诗歌的真正目的是通过美的媒介给人以快乐。

3. The demonic groups include his three masterpieces:*The Rime of the Ancient Mariner*;*Christabel*;*Kubla Khan*. Among the conversational group, "Frost at Midnight" is the most important.

4. Coleridge is one of the first critics to give close critical attention to language.

Ⅳ．乔治·戈登·拜伦 George Gordon Byron（1788～1824）

词语解释和难句分析

1. be a wild but irresponsible profligate　是一个无法无天、不负责任的浪荡子

   passionate temper　激烈的情绪

   to inherit the title of a baron and a large estate.　继承爵位的头衔和大笔财产

   be born lame　生而跛足

   be good at sports　擅长体育运动

   be affected by his club-foot　受到他跛足的影响/羁绊

   to make him sore and angry　使他感到痛苦和恼火

   a very harsh review of this work in *Edinburgh Review*　在《爱丁堡评论》上对这部作品进行了非常苛刻的批评

   to prompt a satirical reply from Byron in heroic couplets　激起/促使拜伦以英雄偶句体做了讽刺性的回答

   to lash the conservative schools of contemporary poetry　鞭挞/抨击当时诗界的保守派

   to show his lasting contempt for what he considered the commonplace and vulgarity of the "Lake Poets"　对他所认为的"湖滨派诗人"之平庸寻常表示了长久的蔑视

2. to take his seat in the House of Lords　在上议院当了议员

   to make vehement speeches　发表激烈讲话

   the first two cantos of *Childe Harold's Pilgrimage*　《恰尔德·哈罗尔德》的头两章

   to narrate his travels in Europe　记述他在欧洲的旅游行记

   long verse tales　长篇叙事诗

   rumors about his incestuous relationship with his half-sister　与他同父异母的妹妹关系过分密切/有乱伦关系的谣言

   doubts about his sanity　对他精神正常的怀疑，怀疑他是否精神健全

   be abused and decried　受到毁谤和谴责，被辱骂和诋毁

3. to establish residence in Venice　定居在威尼斯

   verse drama　诗剧

   in close touch with the Italian patriots　与意大利爱国者有密切联系

   an uprising against the Austrian rule　一场反抗奥地利统治的起义/叛乱

   mock epic　（喜剧）讽刺史诗

4. at the news of the Greek revolt against the Turks　听到希腊反叛土耳其的消息

   to give the insurgent Greeks financial help　为希腊的起义者提供财政援助

   to plunge himself into the struggle for the national independence of Greece　他投身于/亲身参加希腊的民族独立斗争

   to make him commander in chief of their forces　让他当了他们部队的总司令

to mourn over his death   哀悼他的逝世

5. be more or less surrogates of himself   多少带有他自己的影子/有点像他的替身

a gloomy, passionate young wanderer   一位情感丰富的、忧郁的流浪青年

to teem with all kinds of recognizable features of Romantic poetry   充满了各种可以识别的浪漫主义诗歌的特点

outcast figure   被抛弃的/被逐出的/无家可归的人

preoccupation with the remote and savage   对偏远和蛮荒的专注、迷恋

many vivid and exotic descriptive passage on...   许多生动的、具有异国情调的针对……的描写段落

to lament over the fallen Greece   哀悼沦陷了的希腊

to express his ardent wish   表达他的热切的愿望/真诚的祝愿

to glorify the French Revolution and condemn the despotic Napoleon period   高度赞扬法国大革命,抨击暴虐的拿破仑统治时期

to appeal for the liberty of the oppressed nations   呼吁被压迫民族的自由解放

to exalt the great fighters for freedom   颂扬伟大的自由战士

6. be based on a traditional Spanish legend of a great lover and seducer of women   (长诗的)根据是西班牙一个情场高手勾引妇女的传统传奇故事

in the conventional sense   根据传统观念

to invest in Juan the moral positives   花费不少笔墨描写唐璜的正面道德

all the threads of the story woven around him   围绕他编织的所有的线索

to present a panoramic view of different types of society   对各种类型的社会生活进行了全景式的描绘

7. The opening canto of *Don Juan* is a brilliant, vivid analysis of romantic passion and of the youthful ardor that over-idealizes it.   《唐璜》开篇第一章就对浪漫激情和对这种激情过分理想化的青春情欲进行了精彩的、栩栩如生的分析。

8. to describe the siege of Ismail   描写(俄国)对(土耳其)伊兹梅尔城的围攻

the barbarity and blood-lust of war   战争的野蛮、嗜血

the incompetence of the generals   将军们的不称职

the rapaciousness of the rulers who urge the war   发动战争的统治者的贪婪掠夺

9. In the last cantos of the work, Byron's indignation at the self-serving cant of the English aristocracy is supported by a subtle social awareness and a narrative skill which verges on the verse novel.   在这本诗作的最后几章中,拜伦对英国贵族阶级为自己谋私利的伪善言辞的愤慨,由于他敏锐的社会觉悟和近乎写诗体小说的叙述技巧而得到了充分表现。

10. The unifying principle in *Don Juan* is the basic ironic theme of appearance and reality, i.e. what things seem to be and what they actually are.   《唐璜》中统一的原则就是关于事实表象和真实,也即事物似乎是与真实是之关系的基本讽刺主题。

11. And the diverse materials and the clash of emotions gathered in the poem are harmonized by Byron's insight into the difference between life's appearance and its actuality.   该诗所涵盖的各种形式的素材和情感冲突都因拜伦对生活表象和真实有深刻的洞察力和区别力而得到了和谐的统一。

12. With immense superiority in his passion and powers, this Byronic hero would carry on his shoulders the burden of righting all the wrongs in a corrupt society, and would rise single-handedly against any kind of tyrannical rules either in government, in religion, or in moral principles with unconquerable wills and inexhaustible energies.   由于具有巨大的情感和能力的优势,拜伦式英雄会以不可征服的意志和

永远旺盛的精力承担腐朽社会里除暴安良、匡扶正义的重担,会单人独马地起来反抗任何暴政的统治,不论是政府的、宗教的,还是道德原则的。

13. rebellious individuals 叛逆的个人

outgrown social system and conventions 过时的腐朽社会制度

in different guises 以不同的服装/外表/形象

be modeled on the life and personality of Byron himself 模仿拜伦本人的生活和个性

14. be criticized by critics on moral grounds 受到批评家从道德上的抨击

his persistent attacks on "cant political, religious, and moral" 他对政治、宗教和道德上的说假话/伪善言辞所做的持续抨击

the novelty of his oriented scenery 他描写的东方景象的新奇

to use the diction of freedom, copiousness and vigor 措辞自由,有思想、有活力

to bring vivid objects before the reader 把描写的事物生动地展现在读者面前

15. Byron's poetry is like an oratory which hurries the hearers without applause. 拜伦的诗就是没有掌声的慷慨激昂的演说,使听者闻之鼓舞奋进。

16. The glowing imagination of the poet rises and sinks with the tones of his enthusiasm, roughing into argument, or softening into the melody feeling and sentiments. 诗人栩栩如生的想象力随着他热烈的心绪状态而有强弱之别,有时粗加工形成论点,有时精雕细刻成情感的旋律。

17. It was perfected in *Don Juan* in which the convention flows with ease and naturalness, as Colonel Stanhope described:"a stream sometimes smooth; sometimes rapid and sometimes rushing down in cataracts — a mixture of philosophy and slang — of everything." 在《唐璜》中,它(一节八行的意大利讽刺英雄体)得到了完善,这种传统的艺术手法得到潇洒自然的运用,就如克勒尼尔·斯坦和普所描述的:"一条河流,有时平缓畅流,有时迅疾奔流,有时是汇聚一切的大瀑布——哲学和俚语的混合——倾泻而下。"

18. be regarded as the perverted man 被当作性变态者/走上邪路的人

be hailed as the champion of liberty, poet of the people 被热烈赞颂为自由捍卫者,人民诗人

be refused to be buried with his poetic peers 被拒绝与他同等才能的诗人埋葬在一起

to set up a white marble-floor memorial to Lord Byron 为拜伦爵士竖立一块白色大理石的纪念碑

拜伦作品选读

1. 卢德工人之歌 *Song for the Luddites*

词语解释和难句分析

1. As the Liberty lads o'er the sea/Bought their freedom, and cheaply, with blood, 如同大洋彼岸的自由之子(指美国的独立革命)/用鲜血廉价地换得自由,

2. And down with all kings but King Ludd! 打倒一切国王,只要卢德王!

* King Ludd 指 Ned Ludd, 一位莱赛斯特郡(Leicestershire)的工人,据说他 1779 年首先砸碎了工厂里的两台织袜机,从此后捣毁机器、抗议失业的工人就被称为卢德分子或卢德主义者。

3. When the web we weave is complete,/And the shuttle (is) exchanged for the sword, 当我们织的布完工,/把梭子换成利剑,

4. We will fling the winding sheet/O'er the despot at our feet,/And dye it deep in the gore（=blood）he has pour'd. 我们就扔下这裹尸布/盖住这脚下的暴君,/被暴君的血泊浸透（=把裹尸布深深地浸染在暴君的血泊里）。

　＊he has pour'd（=poured）是省略了关系代词 which 的定语从句,修饰 gore。

　＊织的布就用作暴君裹尸布。暴君指的是机器,当时的工人觉悟只能达到这个水平,认为机器是造成他们失业的元凶。

5. Though black as his heart its hue = Though its hue（is）black as his heart /Since his veins are corrupted to mud, 虽然他的污血黑如他的心脏,/因为他血脉已腐败如泥,

6. Yet this is the dew/Which the tree shall renew/Of liberty, planted by Ludd! = Yet this is the dew which shall renew the tree of liberty planted by Ludd! 但就是这血水好比露珠,/可浇灌卢德种下的自由之树,使它青春永驻!

参考译文——姚绍德

卢德工人之歌

海外的自由之子,
已用鲜血"廉价"地购得自由,
而小伙子们,我们呢?
一生不得自由,死也要战斗!
除了卢德王,打倒一切王侯!

当我们把布织好,
梭子换成利剑的时候,
我们将扔下这裹尸布,
盖住脚下的暴君,
在他的鲜血里浸透。

虽然他的血如心脏般黑透,
他的血管似污泥般腐朽;
但这血水却好比露水,
将浇灌我们的自由之树——
为卢德所植,象征自由!

格律和韵律分析

该诗没有固定格律,可以看作是自由体,韵律为 abaab。

2. 希腊诸岛 *The Isles of Greece* 选自《唐璜》第三章

词语解释和难句分析

1. an aristocratic libertine, amiable and charming to ladies 一个讨人喜欢、令女人着迷的贵族风流哥儿

be tossed into the sea and finally cast on the seashore 被抛进大海,最后又被冲上海岸

to die of a broken heart 死于心脏病发作

be sold as a slave to Constantinople 被作为奴隶卖到君士坦丁堡

to take fancy to sb. 爱上某人,对某人喜欢起来

to besiege the town Ismail 围攻伊兹梅尔城

to send news to 送消息给……

be favored by Empress Catherine 得到俄国女皇凯瑟琳(叶卡捷琳娜)的喜爱/支持/帮助

by contrasting the freedom of ancient Greece and the present enslavement 通过对古希腊的自由与现在被奴役的对比……

to appeal to people to struggle for liberty 呼吁人民为自由而斗争

1

2. Where burning Sappho loved and sung, 激情似火的萨福曾在此唱过恋歌,

* Sappho 是古希腊著名女诗人,擅长写情诗和抒情诗。

Where grew the arts of war and peace, = Where the arts of war and peace grew, 在此曾上演过战争与和平的艺术,

Where Delos rose, and Phoebus sprung! 狄洛斯岛在此升起,阿波罗在岛上诞生!

* Phoebus = Phoebus Apollo 太阳神

2

3. The Scian and the Teian muse,/The hero's harp, the lover's lute, 凯俄斯和忒俄斯的诗才,/英雄的竖琴,情人的长笛,

* Scian = of Scio/Chios, 希腊诸岛中的一个岛,是古希腊大诗人荷马(Homer)的出生地,他的《奥德赛》和《伊利亚特》都是英雄史诗,而英雄史诗多用大型乐器竖琴伴奏演唱;而 Teian = of Teos, 为爱琴海中的一个岛,传为古希腊诗人阿那克里翁(Anacreon)的故乡,其作品多为抒情诗和情诗,常用小型乐器如长笛、琵琶伴奏演唱。因为上述原因,故有"凯俄斯和忒俄斯的诗才,英雄的竖琴,情人的长笛"之说。另外,凯俄斯岛也盛产葡萄、橙子,当然还有葡萄酒。

4. Have found the fame your shores refuse:/Their place of birth alone is mute/to sounds... = The "Muse" have found (that) your shore refuse the fame (and) their place of birth alone is mute to sounds (= the fame)... 他们的声名已在你们的海岸绝响,在诗人的故土也早已默默无闻……

5. ... which echo further west / Than your sires' "Islands of the Blest". 而在遥远的西方却回声响亮,/远超过祖先的"乐岛仙乡"。

3

6. look on 旁观,侧视,俯视

Marathon 马拉松,地名,公元前490年古希腊人打败波斯人的地方。

7. And musing there an hour alone,/I dream'd that Greece might still be free; 在那里我独自沉思,/梦想良久,希腊依然还会是自由的地方;

* musing. . . 引导的分词短语作状语,它的逻辑主语就是后面主句的主语"I"。

8. For standing on the Persians' grave,/I could not <u>deem</u> myself a slave. 因为脚踏着波斯人的坟墓,/我无法设想自己会是奴隶。

4

9. sate [古] = sat 坐

rocky brow = the edge of cliff 悬崖边缘,崖顶

look over 俯视

sea-born = rising out of the sea 海生的,突起于海面的

10. He counted them <u>at break of day</u> —/And, when the sun set, where were they? 黎明时分,他还在沙场点兵,/而夕阳西下,他们却在何方?

5

11. And where are they? and where art thou,/My country? 他们现在在哪里? 我的祖国啊,/你现在又在哪里?

* 从上句的过去时态到此句的现在时态,从历史上的他们转到现在的你——祖国,从历史上的威风八面、打败波斯,到今日的沦为土耳其统治下的亡国奴,作者把读者的注意力吸引到现实中来。

12. And must thy lyre, so long divine,/Degenerate into hands like mine? = Must thy lyre, being divine so long, degenerate into hands like mine? 你的弦琴久已不同凡响,/必得败落到我这样的凡夫手中?

6

13. in the dearth of fame 缺少英雄和壮举的平庸时代

fettered race 披枷带锁/被奴役的种族/民族

suffuse v. overspread with colour; redden 因羞愧等原因而脸色变红

14. 'T is something, in the dearth of fame,/Though link'd among a fettered race,/To feel at least a patriot's shame,/Even as I sing, suffuse my face. = Thou linked among a fettered race in the dearth of fame, it is something to feel at least a patriot's shame and suffuse my face even as I sing. 在一个缺少英雄的平庸时代,/虽置身于一个镣铐锁身的被奴役的民族,/至少感到爱国者的羞耻,/即使唱歌也满脸通红,那也算是有价值。

15. For what is left the poet here? = For what is the poet left here? 诗人留在这里是为什么?

For Greeks a blush — for Greeks a tear. = A blush for Greeks — a tear for Greeks. 为希腊人羞愧,为希腊人流泪。

7

16. days more blest 备受神保佑赐福的日子(比喻辉煌往昔)

<u>render back</u> from out they breast 从你的怀抱中归还,交回……

* out 是介词,常与 from 连用。

Thermopylae 德摩比利,又叫温泉关,希腊中部和北部之间的一道关隘。公元前 480 年,列昂尼达(Leonidas)率 300 名斯巴达勇士,在此与波斯军展开一场殊死战斗,最后全部壮烈牺牲。

17. Must we weep o'er days more blest? /Must we but blush? — Our fathers bled. 难道我们只能为辉煌往昔流泪? /难道我们只能脸红羞愧而祖先抛洒热血?

18. Earth! Render back from out thy breast/Aremnant of our Spartan dead! /Of the three hundred grant but three(= but [= only] three of the three hundred),/To make a new Thermopylae! 大地啊! 请从你的怀抱中/送回几个阵亡的斯巴达勇士,/只需个零头,三百个中的三个,/就可重振当年温泉关的雄威!

8

19. And answer, "Let one living head,/But one arise, — we come, we come!" 回答说:"只要有一个活着的人,/挺身而起,——我们就来,就来!"

   * head 指"人"; but = only。

9

20. to strike other chords 另奏其他的乐曲,换一个曲调

21. to fill high the cup with Samian wine (with wine of Samos) 斟满萨莫斯葡萄酒

22. to leave the battles to the Turkish hordes 把战争留给土耳其蛮子/马背上的土耳其人去打吧

   to shed the blood of Scio's vine 让凯俄斯葡萄去流血吧

23. the ignoble call = the dishonourable call 不光彩的号召/召唤

   Bacchanal n. 酒神的信徒,酒徒;adj. of Bocchus 巴克斯的,酒神的(源自希腊神话)

   Hark! Rising to the ignoble call —/How answers each bold Bacchanal! = Listen! How each bold Bacchanal, rising, answers to the ignoble call! 听呵! 每个勇敢的酒徒——/多么踊跃地响应这不光彩的召唤!

10

24. as yet = so far = up to now 到现在为止

   Pyrrhic dance 古希腊模拟战斗的一种战舞,舞者身披盔甲,舞步轻快,为伊庇鲁斯(Epirus)国王皮瑞克斯(Pyrrhicus)所创。

   Pyrrhic phalanx 古希腊伊庇鲁斯国王皮瑞克斯所创的战阵

25. Cadmus 卡德莫斯,腓尼基国王阿格诺尔的儿子,底比斯城邦的缔造者,据说是他把腓尼基字母引进希腊,创造了希腊字母。

26. to mean sth./sb. for... 打算把某物作……用,想要让某人做……

27. Of two such lessons, why forget/The noblier and the manlier one? = Why (do you) forget the noblier and the manlier one or two such lessons? 两门功课中,为什么忘掉/更高贵、更豪迈威武的一种?

   You have the letters Cadmus gave — 你们还有卡德莫斯带来的文字——

   Think ye he meant them for a slave? = Do you think he meant them for a slave? 难道你们认为他是要教亡国奴文化?

11

28. Fill high the bowl with Samian wine!/We will not think of themes like these! 斟满一杯萨默斯美酒!/我们不再想这些话题!

29. It made Anacreon's song divine:/He served — but served Polycrates —/A tyrant; but our masters then/Were still, at least, our countrymen. 美酒使安纳克里翁诗歌神圣:/他也曾侍奉过暴君——/普利克勒提;但当时的主人/毕竟还是我们的同胞。

   * Polycrates 是萨默斯岛的独裁君主,是抒情诗人安纳克里翁的好友,波斯进攻该岛时,诗人曾在普利克勒提身边侍候。

12

30. Chersonese 克森尼斯,现在的加里波利(Gallipoli)半岛,在达达尼尔海峡北部。

   Miltiades 米尔达迪斯,克森尼斯的暴君,在马拉松战役中率领希腊军打败波斯军的统帅。

31. Oh! That the present hour would lend/Another despot of the kind!/Such chains as his were sure to bind. 呵! 但愿今日之情势再天降一个/同样独裁的专制雄主!/用他那样的铁锁把我们捆得牢不可破。

   * That... 是由连词引导的一个表示愿望、感叹的从句,而主句常会略去,这就是一例。

13

32. Suli 苏里,希腊地名,伊庇鲁斯(Epirus)山区的一个山口要隘。拜伦曾在此招募 500 名苏里壮士,参加独立军,并自己支付军饷。

Parga 巴加,苏里地区的一座海滨小城。

Doric = of Dorians,多利安人的。多利安人为希腊人的一支,建立了斯巴达城邦,故又称斯巴达人。

Heracleidan = of Hercules/Heracles,赫丘利的或赫拉克利斯的。赫丘利或赫拉克利斯是希腊神话中的大力神。

33. On Suli's rock, and Parga's shore,/Exists the remnant of a line/Such as the Doric mothers bore; = Such the remnant of a line as the Doric mothers bore exists on Suli's rock, and Parga's shore. 在苏里的山岩,在巴加的海岸,/尚有一个种族的后裔存留,/像是斯巴达母亲的儿孙。

34. And there, perhaps, some seed is sown,/The Heracleidan blood might own. = And there some seed is perhaps sown and might own the Heraleidan blood. 前辈们可能在那里播了种,/继承了赫拉克利斯的血统。

14

35. the Franks 法兰克人,一般指法国人或拉丁人,此处泛指西欧国家的人。

Latin fraud 拉丁国家的诈骗,拉丁国家指西欧国家。

Trust not for freedom to the Franks, 争取自由,别信任西欧人,

They have a king who buys and sells; 他们有一个精于买卖的国王;

36. In native swords, and native ranks, 本国的军队,本国的刀枪,

The only hope of courage dwells; 才是可以寄托的唯一希望;

* to dwell in 在于,居住

37. But Turkish force, and Latin fraud,/Would break your shield, however broad (it is). 土耳其的武力,拉丁人的诈骗,/无论多宽的盾牌都会被砸碎。

15

38. But gazing on each glowing maid, 但凝望着一个个光彩照人的少女,

My own the burning tear-drop laves, = the burning tear-drop laves my own (= my own eyes), 想起来就热泪盈眶,

To think such breasts must suckle slaves. 这样的乳房还得哺育奴隶。

16

39. Place me on Sunium's marbled steep,/Where nothing, save (= except) the waves and I,/May hear our mutual murmurs sweep; 让我登上苏尼姆的大理石悬崖,/别无所有,只有海浪和我,/倾听彼此的低语掠过;

40. There, swan-like, let me sing and die:/A land of slaves shall ne'er (= never) be mine—/ Dash down yon cup of Samian wine! 我要像天鹅唱着歌死亡:/奴隶的国家绝不能是我的祖国——/把那杯萨莫斯的美酒摔掉!

名家译文——查良铮

希腊群岛

1

希腊群岛呵,美丽的希腊群岛!

热情的莎弗在扎里唱过恋歌，
在这里，战争与和平的艺术并兴，
狄洛斯崛起，阿波罗跃出海波！
永恒的夏天还把海岛镀成金，
可是除了太阳，一切已经消沉。

2

开奥的缪斯和蒂奥的缪斯，
那英雄的竖琴，恋人的琵琶，
原在你的岸上博得了声誉，
而今在这发源地反倒喑哑——
呵，那歌声已远远向西流传，
远超过你祖先的海岛乐园。

3

起伏的山峦望着马拉松，
马拉松望着茫茫的海波：
我独自在那里冥想了一时，
梦见希腊仍旧自由而快乐；
因为当我在波斯墓上站立，
我不能想象自己是个奴隶。

4

一个国王高高坐在山头上，
瞭望着萨拉密挺立于海外，
千万只战船停靠在山脚下，
还有多少队伍——全由他统率！
他在天亮时把他们数了数，
但在日落时他们到了何处？

5

呵，他们而今安在？还有你呢，
我的祖国？在无声的土地上
英雄的颂歌如今喑哑了，
那英雄的心也不再激荡！
难道你一向庄严的竖琴
竟至沦落到我的手里弹弄？

6

也好，置身在奴隶民族里，
尽管荣誉都已在沦丧中，
至少，一个爱国志士的忧思，
还使我在作歌时感到脸红；
因为，诗人在这儿有什么能为？
为希腊人含羞，对希腊国落泪。

7

我们难道只对好日子哭泣
和惭愧？——我们的祖先却流血。

大地呵！把斯巴达人的遗骨
从你的怀抱里送回来一些！
哪怕给我们三百个勇士的三个，
让色茅霹雳的决死战复活！

8

怎么还是无声？一切都沉寂？
不是的！你听那古代的英魂
正像远方的瀑布一样喧哗，
他们回答："只要有一个活人
登高一呼，我们就来，就来！"
噫！倒只是活人不理不睬。

9

算了，算了：试试别的调子；
斟满一杯萨摩斯的美酒！
把战争留给土耳其野番吧，
让开奥的葡萄的血汁倾流！
听呵，每一个酒鬼多么踊跃
响应这一个不荣誉的号召！

10

你们还保有庇瑞克的舞步
但庇瑞克的方阵哪里去了？
这是两课：为什么你们偏把
那高尚而刚强的一课忘掉？
凯德谟斯给你们造了字体——
难道他是为了传授给奴隶？

11

斟满一杯萨摩斯的美酒！
让我们且抛开这样的话题！
这美酒曾使阿纳克瑞翁
发为神圣的歌；是的，他屈于
波里克瑞底斯，一个暴君，
但这暴君至少是我们国人。

12

克索尼萨斯的一个暴君
是自由最忠勇的朋友，
那暴君是密尔蒂阿底斯！
呵，但愿我们现在能够有
一个暴君和他一样精明，
他会团结我们不受人欺凌！

13

斟满一杯萨摩斯的美酒！
在苏里的山中，巴加的岸上，

住着一族人的勇敢的子孙，
不愧是到瑞斯的母亲所养，
在这里，也许种子已经播散，
是赫拉克勒斯血统的真传。

14

别相信西方人会带来自由，
他们有一个作买卖的国王；
本土的利剑，本土的士兵，
是冲锋陷阵的唯一希望；
但在御敌时，拉丁的欺骗
比土耳其的武力还更危险。

15

呵，斟满一杯萨摩斯的美酒！
树荫下舞蹈着我们的姑娘，
我看见她们的黑眼睛闪耀；
但是，望着每个鲜艳的女郎，
我的眼就为火热的泪所迷：
这乳房难道也要哺育奴隶？

16

让我登上苏尼阿的悬崖，
在那里，将只有我和那海浪
可以听见彼此的低语漂送，
让我像天鹅一样歌尽而亡；
我不要奴隶的国度属于我——
干脆把那萨摩斯酒杯打破！

格律和韵律分析

细检全诗，各诗节每行都是 4 音步，韵律也都是 ababcc，先列出头两节做具体分析：

1

The ˈisles/of ˈGreece,/ the ˈisles/of ˈGreece!	a
Where ˈbur/ning ˈSa/ppho ˈloved/and ˈsung,	b
Where ˈgrew/the ˈarts/of ˈwar/and ˈpeace,	a
Where ˈDe/los ˈrose,/ and ˈPhoe/bus ˈsprung!	b
Eˈter/nal ˈsu/mmer ˈgilds/them ˈyet,	c
But ˈall,/ exˈcept/their ˈsun,/ is ˈset.	c

2

The ˈSci/ean ˈand/the ˈTei/an ˈmuse,	a
The ˈhe/ro's ˈharp,/ the ˈlo/ver's ˈlute.	b
Have ˈfound/the ˈfame/your ˈshores/reˈfuse:	a
Their ˈplace/of ˈbirth/aˈlone/is ˈmute	b

To 'sounds/which 'e/cho 'fur/ther 'west　　　　　　　　c

　　Than 'your/sires " 'Is/lands of/the 'Blest".　　　　　　c

很明显,绝大多数音步都是抑扬格,因此该诗格律就是四步抑扬格。

主要内容归纳和总结

1. 拜伦出生于英格兰一个古老的贵族家庭,母亲是苏格兰人。他三岁时父亲去世,他 10 岁时继承遗产和爵位,长期随母亲居住在苏格兰,忍受孤贫。他后来在哈罗公学和剑桥大学读书。他天生跛足,却长于体育,但残疾还是带给他一生的烦恼。1811 年,凭借贵族出身,他在参议院谋得议员席位,常发表演说抨击英国政府,同情穷苦人民。他凭借早期的长篇叙事诗《恰尔德·哈罗尔德》(*Childe Harold's Pilgrimage*)一夜成名。

　　拜伦爱憎分明,具有强烈的正义感。他支持欧洲国家的民族独立事业。他游历意大利,与烧炭党的爱国者过从甚密,支持他们反对奥地利统治的起义。他与希腊人民休戚与共,直接投身希腊人民反抗土耳其殖民统治的武装斗争,甚至担任武装部队的司令。他盛赞法国大革命,同时又谴责专制的拿破仑统治。这种火热的情感都反映到他的诗作中,他笔下流淌的都是对人民的同情、对暴君的厌恶和对自由的向往。他的一大贡献还在于他塑造了高傲、神秘、叛逆并带有贵族血统的"拜伦式英雄"(Byronic hero)。

　　拜伦的诗尽管被评论家们说成道德败坏,却在国内外人民中享有盛誉,他在欧洲大陆被冠以"自由的捍卫者"(the champion of liberty)"人民诗人"的美名。由于英国人的偏见,他死后未能在威斯敏斯特大教堂"诗人之角"(Poets' Corner)有一席之地,直到 1969 年,人们重新审视他的伟大,才在那里给他竖起了汉白玉墓碑。他一泻千里的诗才,如泉喷涌的作品,平易近人、优雅流畅的诗句,美轮美奂的东方奇景和拜伦式的英雄形象给读者和后世文学家留下了深刻印象和巨大影响。

2. 拜伦的主要作品:

a. 诗歌

《逃亡者片段》*Fugitive Pieces*（1806）

《悠闲时刻》*Hours of Idleness*（1807）

《英格兰人和苏格兰评论家》*English Bards and Scotch Reviewers*（1809）

《恰尔德·哈罗尔德》*Childe Harold's Pilgrimage*（1812 第一、二章,1816 第三章,1818 第四章与尾声）

《齐伦的囚犯》*The Prizoner of Chillon*（1816）

《别波》*Beppo*（1818）

《唐璜》*Don Juan*（1819～1824）

《审判的幻影》*The Vision of Judgment*（1821）

《岛》*The Island*（1821）

《东方故事集》*Oriented Tales*

b. 诗剧

《曼弗雷德》*Manfred*（1817）

《两个弗斯卡利》*The Two Foscari*（1821）

《该隐》*Cain*（1821）

重要信息句子

1. On the whole, Byron's poetry is one of experience. His heroes are more or less surrogates of himself.

2. *Don Juan* is Byron's masterpiece, a great comic epic of the early 19th century. It is a poem based on a traditional Spanish legend of a great lover and seducer of women.

3. As a leading Romanticist, Byron's chief contribution is his creation of the "Byronic hero," a proud, mysterious rebel figure of noble origin.

V. 珀西·比希·雪莱 Percy Bysshe Shelley（1792～1822）

词语解释和难句分析

1. a conservative man of the landed gentry　一个保守的拥有土地的贵族绅士

   to fag for the bigger boys　听从高年级学生的使唤

   to wander about by himself　独自徘徊

   be more than once brought into trouble by the daring experiments he made.　由于做了许多冒险的实验，不止一次地遇到麻烦

   to write and circulate a pamphlet　写作和发行一本小册子

   The Necessity of Atheism　《无神论的必然性》

   to repudiate the existence of God　否认上帝的存在

   to result in his expulsion from the university　导致他被学校开除

   be disinherited by his headstrong father　被他刚愎自用的父亲剥夺了继承权

   to elope with sb.　与某人一起私奔

   to make an absurdity of selfishness and pride　做出了自私傲慢的荒唐言行

   to free him to legalized his union with Mary　使他获得解放，与玛丽的结合合法化

2. to leave him a bad repute as an "immoralist"　给他留下了一个"不道德"的坏名声

   sb.'s intense consciousness of his own loneliness in life　某人对自己的生活有强烈的孤独意识

   a passionate contemplation of the mystery of death　对死亡的神秘性潜心思考

   to start to develop his acquaintance with sb.　开始与某人不断交往

3. scores of magnificent lyrics　许多壮美的抒情诗

   be cremated on the seashore　在海岸上被火化

   be inscribed/engraved on his tombstone　……被镌刻在他的墓碑上，在他的墓碑上镌刻着……

   Cor Cordium = the heart of all hearts　万心之心

4. to grow up with violent revolutionary ideas　怀着狂热的革命理想长大的

   the existing despotic governments　现存的暴虐的政府

   to show a constant attention to　表现出对……的一贯注意和关心

   to dedicate all his life to　毕生都从事于……，为……奉献一生

   to take interest in social reforms　对社会改革情有独钟

   to loose the evil deep in man's heart　释放出藏于内心深处的邪恶

5. ...so he held a lifelong aversion to cruelty, injustice, authority, institutional religion and the formal shams of respectable society, condemning war, tyranny and exploitation.　所以他一生都深恶痛绝残忍、不公、权势、兼办所谓慈善机构的宗教以及体面社会传统礼仪的虚伪、罪恶的战争、暴政和剥削。

6. So he predicated that only through gradual and suitable reforms of the existing institutions would benevolence be universally established and none of the evils would survive in this "genuine society," where people could live together happily, freely and peacefully. 所以他断言:只有通过对现行社会制度进行渐进的、适当的改革,仁慈善行才会普遍确立,才不会让邪恶存在于这"真诚纯洁的社会",在这样的社会中,人们能够快乐、自由和和平地生活在一起。

    * that 引导的宾语从句是一个倒装句:Only... would benevolence be..., 其正常语序是 Benevolence would be... only...; 关系副词 where 引导的是一个定语从句,修饰 genuine society。

7. It is not only a war cry <u>calling upon</u> all working people to <u>rise up</u> against their political oppressors, but an address to them <u>pointing out</u> the intolerable injustice of economic exploitation. 它不仅是号召劳动人民起来反抗政治压迫者的战斗口号,而且是一次演讲,向他们指出难于容忍的不公正的经济剥削。

    * 分词短语 pointing out ... exploitation 是修饰 address 的定语。

8. war cry 战斗呐喊/口号

    rallying cry 战斗口号

    rallying song 战歌

    to create a Platonic symbol of the spirit of man, a force of beauty and regeneration 创造一种柏拉图式的人类精神的象征,一种美和再生的力量

    to pour forth an exultant song 唱起/传来欢乐的歌

    to suggest to the poet both celestial rapture and human limitation 向诗人表达对天国的痴迷和人生苦短的示意

    to become the embodiments of philistinism and reaction, the enemies of truth 成了平庸和反动的具体体现,成了真理的敌人

9. "Adonais" is an elegy for John Keats whose early death from tuberculosis Shelley believed had been hastened by hostile reviews. "阿多那伊斯"是一首悼念约翰·济慈的挽诗,他过早地死于肺结核,在雪莱看来,敌对的批评加速了他的死亡。

10. Best of all the well-known lyric pieces is Shelley's "Ode to the West Wind"; here Shelley's rhapsodic and declamatory tendencies find a subject perfectly suited to them. 在所有的抒情名诗中,最佳的作品要算雪莱的《西风颂》;在这首诗里,雪莱史诗般激昂慷慨的豪情找到了最合适的宣泄的主题。

    * suited to them = suited to the tendencies, 是过去分词短语作 subject 的定语。

11. <u>be fettered to</u> the humdrum realities of everyday 被束缚在单调乏味的日常现实中

    to have a logic of feeling 具有情感的逻辑

    to lead to a triumphant, hopeful and convincing conclusion 导致一种成功的、顺理成章和令人信服的结论

    be written in the *terza rima* form 以三行诗节、隔行押韵的形式进行创作

    to derive from his reading of Dante 源于他对但丁作品的阅读

12. The nervous thrill of Shelley's response to nature however is here transformed through the power of art and imagination into a longing to be united with a force at once physical and prophetic. 然而,雪莱回应大自然的神经兴奋在这里通过艺术和想象的力量转变为一种渴望,即渴望既与物质的力量也与预言的精神力量相融合。

13. Here is no conservative reassurance, no comfortable mysticism, but the primal amorality of nature itself, with its mad fury and its pagan ruthlessness. 诗里没有审慎的安慰,没有平静的人神灵交,只有大自然本身的无所谓道德是非的原始状态,再加上它疯狂的暴怒和未经教化的冷酷无情。

14. an invocation to a primitive deity 一种对原始神明的祈祷

    A plea to exalt him in its fury and to trumpet the radical prophecy of hope and rebirth 一种在狂暴中

颂扬神明、大声宣告希望和再生的激进的恳求

15. the champion of humanity 人文主义的捍卫者/勇士

be punished to be chained on Mount Caucasus 受到惩罚,被用铁链锁在高加索山上

to suffer the vulture's feeding on his liver 承受被兀鹫啄食他肝脏的痛苦

to reconcile with the tyrant Zeus 与暴君宙斯达成妥协

16. In truth, I was averse from a catastrophe so feeble as that reconciling the Champion with the Oppressor of Mankind. 事实上,我是反对让人类勇士与人类压迫者妥协退让这种软弱的灾难性结局的。

17. to transform the compromise into a liberation 把妥协让步转变为解放

be driven from the throne 被赶下宝座

be an exultant work in praise of humankind's potential 是一部赞颂人类潜力的欢欣鼓舞的作品

to have a reputation as a difficult poet 有深奥难懂的诗人之名

erudite, imagistically complex, full of classical and mythological allusions 博学多才,有意象主义情节,使用丰富的古典和神话典故

to abound in personification and metaphor and other figures of speech 具有丰富的拟人化、暗喻及其他种种修辞手法

雪莱作品选读

1. 致英格兰人 *A Song*: *Men of England*

词语解释和难句分析

1. Men of England, wherefore (*ad.* = for what) plough/For the lords who lay ye (= you) low? = Men of England, why do you plough for the lords who lay you low? 英格兰人,为什么为老爷们耕作,/他们可把你们踩在脚下?

2. Wherefore weave with toil and care/The rich robes your tyrants wear? = Why do you weave the rich robes (which) your tyrants wear with toil and care? 为什么为暴君们辛勤仔细地织造,/让他们穿上豪华的衣袍?

3. 第二诗节四行诗句实际上是一个完整的复合句,正常语序应为:Why (wherefore) do you feed and clothe and save those ungrateful drones from the cradle to the grave while they would drain your sweat — nay, drink your blood? 为何要供养那些忘恩负义的雄蜂,/让它们终生有吃、有穿、有保护,/而它们却榨干了你们的汗——/不,是喝干了你们的血?

   * 原句中 who would...blood? 是定语从句,修饰 drones。

4. 第三节语法结构简单明显,可直白地改写成普通英语:Why do bees of England forge/Many a weapon, chain, and scourge,/(so) That these stingless drones may spoil/The forced produce of your toil? 英格兰的工蜂呵,为何要锻造/许多武器,铁链和钢鞭,/让无刺的雄蜂也能用来逞凶,/劫夺你们被迫劳动的收获?

   * 蜜蜂分工蜂、雄蜂和蜂王,后两种蜂不采蜜,专门负责繁殖后代,工蜂负责干活、保卫;produce = product 产品。

5. Have ye leisure, comfort, calm,/Shelter, food, love's gentle balm? = Have you (Do you have) leisure,

comfort, calm, shelter, food, love's gentle balm? 你们可有安闲、舒适和宁静,/可有吃的、住的、和爱的抚慰?

6. Or what is it ye（＝you）buy so dear/With your pain and with your fear? ＝Or what have you bought so dear at the high price of your sufferings and anxieties? 否则,吃苦、受怕,付出了高昂的代价,/你们究竟得到了什么?

　　＊ ye buy so dear 是定语从句,修饰 it,相当于"你们买到的东西究竟是什么"用反意问句强化语气,表示"你们什么也没得到"。

7. 第五节是"你们播种,别人收获"这种句式的排比;第六节是"你们播种,别让暴君收获"这种句式的排比,都容易看懂。第六节的最后一句结构略有不同:Forge arms—in your defence to bear. ＝ Forge arms — to bear to defend yourself. 造出武器——用来保卫自己。

　　8. Shrink to your cellars, holes, and cells — 蜷缩进你们的地窖、斗室和小房——
In halls ye deck another dwells. ＝ another dwells in halls ye deck. 让别人住进你们装饰的厅堂。

　　＊ ye deck ＝ which you deck 是定语从句,修饰 halls。

9. Why（do you）shake the chains ye wrought（worked/made）? when（you）see/The steel ye tempered glance on ye. 为何要挣脱自铸的铁链? 亲眼见/自打的钢刀寒光照面!

　　＊ ye tempered ＝ which you tempered,是定语从句,修饰 steel, steel 在这里指刀剑,钢制品。when 引导的实际上是时间状语从句,整个句子是 Why do you shake ... when you see...? 这样的结构。

10. With plough and spade and hoe and loom/Trace your grave and build your tomb/And weave your winding sheet — 用犁、锹、锄头和织机/构筑你们自己的坟墓,/织造你们自己的尸衣——

　　＊ 整个句子主语未出现,就是 you"你们",trace（设计）和 weave 是两个并列的谓语动词,with 结构是状语短语。

till fair England be your Sepulchre. 直到美丽的英格兰成了你们的墓穴。

　　＊ 最后两节诗是在告诫和警醒英国劳动人民,不要任由命运安排,要起来斗争、反抗,否则自己的辛勤劳动等于壮大敌人,却把自己送进坟墓。

参考译文——姚绍德

致英格兰人

英格兰人,为什么为老爷们耕种——
他们可是把你们踩在脚下?
为什么辛苦、细心地纺织——
让暴君穿上你们织造的锦袍?

为什么你们要终身辛苦
侍奉那些忘恩负义的雄蜂,
给他们衣食,还要保他们的性命?
他们却榨干你们的血汗!

英格兰工蜂啊,为何要锻造
许多武器,铁链,和镣铐,

让无刺的雄蜂用来掠夺
你们被迫劳动的果实?

你们可有闲暇、舒适和宁静,
可有食、住,和爱情的温柔抚慰?
否则,你们怀着痛苦,怀着恐惧,
究竟买得了什么,价格如此昂贵?

种子你们播,果实别人收;
财富你们创,别人占有之;
你们缝衣袍,别人身上穿,
你们铸武器,别人手中执。

你们播种——但别让暴君收;
你们创造的财富——别让骗子占有;
织出的衣袍——不给懒汉穿,
造出的武器——紧握保自己。

钻进你们的地窖、洞窟和小屋,
让别人住进你们装饰的厅堂;
为什么要挣脱你们自铸的铁链?
应看见自打的钢刀正寒光照面!

用铁犁、铁锹、锄头和织机,
设计和构筑你们的坟茔,
织造你们的尸衣——结果定然是
美丽的英格兰变成了你们的墓地!

格律和韵律分析

本诗的格律是自由的,韵律基本是 aabb/ccdd/...。

2. 西风颂 *Ode to the West Wind*

词语解释和难句分析

1. to eulogize the powerful west wind 赞美强劲的西风
   to enjoy the boundless freedom from reality 享有无限的现实自由
   to gather in this poem a wealth of symbolism 在这首诗里集中使用了多种多样的象征主义手法

to employ a structural art and his powers of metrical orchestration <u>at their mightiest</u> 最大限度地采用结构艺术和韵律协调配合的聪明才智

I

2. O wild West Wind, thou (art) breath of Autumn's being (= life), 呵,狂野的西风,你是秋天生命的气息,

Thou, from whose unseen presence the leaves dead/Are driven, like ghosts from an enchanter fleeing, = The dead leaves are driven from your unseen presence, like ghosts fleeing from an enchanter, 你无形的莅临,枯叶被横扫,/像鬼魅见巫师而逃跑,

3. pestilence-stricken multitudes 像患上瘟疫似的大堆枯叶

　＊ multitudes 大群,大堆,很多

chariot *n.* 双轮翼车,战车;*v.* 用车载送

chariotest *v.* 第二人称单数的古用法,与 thou 相配。

O Thou,/Who chariotest to their dark wintry bed/The winged seeds, = O Thou, Thou chariotest the winged seeds to their dark wintry bed, 呵,秋风,你把飞翔的(带翼的)种子/送进黑暗的冬床,

4. Where they lie cold and low,/Each like a corpse within its grave, 在那里,他们躺在阴冷的深处,/每一颗都像坟墓中的尸体,

Until/Thine azure sister of the Spring shall blow/Her clarion o'er the dreaming earth, 直到你拂过晴空的春风妹妹/吹响号角唤醒沉睡的大地,

　＊ 意大利全年多刮西风,诗中所云为强劲的秋风,而春天则是刮和畅的西风,故互为姐妹。azure *a.* 蔚蓝的,碧空的,苍穹的;clarion *n.* 号角,尖声的喇叭,这里含有复活的意思。《新约·哥林多前书》(15:52)中说:"最后的号角吹起的时候,死人要复活,从此,不朽不灭。"诗人将春天种子的发芽喻为死人的复活,与 Each like a corpse within its grave 相呼应。本诗的末尾,诗人再次采用了复活的意象。

5. and fill/(Driving sweet buds like flocks to feed in air)/With living hues and colours plain and hill: = and fill plain and hill with living hues and colours, driving sweet buds like flocks to feed in air:驱动花蕾羊群觅食般空中飘飞,/使漫山遍野充满鲜活的色彩和芬芳:

　＊ 动词 fill 与前面的 blow 是并列的谓语动词,而 driving 引导的分词短语是作补充说明的状语。

6. Wild Spirit, which (= thou) art moving everywhere;/Destroyer and Preserver; hear, O hear! 呵,狂野的精灵,你吹遍四方,/你肃杀大地,又带来生机;呵,请听!

II

7. Thou on whose (= thine) stream, 'mid (= amid) the steep sky's commotion, 你啊,在你高天的急流涌荡中,

8. Loose clouds like Earth's decaying leaves are shed,/Shook (= shaken) from the tangled boughs of Heaven and Ocean, 流云像大地的败叶凋零,/抖落自海天间纠结的大树虬枝。

　＊ shook from... 应理解为 shaken from...,可看成过去分词短语作状语,说明败叶抖落自何方,如果不是诗的结构需要,shook 是不必要的,...are shed from... 就够了。

9. Angels of rain and lightning: there are spread (= are spread there)/On the blue surface of thine aery surge, 这是雨、电将临先遣的天使,/显现在云海翻腾蔚蓝的表面,

10. Like the bright hair uplifted from the head/Of some fierce Maenad, even from the dim verge/Of the horizon to the zenith's height,/The locks of the approaching storm. = The locks of the approaching storm, like the bright hair ... the zenith's height. 那正在逼近的暴风雨的乱云,/像麦娜德狂暴的亮发竖起,/从遥远昏蒙的地平线,/直竖到九天之顶的中天。

　＊ Maenad 是古罗马神话中酒神巴克斯(Bacchus)的女祭司,常被认为疯狂的女人。

11. Thou dirge/Of the dying year, = Thou art dirge of the dying year,　你是逝去一年的挽歌，

12. To which this closing night will be the dome of a vast sepulchre, = This closing night will be ... to the dying year.　这闭合的夜色为残年的大墓盖上穹顶，

　　(be) vaulted with all thy congregated might (= power/strength)/Of vapours.　穹顶下凝聚/覆盖着你全部的力量。

13. from whose (= vapour's) solid atmosphere/Black rain and fire and hail will burst. = Black rain and fire and hail will burst from...　从浓云密雾的厚实气层中，/将会喷发出黑雨、闪电和冰雹。

Ⅲ

14. Thou who didst (= does) waken from his summer dreams/The blue Mediterranean, = Thou didst waken the blue Mediterranean from his summer dreams,　是你把蓝色的地中海从梦中唤醒。

15. Where he lay,/Lulled by the coil of his crystalline streams,　它本悠闲自得地躺在那里，/晶莹的水流回旋使它安息入眠。

　　* 分词短语 lulled by... 可看成谓语动词 lay 的状语,说明伴随的情况和状态。

16. pumice isle　帕米斯岛,意大利那不勒斯(Naples)附近一个小岛,由维苏威(Vesuvius)火山的熔岩沉积所形成。

　　Baiae's Bay　贝亚湾,古罗马时代的一个著名风景区,位于那不勒斯西端,坎伯尼亚湾附近。1818年,雪莱曾乘船来过这里,后来在给友人的信中说:古代辉煌的废墟像岩石一样立在我们船下透明的水中。(The ruins of its antique grandeur standing like rock in the transparent sea under our boat.)

　　intenser day = intenser daylight　更强烈的日光

17. And saw in sleep old palaces and towers/Quivering within the wave's intenser day,　睡梦中你看到古老的宫殿和塔楼,/在更强烈的波光中荡漾，

18. All overgrown with azure moss and flowers = all palaces and towers grown with...　所有的楼台殿阁都长满青苔和花朵

19. So sweet, the sense faints picturing them! = So sweet they are that one feel faint to picture them!　如此芬芳,美得令人心醉神迷(不知如何描绘)！

　　* so sweet 是 moss and flowers 的后置定语。

20. Thou/for whose path = For thy (= your) path(= passing)　为了你的通行,为给你开道

　　the Atlantic's level powers (= waves)/ Cleave themselves into chasms,　大西洋平缓的波涛/裂成道道深堑。

21. while far below/The sea-blooms and oozy woods which wear/The sapless foliage of the ocean,　而在海洋深处,/海花和泥污的树林披着/大洋里没有汁液的枝叶。

22. know/Thy voice, and suddenly grow grey with fear,/And tremble and despoil themselves: O hear!　听到/你呼啸的声音,顿时吓白了脸,/浑身颤抖,纷纷凋谢:呵,请听！

　　* know 与前面的 wear 和后面的 grow, tremble, despoil 都是 which 即 the sea-blooms and oozy woods 的并列谓语动词。

Ⅳ

23. thou mightest bear = you might carry　mightest 是古英语第二人称单数现在时的用法。

　　to outstrip thy skiey (= sky) speed　超过你空中疾飞的速度

　　to strive with = to contend with　与……竞争

　　in my sore need　在我迫切需要时

　　as then = in my childhood　像那时(儿时)

　　a heavy weight of hour　时间的沉重负担

24. If I were a dead leaf thou mightest bear;/If I were a swift cloud to fly with thee;　但愿我是一片被你

刮起的枯叶,但愿我是一朵随你疾飞的云,

* thou mightest bear 是定语从句,修饰 leaf;注意 if 的译法,在没有结果分句时,if 引导的句子常表示愿望。

A wave to pant beneath thy power, and share/The impulse of thy strength, only less free/Than thou, O Uncontrollable!... = If I were a wave to pant beneath thy power, and share... 但愿我是一个浪波,在你的威力下喘息,/与你的伟力一起冲动,只是自由/不如你,呵,狂放不羁的生命啊!

25. If even/I were as in my boyhood, and could be/The comrade of thy wanderings over Heaven, 假如我还在童年,能/陪伴你同游天外,

As then, when to outstrip thy skiey speed/Scarce (= scarcely) seemed a vision; I would ne'er (= never) have striven/As thus with thee in prayer in my sore need. 那时,超过你的飞行速度/并非幻想;我也不必像现在这样/在紧迫的时刻争着祈求。

26. Oh! lift me as a wave, a leaf, a cloud! /I fall upon the thorns of life! I bleed! 啊! 把我扬起,就当一道浪、一片叶、一朵云! /纵然是跌落在人生的荆棘上,流血!

27. A heavy weight of hours has chained and bowed/One too like thee:tameless, and swift, and proud. 时光的重负捆住了我、压弯了我,/一个太像你的人:傲慢,迅疾,桀骜不驯。

V

28. Make me thy lyre, even as the forest is (thy lyre): 把我当作你的竖琴,甚至像树林一样(也是你的竖琴):

What if my leaves are falling like its own! 要是我像树林一样落叶,又有何妨!

* what if... 表明一种"假如……又怎么样呢?"的意思。

29. The tumult of thy mighty harmonies/Will take from both a deep, autumnal tone,/So sweet though in sadness. 你激起的强大和鸣/将从我和树林中奏出深沉的秋音,/尽管悲凉却很甜美。

30. Be thou, Spirit fierce,/My spirit! Be thou me, impetuous one! = Spirit fierce, be thou my spirit!... 狂暴的精灵,/愿你化为我的精神! 化为我呀,成奋勇的合一!

* Be thou my spirit! 这种句式带有愿望和虚拟假设的含义,类似于 Wish you were my spirit; If you were my spirit...; Were you my spirit...。

31. Drive my dead thoughts over the universe/Like withered leaves to quicken a new birth! 请将我陈腐的思想吹遍天涯,/让它们像你驱动的落叶那样加速新生!

32. And, by the incantation of this verse, 权借这首小诗发挥的魔力,

33. Scatter, as from an unextinguished hearth/Ashes and sparks, my words among mankind! = Scatter my words among mankind, as scatter ashes and sparks from an unextinguished hearth! 把我的话语传遍人间,就像从/未灭的炉中传播灰烬和火星!

34. Be through my lips to unawakened Earth,/The trumpet of a prophecy! = Be the trumpet of a prophecy through my lips to unawakened Earth! 让预言的号角通过我的嘴唇,/把沉睡的大地唤醒!

35. O, Wind,/If Winter comes, can Spring be far behind? 呵,西风啊! /冬天已经来了,难道春天还远吗?

参考译文——姚绍德

西风颂

I

啊,狂野的西风,你是秋天的生命呼吸!
你无形的存在驱赶着枯叶,
像被巫师驱赶的鬼魅,纷纷逃避:
黄,黑,灰,潮红——各色枯叶
像染上瘟疫的一堆:啊,是你,
以翼车把带翅的种子送上黑暗的冬床,
在那里——它们躺在阴冷的深处,
每一颗都像是墓中的尸体,直到
你的春风妹妹在碧空吹响
她的号角,唤醒了睡梦中的大地,
(催发芬芳的花蕾,像羊群觅食般在空中飘飞)
使平野和山峦充满生命的色彩和气息:
狂野的精灵呀,你无处不运行;
你是毁灭的魔鬼呀,也是卫护的神仙;听啊,听!

II

你呀,在你高天的急流涌荡之中,
松散的云絮,像大地的败叶凋零,
抖落自海天缠结的大干虬枝,
那是雨电将临先遣的天使:飘飞在
你高天云海、蔚蓝的表面,
犹如那疯狂女神麦娜德闪亮的怒发竖起,
从地平线昏蒙不清的遥远边际
直到天穹最高的顶点,
正在逼近的暴风雨如卷发穿云。你即
正逝去的残年的挽歌,这四合的
夜色将成为一个巨大陵墓的穹顶,
穹顶下是你凝聚汇集的全部伟力——
这密实雄浑的磅礴水气,将迸发
黑色的暴雨、冰雹和电火:啊来了,你听!

III

是你,将蓝色的地中海从夏日的梦境中
唤醒,而它本悠闲地躺在那里,
晶莹的水流回旋使它安息入眠,
在拜亚海湾的一个浮石小岛边,
睡眠中梦见古老的宫殿和塔楼

在更强烈的波光中荡漾,
宫殿塔楼都长满蔚蓝色的青苔和花朵,
是那样的芬芳,想象一下都会心醉神迷!
为给你开道,大西洋平缓的波涛
豁然开裂成波谷,而在海洋深处,
花藻和泥污的树林,披着
没有液汁的枯萎枝叶,一听说
你的呼啸,顿时吓得脸色灰白,
浑身发抖,叶片自动凋零:哦,你听!

IV

但愿我是一片枯叶被你刮走,
但愿我是一朵流云随你飘飞,
愿我啊,是一朵浪波,随你而喘息,
分享你搏动的伟力,只是不如
你自由,啊,你是何等的无拘无束!
假如我还像童年无忌,假如
能与你结伴同游于天宇,
那时,超越你的行天神速
也并非梦幻,我也就无须如此
急切地向你苦苦祈求。
啊! 扬起我吧,就像扬起水波、树叶和云朵!
我正跌落在生活的荆丛,我正流血!
岁月的重负已锁住、压弯了一个
太像你的人:桀骜不驯,迅疾而自负。

V

请把我当作你的竖琴,就像你演奏森林,
即使我的叶也像树叶一样凋零!
你强劲的和鸣所激起的波澜
将使森林和我奏出深沉的秋音,
纵然悲凉,却很甜蜜。狂暴的精灵,
愿你化作我的精神,化作我呀,成奋勇的合一!
请把我陈腐的思想吹遍天涯,
让它像你驱动的落叶一样催促新生!
权借这首小诗发挥的魔力,
将我的话语传遍人间,就像
从未灭的炉中撒播灰烬和火星!
愿预言的号角,通过我的双唇,
播向还未苏醒的大地! 啊,西风啊,
冬天已经来了,春天还会远吗?

格律和韵律分析

O ˈwild/West ˈWind,/ thou ˈbreath/of ˈAu/tumn's ˈbeing,	a
Thou, from/whose un/seen ˈpre/sence the/leaves ˈdead	b
Are ˈdriven,/ like ˈghost/from an/en·chan/ter ˈfleeing,	a
Yellow,/ and ˈblack,/ and ˈpale,/ and ˈhec/tic ˈred,	b
Pesti/lence-ˈstri/cken ˈmul/ti/tudes:/ O ˈThou,	c
Who ˈcha/riotest/to ˈtheir/dark ˈwin/try ˈbed	d
The ˈwin/ged ˈseeds,/ where ˈthey/lie ˈcold/and ˈlow,	c
Each ˈlike/a ˈcorpse/within/its ˈgrave,/ un'til	d
Thine ˈa/zure ˈsis/ter of/the ˈSpring/shall ˈblow	c
Her ˈcla/rion ˈo'er/the ˈdrea/ming ˈearth,/ and ˈfill	d
(Driving/sweet ˈbuds/like ˈflocks/to ˈfeed/in ˈair)	e
With ˈli/ving ˈhues/and ˈo/dours ˈplain/and ˈhill:	d
Wild ˈSpi/rit, ˈwhich/art ˈmo/ving ˈe/very'where;	f
Des ˈtroy/er and/Pre'ser/ver; ˈhear,/ O ˈhear!	f

取第一段诗的 5 小节作为分析样品,略加分析就可知道,每行诗句都是 5 个音步,全段共 70 个音步,绝大多数音步都是 2 个音节,只有第三行第一音步 are ˈdriven 为 3 个音节,为抑扬抑格;另外,第 7 行的 winged 可有两种读音:[wiŋd]和[wiŋid],前者为单音节,后者为双音节,取后者这一诗行 The ˈwin/ged ˈseeds/, where ˈthey/lie ˈcold/and ˈlow,刚好凑成 5 个音步,每个音步 2 个音节。根据朗读时的自然重音,划出重音,这一段诗有 59 个音步为抑扬格,其他 4 个诗段也大致如此,因此,该诗的格律基本可认为是五步抑扬格。根据诗句的尾韵判断,可知其韵律是 aba/bcb/cdc/ded/ff。

主要内容归纳和总结

1. 雪莱出生于英格兰苏塞克斯郡(Sussex,英格兰旧郡名)一个拥有土地的贵族家庭,从小喜安静、爱思考,先后在伊顿公学和牛津大学学习。在大学期间,他由于宣传无神论,散发自著的小册子《无神论的必然性》(The Necessity of Atheism),批驳上帝存在的说法,因而被开除出校。离校的雪莱成了激进派哲学家威廉·戈德温(William Godwin)的信徒,成了拜伦的密友。他反对私有制,同情劳动人民,主张以革命方式推翻腐朽政府。同时,他又认为罪恶不仅存在于制度,还存在于人的思想,革命成功后,还要进行社会变革,在人的心中注入善良与公正,否则革命还会被毁掉。这些思想即使到今天,也是非常有价值的。

他在游历意大利时的一次风暴中被淹死,终年 30 岁,被葬在罗马,墓碑上镌刻着 Percy Bysshe Shelley, Cor Cordium,意为 the heart of all hearts——万心之心。许多批评家都认为他是最伟大的英国诗人之一,尤指他的抒情诗。他最著名的抒情诗是《西风颂》(Ode to the West Wind);他最伟大的成就是他的四幕诗剧(four-act poetic drama)《解放了的普罗米修斯》(*Prometheus Unbound*);他最伟大的政治抒情诗是《致英格兰人》(*A song:Men of England*)。他一生中的精华作品都是在逝世前的最后四年创作的。

　　他首次把文艺复兴时期意大利诗人但丁的三行诗节隔句押韵法(terza rima)应用于英诗中(《西风颂》)。

2. 雪莱的主要作品:

a. 诗歌

《无神论的必然性》*The Necessity of Atheism*(1811)

《麦布女王:一部哲理长诗》*Queen Mab:A Philosophical Poem*(1813)

《复仇之神,或 孤独之精神》*Alastor, or The Spirit of Solitude*(1816)

《内秀之咏》*Hymn to Intellectual Beauty*(1816)

《勃朗峰》*Mont Blanc*(1816)

《朱利安与麦达罗》*Julian and Maddalo*(1818)

《伊斯兰起义》*The Revolt of Islam*(1818)

《钦契一家》*The Cenci*(1819)

《解放了的普罗米修斯》*Prometheus Unbound*(1819)

《自由颂》*Ode to the Liberty*(1819)

《那不勒斯颂》*Ode to Naples*(1819)

《十四行诗:英格兰1819》*Sonnet:England in 1819*(1819)

《致英格兰人》*A Song:Men of England*(1819)

《西风颂》*Ode to the West Wind*(1819)

《云之歌》*The Cloud*(1820)

《致云雀》*To a Skylark*(1820)

《阿多那伊斯》*Adonais*(1821)

《赫拉斯》*Hellas*(1822)

b. 散文

《诗辩》*A Defence of Poetry*(1822)

重要信息句子

1. Shelley was a quiet and thoughtful boy. Though gentle by nature, his rebellious qualities were cultivates in his early year.

2. In Oxford University, Shelley wrote *The Necessity of Atheism*, repudiating the existence of God.

3. On his tombstone was inscribed "Percy Bysshe Shelley, Cor Cordium," which means "the heart of all hearts."

4. *Ode to the West Wind* is written in the *terza rima* form Shelley derived from his reading of Dante, in which the most famous sentences are "I fall upon the thorns of life! I bleed" and "If Winter comes, can spring be far behind?"

5. Shelley's greatest achievement is his four-act poetic drama, *Prometheus Unbound*. He himself recognized it as "the most perfect of my products."

6. Shelley is one of the leading Romantic poets, an intense and original lyrical poet in the English language.

VI. 约翰·济慈 John Keats (1795~1821)

词语解释和难句分析

1. a livery-stable owner　出租马和马车的小业主/小老板

   his first inclination toward poetry　他对诗歌的早期爱好

   be apprenticed to a surgeon and apothecary　跟一个外科医师和药剂师学徒

   to become a licensed apothecary　成了领有执照的/职业药剂师

   to practice his profession　从事他自己的事业，开业

   to devote himself to poetry　献身于诗歌创作

   be preoccupied with poetry　迷恋诗歌

   to awaken his dormant poetic gift　唤醒他休眠状态的诗歌天赋

   be imitation of the Elizabethan poetry　模仿伊丽莎白时代的诗歌

   the radical journalist and minor poet　激进的新闻工作者和二流诗人

   to cultivate him with a taste for liberal politics as well as the fine arts　培养他对自由民主政治和精美艺术的兴趣爱好

2. to express his own poetic aspirations　表达了他自己诗歌创作的渴望

   moon goddess　月光女神

   to describe his imagination in an enchanted atmosphere　描写了他处于痴迷状态下的想象

   a lovely moon-lit world where human love and ideal beauty were merged into one.　一个可爱的月光照耀的世界，人类之爱与理想的美在那里融为一体。

   to mark a transition phase in Keats' poetry　标志着济慈诗歌的一个转折

   to launch savage attacks on Keats　对济慈发起无礼的攻击

   to declare *Endymion* to be sheer nonsense　宣称《恩底弥翁》为十足的胡话

   the cockney School of poetry　伦敦东区佬诗派

3. the Lake Country　（英国）大湖风景区

   to glory in the grand scenery　对宏伟壮美的景色感到自豪、喜悦

   to become ill with tuberculosis　患了肺结核

   be in trouble about money　钱的方面遇到了问题，经济上遇到困难

4. and to this already overcharged heart something else was added: he fell in love. = and something else was added to this already overcharged heart.　另外一些事情又给他本已负担过重的心脏增加了麻烦/雪上加霜。

5. It was this yearning and suffering that quickened his maturity and added a new dimension to his poetry. 正是这种渴望和痛苦加快了他的成熟，使他的诗歌变得更加丰满。

6. to reach the summit of his poetic creation　达到他诗歌创作的最高峰

   mythical and legendary themes of ancient, medieval, and Renaissance times　古代、中世纪和文艺复兴时期的神话和传奇主题

   be buried in the Protestant cemetery　被埋葬在新教徒公墓

7. At the heart of these poems lies Keats' concern with how the ideal can be joined with the real.　这些诗

歌的核心存在着济慈对理想如何才能与现实结合的思考。

8. the poet's abiding preoccupation with the imagination　诗人的持久不变的对想象的专注

to suggest the undercurrent of disillusion that accompanies such ecstasy　暗示着幻灭的潜流与狂喜相伴

to question the visionary transcendence achieved by art　怀疑通过艺术手法所取得的幻想的超越

9. Here the aching ecstasy roused by the bird's song is felt like a form of spiritual homesickness, a longing to be at one with beauty.　这里鸟鸣所唤起的令人痛苦的欢乐,就像一种精神思归的形式,一种与美统一的渴望。

10. death and rapture which free him into the world of dream　使他获得解脱而进入梦想境界的死亡和升天

＊ which 引导一个定语从句修饰 death and rapture。

11. Opiates and wine at first seem the way to this union and to the attainment of a rapture which transcends the human misery.　起初,鸦片制剂和酒是实现这种统一和超越人类痛苦达到极乐世界的方法。

12. the most effective means to release misery　解脱痛苦最有效的方法

a vehicle to reach paradise　到达天堂的工具

to combine a tingling anticipation with a lapsing towards dissolution　把令人激动的期望与趋向瓦解的流逝相结合

to manage to keep a precarious balance between mirth and despair, rapture and grief　设法保持痛苦和绝望,极乐和悲伤的不稳定平衡

to ascend from the transfigured physical world to the timeless present of the nightingale's song.　从被美化了的物质世界升华到永恒的夜莺歌唱的现实存在。

13. The ultimate imaginative view of "fairy lands forlorn" evaporates in its extremity as the full associations of the last word "toll". The poet backs from his near-loss of selfhood to the real and human world of sorrow and death.　最富想象力的"最无成功希望的仙国"景象,正如最后一个词"丧钟"所产生的充分联想一样,在达致其顶峰时烟消云散。诗人从自我人格的近乎丧失退回到存在悲伤和死亡的人类现实世界。

14. the contrast between the performance of art and the transience of human passion　艺术永恒和人类情感短暂形成的对比

to absorb himself into the timeless beautiful scenery　他自己为永恒的美丽景色所吸引

to exist simultaneously and forever in their intensity of joy　……同时永久地存在于他们极度的欢乐中

be unaffected by time, stilled in expectation　不受时间影响,在期待中定格

15. This is at once the glory and the limitation of the world conjured up by an object art.　这是荣耀和世界的局限同时像中了魔法似的被一件艺术品呈现出来。

16. to celebrate but simplify intuitions of ecstasy　歌颂却又简化了对欢乐的感知

to become a "Cold Pastoral"　变成"冷却了的田园风光"

to present his ambivalence about time and the nature of beauty　表现了他在理解时间和美的本质方面出现了矛盾情绪

17. be sensuous, colorful and rich in imagery　在意象上给人以感官的享受,多彩多姿

to express the acuteness of his senses　表现出他敏锐的感觉

be all taken in to give an entire understanding of an experience　全被吸收/用来全面理解一次体验

to enter the feelings of others:either human or animal　进入别人或别的动物的思想感情

to delight to dwell on beautiful words and phrases which sound musical　喜欢老是思考那些有乐感的词语

to draw diction, style and imagery from works of Shakespeare, ...　从莎士比亚等大诗人那里汲取词语,

学习文风和诗歌意象

18. the mythic world of the ancient Greece 古希腊的神话世界

characterized by exact and closely knit construction, sensual description... 以精确严谨的结构,感官的描写……为其特点

to give transcendental values to the physical beauty of the world 给世界的物质美赋予超越一般常识的价值

one of the indisputably great English poets 英国无可争辩的伟大诗人之一

19. And his realization of the empathic power of the imagination is of the greatest consequence to his work and is a faculty which, as his thought and technique matured, leads him to his most profound insights.
他在诗歌想象方面情感投入的强度意识对他的作品会产生最伟大的结果,这也是一种才能,就像他的思想和技巧变成熟是才能一样,会使他具有最深刻的洞察力。

济慈作品选读

希腊古瓮颂 *Ode on a Grecian Urn*

词语解释和难句分析

1. 本诗是作者看到出土文物希腊古瓮上的装饰画而产生的联想。画面上绿树庭花,笙歌燕舞,抑或是青年男女的婚姻嫁娶,抑或是少男少女的恋情追逐,总之人物风情全都永久地定格在艺术作品上。悠悠岁月千年已过,而古希腊当年的场景,依然鲜活地留存在眼前,使他产生了人生短暂、艺术永存的想法,写了这首诗。诗歌一开始就将古瓮拟人化,对它说话,有如古代诗人对缪斯说话,吁请灵感。

1

2. Thou (art) still unravish'd bride of quietness, 你是宁静中还未失贞的新娘,

* unravish'd = unravished,未遭强暴、未受破损,指古瓮深埋地下未受到破坏,依然完好。

Thou (art) foster-child of silence and slow time, 你是悠悠岁月默默抚育的养女,

* foster-child,领养的孩子。古瓮的创作者斯人已逝,而他的"孩子"(作品)则留给了千年沉寂,悠悠岁月来养育。

3. Sylvan historian, who canst thus express/A flowery tale more sweetly than our rhyme: 林泉史家呀,你能如此铺陈/一个如花的故事,比我们的诗还美:

* 这是作者在对古瓮上的画面讲话。

4. What leaf-fring'd legend haunts about thy shape/Of deities or mortals, or of both,/In Tempe or the dales of Arcady? = What leaf-fringed legend of deities or mortals, or of both haunts about thy shape in ... Arcady? 什么样的传奇枝叶缘边环绕你的形体? /讲的是神耶、人耶,或者亦人亦神? /是太阳神的滕佩,还是田园风光的阿卡狄?

* leaf-fring'd = leaf-fringed 枝叶缘边,是指古瓮上的画用树叶镶边。腾佩(Tempe)是指撒塞莱(Thessaly)和奥林匹斯(Olympus)山之间的腾佩谷,被看成司掌诗歌的太阳神阿波罗(Apollo)的圣地;阿卡狄(Arcady)即阿卡狄亚(Arcadia)山谷,濒临爱琴海,是传统牧歌中象征美好的理想福地。

5. What men or gods are these? What maidens (are) loth? 画中是些什么人? 什么神? 姑娘们怎还不情愿?

What mad pursuit? What struggle to escape? 这是怎么样的狂追呵,怎么样的脱挣?

What pipes and timbrels? What wild ecstasy?　多么美妙的长笛和铃鼓呵,多么疯狂的喜悦?

2

6. 第二节的前四行说明古瓮上所描绘的歌唱和吹笛只是对人的精神而不是对人的感官起作用。

7. Heard melodies are sweet, but those unheard/Are sweeter;　有声的乐曲优美,但无声的乐曲/更美;

　＊ heard 和 unheard 都是定语,修饰 melodies。those unheard = those unheard melodies。

Therefore, ye soft pipes, play on;　因此,你柔情的长笛,尽情地演奏吧!

　＊ play on　继续/持久地演奏下去

8. Not to the sensual ear, but, more endear'd (endeared),/Pipe to the spirit ditties of no tone. = Not to the sensual ear, but pipe to the spirit more endear'd ditties of no tone.　不是奏给感官的肉耳听,而是对着灵魂/演奏更柔情的无声的乐曲。

9. Fair youth, beneath the trees, thou canst not leave/Thy song,　树下的美少年,你的歌声永不停歇,

　＊ canst = can,第二人称单数现在时的古用法,与 thou 连用。thy = your,后跟辅音开头的名词。

nor ever can those trees be bare;　那树上的绿叶也永不会凋落光秃;

10. Bold lover, never, never canst thou kiss,/Though winning near the goal — yet, do not grieve;　大胆的情郎永不能得到一吻,尽管已接近目标——但也不要悲伤;

　＊ win 的后面跟介词、副词或形容词短语时,表示经过努力达到目标、成功的意思。所以,winning near the goal 意指情哥哥好不容易快要够到/吻上心爱的姑娘时却功亏一篑。

11. She cannot fade (= lose her beauty), though thou hast not thy bliss,　你虽未得到痴狂的一吻,她却会容颜不改,

For ever wilt thou love, and she be fair! = Thou wilt love for ever, and she wilt be fair!　你会永远地爱她,她会美丽永在!

　＊ wilt = will

3

12. Ah, happy, happy bough! that cannot shed/Your leaves, nor ever bid the spring adieu;　呵,幸福的树枝! 不会凋落绿叶,/也永不向春天告别;

　＊ to bid … adieu　向……告别/说再见

13. And, happy melodist, unwearied,/ For ever piping songs for ever new;　呵,快乐的乐师,永远不疲倦,/乐曲永长奏,曲调永常新;

14. More happy love! more happy, happy love! / For ever warm and still to be enjoy'd,　幸福的爱呀,格外幸福的爱! /永远的热烈,不尽的享受,

　＊ still（adv.）［古］ = always, often

For ever panting, and forever young;　永远爱得有激情,永远的亢奋年轻;

　＊ panting 喘息,指恋人相会,爱得热烈,充满激情。

15. All breathing human passion far above,/That leaves a heart high sorrowful and cloy'd, = Far above all breathing human passion that leaves a heart high sorrowful and cloyed,　远胜过现实人间一切激动的情爱,/不会有人欲过度的厌倦和离合的忧愁。

　＊ that leaves… cloy'd 是 human passion 的定语从句,直译应为:远胜过一切给人的心灵带来巨大忧愁和厌倦的人间激情。既然“远胜过”,那当然就“不会有”。breathing = living; cloy'd = cloyed = be made weary by excess 由于过度而导致疲劳厌倦。

A burning forehead, and a parching tongue.　(不会有)发烧的头脑、焦渴的舌头。

　＊ 此行也属于上行 that 引导的定语从句,是 leaves 的直接宾语。“不会有”的译法,都是根据前面的 far above,人间的芸芸众生会有人欲过度的表现和烦恼,艺术品上的形象却定格在适可而止的状态保持永恒,因而“超出了”“不会有”真实人间的种种表现。

4

16. 下面的诗行显然说明诗人转动古瓮看到了另一幅画面。

17. Who are these coming to the sacrifice? 这是些什么人来这里祭祀?

18. To what green altar, O mysterious priest,/Lead'st thou that heifer <u>lowing at</u> the skies,/And all her silken flanks with garlands drest? = O mysterious priest, To what green altar dost thou lead that heifer lowing at the skies and drest (= dressed) with garlands all her silken flanks? 直译是:神秘的祭司呀,你要把那头对天哞哞哀叫、光滑的腰身挂满花环的小牛牵到哪座绿色的祭坛去呀?

    * lowing 和 drest 引导的两个分词短语都是 heifer 的定语; dost 和 lead'st (= leadest) 都是古用法第二人称单数现在时态,与 thou 相配。

19. What little town by river or sea shore,/Or mountain-built with peaceful citadel,/<u>Is emptied of</u> this folk, this pious morn? 那依山傍海或傍河的,是怎样的一座小城?/山崖上还静立着一座城堡,/倾城百姓(全离城)去往神坛,在这个虔诚的清早?

20. And, little town, thy streets for evermore/Will silent be; = And little town, thy streets will be silent for evermore; 小城,你的街道将永远寂静;
    and not a soul to tell/Why thou art desolate, can e'er return. = and not a soul can ever return to tell why thou art desolate. 没一个人会回来讲述/你为何变得如此荒凉。

5

21. O Attic shape! Fair attitude! with brede/Of marble men and maidens overwrought, = O Attic shape! Fair attitude! <u>overwrought with</u> brede of marble men and maidens, 呵,雅典式的形状!美好的姿态!/饰满大理石雕刻的(人流如织/摩肩接踵的)男人和少女,
    With forest branches and the trodden weed; 还有森林的树枝和践踏过的青草;

22. Thou, silent form, dost tease us out of thought/As doth eternity: Cold Pastoral! 你,沉默的形体,引我们超脱尘虑,/犹如永恒——冷凝的牧歌——所启示!

22. When old age shall this generation waste, = When old age shall waste this generation, 当老迈把我们这代人耗尽,
    Thou shalt remain, in midst of other woe/Than ours, a friend to man, to whom thou say'st, = In midst of other woe than ours, thou shalt/remain a friend to man, to whom thou say'st, 在不同于我们的别样的悲苦中,你依然是/人类的朋友,你对他们说——

24. "Beauty is truth, truth beauty," — that is all/Ye know on earth, and all ye need to know. "美即是真,真即是美"——这就是世人/你们所知和须知的一切!

参考译文——姚绍德

希腊古瓮颂

1

你是宁静中保持着童贞的新娘,
你是悠悠岁月默默抚育的养女,
林泉史家呀,你竟如此铺陈
一个如花的故事,比我们的诗还美:
什么枝叶镶边的传奇环绕你的形体?

讲的是神耶？人耶？或是亦人亦神？
是阿波罗的滕佩，还是田园风光的阿卡狄？
这是些什么人，什么神？姑娘怎还不情愿？
怎样热烈的狂追？怎样竭力的挣脱？
多么美妙的风笛、铃鼓啊，多么疯狂的喜悦？

2

有声的乐曲悦耳，无声的乐曲更美；
尽情地演奏吧，演奏你柔情的风笛，
不是对感官的肉耳，而是对灵魂
奏出更令人爱的、无声的乐曲：
树下的美少年，你歌声永不会停歇，
那树上的绿叶，也永不会凋零干净：
大胆的情哥哥，你永远吻不着妹妹，
虽说只差一点点——不过你可别伤悲，
你虽不能得一次极乐，她却会容颜不改，
你会永远爱她，她会美丽永在！

3

啊，幸福的树枝！永不凋落绿叶，
也永不向春光告别；
幸福的乐师，永远不疲倦，
风笛永长奏，曲调永长新；
只能是更幸福、更加幸福的爱情啊！
永远的热烈，不尽的享受，
永远有激情，永远亢奋年轻；
远胜过现实人间一切激动的情爱，
不会有人欲过度的心灵厌恶和痛苦，
额头不发烫，喉舌不焦渴。

4

来祭祀的都是些什么人？
神秘的祭司啊，你要把小牛
牵到哪座绿色的祭坛——
它正对天哞哞地哀鸣，
花环挂满它那光滑的腰身？
那依山傍河或傍海的是什么小城，
山崖上还屹立着宁静的城堡，
城里人都走空了，在这个虔诚的清早？
小城啊，你的街道将永远寂静，
没一个人会回来言讲——
你为何变得如此荒凉。

5

啊，好个雅典的形态！优美的身姿！
你身上雕满了大理石的少女和靓男，
还有森林树枝和践踏过的草地；

你静默无言,引我们超脱尘世的思虑,
启示如永恒——这冷凝的牧歌!
等老迈耗尽我们这一代,
在别样的悲苦中,你依然是
人类的朋友,你会对他们说
"美即是真,真即是美"——这就是
你们世人所知和须知的一切。

格律和韵律分析

全诗共 5 节,取第一节做格律、韵律分析的样板。

Thou ˈstill/unˈra/vishˈd ˈbride/of ˈqui/etˈness,	a
Thou ˈfos/terˈchild/of ˈsi/lence and/slow time,	b
ˈSylvan/hisˈto/rian, ˈwho/canst thus/exˈpress	a
A ˈflowe/ry ˈtale/more ˈsweet/ly ˈthan/our ˈrhyme:	b
Whatˈleaf/-fringˈd ˈle/gend ˈhaunts/aˈbout/thy ˈshape	c
Of ˈde/ities/or ˈmor/tals, or/of ˈboth,	d
In ˈTem/pe ˈor/the ˈdales/of ˈAr/caˈdy?	e
What ˈmen/or ˈgods/are ˈthese? What ˈmai/dens ˈloth?	d
What ˈmad/purˈsuit? /What ˈstrug/gle to/esˈcape?	c
What ˈpipes/and ˈtim/brels? ˈWhat/wild ˈec/stasy?	e

这节诗共 10 行,据上述分析可知,每行 5 个音步,每个音步均为 2 个音节。从上面重音节的标注可知,大部分音步都是轻重音节,抑扬格。因此,此节诗格律为五步抑扬格,韵律为 ababcdedce。

主要内容归纳和总结

1. 约翰·济慈出生于伦敦一个出租马和马车的小业主家庭,9 岁丧父,15 岁丧母。他未读过大学,曾跟外科医生、药剂师当学徒,并有营业执照,却从未真正开业。因酷爱斯宾塞、弥尔顿和荷马的作品,他转而献身于诗歌创作,初期的作品既有伊丽莎白时代的文学元素,也有当时激进新闻工作者的政治影响。

他最优秀的诗集《拉米亚、伊莎贝拉、圣爱格尼斯节前夕及其他诗歌》(*Lamia*, *Isabella*, *The Eve of St. Agnes*, *and Other Poems*)中的三首标题诗都与神话传奇有关,表达了他将理想与现实、想象与实际、男人与女人结合起来的思考。这部诗集中还包括他最成熟的作品——四首颂诗:《忧郁颂》《希腊古瓮颂》《夜莺颂》《普赛克颂》。尽管他对资本主义社会现实不满,但他的诗歌却追求唯美,逃避现实,创作素材多取自神秘的上古时期和文艺复兴时期的典故。

济慈想象力极强,常将感觉甚至幻觉入诗,转化成绝美的诗句,写透了人乃至动物的心灵,从抒情诗到叙事诗,他留给人们大量体裁迥异的作品(different types or forms of literature)。

2. 济慈的主要作品:
《读恰普曼译荷马》*On First Looking into Chapman's Homer* (1816)
《诗集》*The First Volume of Poems* (1817),其中包括名诗:
《睡与诗》Sleep and Poetry

《安狄米翁》*Endymion*（1818）

《拉米亚、伊莎贝拉、圣爱格尼斯节前夕及其他诗歌》*Lamia*，*Isabella*，*The Eve of St. Agnes*，*and Other Poems*（1820），其中包括他的四大颂诗：

* 《忧郁颂》*Ode on Melancholy*（1819）

* 《夜莺颂》*Ode to a Nightingale*（1819）

* 《普赛克颂》*Ode to Psyche*

* 《希腊古瓮颂》*Ode on a Grecian Urn*

《秋日颂》*To Autumn*（1819）

《希波里恩》*Hyperion* 未完稿

重要信息句子

1. The four odes are generally regarded as Keats' most important and mature works. 四大颂诗被普遍认为是济慈最重要和最成熟的作品。

2. His lyric masterpiece is *To Autumn*. 《秋日颂》是他抒情诗的杰作。

3. "Ode on an Grecian Urn" shows the contrast between the permanence of art and the transience of human passion. 《希腊古瓮颂》展示了艺术永久和人情短暂之间的对比。

4. "Ode to a Nightingale" expresses the contrast between the happy world of natural loneliness and human world of agony. 《夜莺颂》表述了快乐秀美的自然世界和痛苦的人类世界的比较。

VII. 简·奥斯汀 Jane Austen（1775～1817）

词语解释和难句分析

1. be brought up in an intelligent but restricted environment 在一个学识氛围浓厚、但生活空间狭小的家庭环境中成长起来

 be a rector and a scholar with a good library 是圣公会的一个教区长，一个拥有一座很好的图书馆的学者

 to acquire a thorough knowledge of eighteenth-century English literature 对18世纪的英国文学获得了透彻的了解

 to live a quiet, retired and, in public terms, uneventful life 过着一种安静的、离群索居的生活，用老百姓的话说，就是没有是非烦扰的生活

 to write novels for her family entertainment 她写小说是为了家庭娱乐消遣

 be published anonymously due to the prejudice against women writers 考虑到对女作家的偏见，（她的小说）以匿名的方式出版

2. six complete novels 6部完成了的小说

 to satirize those popular Gothic romances 讽刺那些流行的哥特式骑士抒情诗

 to deal with the romantic entanglements of their strongly characterized heroines 描写他们（这些小说中）性格鲜明的人物浪漫主义的感情纠葛

to present the antithesis of worldliness and unworldliness　对世俗和非世俗进行了对照

to give the thought over self-deceptive vanity　表现出自欺欺人的虚荣的思想

to contrast the true love with the prudential calculations　把真正的爱情与精打细算的爱情进行对照

3. to hold the ideals of the landlord class　怀着地主阶级的理想

to <u>show her firm belief in</u> the predominance of reason over passion　她对理性支配情感表现出坚定的信仰

the sense of responsibility　责任感

good manners and clear-sighted judgment over Romantic tendencies of emotion and individuality　良好的言谈举<u>止</u>和对浪漫主义情感和个性的目光敏锐的判断

to express a discriminated and serious criticism of life　表达出对生活的一种有区别的严肃的批判

to expose the follies and illusions of mankind　揭露人的愚蠢和幻想

to show comtemptuous feelings towards snobbery, stupidity, worldliness and vulgarity　显示出对势利、愚蠢、市侩和庸俗的蔑视的情感

to uphold those traditional ideas of order, reason, proportion and gracefulness in novel writing　在小说创作中,赞成有序、理性、均衡和典雅等传统的想法

4. It is her conviction that a man's relationship to his wife and children is at least as important a part of his life as his concerns about his belief and career.　她坚定地相信,一个人与妻子、孩子的关系至少要被看得与他的信仰和事业同等重要。

5. main literary concern　主要的文学主题

a man's talents, nature and temper　人的才能、秉性和脾气

at moment's of crisis　在生死存亡的危急时刻

the most trivial incidents of everyday life　日常生活中最琐碎的小事

6. be preoccupied with　专注于

in their pursuit of　他们追求……,在他们对……的追求中

be categorized into　被分类成……

to marry for material wealth and social position　为追求物质财富和社会地位而结婚

to marry just for beauty and passion　只为美貌和人欲的激情而结婚

to marry for true love with a consideration of the partner's personal merit as well as his economical and social status　为真爱而结婚,但也要考虑对方的个人美德以及经济地位和社会地位

7. subject matter　主题

character range　人物阶层

the social setting　社会背景

be restricted to the provincial life　受到当地地方生活的限制

landed gentry families　拥有土地的贵族家庭

(there is) little reflection on the events that stirred the whole Europe at the time　几乎没有反映当时激荡整个欧洲的大事件

no thrilling adventures　没有令人惊悚的冒险

no romantic reveries　没有浪漫主义的幻想/妄想

to result from an observation of a quiet, uneventful and contented life of the English country　是由于对英国乡村安静、波澜不兴和心满意足的生活的观察

to portray them with absolute accuracy and sureness　绝对准确可靠地描述它们

8. It is no exaggeration to say that...　可以毫不夸张地说……

9. <u>be originally drafted as</u> "First Impression"　初稿名为……,原名为……

to <u>tell of</u> a major concern of the novel　讲明这本小说的主要内容

as is shown here by those of Elizabeth　就像伊丽莎白的"第一印象"所表现的那样(是错误的)

＊ those 即句中前面所说的 the first impressions。

to find something about herself：her blindness, partiality, prejudice and absurdity　发现她自己的一些问题：盲目、偏颇、偏见和荒谬

10. The structure of the novel is exquisitely deft, the characterization in the highest degree memorable, while the irony has a radiant shrewdness unmatched elsewhere.　小说的结构极为灵巧,人物塑造最令人难忘,而反语冷嘲则闪烁着无可匹敌的机敏。

11. the exhilarating suspense of the relationship between Elizabeth Bannet and Darcy　在伊丽莎白与达西的关系上令人兴奋的悬念

    delicate probing of the values of the gentry　对中上阶级的价值观进行仔细的探讨

    self-esteem = self-respect　自尊

    to avoid the wretchedness of aging spinsterhood　避免老处女身份的不幸和烦恼

    the dangers of feckless relationships unsupported by money　没有金钱支撑的无效婚姻关系的危险性

    monstrous snob　极端荒谬的势利小人

    to parody erroneous views of marriage and class　嘲弄错误的婚姻观点和阶级观点

12. trenchant observation and in meticulous detail　敏锐的观察和对细节的一丝不苟

    to learn lessons through tribulation　通过经历的磨难和忧伤吸取教训

    to particularized the most minor characters vividly　详细地把不太重要的次要人物描写得栩栩如生

    to bring the English novel to its maturity　使英国小说走向成熟

13. Even the most minor characters are vividly particularized in Austen's lucid style.　即使是不太重要的次要人物,奥斯汀也以清晰的文风详细地把他们描写得栩栩如生。

14. All these show a mind of the shrewdest intelligence adapting the available traditions and deepening the resources of art with consummate craftsmanship.　所有这些都表现了一种精明睿智的思想,既适应有益的艺术传统,又以极高的艺术技巧对创作素材进行了深入的挖掘和探索。

简·奥斯汀作品选读

《傲慢与偏见》Pride and Prejudice 第一章节选

词语解释和难句分析

1. be skeptical of conventional marriage　怀疑传统的婚姻

   to have no good words for his beautiful daughters　对自己漂亮的女儿们从未好言相待/从未给过好脸

   a beautiful but empty-headed, snobbish and vulgar woman　一个美丽但没有头脑,势利而庸俗的女人

   cold disposition　冷漠的脾性

   to make a bad impression on the local people　给当地的人留下不好的印象

   to slight Elizabeth and hurt her dignity by refusing to dance with her　拒绝与伊丽莎白跳舞,冷落了她,伤了她的尊严

   to try to bring down his pride　竭力挫折/打击他的傲气

   to make acquaintance with　与某人结识,开始熟悉……

   a cold-blooded, selfish man　一个冷血自私的人

   be responsible for the separation of Bingley and Jane　对宾莱和简未能结合承担责任

to explain his justified low opinion of the Bennet family　解释他对班内特一家口出微词的缘由

a vain, wicked-minded man　一个爱慕虚荣的、卑鄙下流的人

to <u>set on</u> a tour to Derbyshire　到德比郡做一次旅游

to pay a visit to Pemberley　参观了彭伯莱花园

impaired relationship　受到损伤的关系

be well on the way to improvement　正在顺利修复/改善的过程中

be summoned home　被叫回/召回家

through the generous intervention of Darcy　通过达西的慷慨介入/斡旋

to have them properly married　使他们体面结婚

to get out of the disgrace　避免丢人出丑

2. The revelation of Darcy's generous help further <u>assures Elizabeth of</u> his feelings towards herself and at the same time makes her realize how truthful his accusation of lowliness of her family is.　达西慷慨相助的启示进一步使伊丽莎白相信他对自己的真心,同时,使她认识到过去他对自己家庭评价不高多么符合事实。

3. As Elizabeth <u>is meditating on</u> the hopeless situation of her union with Darcy, Lady de Bourgh, aunt of Darcy, comes to Longbourn, on hearing some rumor, to <u>force Elizabeth into</u> a promise of never consenting to marry Darcy.　当伊丽莎白正在为自己与达西结合无望的境况沉思的时候,达西的姑母德·鲍夫人,听到了一些谣传,来到了朗伯恩强迫伊丽莎白答应绝不会同意嫁给达西。

4. out of anger and <u>contempt for</u> the arrogant and bad-mannered lady　出于对这个傲慢的、坏脾气的女人的愤怒和蔑视

with the indignation　怀着义愤

to give him a picture of a disrespectful, ill-mannered Elizabeth　向他描述了一个不懂礼貌、举止粗鲁的伊丽莎白

to enlighten him about the young lady's heart　使他得到启示,了解了这年轻女子的心

to make a second proposal　再次求婚

5. bachelor *n.* 年轻单身男子；Bachelorette *n.* 年轻单身女子

servile clergyman　奴颜婢膝的牧师

heir to the Bennets' property　班内特家财产的继承人

to propose to Elizabeth　向伊丽莎白求婚

the thoughtless couple　没头脑的一对(恋人/夫妻)

6. a truth <u>universally acknowledged</u>　一个举世公认的真理

a single man <u>in possession of</u> a good fortune　拥有大笔财产的单身汉,很有钱的单身男子

in want of　想要,缺少,缺乏

<u>be</u> so well <u>fixed in</u> the minds of...　深深地植根于……的思想中,深入……的思想

some one or other　不是这个,就是那个;总有一个

7. However little known the feelings or views of such a man may be on his first entering a neighborhood, this truth <u>is so well fixed in</u> the minds of the surrounding families, that he is considered as the rightful property of some one or other of their daughters.　不管对一个初来乍到的男子的心思了解得多么少,左邻右舍心里的这条真理却是根深蒂固的:他就是自己的某个女儿的合法财产。

to have no objection to doing sth.　不反对做某事

8. be invitation enough = be encouraging enough　(对做某事)是足够的鼓舞

to come down on Monday in a chaise and four to see the place　周一乘四匹马拉的双轮马车来此看地方/看房子

be so much delighted with sth.　对某事非常喜欢/满意

to take possession before Mechaelemas　要在米迦勒斯节前入住

to take possession of...　占据、拥有、控制、入住……

to be in the house　打算就要入住那房子了

9. no occasion for... = there is no reason for...　没有理由做某件事

　to send them by themselves　打发她们自己去

10. My dear, you flatter me. I certainly <u>have had my share of beauty</u>, but I do not pretend to be any thing extraordinary now. When a woman has five <u>grown up</u> daughters, she ought to <u>give over thinking of</u> her own beauty.　亲爱的，你吹捧我了。我的确曾经美丽过，不过现在我却不能装嫩（假装有什么出类拔萃的地方），一个女人如果五个女儿都长大了，就不该再考虑自己漂亮不漂亮了。

11. It is more than I <u>engage for</u>, I assure you.　老实对你说，那不是我分内的事。/可以肯定，那超出了我该做的范围。

12. Only think what an establishment it would be for one of them.　只要想一想对他们当中的任一个人（女儿）都会是多么好的（安身立命的）归宿！

13. on that account = on account of that　考虑到那一点/由于那个原因

　be over scrupulous surely　确实过于细心/认真了

　to <u>assure him of</u> my hearty consent to his marrying whichever he chooses of the girls　让他放心，不管他选中哪一个女儿，我都心甘情愿地赞同他娶她

　to <u>throw in</u> a good word for my little Lizzy　为我的小丽萃多说几句好话

　be not half so handsome as Jane, nor half so good humored as Lydia　相貌不及简一半漂亮，性情也不及莉狄亚一半好

　to give her the preference　对她有所偏爱

14. They have none of them much to recommend them.　她们没一个人有足以推荐她们的东西。/她们没有一个人值得推荐。

15. to have something more of quickness than her sisters　有些方面比她的姐妹聪明些

　to take delight in vexing sb.　故意气恼某人，以气恼某人为乐

　to <u>have no compassion on</u> my poor nerves　对我的神经衰弱一点也不体谅/同情

　to have a high respect for your nerves　体谅你的神经衰弱

　to mention them <u>with consideration</u> these twenty years　你正儿八经地提你的神经衰弱已经提了20年了。

　to <u>get over</u> your poor nerves　克服你的神经衰弱，使你的神经衰弱得到康复

　depend upon it = don't worry about it = you are sure　别担心/请放心

　so odd a mixture of quick parts, sarcastic humor, reserve, and caprice　一个时而插科打诨、挖苦嘲笑，时而深藏不露、阴晴不定的复杂情感的奇怪混合体

　a woman of mean, understanding, little information, and uncertain temper.　一个智力平庸、孤陋寡闻、脾气多变却又能通情达理的女人。

16. Her mind was less difficult to develop.　她的想法不太难/容易捉摸。

17. When she was discontented she <u>fancied herself nervous</u>.　当她碰到不满意的事，就想当然地以为自己得了神经衰弱。

18. Its solace (= the comfort of her life) was visiting and news.　她的生平乐事就是串门拉呱，打听新闻。

主要内容归纳和总结

1. 简·奥斯汀出生于英格兰斯蒂文顿(Steventon)一个圣公会教区长的家庭,属于书香门第,父亲有自己的私人图书馆,她从小就徜徉在书海中,受过良好的家庭教育。她悠闲平静的生活,狭小的社交范围,使她的创作素材也十分狭窄,主题、角色、背景和情节都离不开 18 世纪英国乡村中产阶级的生活,三四口之家的日常生活舞会、茶点、野餐以及无关风雨的家长里短和闲言碎语。她从不把人物放到生死攸关的危急时刻来塑造,欧洲的革命风暴在她的作品中没有一丝痕迹,她的作品像是激情澎湃的浪漫主义时期的一股温婉的清流。

奥斯汀是浪漫主义时期的一个现实主义作家,她继承了新古典主义风格,坚持理性、秩序和典雅的原则,强调理智高于情感,责任、礼节和公正高于个人主义。这些理性思想表现在她作品描写的爱情上,就是纯粹为利益结婚与根本不考虑利益而结婚都是不对的,虚幻的浪漫激情的婚姻是靠不住的。

奥斯汀的作品故事构思精巧细密,人物性格和心理活动刻画得细腻准确,同时代的作家在这一点上无人可以与之匹敌。

2. 奥斯汀一生写过 6 本完成了的小说,可分为两个创作时期

a. 1795 ~ 1798 为第一阶段, 完成 3 部小说,15 年后出版

《理智与情感》*Sense and Sensibility*(1811)

《傲慢与偏见》*Pride and Prejudice*(1813)

《诺桑觉寺》*Northanger Abbey*(1818)

b. 1811 年《理智与情感》出版之后,她开始了创作的第二阶段,完成 3 部小说

《曼斯菲尔德花园》*Mansfield Park*(1814)

《爱玛》*Emma*(1815)

《劝告》*Persuasion*(1818)

另外还有 3 部未完成的小说:

《沃特森一家》*The Watsons*(1923)

《一部小说的未完成部分》*Fragment of a Novel*(1925)

《小说的构思》*Plan of a Novel*(1926)

重要信息句子

1. Generally speaking, Jane Austen was a writer of the 18th century, though she lived mainly in the 19th century.

2. Austen's main literary concern is about human beings in their personal relationships.

3. As a novelist Jane Austen writes within a very narrow sphere.

4. It is no exaggeration to say that within her limited sphere Jane Austen is unequaled.

5. The works of Jane Austen, at once delightful and profound, are among the supreme achievements of English literature.

6. Jane Austen tries to say, in *Pride and Prejudice*, that it is wrong to marry just for money or for beauty, but it is also wrong to marry without it.

英国浪漫主义时期文学同步练习与答案

1. The Romantic Period of English literature is said to have begun in 1798 with the publication of Wordsworth and Coleridge's _____ and to have ended in 1832 with Sir Walter Scott's death and the passage of the first _____ in the Parliament.
   a. *Songs of Innocence*/Bill of Right
   b. *Lyrical Ballads*/Reform Bill
   c. *Don Juan*/Declaration of Rights of Man
   d. *Ode to the West Wind*/Reform Bill

2. During this period, the biggest social change in English history was _____.
   a. the agricultural mechanization
   b. the transfer of large masses of the population from the countryside to the town
   c. that some people emigrated to the colonies
   d. the Enclosures

3. _____ published two books that electrified Europe – *Du Contrat Social* and *Emile* (1762), provided necessary guiding principles for the French Revolution; _____ *Declaration of Rights of Man* (1791 ~ 1792) and the storming of Bastille aroused great sympathy and enthusiasm in the English liberals and radicals; And then _____ urged the equal rights for women in her *A Vindication of the Rights of Woman* (1792), thus setting out the earliest exposition of feminism.
   a. Jean-Jacques Rousseau/Thomas Paine's/Marry Wollstonecraft
   b. Edmund Burke/William Godwin's/William Cobbet
   c. Jean-Jacques Rousseau/Edmund Burke's/Marry Wollstonecraft
   d. Marry Wollstonecraft/William Cobbet's/William Godwin

4. The Romantic Movement expressed a more or less _____ toward the existing social and political conditions that came with industrialization and the growing importance of the bourgeoisie.
   a. positive attitude
   b. negative attitude
   c. support
   d. indifferent attitude

5. The Romantic period is an age of _____.
   a. reason
   b. prose
   c. drama
   d. poetry

6. Where their predecessors saw man as a social animal, the Romantics saw him essentially as an _____ in the _____ state.
   a. type character/collective
   b. real man/social
   c. individual/solitary
   d. abstract person/imaginary

7. Where the Augustans emphasized those features that men have in common, the Romantics emphasized _____.
   a. the individuality of a man
   b. the outer world of social civilization
   c. the inner world of the human spirit
   d. imagination

8. Imagination, defined by Coleridge, is the vital faculty that creates new whole out of _____.
   a. objective truth
   b. social reality
   c. individual idea
   d. disparate elements

9. Nature, for the most influential 18th-century writers, was more something _____ than something _____. But for the Romantics it is just the opposite.

a. rational/imaginary   b. in order/out of order

c. to be seen/to be known   d. to be known/to be seen

10. Wordsworth, Coleridge and Southey chose to live _____ so as to escape from the "madding crowd," while Byron and Shelley rejected the entire English society by _____.

     a. in the rural area/underlife   b. in the mountainous area/living in solitude

     c. by the lakeside/their self-inposed exile   d. on the island in the sea/fishing alone

11. _____ is also a great age of prose. Newspapers, magazines and periodicals run by private enterprises started to flourish in this period.

     a. The Neoclassical period   b. The Romantic period

     c. The Modernist period   d. The Victorian period

12. The two major novelists of the Romantic period are _____ and _____.

     a. William Hazlitt/Charles Lamb   b. Thomas De Quincey/Jane Austen

     c. Walter Scott/Charles Lamb   d. Jane Austen/Walter Scott

13. In the Romantic period, there was a great critic on Shakespeare, Elizabethan drama, and English poetry, who is _____.

     a. Walter Scott   b. William Hazlitt

     c. Percy Bysshe Shelley   d. Charles Lamb

14. As one phase of the Romantic movement, _____ have _____, _____, and _____ as its principal elements.

     a. Romance/knight/beauty/adventure

     b. lyrical ballads/emotional expression/rhythm/rhyme

     c. prose/comment/narration/exposition

     d. Gothic novel/violence/horror/the supernatural

15. _____ is central to Blake's concern in the *Songs of Innocence* and *Songs of Experience*.

     a. Social development   b. Future prospect

     c. Childhood   d. Belief

16. In his later period, Blake wrote quite a few prophetic books, among them are _____ and _____.

     a. *The Book of Urizen/The Book of Los*

     b. *The Four Zoas/Marriage of Heaven and Hell*

     c. *The Book of Urizen/The Mysteries of Udolpho*

     d. *The Book of Los/Spirit of Nature*

17. In the following years of the French Revolution, the Jacobin terror and the French invasion of other European countries fully revealed that the desire for Liberty had been swallowed up by the desire for _____.

     a. Conquest   b. Domination

     c. Massacre   d. Empire

18. _____ and _____ collaborated on a book of poems entitled *Lyrical Ballads*, first published in 1798 and marking the beginning of the Romantic period of English literature.

     a. Samuel Taylor Coleridge/John Keats

     b. John Keats/William Wordsworth

     c. William Wordsworth/William Blake

     d. William Wordsworth/Samuel Taylor Coleridge

19. Wordsworth had a long poetic career. His first volumes were _____.

a. *Lyrical Ballads*

b. *Descriptive Sketches, an Evening Walk*

c. *Don Juan*

d. *Ode to the West Wind*

20. According to the subjects, Wordsworth's short poems can be classified into groups: _____ and _____.

    a. poems about deities/poems about death

    b. poems about nature/poems about human life

    c. poems about eternality/poems about universe

    d. poems about afterlife/poems about meditation on the earth

21. Wordsworth is regarded as a(n) "_____."

    a. expert to express emotion

    b. worshipper of God

    c. narrative poet

    d. worshipper of nature

22. Wordsworth thinks that _____ is the only subject of literary interest.

    a. uneventful life

    b. common life

    c. violent revolution

    d. social change

23. Wordsworth is a poet in memory of _____. To him, life is a _____. Its beginning finally turns out to be its end.

    a. the past/review of the past

    b. his own dreamland/subjective existence

    c. the past/cyclical journey

    d. his childhood/recurrence of fairy tales

24. _____ wrote his major prose work, *Biographia Literaria*, a series of autobiographical notes and dissertations on many subjects.

    a. Samuel Taylor Coleridge

    b. Percy Bysshe Shelley

    c. John Keats

    d. George Gordon Byron

25. Coleridge's poems can be divided into two groups: the demonic and the conversational. The masterpiece (s) of the former is/are _____; and of the latter is/are _____.

    a. *Frost at Midnight* // *Kubla Khan/Christabel/The Rime of the Ancient Mariner*

    b. *Ode on the Ancient Grecian Urn/Kubla Khan* // *Ode to Liberty/Christabel*

    c. *Prometheus Unbound/Kubla Khan* // *Frost at Midnight*

    d. *Kubla Khan/Christabel/he Rime of the Ancient Mariner* // *Frost at Midnight*

26. In his *Biographia Literaria*, Coleridge denies Wordsworth's claim that there is no essential difference between _____ and _____.

    a. the language of poetry/the language spoken by common people

    b. the language of poetry/the language of other forms of literature

    c. the language of poetry/the language of prose

    d. the novel story/the plot of a drama

27. Which one's publication of Byron's works first made him say "I awoke one morning and found myself famous."? _____.

    a. Long verse-tales *Oriented Tales*

    b. Narrative poem *The Prisoner of Chillon*

    c. *Childe Harold's Pilgrimage*

    d. Verse drama *Manfred*

28. On the whole, Byron's poetry is one of experience. His heroes are more or less _____.

    a. his family member

    b. his acquaintance

    c. surrogates of himself

    d. his comrades sharing the same views

29. *Don Juan* is Byron's masterpiece, a great comic epic of the early 19th century. It is a poem based on a traditional _____ of a great lover and seducer of women.

a. English epic
b. Spanish legend
c. French novel
d. Greek comedy

30. As a leading Romanticist, Byron's chief contribution is his creation of the "Byron's hero," a proud, mysterious _____.

a. rebel of noble origin
b. patriot defending his country
c. knight agaist evil force
d. hermit hard to see

31. Except writing a lot of poems, Percy Bysshe Shelley wrote a prose essay about poetic theory — _____, and a pamphlet about world outlook — _____, repudiating the existence of God.

a. *The Necessity of Atheism/A Defence of Poetry*

b. *Hymn to Intellectual Beauty/A Defence of Poetry*

c. *A Defence of Poetry/Inquiry Concerning Political Justice*

d. *A Defence of Poetry/The Necessity of Atheism*

32. Best of all the well-known lyric pieces is Shelley's _____.

a. *Ode to Liberty*
b. *Ode to Naples*
c. *Ode to the West Wind*
d. *Prometheus Unbound*

33. Shelley's greatest achievement is his _____.

a. four-act poetic drama, *Prometheus Unbound*

b. well-known lyrics, *Ode to the West Wind*

c. prose essay, *A Defence of Poetry*

d. political pamphlet, *The Necessity of Atheism*

34. Among John Keats' poems, the most important and mature are four great odes: *Ode on Melancholy*, _____, _____, *Ode to Psyche*.

a. *Ode to Liberty/Ode to Naples*
b. *Ode on a Grecian Urn/Ode to a Nightingale*
c. *Ode on a Grecian Urn/Ode to Autumn*
d. *Ode to the West Wind/Ode to a Nightingale*

35. Keats' lyric masterpiece is _____.

a. *Ode to the West Wind*
b. *Ode on a Grecian Urn*
c. *To Autumn*
d. *Ode to Nightingale*

36. In Keats' works, _____ shows the contrast between the permanence of art and the transience of human passion.

a. *Ode on Melancholy*
b. *Ode on a Grecian Urn*
c. *To Autumn*
d. *Ode to Psyche*

37. In her lifelong career, Jane Austen wrote altogether six complete novels, which are _____, _____, *Northangers Abbey*, *Mansfield Park*, _____, *Persuasion*.

a. *The Watsons/Pride and Prejudice/Plan of a Novel*

b. *Sense and Sensibility/Emma /Fragment of a Novel*

c. *Sense and Sensibility/Pride and Prejudice/The Watsons*

d. *Sense and Sensibility/Pride and Prejudice/Emma*

38. Austen's main literary concern is about human beings in their _____. She shows a human being in her novels always _____.

a. personal relationships/at moments of crisis

b. families/in the most trivial incidents of everyday life

c. neighborhood/at moments of crisis

d. personal relationships/in the most trivial incidents of everyday life

39. In her study of human beings of daily life, Austen is particularly preoccupied with the relationship between _____.

    a. landlord and peasants   b. mother and her daughters

    c. women in love   d. men and women in love

40. Through the description of her characters' pursuit of marriages, Jane Austen tries to say _____.

    a. it is wrong to marry just for money

    b. it is wrong to marry just for beauty

    c. it is wrong to marry just for passion or sexual need

    d. it is wrong to marry just for money or for beauty, but it is also wrong to marry without it

41. The Romantic Movement expressed a more or less _____ attitude toward the existing social and political conditions.

    a. positive   b. negative

    c. neutral   d. indifferent

42. It is _____ who established the cult of the individual and championed the freedom of the human spirit.

    a. Jean-Jacques Rousseau   b. Johann Wolfgang von Goethe

    c. Edmund Burke   d. Thomas Paine

43. In *Marriage of Heaven and Hell* (1790), the word "marriage", to Blake, means the _____.

    a. subordination of the one to the other   b. co-existence of the conflicting parts

    c. reconciliation of the contraries   d. fighting of the conflicting parts

44. Blake began writing poetry at the age of 12, and his first printed work is _____, which is a collection of youthful verse.

    a. *Songs of Experience*   b. *Songs of Innocence*

    c. *Marriage of Heaven and Hell*   d. *Poetical Sketches*

45. In his poem, "The Chimney Sweeper" (from *Songs of Experience*), Blake depicted the miseries of the child sweepers in order to reveal the _____ of Christianity.

    a. great ideals   b. false ideals

    c. magic power   d. true faith

46. Adonais is an elegy for _____ whose early death from tuberculosis Shelley believed had been hastened by hostile revisions.

    a. Byron   b. Keats

    c. Tennyson   d. Blake

47. In the poem, "She Dwelt among the Untrodden Ways," Wordsworth writes: "A violet by a mossy stone/ Half hidden from the eye!" The figure of speech used in the two lines is _____.

    a. metaphor   b. personification

    c. simile   d. metonymy

48. The _____ are generally regarded as Keats's most important and mature works.

    a. odes   b. lyrics

    c. epics   d. elegy

49. Shelley's _____ and *The Cenci*, Byron's _____, and Coleridge's *Remorse* are generally regarded as the best verse plays in the Romantic period.

    a. *Prometheus Unbound/ Cain*   b. *Cain/ Manfred*

    c. *Prometheus Unbound/ Manfred*   d. *Waverley/ Cain*

50. Among Coleridge's _____ group of poems, *Frost at Midnight* is the most important.

a. conversational   b. Romantic

c. demonic   d. lyrical

51. After reading the first chapter of *Pride and Prejudice*, we come to know that Mrs. Bennet is a woman of _____.

    a. simple character and mean understanding

    b. simple character and quick wit

    c. intricate character and quick talent

    d. intricate character and great talent

52. In the conversation with Mrs. Bennet in Chapter One of *Pride and Prejudice*, Mr. Bennet uses a _____ tone and sarcastic humour.

    a. solemn   b. harsh

    c. intimate   d. teasing

53. In his poem, "Ode to the West Wind", Shelley intends to present his wind as a central _____ around which the poem weaves various cycles of death and rebirth — seasonal, vegetational, human and divine.

    a. concept   b. metaphor

    c. symbol   d. metonymy

54. William Wordsworth, a romantic poet, advocated all the following EXCEPT _____.

    a. the using of everyday language spoken by the common people

    b. the expression of the spontaneous overflow of powerful feelings

    c. the humble and rustic life as subject matter

    d. elegant wordings and inflated figures of speech

55. In the poem "She Dwelt among the Untrodden Ways", the ending lines go like this: "But she is in her grave, and, oh,/The difference to me!" The word "me" in the quoted lines may probably refer to _____.

    a. the poet   b. the reader

    c. her lover   d. her father

56. In S. T. Coleridge's poem "Kubla Khan", "A sunny pleasure dome with caves of ice" _____.

    a. refers to the place where Kubla Khan's father once lived

    b. vividly describes a building of poor quality

    c. is the gift given to a beautiful girl called Abyssinian

    d. symbolizes the reconciliation of the conscious and the unconscious

57. Which of the following is NOT a quality of the west wind described by Shelley in his poem "Ode to the West Wind"? _____.

    a. Wild   b. Tamed

    c. Swift   d. Proud

Keys: bbabd/cadcc/bdbdc/addbb/dbcad/accba/dcabc/bdddd/bacdb/baaaa/adcdc/db

第四章 维多利亚时期 The Victorian Period

词语解释和难句分析

1. to coincide with the reign of Queen Victoria　与维多利亚女王执政的时间恰好相符

   to pass the political power from the decaying aristocrats into the hands of middle-class industrial capitalists　把政治权力从腐败的贵族手中转移到中产阶级实业家手中

   to gear up/down　换挡增速/减速

   spinning looms　织布机

   textile factories　纺织厂

   printing machines　印刷机

   be accumulated from expanding its foreign trade markets and from exploiting its huge-sized colonies　通过扩大外贸市场、剥削幅员广阔的殖民地人民而累积起来

   to reach its highest point of development as a world power　达到了作为世界强国发展的顶峰

   to crowd in the dirty and insanitary slums　拥挤在肮脏、不卫生的贫民窟

   the new Poor Law of 1834 with its workhouse system　1834 年颁布的涉及济贫院体系的新济贫法

   to give rise to the Chartist Movement　产生了人民宪章运动

   to get themselves organized　把他们自己组织起来

   to bring forth the People's Charter　产生/推出了"人民宪章"

   to better living and working conditions　改善生活条件和工作条件

   to make appeals to the government　向政府发出呼吁

   to sweep over most of the cities　席卷/横扫大多数城镇

   to bring some improvement to the welfare of the working class　为工人阶级的福利带来了一些改进

2. to settle down a time of prosperity and relative stability　安顿下来过了一段繁荣昌盛和相对稳定的日子

   with the Industrial Revolution in full swing　随着工业革命的充分展示

   be well ahead of others in development　在发展过程中充分领先于其他人

   be characterized by prosperity, respectability and material progress　以昌盛、受人尊敬和物质进步为特点

   to try to live up to a national spirit of earnestness, respectability, modesty and domesticity　竭力符合认真、体面、谦逊和爱家的民族精神

   with Queen herself as the epitome of such virtues　以女王本人作为那些道德的象征

   to become the predominant preoccupation in literary works　在文学著作中,变成了主要关注点

3. to hurt the British monopoly in trade and commerce　伤害了英国在商贸中的垄断地位

   the spiritual prop for the national consolidation　国家巩固的精神支柱

   to begin to lose its glamour　开始失去它的魅力

   be replaced by a more "loose and dissipating one"　被一个更加松散和放荡的人所取代

4. This fin-de-siecle sentiment was best reflected in the works of such aestheticists as Oscar Wilde and Walter Pater, both notorious advocators of the theory of "art for art's sake."　这种颓废派的伤感情绪在像王尔德和派特这样的唯美主义作家的作品中得到了最充分的反映,他们就是所谓的"为艺术而艺术"

理论的倡导者。

5. drastically shake people's religious convictions　猛烈地动摇了人们的宗教信仰

religious collision　宗教冲突

be intensified by the disputes over evolutionary science　为关于科学进化论的争论所强化

The Origin of Species　《物种起源》

The Descent of Man　《人类的进化》

In Memoriam　《悼念》

to record his own experience of religious uncertainties before the falling faith in god　记录了他对神的信仰崩溃之前自己对宗教怀疑的体验

be put to the test by the criterion of utility　被拿来接受实用标准的检验

the Bible and the Evangelical Orthodoxy　《圣经》和四福音书的正统信仰

an outmoded superstition　一种过时的迷信

be tested by the principle of utility　受到功利主义原则的检验

church service　教堂礼拜

real devotion　真正的虔诚

to hold a special appeal to the middle-class industrialists　对中产阶级的实业家具有特别的感染力

to criticize the Utilitarian creed　批判实用主义/功利主义的信条

its depreciation of cultural values　它(实用主义)对文化价值的贬低/轻视

its cold indifference towards human feelings and imagination　它(实用主义)对人类情感和想象力的冷漠态度

6. to take on its quality of magnitude and diversity　呈现出既宏大又多种多样的特点

many-sided and complex　多侧面的、复杂的

to reflect both romantically and realistically the great changes that are going on in people's life and thought　对人们的生活和思想正在发生的巨大变化进行了既浪漫主义又现实主义的反映

7. the most vital and challenging expression of progressive thought　先进思想的最重要、最令人感兴趣的表现

the critical realists　批判现实主义者

to stick to the principle of faithful representation　坚持重视表现的原则

to share one thing in common　在一件事上有共同点

the inhuman social institutions　不人道的社会制度/习俗

the decaying social morality as represented by the money-worship and Utilitarianism　诸如拜金主义和实用主义所表现出来的腐败社会道德

to awaken the public consciousness to the social problems　唤醒大众对社会问题的认识/觉悟

to start putting all the actions inside　开始在人的内心世界采取行动,即描写人物的心理活动

all sorts of social iniquities　各种不公正的社会行为

to come to question and attack the Victorian conventions and morals　渐渐地开始怀疑和抨击维多利亚王朝的传统和道德准则

8. a host of great prose writers　许多伟大的散文作家

to join forces with the critical realist novelists　加入了批判现实主义作家的大军

to become very influential in the ideological field　在思想领域变得很有影响

historical accounts　历史叙述

religious dissertations　宗教方面的论文

to constitute a formidable force of influence upon the whole society　对整个社会形成巨大的影响力

Carlyle's *Sartor Resartus*, *The French Revolution*, *Chartism* 卡莱尔的《萨特·雷萨特》《法国大革命》和《宪章主义》

Macaulay's *History of England* 麦考利的《英国史》

Ruskin's five-volumed *Modern Painters* 卢斯金的五卷本《现代画家》

9. be mainly characterized by experiments with new styles and new ways of expression 以进行新文体和新表现手法试验为其创作特征

to create the verse novel by adopting the novelistic presentation of characters 采取小说中常见的人物表现手法来创作诗体小说

to transfer the thematic interest from mere narration of the story to revelation and study of characters' inner world 把主题的取向从只是故事的叙述转移到对人物内心世界的揭示和研究上来

to bring to the Victorian poetry some psycho-analytical element 给维多利亚时代的诗歌带来了一些心理分析的元素

10. to truthfully represent the reality and spirit of the age 忠实地表现那个时代的现实和精神

the high-spirited vitality 百折不挠/昂扬的活力

the down-to-earth earnestness 脚踏实地的认真

the good-natured humor and unbounded imagination 善意的幽默和毫无束缚的想象

to pave the way for the coming century 为即将来临的世纪铺平了道路

to witness their bumper harvest 见证了它们极为成功的收获

主要内容归纳和总结

1. 英国文学上的维多利亚时期与维多利亚女王的执政时期恰好相符(1836~1901)。

2. 维多利亚时期经济空前发展,政治也发生重大变化。1932年通过《改革法案》(Reform Bill)后,政权从没落贵族转移到新兴的资产阶级手中。工业革命使英国变成了"世界的工厂"。

3. 工人失业和生活、工作条件的恶化导致人民宪章运动(the Charter Movement)的发生。

4. 科学发现和技术发明导致了国家的工业化、机械化和交通运输等各方面的现代化。

5. 思想上,维多利亚时代发生了根本性的变化。达尔文(Darwin)进化论动摇了人们对上帝的信仰,教堂礼拜(religious service)变成了一种形式,而不是真正的信仰(real devotion)。功利主义(utilitarianism)盛行,一切都要经过实用的标准(criterion of utility)检验,人情冷漠,道德沦丧。

6. 维多利亚时代是一个小说的时代,巨星层出不穷,狄更斯(Dickens)、萨克雷(Thackeray)、勃朗特姐妹(the Brontë sisters)等基本上都是批判现实主义作家;诗歌处于各种文体和表达形式试验革新的阶段,罗伯特·布朗宁(Robert Browning)和阿尔弗雷德·丁尼生(Alfred Tennyson)是这一时期诗人改革者的代表人物。

重要信息句子

1. Victorian literature, as a product of its age, naturally took on its quality of magnitude and diversity.

2. Victorian literature, in general, truthfully represents the reality and spirit of the age. The high-spirited vitality, the down-to-earth earnestness, the good-natured humor and unbounded imagination are all unprecedented.

3. This period can be said an age of novels, in which the novel became the most widely read and the most

vital and challenging expression of progressive thought.

4. The poetry of this period was mainly characterized by experiments with new styles and new ways of expression.

I. 查尔斯·狄更斯 Charles Dickens（1812～1870）

词语解释和难句分析

1. a petty navy office clerk　一个海军小军官

   blacking factory　鞋油厂

   to paste labels on blacking bottles　在黑色鞋油瓶上贴标签

   the hardship and suffering <u>inflicted upon</u> the sensitive young Charles　年轻敏感的查尔斯所遭受的艰辛和痛苦

   ＊inflicted upon...　意为"强加在"，引导一个过去分词短语作定语。

   to leave an everlasting bitter remembrance in his later life　给他的晚年生活留下了永久的痛苦记忆

   a Parliamentary reporter for newspapers　为几家报纸做议会活动报道的记者

   to lay a good foundation for...　为……打下良好基础

2. to write occasional sketches of London　写一些关于伦敦的随笔速写

   be appeared/published in monthly installments　以月刊分期连载的方式出版

   an enthusiastic participant and organizer of some charity activities　一些慈善活动的热情的参与者和组织者

   to do a lot of recitation of his own works　多次朗诵他自己的著作

3. to hate the <u>state apparatus</u>　憎恨国家机器

   the fundamental solution to the social plights　社会困境的根本解决办法

   to try to retain an optimism with wishful thinking　竭力保持一厢情愿的乐观主义

   to express a helpful indignant protest　表达一种无奈的激愤的抗议

   to effect some reform or amelioration　（从而）实现/产生某种变革或改善

4. to set out a full map and a large-scale criticism of the 19th century England　对19世纪的英国发动全面的、大规模的批判

   products of bursting fantasy　突发奇想的产物，一时灵感驱动的作品

   petty-bourgeois urban world　城市小资产阶级社会

   to know <u>under the skin</u>, from its prestigious absurdity to its most sordid squalor　对（城市小资产阶级）有实质性的了解，从它的诡诈荒唐到它的卑鄙肮脏

   the dehumanizing workhouse system　丧失人性的孤儿院制度

   the dark, criminal underworld life　黑暗、罪恶的下层社会

   be enslaved at the master's house　在校长的家里被当作奴隶使唤

   legal fraud　法律欺诈

5. Here, the techniques, both of the fiction itself and of the social criticism embodied within it, are relatively straightforward and the objects of his attack are easily recognizable, and once the abuse has been overcome, the way is open to a happy conclusion.　在这些作品中，虚构本身的技巧以及虚构当中所

体现的社会批判的技巧都比较直截了当,抨击的目标也容易确认,而一旦凌辱伤害得到克服,故事线索的发展就是快乐的结局。

6. a mixture of the contemporary and the recollected past　当代和过去的回忆相混合

   double-or multiple-plotted (stories)　双线或多线的情节构思

   as metaphors for a repressive social psychology　作为压抑的社会心理的比喻说法

   with the exception of　除……之外

   most fundamental social institutions and morals　最基本的社会制度和道德准则

   the legal system and practices　法律体系和执法行为

   to aim at devouring every penny of the clients　旨在吃掉/掏光客户的每一分钱

   governmental branches　政府部门

   to run an indefinite procedure of management of affairs　实行一种变化不定的事务管理程序

   the overwhelming social environment　压抑的/令人窒息的社会环境

   to bring moral degeneration and destruction to people　使得人们道德蜕化和崩溃

7. The attack now becomes more urgent and passionate, and this urgency creates novels of great compactness and concentration.　这时作者笔下展开的抨击更加趋于急促紧张和情绪激烈,这种急迫的情绪使得创作的小说带有很大的凝缩感。

8. to explore more bleakly a bleaker world　以更为严峻的态度来探讨一个变得更为冷酷的世界

   be constantly inhibited by the consciousness of the unfunny side of life　(他的笑声)常常因意识到生活还有不快之处而被抑制

   a master story-teller　一个讲故事的大师

   to engage the reader's attention and hold it to the end　(从一开始就)吸引住读者的注意力,一直到最后

   a result of years' intimacy and rich imagination　多年亲密接触和丰富想象力的结果

   for his adeptness with the vernacular and large vocabulary　由于他擅长运用地方语言,并拥有巨大的词汇量

   character-portrayal　人物描写

9. Among a vast range of various characters, marked out by some peculiarity in physical traits, speech or manner, are both types and individuals. = Among a vast range of various characters, both types and individuals are marked out by some peculiarity in physical traits, speech or manner. 在他所描写的形形色色的人物中,根据其生理特征、讲话或言谈举止方面的某种特点,就可以分别出类型人物和个性人物。

10. his best-depicted characters　他描写得最好的人物

    horrible and grotesque characters　可怕的、奇形怪状的人物

    be true to life and be larger than life　忠实于生活,高于生活

    with some particular features exaggerated and highlighted, exposed to the degree of extremity　把某种特征夸大、突出,暴露到极致

11. be characterized by a mingling of humor and pathos　以幽默与同情相混合为特点

    to achieve a dramatic effect　取得一种喜剧效果

    to ridicule his personal defects　嘲笑他的个人缺陷

    to be light-heartedly jocular or bitterly satirical　轻松愉快地开玩笑或者犀利地讽刺

    to produce roaring laughter or understanding smiles　令人捧腹大笑或者会心一笑

    the death-bed scenes of sb.　某人临死时的情景

    to strike people to the heart　(痛苦)深刺人心,使读者感到痛彻心扉

    to wring an extra tear from the audience　从观众/读者眼里挤出更多眼泪

to indulge himself in excessive sentimental melodrama and spoil the story　他过度沉湎于悲情剧的描写,破坏了故事的连贯性

狄更斯作品选读
《雾都孤儿》*Oliver Twist* 第三章

词语解释和难句分析

1. be maltreated and constantly starved　受到虐待,并经常挨饿

   to ask for more gruel　想多要点粥/要求再给点儿粥

   be sent to an undertaker to work as an apprentice　被送给一个丧事承办人当学徒

   unable to bear the bullying from...　不能忍受来自……的欺负

   to fall into the hands of a gang of thieves　落入一帮盗贼之手

   thieves' den　贼窝,贼巢

   be rescued for a time by the kind-hearted Mr. Brownlow　有一次被好心的布朗罗先生所救

   be forced to help a burglar in a burglary　被迫在一次偷盗活动中当一个盗贼的助手

   protégée　女被保护人

   to bring him back to health　使他恢复健康

   half-brother　同父异母或同母异父的兄弟

   be adopted by...　被……所收养/采用

   the self-important beadle of the workhouse　自以为了不起/妄自尊大的济贫院教区执事

   to conspire with sb.　与某人密谋/搞阴谋

   to become an inmate of the workhouse over which he formerly ruled　变成了他自己以前掌控的济贫院的收容人员

2. the author's intimate knowledge of people of the lowest order　作者对社会底层人民的深刻了解

   the first grotesque figure　(作者描写的)第一个丑陋的人物

3. be punished for that "impious and profane offence of asking for more"　因"要求多给点儿粥这种逆天渎神的罪行"而受到惩罚

   be able to afford a smile now and then　偶尔可以付之一笑

   ＊can/be able to 后接 afford,常表示"买得起""经受得起"的意思。

   the pitiable state of the orphan boy　这孤儿值得同情的处境

4. the cruelty and hypocrisy of the workhouse board　济贫院理事会的残忍和伪善

5. ..., Oliver remained a close prisoner in the dark and solitary room to which he had been consigned by the wisdom and mercy of the board.　根据英明仁慈的理事会下的命令,奥利弗依旧被单独禁闭在一间阴暗的小屋里。

   ＊to which...引导的是 room 的定语从句,be consigned to... by...,由……委托/交付给……,即由……下令交给……处理的意思。

6. at first sight　乍一看,粗看起来

   once and for ever　永久

   to entertain a becoming feeling of respect for the prediction of the gentleman　对那位绅士的预测抱有适当的尊重

to tie... to...　把……系到……上

to attach... to...　把……连接/系到……上

7. It appears, at first sight, not unreasonable to suppose that, if he had entertained a becoming feeling of respect for the prediction of the gentleman in the white waistcoat, he would have established that sage individual's prophetic character, once for ever, by tying one end of his pocket-handkerchief to a hook in the wall, and attaching himself to the other.　乍看起来,这种猜测也不无道理,即奥利弗如果能对那位穿白背心绅士的预测抱有适当尊重的话,只需把手帕的一端系住墙上的挂钩,另一端系住自己的脖子,本来是可以确立这位贤哲预言不爽的声誉的。

8. To the performance of this feat, however, there was one obstacle: namely, that pocket handkerchiefs, being decided articles of luxury, had been, for all future times and ages, removed from the noses of paupers by the express order of the board in council assembled, solemnly given and pronounced under their hands and seals.　然而,要实现这一壮举,还存在一个障碍,那就是手帕确定无疑是个奢侈品,经理事会全体会议的特别程序通过并签名盖章、郑重宣布:此后,手帕就永远离开贫民的鼻子了。

　　* 注意句中的几个状语短语的用法和含义。

9. There was a still greater obstacles in Oliver's youth and childishness.　还有更大的障碍,就是奥利弗的年幼无知。

10. dismal night　阴郁的夜晚

　　to spread his little hands before his eyes to shut out the darkness　张开他的小手,蒙住眼睛,挡住黑暗。

　　crouching in the corner　蜷伏在墙角

　　ever and anon waking with a start and tremble　不时地一惊或一颤醒来

　　drawing himself closer and closer to the wall　他把身体缩起来越来越紧地贴在墙上

11. Let it not be supposed by the enemies of "the system," that...　可别让这套"体制"的反对者们认为……

　　* it 为形式宾语,that... 为真正的宾语从句,即 it = that...。

12. the period of his solitary incarceration　被单独关押/禁闭的那段时间

　　be denied the benefit of exercise, the pleasure of society, or the advantages of religious consolation 被剥夺身体锻炼的益处,社交活动的快乐,或宗教慰藉的好处

　　to perform his ablutions every morning every morning under the pump　每天早晨都在唧筒下做净体仪式

　　to cause a tingling sensation to pervade his frame by repeated applications of the cane　用藤杖不断抽打,使全身都感到刺痛

　　be there sociably (= publicly) flogged as a public warning and example　在那里当众挨鞭打,以儆效尤

　　so far from being denied the advantages of religious consolation　远未被/根本谈不上剥夺宗教慰藉的益处

　　to console his mind with, a general supplication of the boys　倾听男童们的集体祷告,以慰藉他自己的心灵

　　containing a special clause, therein inserted by the authority of the board　包含一条由理事会当权者加进去的特别条款

　　to entreat to be made good, virtuous, contented, and obedient.　祈求上帝保佑他们成长为高尚、有道德、知足和顺从的好孩子

　　to be guarded from the sins and vices of Oliver Twist　防止犯奥利弗的罪行

13. ..., whom the supplication distinctly set forth to be under the exclusive patronage and protection of the powers of wickedness　祷告词中明确阐明他(奥利弗)就得到了邪恶势力的支助和庇佑

　　* to set forth sb. to be under...　阐明某人受到……

14. to be an article direct from the manufactory of the very Devil himself.　它本身就是直接从魔鬼的工厂里炮制出来的

15. It chance one morning, while..., that...　一天早晨,正当……的时候,恰巧……

be in this auspicious and comfortable state　处于这种吉祥如意、万事随心的状态

deeply cogitating in his mind his ways and means of paying certain arrears of rent　脑子里正仔细地盘算着用什么办法交付所欠的房租

sb.'s most sanguine estimate of his finances　某人最乐观的财政估计/状况

within full five pounds of the desired amount　所需的整五镑款子

in a species of arithmetical desperation　陷于解不开一道算术题的绝望中

be alternately cudgeling his brains and his donkey　他用根短棍轮换着敲打自己的脑袋和驴

the bill on the gate　门上的告示

16. in a state of profound abstraction　正在遐想的状态中出神

be destined to be regaled with a cabbage-stalk or two　目的是想得到一两棵白菜的犒赏

to dispose of the two sacks of soot with which the little cart was laden.　把车上装的两袋烟灰处理掉

be laden with　载满……

to jog onward　慢悠悠地往前进

17. to growl a fierce imprecation on the donkey generally　凶狠地吼着诅咒驴子,含糊不清,不知骂啥

to beat in any skull but a donkey's　除了驴以外,可砸碎任何畜生的脑壳

to catch hold of the bridle　抓住缰绳

to give his jaw a sharp wrench　对它下巴猛力一勒

18. by way of gentle reminder that he was not his own master　作为温和的提醒:它可不能自己做主

just to stun him till he came back again　就是要打昏它,让它在自己回来前醒不过来

19. with his hands behind him　双手背在身后

after having delivered himself of some profound sentiments in the board room　他在理事会办公室抒发了一番高深的感慨之后

be exactly the sort of master Oliver Twist wanted　正是适合奥利弗的那种主人

to peruse the document　阅读那文告

as to the boy it was encumbered　至于那个孩子,有了他就等于五镑钱多了个负担/累赘/附加条件;至于作为附加条件的那个孩子

＊it 指的是前面讲的 five pounds。

the dietary of the workhouse　济贫院的食谱/伙食

just the very thing for register stoves　正是进出带暖气片炉灶的适当人选(个头小)

to spell the bill through again　又把那告示拼读了一遍

touching his fur cap in token of humility　他手碰碰帽子,表示谦恭/作谦恭的象征

to accost the gentleman in the white waistcoat　与那位穿白背心的绅士搭讪起来。

＊小说中这段对话,由于甘菲尔德先生没有文化,说话吞音,直录下来就有很多错字,甚至语法错误,阅读时注意改正。

20. This here boy, sir, wot the parish wants to 'prentis, = What the parish wants this boy here to apprentice?　教堂想要这孩子去学徒吗?

21. with a condescending smile　带着一种恩赐似的微笑

What of him? = What do you think of him?

to learn a light pleasant trade　学会一门轻松愉快的行当

to linger behind　在后面拖延/磨蹭了一会儿

as a caution not to run away in his absence　作为他离开时不得跑开的警告

a nasty trade　肮脏的交易

22. That's acause they damped the straw afore they lit it in the chimney to make 'em come down again = That's because they damped the straw before they lit it in the chimney to make them come down again. 那是因为他们再次在烟囱里点火赶男孩下来时，先把草弄湿了。

23. vereas smoke ain't o' no use at all in making a boy come down, for it only sinds him to sleep, = whereas smoke is not of use at all in making a boy come down, for it only sinks him to sleep, 而用烟熏使男孩下来是一点用也没有的，因为那只能使他们发困想睡觉

24. There's nothing like a good hot blaze to make 'em (= them) come down vith (= with) a run.   没有什么比火焰更能使他们飞跑下来。

25. to stick in the chimney   在烟囱里被卡住
    to make them struggle to extricate themselves   使他们拼命挣脱

26. but his mirth was speedily checked by a look from Mr. Limbkins.   但他的笑容很快就被林伯金斯先生的目光制止了

27. These only chanced to be heard, indeed, on account of their being very frequently repeated with great emphasis.   只有这些话碰巧被听到，真的，原因还是它们被重复强调的次数太多的缘故。

28. at length = at last   最后
    to resume their seats and their solemnity   重新坐回座位，恢复他们庄严的神态
    to labour under the slight imputation of having bruised three or four boys to death already   为自己把三四个男孩儿殴打致死的小小污点而苦恼担心
    it occurred to him that...   他（突然）想到……
    in some unaccountable freak   由于某种说不清的怪念头/突发奇想
    extraneous circumstance   意外的情况，题外的枝节
    be very unlike their general mode of doing business   违背了他们一贯的做事原则
    to have no particular wish to revive the rumour   实在不愿重提那些流言蜚语

29. his countenance brightened as...   当……的时候，他的表情豁然开朗

30. Don't be too hard on a poor man.   对一个穷人不要太苛刻。

31. for good and all   永久
    to split the difference   折中，妥协
    not a farthing more   一分钱都不能再加了（a farthing = 1/4 penny 便士）

32. You're desperate hard upon me.   你对我卡得也太紧了。

33. He'd be cheap with nothing at all, as a premium.   一点酬金都没有，他也太便宜了。

34. to give an arch look at the faces round the table   狡黠地看了一眼桌子周围的几张脸

35. Mr. Bumble was at once instructed that Oliver Twist and his indentures were to be conveyed before the magistrate, for signature and approval, that very afternoon.   就在那天下午，班布尔先生接到通知把奥利弗和他的学徒期约同时送达地方官，申请签名批准。

36. in pursuance of this determination   为了贯彻这一决定
    be released from bondage   解释禁闭
    be ordered to put himself into a clean shirt   被命令穿上一件干净的衬衫
    holiday allowance   假日津贴
    at the tremendous sight   看到这惊人的景象
    to kill him for some useful purpose   杀了他做某种用场
    to fatten him up in that way   以哪种方法把他喂肥

37. in a tone of impressive pomposity   以令人敬畏的自负的语调
    be so many parents to you   就都像你的父母

to prentice you　教你手艺

to set you up in life　供你生活,把你养大成人

to make a man of you　使你成个男子汉

all for a naughty orphan　全都是为了一个淘气的孤儿

38. to pause to take breath　停下来喘了口气

   after delivering this address in an awful voice　用威严的语调做了上述讲话之后

   for it was gratifying to his feelings to observe the effect　看到这种效果,他在感情上已十分满足

   to wipe your eyes with the cuffs of your jacket　用你夹克衫的袖口擦去泪水

   both of which injunctions Oliver promised to obey　前面说的两个指令,奥利弗答应全都照办

   the rather　更有甚者,更不用说

   to throw in a gentle hint　加了一个委婉的暗示

39. There were no telling what would be done to him.　不用说会怎么对待他。

40. He was admonished by Mr. Bumble to stay there until he came back to fetch him.　他受到班布尔先生的警告,要待在那里,直到他回来领他。

41. with a palpitating heart　怀着一颗惴惴不安的心

   at the expiration of...　直到……的时间/截止期

   to thrust in his head　他伸进头来

   be unadorned with the cocked hat　歪戴着帽子,不加修饰

   to put on a grim and threatening look　装出/显出一副狰狞可怕的样子

42. to face at this somewhat contradictory style of address　面对这有点儿相互矛盾/忽阴忽阳的讲话语气

   an adjoining room　比邻/隔壁的房间

   two old gentlemen with powdered heads　两个头上敷了粉的老绅士

   to peruse a small piece of parchment which lay before him　仔细阅读一小张展开在他面前的羊皮纸文件

   with the aid of a pair of tortoise-shell spectacles　借助于/靠一副玳瑁眼镜(的帮助)

   a partially washed face　胡乱洗了一把的脸

   bluff-looking men　样子粗鲁的人

   in top-boots　穿着高通靴

   to lounge about　百无聊赖地闲逛,懒散地踱来踱去

43. to doze off over the little bit of parchment　趴在那一小张羊皮纸上打盹

   be stationed by Mr. Bumble in front of the desk　被班布尔先生安排站在那张桌子前面

   to pull sb. by the sleeve　拉某人的袖子

   the last-mentioned old gentleman　上面提到的那位老绅士

   to rouse himself and make his best obeisance　他振作了一下精神,毕恭毕敬地鞠了一躬

44. Whether all boards were born with that white stuff on their heads, and were boards from thenceforth on that account.　是但凡理事老爷的头上都有那白东西,还是正因有了那白东西才做了理事老爷?

   ＊ on that account = on account of that　因为那个缘故

45. to dote on...　溺爱,过分喜爱

   to give sb. a sly pinch to intimate that he had better not say he didn't.　偷偷地拧了某人一下,向他暗示最好别说他不愿意

46. an honest, open-hearted man　一个诚实、直率的老实人

   to turn his spectacles in the direction of the candidate for Oliver's premium.　他把视线转向那个想领走奥利弗得到酬金的候选人

his villainous countenance　他凶恶的表情

a regular stamped receipt for cruelty　鲜明地打下了凶残的印记

half blind and half childish　眼力不济,想法单纯

be not reasonably expected to discern what other people did　不可理所当然地指望他能辨别其他人所能辨别的事物

47. If we was to bind him to any other trade tomorrow, he'd run away simultaneous, your worship. 如果我们明天逼他去学其他任何行当,他绝对会立刻逃跑的。

　　* 这是一个虚拟语态的句子,平常多用 If we were...,主语为单数时,were 和 was 均可,此处主语为复数,却用 was,似不多见。句子最后的 simultaneous 似应为 simultaneously。

48. "When I says I will, I means I will," replied Mr. Gamfield doggedly.　"我说到做到。"甘菲尔德先生语气倔强地回答。

　　* 句中 says 应为 say, means 应为 mean。类似的语法和读音上的错误还有不少,说明了甘菲尔德先生文化水平较低。

49. with an ugly leer　丑恶地斜睨了一眼

fixing his spectacles more firmly on his nose　把眼镜在鼻梁上架得更稳点儿

to dip his pen into the inkstand　他把笔尖伸进墨水瓶

be straightway hurried off　被直接送/带走

as a matter of course　作为必然的结果,理所当然

to look all over his desk for it without finding it　目光越过了办公桌向前寻找,结果未找到

despite all the admonitory looks and pinches of Bumble　不顾班布尔警告的目光和拧掐

the repulsive countenance of his future master　他未来主人的令人厌恶的表情

too palpable to be mistaken　那么容易察觉,绝不会看不出来/被看错

50. to attempt to take snuff with a cheerful and unconcerned aspect　想要以一种轻松愉快、漫不经心的样子吸吸鼻子

to lean over the desk　向桌子俯下身子

to start at the sound　听到这声音吃了一惊

laying aside the paper　把手里的纸放到一旁

leaning forward with an expression of interest　满怀好奇地向前俯下身去

51. Oliver fell on his knees, and clasping his hands together, prayed that they would order him back to the dark room — that they would starve him — beat him — kill him if they pleased — rather than send him away with that dreadful man. 奥利弗双膝跪下,两手合握哀求他们还把他关回黑屋,饿他,打他,假如高兴杀他也可以,就是不要把他送给这个可怕的人。

raising his hands and eyes with most impressive solemnity　他举起手,翻翻眼,带着一副很威严的神情

one of the most bare-facedest of all the artful and designing orphans　所有的狡诈和心术不正的孤儿中最厚颜无耻者之一

to give vent to this compound adjective　用这个复合形容词来发泄自己的诅咒/情感

be incredulous of his having heard aright　(简直)不相信自己清清楚楚听到的东西

be stupefied with astonishment　惊得目瞪口呆,吃惊得发懵

a moral revolution　简直是道德颠覆/纲常大乱

to nod significantly　意味深长地点点头

52. to refuse to sanction these indentures　拒绝批准这些契约

to toss aside the piece of parchment　把那张羊皮纸文件扔在一边

to form the opinion that...　形成某种看法,认为……

be guilty of improper conduct　负有行为不当的罪责

on the unsupported testimony of a mere child　仅仅根据一个孩子的不实之词/未经证实的话

be not called upon to pronounce on the matter　未被要求/不必对此事发表意见

53. be drawn and quartered into the bargain　受到五马分尸的惩罚

to shake his head with gloomy mystery　他阴郁而神秘地摇头

to come to(no) good　（没）有好结果

to seem to be a wish of a totally opposite description　双方的愿望似乎是性质上完全对立的/背道而驰的

54. be once more informed that ...　又一次听悉……

to take possession of　占有,拥有

主要内容归纳和总结

1. 查尔斯·狄更斯出生于英格兰一个海军小军官家庭,因为家贫他 10 岁即进入鞋油厂当童工,17 岁进入新闻界,做专门报道议会活动的报纸记者,这使他有机会接触法律和政治生活的内幕及社会各界的人物。这些生活经历为他后来的小说创作奠定了基础。

狄更斯是伟大的批判现实主义作家,他以揭露和抨击社会不公、虚伪、腐败与贫穷为己任。他对社会的批判有一定的局限性,他一方面痛恨国家机器和邪恶势力,另一方面又盲目乐观,寄希望于社会改良,所以他的前期作品总有乐观主义的期待,后期小说则表现出一种无助的愤慨和反抗。

2. 狄更斯文学创作的艺术特点

a. 他具有非凡的讲故事能力,由于是亲身经历,又善用方言土语,所以故事的背景被表现得活灵活现,使读者读了第一页,就会欲罢不能,一直读到最后一页。

b. 他特别善于刻画各种各样的人物形象,从残酷盘剥济贫院(workhouse)儿童的教区执事(beadle)班布尔(Bumble)到穷困潦倒还总不忘说大话的幽默善良的麦考伯先生(Mr. Micawber),从唆人为盗的黑社会头子费根(Fagin)到心地善良、气质如兰的罗丝小姐(Miss Rose),个个形象鲜明,令人难忘。他刻画得最鲜活生动的要算那些纯真无辜而又深受迫害的儿童,引起读者极大的同情。

c. 他善于将幽默与哀伤交汇起来,幽默时叫人捧腹大笑,悲情时让人潸然泪下,笔下总能创造出令人动情的故事来。

3. 狄更斯是英国文学史上能与莎士比亚比肩的文学巨匠。

4. 狄更斯的主要作品:

《勃兹速写》Sketches by Boz（1816）

《匹克威克外传》The Posthumous Papers of the Pickwick Club（1836～1837）

《雾都孤儿》(又名《奥利弗·退斯特》) Oliver Twist（1837～1838）

《尼古拉斯·尼克尔贝》Nicholas Nickleby（1838～1839）

《大卫·科伯菲尔》David Copperfield（1849～1850）

《马丁·瞿术伟》Martin Chuzzlewit（1843～1845）

《董贝父子》Dombey and Son（1846～1848）

《双城记》A Tale of Two Cities（1859）

《荒凉山庄》Bleak House（1852～1853）

《小多利特》Little Dorrit（1855～1857）

《艰难时事》Hard Times（1854）

《孤星血泪》(又名《远大前程》) Great Expectations（1860～1861）

《我们共同的朋友》Our Mutual Friend（1864～1865）

重要信息句子

1. Dickens is one of the greatest critical realist writers of the Victorian Age.

2. In his works, Dickens sets out a full map and a large scale criticism of the 19th century England, particularly London.

3. Charles Dickens is a master story-teller. With his first sentence, he engages the reader's attention and holds it to the end.

4. Dickens' works are also characterized by a mingling of humor and pathos.

II. 勃朗特姐妹 The Brontë Sisters:夏洛特 Charlotte (1816~1855),艾米莉 Emily (1818~1848),安妮 Anne (1820~1849)

词语解释和难句分析

1. to work either as teacher or governess in some private families. 要么去学校做教师工作,要么去做私人家庭教师

   to leave hardly any trace on Emily 给艾米莉几乎没有留下任何痕迹

   this passionate yet one-sided love 这种非常动情的、却又是单相思的爱

   be later recounted in her works 后来就复述到她的著作中

2. to design their own device for solace and comfort 创造出她们自己的种种设计,以寻求安慰

   the vast, rough, untouched moorland wilderness 广漠、崎岖、处于原始状态的高沼地荒原

   a rather reserved and simple girl 一个相当含蓄、简单的女孩儿

   be very much a child of nature 性情非常像个孩子

3. This was especially so with Emily. 艾米莉尤其如此。

4. to read omnivorously 博览群书,无所不读

   recordings of brilliantly contrived adventures in *Angrian* 在小说《安格里昂》中,描述了她们构思出来的精彩绝伦的冒险故事

   at sb.'s initiative 在某人的倡导/发动下

   be published at their own expense 她们自费出版

   to receive little attention 没引起什么注意

   to win immediate success 立即大获成功

5. to die of consumption 死于肺痨

   a work about the industrial troubles between the mill-owners and machine-breakers 一部描写工业领域磨坊主人与砸毁机器的工人之间矛盾冲突的著作

   her most autobiographical work 她的最具自传性质的著作

   the struggle of an individual consciousness towards self-realization 一个人实现自我价值的自觉的奋斗

6. be brought up with strict orthodoxy 以严格的正统观念培养起来

to <u>stick to</u> the Puritanical code　坚守清教徒的道德标准

to despise worldly ambition and success　鄙视世俗的所谓雄心和成功

be marked throughout by an intensity of vision and of passion　（作品）处处都显示出丰富的想象,洋溢着强烈的激情

by <u>resorting to</u> some elements of horror, mystery and prophesy　借助/采用一些恐怖、神秘和预言的元素

to recreate life in a wondrously romantic way　以令人惊叹的浪漫主义手法重新诠释生活

7. All this renders her works a never dying popularity.　所有这些都赋予她的作品永远不灭的魅力/使她的作品永远受到大众的喜爱。

夏洛特·勃朗特作品选读
《简爱》*Jane Eyre* 第二十三章节选

词语解释和难句分析

1. the titular heroine　与书同名的女主人公

   in an outbreak　一次情感爆发,一次大发脾气的时候

   to fight back　回击,还手

   to get rid of this eye-sore　拔去这个眼中钉

   a charity school for the orphaned or unwanted children　一所为成为孤儿或者无人认领的儿童而建立的慈善学校

   a grim-looking, energetic, quick-tempered but an understanding middle-aged man　一个面貌冷峻、精力充沛、脾气暴躁却又能理解别人的中年男子

   be attracted to the little plain governess for her quick-wit, loving heart and self-dignity　因其智慧、爱心和自尊而为那瘦小平常的家庭女教师所吸引

   be canceled <u>on the ground that</u> ...　由于……而终止/取消

   be raving mad　是个胡言乱语的疯子

   to <u>flee into</u> the moorland　逃进高沼地荒原

   to <u>devote himself solely to</u> God　把自己的一切都奉献给上帝

   to accompany him to India for missionary work　陪伴他去印度传教

   (be) desperate of her union with Rochester　对她与罗切斯特的结合感到无望

   be about to accept John's loveless proposal　差一点接受约翰无爱的求婚

   to hear Rochester calling for her　（心灵里如同）听到了罗切斯特对她的召唤

   following her own heart, ...　响应自己心灵的呼唤

   the burn-down Thornfield Hall　被大火烧成灰烬的桑菲尔德庄园

   a blind but free man　成了一个盲人,但已是自由身

   be finally united and live happily <u>ever after</u>　最终结合在一起,从此后过着幸福的生活

2. the religious hypocrisy of charity institutions　宗教界慈善机构的伪善

   be trained, through constant starvation and humiliation, to be humble slaves　由于经常挨饿和蒙受屈辱,被训练成谦卑的奴隶

   the social discrimination Jane experiences　简经历的社会歧视

as a dependent（＝dependant）at her aunt's house　作为她舅母家的一个受抚养人

the false convention as concerning love and marriage　关于爱情和婚姻的虚伪的传统习俗

an intense moral fable　一个情感热烈的道德寓言

to undergo a series of physical and moral tests to grow up　经受了一系列肉体和道德的双重考验才成长起来

3. an orphan child with a fiery spirit and a longing to love and to be loved　一个性烈如火,渴望爱和被爱的孤儿

to cut a completely new woman image　给人以一个全新的女性形象

to struggle for recognition of their basic rights and equality as a human being　为争取人的基本权利和平等得到承认而奋斗

to bring her to the heart of the audience　把她的形象带到观众的心里

be aware that her love is out of the question　意识到她的爱情是绝不可能了

4. Jane's passionate protestation is typically hers.　简那充满激情的抗争是她所特有的。

5. to send my little friend on such weary travels　要把我的小朋友送上如此累人的旅程

be akin to　与……相似

to risk no sort of answer　没敢回答

6. (be) tightly and inextricably knotted to a similar string situated in the corresponding quarter of your little frame　与你小小身躯同一部位相似的弦牢固难分地缠结在一起

boisterous channel　奔腾咆哮的海峡

to come broad between us　将我们远远地分隔开

7. That cord of communion will be snapt.　那根思想交流的弦就会崩断。

8. to have nervous notion　紧张地想/思考

to take to bleeding inwardly　开始内心流血了

to sob convulsively　猛烈地抽泣起来

to repress what I endured no longer　我本来强忍着的(眼泪)再也忍不住了

be obliged to yield　被迫妥协退让(指前面所说的眼泪抑制不住任其流淌)

be shaken from head to foot with acute distress　因剧烈的痛苦从头到脚都颤抖了起来

to express an impetuous wish that...　表达一个冲动的愿望

the vehemence of emotion, stirred by grief and love within me　我内心的悲伤和爱激起/煽起的强烈情感

be claiming mastery, and struggling for full sway　逐渐占了上风/拥有优势,竭力要支配一切

asserting a right to predominate　掌握主宰权

9. be not trampled on　没有遭人践踏/蹂躏

be not petrified　没有僵化,没有丧失活力

be buried with inferior minds　被埋没在志向低劣的人之中

be not excluded from every glimpse of communion with what is bright, and energetic, and high　没有被排斥于同光明、充满活力的高尚的人交流的一切机会之外

10. I have talked, face to face, with what I reverence; with what I delight in — with an original, a vigorous, an expanded mind.　我面对面地同我敬重、喜欢的人——同一个独特、活跃、博大的心灵交谈过。

11. ... and it strikes me with terror and anguish to feel I absolutely must be torn from you for ever.　一想到必定会永远与你分开,我就感到恐怖和痛苦。

* it ＝ to feel..., it 为形式主语,不定式短语 to feel... 才是真正的主语。

* to strike sb. with　使某人感到……

12. to set his teeth　紧咬着牙齿

to keep the oath　信守誓言

be roused to something like passion　情绪激动起来

to become nothing to you　对你来说是个无足轻重的人

to have my morsel of bread snatched from my lips　让别人把一块面包从我嘴里抢走

to have my drop of living water dashed from my cup　让别人把我杯子里的一滴活命水泼掉

be soulless and heartless　没有灵魂,没心没肺

to have as much soul as you　心灵与你同样丰富

full as much heart（as you）　心胸与你同样充实

to gift me with some beauty　恩赐给我一点美貌

mortal flesh　血肉之躯

to enclose me in his arms and gather me to his breast　用胳膊抱住我,搂在怀里/胸前

13. as good as a married man　相当于一个结过婚的人

to wed to one inferior to you　与一个远不如你的人举行婚礼

to have no sympathy with　与……不能志同道合/意气相投

to sneer at her　讥笑她

to scorn such a union　鄙视,嘲笑

to have spoken my mind　说了心里话

like a wild, frantic bird that is rending its plumage in its desperation　像一只发疯的野鸟绝望地撕扯自己的羽毛

14. No net ensnares me.　没有任何网能罩得住我。

a free human being with independent will　一个具有独立意志的自由人

to exert the independent will to leave you　就是运用这种独立意志要离开你

15. Another effort set me at liberty.　又一次挣扎,我挣脱了自己。

to stand erect before him　直挺挺地站在他面前

to offer you a share of all my possessions　提议你分享我整个财产的一部分

to play a farce　表演一场闹剧

to laugh at the farce　对这种闹剧付之一笑

to pass through life at my side — to be my second self, and best earthly companion　在我身边度过一生——做我的另一半,我尘世最好的伴侣

16. to abide by　遵循,坚守

a waft of wind　刮过的一阵风

to come sweeping down the laurel-walk　（风）刮过月桂小路

through the boughs of the chestnut　吹过/穿过栗树枝

to wander away — away — to an indefinite distance　飘走了——飘走了——飘到天涯海角

be torn away and can not return　被拉走,再不会回来了

17. to summon you as my wife　请求你做我的妻子

to come hither = to come here　来这里

to rise and with a stride reach me　站起来,一个箭步走到我跟前

to writhe myself from his grasp　扭动着身子要挣脱他

to have no faith in...　对……一点也不信任

not a whit = not at all　一点也不

little skeptic　疑神疑鬼怀疑一切的小东西

to have taken pains to prove　煞费苦心地想要证明

to cause a rumour to reach her that 放出一个谣言让她知道……

to present myself to see the result 我把自己装扮起来去看结果

you almost unearthly thing 你简直就是个小精灵

to entreat（you）to accept me as a husband 恳求你接受我做你的丈夫

18. I ejaculated：beginning in his earnestness — and especially in his incivility — to credit his sincerity. 我突然惊叫起来：由于他的认真，尤其是他的粗鲁言行，我开始相信他的诚意了。

    ＊ beginning to credit his sincerity. 要连起来看，介词短语 in his earnestness 和 in his incivility 表示原因。

19. to read your countenance 想要看清你的表情

    Read on：only make haste，for I suffer. 看吧：只是要快点，因为我难受。

20. There：you will find it scarcely more legible than a crumpled，scratched page. 那，你所看到的脸不会比一页揉皱、抓破了的纸更容易看清/你所看到的只能是一张揉皱了、抓破了的纸。

21. There were strong workings in the features. 面部表情产生强烈的抽搐。

22. give me my name 叫我的名字

    speaking in my ear as his cheek was laid on mine 他的脸贴着我的脸，嘴对着我耳朵说

艾米莉·勃朗特作品选读

《呼啸山庄》*Wuthering Heights* 第十五章节选

词语解释和难句分析

1. be seldom away from home 很少离家外出

   be much more a genius than her elder sister 比她的姐姐更有（文学）天赋

   a surprisingly simple，strong but reserved person 一个极其单纯、个性极强而又非常内向的人

   be rather shy in society 对社交非常害羞

   to have a passionate love for the wilderness of the moor in all seasons 对高沼地一年四季的荒野怀有深情的爱

   be very much a child of nature 非常像大自然的孩子

2. mostly devoted to the matter of nature with its mysterious workings and its unaccountable influence upon people's life 大多作品都着力于大自然的主题，描述它的神秘运行以及它对人生活难以说明的影响

   works of strange sublimity and beauty 表现出独特的崇高和美的著作

   be ample proof for... 是证明……的充分证据

   a young，reclusive woman 一位僻居遁世的年轻女士

3. an intruding stranger 一个陌生的外来者

   a bluff prosperous Yorkshire farmer 一个粗率、富有的约克郡农夫

   up in the folds of the moor 突出在荒原的怀抱之中

4. Wuthering is Yorkshire dialect for "weathering," which is indicative of "the atmospheric tumult to which its station is exposed to in stormy weather". wuthering 是 weathering 的约克郡方言发音，意思是山庄暴露在暴风雨的喧嚣之中。

   ＊ weathering 意指一年四季风霜雨雪的侵蚀。

5. a sallow, rugged foundling　一个面黄肌瘦、衣衫褴褛的弃儿

　　out of jealousy of his father's fondness for the waif　出于对他父亲偏爱这小流浪儿的嫉妒

　　to degrade Heathcliff in every way he can　他想尽一切办法侮辱歧视希斯克利夫

　　to grow brutal and sullen　长成了冷酷和郁郁寡欢的性格

　　to take his revenge on Hindley　对辛德莱实施他的报复

　　tormented by her love for her husband and her overwhelming passion for Heathcliff　（凯瑟琳）为她对丈夫的爱和对希斯克利夫压倒一切的深情（这割舍不掉的双重情感）所折磨

　　in giving birth to a daughter　在生女儿的时候

　　be driven mad at her death　为凯瑟琳的死而发疯

　　to hasten his revenge on people of both houses　加速了他对两大庄园的人的报复

　　to have hindered his union with Catherine　曾经阻碍他与凯瑟琳结合

　　to reduce Hindley to a gambler and a drunkard　使辛德莱沦为一个赌徒和酒鬼

　　by marrying Cathy to his sickly son Linton　通过让凯茜嫁给自己的病儿子林顿的手段

　　in due time　在适当时机

　　to drive sb. to death　将某人逼死

　　to have sb. at his mercy　使某人在他的掌握之中

　　to take another turn　事情又发生了转折

　　to starve himself to death　把他自己饿死

6. a story about a poor man abused, betrayed and distorted by his social betters because he is a poor nobody.　一个关于穷人被社会地位比他高的人虐待、背叛和扭曲的故事，境遇如此，原因就在于他是个无足轻重的穷人

　　a temporary tenant at Grange　格兰治庄园的一位临时房客

　　to give an account of　叙述

7. While the central interest is maintained, the sequence of its development is constantly disordered by flashbacks.　在小说的中心线索维持不变的情况下，情节的发展顺序常常被闪回所颠倒。

8. to make the story all the more enticing and genuine　使得情节更加吸引人和真实

　　be fully shown in this agonizing scene　在这撕心裂肺的痛苦情景中得到了淋漓尽致的展示

9. with straining eagerness　全神贯注，急切地渴望

　　not hit the right room directly　没有立刻找对房间

　　to motion me to admit him　用手势示意我带/让她进来

　　in a stride or two　一两个大步

10. to loose his hold　松开他的拥抱

　　to look into her face　正面看她的脸

　　for downright agony　由于彻骨的痛苦

11. The same conviction had stricken him as me, from the instant he beheld her, that there was no prospect of ultimate recovery there — she was fated, sure to die.　从看到她那一瞬间起，他就感到了一种突袭而来的绝望，与我一样，确信她一点康复的希望都没有了——她已命中注定，一定要死了。

　　* conviction　信念，相信，与后面的 that 从句是同位语，可直译为：他一看到她就产生了与我一样的想法，认为她活不了了，必死无疑。

12. in a tone that did not seek to disguise his despair　以一种毫不掩饰绝望的声调

　　to bring tear into his eyes　使他热泪盈眶

　　to return his look with a suddenly clouded brow　脸色突变阴郁，回应/面对他的目光

13. Her humor was a mere vane for constantly varying caprices.　她的思想变化不定，脾气就是风向标。

14. to break my heart   伤心欲碎

   to bewail the deed to me   因对我的所作所为而哭哭啼啼/伤心落泪/悲伤遗憾

   to thrive on something   因某事而发达了

   to kneel on one knee to embrace her   单腿跪下把她抱在怀里

15. be wretched to lose her   因失去她而感到难过

   to wrench his head free, and grind his teeth   猛地把头一摆,挣脱了她的手,牙齿咬得格格响

   to a cool spectator   对一个冷眼旁观的人来说

   (heaven) be a land of exile to her   (天堂)对她来说,就是一块流放地

   to cast away her mortal character with her mortal body   把她凡人的性格连同她凡人的躯体一起抛掉

   scintillating eyes   闪闪发亮的眼睛

   to retain, in her closed fingers, a portion of the locks she has been grasping   在她紧握的手指中间,还攥着一缕她一直紧握不放的头发

16. ... and so inadequate was his stock of gentleness to the requirements of her condition, that on his letting go, I saw four distinct impressions left blue in the colourless skin. = ... and his stock of gentleness was so inadequate to the requirements of her condition that ... in the colourless skin.   他所储存的柔情不足以适应她健康状况的需求,以至于他一松手,我就看到了四个清晰的紫痕留在了她没有血色的皮肤上。

17. be possessed with a devil   着了魔了,中了邪了

   to talk in that manner to me, when you are dying   你就要死的时候,还那样跟我说话

   be branded in my memory, and eating deeper eternally   被铭刻在我的记忆中,会越来越深地永远地啮咬着我

18. Catherine, you know that I could as soon forget you as my existence.   凯瑟琳,你知道只要我活一天,就不会忘记你。/即使死了也不会忘了你。

   * 直译为"我会像忘了自己的存在一样忘了你",而自己的存在是忘不了的,所以是说"只要我活一天,就不会忘了你"。

19. Is it not sufficient for your infernal selfishness, that while you are at peace I shall writhe in the torments of hell?   当你得到安息的时候,我还要在地狱的折磨里备受煎熬,难道这对你那魔鬼般的自私心还不够吗?

20. "I shall not be at peace," moaned Catherine, recalled to a sense of physical weakness by the violent, unequal throbbing of her heart, which beat visibly, and audibly, under this excess of agitation.   "我不会得到安息的,"凯瑟琳呜咽着,又感到一阵由于心脏不规则的激烈跳动引起的虚弱,她的心因这阵过分的激动而砰砰乱跳,胸脯不停地起伏。

   * which引导的非限制性定语从句进一步描述her heart的情况。visibly和audibly是"胸脯起伏"和"砰砰乱跳"的翻译依据。

21. to say nothing further till the paroxysm was over   再没说什么,直到这阵发作平息

   to nurse anger   把气憋在心里,心里老想着生气

   harsh words   尖刻的话语/言词

   be livid with emotion   因情绪激动而脸色发青

   to bend round to look at him   转过脸来看着他

   addressing me in accents of indignant disappointment   以一种愤慨的失望的口气对我说

22. He would not relent a moment to keep me out of grave!   他就不肯发发善心让我晚一点进坟墓!

23. the thing that irks me most   最使我厌烦的东西

   be wearying to escape into that glorious world   正渴望逃进那美好的世界

not seeing it dimly through tears, and yearning for it through the walls of an aching heart　不是泪眼模糊地遥望它,也不是隔着痛苦的心房之高墙渴望它

be incomparably beyond and above you all　超越你们,高高地在你们之上,谁也比不了

24. to support herself on the arm of the chair　依靠椅背支撑着自己

at that earnest appeal　对那真挚的恳求

looking absolutely desperate　完全不顾一切的神情

to flash fiercely on her　目光炯炯地盯着她。

25. His breast heaved convulsively.　他胸部猛烈地起伏着。

to hold asunder　相对而立,分开站立

to make a spring　向前一扑/跳

be locked in an embrace　死死地抱在一起

to my eyes　在我看来

to seem directly insensible　似乎立即失去知觉了

to fling himself into the nearest seat　他猛地一下坐进最近的椅子里

on my approaching hurriedly to ascertain if she had fainted　我急忙走近想看清她是否已晕过去了

to gnash at me　对着我咬牙切齿

to foam like a mad dog　嘴里吐着白沫,像一只疯狗

to gather her to him with greedy jealousy　怀着贪婪的嫉妒,他把她紧紧地抱住

not feel as if I were in the company of a creature of my own species　我感觉似乎不是在与一个自己的同类为伴

to stand off　站在一旁

to hold my tongue, in great perplexity　我一言不发,心里慌恐万分

26. to relieve me a little presently　立刻使我轻松了一点儿

to put up her hand to clasp his neck　伸出她的一只手搂住他的脖子

to bring her cheek to his　把她的脸贴在他的脸上

to cover her with frantic caresses　不停地发疯似的亲吻/爱抚她

27. to betray your own heart　出卖/背叛你自己的心

to wring out my kisses and tears　逼/挤出我的吻和眼泪

to blight you　毁灭你,使你枯萎

28. I have not one word of comfort — you deserve this.　我可没有一句安慰的话给你——你自作自受/罪有应得。

29. What right — answer me — for the poor fancy you felt for Linton?　你有什么权力离开我——回答我——就因为你对林顿的那一点可怜的空想?

30. Because misery, and degradation, and death, and nothing that god or Satan could inflict would have parted us, you, of your own will, did it.　因为痛苦、屈辱和死亡,以及上帝或撒旦所能施加的一切手段都不能把我们拆散,而你,出于你自己的意愿,却做到了。

31. So much the worse for me, that I am strong. = It is so much the worse for me that I am strong. 对我来说那就更糟,因为我现在身强力壮。(含义是:你一死,什么痛苦也没了;而我还要忍受这令人心碎的痛苦很久很久。)

32. Oh, God! Would you like to live with your soul in the grave?　呵,上帝呵! 当你的灵魂已进入坟墓的时候,还想活下去吗?

33. to upbraid you　责怪你

on a great occasion like this　在想这样不寻常的场合

to return from his errand　完成了他的差事回来了

to distinguish... by the shine of the westering sun up the valley　凭借西斜的夕阳照耀在山谷的光辉，可以看清/辨认……

a concourse thickening outside Gimmerton chapel porch　从吉默顿教堂走廊走出来的人越来越多

to groan a curse　像呻吟似的发出一声诅咒

to strain sb. closer　把某人抱得更紧

ere long = before long　不久之后

34. passing up the road towards the kitchen wing　沿着大路朝厨房旁边走过来

to saunter slowly up　悠闲地慢慢走过来

to enjoy the lovely afternoon that breathed as soft as summer　享受那个和煦宜人、散发着夏日气息的下午

please stay among the trees till he is fairly in　请在树林里待着，等他进屋以后再走

seeking to extricate himself from his companion's arms　想要从他伴侣的手臂中挣脱出来

the alarmed intruder　受惊的闯入者/外来者

to unfix her fingers by the act　想借此动作挣开她的手指

to cling fast, gasping　紧紧地抱/缠在一起，喘息着

mad resolution　疯狂的决心

35. If he shot me so, I'd expire with a blessing on my lips.　如果他开枪就这样打死我，我也会在嘴唇上带着你的祝福而离去。

　　* expire　v. 断气，死亡

主要内容归纳和总结

1. 勃朗特姐妹出生于一个爱尔兰裔的英国家庭，父亲是约克郡赫华斯（Haworth）的一个牧师。她们幼年时曾被送入为神职人员女儿专设的女校，那里的恶劣生活条件就成了夏洛特《简·爱》（*Jane Eyre*）里洛伍德学校的原型。长大后，为创建自己的学校，夏洛特和艾米莉还到布鲁塞尔去学习外语。在那里，夏洛特爱上了一位德语教授，这段无果的恋情成了她后来的小说《维莱特》（*Villette*）的素材。

　　三姐妹均有文学天赋，曾有评论家言，以二姐艾米莉为最。然而天不假年，二姐三妹很年轻时，就过早离世。尽管如此，她们依然有惊人之作留存于世，尤其是艾米莉的《呼啸山庄》（*Wuthering Heights*），文笔奇诡，有浓郁的哥特式（Gothic）小说风味。大姐夏洛特创作时间相对较长，作品较多，以《简·爱》影响最大。

　　夏洛特最擅长描写中产阶级的职业女性，特别是家庭教师，善于塑造具有强烈感情和超凡个性的角色，也时常以浪漫主义手法重新诠释生活。她作品的主题几乎都是个人自觉地为实现自我价值而奋斗，她小说中的女主人公最大的快乐都来自做了一些自我牺牲或克服了个人弱点后获得的幸福。另一方面，她的作品也对英国上流社会的残酷、虚伪和种种丑恶现象做了真实的再现。

2. 勃朗特姐妹、姐弟早期合著：

夏洛特和弟弟布伦威尔（Branwell）合著小说《安格里昂》*Angrian*

艾米莉和安妮合著小说《刚朵儿》*Gandal*

夏洛特、艾米莉、安妮合著诗集《诗集》*Poems by Currer, Ellis and Action Bell*

3. 夏洛特的主要作品：

《简·爱》*Jane Eyre*（1847）

《雪莉》*Shirley*（1849）

《维莱特》*Villette*（1853）

4. 艾米莉的主要作品：

《呼啸山庄》*Wuthering Heights*（1847）

《教授》The Professor（1854 出版）

另有 193 首抒情诗，她在诗歌方面的天赋更高。

5. 安妮的主要作品：

《阿格尼斯·格雷》*Agnes Grey*（1847）

《维尔德费尔·霍的佃户》*The Tenant of Wildfell Hall*（1848）

重要信息句子

1. Social life was very limited for the Brontë children.

2. Charlotte's works are all about the struggle of an individual consciousness towards self-realization，about some lonely and neglected young women with a fierce longing for love, understanding and a full, happy life. 夏洛特的著作都是关于个人实现自我价值的自觉奋斗的故事,也是关于一些孤独、被冷落的年轻妇女渴望爱情、理解和完美幸福生活的故事。

3. In Charlotte's mind, man's life is composed of perpetual battle between sin and virtue, good and evil. All her heroines' highest joy arises from some sacrifice of self or some human weakness overcome. 依夏洛特的想法,人的生活是由罪孽与美德,善与恶之间永久的斗争组成的。所有女主人公的最大快乐都产生于自我牺牲或对某些人性弱点的克服。

Ⅲ. 阿尔弗雷德·丁尼生 Alfred Tennyson（1809～1892）

词语解释和难句分析

1. to voice the doubt and the faith, the grief and the joy of the English people in an age of fast social changes 表达了社会剧变的时代英国人民的怀疑和信仰,悲伤和快乐

to show a flair for poetry 展示了诗歌方面的天赋和才华

an attraction to oriental themes 对东方主题的兴趣,迷恋东方主题

the Trinity College, Cambridge 剑桥大学三一学院

be drawn to a circle of brilliant young men, known as "the Apostles" 被引入了一个名叫"使徒党"的青年才俊的团体

to publish his first signed work 出版了他第一本署名著作

the elaborate texture, the splendid coloring and the dreaming melancholy 精致的构思,绚丽的文采和梦幻般的忧郁

2. beautiful in melody, and rich in imagery 韵律优美,意象/形象丰富

to receive very harsh and hostile criticism 收到尖刻而敌意的批评

to throw the young poet into deep sorrow and gloom　使得年轻诗人陷入极度的悲伤和消沉之中

to nurse his bleeding heart and <u>devoting himself to</u> the task of perfecting his art　医治心头的创伤,全力完善他的艺术技巧

the dramatic monologue　戏剧独白

the epic narrative　叙事史诗

the exquisite idylls　精美的田园诗

blank verse　无韵诗

3. be appointed the Poet Laureate　被授予桂冠诗人

to <u>dwell on</u> the personal bereavement　停留在/总是思考个人逝去的亲友

an elaborate and powerful expression of the poet's philosophical and religious thoughts　对诗人的哲学和宗教思想所做的强有力的、精致的表达

his doubts about the meaning of life, the existence of the soul and the afterlife, and his faith in the power of love and the soul's instinct and immortality　他对人生的意义、灵魂和人死后来生是否存在的怀疑,以及对爱情的力量和灵魂的本能和不朽的信仰

religious reflections　宗教思考

the familiar <u>trance-like experience</u>, mellifluous rhythm and pictorial descriptions　不拘泥形式、使人迷茫的经历,流畅悦耳的韵律和形象化的描写

4. to publish a monodrama　出版一部单人剧/独角戏

the amazing poetic freshness and inspiration　令人惊叹的诗意的新颖和灵气

his most ambitious work　他的最雄心勃勃的著作

the Celtic legends of King Arthur and his knights of the Round Table　凯尔特人的亚瑟王和圆桌骑士的传奇

to restore order and harmony out of chaos　从混乱中恢复秩序和和谐

<u>be disillusioned by</u> the faithlessness of Queen Guinevere and the betrayal of his round table knights　(他)为圭尼维亚王后的不贞和圆桌骑士的背叛而感到万念俱灰

to cherish his faith in God　他怀着对上帝的信仰

a modern interpretation of the classic myth　对古典神话的现代诠释

the rise and fall of King Arthur　亚瑟王的沉浮兴衰

to represent a cyclic history of western civilization　表现了西方文明的周而复始的历史

5. to have the natural power of linking visual pictures with musical expressions　有一种天然的把视觉形象与音乐表现联系在一起的能力

to have perfect control of the sound of English, and an excellent choice and taste of words　对英语的音律和词语的选择都驾驭自如,有极高的品位

be rich in poetic images and melodious language　诗歌意象丰富、音律优美

<u>be noted for</u> its lyrical beauty and metrical charm　以抒情优美、富有韵律魅力著称

products of a long and rich English heritage　历史悠久、积淀丰厚的英语文化传统的产物

to manifest all the qualities of England's great poets　表现了英格兰伟大诗人的一切特征/成就

the natural simplicity　自然简洁

the narrative vigor　叙事如生,充满活力

be evident on <u>successive pages</u> of Tennyson's poetry　在丁尼生的后续诗篇中都是得到鲜明体现的

丁尼生作品选读

1. 拍击,拍击,拍击 *Break*, *Break*, *Break*

词语解释和难句分析

1. 此诗发表于 1842 年,为悼念剑桥大学时的同窗好友、妹妹的未婚夫亚瑟·哈勒姆(Arthur Hallam)而作。哈勒姆在去维也纳的旅途中不幸亡故,引起丁尼生长久的悲伤和怀念,1850 年还发表了长篇挽诗《悼念》(*In Memoriam*)。

   这首诗是作者的触景生情之作,他看到海波拍岸,渔舟唱晚,孩童嬉戏,世事如常,不由得想起了故人,想起了与故人的往昔深情,一言一笑,不禁成诗。

2. Break, break, break,/On thy cold grey stone, O sea!   啪——啪——啪——/哦,海浪向你灰冷的岩石拍击!

   ＊第一行三个 break,只有三个音节,并不能独立构成三个音步,每个 break 后都有一个较长的停顿,正是这三个停顿的帮助,使第一行读起来有了三个音步的节奏感。

3. And I would (＝wish) that my tongue could utter/The thoughts that rises in me.   但愿我能振舌呼喊/发泄心头涌动的情怀。

4. O, well for the fisherman's boy,/That he shouts with his sister at play!   ＝O, it would be well for...   哦,多快乐呀,这渔家童子/喊叫着与妹妹嬉戏玩耍!

   ＊it＝that...从句,it 为形式主语,that...从句为真正的主语从句。下两行诗句结构相同。

5. O, well for the sailor lad,/That he sings in his boat on the bay!   哦,多快乐呀,那驾舟少年,/在海湾里荡桨放歌!

6. And the stately ships go on/To their haven under the hill;   一艘艘船舶威严驶来/昂然进入山下的港湾;   But O for the touch of a vanished hand,/And the sound of a voice that is still!   而我——多想再握那消逝的手,/多想再听那已沉寂的声音!

   ＊O for＝How I wish for...

7. Break, break, break,/At the foot of thy crags, O sea!   啪——啪——啪——/哦,海浪向悬崖的脚下拍击!

   But the tender grace of a day that is dead/Will never come back to me.   但往昔的美好情谊已成记忆,/永不会再回到我身边来。

   ＊a day that is dead＝a day/the days that has/have passed. 指已经逝去的岁月。

参考译文——姚绍德

拍击,拍击,拍击

啪——啪——啪——
海浪拍向你冰冷的灰石!
但愿我能鼓舌呼喊

喊出我心头涌动的情怀。

多快乐呀,那渔家童子,
呼叫着与妹妹玩耍嬉戏!
多快乐呀,那驾舟少年,
在海湾里荡桨放歌!

一艘艘威严的船舶驶来,
昂然驶入悬崖下的港湾,
而我呀,多想再摸一下那逝去的手,
多想再听一次那沉寂了的声音!

啪——啪——啪——
啊大海,拍击在你悬崖的脚下!
但往昔的美好情谊已逝,
再不会回到我身边。

格律和韵律分析

'Break, / 'break, / 'break,	a
On 'thy/cold grey 'stones, /O 'sea!	b
And I 'would/that my 'tongue/could 'utter	c
The 'thoughts/that 'arise/in 'me.	d
O, 'well/for the 'fish/erman's 'boy,	a
That he 'shouts/with his 'sis/ter at 'play!	b
O, 'well/for the 'sai/lor 'lad,	c
That he 'sings/in his 'boat/on the 'bay!	d
And the 'state/ly 'ships/go 'on	a
To their 'ha/ven 'un/der the 'hill;	b
But 'O/for the 'touch/of a 'va/nished 'hand,	c
And the 'sound/of a 'voice/that is 'still!	b
'Break, / 'break, / 'break,	a
At the 'foot/of thy 'crags, / O 'sea!	b
But the 'ten/der grace/of a 'day/that is 'dead	c
Will 'ne/ver come 'back/to 'me.	d

根据上述音步的划分和重音的标注,可得出如下几个结论:

a. 除了第三节和第四节的第三行诗句为 4 个音步外,所有诗行均为 3 个音步。

b. 第一和第四诗节的第一行 3 个 break 为不完整的 3 个音步,它们的不完整由 3 个较长的停顿来弥补,作为补充音节,相当于使得每个音步有了 2 个音节。

c. 大多数音步为 2 个音节、抑扬格,也有部分音步为 3 个音节、抑抑扬格,其他例外较少。

d. 全诗格律为三四音步抑扬格,适当伴有抑抑扬格。

e. 诗的韵律为 abcb 型,偶数句押韵。

2. 越过沙洲 *Crossing the Bar*

词语解释和难句分析

1. "Crossing the Bar"意味着跨越生死的界限,离开人生的世界到另一个世界去。这是作者晚年的作品,表达了作者"生死一旅程"的坦然无畏的人生观,对上帝和来世抱有坚定信仰,但又对死亡(death)和 来世(afterlife)感到无知,带有想要探索的渴望。诗中的 sunset, evening star, twilight, evening bell 是生命结束的象征;而 sea, tide, deep, flood 都象征着生命。

2. Sunset and evening star,　夕阳西下,晚星初现,

   And one clear call for me!　一个清晰的声音对我呼唤!

   And may there be no moaning of the bar,　但愿沙洲不要悲伤地呜咽,

   When I put out to sea.　在我驾舟出海的时刻。

3. But such a tide as moving seems asleep,　波动的海潮似人在安眠,

   Too full for sound and foam,　潮涨得太满反而无声无息/没有声音、没有泡沫,

   When that which drew from out the boundless deep　大潮本来自无涯的深渊

   Turns again home.　如今又如游子的回归。

   * 第三、四行可解析为:When that turns again home, which drew from out the boundless deep. 其中 that 指的是前面的 tide, which 引导的是它的定语从句。意思是潮涨潮落皆源自无涯深渊,比喻人的生死如同出门和回归。注意 turns 和 drew 时态上的不同,"潮涨自深渊"是"过去",用 drew;"潮落"是"现在",用 turns。turns 是 that 的谓语动词。when 引导的是一个时间状语从句,说的是潮涨到顶点回落时声息皆无的景象,前两行才是主句。

4. Twilight and evening bell,　黄昏时刻,晚钟响起,

   After that the dark!　此后是夜的黑暗!

   And may there be no sadness of farewell,　但愿没有告别的悲伤,

   When I embark;　在我起航之际;

5. For though from out our bourne (= boundary) of Time and Place/The flood may bear me far, = For though the flood may bear me far from out our bourne of Time and Place,　虽然海潮要带我去远方,超越我们时空的界限,

6. I hope to see my Pilot face to face/When I have crossed the bar.　但希望亲眼见到领航人,就在越过沙洲之后。

   * 这一节说明了诀别去、莫悲伤的原因,就是越过生死界限之后,可以面对面见到一生信仰的上帝,表现了作者宗教信仰的虔诚。Pilot,领航人,指路人,这里指上帝。

参考译文——姚绍德

越过沙洲

夕阳西下，晚星初现，
一个清晰的声音对我呼唤！
但愿沙洲莫悲泣，
任我驾舟出海去，

波动的海潮像是悠然入睡，
涨得太满反而无声无息，
大潮本涨至无边的深渊，
如今又如游子归去。

黄昏时分，晚钟响起，
此后便是那种黑暗！
但愿没有告别的伤悲，
在我登舟起航之际；

越过尘世的时空之界，
大潮会载我向遥远的境地，
但我渴望面见生命的"舵手"——
当我越过沙洲之后。

格律和韵律分析

这首诗的一、三两节为3342音步，二、四两节为5352音步。多数音步为抑扬格，少数为抑抑扬格，其他的就更少了，因此，此诗可以认为是没有严格格律的自由体诗，韵律为abab/cdcd/efef/ghgh，参见下面具体的音步划分和重音标注。

Sun·set/and ·e/vening ·star,   a
And ·one/clear ·call/for ·me!   b
And may ·there/be ·no/·moaning/of the ·bar,   a
When I ·put/out to ·sea,   b

But ·such/a ·tide/as ·mo/ving ·seems/a·sleep,   c
Too ·full/for ·sound/and ·foam,   d
When ·that/which ·drew/from ·out/the ·bound/less ·deep   c
·Turns a/gain ·home.   d

Twi·light/and ·e/vening ·bell,   e

And ·a/fter that/the ·dark!   f

And may ·there/be ·no/·sadness/of ·farewell,   e

When·I/em·bark;   f

For ·though/from ·out/our ·bourne/of ·Time/and ·Place   g

The ·flood/may ·bear/me ·far,   h

I ·hope/to ·see/my ·Pi/lot ·face/to ·face   g

When I ·have/crossed the ·bar.   h

3. 尤利西斯 *Ulysses*

词语解释和难句分析

1. 此诗于 1833 年作者的好友哈勒姆去世后不久写成,但发表于 1842 年。丁尼生曾自注说,此诗是"在失落感之下写成,一切都消逝了,但仍必须以战斗到底的姿态去度过平静的生活"。诗人通过戏剧独白的形式,借尤利西斯之口,表达了人类的也是他自己的不断追求的热望。

   尤利西斯(Ulysses)是荷马(Homer)史诗《奥德赛》(*Odyssey*)中主人公奥德修斯(Odysseus)的希腊名。奥德修斯是古希腊的伊萨卡(Ithaca)岛国的国王,在荷马史诗中他参加了特洛伊战争,10 年征战破城之后,又历经千辛万苦,在海上航行了 10 年,才回到自己的王国,重新控制了这个国家,杀死了前 20 年中不断向他贤惠的妻子珀涅罗珀(Penelope)求婚骚扰的人,一家人其乐融融。但丁尼生没有采用这个版本,而是采用了但丁《神曲·地狱篇》中的另一版本,描写尤利西斯不安于老婆孩子热炕头的平庸生活,又率领他的老部下扬帆远航,踏上向西航行的探索旅程。

2. 诗的开头 5 行,是一个完整的句子,基本句架是 It little profits that ...,it 为形式主语,that 从句为真正的主语从句。

3. It little profits that... = It profits little that... = It is no good that...   毫无益处,没有意思

   by this still hearth   静坐炉边

   among these barren crags   置身于荒凉岩石之中;周围巉岩乱石,一片荒凉(待在荒凉的伊萨卡岛上)

   match'd (= matched) with an aged wife   与老妻做伴

4. to mete and dole unequal laws unto a savage race   给一个野蛮的种族论罪量刑、发布各种不同的奖惩法令

   * mete = measure 衡量,计量; dole = give 发布,给予

   that hoard, and sleep, and feed, and know not me.   他们只知聚敛钱财,贪吃贪睡,根本不知道我是谁

   * that... 从句为 savage race 的定语从句。

5. to rest from travel   中途停止旅程

   to drink life to the lees   痛饮人生,直到汲尽生命的最后余沥/尝尽人生的滋味

6. thro' scudding drifts = through scudding drifts   穿过疾飞奔腾的阵雨,挟狂风暴雨

   to vex the dim sea   把大海搅得天昏地暗/搅动昏暗的大海

   * vext = vexed   使激荡/汹涌

   on shore, and when thro' scudding drifts the rainy Hyades vext the dim sea.   不论在陆地,还是(在海上)当雨神亥亚迪斯挟狂风暴雨搅得大海天昏地暗的时候(都享过大福,遭过大罪)

7. I am become a name　我已成了一个虚名

　＊ am become＝have become，前者强调目前的状态，后者强调目前的结果，意思差不多。尤利西斯离家日久，百姓对他已很陌生了。

8. For always roaming with a hungry heart/Much have I seen and known；　因为我总是带着一颗饥渴的心四处漫游，所以我已看了很多，也知道很多，见闻广博；

9. Myself not least, but honour'd of them all. ＝ Myself is not least important, but honoured of them all. 我本人并非无足轻重，而是深受他们大家的尊敬。

10. And drunk delight of battle with my peers. ＝ I have drunk...with... 我曾和我的战友们畅饮战斗的快乐。

11. the ringing plains of windy Troy　特洛伊那风云叱咤的平原/呼啸的多风的平原

　an arch where-thro'/Gleams that untravell'd world ＝ an arch through which that untraveled world gleams. 一道未曾涉足的世界在其中闪烁的拱门

12. How dull it is to rust unburnish'd, not to shine in use!　弃置不用、任其生锈，而不在使用中发光，是多么愚蠢！

　＊ unburnish'd＝unburnished　未擦亮/打磨/抛光的

13. As tho'（＝as though）to breathe were life.　仿佛有口气就算生命。

14. Life piled on life were all too little,　几辈子的生命叠加也全无价值，

15. and of one to me/little remains ＝ and little of one (life) remains to me.　而我只有一次的生命也所剩无几

16. but every hour is saved from that eternal silence, something more, a bringer of new things.　但每一个小时都是从永恒的沉寂（死亡）中抢来的，而且，都是创造新事物的机遇/都可以带来新事物

　＊ a bringer of new things 是 is 后面的表语成分。

17. and vile it were for some three suns to store and hoard myself ＝ and it were vile to store and hoard myself for about three years.　把我自己封藏三年是可悲可叹的/可悲的是把……封藏三年使韶光消逝

　＊ 用 were 表明虚拟语气。

　this grey spirit yearning in desire to follow knowledge　白发老人渴望追求知识的这颗热切的心/这种热烈的精神

　＊ 此短语与 myself 一样都是不定式 to store and hoard 的宾语。故而整个长句可译为：可悲的是我自己和我这颗老骥伏枥渴求知识的雄心被封存了三年之久，使我就像一颗陨星坠落到人类思想的范围之外。

　＊ 但丁版本的奥德修斯在特洛伊战争胜利之后，回到伊萨卡待了三年，才又重新开始新的航程和探索之旅。这里所说的封存了三年就是指这三年，把白发雄心、志在千里的老英雄困在家里，当了三年"家庭妇男"。

18. This is my son, mine own Telemachus ＝ my own Telemachus　这是我儿子，我的忒勒马科斯

　＊ mine 的古代用法也可以作形容词性物主代词，用在元音和 h 之前或名词之后，等于 my。

　to whom I leave the scepter and the isle　我把权杖和岛国留给他

　＊ 此为 Telemachus 的后置定语从句。

　(be) well-loved of me, discerning to fulfill this labour　（他）深受我的宠爱，有见识、有能力担此重任

　＊ 过去分词短语和现在分词短语都是 Telemachus 的后置定语。

　by slow prudence to make mild a rugged people　以循序渐进的谨慎步骤教化/驯服一个粗鲁的民族

　＊ to make mild sth. ＝ to make sth. mild.

　(to) subdue them to the useful and the good　使他们归化文明，懂得良善，学会生聚

　＊ 三个不定式短语 to fulfill.../to make mild.../to subdue…都是跟在 discerning 后面的并列短语，

说明他有能力做的几件事情。

19. be most blameless　最无可指责

（be）centered in the sphere of common duties　集中精力/专心致力于公务职责

（be）decent not to fail in offices of tenderness　做事平和得体以免公务处理有失仁厚

＊注意短语 to fail of tenderness（in offices）。

(to) pay meet（＝suitable）adoration to my household gods　对宗庙应有正常的礼敬和祭祀

整个句子可理解为 He is most blameless, when I am gone, he will be centred..., decent not to fail ..., and will pay...。

20. to puff her sail　扬起/张满她的风帆

21. There gloom the dark broad seas. ＝The dark broad seas gloom there.　辽阔的大海阴暗了下来。

22. souls that have toiled, wrought（＝worked）, and thought with me　曾与我同辛劳、同工作、且志同道合的人

＊souls ＝my mariners, 有两个 that 引导的定语从句, 此其一, 下一个也是。

（souls）that ever with a frolic welcome took the thunder and the sunshine, and opposed free hearts, free foreheads　他们曾乐观地迎战雷电、烈日, 对抗各种偏激情绪和蛮干思想

Old age hath yet honour and his toil.　（我们虽已年老,）但老人也有他的荣誉和要操劳的事情。

23. But something ere（＝before）the end,/Some work of noble note, may yet be done,　但生命结束前, 总还得有点作为, 做一些高尚的工作,

Not unbecoming（＝incompetent/unfit）men that strove with Gods.　够格/不辱没做与神抗争过的人。

24. The long day wanes; the slow moon climbs;　漫长的白昼在消逝, 蹒跚的月亮爬上来;

the deep/Moans round with many voices.　大海向四周发出各种深沉的呻吟。

my friends,/'Tis（＝It is）not too late to seek a newer world.　我的朋友, 寻找新世界永不会太迟。

25. to push off　（开船）出发吧

sitting well in order　各就各位, 按序坐好

to smite the sounding furrows　击水破浪

26. for my purpose holds/ to sail beyond the sunset, and the baths/of all the western stars, until I die.　因为我的目标就是驶过落日, 驶过西天群星照耀/沐浴的大海, 矢志不渝, 到死方休。

27. It may be that the gulfs will wash us down;　也许海底深渊要把我们吞没;

It may be（that）we shall touch the Happy Isles,　也许我们就要到达极乐仙岛,

And see the great Achilles, whom we knew.　见到伟大的阿喀琉斯, 我们的老友。

28. Tho'（＝though）much is taken, much abides（vi）;　虽然已失去不少, 留下的却还很多;

and tho'/We are not now that strength which in old days/Moved earth and heaven;　虽然/我们现在的力气不比从前/——撼天动地;

that which we are, we are; ＝we are that（＝the strength）which we are.　但今天, 我们依然有威力/今天有今天的威力。

（we are）One equal temper of heroic hearts,　我们有英雄心, 有同样英雄的性格,

29. Made weak by time and fate, but strong in will/To strive, to seek, to find, and not to yield.　虽然被时光和命运削弱, 但意志依然坚强,/要去奋斗, 去求索, 去发现, 就是不屈服。

＊made weak by... ＝though we are made weak by..., but we are strong..., 语法上相当于分词短语作让步状语; 另外, to strive,... 等四个不定式在语法上是 will 的定语短语, 如果直译, 应为: 但奋斗、求索、发现和不屈服的意志依然坚强。

参考译文——姚绍德

尤利西斯

这事想来真是太无意趣——
我,一位无所事事的国王,
置身于荒岛嶙岩之中,
偎着老妻,傍着火炉,
只为一个野蛮的民族,
颁布些定罪量刑的法令,
而他们只知聚财、睡觉和吃喝,
从不知有我为谁。

我不能中断旅程、安享清闲:
我要痛饮人生,尝尽人生余味:
多少年来,我享受过极乐和大苦,
或有爱我者相伴,或者独自承受;
不论在陆地,还是在海上——
雨神亥亚迪斯挟狂风暴雨
把大海搅得天昏地暗的时候。
而现在呀,我只是虚名一个!
我曾如饥似渴、到处漫游,
因而我见闻广博;多少个
名城大都,各色人种,礼仪气候
乃至议会政府,都曾亲历目睹。
我自己也并非无足轻重,
而是深受他们的尊重和礼遇。
我曾长途远征——
鏖战在疾风呼啸的特洛伊平原,
与战友们痛饮战斗的欢欣。
凡我所遇,我便与之融为一体;
而一切经验就像一座拱门,
前方未曾涉足的世界,
在门里闪耀着诱人的光辉,
我渐行,它渐远,永远永远
够不着它隐退的边际。
但就此停歇,终止探索之旅,
宁可生锈而不磨砺,
也不在使用中发出光辉,
这是何等的无聊和愚昧!

仿佛有口气就算生命!
几辈子的生命叠加都太无意义,
而我只有一次的生命已所剩无几:
每一小时都抢自那永恒的寂静,
都是创造新事物的机遇。
可悲呀,实在是可悲! ——
竟把我自己封存了三年,
虚负了老骥伏枥宏图志,
虚负了白发老人求知欲,
徒使得热切雄心似陨星——
坠落出人类思想最远的边界。

这里自有我的儿子,我的
忒勒马科斯继承大任,
我将把权杖和岛国授予他——
我最亲爱的人,他的见识和能力
足以胜任。以循序渐进的耐心,
驯化一个野蛮的民族;
通过温和灵活的步骤,
使他们归化为懂得生计的良善。
我走之后,他会无可挑剔,
集中精力,专心公务,
他处事平和得体,以免有失仁厚,
宗庙祭祀也都会正常进行。
他做他的国王,我做我的航行。
我们各管其事,职责分明。

那里就是港口,舰船正扬帆待发,
辽阔的大海正阴沉下来。
我的水手,都与我志同道合,
是一起经历过大风大浪的弄潮儿;
都曾乐观地迎战过雷电、烈日,
对抗过种种偏颇人思想和激动情绪
——如今虽说年已老迈,但老人
也有他们的荣誉和操劳的事情。
死亡会结束一切,
但结束前总得有点作为,
做点高尚的事情,
够格做个与众神抗争过的人。
灯光开始在山岩上闪烁;
漫长的白昼消逝,月亮慢慢爬上来;
大海向周围发出各种深沉的呻吟。
来吧,我的朋友,

寻求新世界还不算太晚。

开船出发吧，各就各位坐好，

摇桨破浪前进！我的目标是——

扬帆一直驶过落日，驶过

西方群星沐浴的大海，直到生命终止。

也许海底深渊会把我们吞没，

也许我们会到达神仙天堂——快乐岛，

见到伟大的阿喀琉斯——我们的老友。

虽然失去的已经很多，留下的却还不少；

虽然我们的力气不比从前——撼天动地，

但今天我们自有今天的神威；

同样的英雄性格，同样的英雄心，

人虽被岁月和命运削弱，

意志却依然坚强，

要奋斗，要探索，要发现，

就是不屈服！

* 这首诗没有固定的格律和韵律，属于自由体诗。

主要内容归纳和总结

1. 阿尔弗雷德·丁尼生出生于英格兰林肯郡（Lincolnshire）一个有学识的神职人员家庭。他的诗作传达了处在社会大变革时期的英国人民内心的困惑与信仰、痛苦与欢乐。

　　他少年时期便显露诗歌才华，在剑桥读书期间，便出版了自己的第一本诗集《抒情诗集》（*Poems, Chiefly Lyrical*），其精致的构思，绚丽的华彩及梦幻般的伤感都预示着一位伟大诗人的诞生。在大学他加入了使徒党（the Apostles），与党的领导人哈勒姆（Arthur Henry Hallam）友谊甚笃，为哀悼哈勒姆的英年早逝，他写下了一生中最伟大的作品《悼念》（*In Memoriam*），诗中深邃的思想（profound thoughts），如梦如幻的意境（trance-like experience），悦耳的韵律（mellifluous rhythm）和如画的描写（pictorial description）都足以使它成为英国文学史上最优秀的挽诗（elegy）。

　　丁尼生的突出特点是善于将可视的风景图画与极富乐感的语汇及多姿多彩的情感非常自然地糅合在一起（linking visual pictures with musical expressions, and these two with the feelings）能够集前辈诗人之所长，形成自己作品的独特美丽。直到暮年，他依然文思未竭，写出像《跨越沙洲》这样新颖而富有灵气的作品。

2. 丁尼生的主要作品：

《兄弟诗集》*Poems by Two Brothers* (1827)

《抒情诗集》*Poems, Chiefly Lyrical* (1830)

《诗集》*Poems* (1832)

《诗集》卷二 *Poems Vol. 2* (1842)，内收：

* 戏剧独白（dramatic monologue）:《尤利西斯》*Ulysses*

* 叙事史诗（epic narrative）:《摩尔特·亚瑟》*Morte Arthur*

* 田园诗（idylls）:《朵拉》*Dora*;《园丁女儿》*The Gardener's Daughter*,等等

* 无韵体诗（blank verse）:《公主》*Princess* (1847)

* 诗体日记(poetic diary):《悼念》*In Memoriam*(1850)一部分为悼念好友哈勒姆的挽诗和缅怀诗歌,大多为专门表达作者哲学思想和宗教思想的诗歌,为作者最伟大的作品。
* 单人剧或独角戏(monodrama):《摩德抒情短歌集》*Maud, a Collection of Short Lyrics*(1855);《里兹帕》*Rizpah*

《伊诺克·阿顿》*Enoch Arden*

《魔法师与灵光》*Merlin and the Gleam*

《越过沙洲》*Crossing the Bar*

《国王诗歌集》*Idylls of the King*(1842~1885)讲述凯尔特人传奇亚瑟王和圆桌骑士的故事,由12卷叙事诗组成,为丁尼生最雄心勃勃的作品,花了他30多年的时间。

重要信息句子

1. Alfred Tennyson is certainly the most representative, if not the greatest, Victorian poet.
2. This year (1850) also saw the publication of his greatest work *In Memoriam*.
3. Tennyson's poetic career is also marked out by *Idylls of the King* (1842~1885), his most ambitious work which took him over 30 years.
4. Tennyson is a real artist. He has the natural power of linking visual pictures with musical expressions, and these two with the feelings.

IV. 罗伯特·勃朗宁 Robert Browning (1812~1889)

词语解释和难句分析

1. be acknowledged by many as the most originated poet of the time 被许多人认为是当时最富有独创性的诗人

   to receive his education mainly from his private tutor 主要是接受私人导师的教育

   to give him freedom to follow his own interest 给了他按照自己兴趣发展的自由

   to read widely and voraciously 贪婪地广泛阅读;广泛阅读,狼吞虎咽

   be fond of the most profound, obtuse and mystic 喜爱阅读最深刻、最令人费解和神秘主义的书籍

   without having to worry about his sustenance 他不必担心自己的生计/生活资料

2. The apparent modeling on Shelley's personal style and an easily detectable intense self-consciousness of the author brought about great embarrassment upon Browning. 对雪莱个人风格的明显模仿与作者清晰可辨的强烈自我意识给布朗宁的创作带来了尴尬和窘迫。

3. to go too far in self-correction 矫枉过正

   to become so obscure as to be hardly readable 变得非常晦涩、难以读懂

   too many subtle analyses and too few actions (剧作)分析过多过细,动作表演太少

4. frustrating experiences 经受挫折的经历

   a fortune in disguise 无形的财富

to develop a literary form that suits him best　开发一种最适合他的文学形式

to give full-swing to his genius　充分发挥他的天才

the dramatic monologue　戏剧独白

a semi-invalid　一个半残废的人

be strictly confined home by her domineering father　被她专横跋扈的父亲严格地禁锢在家里

be accused of having an affair with a young priest　被指控与一个年轻的神父有染/通奸

to help her in her flight from the sadistic husband　帮助她逃离性虐待狂的丈夫

participants and spectators　参与者和旁观者

the goldsmith's technique of alloying gold in making rings　金匠铸合金制作戒指的技巧

hard truth　铁的事实,不可改变的事实

be not workable in making rings　不能加工成戒指

be alloyed with other materials　与其他物质/材料铸成合金

the alloying ingredients　制合金的材料/成分

to bring the dead truth to life　给生活带来铁打的真理

5. his old defects of obscurity and mannerism　他晦涩难懂、矫揉造作的老毛病

to reach its maturity and perfection　达到它成熟和完美的阶段

to choose a dramatic moment or a crisis　选择最富戏剧性或最关键的时刻

in listening to those one-sided talks　在倾听那些单人独白的谈话

to form their own opinions and judgments about the speakers personality　形成他们自己对说话人个性的看法和判断

to reveal bit by bit his cruelty and the possessiveness　一点一点地把他的残忍和占有欲揭露出来

the Duke's own defensive words　这位公爵自己的辩护言辞

to betray and condemn himself　暴露和谴责他自己

6. To Browning, the dramatic monologue is an ingenious means to exploit his literary gift without getting too personal.　对布朗宁来说,戏剧独白是一种不用过多个人介入就可开发自己文学天才的聪明方法。

7. to keep a good distance from his characters　与他所创作的人物保持一定的距离

to belong to the remote history, or just the fantastic world　属于遥远的历史,或者属于幻想的世界

to share nothing with him both in personality and in attitudes toward life　在个性和生活态度两方面与他毫无关系

to put his spirit, his vigor and energy into these characters　把他的精神、活力和精力都灌输到这些人物身上

to possess a good knowledge about man's psychology and nature　对人的心理和本性有深刻的理解

8. The syntax is usually clipped and highly compressed. The similes and illustrations appear too profusely. The allusion and implications are sometimes odd and farfetched. All this makes up his obscurity.　句子结构通常被剪辑和高度压缩。比喻和例证的使用过滥。有时典故和暗示的使用荒诞古怪、牵强附会。所有这一切造成了他作品的晦涩难懂。

9. idiosyncrasy　个人习性,习惯的表现手法/风格

be like a weather-beaten pioneer　像一个饱经风霜的开拓者

to beat a track through the jungle　在丛林中开辟出一条路来,披荆斩棘

10. The rough, grotesque and disproportionate appearance, the non-poetic jarring diction and the clumsy rhythms fit marvelously a life that is just as imperfect and incongruous.　粗糙、怪诞、比例不协调的形象,没有诗味儿的不雅措辞和粗陋的节奏正符合不完美、不和谐的真实生活。

to entertain the reader with the usual acoustic and visual pleasures　使读者享受到通常的视听娱乐

be supposed to keep sb. alert, thoughtful and enlightened 应当使某人保持警觉,善于思考,摆脱偏见和迷信/得到文明的启示

罗伯特·勃朗宁作品选读

1. 我的前公爵夫人 *My Last Duchess*

词语解释和难句分析

1. 本诗特定的剧情环境是费拉拉公爵正带领女方派来与他商谈婚事的使者在公爵府邸楼上观赏他收藏的艺术珍品,他们停在前公爵夫人像前,由公爵向使者讲述这幅画像绘成的原委,以及他对未来的公爵夫人娘家陪嫁的要求,暴露了他的狭隘、凶残和贪婪。整个故事和人物的思想都是通过他自己向别人讲述的独白展示出来的。

   作品取材于文艺复兴时期意大利濒临亚得里亚海的费拉拉公国第五位公爵阿方索二世(Alfonso Ⅱ)的记载。阿方索第一个妻子露克丽吉亚(Lucrezia)是美第奇家族科西摩一世(Cosimo I de Medici)的女儿,于1558年14岁时嫁给了阿方索,三年后去世。当时曾有人怀疑她是被毒死的。不过,费拉拉并未留下这位公爵夫人的任何画像。她死后不久,阿方索又筹划迎娶斐迪南一世之女芭芭拉为妻,芭芭拉的父亲已故,因而受她的叔父奥地利蒂罗尔伯爵(the Count of Tyrol)的监护。蒂罗尔伯爵派了因斯布鲁克的尼古拉·马得鲁兹作为使者前来与费拉拉商谈这桩婚事。这一原始资料就成了勃朗宁这首诗的创作素材。

2. I call that piece a wonder, now. = I call that piece of picture a wonder, now. 现在我称那幅画为一个奇迹。

   Frà Pandolf's hands worked busily a day (虚构的名画家)潘道夫的圣手忙碌了一整天才完成。

3. Will't please you sit and look at her? = Will it please (that) you sit and look at her? 你愿意坐下来看看她吗?

4. by design = on purpose 故意

   never read that... but.., = never understand that... except... 除了……没有能理解……

5. for never read/Strangers like you that pictured countenance,/The depth and passion of its earnest glance, = for strangers like you could never understand... 因为像你这样的陌生人,/没有能理解那画上的表情的,/没有能看懂那真挚眼神中的深邃和热情的。

   * never read 有两个并列的宾语短语,一是 that pictured countenance,二是 the depth and passion of its earnest glance。

6. But to myself they turned and seemed as they would ask me, if they durst (= dare),/How such a glance came there; 他们只有转向我,似乎要问我——如果敢问的话——/怎么会有这样的眼神?

7. so, not the first/Are you to turn and ask thus = so you are not the first one to turn and ask thus. 所以,你并非第一个/转头这样问我的人。

8. (since none puts by/The curtain I have drawn for you, but I) = since none but I puts by the curtain I have drawn for you. 因为除我之外,/没有人会替你拉开画上的帘幕。

   * I have drawn for you 是省略了关系代词的定语从句,修饰 the curtain。

9. 'twas (= it was) not/Her husband's presence only, (that) called that spot/Of joy into the Duchess' cheek: 不仅仅是/她丈夫的来到,唤起了/公爵夫人脸上的笑容:

10. perhaps/Frà Pandolf chanced to say "Her mantle laps/Over my lady's wrist too much," or "Paint/Must never

hope to reproduce the faint/Half-flush that dies along her throat": 也许/潘道夫偶然说过"她的披风/把手腕盖得太多了",或者/"一直红到脖子才隐约淡去的红晕,/绝不能指望颜料能够再现"

11. such stuff/Was courtesy, she thought, and cause enough/For calling up that spot of joy. = She thought that such stuff ..., and cause ... 这样的无聊话/她也当成殷勤美意,竟使她欢容满面/成为她喜形于色的原因。

    * cause *n.* 原因(was 的表语)

12. too soon made glad, too easily impressed = be made glad too soon, and be impressed too easily   (某人)太容易被哄高兴/讨其欢心,也太容易感动

13. she liked whate'er/She looked on, and her looks went everywhere.   她看到什么就喜欢什么,/而她偏又喜欢到处乱看。

    'twas all one! = It was all the same!   (她)对什么都一样/什么都喜欢!

14. My favor (= gift) at her breast,   不论是佩在胸前的我给她的礼物,
    The dropping of the daylight in the West,   还是夕阳西下的落日余晖,
    The bough of cherries some officious fool/Broke in the orchard for her   傻子殷勤,/为她从园中折下的那枝樱桃,

    * some officious fool broke in ... 是省略了关系代词的定语从句,修饰 the bough of cherries。

    the white mule/She rode with round the terrace   还有她/骑着绕行庭院的白骡
    — all and each/Would draw from her alike the approving speech,/Or blush, at least.   ——所有这一切,/都同样会得到她的赞美,/至少会引起她脸泛红晕。

15. as if she ranked/My gift of a nine-hundred-years-old name/ With anybody's gift.   仿佛她把我/赐她的具有 900 年历史家声的礼物/与任何寻常人的赠品等量齐观

16. Who'd stoop to blame/This sort of trifling? = Who would lower oneself to blame this sort of frivolousness?   谁愿意屈尊/去指责这轻浮的举止?

17. Even had you skill/In speech — (which I have not) — to make your will/Quite clear to such an one. = Even you had skill in speech ... to make your will quite clear to ...   即使你有语言天赋/(而我却没有)能把你的意志/向这样一个人讲清楚。

18. here you miss,/Or there exceed the mark   你这儿有点欠缺,/那儿又过了线
    and (even) if she let/Herself be lessoned so, nor plainly set/Her wits to yours, forsooth (= indeed),
    and made excuse —   即使她肯/听人教训,也丝毫不与你争辩,/确实,也不找任何借口——

    * set one's wits to sb. else's 与别人争辩/斗智;set one's wits to sth. 开动脑筋应付某事

19. E'en (= even) then (there) would be some stooping;   即便如此,依然有失身份;
    Will't please you rise? = Will it please that you rise?   请你起身好吗?
    The Count your master's known munificence is ample warrant that no just pretense of mine for dowry will be disallowed;   你的主人——伯爵大人闻名的慷慨就是充分的保证:我对嫁妆的任何合理的要求都不会遭到拒绝。

    * pretense = claim   要求,虚假的理由

20. Though his fair daughter's self, as I avowed at starting, is my object.   当然了,她美貌的女儿本身才是我追求的目标,一开始我就声明了。

21. Neptune   尼普顿,希腊神话中的海神。
    taming a sea horse   驯服海马
    Claus of Innsbruck   因斯布鲁克的克劳斯,这是诗人臆造的著名雕塑家。Innsbruck 现实中为奥地利西部一个城市的名字。
    to cast the rarity in bronze for me   为我特制的这座青铜雕塑珍品

参考译文——姚绍德

我的前公爵夫人

（费拉拉）

墙上画的便是我的前公爵夫人，
看起来她就像活着一样。如今，
我称它为奇迹：潘道夫的大手笔
忙碌了一天，从此她就在那儿站立。
你愿坐下来仔细看看她吗？
我有意提到画家潘道夫，
是因为像你这样的陌生客
根本看不懂画中的表情，看不懂
那眼神中的真挚、深邃和激情。
没有一个不转向我（因为只有我
才能把画上的帘幕拉开），
他们那些想问而不敢问的，
似乎全都想弄明白——
公爵夫人何以有这样的眼神？
所以，回头问我者，你非第一人。
先生，不仅仅是她丈夫的来到，
能使公爵夫人绽开笑容，就是
潘道夫的随口之言："夫人的披风
把她的手腕盖得太多"，以及
"任何颜料都不能再现她
向颈部淡去的那丝红晕"，
这样的无聊话也被她当成美意，
足以激起她心花怒放。她那颗心呀——
唉，怎么说呢？——太容易讨她欢心，
也太容易使她动心。她看什么都喜欢，
眼睛又偏爱到处看。
先生，她对什么都一样！
不论是佩在胸前的我给她的赠品，
还是夕阳西下时的落日余晖，
傻子殷勤，为她从园中折的那枝樱桃，
还有她骑着绕行花圃的白骡——
所有这一切，都同样会得到她的赞美，
至少会使她脸上泛起红晕。
她感激人，这很好！
但不知怎的总觉得她竟不分贵贱，

把我 900 年历史豪门给她的礼物，
与任何不相干的人的赠品并列。
谁愿意屈尊去谴责这种轻浮举止？
即使你有口才——而我没有——
能把你的意志向这样的人说清。
"你就这点或那点令我讨厌；
你这里差点儿，那里又过了线。"——
即使她愿受教训，也显然不作争辩，
托词和借口，什么都没有——即使这样，
我也觉得屈尊降贵、有失身份；
于是我做出抉择：绝不失身份！
啊，先生，她总是在慷慨地微笑！
当我从她身边走过，她无疑会微笑；
可谁人从她身边走过又得不到这样的笑？
事情发展至此，我发出了命令；
于是所有的微笑都一起终止。
她站在那儿，像活着一样。
你可否站起？我们要会见楼下的访客。
有句话我要再次重申——你主人——
伯爵先生的慷慨之名是婚约的充分保证，
他绝不会拒绝我对嫁妆的任何合理要求。
当然了，正如我开头的声明，
他美貌的小姐本身才是我追求的目标。
嘿，我们一起下楼吧，先生。
但请注意一下这青铜塑像——
海神尼普顿正驯服海马呢！
这可是件珍奇的收藏，
是因斯布鲁克的克劳斯为我特制的！

格律和韵律分析

这首诗格律和韵律是比较规则的，先列出开头 10 行诗作代表性分析：

> That's ˈmy/last ˈDu/chess ˈpain/ted ˈon/the ˈwall,　　　　a
> ˈLooking/as ˈif/she ˈwere/aˈlive,/ I ˈcall　　　　a
> That ˈpiece/a ˈwon/der, ˈnow:/ Frà ˈPan/dolf's ˈhands　　　b
> Worked ˈbu/sily/a ˈday,/ and ˈthere/she ˈstands.　　　b
> Will'ˈt ˈplease/you ˈsit/and ˈlook/at ˈher? / I ˈsaid　　　c
> "Frà ˈPan/dolf" by/deˈsign,/ for ˈne/ver ˈread　　　c
> ˈStrangers/like ˈyou/that ˈpic/tured ˈcoun/tenance,　　　d
> The ˈdepth/and ˈpa/ssion of/its ˈear/nest ˈglance,　　　d
> ˈBut to/myˈself/they ˈturned/(since ˈnone/puts ˈby　　　e
> The ˈcur/tain ˈI/have ˈdrawn/for ˈyou,/ but ˈI)　　　e

从上述分析可以看出,每行诗都是 5 音步,每个音步都是 2 个音节,绝大多数音步都是轻重音节,即抑扬格,所以这首诗为五步抑扬格;韵律为英雄偶句体,每两行押一个尾韵,即 aabbccddeeff...。

2. 夜半相会 *Meeting at Night*

词语解释和难句分析

1. 本诗最初载于 1845 年版《戏剧罗曼司》(*Dramatic Romance and Lyrics*),在《夜与晨》(*Night and Morning*)的标题下与《清晨分别》(*Parting at Morning*)合为一诗,直到 1849 年的版本中才分为两首独立的诗。

　　两首诗的立意和写法都突破了前人的窠臼。《夜半相会》不写恋人相会的缠绵,而写深夜海陆兼程赶去与恋人相会以及突然相逢一刹那的情景;后一首《清晨分别》的立意就更加独特了,不写恋人分别时的柔肠寸断,而写一夜销魂之后的顿悟:太阳前面是金色的大道,自己还有男人的世界——事业和理想。

2. And the startled little waves that leap/In fiery ringlets <u>from</u> their sleep　浪花儿朵朵从睡梦中惊起,/化作无数粼光闪耀的小圈。

　　* in fiery ringlets 指月光下,波光粼粼,火花闪亮。这是主人公将与恋人相会无限欢愉的意象。

3. I <u>gain</u> the cove with pushing prow,　我迅速推进的船头<u>到达</u>了海湾,

　　And <u>quench</u> its speed i'(= in) the slushy sand.　在泥泞的沙滩中稳稳/缓缓刹住。

4. Then a mile of warm sea-scented beach;/Three fields to cross till a farm appears;　走过了一英里暖融融带腥味的海滩,/又越过三块田才看到农庄;

5. a tap at the pane　手指在窗玻璃上轻弹

　　the quick sharp scratch/And blue spurt of a lighted match,嚓的一声刮擦,/火柴冒出了蓝色的火焰,

　　* lighted match 指擦燃/点着了的火柴

6. A voice <u>less</u> loud, through its joys and fears,/ <u>Than</u> the two hearts beating each to each!　惊喜之中一声快乐的呼喊,/顷刻间融入了两颗心更强烈的跳动!

参考译文——姚绍德

夜半相会

1

灰暗的大海,黑黑长长的陆地,
大大的一弯黄月低悬天边;
微小的浪波从睡梦中惊跳而起,
化作粼光闪耀的小圈无数。
我驾小舟驶进海湾,
在泥泞的沙滩上缓缓停住。

2

闻着海腥走过一哩暖暖的海滩，

又穿过三块田才见到农庄；

轻叩玻璃窗，咻啦一声响，

点亮的火柴闪出蓝光，

无穷惊喜，一声轻呼，

掩不住两颗心跳得更欢！

格律和韵律分析

这首诗分两节,取第一节做格律和韵律分析如下:

The ˈgrey/sea and/the ˈlong/black ˈland；　　　　　　a

And the ˈyel/low ˈhalf/-moon ˈlarge/and ˈlow；　　　　b

And the star/tled ˈlit/tle ˈwaves/that ˈleap　　　　　c

In ˈfie/ry ˈring/lets from/their ˈsleep,　　　　　　　c

As I ˈgain/the ˈcove/with ˈpu/shing ˈprow,　　　　　b

And ˈquench/its ˈspeed/ i' the ˈslu/shy ˈsand.　　　　a

根据上述音步的划分和重音的标注,每行诗有 4 个音步,这节诗共有 24 个音步。除了 4 个音步为抑抑扬格(加下划线)、2 个为抑抑格(阴影部分)以外,绝大多数音步为抑扬格,所以此诗为四步抑扬格。根据诗行尾韵的押韵规则可断定此诗的韵律为 abccba,又称搂抱韵。

3. 清晨分别 *Parting at Morning*

词语解释和难句分析

1. Round the cape of a sudden came the sea, = Round the cape the sea came of a sudden,　绕过海角,眼前大海突现,

   And the sun looked over the mountain's rim：　朝阳初露,越过了山脊：

2. And straight was a path of gold for him, = And a path of gold was straight for him,　对太阳,前程通畅,展现着一条金色的大道,

   ＊ him 即 the sun。

   And the need of a world of men for me. = And the need for me is a world of men.　而我,需要一个男人的世界!

   ＊ 所谓"男人的世界"是指男人的事业、理想和抱负(暗含"不只是爱人的迷恋、销魂"之意)。for him 和 for me 是对比的表意。

参考译文——姚绍德

清晨分别

绕过海角,眼前大海突现,
朝阳初露,越过了山脊:
太阳下是一条金色的大道,
而我,则需要开拓男人的世界。

格律和韵律分析

Round the ꞌcape/ of a ꞌsu/dden ꞌcame/the ꞌsea,   a

And the ꞌsun/looked ꞌo/ ver the ꞌmoun/tain's ꞌrim: b

And ꞌstraight/ was a ꞌpath/of ꞌgold/for ꞌhim,   b

And the ꞌneed/of ꞌworld/of ꞌmen/for ꞌme.   a

这首诗每行为 4 个音步,共 16 个音步,其中阴影部分的 7 个音步为抑抑扬格,其余 9 个音步均为抑抑扬格,故这首诗的格律为四步抑抑扬格。看尾韵可知该诗的韵律为 abba。

主要内容归纳和总结

1. 罗伯特·勃朗宁出身豪门,父亲的私人书库为他的文学慧根提供了充足的营养,他年纪轻轻就出版了诗集,但先是失于模仿过多,后又过于独创,晦涩难懂。他退而尝试戏剧创作,却又分析多于情节,不能成功。但这并没有使他气馁,反而认真总结,找到了最适合他自己的文学形式——戏剧独白(dramatic monologue),使他的文学天赋得以充分发挥,出版的诗集一部接着一部。《指环与书》(*The Ring and the Book*)是他的代表作品,使他成为英国最伟大的诗人之一。

   勃朗宁的名字是与"戏剧独白"的诗歌联系在一起的。在这些诗作中,他总能选择最富戏剧性或最紧要的时刻,让角色滔滔不绝地讲出他们的经历和思想,有时会由几个参与者或旁观者分别从不同角度来讲述(如《指环与书》),既塑造了人物形象,又揭示了主题。

   勃朗宁如旷野莽林中的拓荒者,文风粗犷,措辞不够优雅,节奏缺乏音乐性,常被人们与丁尼生比较,后者是精雕细刻的唯美主义"雕塑家"。另外,说到勃朗宁,别忘了勃朗宁夫人,伊丽莎白·芭瑞特(Elizabeth Barrett),她虽身体残疾,却是位杰出的诗人,她的诗集《葡萄牙十四行诗》(*Sonnets of the Portuguese*)是著名的爱情诗集。

2. 罗勃特·勃朗宁的主要作品,带 * 的为其代表作:

   《保林》*Pauline*(1832)

   《斯特拉福德》*Stratford*(1837)

   《索德罗》*Sordello*(1840)

   *《戏剧与抒情》*Dramatic Lyrics*(1842)

   *《戏剧罗曼司》*Dramatic Romances and Lyrics*(1845)

*《铃铛与石榴》*Bells and Pomegranates*（1846）
*《男人和女人》*Men and Women*（1855）
*《戏剧人物》*Dramatic Personae*（1864）
*《指环与书》*The Ring and the Book*（1868～1869）
*《戏剧田园诗》*Dramatic Idylls*（1880）
《我的前公爵夫人》*My Last Duchess*
《主教安排他的坟墓》*Bishop Orders His Tomb*
《鲍菲莉亚的情人》*Porphyria's Lover*
《一位文法学家的葬礼》*A Grammarian's Funeral*
《比芭走过》*Pippa Passes*

重要信息句子

1. In 1869 *The Ring and the Book*, his masterpiece, came out. It finally established Browning's position as one of the greatest English poets.
2. The name of Browning is often associated with the term："dramatic monologue." Although it is not his invention, it is in his hands that this poetic form reaches its maturity and perfection.
3. His poetic style belongs to the twentieth century rather than to the Victorian age.

V. 乔治·艾略特 George Eliot（1819～1880）

词语解释和难句分析

1. pseudonym   笔名,假名
   an estate agent's family   地产商/地产代理人的家庭
   to show no evidence of special talent   没有显示出特别的天赋
   extraordinary intelligence   过人的聪慧
   be acknowledged both at home and at school   不仅在家里而且在学校里都得到了承认
   be brought up with the strict orthodox teaching   在成长过程中受到严格的正统教育
   bookish girl   书卷气的姑娘
   to devote herself to a diligent study of the Scripture   潜心钻研圣经的经文
   be forced to drop school on account of her mother's death   由于母亲的去世而被迫辍学
   to enlarge her study from the church history and theological doctrine to wider, more philosophical issues
   她从研究教会历史和神学教义扩展到研究更为广泛、更富有哲学性的题目
   to bring her into collision with her family   促使她与家庭发生冲突
   to threaten permanently to separate her from her family   威胁着/预示着要永久与她的家人断绝往来
   her dramatical departure from the social convention   她极大地背离了社会习俗
   her common-law marriage with...   她与……的同居/事实婚姻
   the unhappily married critic and publicist   这位婚姻不幸的批评家和出版商

to result in their 25 years <u>alienation from</u> the respectable society　导致他们与这个体面的传统社会长达 25 年的疏离/格格不入

2. to open up for George Eliot a completely new prospect　为乔治·艾略特展现了一个全新的前景

to bring her into contact with many famous men of the time　使她得以与当时许多著名作家进行接触

to find herself <u>ranking high among</u> the great writers　发现自己已跻身于伟大作家之列

Ludwig Feuerbach's groundbreaking *The Essence of Christianity*　路德维希·费尔巴哈的开天辟地的《基督教的精髓》

to <u>embark on</u> a flourishing enterprise as a novelist　开始了作为小说家的欣欣向荣的事业。

be later published in book form under the title of *Scenes of Clerical Life*　后来以"牧师生活一瞥"为题出版成书

<u>be notable for</u> their realistic details, pungent characterization and high moral tone　以他们的现实主义的细节、敏锐的人物刻画和很高的道德基调而著称

a full elaborately documented story of Florence　一部关于佛罗伦萨的详细的纪实文学

a panoramic book considered by many to be her great achievement　一部被许多人认为是她最伟大创作成就的反映生活的全景图

a preachment against anti-Semitism　一部反闪米特主义的布道文

to constitute a formidable body work from a woman <u>frail in health</u> and working constantly <u>under the apprehension of</u> failure or worthlessness　（这些作品）构成了一个数量可观、质量出类拔萃的著作群体，而这些著作竟出自一位体弱多病，一边勤奋笔耕一边还担心着是否会失败、是否没有价值的女作家之手

to <u>bring about a kind of reconciliation with</u> her family and the society　结果使她与家庭和社会达成了某种妥协

be never able to <u>cast off</u> a sense of depression and dreariness left by Lewes' death　绝不能摆脱刘易斯之死带给她的消沉和沮丧

be refused burial in Westminster Abbey by a pious dean <u>on account of</u> her personal life　鉴于她个人生活的原因而被拒绝埋葬在威斯特敏斯特大教堂

be working at something new　有所创新

to set sth. into motion　发动，开动，使……运动起来

3. By joining the worlds of inward propensity and outward circumstances and showing them both operating in the lives of her characters, she initiates a new type of realism and <u>sets into motion</u> a variety of developments, leading in the direction of both the naturalistic and psychological novel.　她把内心活动和性格倾向与外部环境结合在一起，表现在人物创作和塑造之中，开创了一种新型的现实主义，并进行了各种各样的探索，逐步朝自然主义和心理分析小说的方向发展。

4. instinctively analyzing and generalizing to discover the fundamental <u>truth about</u> <u>human life</u>　本能地进行分析和推理以发现人生的根本真谛

to present the inner struggle of a soul　表现一个人内心的思想斗争

to reveal the motives, impulses and hereditary influences which govern human action　揭示那些驾驭人类行动的动机、冲动和遗传影响

to humanize a sense of human dignity with a sense of human limitations　对人类的尊严与人类的局限进行协调平衡

the need of the individual for expansion and growth　个人扩大和发展的需要

to be brought into harmony with a sense of social responsibility　与社会责任感协调起来

to <u>lose sight of</u> the limits to the exercise of individual power　忽视/看不到个人能力发挥的局限性

to insist on the need to cultivate the strength of will and the necessity to return to the routine of life 坚持认为必须培养人的意志力和回归平淡的日常生活

5. As a woman of exceptional intelligence and life experience, George Eliot shows a particular concern for the destiny of women, especially those with great intelligence, potential and social aspirations, such as... 作为一个智力过人又有丰富的生活经验的女人,乔治·艾略特对妇女的命运表现出特别的关心,尤其是那些具有伟大智慧和潜力又渴望进入社会的女人,例如……

6. the pathetic tragedy of women 女人的令人同情的悲剧
   to lie in their very birth 与生俱来
   to depend on men for sustenance 靠男人维持生计
   to fulfill the domestic duties expected of them by the society 完成社会期望与她们的家庭职责

7. Every woman is supposed to have the same set of motives, or else to be a monster. 据说每个女人都有同样的一套想法/动机,否则就是个怪物。

8. You may try — but you can never imagine what it is to have a man's force of genius in you, and yet to suffer the slavery of being a girl. 你可以努力——但是你永远不能想象你作为男人天生的优势,也永远不能想象作为女人要遭受多少奴役。

   ＊ what it is to have ... and yet to suffer ... 是 imagine 的宾语从句,句中 it 是形式主语,to have ... and to suffer ... 两个不定式短语是真正的主语,可直译为:男人所拥有的天生优势和作为女人所遭受的奴役(是什么)。

乔治·艾略特作品选读

米德尔玛琪镇 *Middlemarch* 第三十章节选

词语解释和难句分析

1. provincial life 乡村地方生活
   to provide a panoramic view of life in a small English town 对英国一个乡村小镇做了全景式的描绘
   be mainly centered on the lives of... 主要集中在……的生活方面
   both fail in achieving their goals owing to their own vulnerabilities 由于自己的脆弱,她们没有达到目的

2. a beautiful, intelligent young lady of an "ardent and theoretic nature" 一位美貌、聪慧、既热烈又理性的青年女子
   be not satisfied with the common fate of gentle-women 不满足普通的贤良淑女的命运
   be full of manly, lofty ideas 心中充满了男子汉般的宏伟理想
   the elderly pedant 年长的老学究
   in his pursuit of the fundamental truth about Christianity 追求/探究基督教的真谛
   to find herself totally disillusioned as to... 发现自己对……的希望完全破灭了
   to retrieve her error 补救自己的过错
   be content with giving him her "wifely help" and exercising a "diffusive influence" upon those around 满足于对丈夫尽妻子之责,对周围的人施加影响/满足于相夫教子、睦邻交友

3. spot of commonness 凡夫俗子的通病
   to induce him to marry the beautiful, "accomplished" "flower," Rosamond Vincy 诱使他娶了美丽、

擅长社交的"鲜花",罗莎蒙·温西

to turn out a destroyer of men　结果却是毁了男人生活的(女)人

4. Her extravagant way of life costs him not only a <u>promising</u> <u>career</u> as a great scientist but also loss of his <u>professional conscience.</u>　她奢侈的生活方式不仅毁掉了他作为科学家前程似锦的事业,而且还使他丧失了职业良心。

5. <u>be intertwined with</u> the two stories　与这两个故事情节缠绕在一起

the mysterious and guilty past life of the rich banker　这位富有的银行家神秘而愧疚的过去

the death of the old miser　老守财奴/吝啬鬼的死

their distinctive personalities　他们各不相同的个性

their multitudinous opinions and behaviors　他们各种各样的想法和行为

6. to bury himself in the library　他整日埋头在图书馆里

<u>be but</u> the first taste of bitterness and disappointment for the youthful and hopeful Dorothea　仅仅是这位既年轻又心高气傲的朵罗茜第一次尝到苦果和感到失望

to find herself <u>shut up</u> in the cold, lifeless Lowick Manor　发现自己被关在冷清的、毫无生气的洛维克庄园里/发现自己成了凄清、沉闷的洛维克庄园的笼中鸟

＊ shut up 是过去分词短语作 find 的宾补。

7. All times are good to seek your wedded home/Bringing a mutual delight. 天天都可以作你们的喜日,享受爱巢带给你们的欢乐。

＊ 从语法上讲,bringing a mutual delight 是作 wedded home 定语的分词短语。

8. Why, true. ＝ Oh, it's really true!　啊,的确如此!

The calendar hath (＝ has) not an evil day/For souls <u>made one by love</u>,　对由爱情结成一体的两颗心(来说),日历上没有不祥的日子。

＊ made one by love 为过去分词短语作 souls 的定语。

9. and even death/Were sweetness, if it (＝ death) came like rolling waves/While they two clasped each other, and foresaw/no life apart.　当他们紧紧拥抱在一起,心知/今生绝不再分离,/即使一起死去/也感到快乐,/哪怕死亡的浪潮滚滚而来。

10. wedding journey ＝ honeymoon travel　蜜月旅行

to descend at the door　在门口下来/下车

to pass from her dress-room into the blue-green boudoir　经由她的更衣室进入蓝绿色的客厅

the long avenue of limes lifting their trunks from a white earth　长长的林荫道两旁,酸橙树挺立在白茫茫的(积雪覆盖的)大地上

spreading white branches against the dun and motionless sky　白色的树枝伸向阴沉灰暗的毫无生气的天空

to shrink in uniform whiteness and low-hanging uniformity of cloud　缩成浑然一片的白色的低悬的云团

the stag in the tapestry　挂毯上的牡鹿

in his ghostly blue-green world　在他阴森的蓝绿世界里

the volumes of polite literature in the bookcase　书架上的一卷卷古希腊和古罗马的经典文学书籍

to look more like immovable imitations of books　看起来更像不能翻页的书的模型

11. The bright fire of dry oak-boughs burning on the dogs seemed an incongruous renewal of life and glow—like the figure of Dorothea herself as she entered carrying the red-leather cases containing the cameos for Celia.　(壁炉里)干燥的栎树枝在铁架上熊熊燃烧,发出了明亮的光焰,就像朵罗茜走进房间的身形一样,带来了与周围景象不协调的生机和温暖。她手里拿着几个红皮匣,里面装着送给西莉亚的彩雕宝石。

12. be glowing from her morning toilette as only healthful youth can glow　经过清晨的梳妆打扮,她显得容光焕发,只有健康的青春才会放射出这样的光辉

gem-like brightness on her coiled hair and in her hazel eyes　她卷成圈圈的头发和灰色的眼睛里都像宝石一般闪闪发光

warm red life in her lips　她的嘴唇散发着殷红的温暖的活力

13. Her throat had a breathing whiteness above the differing white of the fur which itself seemed to wind about her neck and cling down her blue-grey pelisse with a tenderness gathered from her own, a sentient commingled innocence which kept its loveliness against the crystalline purity of the out-door snow.　她的喉咙洁白而带有呼吸的律动,露出在围着脖子的皮毛的另一种不同的白色之上,这白色的皮毛顺着她青灰色的毛领大衣垂延而下,带着一种发自她本身的温柔,一种可以感觉到的温柔中的纯真,在门外晶莹白雪的衬托下,纯真之中还透着娇嗔可爱。

14. to lay the cameo-cases on the table in the bow-window　把彩雕珠宝盒放在拱形窗下的桌子上

be absorbed in looking out on the still, white enclosure which made her visible world　她被深深吸引住了,注视着外面静谧的、银装素裹的封闭的小天地——一个她所能看到的世界

＊ which made her visible world 暗指朵罗茜老夫子一般的丈夫把她一人留在房间里,她新婚宴尔就遭受冷落,这里把女主角内心跃动的青春与似乎被禁锢的狭小天地进行了对比。

15. to complain of palpitation　抱怨心跳得慌

be giving audience to his curate Mr. Tucker　接见他的助手特克先生

by and by　不久,过了一会儿

in her/the quality of bridesmaid as well as sister　以女傧相以及姐姐的身份……

16. There would be wedding visits received and given　会有新婚佳期接待宾朋、走亲访友等种种交际应酬

17. in continuance of that transitional life understood to correspond with the excitement of bridal felicity　在接下来的被认为是与新婚快乐的兴奋相对应的过渡阶段

keeping up the sense of busy ineffectiveness, as of a dream which the dreamer begins to suspect　保持一种忙忙碌碌却无所作为的感觉,就像是一场美梦,而做梦人自己都开始怀疑这梦了

＊ as of a dream = as the sense of a dream　与做梦的感觉一样

contemplated as so great beforehand　以前曾被考虑得非常伟大

the white vapour-walled landscape = the landscape covered with snow　白雪笼罩/覆盖下的景色

the clear heights where she expected to walk in full communion　她曾指望(与丈夫)达到充分的心神交融,共同跨越这通畅的高地

＊ to walk the clear heights　相互扶持,共同走过这畅通无阻的高地

18. The delicious repose of the soul on a complete superior had been shaken into uneasy effort and alarmed with dim presentiment.　着落在一个长者身上的美好寄托已经发生动摇,变成了不安的挣扎和不祥的预感所带来的惊恐。

19. When would the days begin of that active wifely devotion which was to strengthen her husband's life and exalt her own?　那种积极做出妻子的贡献的日子,那种既能协助丈夫又能提高自己生活意义的日子,何时才能来到呢?

＊ of that active wifely devotion 是 days 的定语成分,后面又带有 which 引导的定语从句,比较长,如果把 begin 放在最后,则主语太长,谓语太短,头大尾小。

20. Never perhaps, as she had perceived them (= the days).　永不会到来,永不会像她原来想象的那样到来。

21. in this solemnly pledged union of her life　在她作过庄严宣誓的婚姻/共同生活中

to present itself <u>in some new form</u> of inspiration　以新的形式(使自己)给人以启示

the low arch of dun vapour　雾气充斥、阴沉低垂的苍穹

the stifling oppression of the gentlewoman's world　那种贵夫人世界令人窒息的沉闷压抑。

22. Where the sense of <u>connection with</u> a manifold pregnant existence had to <u>be kept up</u> painfully as an <u>inward vision</u>, instead of coming from without (*n.*) in claims that would have <u>shaped</u> her energies.　在那里,要感受丰富多彩、有意义的生活(与丰富多彩、有意义的生活相联系的感受),只能作为一种内心憧憬而痛苦地保存,这种憧憬不是来自本可体现/发挥她能力、活力的任何外在要求(外部不要求她有这种憧憬,不要求她发挥能力和活力)。

　　＊ without in claims 外部要求。that 从句是 without 的定语从句。

23. to <u>leave off</u> learning morning lessons and practicing silly rhythms on the hated piano　放弃/中断早晨攻读功课,放弃/中断在可恨的钢琴上练习什么愚蠢的旋律

to <u>bring guidance into</u> worthy and imperative occupation　引导人们去做有价值的和必须去做的工作

to <u>free her from</u> the gentlewoman's oppressive liberty　使她从淑女贵妇压抑的无所事事(所谓"自由")中解脱出来。

to <u>fill</u> her leisure <u>with</u> the ruminant joy of unchecked tenderness　闲暇时光,尽情地回想和享受新婚蜜月柔情似水春光无限的快乐

her blooming full-pulsed youth　她鲜花盛开似的跃动的青春

in a moral imprisonment　受到精神禁锢

to <u>make itself one with</u> the chill, colourless, narrowed landscape　使自己(她跃动的青春)与周围阴冷、单调、狭隘的景象一致起来

shrunken furniture　收缩了的家具

the never-read books　从未打开读过的书

the ghostly stag in a pale fantastic world　一个苍白、幻觉般的世界里幽灵似的牡鹿

be vanishing from the daylight　正在日光中消失

24. to feel <u>nothing but</u> the dreary oppression　只感到沉闷单调的压抑

keen remembrance　深刻的记忆

transient and departed things　转瞬即逝的往事

a solitary cry　孤独的呼喊

the struggle out of a nightmare　摆脱噩梦的挣扎

25. All existence seemed <u>to beat with a lower pulse than</u> her own,...　一切事物的脉搏似乎都不如她的强烈。

26. Each remembered thing in the room was <u>disenchanted</u>, was <u>deadened</u> as an <u>unlit transparency</u>, till her wandering gaze came to the group of miniatures, and there at last she saw something which had gathered new breath and meaning.　房间里每一件记得的东西都失去了魅力,都像没点亮的透明画那样失去了生命,直到后来,她恍惚的眼光落到了几张小型画像上,才终于看到了某种蕴集着新的气息和新的意义的事物。

27. to have a headstrong look, a peculiarity difficult to interpret　带有任性而固执的眼神,一种难以理解的独特气质

to taste the salt bitterness of her tears in the <u>merciful</u> silence of the night　在向她祖怀示悯的安详静夜之中,体味到了眼泪的苦涩

to pass over <u>breadths of</u> experience　经历了丰富的体验

to have a ear for her　准备听她诉说

to be sending out light　正在/正要发(出闪)光

28. ... the face was masculine and <u>beamed on</u> her <u>with that full gaze</u> which tells her on whom it falls that she is <u>too</u> interesting for the slightest movement of her eyelid <u>to</u> pass unnoticed and uninterpreted. 那张脸具有男人的刚毅,正全神贯注地看着她,对她微笑,(这眼神)似乎在告诉她(自己所发生的事):她眼睑的极其细微的活动,都会使她变得非常有趣,不能不被注意和猜测。

  ＊ it falls on sb. that ... 在某人身上发生了这样的事:……;on whom it falls = to whom it happens, whom 就是指具有那张脸的画像上的人。

主要内容归纳和总结

1. 乔治·艾略特,玛丽·安·伊万斯(Mary Ann Evans)的笔名(pseudonym)。她出生在英格兰沃里克郡(Warwickshire)的一个地产商的家庭,从小就受到家庭和学校老师严格的正统教育,精研了《圣经》经文。后来,她家搬至考文垂(Coventry),受到几位自由主义思想家的影响,她从宗教转而研究哲学,拒绝再进教堂,甚至与已婚出版商乔治·亨利·刘易斯同居,这一连串叛逆行为使她与家庭断绝来往长达 25 年。

    在考文垂,她结识了《威斯特敏斯特评论报》的老板约翰·查普曼,成为该报的编辑和撰稿人,因而有幸接触到当时的大文豪狄更斯、萨克雷、卡莱尔等,受到教诲和鼓舞,39 岁时开始了文学创作生涯,凭着过人的文学才华,很快跻身于大文豪之列。

    <u>她的三部代表作品</u>《亚当·彼得》(*Adam Bede*)、《弗洛斯河上的磨坊》(*The Mill on the Floss*)、《织工马奈》(*Silas Marner*)真实细腻的现实主义描写,显示了她对英国乡村生活的熟悉和切身体验。1872 年,《米德尔玛琪镇》(*Middlemarch*)问世,被认为是她最杰出的作品。

2. <u>她的作品可概括为两个主要特点</u>:1)将自己的内心世界与外在环境结合起来,并把二者注入对角色的塑造之中,开创了一种新型的现实主义,并朝着自然主义与心理分析小说的方向发展;2)作为女性作家,她尤其关心女性的命运,特别是那些渴望步入社会的女性,如《米德尔玛琪镇》中的朵罗茜(Dorothea),《弗洛斯河上的磨坊》中的麦琪·图利沃(Maggie Tulliver),以及《罗摩拉》中的同名女主角罗摩拉(Romola)等都表现了女性的人生追求和与命运的抗争。

3. 乔治·艾略特的主要作品:

a. 英文翻译作品

《耶稣传》*Life of Jesus* 译自德国基督教神学家斯特劳斯(Strauss)的作品

《基督教的精髓》*The Essence of Christianity* 译自德国哲学家路德维希·费尔巴哈(Ludwig Feuerbach)的作品

《伦理学》*Ethics* 译自荷兰哲学家斯宾诺莎(Spinoza)的作品

b. 小说创作

《牧师生活一瞥》*Scenes of Clerical Life* (1857)

《亚当·彼得》*Adam Bede* (1859)

《弗洛斯河上的磨坊》*The Mill on the Floss* (1860)

《织工马奈》*Silas Marner* (1861)

《罗摩拉》*Romola* (1863)

《菲利克斯·霍尔特,一个激进派》*Felix Holt, the Radical* (1866)

《米德尔玛琪镇》*Middlemarch* (1872)

《丹尼尔·德隆达》*Daniel Deronda* (1876)

c. 讽刺散文集

《古希腊逍遥派哲学家的印象》*The Impressions of Theophrastus Such*

重要信息句子

1. In 1857, George Eliot wrote her first three stories which were later published in book form under the title of *Scenes of Clerical Life*（《牧师生活一瞥》）.

2. Her three most popular novels, *Adam Bede*（1859）, *The Mill on the Floss*（1860）and *Silas Marner*（1861）were all drawn from her lifelong knowledge of English country life and notable for their realistic details, pungent characterization and high moral tone. 她的三部最受欢迎的小说《亚当·彼得》《弗洛斯河上的磨坊》和《织工马奈》都是取材于她长期生活并非常熟悉的英国农村生活，以其现实主义的细节、敏锐的人物刻画和道德高调而著称。

3. *Felix Holt, the Radical*（《菲利克斯·霍特，一个激进派》）was her only novel on politics.

4. *Middlemarch*, a panoramic book, is considered by many to be George Eliot's greatest achievement.

VI. 托马斯·哈代 Thomas Hardy（1840~1928）

词语解释和难句分析

1. be apprenticed to a famous architect　跟一个著名的建筑师当学徒

   to win two prizes for essays on architectural subjects　两次获得建筑主题的论文奖

   his desired profession　他理想的职业

2. impressive ceremonies　感人的/激动人心的葬礼

   be set in Wessex　以威塞克斯郡为背景，背景设在威塞克斯郡

   the vicissitudes of people　人们命运的变化

   (be) menaced by the forces of invading capitalism　受到侵入的资本主义的威胁

   novels of character and environment　以角色、环境为纲的小说

3. the keynote of his novels　他的小说的主调

   to try to find a way out of the wild, dull, and backward rural world　试图找到一条出路摆脱荒凉、愚昧、落后的农村世界

   to try to flee but is drowned in a big storm　想要逃走却在暴风雨中被淹死了

   to reveal the conflict in a deeper and fuller sense　更深刻更全面地揭示了这种冲突

   a self-sufficient man　一个自给自足/过分自信的人

   to carry out his mayor's duty in an old-fashioned way　以陈旧过时的方式履行市长职责

   a decent and shrewd merchant　一位体面、精明的商人

   a modern man in every sense　一个完全的现代人

   as a matter of course　理所当然，作为必然的结果

   the vulnerable rural life-style　脆弱的农村生活方式

   be uprooted by industrialization　被工业化连根拔除

   be touched by the integrity and fullness of his being　为她做人的正直和完美所感动

   be at odds with the nouveau like Alec　与阿里克这样的新富发生矛盾冲突，不赞同阿里克这样的新富

be cornered by the traditional social morality　被传统的社会道德逼入死角/困境/逼得走投无路

to return to the former destructive way of life　回到以前那种缺乏建设性的生活方式

to kill their own will and passion　扼杀他们自己的意愿和激情

4. be often regarded as a transitional writer　常常被认为是承前启后的/过渡性的作家

be intellectually advanced and emotionally traditional　艺术技巧上先进/现代，情感上传统

apparent nostalgic touch　明显的怀旧情怀

5. Man's fate is predeterminedly tragic, driven by a combined force of "nature," both inside and outside.　人的悲剧命运早有前定，从内到外都受到自然环境和人的"天性"两方面力量的驱动。

6. be inevitably bound by his own inherent nature and hereditary traits　不可避免地受到他自身的天性和遗传特质的束缚

to prompt him to go and search for some specific happiness or success　促使他去追求某种具体的幸福和成功

to set him in conflict with the environment　使他陷入与环境的冲突之中

be shown as some mysterious supernatural force, very powerful but half-blind, impulsive and uncaring to the individual's will, hope, passion or suffering　表现为某种神秘的超自然力，非常强大，却又有点盲目、冲动，根本不在意个人的意愿、希望、感情或痛苦

to play practical joke upon...　在实践中捉弄/笑话……

to produce a series of mistimed actions and unfortunate coincidences　创造一系列不合时宜的动作和不幸的巧合

to prove impotent before fate　证明人类在命运面前的无能为力

ordained destiny　注定的命运

to earn him a reputation as a naturalistic writer　他为自己赢得了自然主义作家的名声

7. the irrational, hypocritical and unfair Victorian institutions, conventions and morals　非理性的、伪善的和不公正的维多利亚体制，传统习俗和道德准则

to strangle the individual will　扼杀/压制个人的意志

the old rural value of responsibility and honesty　以诚实可敬为特点的传统农村价值观

the new utilitarian commercialism　新的实用主义的商业化

be all closely set in a realistic background true to the very time and the very place　全都设定在与具体的时间、具体的地点相符合的现实背景中

8. a meditative story-teller or romancer　长于思考的讲故事的高手或传奇作家

to assume the form of life and become a most powerful, forbidding force with its own life and will　（自然）以生命的形式呈现，成为一种具有自己的生命和意志的、最强大的、令人生畏的力量

their desperate struggle for personal fulfillment and happiness　他们追求个人完善和个人幸福的不顾一切的奋斗

to possess a kind of exquisitely sensuous beauty　具有一种精致的感观美

the rustic dialect　乡土方言

to fit well into their perfectly designed architectural structures　与这些作品完美构思的艺术结构非常匹配

a conscientious artist　一位勤勤恳恳、按良心办事的艺术家

托马斯·哈代作品选读

《德伯家的苔丝》*Tess of the D'Urbervilles* 第十九章节选

词语解释和难句分析

1. to <u>claim kinship with</u> the sham, a dandy but rich D'Urbervilles　去与一个假冒德伯家族成员的冒牌货但却非常富有的花花公子认亲

   to seduce Tess and impregnate her　诱奸了苔丝,使她怀了孕

   to <u>give birth to</u> a baby　生下一个婴儿

   to leave home to work on a dairy farm　离家到一个奶牛场工作

   to <u>make a confession about</u> his past dissipation　坦白他过去的放荡行为

   to bear the harshest insult　承受最难忍的侮辱

   to <u>transfer</u> the whole burden of the family <u>on</u> her　把整个的家庭重担都转嫁到她身上

   <u>putting</u> all the blames of her unhappiness <u>on</u> Alec　把她一切不幸的罪责全都压到阿里克的头上

2. a fierce attack on the hypocritical morality of the bourgeois society　对资产阶级虚伪的道德观进行猛烈的抨击

   be brought up with the traditional idea of womanly virtues　由传统的妇德观念培养出来

   agents of the destructive force of the society　社会破坏力的象征

   the misery, the poverty and the <u>heartfelt pain</u> she suffers　她所承受的悲惨的境遇、贫穷和刻骨铭心的痛苦。

   ＊ she suffers = which she suffers,是一个定语从句。

   to <u>give rise to</u> a most bitter cry of protest and denunciation of the society　导致对社会发出抗议和声讨的最愤怒的呼喊

3. Coincidence <u>adds one</u> "wrong" <u>to another</u> until she <u>is caught up in</u> a dead-end.　巧合使得"错误"一个连着一个,直到她陷入死亡的绝境。

4. Justice was done, and <u>the President of the Immortals</u> had ended <u>his sport with</u> Tess.　正义得到了伸张,上帝(众神之首)与苔丝的游戏结束了。

5. Chapter XIX, Phase Three, The Rally　(小说)第三部,第十九章:重新振作

6. Tess gradually <u>rides off</u> her recent misfortune and unconsciously <u>gives herself up to the</u> <u>attraction of</u> Angel Clare.　苔丝渐渐赶走了近来的不幸,不知不觉迷上了安吉尔·克莱尔。

   ＊ give oneself up to　陷入,献身于,从事,专注于

7. to present themselves without fancy or choice　它们没有喜爱或没有选择地走到人的面前

   to <u>show a fondness for</u> a particular pair of hands　对特定的某双手表现出喜爱

   sometimes carrying this predilection (= preference) <u>so far as to</u> refuse to stand at all except to their favourite　有时这种偏爱还很强烈,(以至于)不是它们喜爱的人,就不肯站下来让人挤奶

   be unceremoniously kicked over　被毫不客气地踢翻

8. to insist on <u>breaking down</u> these partialities and aversions by constant interchange since　坚持用不断交换的方法打破这种好恶(偏爱和反感)的习惯

   in the event of　如果……发生,万一

   (sb.) be placed in a difficulty　某人就不好办了/难办了

9. The maids' private aims, however, were the reverse of the dairyman's rule, the daily selection by each damsel of the eight or ten cows to which she had grown accustomed rendering the operation on their willing udders surprisingly easy and effortless. 然而,挤奶女工私下的目的就与奶场主的规则相反了,每个少女每天选择八到十头自己挤惯了的奶牛,给听话的奶头挤奶既容易又不费力。

10. compeers:partners; comrades; companies. 同事,伙伴
    to have a preference for her style of manipulation 喜欢她的操作(挤奶)方式
    to have become delicate from the long domiciliary imprisonments 由于长时间闭门不出(手指)都变得娇嫩了
    to subject oneself to the domiciliary imprisonment at intervals 不时把自己关在家里
    be glad to meet the milcher's views 乐意顺从奶牛的意愿
    the teats as hard as carrots 硬得像萝卜的奶头
    to give down to her with a readiness that made her work on them a mere touch of the fingers (奶牛)在她面前很容易下奶,这使得她为它们挤奶时,只需要指头碰一碰奶头就可以了
    to endeavour conscientiously to take the animals just as they come 尽力为经过面前的奶牛认真挤奶
    excepting the very hard yielders 除非是非常顽固的犟牛

11. a curious correspondence between the ostensibly chance position of the cows and her wishes in this matter 表面上看似偶然的奶牛出现的位置与她(对此)所希望的令人惊讶地一致
    not be the result of accident 不是出于偶然
    to lend a hand in getting the cows together 帮助把奶牛聚拢在一起
    to turn her eyes full of sly inquiry upon him 她转过脸去向着他,眼里充满了狡黠/心照不宣的疑问
    to rest against the cow 靠在奶牛身上
    to rest one's head on the pillow 头倚在枕头上

12. in making the accusation, symptoms of a smile gently lifted her upper lip in spite of her 在指责的同时,不由自主地微启上唇露出了笑容

13. (be) unaware of her grave reasons for liking this seclusion 没有意识到她乐意待在这隐蔽的地方的重要原因

14. She had spoken so earnestly to him, as if his presence were somehow a factor in her wish. 她跟他说话时那么认真,仿佛他的出现是他所希望的/仿佛他在这里也是她愿意待在这里的一个原因。

15. to have disclosed to him her discovery of his considerateness (她)已经在他面前表露了一个事实:她已经看出他对自己的关切体贴了

16. ..., the atmosphere being in such delicate equilibrium and so transmissive that inanimate objects seemed endowed with two or three senses, if not five. (夏日的夜晚)四野的空气宁静到了极致,还不断弥漫扩展,就连无生命的物体也似乎有了两三种知觉——如果不是五种。
    to feel close to everything within the horizon 地平线以内,万物都感到很近
    the strumming of strings 琴弦的弹拨声,错落的琴声

17. The soundlessness impressed her as a positive entity rather than the mere negation of noise. 这无声的寂静在她看来/给她的印象不是万籁的虚无,而是一个积极的实体存在。

18. Dim, flattened, constrained by their confinement, they had never appealed to her as now, when they wandered in the still air with a stark quality like that of nudity. 由于环境的限制,那琴声微弱、刻板而拘束,从来没有像现在这样吸引她,现在这琴声正在宁静的空气中飘荡,质朴无华,像裸露着身子一样毫无修饰。

19. Far from leaving, she drew up towards the performer, keeping behind the hedge that he might not guess her presence. 别说离开,她甚至朝演奏者/弹琴人走去,躲在树篱后面,使他猜不到她的存在。

20. the outskirt of the garden　花园的外围/边缘

　　to find oneself in　发现自己置身于/在……

　　be left uncultivated for some years　无人栽培,任其自然生长好多年了

　　be rank with juicy grass　(地里)长满汁液饱满的野草

　　to send up mists of pollen at a touch　(植物)一碰就散发出雾状的花粉

　　(be rank) with tall blooming weeds emitting offensive smells　野草繁茂,长得很高,野花散发着呛人的气味

　　(hues) to form a polychrome as dazzling as that of cultivated flowers　形成一个色彩缤纷的景象,与人工培植的花朵一样艳丽、灿烂

21. She went stealthily as a cat through this profusion of growth,　她像只猫一样悄悄地穿过丛生的茂草

　　gathering cuckoo-spittle on her skirts,　裙子上沾上了杜鹃的黏液,

　　cracking snails that were underfoot,　脚下踩碎了蜗牛,

　　staining her hands with thistle-milk and slug-slime,　手上沾上了蓟草浆和蛞蝓液,

　　and rubbing off upon her naked arms sticky blights　因为摩擦使得裸露的手臂沾上了黏糊糊的树莓(使植物枯萎的萎菌)

　　which, though snow-white on the apple-tree trunks, made madder stains on her skin;　树莓在苹果树干上虽然是雪白的,沾在她皮肤上却形成许多茜红的斑点;

　　*上面是一个完整的句子,gathering, cracking, staining 和 rubbing 引导四个并列的分词短语作状语,其逻辑主语都是 she。最后一行的 which 引导一个定语从句,修饰 sticky blights。

22. to draw quite near to Clare　走得离克莱尔很近了

　　still unobserved of him = being still unobserved of him　依然没有被他看见

　　be conscious of neither time nor space　没有意识到/忘了时间和空间

　　be producible at will by gazing at a star　凝望星星就会自然/不由自主地产生想法

　　(exaltation) to come without any determination of hers　(灵魂的升华)不期而至地出现在她身上

　　to undulate upon the thin notes of the second-hand harp　随着那只旧竖琴轻微细弱的音符而心潮起伏

　　to pass like breezes through her　像微风浸润她的身体

　　the floating pollen　漂浮的花粉

　　to seem to be his notes made visible　似乎是他弹出的可见的音符

　　to seem to be weeping of the garden's sensibility　似乎是花园动情/多愁善感的哭泣

23. Though near nightfall, the rank-smelling weed flowers glowed as if they would not close for intentness, and the waves of colour mixed with the waves of the sound.　虽然夜幕降临,但气味难闻的野花依然鲜艳夺目,仿佛它们倾听琴声入了迷而不肯闭合,一波波的色彩和一阵阵的琴声融汇在一起。

24. be derived from a large hole in the western bank of the cloud　(照耀的光线)来自西方云层中的一个大洞

　　like a piece of day left behind by accident　偶然遗忘/留下的一片白昼

　　to conclude his plaintive melody　结束他伤心的乐曲(不再继续弹奏)

　　to come round the fence desultorily　沿着篱笆信步走来

　　be rambling up behind her　正漫步走向她背后

　　to move away furtively, as if hardly moving at all　悄悄地走开,仿佛一点动作也没有

　　her light summer gown　她浅色的夏季长裙

　　be some distance off　待在一定的距离之外

　　to draw off in that way　那样离开/逃走

not of outdoor things = I'm not afraid of outdoor things.　不害怕外面的东西

What of? = What are you afraid of?　你在怕什么?

25. I couldn't quite say. = I couldn't make it clear.　我说不清楚。

26. The milk turning sour? = Are you afraid of the milk turning sour?　你怕牛奶变酸吗?

27. Life in general? = Are you afraid of life in general?　你是总体上怕生活吗?

28. tell me in confidence　私下里跟我讲,给我说说心里话

inquisitive eyes　探询的眼睛

just all in a line　全都排成一队

getting smaller and smaller as they stand farther away　随着越来越远,它们变得越来越小

Beware of me!　对我小心点儿!

to raise up dreams with your music　你的乐曲唤醒了许多梦想

to drive all such horrid fancies away　驱除所有这些可怕的幻想

be surprised to find this young woman shaping such sad imagines　吃惊地发现这个年轻姑娘内心的意象居然如此忧伤

to have just that touch of rarity about her　对她身边之事竟有如此罕见的感触

29. He was surprised to find this young woman — who though but (= only) a milkmaid had just that touch of rarity about her which might make her the envied of her housemates — shaping such sad imagines.　他吃惊地发现这个年轻姑娘内心竟有如此忧伤的想象,虽然只是一个挤奶女工,对身边之事竟有如此罕见的感触,这可能会使得住在一起的伙伴羡慕不已。

　＊ shaping such sad imagines 是跟在 young woman 后面的宾语补足语。

30. She was expressing in her own native phrases — assisted a little by her Sixth Standard training — feelings which might almost have been called those of the age: the ache of modernism.　靠着六年标准化教育训练的一点儿帮助,她用家乡的地方语言,表达了几乎可以说是那个时代的感受:现代主义的痛苦。

　＊ feelings 是 expressing 的宾语;assisted...为过去分词短语作状语,those 即 feelings。

31. The perception arrested him less when he reflected that what are called advanced ideas are really in great part but (= only) the latest fashion in definition — a more accurate expression, by words in logy and ism, of sensations which men and women have vaguely griped for centuries.　当他想到所谓先进思想实际上大部分只是最新潮流的定义,只是用什么"论",什么"主义"更准确地表达男女大众早就模模糊糊体会了好几个世纪的感觉,这种感受就不再使他感到多么惊奇,不太吸引他了。

32. It was strange that they (= those feelings) should have come to her while yet so young.　令人惊奇的是苔丝还如此年轻就有这些感受。

33. There was nothing to remind him that experience is as to intensity, and not as to duration.　没有什么可以提醒他,让他明白:人生体验在于感受的强烈,而不在于年龄(时间的长短)。

　＊ as to　根据,在于

34. Tess's passing corporeal blight had been her mental harvest.　苔丝经受的肉体摧残成了她精神上的收获。

　＊ 此句的主语是带逻辑主语的动名词短语 Tess's passing corporeal blight。

35. on her part　从她这方面来看

above physical want　不受物质匮乏的影响,衣食无忧

to look upon it as a mishap to be alive　视活着为不幸

for the unhappy pilgrim herself　对她本人这个不幸的朝圣者

to descended to the Valley of Humiliation　堕入耻辱之谷

to feel with the man of Uz 　与乌兹老人(Job)有同样的感情

36. My soul chooseth strangling and death rather than my life. I loathe it; I would not live always. 　我的灵魂选择窒息而死而不是活着。我厌恶活着,我不愿长存。

37. out of his class 　脱离他的阶级

　　like Peter the Great in a shipwright's yard 　像彼得大帝去造船厂一样

　　be obliged to milk cows 　被迫/不得不挤牛奶

　　a rich and prosperous dairyman 　一个富有的、事业兴旺的奶牛场场主

　　a breeder of cattle 　(养牛的)畜牧业老板

　　commanding like a monarch his flocks and his herds, his spotted and his ring-streaked, his men-servants and his maids 　像君主一样指挥他的羊群、牛群,有花点的和环形条纹的,还有他的男仆和侍女

38. At times, however, it did seem unaccountable to her that a decidedly bookish, musical, thinking young man should have chosen deliberately (= on purpose) to be a farmer, and not a clergyman, like his father and brothers. 　不过,有时她似乎无法理解一个明显有书生气的、懂音乐、有思想的青年人竟然有意要当个农民,而不是像他父兄那样做牧师。

39. neither having the clue to the other's secret 　彼此都不了解对方的秘密

　　be puzzled at what each revealed 　对彼此的表现感到迷惑不解

　　to await new knowledge of each other's character and moods 　等待着更多地了解对方的性格和脾气

　　to pray into each other's history 　打听/窥探对方的历史/经历

　　to bring to him one more little stroke of her nature, and to her one more of his 　(每一天)都让他和她多了一点对对方性格的了解/多了解一点对方性格的表露

　　to lead a repressed life 　过一种克制的生活

　　to little divine... = to divine little the strength of her own vitality 　(她)没能预计到/低估了自己强大的生命活力

主要内容归纳和总结

1. 托马斯·哈代出生在英格兰南部多塞特郡的首府多切斯特(Dorchester),父亲是个泥瓦匠(mason),在哈代后来的许多小说中,他的故乡以威塞克斯(Wessex)的名字出现,作为故事发生的背景。随着哈代的成名,威塞克斯(Wessex)名动天下。

　　他青少年时做过建筑师,并发表过专业论文。后来由于他的小说《计出无奈》(*Desperate Remedies*)、《格林伍德林荫下》(*Under the Greenwood Tree*)、《远离尘嚣》(*Far From the Madding Crawd*)接连出版,大获成功,他终于放弃建筑业,正式开始自己的文学创作生涯。

　　处于世纪之交的哈代是一位承前启后的作家。在写作技巧方面他属于新派,而在情感上他却十分传统,对作品中传统型角色总是寄予深切同情,相信天性(inherent nature)、遗传(hereditary traits)和超自然的力量(supernatural power),悲观主义情绪(pessimistic mood)笼罩了哈代后期的所有作品,使他成为著名自然主义作家。哈代同时又是个批判现实主义作家(writers of critical realism),对失去理性的(irrational)、扭曲人性的(abnormal humanity)维多利亚时代的国家机器、法规制度和道德标准(Victorian institutions, conventions and morals)进行了尖锐的批判和公开的挑战。

　　他是人生和人性的分析家,但他只将人性忠实地展现出来,像画家临摹,却不问为什么和怎么办,一切留给读者自己去思考,他本人是个思想者,也总是引导读者去思想。他的小说结构完美,人物形象令人难忘,语言带有浓郁的乡土气息,充满诗情画意。

　　哈代不仅是伟大的小说家,同时还是伟大的诗人。他一生勤奋创作了23年,创作小说10部,

诗集 8 部,共 918 首诗。

2. 哈代的主要作品,未特别说明者皆为小说,加＊者为威塞克斯 Wessex 小说:

《计出无奈》*Desperate Remedies*（1871）

《格林伍德林荫下》*Under the Greenwood Tree*（1872）

《远离尘嚣》*Far from the Madding Crowd*（1874）

＊《还乡》*The Return of the Native*（1878）

＊《号兵长》*The Trumpet Major*（1880）

＊《卡斯特桥市长》*The Mayor of Casterbridge*（1886）

＊《林地居民》*The Woodlanders*（1887）

＊《德伯家的苔丝》*Tess of the D' Urbervilles*（1891）

＊《无名的裘德》*Jude the Obscure*（1896）

《塔上二人》*Two on a Tower*（1882）

《意中人》*The Well-beloved*（1892～1897）

《列王纪》*The Dynasts*（1904～1908）长篇史诗剧

《诗集》*Poems* 共 8 部,918 首,《列王纪》是其中一首长篇史诗剧。

重要信息句子

1. In 1871, his <u>first novel</u> *Desperate Remedies*（《计出无奈》）was published and well received. However, the <u>real success</u> came with *Under the Greenwood Tree*（《格林伍德林荫下》）（1872）. The publication of *Far from the Madding Crowd*（《远离尘嚣》）in 1874 <u>finally enabled him to give up architecture for writing</u>.

2. In 1928, this <u>last important novelist and poet of the 19th</u> century died.

3. Living at the turn of the century, Hardy is often regarded as a transitional writer, intellectually advanced and emotionally traditional.

4. Hardy is not an analyst of human life or nature like George Eliot, but a meditative story-teller or romancer. He tells very good story about very interesting people but seldom stops to ask why.

英国维多利亚时期文学同步练习与答案

1. The Victorian period of English literary history is _____.

   a. from 1798 to 1832　　　　　b. from 1660 to 1798

   c. from 1836 to 1901　　　　　d. from the 14th to mid-17th century

2. Reform Bill of 1832 passed the political power from _____ into the hands of _____.

   a. the middle-class industrial capitalists/the working class

   b. the aristocrats/the middle-class industrial capitalists

   c. the rural peasants/the city proletariats

   d. the king/the vassals

3. In _____ of 1836～1848, the English workers got themselves organized to demand basic rights and better living and working conditions.

   a. the Industrial Revolution　　　　b. Reform of Bill

c. Bill of Right

d. the Chartist Movement

4. Ideologically, the Victorians experienced fundamental changes. Darwin's _____ shook the theoretical basis of the traditional faith in Christianity.

    a. evolutionary science

    b. utilitarianism

    c. new anthropology

    d. religious uncertainties

5. Victorian literature, as a product of its age, naturally took on its quality of _____.

    a. reason or ration

    b. romanticism

    c. magnitude and diversity

    d. realism

6. Although writing from different points of view and with different techniques, writers in the Victorian Period shared one thing in common, that is, they were all concerned about _____.

    a. the love story between the rich and the poor

    b. the techniques in writing

    c. the fate of the common people

    d. the future of their own country

7. According to D. H. Lawrence, _____ was the first novelist that "started putting all the actions inside"?

    a. Robert Browning

    b. Thomas Hardy

    c. Charles Dickens

    d. George Eliot

8. Victorian literature, in general, truthfully represents _____ and _____ of the age.

    a. the reality/the spirit

    b. the high-spirited vitality/the down-to-earth earnestness

    c. the good-natured humor/unbound imagination

    d. the values/the ambition

9. In his _____, Charles Dickens attacks the dehumanizing workhouse system and the dark, criminal underworld life.

    a. *Dombey and Son*

    b. *David Copperfield*

    c. *The Pickwick Paper*

    d. *Oliver Twist*

10. In *Nicholas Nickleby*, the children in Yorkshire School are not taught anything but actually _____.

    a. enslaved at the master's house

    b. the members of church choir

    c. run errands for their teachers

    d. the real owners of the school

11. The money-worship that dominates people's life, corrupts the young and brings tragedy to Mr. Dombey's family in _____ and _____.

    a. *The Pickwick Paper/David Copperfield*

    b. *Martin Chuzzlewit/Dombey and Son*

    c. *Great Expectations/Oliver Twist*

    d. *The Old Curiosity Shop/David Copperfield*

12. All of the works, with the exception of _____, present a criticism of the more complicated and yet most fundamental social institutions and morals of the Victorian England.

    a. *Our Mutual Friend*

    b. *Great Expectations*

    c. *A Tale of Two Cities*

    d. *Bleak House*

13. Legal fraud in _____ and the debitor's prison in _____ are both the social evils Charles Dickens attack.

    a. *Oliver Twist/Great Expectations*

    b. *Nicholas Nickleby/The Pickwick Paper*

    c. *The Pickwick Paper/David Copperfield*

    d. *Bleak House/Dombey and Son*

14. In the novel of _____, Dickens criticizes the legal system and practices that aim at devouring every penny of the clients.
    a. *Hard Times*　　　　　　　　　　　b. *Little Dorrit*
    c. *Oliver Twist*　　　　　　　　　　　d. *Bleak House*

15. In *Hard Times*, Dickens attacks _____ that rules over the English educational system and destroys young hearts and minds.
    a. bourgeois commercialism　　　　　　b. religious hypocrisy
    c. the utilitarian principle　　　　　　d. political corruptness

16. Dickens's works are also characterized by a mingling of _____ and _____. He seems to believe that life is itself a mixture of _____ and _____.
    a. joy/grief/humor/pathos
    b. humor/pathos/joy/grief
    c. truth/friction/the realistic/the gothic
    d. storytelling/characterization/truth/illusion

17. In the following figures, _____ is Dickens's first child hero.
    a. Fagin　　　　　　　　　　　　　　b. Mr. Brownlow
    c. Oliver Twist　　　　　　　　　　　d. Bill Sikes

18. No one who has ever read the death-bed scenes of little Nell in _____ and little Paul in _____ can forget them. The pain strikes people to the heart.
    a. *Bleak House/Little Dorrit*　　　　　b. *Oliver Twist/The Old Curiosity Shop*
    c. *Great Expectations/Hard Times*　　　d. *The Old Curiosity Shop/Dombey and Son*

19. Which of the following comments on Charles Dickens is wrong? _____
    a. Dickens is one of the greatest critical realist writers of the Modern period.
    b. His serious intention is to expose and criticize all the poverty, injustice, hypocrisy and corruptness he sees all around him.
    c. The later works show the development of Dickens towards a highly conscious artist of the modern type.
    d. *A Tale of Two Cities* is one of his later works.

20. When studying foreign languages in Brussels, Charlotte experienced a passionate yet one-sided love with her married German professor, which was later recounted in her novel _____.
    a. *The Professor*　　　　　　　　　　b. *Villette*
    c. *Jane Eyre*　　　　　　　　　　　　d. *Shirley*

21. Charlotte's works are famous for the depiction of _____.
    a. the life of the middle-class working women
    b. the rural landlord family
    c. the women's pursuit for freedom, equality, independence, and real love
    d. love and nature

22. In Charlotte's mind, man's life is composed of perpetual battle between _____ and _____, _____ and _____.
    a. sin/virtue/good/evil
    b. individual consciousness/self-realization/orthodoxy/rebellion
    c. the lonely/longing for love/tradition/reform
    d. kind/wicked/men/women

23. Brought up with strict orthodoxy, Charlotte usually stuck in her works to _____.

a. the morals of feudalism

b. the morality of Catholic Church

c. the Puritanical code

d. the traditional principles of behaviour

24. _____ is the first important governess novel in the English literary history.

a. *Jane Eyre*

b. *Emma*

c. *Wuthering Heights*

d. *Middlemarch*

25. "Do you think, because I am poor, obscure, plain, and little, I am soulless and heartless? ... And if God had gifted me with some beauty, and much wealth, I should have made it as hard for you to leave me, as it is now for me to leave you." The above quoted passage is most probably taken from _____.

a. *Great Expectations*

b. *Wuthering Heights*

c. *Jane Eyre*

d. *Pride and Prejudice*

26. *Wuthering Heights* is the story about two families and an intruding stranger. The two families are _____ and _____; The intruding stranger is _____.

a. The Copperfield family/the Micawber family/Heathcliff

b. The Oliver family/the Dombey family/Hindley

c. The Pickwick family/the Linton family/Edgar

d. The Earnshaw family/the Linton family/Heathcliff

27. Which statement about Emily Brontë is NOT true? _____

a. She was famous for her *Wuthering Heights*.

b. She wrote 193 poems.

c. She lived a very short life.

d. Her masterpiece is noted for its optimistic tone.

28. The sentences "And now he stared at her so earnestly that I thought the very intensity of his gaze would bring tears into his eyes; but they burned with anguish, they did not melt" are found in _____.

a. *Wuthering Heights* by Emily Brontë

b. *Jane Eyre* by Charlotte Brontë

c. *Gulliver's Travels* by Jonathan Swift

d. *Paradise Lost* by John Milton

29. In *Wuthering Heights* as a love story, the passion between _____ proves the most intense, the most beautiful and at the same time the most horrible.

a. Edgar and Catherine

b. Heathcliff and Catherine

c. Heathcliff and Cathy

d. Heathcliff and Esabella

30. _____ is the most representative Victorian poet. His poetry voices the doubt and the faith, the grief and the joy of the English people in an age of fast social changes.

a. Robert Browning

b. Alfred Tennyson

c. Thomas Hardy

d. George G. Byron

31. In the 2nd issue of *Poems* published in 1842 were collected his dramatic monologue "_____," the epic narrative "Morte d' Arthur," and the exquisite idylls "Dora" by Tennyson.

a. *The Princess*

b. *Ulysses*

c. *In Memoriam*

d. *Crossing the Bar*

32. What is Tennyson's greatest work which is an elegy on the death of Hallam, his dearest friend? _____.

a. *Ulysses*

b. *The Princess*

c. *Idylls of the King*

d. *In Memoriam*

33. The most important characteristic in *Ulysses* by Alfred Tennyson is _____.
   a. excellent choice of words
   b. use of the dramatic monologue
   c. mastering of language
   d. excellent metaphor

34. In Tennyson's most ambitious work *Idylls of the King*, the rise and fall of King Arthur is meant to represent _____.
   a. a cyclic history of western civilization
   b. a reproduction of the old legend
   c. a modern interpretation of the classic myth
   d. the rise and fall of the Victorian values in the people

35. "I will drink/life to the lees." In the quoted line *Ulysses* is saying that he _____ till the end of his life.
   a. will keep traveling and exploring
   b. will go on drinking and being happy
   c. would like to toast to his glorious life
   d. would like to drink the cup of wine

36. Which one established his position as one of the greatest English poets in Robert Browning's works? _____.
   a. *Pauline*
   b. *Sordello*
   c. *Dramatic Romance*
   d. *The Ring and the Book*

37. According to the symbolism of the title of *The Ring and the Book*, a poet's _____ are just the alloying ingredients.
   a. original creation
   b. creativity
   c. fancy and imagination
   d. figure of speech

38. Although _____ is not his invention, it is in his hands that this poetic form reaches its maturity and perfection.
   a. dramatic monologue
   b. epic narrative
   c. lyrical ballads
   d. blank verse

39. Whose poetic style in Victorian poets belongs to the 20th century rather than to the Victorian age, presenting rough, grotesque and disproportionate appearance? _____.
   a. Alfred Tennyson's
   b. Robert Browning's
   c. George Eliot's
   d. Thomas Hardy

40. A contemporary of Alfred Tennyson, _____ is acknowledged by many as the most original and experimental poet of the time.
   a. Thomas Carlyle
   b. Thomas B. Macaulay
   c. Robert Browning
   d. T. S. Eliot

41. "Self-conceited", "cruel" and "tyrannical" are most likely the names of the characters in _____.
   a. Robert Browning's *My Last Duchess*
   b. Christopher Marlowe's *Dr. Faustus*
   c. Shakespeare's *Love's Labour's Lost*
   d. Sheridan's *The School for Scandal*

42. Robert Browning's style is _____.
   a. identical with that of the other Victorians
   b. similar to that of Tennyson

c. perfectly artistic

d. rough and disproportionate in appearance

43. "She smiled, no doubt,/Whenever I passed her.../...This grew; I gave commands; /Then all smiles stopped together." The quoted lines imply that she _____.

a. obeyed his order and stopped smiling at everybody including the duke

b. obeyed his order and stopped smiling at anybody except the duke

c. refused to obey the order and never smiled again

d. was murdered at the order of the duke

44. Robert Browning's best-known dramatic monologue is _____.

a. *Meeting at Night*   b. *Parting at Morning*

c. *My Last Duchess*   d. *The Ring and the Book*

45. As a woman of exceptional intelligence and life experience, George Eliot shows a particular concern for _____.

a. the destiny of women

b. her social responsibility

c. human limitations

d. the need of the individual for expansion and growth

46. Which of the following descriptions of Thomas Hardy is wrong? _____

a. Most of his novels are set in Wessex.

b. *Tess of the D'Urbervilles* is one of the most representative of him as both a naturalistic and a critical realist writer.

c. Among hardy's major works, *Under the Greenwood Tree* is the most cheerful and idyllic.

d. From *The Mayor of Casterbridge* on, the tragic sense becomes the key note of his novels.

47. *Middlemarch* is considered to be George Eliot's greatest novel, owing to all the following reasons EXCEPT _____.

a. it vividly depicts English country life

b. it probes into perpetual philosophical thoughts

c. it provides a panoramic view of life

d. it reveals women's true feelings

48. Most of Hardy's novels are set in _____, the fictional primitive and crude rural region that is really the home place he both loves and hates.

a. Yorkshire   b. Wessex

c. London   d. Manchester

49. "The floating pollen seemed to be his notes made visible, and the dampness of the garden the weeping of the garden's sensibility." The quoted sentence is suggestive of _____.

a. the richness of the music in the garden

b. the beauty of the scenery in the garden

c. the great power of the music in affecting the environment

d. the harmony and oneness of the music, the garden and the heroine Tess

50. "Every day, every hour, brought to him one more little stroke of her nature, and to her one more of his", the sentence is found in _____.

a. *Middlemarch* by George Eliot

b. *Tess of the D'Urbervilles* by Thomas Hardy

    c. *Jane Eyre* by Charles Dickens

    d. *Wuthering Heights* by Emily Brontë

51. The author of writing *The Return of the Native* is _____.

    a. Thomas Hardy   b. D. H. Lawrence

    c. Robert Browning   d. Alfred Tennyson

52. Which of the following best describes the protagonist of Thomas Hardy's *The Mayor of Casterbridge*? _____

    a. He is a man of self-esteem.   b. He is a man of self-contempt.

    c. He is a man of self-confidence.   d. He is a man of self-sufficiency.

53. _____ not only continued to expose and criticize all sorts of social iniquities, but finally came to question and attack the Victorian conventions and morals.

    a. George Eliot   b. Thomas Hardy

    c. D. H. Lawrence   d. Charles Dickens

54. Who is the last important novelist and poet of the 19th century? _____.

    a. Robert Browning   b. Charlotte Brontë

    c. Thomas Hardy   d. T. S. Eliot

55. Dickens takes the French Revolution as the background of the novel _____.

    a. *Great Expectations*   b. *A Tale of Two Cities*

    c. *Bleak House*   d. *Oliver Twist*

56. The title of Alfred Tennyson's poem "Ulysses" reminds the reader of the following EXCEPT _____.

    a. the Trojan War   b. Homer

    c. quest   d. Christ

57. The character Rochester in *Jane Eyre* can be termed as a _____.

    a. conventional hero   b. Byronic hero

    c. chivalrous aristocrat   d. Homeric hero

58. Mr. Micawber in *David Copperfield* and Sam Well in *Pickwick Paper* are perhaps the best _____ characters created by Charles Dickens.

    a. comic   b. tragic

    c. round   d. sophisticated

59. The typical feature of Robert Browning's poetry is the _____.

    a. bitter satire   b. larger-than-life caricature

    c. Latinized diction   d. dramatic monologue

60. In *Tess of the D' Urbervilles*, Thomas Hardy resolutely makes a seduced girl his heroine, which clearly demonstrates the author's _____ of the Victorian moral standards.

    a. blind fondness   b. total acceptance

    c. deep understanding   d. mounting defiance

61. "The dehumanizing workhouse system and the dark, criminal underworld life" are the right words to sum up the main theme of _____.

    a. *David Copperfield*   b. *A Tale of Two Cities*

    c. *Oliver Twist*   d. *Bleak House*

62. "... and then how they met I hardly saw, but Catherine made a spring, and he caught her, and they were locked in an embrace..." In the quoted passage, Emily Brontë tells the story in _____ point of view.

    a. first person   b. second person

    c. third person limited   d. third person omniscient

63. Which of the following statements is not a typical feature of Charles Dickens? _____

    a. He sets out a large-scale criticism of the inhuman social institutions and the decaying social morality.

    b. His works are characterized by a mingling of humor and pathos.

    c. The characters portrayed by Dickens are often larger than life.

    d. He shows a human being not at moments of crisis, but in the most trivial incidents of everyday life.

64. In the statement "— oh, God! Would you like to live with your soul in the grave?" the term "soul" apparently refers to _____.

    a. Heathcliff himself   b. Catherine

    c. one's spiritual life   d. one's ghost

65. In the clause " As Mr. Gamfield did happen to labor under the slight imputation of having bruised three or four boys to death already...", the word "slight" is used as a(n) _____.

    a. simile   b. metaphor

    c. irony   d. overstatement

Key: cbdac/cdada/bccdc/bcdab/aacac/ddabb/bdbaa/dcabc/addda/dbbdb/adbcb/dbadd/ccdbc

第五章 现代时期 The Modern Period

词语解释和难句分析

1. to lead to great gains in material wealth 导致物质财富大量增加

   to come into the monopoly stage of capitalism 进入垄断资本主义阶段

   the sharpened contradictions between socialized production and the private ownership 社会化大生产和私人所有(制)之间的尖锐矛盾

   economic depressions and mass unemployment 经济萧条和大规模失业

   the gap between the rich and the poor 贫富差距

   to crown it all 更糟糕的是,更使人高兴的是

   the postwar economic dislocation and spiritual disillusion 战后经济的混乱和精神幻灭

   to produce a profound impact on... 对……产生深刻的影响

   the prevalent wretchedness in capitalism 资本主义普遍存在的苦难不幸

   the disintegration of the British Empire 大英帝国的解体

   the once sun-never-set Empire 曾经的"日不落"帝国

2. to give rise to all kinds of philosophical ideas 产生了各种各样的哲学

   to inspire them to make dauntless fight for their own emancipation 鼓舞人们为自身的解放进行无畏的斗争

3. The social Darwinism, under the cover of "survival of the fittest," vehemently advocated colonialism or jingoism. 社会达尔文主义打着"适者生存"的招牌,激烈主张殖民主义或沙文主义。

   ＊ under the cover of 以……为借口,在……的掩护下

4. to stress the importance of will and intuition 强调意志和直觉的重要性

   to go further against rationalism 进一步反对理性主义

   to advocate the doctrines of power and superman 主张强权和超人的教条

   to establish his irrational philosophy 建立他(亨利·柏格森 Henry Bergson)的非理性哲学

   to put the emphasis on creation, intuition, irrationality and unconsciousness 强调创造、直觉、非理性和无意识

5. to rise out of skepticism and disillusion of capitalism (现代主义)产生于对资本主义的怀疑和幻灭

   the appalling shock of the 1st World War 第一次世界大战带来的恐惧和震惊

   to incite writers to make new explorations on... 激发作家对……进行新的探索

6. to herald modernism 预示现代主义的来临

   to converge into a mighty torrent of modernist movement towards the 1920s 到20世纪20年代,汇成了现代主义的巨大洪流

   to sweep across the Europe and America 横扫欧洲和美洲

   be curbed in the 1930s 在20世纪30年代受到了遏制

   surrealism, Dadaism, imagism, existentialism, stream of consciousness, and theater of the absurd 超现

实主义,达达主义(颓废派文艺思想),意象主义,存在主义,意识流,以及荒诞戏剧

to rise with the spur of the existentialist idea　因受到存在主义思潮的激励而兴起

7. the distorted, alienated and ill relationships between man and nature, man and society, man and man, and man and himself　人与自然,人与社会,人与人以及人与自己的被扭曲的、被疏远的、病态的关系

to concentrate more on the private than on the public, more on the subjective than on the objective 更注重描写个人而非公众,更注重描写主观而非客观

be concerned with the inner being of an individual　关注个人的内心活动

to pay more attention to the psychic time than the chronological one　更多地关注心理上的时间,而不是现实的顺序时间

8. a reaction against realism　对现实主义的反动/反叛

to exclude from its major concern the external, objective, material world = to exclude the external, objective, material world from its major concern　(现代主义)不太关注外在的、客观的、物质的世界

to cast away almost all the traditional elements in literature　几乎抛弃所有传统的文学元素

chronological narration　按时间顺序进行的叙述

be labeled as anti-novel, anti-poetry and anti-drama　被贴上反小说、反诗歌、反戏剧的标签

9. to express his strong sympathies for the suffering poor and his bitter disgusts at the social evils　表达了他对受苦受难的穷人的强烈的同情和对社会邪恶的深恶痛绝

the appalling brutality of the war　这场战争的害人的野蛮和残忍

to fight against the romantic fuzziness and self-indulged emotionalism　反对浪漫派的模糊、放纵情感的无病呻吟

to use hard, clear and precise images in poems　采用真实可靠、清晰准确的诗歌意象

10. to start to turn the left　开始向左倾

to express in their poetry a radical political enthusiasm and a strong protest against fascism　他们的诗歌中表达了一种激进的政治热情和对法西斯主义的强烈的抗议

to explicitly reject the modernist influence　公开反对现代主义的影响

11. A multiplicity of choices opened to both the poet and the reader　(创作风格上)诗人和读者都趋于多样化的选择

12. to move into more individual styles　转向更注重个性化的风格(而非什么潮流)

the three trilogies of Galsworthy's Forsyte novels　高尔斯华绥的福塞特世家小说三部曲

to make realistic studies of the aspirations and frustrations of the "Little Man"　对"小百姓"的雄心壮志和挫折失败进行了现实主义的探究

to present a vivid picture of the English life in the industrial Midlands　对英格兰中部工业地区的生活进行了生动的描绘

13. be eclipsed by the rapid rise of modernism in the 1920s　在20世纪20年代被现代主义的迅速崛起所掩盖/弄得黯然失色

with the strong swing of leftism in the 1930s　随着20世纪30年代文学的左翼化/左派运动

to turn their attention to the urgent social problems　他们把注意力转移到紧迫的社会问题上

to enrich the traditional ways of creation by adopting some of the modernist techniques　借鉴某些现代主义的技巧来丰富传统的创作方法

be touched by a pessimistic mood　带有悲观主义的情绪/受到悲观主义的影响

be preoccupied with the theme of man's loneliness　专注于描写人的孤独情绪

be shaped in different forms　呈现不同的形式

to give a direct portrayal of... 直接描写……

by singing highly of the heroic struggles against capitalism waged by the working class 通过歌颂工人阶级掀起的反对资本主义的英勇斗争

14. a group of young novelists and playwrights with lower-middle-class or working class background 一大群中下层阶级或者工人阶级背景的青年小说家和剧作家

to demonstrate a particular disillusion over the depressing situation 对萧条的形势表现出一种特别的幻想破灭的情感

to launch a bitter protest against the outmoded social and political values 对过时的社会和政治价值观发表尖锐的抗议

to portray unadorned working-class life 描写朴素的工人阶级生活

be merged and interpenetrated with modernism 与现代主义相互融合、相互渗透

to appear in a new face with... 以……的新面貌出现

15. With the notion that multiple levels of consciousness existed simultaneously in the human mind, that one's present was the sum of his past, present and future, and that the whole truth about human beings existed in the unique, isolated, and private world of each individual, writers like Dorothy Richardson, James Joys... concentrated all their efforts on digging into the human consciousness. 像多罗西·理查德森、詹姆斯·乔伊斯……这样的作家认为：人的思想中同时存在着多层次的意识，人的表现是他过去、现在和未来的集中体现（总和），人的真情就存在于每个人独特、孤立和私密的世界里，因此他们都竭力挖掘人的各种潜意识。

16. unprecedented stream-of-consciousness novels 空前的意识流小说

his encyclopedia-like masterpiece 他百科全书式的杰作

to present a fantastic picture of the disjointed, illusory, and mental-emotional life of Leopold Bloom 对利奥波尔德·布鲁姆的支离破碎、没有逻辑、虚幻的精神世界和情感生活进行了幻想式的展现

the symbol of everyman in the post-War 1 Europe 一战后所有欧洲人的形象代表

subject matter 主题

their symbolic or psychological presentation of the novel 它们在小说中的象征性的或者心理分析的表现

a novel of decidedly symbolist aspirations 一部明显是关于象征主义雄心壮志的小说

to set up, within a realistic story, a fable life of moral significance 在现实主义的故事情节中建立一个道德寓言

to lay in the tracing of the psychological development of his characters 在于追寻他的人物心理发展的轨迹

life impulse 生命的冲动

the primacy of man's instinct 人类的第一本能

to cause distortion or perversion of the individual's personality 引起人的个性的扭曲或变态

the alienation of the human relationships and the perversion of human nature 人际关系的疏远冷漠和人性的变态反常

the desires for power and money 追求权力和金钱的欲望

the shams and frauds of middle-class life 中产阶级生活的虚伪和欺诈

to turn men into inhuman machines 把人变为无人性的机器

17. to come to a decline 走向衰弱

to have another upsurge with the rise of existentialism 随着存在主义的兴起，又形成一次高潮

be examples of the plays inspired by social criticism 戏剧创作中充满了社会批判之灵气的典范

to dramatize social and ethical problems　将社会问题和伦理问题戏剧化/用戏剧来表现社会问题和伦理问题

18. with their joint efforts　在他们的共同努力下

to start an Irish dramatic revival　开始爱尔兰戏剧的复兴/复苏

to desire to restore lyrical drama to popularity　想要让抒情诗剧重新受到欢迎/得到普及

with the heroic portrayal of spiritual truth as his main concern　把英雄的精神世界(实质)的描写作为他的主要关切

introducing Irish myths and folk legends　(在戏剧创作中)引入爱尔兰神话和民间传奇故事

be among the best of his poetical achievement　达到他诗歌作品的最佳成就

19. By adopting the vivid figurative language of the Irish peasantry, Synge brought vigor, ironic humour, and dramatic pathos to the Irish stage.　辛格采用爱尔兰农民生动形象的语言,给爱尔兰的戏剧舞台带来生气、嘲讽的幽默、和戏剧性的悲情。

20. to regard drama as the best medium of poetry　认为戏剧是诗歌的最佳媒介

in spite of its primarily religious purpose　尽管它主要是宗教的目的

21. His exuberant though poetically commonplace verse drama, *The Lady's Not For Burning*, attracted delighted audience.　他的生气勃勃的诗剧《不该烧死她》,尽管诗写得平常,但却吸引着快乐的观众。

22. the Theater of Absurd　荒诞剧

to express a mood of restlessness, anger and frustration, a spirit of rebelliousness, and a strong emotional protest against the existing social institutions　表达了一种不安、愤怒和挫折的情绪,一种反叛的精神,以及对现实的社会制度强烈的抗议

unrelentingly condemned the contemporary social evil　无情地抨击当时的社会邪恶

to become known as the first "Angry Young Man"　作为"愤怒的青年"的第一人而闻名于世

主要内容归纳和总结

1. 现代主义的起源是怀疑论(skepticism)和对资本主义的幻想破灭(disillusion of capitalism)。一战的毁灭性灾难摧垮了人们对维多利亚时代道德标准的信奉,科技进步和非理性哲学(irrational philosophy)使作家们对人性和人际关系进行新的探索。

2. 现代主义的理论基础

非理性哲学和精神分析原理(theory of psycho-analysis)是现代主义的理论基础。许多思想家都推动了非理性哲学的发展。德国哲学家亚瑟·叔本华(Arthur Schopenhauer)的悲观主义(pessimism)和反理性哲学强调人的意愿与直觉(will and intuition)的重要性;尼采(Friedrich Nietzsche)进一步反对理性主义和基督教精神,推崇强权与霸权(power and hegemony);亨利·柏格森(Henry Bergson)则创立了自己的非理性哲学,强调创造力、直觉、非理性和无意识;弗洛伊德(Freud)的精神分析法也改变了人们对人性的看法。

3. 现代主义文学的特点

现代主义文学是对现实主义的反叛,是对传统文学观念的反叛。它反理性,排斥外在的客观物质世界(objective material world),而这些正是现实主义创作的根基和源泉;现代主义文学倡导新形式、新手法的自由试验,丢掉了故事(story)、情节(plot)、人物(character)、冲突(conflict)、高潮(climax)、结局(end)等几乎所有传统的文学元素,因此常被贴上反小说、反诗歌、反戏剧的标签(be labeled anti-novel, anti-poetry and anti-drama)。

现代主义文学的<u>主题</u>反映人与自然、人与社会、人与人、人与自我之间被扭曲的、病态的关系。作家注重写个人而非公众,写主观而非客观,重内心世界而非客观外界,重心理时间而非实际时间(pay more attention to the psychic time than the chronological one),因此作品中过去、现在、未来都混合在一起在人的意识中出现;现代主义小说致力于挖掘人类各种潜意识(subconsciousness),开创了史无前例的意识流小说(stream-of-consciousness novel);现代主义文学反对无病呻吟的浪漫与激情(the romantic and self-indulged emotionalism),提倡创作的新思想,使用寻常百姓的语言,将清新准确的形象引入诗歌。

4. 现代主义文学主要流派

　　a. 20 世纪前 30 年的现代主义

　　　　表现主义(Expressionism):强调自我表现,反对文艺的目的性。

　　　　超现实主义(Surrealism):一种以下意识、梦幻、本能为创作源泉的文艺流派。

　　　　未来主义(Futurism):1) 20 世纪初起源于意大利的现代西方文艺思潮,宣扬极端民族主义,否定一切文化遗产和传统,主张未来艺术应表现现代机械文明的速度、暴力等;2)认为预言(prophecy)能在未来实现(be made real)。

　　　　达达主义(Dadaism):20 世纪初起于苏黎世并在西方流行的一种虚无主义(nihilism)的文艺流派,完全抛弃传统,靠幻觉、抽象等方法进行创作。

　　　　意象主义(Imagism):20 世纪初由美国诗人埃兹拉·庞德(Ezra Pound)等发起的一种英美诗歌流派,主张使用自由体创作,表达一种瞬间的直觉和思想。

　　　　意识流小说(the Stream-of-consciousness novel):用看似混乱无序的意识流动或内心独白(而实质智力有序)表达复杂人物的情感世界就是小说创作中的意识流手法。意识流小说有三个共同假设:1)人类实质是存在于思想情感的过程中,而不是存在于外部世界中;2)这种思想情感的过程是支离破碎、无逻辑的;3)决定人思想情感变化轨迹的正是这种自由奔放的精神联系,而不是其逻辑关系。

　　b. "二战"后复兴的现代主义或后现代主义(post-modernism)

　　　　存在主义(Existentialism):即生存主义,认为存在不是客体,而是主体,强调个人存在是一切其他存在的根据。它有个独特的思想:"世界是荒诞的(absurd),人类生活很痛苦。"并由此产生出荒诞戏剧(theater of the absurd)黑色幽默(black humor)。

5. 现代主义文学兴起的时代和代表作家

　　20 世纪 20 年代现代主义的改革洪流席卷欧美,杰出的代表人物有卡夫卡(Kafka)、毕加索(Picasso)、庞德(Pound)、韦伯恩(Webern)、T. S. 艾略特(T. S. Eliot)、詹姆斯·乔伊斯(James Joyce)和弗吉尼亚·伍尔夫(Virginia Woolf)。20 世纪前 30 年是现代主义的黄金时期,从 30 年代开始,现代主义式微,现实主义开始回归。

　　诗歌方面:代表人物有托马斯·哈代(Thomas Hardy),埃兹拉·庞德(Ezra Pound),T. S. 艾略特(T. S. Eliot),威廉·巴特勒·叶芝(William Butler Yeats)。

　　小说方面:多罗西·理查德森(Dorothy Richardson)的《朝觐》(*Pilgrimage*),詹姆斯·乔伊斯(James Joyce)的《尤利西斯》(*Ulysses*),弗吉尼亚·伍尔夫(Virginia Woolf)的《黛洛维夫人》(*Mrs. Dalloway*)为现代主义的典型代表。D. H. 劳伦斯(D. H. Lawrence)的作品虽然保留了现实主义传统,但也用了大量心理分析和象征手法等现代主义技巧,如《虹》(*Rainbow*),《恋爱中的女人》(*Women in Love*),E. M. 福斯特(E. M. Forster)的《印度之行》(*A Passage to India*)也是一例。

　　戏剧方面:奥斯卡·王尔德(Oscar Wilde)和萧伯纳(G. B. Shaw)可以认为是英国现代戏剧之先锋,但他们并未对传统技法与形式进行大幅度改革,从批判现实的角度说来,他们是现实主义剧作家。继承他们批判现实主义传统的还有约翰·高尔斯华绥(John Galsworthy),通过社会与伦理问题的戏剧化,他在戏剧上取得了耀眼的成就,《银盒》(*The Silver Box*)与《抗争》(*Strife*)便是很好的例证。叶芝从爱尔兰神话中取材,创作了不少诗剧,但因缺少戏剧性,未产生很大效果。J. M. 辛格(J. M. Synge)用鲜活的爱尔兰乡村语言创作了很多成功的幽默剧、悲剧和喜剧,最著名的是《西方的花花公子》(*The Playboy of the Western World*)。30 年代,艾略特创作了诗剧《教堂里的谋杀》(*Murder in the Cathedral*)。50 年代,英国戏剧出现重大变革,工人阶级戏剧表达了对现存制度的叛逆和愤怒,约翰·奥斯博恩(John Osborne)的作品《愤怒的回顾》(*Look Back in Anger*)为其代表作品,使他成为第一位"愤怒的青年"(Angry Young Man)。荒诞派戏剧(Theater of Absurd)是一些特立独行的戏剧,描写腐朽孤独的世界里毫无意义的人生,塞缪尔·贝克特(Samuel Beckett)的代表作《等待戈多》(*Waiting for Godot*)是荒诞派戏剧中最有影响力的作品。

6. 借鉴了现代主义手法的现实主义作家和作品

    20 世纪 30 年代,小说家们开始转向严峻的现实问题,现实主义之风代替了现代主义,但作家们借鉴一些现代主义的创作手法,拓宽了传统的创作之路,使现实主义中带上了悲情主义色彩。代表作家和作品有奥尔德斯·赫胥黎(Aldous Huxley)的《勇敢的新世界》(*Brave New World*)和乔治·奥威尔(George Orwell)的《一九八四》(*Nineteen Eighty-Four*),两者都属于社会讽刺小说,尤其是后者,把极权统治无处不在地监控着人们一切言行的情景做了形象的表现。伊夫林·沃(Evelyn Waugh)的《一把尘土》(*A Handful of Dust*)是讽刺上流社会的戏剧小说。格拉汉姆·格林(Graham Greene)的《权利与光荣》(*The Power and the Glory*)为天主教小说。最突出的是出现了一批工人阶级作家,反映工人阶级的生活状况和他们与资产阶级的斗争。其中最著名的是苏格兰作家路易斯·吉本(Lewis Grassic Gibbon),代表作是他的三部曲(trilogy)《日落之歌》(*Sunset Song*)《云》(*Cloud Howe*)和《灰色花岗岩》(*Grey Granite*)。

重要信息句子

1. Modernism rose out of skepticism and disillusion of capitalism.

2. The French symbolism, appearing in the late 19th century, heralded modernism.

3. Modernism takes the irrational philosophy and the theory of psycho-analysis as its theoretical base.

4. Modernism, in many aspects, a reaction against realism. It rejects rationalism, which is the theoretical base of realism.

5. The first decades of the 20th century were golden years of the modernist novel. The theory of Freudian and Jungian psycho-analysis played a particular important role in stimulating the technical innovations of novel creation.

6. The 1930s witnessed the decline of modernist novels and the revival of poetic drama in England.

7. The English dramatic revolution in the 1950s developed in two directions: the working-class drama and the Theater of Absurd.

8. The most original playwright of the Theater of Absurd is Samuel Beckett, whose first play *Waiting for Godot*.

9. John Osborne angrily, violently condemned the contemporary social evils in his play *Look Back in Anger* (1956), and became known as the first "Angry Young Man" for his bringing vitality to the English theater.

I. 乔治·萧伯纳 George Bernard Shaw (1856～1950)

词语解释和难句分析

1. to work in a land-agent's office 在地产经纪商的事务部门工作

   to collect rents 收租金

   to have much contact with the poor people 与穷人有大量的接触

   to devote much of his time to self-education 投入很多时间进行自学

2. to bring him profit and fame 给他带来了收益和名声

   to come under the influence of Henry George and William Morris 开始受到亨利·乔治和威廉·莫里斯的影响

   to take an interest in socialist theories 对社会主义理论产生兴趣

   the emancipation of land and industrial capital from individual and private ownership 土地和工业资本从个人和私人所有制中获得解放

   to have a distrust of the uneducated working class 不信任没有文化的工人阶级

   to shoulder this task 肩负这项重任

   to bring about evolutionary socialism by legal and democratic means,... 通过合法的民主的方法逐步进入社会主义

   to break out of the snobbish intellectual isolation 产生了知识界自命不凡的孤立主义/孤芳自赏

3. about a world-famous prize fighter marrying a priggishly refined lady of property 讲的是一个世界闻名的杰出战士与一个古板的、过分考究的富婆的婚姻故事

   apprenticeship for his later dramatic writing 他后来戏剧创作的见习期/学徒期

   to direct his attacks on the Neo-Romantic tradition and the fashionable drawing-room drama 抨击的矛头指向新浪漫主义传统和时髦的画室话剧

   decadent aesthetic artists 颓废的唯美主义艺术家

   the "well made" but cheep, hollow plays which filled the English theater 充斥着英国戏剧舞台的虽然精雕细琢而实际浅薄空洞的戏剧

   to meet the low taste of the middle class 满足中产阶级的低级趣味

   to serve social purposes 为社会服务

4. be put on by the Independent Theater Society 在独立剧社上演

   be produced in New York 在纽约上演

   to touch upon a variety of subjects 涉及各种各样的主题

   be directed to/towards... 指向……,针对……

5. As he wrote in his preface to the "Plays Pleasant", he could "no longer be satisfied with fictitious morals and fictitious good conduct, shedding fictitious glory on robbery, starvation, disease, crime, drink, war, cruelty, and all other commonplaces of civilization which drive men to the theater to make foolish pretense that such things are progress, science, morals, religion, patriotism, imperial supremacy, national greatness and all the other names the newspaper calls them." 正如他在《快乐戏剧》的前言中所说,他

"不再满足于虚构的道德规范和虚构的优良品行,(不再愿意)把虚构的光辉抛撒给抢劫、饥饿、疾病、犯罪、酗酒、战争、残忍,以及文明中一切平庸的东西,这平庸驱使人们到剧院去做愚蠢的吹嘘说:所有上述种种(社会弊病)都是进步、科学、道德规范、宗教、爱国主义、帝国的至高无上、民族的伟大以及报纸上其他一切溢美之词的具体表现"。

6. a grotesquely realistic exposure of slum landlordism　对贫民窟地主土地所有制所做的风格怪异的现实主义暴露

to keep an eye on the contemporary society　密切注意当时的社会

to create superior beings to be equal to God　创作可与上帝媲美的高级人类

to solve all the metaphysical problems of the human society　解决人类社会各种玄奥的问题

to write plays on miscellaneous subjects　进行了多方面主题的戏剧创作

be about the ignorance, incompetence, arrogance and bigotry of the medical profession　关于医学专业方面存在的无知、无能、自负和偏执

7. *Too True to Be Good* is a better play of the later period, with the author's almost nihilistic bitterness on the subjects of the cruelty and madness of World War I and the aimlessness and disillusion of the young. 《难以置信》是他后期戏剧创作中较好的作品,作者对第一次世界大战的残忍和疯狂以及年轻人的彷徨和幻灭(这样的主题)进行了近乎虚无主义的嘲讽。

8. be termed as problem plays　被称作"问题剧"

indignation against oppression and exploration, against hypocrisy and lying, against prostitution and slavery, against poverty, dirt and disorder　对压迫和剥削的愤慨,对虚伪和谎言的愤慨,对卖淫和奴役的愤慨,对贫穷、肮脏和混乱无序的愤慨

9. to make the trick of showing up one character vividly at the expense of another　玩弄技巧、活灵活现地去展示/炫耀一个人,而不惜牺牲另一个人作陪衬/以牺牲另一个人为代价

to impinge an unconventional character upon a group of conventional social animals, so as to reveal at every turn stock notions, ...　把一个反传统的人物置于一群传统的社会动物之中进行打击,以便时时处处揭露陈腐的观念

be constructed around the inversion of a conventional theatrical situation　(剧本)是在传统的戏剧情节的基础上倒转错位,进行解构

an integral part of an interpretation of life　诠释生活的种种方法之一

to refuse to live on his fiancée's tainted dowry　拒绝靠未婚妻的不洁的陪嫁生活

10. The "deceived" husband is not outraged by his wife's extra-curricular friendship with a youthful poet, but is outraged instead by the poet's feigned indifference to the charms of his wife, thus producing a strong effect of irony.　那位"被欺骗的"丈夫并未被妻子与一个青年诗人的婚外情所激怒,却为这个诗人对妻子的魅力假装视而不见感到愤愤不平,于是强烈的讽刺效果就产生了。

11. not to work by plots　不靠情节取胜

the disregarded backbone to one long, unbroken conversation　一段不间断的长对白的被忽视了的线索/骨架

the dialogue and the interplay of the minds of the characters　人物对话和思想活动

to maintain the interest of the audience　一直吸引着观众/使观众感兴趣

the unrolling of plot　戏剧情节的展开

the operation of the spirit of discourse　人物对白体现的思想内涵

乔治·萧伯纳作品选读

《华伦夫人的职业》Mrs. Warren's Profession 第二幕节选

词语解释和难句分析

1. resigning herself to an evening of boredom　忍受一个烦闷的夜晚

   to rattle on　喋喋不休,咋咋呼呼说个不停

   a regular good-for-nothing　一个十足的饭桶,一个一无所能/没有出息的人

   to have to get rid of him　必须摆脱他

   not to be good for much either　也好不了多少,算不了什么

   be galled by Vivie's indifference　被薇薇的无动于衷/漠然无视伤了感情

   to make up your mind to see a good deal of Sir George Crofts　下定决心好好看看乔治·克拉夫兹

   be quite unmoved　无动于衷

   the paper knife on her chatelaine　她腰间钥匙链上的裁纸刀

2. it has never occurred to sb. that...　某人从未曾想到过……

3. a great little person at school　学校一个小小的人物

   loosing no time　一刻不停,一点时间也不浪费

   to get that tripos or whatever you call it　得了(剑桥的)那个学位或者别的什么

   to put up with the airs in you　忍受你神气活现的样子

4. What is that way of life which you invite me to share with you and Sir George Crofts, pray?　你请我与你和乔治·克拉夫兹先生共享什么生活方式?

5. I shall do something I'll be sorry for after, and you (will be sorry) too.　我会做出事后我要后悔你也要后悔的事情。

6. Let us drop the subject until you are better able to face it.　这个话题我们先放一放,等你能够面对它时再谈。

7. You want some good walks and a little lawn tennis to set you up.　你需要多散散步,打打草地网球,好恢复健康。

8. out of condition = poor health　身体很糟,健康状况很差

   be not able to manage twenty yards uphill without stopping to pant　不停下来喘气就不能爬上20码小山坡

   anything but crying = never cry　千万别哭

9. How can you be so hard on me? Have I no right over you as your mother?　你怎么能对我那么狠心?作为母亲我也无权管你吗?

10. to speak to me as no woman in authority over me at college dare speak to me　学校里有权管我的女人,还没有一个敢像你这么对我说话

    to dictate my way of life　支配/主宰我的生活方式

    to force on me the acquaintance of a brute whom anyone can see to be the most vicious sort of London man about town.　强迫我与一头野兽相识,任何人都能看出他是伦敦城里最邪恶的那种人。

    to give myself the trouble to resist such claims　自己劳神抵制这样的权利

    to throw herself on her knees　一下子跪了下来

11. You cant mean to turn on me! It's not natural.　你不要冲我发火/突然用语言攻击我! 这是不应该的。

12. to trifle with me about this　在此事上对我耍花招/戏弄我的感情

    to have the contaminated blood of that brutal waster in my veins　我的血管里流着那个野蛮的无形浪子的肮脏的血液

    on my oath　我发誓

13. Vivie's eyes fasten sternly on her mother as the significance of this flashes on her.　薇薇的眼睛牢牢地盯着母亲,仿佛她突然明白了这话中的含义。

    ＊it flashes on sb. that...　某人突然明白.....

14. to bury her face in her hands　她双手捂面

    to take down her hands and look up deplorably at Vivie　她放下手,可怜巴巴地看着薇薇

    to pull yourself together　振作起来,精神一点

15. What sort of woman are you?　你是个什么样的女人?

    The sort the world is mostly made of, I should hope. Otherwise I don't understand how it gets its business done.　与构成世界的大多数女人一样,我希望是。否则,我就不明白世界万物是怎么运行的。

    ＊the world is mostly made of 是 the sort 的定语从句,完整的句子应是 I'm the sort the world is mostly made of。

16. Youre very rough with me.　你对我太狠了。

17. She suddenly breaks out vehemently in her natural tongue — the dialect of a woman of the people — with all her affections of maternal authority and conventional manner gone, and an overwhelming inspiration of true conviction and scorn in her.　她突然猛烈地爆发了,恢复了她本来的语调———一个妓女的语调———她那带着母亲权威的钟爱之情和传统的言谈风度全都抛掉了,语调中带着一股自信和嘲讽、一股压倒一切的气势。

    ＊an overwhelming inspiration of... 应为前面介词 in 的宾语,与 her natural tongue 并列。

18. to put up with the injustice of it　忍受这种不公

    to boast of/about what you are to me　向我吹嘘你是个什么人物

19. Shame on you for a bad daughter and a stuck-up prude!　作为一个女儿,这么不孝顺,这么盛气凌人,你真不害臊!

20. to ring rather woodenly and even priggishly against the new tone of her mother　比起她母亲的新的语调,听起来很呆板,甚至于太正经

    to set myself above you in any way　千万不要认为我把自己摆在你之上

    to attack me with the conventional authority of a mother　(你)用一个母亲的传统权威攻击我

    to defend myself with the conventional superiority of a respectable woman　(我也要)用一个有尊严的女人的传统的优越感捍卫自己

    to respect your right to your own opinion and your own way of life　尊重你保留自己意见和自己生活方式的权利

21. Frankly, I am not going to stand any of your nonsense; and when you drop it I shall not expect you to stand any of mine.　坦白地说,我不想忍受你的胡说八道;假如你不谈这事,我也不想让你忍受(我的胡说八道)。

22. but she can choose between rag-picking and flower-selling, according to her taste.　但她可以根据自己的品位在捡破烂和卖花之间选择

23. The people who get on in this world are the people who get up and look for the circumstances they want,

if they cant find them, make them. 在这个世界上出人头地的就是那些奋发上进、寻找他们追求的机遇的人,如果找不到机遇,他们就创造机遇。

24. She plants her chair farther forward with brazen energy, and sits down. Vivie is impressed in spite of herself. 她一副厚颜无耻挺来劲样子,把椅子往前使劲挪了挪,然后坐下。薇薇不由自主地被触动了

25. to have a fried-fish shop down by the Mint 在铸币局旁边有一个炸鱼铺

be both good-looking and well made 长得又好看发育得又好

a well-fed man 吃得很讲究的人

undersized, ugly, starved looking, hard working, honest poor creatures 矮小、丑陋、一副饿死鬼样子的干活卖力、老实巴交的小可怜虫

26. Liz and I would have half-murdered them if mother hadn't half-murdered us to keep our hands off them. 要不是母亲把我们打得半死、不准我们碰她们,丽兹和我早就把她们打得半死。

27. be always held up to us as a model 一直被确立为我们的榜样

victualling yard 食品供应站

to take to drink 染上了酒瘾,酗酒

to have more spirit (= courage) 有更多的勇气

28. We both went to a church school — that was part of the ladylike airs we gave ourselves to be superior to the children that knew nothing and went nowhere. 我们两人到一家教会学校上学,使我们具有了一点贵妇人的风度,显得比什么也不懂、哪儿也没去过的孩子多点儿气质。

29. to get me a situation as a scullery maid in a temperance restaurant 给我在一家禁酒的餐馆里找了一份洗碗女工的活儿

to send out for (= provide) anything you liked 提供任何你想要的东西

be unable to/can hardly keep myself awake （几乎)睁不开眼

to come up for a half of Scotch but Lizzie 只有丽兹来为她要了半份苏格兰威士忌

30. chaperones of girls at the county ball 未婚女孩儿参加郡舞会的年长女伴/临场女监护人

a first-rate business woman 第一流的职业女性

never let herself look too like what she was 绝不让人从外表上看出她的真实身份/老底

never lost her head or threw away a chance 从不丧失理智或放弃一次机会

for other people's profit 为别人赚钱

31. So she lent gave me a start; and I saved steadily and first paid her back, and then went her partner. 于是从她借钱给我起,我不停地攒钱,先还了她的借款,后又与她搭伙。

32. to become a worn-out old drudge 变成一个被榨干的老苦役/老太婆

saving money and good management 攒钱和经营有方

to have a turn for music, or the stage 有音乐天赋,或表演才能

our appearance and our turn for pleasing men 我们的相貌和讨男人喜欢的天赋

to trade in our good looks 拿我们的姿色做生意

to employ us as shopgirls, or barmaids, or waitresses 雇佣我们做女店员、酒吧女郎或女招待

to get all the profits instead of starvation wages 获得全部的利润,而不是难以糊口的报酬

be quite justified from the business point of view 从做生意的观点来看是很有道理的

to catch some rich man's fancy 赢得某个富人的欢心,使某个富人(对你)着迷

to get the benefit of his money by marrying him 以嫁给他的方式从他的钱财中获得好处

33. as if a marriage ceremony could make any difference in the right or wrong of the thing 仿佛一个结婚仪式能使这件事的是与非有所不同

to make me sick　使我恶心

drunken waster of a woman that thinks her luck will last for ever　自以为永远有好运的女酒鬼

34. If theres a thing I hate in a woman, it's <u>want of character</u>.　如果说女人身上有什么我恨的东西,那就是缺乏/没有个性。

35. Isnt it part of what you call character in a woman that she should greatly dislike such a way of making money?　一个女人理应极其厌恶这样一种赚钱方式,难道不也是你所说的女人个性的组成部分吗?

　　* it = that she should greatly dislike … money, it 为形式主语, that 从句为真正的主语。

36. not give a straw　毫不在乎

　　not give two straws　毫不在乎

37. (She is) having to try to please some man that she doesnt <u>care two straws for</u>　(她)不得不竭力讨好/取悦某个她根本不喜欢的男人

38. Some half-drunken fool that thinks he's <u>making himself agreeable</u> when he's <u>teasing</u> and worrying and disgusting a woman so that hardly any money could pay her for <u>putting up with</u> it.　一些喝得半醉的傻瓜以为自己讨人喜欢,而实际上当他在戏弄、骚扰和恶心一个女人的时候,多少钱都偿付不了她的忍受和煎熬。

　　* hardly any money could pay…　几乎没有钱可以偿付……

39. to <u>bear with</u> disagreeables and take the rough with the smooth　逆来顺受,忍受那些心所不愿的事情,苦与乐都得承受

　　a bed of roses　称心如意的境遇,安乐窝

40. though to hear the pious people talk you would suppose it was <u>a bed of roses</u>　不过听那些虔诚的人们说起来,你会以为那是令人称心如意的安乐窝呢

　　* to hear the pious people talk = it, 是 suppose 的真正的宾语, it 是形式宾语。

41. be well conducted and sensible　举止得体,头脑理智

　　be worth while　值得(做)的

　　to <u>take to</u> it　喜欢干这事,沉湎于某事之中

　　to give my daughter a first-rate education　让我女儿享受第一流的教育

　　in the gutter　待在贫民窟,过着贫穷和有损人格、降低身份的生活

　　be looked up to　受到崇敬,被人仰视

　　nothing to <u>look forward to</u> but the workhouse infirmary　没什么可指望的了,只有收容所的诊所

　　be led astray by people　被人领偏了路/领错了方向

42. The only way for a woman to provide for herself decently is for her to be good to some man that can afford to be good to her.　一个女人能给自己提供体面生活的唯一途径就是对一个经济上有能力对她好的男人好。

43. If she's in his own station of life, let her make him marry her; but if she's far beneath him he cant expect it: why should she (expect)?　如果她与他生活在同样的社会地位,她就该让他娶了她;但是如果她的社会地位比他低得多,她就不要指望嫁他了:她怎么能指望呢?

44. to tell you straight　直截了当地告诉你

　　to tell you crooked (= dishonest, not straight-forward)　拐弯抹角地告诉你

45. It's only good manner to be ashamed of it.　对此感到羞愧只不过是良好教养的表现而已。

46. It's expected from a woman.　那是(大家)对女人的希望。

47. be angry with me for <u>plumping out</u> the truth about it　对我照直说出事情的真相非常生气

48. She <u>used to</u> say that when every woman could learn enough from what <u>was going on</u> in the world before

her eyes, <u>there was no need to</u> talk about it to her. 以前她常说,当每一个女人都能从眼前发生的世事人情中,学习到足够多东西的时候,就没有必要对她谈这件事了。

49. to have the true instinct of it 对此有真正的本能
    be always a bit of a vulgarian 总是有点儿粗俗
    to have just her ladylike determined way 就是有她的贵妇人似的行事果断的范儿

50. But I cant stand saying one thing when everyone knows I mean another. What's use in such hypocrisy? 但是,我忍受不了言不由衷,我嘴上这么说,而大家却都知道我想说的是另一个意思。这样的虚伪有什么用?

51. to manage everything so respectably 把一切都办得很体面

52. I never had a word against us 从未听到有人对我们说三道四

53. to stretch herself lazily 她伸了个懒腰
    be thoroughly relieved by her explosion 由于爆发,她彻底放松下来
    be placidly ready for her night's rest 她很镇定地准备睡觉

54. Whatever would they think of us! = If I talked about it, whatever would they think of us! (如果我谈这事,)他们会怎么想我们呢!

55. Better <u>let in</u> some fresh air before locking up. = I'd better let in … 最好在关门前放进一些新鲜空气。

56. to draw aside the curtains of the window 把窗帘拉至一边
    with a perfunctory glance at the scene 漫不经心地看了一眼外面的景色
    dont catch your death of cold from the night air 晚上湿气重,别着了凉
    to have got completely the better of 已经完全胜过了我
    to get the worst of it from Liz 输给丽兹
    to give in to it 对此让步
    Blessings on my own dearie darling! 保佑/祝福我亲爱的孩子!

57. The landscape is seen <u>bathed in</u> the radiance of the <u>harvest moon</u> rising over Blackdown. 布莱克当,秋月中天,原野风光全都沐浴在月色的银灰之中。

58. She embraces her daughter protectingly, instinctively <u>looking upward</u> for divine sanction. 她抱住女儿,好像在保护她,本能地仰起头来,祈祷上帝的保佑。

主要内容归纳和总结

1. 乔治·萧伯纳,莎士比亚之后最伟大的剧作家,出生在爱尔兰都柏林,父母为英格兰人。离开中学后,他曾在一家房地产公司负责收房租,对贫苦百姓的生活有深刻了解。20 岁时他到伦敦,在各大图书馆中博览群书,打下文学功底。

  1884 年,他加入费边社(the Fabian Society),开始研究马克思的社会主义理论,认为必须把土地和工业生产资料从私人占有者手中解放出来,但如何实现这一目标,他却不同意马克思主义观点,他反对暴力革命,不相信没受过良好教育的工人阶级,陷入改良主义的窠臼。他一方面渴求新世界,另一方面又无法打破知识分子的局限,苦闷得很。

  他虽然也写过 5 部小说,但主要的成就在戏剧方面。

2. 萧伯纳戏剧的思想艺术特点
a. 从内容到结构,都是现实主义的,尽管也吸收了一些现代主义手法。作品注重剖析社会现实问题,多被认为是"问题剧"(problem plays),只表达一种情感"愤怒",对社会不公的愤怒。
b. 衬托(set off by contrast)——为表现这一方面,不惜牺牲所有其他方面来烘托它。

c. 对传统的常情、逻辑进行颠覆错位(an inversion of a conventional theatrical situation),常把传统认识中的英雄塑造成恶棍,而把传统认识中的恶棍塑造成英雄。在《鳏夫的房产》(*Widowers' Houses*)中,贵族出身的男主角本来清高地拒绝依赖未婚妻、房地产商女儿来路不正的嫁妆生活,结果却发现自己的收入更不干净。在《她是怎样欺骗丈夫的》(*How She Lied to Her Husband*)中,被骗的丈夫不对自己的妻子与青年诗人的婚外情感到愤怒,却对青年诗人(假装)不为自己妻子的魅力所动而愤怒异常,讽刺之辛辣,非常罕见。

d. 萧伯纳的戏剧不以情节取胜,生动精彩的对白超越了情节,这才是他吸引读者的法宝。

3. 萧伯纳著有剧作 54 部,主要作品有:

《鳏夫的房产》*Widower's Houses*(1892)

《康蒂姐》*Candida*:*A Mystery*(1895)

《华伦夫人的职业》*Mrs. Warren's Profession*(1893~1898)

《追求女性的人》*The Philanderer*(1893)

《武器和人》*Arms and the Man*:*An Anti-Romantic Comedy*(1894)

《恺撒与克莉奥佩特拉》*Caesar and Cleopatra*(1898)

《你永远说不准》*You Never Can Tell*(1899)

《人与超人》*Man and Superman*(1904)

《英国佬的另一个岛》*John Bull's Other Island*(1904)

《芭芭拉上校》*Major Barbara*(1905)

《结婚》*Getting Married*(1908)

《不合适的婚姻》*Misalliance*(1910)

《医生的两难选择》*Doctor's Dilemma*(1906)

《卖花女》或《皮格马利翁》*Pygmalion*(1912)

《法尼的第一场戏》*Fanny's First Play*(1911)

《圣女贞德》*Saint Joan*(1923)

《回归马士撒拉》*Back to Methuselah*(1921)

《苹果车》*The Apple Car*(1929)

《难以置信》*Too True to Be Good*(1932)

另著有小说和戏剧评论,最著名的有:

《卡歇尔·拜伦的职业》*Cashel Byron's Profession*(1886)

《九十年代戏剧评论集》*Our Theaters in the Nineties*(1931)

重要信息句子

1. G. B. Shaw's career as a dramatist began in 1892, when his first play *Widower's Houses* was put on by the Independent Theater Society.

2. One feature of Shaw's characterization is that he makes the trick of showing up one character vividly at the expense of another. Another feature is that Shaw's character are the representatives of his ideas, point of view.

3. Shaw's plays have plots, but they do not work by plots. It is the vitality of the talk that takes primacy over mere story.

II. 约翰·高尔斯华绥 John Galsworthy (1867~1933)

词语解释和难句分析

1. to practice the law　从事法律工作,开办律师事务所

   to publish his first book under the pseudonym of...　以……为笔名出版了他第一部著作

   to establish him as prominent novelist and playwright in the public mind　在大众心目中确立了他作为一个杰出的小说家和剧作家的突出地位

   to complete *The Forsyte Saga*, his first trilogy　完成他第一个三部曲：福塞特世家

   be essentially a bourgeois liberal, a reformist　本质上是一个资产阶级自由主义者,一个改革家

2. be preoccupied with　专注,关注

   to appear in contrast　以相互对立而出现

   a dull, parasitic and inhuman class of the rich　愚钝的、无人性的、寄生虫一样的富人阶级

   be against any kind of change　反对任何的变革

   be bent on reforming things　精力集中/专注于改革的事情

   to battle for many liberal causes, from women's suffrage to the abolition of censorship　为种种自由事业而斗争,从妇女的选举权到审查制度的废除

   be both a moralist and a critic　既做道德家, 又做批评家

   to keep balance between the rich and the poor　在穷人和富人之间保持平衡

   be designed to help improve the status quo　目的就是要对改变现状有所帮助

3. to admire Tolstoy for the depth of insight and the breadth of character drawing　欣赏托尔斯泰深刻的洞察力和人物描写的雄浑阔大

   focusing on plot development and character portrayal　着力于情节发展和人物描写

   to learn about the essentials of style　学习问题的实质

   to make an impartial presentation of the social life in a documentary precision　以文献资料般的精确,对社会生活做了全面的展现

   to dauntlessly lay bare the true features of the good and the evil of the bourgeois society　无所畏惧地对资产阶级社会善恶是非的真实面貌进行了揭露

   to write in a clear and unpretentious style with a clear and straightforward language　用明确直白的语言和清楚明白、毫不做作的风格写作

高尔斯华绥作品选读

《财主》*The Man of Property*

词语解释和难句分析

1. the ups and downs of the Forsyte family　福塞特家族的兴衰沉浮

to center itself on the Soames-Irene-Bosinney triangle 集中描写索姆斯—艾琳—波辛尼之间的三角恋爱

the accumulation of wealth 财富的累积

to love art and cherish noble ideals of life 喜欢艺术和崇尚高尚的生活理想

to come to enjoy a great deal of each other's company 两人逐渐喜欢待在一起

to sue Bosinney at the court for spending more money than stipulated 以花费超出协议规定为由将波辛尼告上法庭

2. the predominant possessive instinct/desire of the Forsytes 福塞特家族明显的占有欲

with the underlying assumption that... 以假定……为基础的

the inhuman sense of property 没有人性的财产观念

to change into a more tolerant tone 转变成比较宽容的笔调

finally to become a distinctly sentimental tone 最后变成了明显的感伤主义语调

3. The theme of this novel is that of the predominant possessive instinct of the Forsytes and its effect upon the personal relationships of the family with the underlying assumption that human relationships of the contemporary English society are merely an extension of property relationships. 这部小说的主题关系到福塞特家族明显的占有欲及其对家庭成员个人关系的影响,这个家庭的基本观念是:当时英国社会的人际关系仅仅是财产关系的延伸。

4. one mockturtle = one mock turtle soup 一份假甲鱼汤

one oxtail = one oxtail soup 一份牛尾汤

two glasses of port = two glasses of port wine 两杯波特酒

to get heavy English food 享受丰盛的英格兰式的食物

5. There was something unpretentious, well-flavoured, and filling about it. 这里的菜实惠、味道好,可以让人吃饱喝足。

6. be corrupted by the necessity for being fashionable 受到追求时髦的必然性的影响

the trend of habits (have been) keeping pace with an income that would increase 习惯的取向一直与收入的增长保持同步

to hanker moments after the tasty flesh-pots of his early days 对当年(在这里)享受美味肉食的时光依然渴望

be served by hairy English waiters in aprons 毛发浓密、穿着围裙的男侍者在一旁侍候

three round gilt looking-glasses 三个圆形金边的镜子

above the line of sight 在视线的上方

to do with away the cubicles 取消小隔间

to have your chop and prime chump 享受你的排骨和头等的羊羔肉

7. to tuck the top corner of his napkin behind the third button of his waistcoat 把餐巾的上角塞在背心第三个纽扣里面

to relish his soup 品尝他的汤

to wind up the estate of an old friend 为一个老朋友清查地产

after filling his mouth with household bread, stale, ... 面包塞满一嘴,感到变味了

8. there'll be a lot that'll want seeing to 有很多事需要照料/办理

9. (not) have anything said against her (不愿)让人说她的坏话

rousing himself from his reverie over the soup 他喝汤正喝得出神,突然醒悟过来

* reverie over 对着……沉思/遐想/出神

to take one of his rapid shifting surveys of surrounding facts 他迅速地扫视了一下周围的情况

10. to show you over　领你看(房子)

to go and see by myself what sort of a job he's made <u>finishing off</u>　亲自去看看有什么事情叫他完成

to <u>drive round</u> and pick you both <u>up</u>　坐马车来接你们俩走

to sign to the waiter to bring the bill　打手势叫侍者拿账单来结账

11. They parted at St. Pauls, Soames branching off to the station, James taking his omnibus westwards.　他们在圣保罗大教堂分手,索姆斯拐到去火车站的路上,詹姆士乘公共马车向西去。

　　* Soames branching off...和 James taking...是两个独立分词短语作补充说明的状语,主句是开头的 They parted at St. Pauls。

12. to secure the corner seat next the conductor　坐上紧挨售票员的那个角落上的座位

to <u>have no business to</u> be using up his air　没有理由用光他的空气

to turn over a new leaf　翻过新的一页,改过自新

not to stand very much more of her goings on　对她的所作所为已忍无可忍

13. A word in time saved nine　及时的一句话,省却以后无数唇舌

14. <u>It didn't occur to him to</u> define what he meant by her "goings on".　他没有想他那句"(她的)所作所为"指的是什么。

15. James had more than his common share of courage after lunch.　午餐后詹姆士有了比平日更多的勇气。

16. to order out the barouche　下令出动马车

<u>with special instructions that</u> the groom was to go too　特别叮嘱/附带加了句小马夫也要跟着去

to prevent any chance of being denied entrance　防止遭到拒绝/进不去

to <u>astonish the observers of</u> his long figure and absorbed expression　他的高个儿和专注的神情使看到的人感到吃惊

to go forthwith (*ad.*) into the drawing-room without permitting this to be ascertained　一刻也不延迟,立即走进画房,不待别人弄清来意

seating at the piano with her hands arrested on the keys　坐在钢琴旁边,两只手放在琴键上

hoping at once to enlist her sympathy　希望立刻赢得她的同情

to come with me <u>for a drive</u>　来,跟我出去走走/兜兜风

spluttering out his words very quick　他噼里啪啦很快地说

17. The horses want exercise.　马需要遛遛/活动活动。

18. to hang back = to hesitate　犹豫不决,踌躇不前

to brood over　担心/默默地想着……

to show him more affection　对他更亲热一点

be really <u>in command of</u> the situation　真正掌控着局面

19. She could not <u>put him off</u>; nor would she <u>make a scene</u> in public.　她既不能拒绝/不理会,也不能公开闹事/大吵大闹。

20. What are you about? = What do you mean?　你什么意思/你想要说什么?

21. to catch the words　听清了几个字/一句话

22. What's that <u>got to do with it</u>?　这又有什么关系呢?

　　* 画线部分是过去分词短语作 that 的定语,直译是:与此有关的是什么呢?

23. It's not as if you had anything of your own.　这不同于你有嫁妆陪嫁。/要是你有嫁妆,那就不同了。

24. not to <u>make out</u> the expression on her face　没有看懂她脸上的表情

(a tear) to steal down her cheek　眼泪悄悄地流下脸颊

to feel a choke rise in his own throat　感到喉咙里有个东西堵着

to behave yourself　学好，行为得体

be more of a wife to him　待他要更像个妻子

to disconcert him　令他不安

25. It was not the silence of obstinacy, rather that of acquiescence in all that he could find to say.　那与其说是抗拒的沉默，不如说是对他能想到能说出来的话的一种默认。

　　＊第一个 that＝silence。

26. to feel as if he had not had the last word.　感到话还未说完/还有话要说

ruminating over his rebuff　反复思考他遭到的冷遇/峻拒

not to stand a great deal more of this sort of thing　对这种事情再也不能忍受了/忍无可忍

to have nobody but yourself to blame　只怪你自己，不怪别人

to bend her head with a little smiling bow　她低下头来，含着微笑鞠躬

be very much obliged to sb.　非常感谢某人

the bright hot morning　早晨晴好炎热

a grey, oppressive afternoon　下午变得阴沉压抑

a heavy bank of clouds, with the yellow tinge of coming thunder　一堆浓密的乌云，黑中带黄，带有雷雨来临的气息

without the smallest stir of foliage　树叶一动不动

a faint odour of glue from the heated horses　跑热了的马，身上散发出一种轻微的胶黏气息

to cling in the thick air　凝聚在混浊的空气中/在浑浊的空气中久久不散

to exchange stealthy murmurs on the box　在车厢里悄悄低语

to James' great relief　使詹姆士大大松了一口气

27. The silence and impenetrability of this woman by his side, whom he had always thought so soft and mild, alarmed him.　身边的这个过去一直被他认为温和柔顺的女人，始终沉默不语，风雨不透，使他惊恐。

28. (a shudder) to run down James' spine　（一个寒噤）直通到脊梁骨

not to restrain an exclamation of approval　禁不住一声赞叹/喝彩

the dull ruby tiles　暗红色的瓷砖

be of the best quality　有最好的质量

to extend from the foot of the walls to the verge of a circular clump of tall iris plants　（瓷砖）从墙根一直延伸到圆圆的一团高高的鸢尾草边缘

surrounding in turn a sunken basin of white marble filled with water　（鸢尾草）又围在一个埋在地下盛满水的白色大理石盆周围

29. He admired extremely the purple leather curtains drawn along one entire side, framing a huge white-tiled stove.　他极为欣赏地拉起整整遮盖了一面墙的紫色皮帘，刚好为一个白色瓷砖砌的大炉子镶了边框/做了背景。

30. the central partitions of the skylight　天窗的中央部分

be slide back　被打开/拉开

to spy the tracery on the columns　仔细察看柱子上的装饰条纹

to draw the curtains asunder and disclose the picture-gallery　把窗帘向两边拉开，露出里面的画廊

to go on throwing open doors, and peeping in　把门陆续打开，向里窥视

(everything) be in apple-pie order, ready for immediate occupation　一切都布置得井井有条，可立即入住

31. Evidently, no pains had been spared. 很明显,没省一点功夫/没一点儿偷工减料。

32. to feel vaguely alarmed 感到隐隐的担忧,着急

   to make an attempt to smooth things over 竭力纾解矛盾,摆平事端

   frowning face 皱眉蹙额的面容,愁眉苦脸的样子

   making off after his son 他跟在儿子后面,出门离开

33. In his agitation, James spoke his thoughts aloud. 一急之下,詹姆士把心里的话说了出来。

34. her face not like the face he knew of her 她的脸再不是他所熟悉的旧日模样

   to hasten up to his son 急忙走到他儿子面前

   be pacing the picture gallery 正在画廊里踱步

   to look at him with his supercilious calm unbroken 眼睛看着他,依然不变的是傲然的沉默

   so much the worse for him this time 这次对他可没那么客气了

   edging himself in front 抢到前面,使自己位于前边

35. Don't get caught in the storm! 别赶上雷雨啊!

36. the sight of Irene's face = seeing Irene's face 看见艾琳的脸色(不好)

   to escort her towards the carriage 陪伴/护送她去车厢

37. Nothing in this world is more sure to upset a Forsyte than the discovery that something on which he has stipulated to spend a certain sum has cost more. 对于福塞特家族的人来说,没有什么能比发现一件事情实际的花销超过了他计划规定的数额更使他恼火的了。

38. for upon the accuracy of his estimates the whole policy of his life is ordered = for the whole policy of his life is ordered upon the accuracy 因为他整个人生的大政方针都是根据这种精密的计算来安排的

39. If he cannot rely on definite values of property, his compass is amiss; he is adrift upon bitter waters without a helm. 如果他不能依靠财产的固定价值来计算,他就失去了一切的准绳/方向盘出了问题;他就会像一条无舵的小船,漂流在茫茫的苦海中。

40. After writing to Bosinney in the terms that have already been chronicled, Soames had dismissed the cost of the house from his mind. 在索姆斯写信给波辛尼讲定了已记录在案的协议条款之后,他再也没有认真考虑过房子的费用。

41. to have made the matter of the final cost so very plain that ... 已把最终价格的问题讲得那样清楚明白以至于……

   to have grown white with anger 已经气得浑身发冷

   to have put himself completely in the wrong 完全错了,怎么也说/赖不过去了

   to make an ass of sb. 愚弄某人,使某人出洋相

   to make an ass of oneself 做蠢事,闹笑话,出洋相

   all the rancour and hidden jealousy that had been burning against him for so long 对他如火中烧的长期积怨和暗藏的嫉妒

   be focused in rage at this crowning piece of extravagance 面对这件登峰造极的奢侈浪费,一下子发泄了出来

42. To preserve property — his wife — he had assumed it (= the attitude), to preserve property of another kind he lost it now. 为了保全财产——保全他的妻子——他假装那个样子,为了保全另一种财产,他原形毕露/剥去了伪装。

43. and I suppose you're perfectly contented with yourself. But I may as well tell you that you've altogether mistaken your man! 我想你一定很满意/得意。但我不妨告诉你,你完全看错了(主)人。

44. to have made himself liable for that extra four hundred (自己的行为)使他对超出预算的四百英镑承担(法律)责任

at all events　无论如何

to make it good　对此做出赔偿，在此事上取得成功

be altering the lace on a collar　摆弄着一个衣领的花边

to go up to the mantelpiece, and contemplating his face in the mirror　走到壁炉前,看着镜子里自己的脸出神/端详着镜子中自己的脸

to make a fool of himself　使自己出丑,与自己过不去

a mere trifle, quite beneath your contempt — four hundred pounds　仅仅是一笔小钱,不值你一笑——400 英镑

unconsciously taking a china cup from the mantelpiece, clasped his hands around it, as though praying　无意中从壁炉板上拿起一个瓷杯,双手抱握,像在祈祷

her eyes darkening with anger　她的目光因愤怒而阴沉下来

45. to take no notice of the taunt　不理会这嘲讽/奚落

to carry on a flirtation with sb.　与某人调情/有暧昧关系

the sight of (= seeing) her inscrutable face　看着她神秘的、无法臆测的面部表情

the thought (= thinking) of all the hundreds of evenings he had seen her sitting there like that　想到无数个夜晚他总是看到她像这样在那里坐着

to enrage him beyond measure　使他怒不可遏(超出了界限)

clenching his fingers so hard that he broke the fragile cup　他手指使劲一握,把脆弱的茶杯捏碎了

to bring you to your sense　使你清醒,使你明白

to turn on his heel　他转过身去

主要内容归纳和总结

1. 约翰·高尔斯华绥出身于上流社会家庭,曾在哈罗公学和牛津大学读书,做过律师,后转攻文学,取得成功。他的小说《财主》(*The Man of Property*)和剧作《银盒》(*The Silver Box*)使他进入著名小说家和剧作家的行列。

　　高尔斯华绥是个自由主义和改良主义者(liberalist and reformist),其作品中展现的多是贫富两个阶级之间的斗争,而他的同情总是在穷人一边。但他总想以调和的方法(reconciled method)解决阶级矛盾,不愿诉诸激进的革命。

　　高尔斯华绥是传统型作家,是狄更斯(Dickens)、萨克雷(Thackeray)等维多利亚时期(Victorian Period)优秀文学家的继承者。他的写作技法比较保守,严格把握情节的发展和角色的描写,对社会生活的展现竭力做到全面、精确,如同文献资料(documentary precision)一般。在他的作品中讽刺与幽默无处不在,语言风格清晰、直白、毫不做作(clear, straightforward and unpretentious style)。

2. 高尔斯华绥的主要作品:

《来自四个吹奏者》*From the Four Winds* (1879)

《银盒》*The Silver Box* (1906)

《福塞特世家三部曲》第一部 *The Forsyte Saga Trilogy I*

《财主》*The Man of Property* (1906)

《骑虎难下》*In Chancery* (1920)

《出租》*To Let* (1921)

《福塞特世家三部曲》第二部 *The Forsyte Saga Trilogy II*

《现代喜剧》*A Modern Comedy* (1929)

《福塞特世家三部曲》第三部 *The Forsyte Saga Trilogy III*
《篇章末尾》*End of the Chapter*（1934）

重要信息句子

1. John Galsworthy's first book is *From the Four Winds* published in 1897 and his first play is *The Silver Box* (1906).
2. He regarded human life as a struggle between the rich and the poor.

III. 威廉·巴特勒·叶芝 William Butler Yeats（1865～1939）

词语解释和难句分析

1. Irish folklore, Celtic legends, and Gaelic sagas　爱尔兰民间故事,凯尔特传奇,以及盖尔英雄传奇
   to organize the Irish National Dramatic Society　组织爱尔兰民族剧社
   to open the Abbey Theater　开办教堂/寺院剧院
2. to go through several different stages　经历几个不同阶段
   to take an active interest in nationalist poetics　对民族主义诗学有浓厚的兴趣
   a fiery freedom fighter　热情似火的自由战士
   to turn out to be fruitless　最后无果而终
   be denounced by the Dublin middle class as being anti-religious　被都柏林的中产阶级斥之为反宗教
   be apparently disillusioned with the state of the Irish National Movement　对爱尔兰民族运动的状态感到失望
   to turn to praise the refinement of the aristocratic life　转而歌颂贵族生活的精致
   moderate nationalist　中庸/温和的民族主义者
3. not content with any dogma in any of the established religious institutions　对现行的/既定的宗教制度的任何教条都感到不满意
   mystical system of belief　神秘的信仰体系
   cyclical history over the modern conception of progress　以现代进步观念为基础的历史循环论
4. He believed that history, and life, followed a circular, spiral pattern consisting of long cycles which repeated themselves over and over on different levels.　他认为历史和生活都遵循一种循环的螺旋形的运行模式,这种模式由不同水平上重复出现的漫长周期所组成。
5. Symbols like "winding stairs," "spinning tops," "gyres" and "spirals" were part of his elaborate theory of history, which had obviously become the central core of order in his great poems.　像"旋转楼梯""陀螺""回旋"和"螺旋"这些象征符号都是他精致的历史理论的组成部分,已经成了他伟大诗歌的核心法则。
6. to disagree with the idea of "art for art's sake"　不同意"为艺术而艺术"的观点
   (literature) not be an end in itself but the expression of conviction and the garment of noble emotion

（文学）本身并不是目的,而是对信仰的表达和抒发高尚情操的载体/外衣

to recreate a specifically Irish literature 重建具有爱尔兰独特风格的文学

to <u>fill</u> the people <u>with</u> national aspirations <u>in striving for</u> a new Ireland 给人民灌输/点燃了争取建设新爱尔兰的民族理想/抱负

only by expressing primary truth in ways appropriate to this country 只有以适合这个国家国情的方法来表达基本真理,……

to <u>restore to</u> the modern Ireland the "unity of culture" = to restore the "unity of culture" to the modern Ireland 使现代的爱尔兰重新实现"文化的统一"

to <u>bring an end to</u> his country's internal division and suffering 结束他的国家的内部分裂和受苦受难的局面

7. starting in the romantic tradition and finishing as a matured modernist poet 从继承浪漫主义传统开始,到成为一个成熟的现代主义诗人结束

to have dreamy quality, expressing melancholy, passive and self-indulgent feelings （早期诗歌)具有梦幻气质,表达了忧郁、被动和自我放纵的情感

8. Yeats has achieved suggestive patterns of meaning by a careful counterpointing of contrasting ideas or images like human and fairy, natural and artificial, domestic and wild, and ephemeral and permanent. 叶芝把反差较大的思想或意象进行仔细的对比,成功地掌握运用意义暗示的技巧,比如人与仙,天然与人工,家养与野生,以及昙花一现与天长地久。

9. be closely woven, easy, subtle and musical （诗歌)构思绵密,自如微妙,富有音乐感

to give the poem a <u>haunting quality</u> 赋予诗歌一种令人难忘/长系心头的神韵

to make something peculiarly effective out of the contrast between human activities and the strangeness of nature 从人的活动和自然的奇特之间的反差中创造出某种具有独特效果的东西

* peculiarly effective 是 something 的后置定语。

the overall style of his early poetry 他早期诗歌的总体风格

be delicate with natural imagery, dream-like atmosphere 意象精巧自然,氛围如梦如幻

10. His <u>disgust</u> at the bourgeois philistinism soured his political optimism, leaving him a disillusioned patriotic sentiment. 他对资产阶级庸俗市侩的厌恶浇灭了他政治上的热情,空留下一个希望破灭的爱国主义情怀。

11. his long-cherished but hopeless love for . . . 他对……的长久但是无望的爱情

to bring him only suffering and bitterness 带给他的只有痛苦

to <u>respond to</u> Nietzsche's works with great excitement 非常激动地与尼采的著作发生共鸣

to <u>come under</u> the influence of French symbolism 受到法国象征主义的影响

12. to give a significance to the ordinary events of life in his poetry 他的诗歌给生活中的普通事物赋予重要意义

metaphysical wit and symbolic vision 玄学派的机智和象征主义的幻象

be <u>on his way</u> to modernist poetry 正在走向现代主义诗歌(的创作)道路

with scornful irony 带着轻蔑的冷嘲

to assault the bourgeois philistines and their meanness of spirit and selfish materialism 攻击资产阶级的庸俗市侩、灵魂卑劣以及自私自利的物质主义

13. The scorn so pervasive before was gone. 以前无处不在的轻蔑和讽刺现在不见了。

14. to <u>yearn</u> to move away from the sensual world of growth and change. 渴望逃离不断发展变化的世俗社会

to <u>turn to</u> the great subjects of dichotomy 转向一分为二的大主题

to bring constant tensions in his works and reveal the human predicament　（一分为二）不断给他的作品增加紧张情绪,揭示了了人的困境

14. Being <u>at the junction of</u> East and West, the city became <u>a refuge from</u> time, and, at once, purgatory and paradise, <u>a haunt of</u> spirit, symbolizing <u>the unity of the opposites</u>. 　（拜占庭）这座城市,位于东西方的交接之处,成为逃避时光流逝,同时也是逃避炼狱和天堂的庇护所,它也是神鬼精灵的显现出没之地,象征着对立统一。

　　﹡ a haunt of spirit 与 a refuge from … 是 became 的并列宾语。

15. "Once out of nature," or dead, the old man in "Sailing to Byzantium" will be gone into the "Monuments of unaging intellect", the "artifice of eternity" where art arrests change. 《驶向拜占庭》一诗中的那位老人,一旦脱离凡尘,或者死去,就要载进"知识长青的纪念碑",进入"艺术的永恒"境界,在那里艺术亘古不变。

　　﹡ the "artifice of eternity"是前面的"Monument of unaging intellect"的同位语,后面 where 引导的定语从句中, arrest 意为抑制,阻止。

16. His great works of art, which are needed now to carry him beyond the sensual world, to transform him into a golden bird, would <u>sing of</u> time, "Of what is past, or passing, or to come." 他的伟大艺术作品,今天可度他超脱尘俗、变为金鸟,常常要歌唱时光,"歌唱过去、现在和未来"。

17. to <u>express</u> a tragic sense of history <u>as</u> a series of patterns of behavior and action　把历史的悲剧感/悲情表现为一系列的行为模式

　　be raped by Zeus <u>in the form</u> of swan　被宙斯化装成天鹅强奸了

　　to <u>give birth to</u> two eggs　产下两个鹅蛋

　　to <u>lay the foundation</u> of modern Europe　为现代欧洲文明的出现打下基础

18. to write more than 20 plays <u>in stretch of</u> 48 years　在48年中他创作了二十多部戏剧

　　to <u>consider it as</u> an appropriate symbol of the activities <u>to</u> which Gonne <u>had dedicated her life</u>　认为这部剧(《凯瑟琳的伯爵夫人》)准确地反映了(他的恋人)歌妮为之献身的民族解放运动

　　to <u>promise glory to</u> those who <u>make sacrifice in</u> their fight　承诺给那些在斗争中牺牲的人以崇高的荣誉

　　with techniques <u>borrowed from</u> the Japanese Noh plays　借用日本"能乐"剧的表演技巧

　　to anticipate the abstract movement of modern theater　为现代抽象戏剧运动的先声

　　be enjoyed more for the beauty of their language than for <u>dramatic situations</u>　（他的戏剧）为人所欣赏的更多的是他优美的语言,而不是他的戏剧情节

叶芝作品选读

1. 茵尼斯弗利岛 *The Lake Isle of Innisfree*

词语解释和难句分析

1. 茵尼斯弗利岛位于爱尔兰西部叶芝母亲的故乡斯莱戈(Sligo)附近的洛吉尔(Lough Gill)地方,叶芝年轻时曾在那里住过。这首诗显然受到美国作家梭罗(Henry David Thoreau)散文集《瓦尔登湖》(*Walden*)的影响,梭罗曾在马萨诸塞州新康科德的瓦尔登湖畔结庐而居,独享自然美景。诗中茵尼斯弗利岛就是宁静的隐居之地的象征。

2. I will arise and go now　《圣经新约·路加福音》中有"I will arise and go to my father",这句诗是对圣

经语言的模仿。

And a small cabin build there, of clay and wattles made: = And build there a small cabin made of clay and wattles. 用泥巴和篱笆条在那里建一座小房

3. Nine bean-rows will I have there, a hive for the honeybee = I will have there nine bean-rows and a hive for the honeybee. 我要有九排芸豆架,一个蜜蜂巢。

And live alone in the bee-loud glade 独自住在蜜蜂嗡嗡叫的林间空地上

4. for peace comes dropping slow 因为宁静慢慢地降临。

＊这里有形容"宁静"是一点一滴慢慢凝集而成的意思。

Dropping <u>from</u> the veils of the morning <u>to</u> where the cricket sings "宁静"随面纱般的晨雾而来,落向蟋蟀歌吟的地方。

5. There midnight's all a glimmer, and noon (is) a purple glow. 子夜一片闪光,正午紫光如燃。

＊子夜时,月色照射湖面,一片闪亮;正午时,骄阳似火,使湖面一片紫红。

And evening (is) full of the linnet's wings. 暮色里,到处飞舞着红雀的翅膀。

6. I hear lake water lapping with low sounds by the shore. 我听见湖水轻声拍打着湖岸。

＊lapping... 为分词短语,作 hear 的宾补。

to stand on the roadway, or on the pavements grey = or on the grey pavements 不论是站在大马路上,还是在灰色人行道上

I hear it in the <u>deep heart's core</u>. 我心灵深处总听见那波涛的声音。

＊说明作者身在闹市,仍然怀念着那幽静的湖泊。

参考译文——姚远

茵尼斯弗利岛

我要动身,去往茵尼斯弗利岛,
用黏土和篱笆条,傍湖筑小居;
九排芸豆架,一个蜜蜂房,
独自林间住,蜂鸣在耳旁。

我会得到安宁,安宁会慢慢降临,
像面纱般的晨雾,落向蟋蟀歌吟处;
子夜一片湖光月色,正午一片骄阳紫光,
傍晚到处是红雀飞舞的翅膀。

我要动身去,动身去湖岛,
涛声日夜响耳边,波浪拍湖滨;
我站在车行路,或灰色的人行道,
湖水的声声拍击,都激荡在我心灵深处。

格律和韵律分析

I will a·rise/and go ·now/, and ·go/to ·In/nis·free,	a
And a small ·ca/bin build ·there,/ of ·clay/and ·wat/tles ·made;	b
Nine bean-·rows/will I ·have/there, a ·hive/for the ·ho/ney·bee,	a
And ·live/a·lone/in the ·bee/-loud ·glade.	b
And I ·shall/have some ·peace/there,for ·peace/comes ·drop/ping ·slow,	c
·Dropping/from the ·veils/of the ·mor/ning to ·where/the ·cri/cket ·songs;	d
There ·mid-night's/all a ·glim/mer,and ·noon/a ·pur/ple ·glow,	c
And ·eve/ning ·full/of the ·lin/net's ·wings,	d
I will a ·rise/and go ·now,/for ·al/ways ·night/and ·day,	e
I ·hear/lake ·wa/ter ·lap/ping with ·low/sounds by/the ·shore;	f
While I ·stand/on the ·road/way,or ·on/the ·pave/ments ·gray,	e
I ·hear/it in/the ·deep/heart's ·core.	f

根据上面的格律划分可以看出,第一节4行诗为5554音步,共19个音节,其中抑扬格为10个,抑抑扬格为7个,只有And a small ·ca/(bin)和I will a ·rise是2个抑抑抑扬格。第二节4行诗为5654音步,共20个音步,其中抑扬格为10个,抑抑扬格为9个,抑扬抑格为1个。第三节4行诗为5654音步,共20个音步,其中抑扬格为12个,抑抑扬格为6个,抑抑格为2个。综上可知,全诗12行诗,7行为5个音步,3行为4个音步,2行为6个音步,5音步诗行占大多数。总共59个音步,32个为抑扬格,22个为抑抑扬格,1个为抑扬抑格,2个为抑抑格,2个为抑抑抑扬格,抑扬格占大多数。因此这首诗的格律为五步抑扬格。根据尾音押韵规则,很容易看出这首诗的韵律为abab/cdcd/efef。

2. 走过黄柳园 *Down by the Salley Gardens*

词语解释和难句分析

1. 此诗原名《老歌重唱》(*An Old Song Resung*),叶芝还做了脚注:"这是对一首老农妇记忆中残缺不全的三行诗老歌的再创作尝试,这位老农妇住在爱尔兰斯莱戈(Sligo)地区巴莱索德尔(Ballysodare)的一个村子里,她常常在心里唱这首歌。"

2. Down by the salley gardens my love and I did meet; = Coming down by... meet; 来到黄柳园畔,我与爱人相遇;

3. She bid me take love easy, ... 她劝/求我自自然然地及时相爱,不要心有所忌,不要太过严肃/一切随缘,不要太过急切;

4. But I, being young and foolish, <u>with her would not agree</u>. = But being young and foolish, I would not <u>agree with her</u>. 可我当时年轻糊涂,未听她意见。

5. And on my leaning shoulder she laid her snow-white hand. = And she <u>laid</u> her snow-white hand <u>on</u> my

leaning shoulder. 我斜肩相倚,她雪白小手,轻搭我肩。

6. She bid me take life easy, as the grass grows on the weirs; 她劝我对生活要自然随意,就像是堤堰上的青草漫长;

7. and now am full of tears = and now I am full of tears. 如今我后悔呀涕泪双流。

参考译文——姚远

走过黄柳园

我和爱人相遇在黄柳园畔;
她雪白的小脚,款款走过柳园。
她劝我爱情随缘,如树枝长叶般自然;
可我年轻糊涂,心里不曾同意。

我和爱人站立在河边田野,
她雪白的小手,轻搭在我肩。
她劝我生活随意,如草生堤堰并非刻意;
可当时年轻糊涂,如今我泪流涟涟。

格律和韵律分析

'Down by/the 'sal/ley 'gar/dens my 'love/and 'I/did 'meet; a

She 'passed/the 'sal/ley 'gar/dens with 'lit/tle 'snow/-white 'feet. a

She 'bid/me 'take/love 'ea/sy, as/the leaves 'grow/on the 'tree; b

But 'I,/ being 'young/and 'foo/lish, with her/would 'not a'gree. b

In a 'field/by the 'ri/ver my 'love/and 'I/did 'stand, c

And on my 'lea/ning 'shoul/der she 'laid/her 'snow-/white 'hand. c

She 'bid/me 'take/life 'ea/sy, as/the grass 'grows/on the 'weirs; d

But 'I/was 'young/and 'foo/lish, and 'now/am 'full/of 'tears. d

这首诗的格律不够严谨,第一节每行 6 音步,而第二节却又变成 5566 音步,抑扬格占多数,为主调格,抑抑扬格也不少,但依然是非主调格。第二节第二行第一音步 and on my 'lea/ning 中的 and on 可约音为[dɔn],形成抑抑扬格。全诗基本上是六步抑扬格,格律的不规则并未影响诗的韵律美,韵律是严格的 aabb 型,读起来非常优美。

主要内容归纳和总结

1. 叶芝(W. B. Yeats)出生于都柏林一个盎格鲁－爱尔兰新教徒家庭(Protestant family),童年时代在伦敦的学校和他母亲的故乡斯莱戈(Sligo)县度过。中学毕业后,他考入都柏林艺术学院,走上诗歌创作之路。曾与格利高里夫人(Lady Gregory)和约翰·辛格(John Synge)合作组建了爱尔兰民族剧社(Irish National Society),并建成寺院剧场(Abbey Theater)。他是个温和的民族主义者,憎恶英格兰的压迫,却不赞成民众暴动。

他不满任何宗教教条,建有自己的一套信仰。他认为历史与人生都是周期性的、螺旋式的,各种现象都是重复出现的,他诗歌中的历史总是以"旋转楼梯""螺旋"来比喻。在后期,他反对唯美主义(aesthetic)的"为艺术而艺术"(arts for art's sake),认为艺术的目标是为了表达信仰和抒发高尚情操。

总的来说,在艺术上,他经历了一个从浪漫主义到现代主义的过程。早期的作品以凯尔特人传奇(Celtic legend)和民间传说(local folktales)为主要内容,多带有梦幻色彩(dreamy quality)、忧郁伤感的情怀(melancholy)和被动的自我放纵(passive self-indulgence);在艺术技巧上,他把反差鲜明的思想或意象进行对比(counterpointing of contrasting ideas or images),语言结构细密而微妙,极富音乐感。中后期,由于恋情的挫折,他在诗歌创作思想上受到约翰·邓恩(John Donne)、庞德(Ezra Pound)和T. S.艾略特(T. S. Eliot)的影响,早期被动的梦幻被愤怒、失望和辛辣的讽刺所代替,风格既凝练简洁又丰富多彩(simple and rich),既口语化又十分郑重(colloquial and formal),具有形而上学的机智和象征主义的幻象(metaphysical wit and symbolic vision)。

他的艺术生命非常长,从19世纪80年代到20世纪30年代,整整半个世纪,创作不断。1923年,他因诗歌创作的辉煌成就获得诺贝尔文学奖。

2. 叶芝的主要作品:

a. 早期阶段(19世纪后期的几十年):主题出自凯尔特人传奇、爱尔兰民间故事以及历史英雄故事。诗歌的总体风格是意象精巧自然,氛围如梦如幻,富有韵律美感。代表作品有:

《玫瑰诗集》*The Rose* (1893)

《茵尼斯弗利岛》*The Lake Isle of Innisfree* (1893)

《梦想仙境的人》*The Man Who Dreamed of Fairyland*

《俄伊欣的漫游及其他诗歌》*The Wanderings of Oisin and Other Poems* (1889)

《芦苇中的风》*The Wind Among the Reeds* (1899)

b. 中期阶段(1900~1926):政治热情幻灭,爱情失败,艺术上受法国意象主义、美国庞德和T. S.艾略特现代主义的影响,诗歌创作逐步由传统转向现代主义。代表作品有:

《在七片树林里》In the Seven Woods (1904)

《绿头盔及其他》*The Green Helmet* (1910),其中包括:

*《没有第二个特洛伊》*No Second Troy*

《责任》*Responsibilities* (1914)

《库尔庄园的野天鹅》*The Wild Swan at Coole* (1919)

《幻象》*A Vision* (1926)

c. 晚期阶段(1926~1939):作品失去了往日的轻蔑的讥讽,思想更加幻灭,转而追求时光和艺术的永恒,尤其把一分为二(dichotomy)广泛用于主题,形成了激烈、复杂和象征主义的风格。代表作有:

《塔》*The Tower* (1928),其中包括:

*《驶向拜占庭》*Sailing to Byzantium*

*《丽达和天鹅》*Leda and the Swan*

*《在学童们中间》*Among School Children*

《旋梯及其他》*The Winding Stair* (1933)

《三月的圆月》*A Full Moon in March* (1935)

《最后的诗歌和两个剧本》*Last Poems and Two Plays* (1939)

d. 诗剧二十多部,代表作有:

《凯瑟琳伯爵夫人》*The Countess of Cathleen*

《心欲的土地》*The Land of Heart's Desire* (1894)

《布满阴影的水城》*The Shadowy Waters* (1900)

《炼狱》*Purgatory* (1935)

重要信息句子

1. Yeats' poetic achievement stands at the center of modern literature.
2. During his last stage of poetic creation, Yeats yearned to move away from the sensual world of growth and change, and to enter the timeless, eternal world of art and intellect. Yeats came to realized that eternal beauty could only live in the realm of art.

Ⅳ. 托马斯·斯特恩·艾略特 Thomas Stearns Eliot (1888~1965)

词语解释和难句分析

1. Indian mystical philosophy of Buddhism 印度神秘的佛教哲学

   to serve as the assistant editor of *The Egoist*, a magazine advocating Imagism 在一家主张意象主义的刊物《自我主义者》做助理编辑

   to appear in the first number of *The Criterion* 刊登在《标准》杂志的第一期上

   a devout member of Anglican Church 英国国教/圣公会虔诚的会员

   to busy himself with… 他忙于……

   the Nobel Prize and the Order of Merit 诺贝尔奖和功绩勋章

2. as a young man with bitter disillusionment and with boldness in handling of language 作为一个经历过幻灭痛苦、却能大胆勇敢地驾驭语言的青年

   to explore various aspects of decay of culture in the modern Western world 探讨现代西方世界文化颓败的各个方面

   to express a sense of the disintegration of life 表达生命崩溃的感觉

   be dominated by the dark horror of an earthly hell 被人间地狱的黑暗恐怖所笼罩

   to reminisce about his lost power to live and his lost hope of spiritual rebirth 缅怀/回想他逝去的活力（生活力量）和精神复苏的希望

   be heavily indebted to James Joyce in terms of the stream-of-consciousness technique 在运用意识流的技巧方面很大程度上得益于/受惠于詹姆斯·乔伊斯

   ＊ be indebted to 欠……,得益于/受惠于……,感激……

   be an advance over *Prufrock* and a prelude to *The Waste Land* 比《普鲁弗洛克》更进一步,可谓《荒原》的序曲

   to point up the continuity of Eliot's thinking 强调/保持艾略特思想的连续性

to <u>bear</u> a strong thematic <u>resemblance to</u> *The Waste Land* 主题上与《荒原》非常一致

to wait for death to <u>liberate them into</u> a kind of purgatory 等待死亡以超度自己到一种炼狱中去

3. <u>be hailed as</u> a landmark and a model of English poetry 被歌颂为现代英语诗歌的里程碑和典范

with bold innovations in versification and style 在诗体韵律和文体风格方面进行大胆革新

to present <u>a panorama of</u> physical disorder and spiritual desolation in the modern Western world 全面地展现了现代西方社会的物质错乱和精神空虚

to reflect the <u>prevalent</u> mood of disillusionment and despair of a whole post-war generation 反映了整个战后一代人盛行的幻灭和绝望的情感

4. to lose the knowledge of good and evil 失去了善恶是非的观念

to live a sterile, meaningless life 过着枯燥乏味、毫无意义的生活

to <u>connect</u> the "unreal city" <u>with</u> the city of the dead, and modern London with Dante's Hell 把"虚幻城"与死者城,现代伦敦与但丁笔下的炼狱联系起来

5. Hurry up please its time. = Hurry up its time to close. 打烊了,请离开。

6. A picture of spiritual emptiness is presented with the reproduction of a contemporary pub conversation between two cockney women. 通过再现伦敦东区的两个女人在现代酒吧里的谈话,表现了人们精神空虚的一幅画面。

7. to express a painfully elegiac feeling by <u>juxtaposing</u> the vulgarity and shallowness of the modern <u>with</u> the beauty and simplicity of the past 把现代的粗俗浅薄与过去的美丽单纯并列比较,表达沉痛的哀悼之情

an emblem of futile worries over profit and loss, youth and age 对利益得失和年轻衰老做徒劳计较的象征

8. What was once ritualistic and meaningful is now despairing and empty. 过去曾经是体面规矩和内涵丰富的东西,现在则变得令人绝望和空洞无物。

9. With the curative and baptismal power of the water images, the drowned Phoenician Sailor also recalls the rebirth of the drowned god of the fertility cults, thus giving an instance of the conquest of death. 由于水的治疗和洗礼,被淹死的腓尼基水手也想起了有膜拜丰收的神仙被溺死而复生的故事,从而例证了死亡是可以征服的。

 * the water images 化身为水的诗歌意象,水的形象

10. be <u>derived from</u> an Indian myth 源于/取材于一个印度神话

 the supreme <u>Lord of the Creation</u> 至高无上的造物主

 various elusive suggestions of hopes 各种难以捉摸的希望的暗示

 to project the possibility of regeneration 反映复活再生的希望/可能性

11. a poem concerned with the spiritual breakup of a modern civilization 一首表达现代文明精神崩溃的诗歌

 a reflection of the 20th-century people's disillusionment and frustration in a sterile and futile society 反映了身处枯燥乏味和毫无意义的荒原社会中的 20 世纪的人的幻灭和挫折情感

12. to reflect his <u>allegiance to</u> the Church of England 反映了他对英国国教的忠诚

 based on the Christian dogmas of incarnation and resurrection 在基督化身和复活这一宗教教义的基础上

 the <u>quest for</u> the immortal element, the stillness within time or history 寻求不朽的元素,寻求时间或历史中的恒定

 quite <u>in contrast to</u> the despair and suffering of the early works 与早期作品中的绝望和痛苦形成鲜明的反差/对比

13. some fragmentary pieces　一些残缺不全、未完成的作品

五部完整(无缺)的剧作

Canterbury Festival　坎特伯雷节

be concerned with the death and martyrdom of Thomas Becket　主题是关于托马斯·贝克特以身殉教的内容

＊托马斯·贝克特是坎特伯雷大教堂的大主教,因反对亨利二世控制教会而遭杀害,从而被宗教界尊崇为圣人。

to lie not in the violent killing of St. Thomas but in his inner conflict with various temptations　(剧本的焦点)不在圣托马斯被暴力杀害,而在他面对各种诱惑时的内心冲突

the temptation to accept his martyrdom for the wrong reason　因为荒唐的理由而接受诱惑,甘愿牺牲他自己

be marked by the sharp, irregularly assorted stresses, four to a line　(句中对白的)特点是重音多样,一行四重音,尖利,不规则

＊be marked by　以……为特点

to mimic the versification of *Everyman*　模仿《每个人》的诗体韵律

the most coherent drama　相互连贯的最完美的剧情

to divest of all deception and distraction　脱下伪装,摆脱干扰

to set out on a lonely journey towards union with the divine　独自踏上旅程,与神团聚

instead of the rich, highly colored language of the choruses in *Murder in the Cathedral*　《教堂里的谋杀》没有采用合唱队富丽华彩的语言

14. His three later plays are also concerned with the subject of spiritual self-discovery but in the form of a sophisticated modern social comedy.　他后期的三个剧本主题也是关于精神的自我觉醒,但形式上却是现代世俗的社会喜剧。

15. to express the ideas and actions of modern society with new accents of the contemporary speech　用当代口语的特点表达现代社会的思想行为

to express his doctrine of impersonality　表达他非个性化的主张

to remain "inert" and "neutral" towards his subject matter　(作者的思想)对创作的题材要保持"惰性"和"中立"

keeping a gulf between the man who suffers and the mind which creates　笔下描写的受苦之人与创造作品的作者之间保持一定距离/一道鸿沟

to have occupied a position of distinction　已经拥有卓越的地位

16. His wasteland derogation of the civilized world was the precise expression of the young people after the First World War.　他所描写的文明世界如荒原般败落,准确地表现了一战以后年轻人的思想状况。

17. The horror and menace, the anguish and dereliction, and the futility and sterility in his poetry has been afflicting all sensitive members of the postwar generation.　他诗歌中所表现出来的恐惧和威胁,痛苦和遗弃,徒劳和空虚都在战后一代敏感的年轻人心中引发了痛苦的情感煎熬。

18. to have himself well-established　他已功成名就

his authoritative habit of mind　他头脑里形成习惯的权威意识

to turn him to the choice of conservatism and a hierarchic society　使他转而选择保守主义和等级制社会

his conversion to Anglicanism　他转而皈依圣公会/英国国教

in favor of the divine order against the anarchic chaos　支持宗教秩序,反对无政府主义的混乱

19. Eliot came to believe that the illness of the modern world was the sum of individual souls, and that the cure could only be obtained by the change of the individual souls through the religious salvation.　艾略特逐步认识到现代社会的弊病就是(作为社会成员的)每个个体灵魂弊病的总和,社会弊病的救治只有通过宗教救赎改变每个人的灵魂才能完成。

the quest for stability, for order, and for the maintaining of the bourgeois status quo　对稳定、秩序和维护资产阶级现状的追求

T. S. 艾略特作品选读

J. A. 普鲁弗洛克的情歌 *The Love Song of J. Alfred Prufrock*

1. to present the meditation of an aging young man over the business of proposing marriage　表现了一个大龄青年对求婚问题的思考

the speaker's incapability of facing up to love and to life in sterile upper class world　讲话人不能正视爱情和空虚的上流社会的生活

be neurotic, self-important, illogical and incapable of action　神经过敏,妄自尊大,违背常理,不善于实际行动

be caught in a sense of defeated idealism and tortured by unsatisfied desires　陷入理想主义失败的挫折感,经受着愿望得不到满足的煎熬和痛苦

2. The setting of the poem resembles the "polite society" of Pope's "The Rape of the Lock," in which a tea party is a significant event and a game of cards is the only way to stave off boredom.　这首诗的背景与蒲伯《夺发记》里的"文明社会"相似,里面的一次茶会都是有意义的事件,打牌也成了排解无聊的唯一方法。

3. The poem is intensely anti-romantic with visual images of hard, gritty objects and evasive hellish atmosphere.　这首诗以坚实可感的物体的视觉形象和难以捉摸的地狱似的氛围为其特点,带有强烈的反浪漫主义色彩。

4. you and I　这首诗采用的是戏剧独白的形式,表面上的两个人"你"和"我"实际是"自我"中的一部分对另一部分的讲话。"我"代表感性肉体,"你"代表理性灵魂。"我"对"你"的诉说,是情感向理智的诉说。从普鲁弗洛克独白中的旁征博引可看出,他是一个中年知识分子,正打算向他所追求的女子求婚,但又陷入冥思苦想,犹豫不决,担心遭到拒绝,充满了苦闷和彷徨。Love song 暗示传统的人类情感;而人物名字 Prufrock 却暗示着对情感的束缚,它由 prude 和 frock 两词合成,前者暗示 prudence (谨慎);后者可能有 frock coat (男人的外套)之意,本能的情感与理性和现实的束缚隐含其中。

5. When the evening is spread out against the sky/Like a patient etherized upon a table;　夜色在天空铺开/像病人施了乙醚躺在手术台;

＊暗示普鲁弗洛克的麻木、顺从和无助。

6. Let us go, through certain half-deserted streets,/The muttering retreats/Of restless nights in one-night cheap hotels/And sawdust restaurants with oyster shells:　我们走吧,穿过行人稀少的街道,/穿过人声嗡嗡、一夜难眠的投宿处,/那只宿一夜的廉价旅店/还有满地牡蛎壳和锯木屑的小饭馆。

＊through 后面有 streets 和 retreats 两个并列宾语,in...hotels and...restaurants 是 retreats 的定语。

7. Streets that follow like a tedious argument/Of insidious intent/To lead you to an overwhelming question...　街道蛛网连结,/像居心叵测的冗长辩论,/引你向一个压倒一切的问题……

＊这个问题就是他敢不敢于听从真实情感的驱使,向自己所爱的女人求婚,敢不敢高唱情歌。

8. In the room the women come and go/Talking of Michelangelo.　屋子里的女人来来去去,/谈论着米开朗琪罗

　＊他来到了要拜访的地方,敢不敢向这些附庸风雅的女人中的自己的情人求婚呢?

9. The yellow fog that rubs its back upon the windowpanes,　黄雾在玻璃窗上蹭者脊背,

The yellow smoke that rubs its muzzle on the windowpanes,　黄烟在玻璃窗上蹭着嘴,

Licked its tongue into the corners of the evening,　舌尖舔进黄昏的各个角落,

Lingered upon the pools that stand in drains,　闲荡在阴沟的积水上,

　＊that 引导的是主语 the yellow fog/smoke 的定语从句,真正的谓语动词是 17 至 22 行中的 licked, lingered, slipped, let, made, curled。

Let fall upon its back the soot that falls from chimneys, ＝ Let the soot that... fall upon its back,任凭烟囱里的烟灰落在它的背上,

Slipped by the terrace, made a sudden leap,　它偷偷溜过阳台,突然纵身一跃,

And seeing that it was a soft October night,/Curled once about the house, and fell asleep.　发现 10 月的夜色如此柔和,在房子近旁蜷曲身子睡着了。

　＊Seeing... night 是一个现在分词短语作状语,分词短语的逻辑主语当然是主句的主语,也就是被形象化为黄猫的 the yellow fog/smoke。

　＊猫的意象反映着普鲁弗洛克的内心波澜和犹豫不决。

10. And indeed there will be time/For the yellow smoke that slides along the street,/Rubbing its back upon the windowpanes;　沿长街滑行的黄烟/的确还有时间/在窗玻璃上蹭蹭脊背;

11. There will be time to murder and create,/And time for all the works and days of hands/That lift and drop a question on your plate;　还有时间去杀戮和创造,/还有时间给双手天天劳作/把你盘中的问题拿起又放下;

12. (There will be) Time for you and time for me,/And time yet for a hundred indecisions,/And for a hundred visions and revisions,/Before the taking of a toast and tea.　你有时间,我也有时间,/还有时间做一百次的犹疑,/还可做一百次的幻想和修正,/就在取烤面包和茶水之前(＝然后再去取烤面包和茶水)。

　＊上述三条中的"还有时间"充分反映了普鲁弗洛克向女人求婚前的畏难不前、优柔寡断、自我原谅和拖拉延宕的情绪。前面用庄重的语气,给人以大事即将发生的期待,但最后出现的却是吃烤面包、饮茶之类的小事,这样的描写旨在说明主人公总在躲避触及那真正的大事。

13. And indeed there will be time/To wonder, "Do I dare?", "Do I dare?"/Time to turn back and descend the stair,/With a bald spot in the middle of my hair —　的确还有时间/问一下自己,"我可敢?""我可敢?"/(即使在上楼)还有时间转身走下楼梯,/暴露那头发中心的秃顶——

14. My morning coat, my collar mounting firmly to the chin,/My necktie rich and modest, but <u>asserted by a</u> simple pin —/(They will say: "But how his arms and legs are thin!")　我早晨的外套,硬领紧抵下巴,/我的领带贵重而不奢华,别着朴素的领针——/(他们会说:"他的胳膊腿多细!")

15. In a minute there is time/For decisions and revisions which a minute will reverse.　一分钟内还有时间做决定和修改,/一分钟后也许会完全推翻。

　＊上述三条说明了主人公内心充满了挫折感和失败情绪,一事未做,先想失败,踌躇不前。

16. I have <u>measured out</u> my life with coffee spoons;　我曾用咖啡勺慢慢量尽/消耗我的生命;

　＊与前面的两个诗行一起,表现了他所在的那个上流社会的无聊生活。

17. I know the voices dying with <u>a dying fall</u>/Beneath the music from a farther room.　随着远处房间飘来的乐声渐渐消沉,/我知道人声也在衰弱、消失。

　＊a dying fall 指音乐的逐渐消沉的音调。莎士比亚《第十二夜》中,奥西诺伯爵高叫音乐太响,后

来又注意到:"That strain again! It had a dying fall." ("又奏起这个调子来了! 它有一种渐渐消沉下去的音调。")

18. So how should I presume? 这样我又怎敢冒昧?

19. The eyes that fix you in a formulated phrase,/And when I am formulated, sprawling on a pin,/When I am pinned and wriggling on the wall, ... 那些眼睛盯着你,以公式化的词语评定你,/而我一旦被评定,就被别针固定,/我被钉在墙上,拼命挣扎……

    * 这里 the eyes 是这一节第一行"我已熟悉了这些眼睛,我全都熟悉了——"中的"眼睛"的同位语,that 引导的是其定语从句。下一诗节里的 arms that ... 也是同样的结构。

20. Then how should I begin/To spit out all the butt-ends of my days and ways? 那我又怎样开始/吐尽我生活和习惯的烟蒂?

    * 这几行诗暗示那些女人对主人公已经有了固定的看法,他用咖啡勺量尽自己的生命,自己又被女人的眼睛衡量,令他不敢造次。

21. Arms that are braceleted and white and bare/(But in the lamplight, downed with light brown hair!) (我已熟悉了它们,这些)戴着手镯的,雪白裸露的胳膊/(在灯下却显出淡褐色的绒毛!)

22. Is it perfume from a dress/That makes me so digress? 是不是衣裙上的香水味/使得我语无伦次? * digress vi. wander away 转向,背离;to digress away 偏题

23. Arms that lie along a table, or wrap about a shawl. 手臂搁在桌上,缠绕着披巾。

24. Shall I say, I have gone at dusk through narrow streets/And watched the smoke that rises from the pipes/Of lonely men in shirt-sleeves, leaning out of windows? 我是否该说,黄昏时分我穿过狭窄街道,/孤独的男人们套着衬衫探身窗外,/我看到他们的烟斗在往上冒烟?

25. I should have been a pair of ragged claws/Scuttling across the floors of silent seas. 我应是一对凹凸不平的蟹螯,/急促地爬过沉寂的海底。

    * 上述两条反映了普鲁弗洛克在爱情探求方面的优柔寡断。他由于吃不到葡萄,就觉得葡萄酸,并以此来自慰,所以他看到了已婚男人同样孤独,不是在妻子的怀里获得快慰,而是独自凭窗惆怅地抽烟。于是他觉得婚姻对他不合适,自己还是像螃蟹那样独来独往、自由爬行的好。

26. And the afternoon, the evening, sleeps so peacefully! /Smoothed by long fingers,/Asleep ... tired ... or it malingers,/Stretched on the floor, here beside you and me. 午后,夜晚,睡得多安然! /在纤长的手指安抚下,/困了…… 累了……或者装病,/躺在地板上,在你我身旁。

    * 这里的 long fingers 指薄暮时分,各种影子变长,犹如纤长的手指。you and me 即自我的灵与肉,实为一人。诗中普鲁弗洛克又羡慕上了夜晚的无忧无虑。

27. Should I, after tea and cakes and ices,/Have the strength to force the moment to its crisis? 我是否会,用过茶点和冰激凌之后,/有勇气把那事情/时刻推进到成败的关键?

28. But though I have wept and fasted, wept and prayed,/Though I have seen my head (grown slightly bald) brought in upon a platter,/I am no prophet — and here's no great matter; 虽然我已哭泣、斋戒和祈祷,/虽然我看到我的头(微秃)摆在盘里端上来,/但我不是先知——事情也并不伟大;

    * 诗里有种暗示:普鲁弗洛克试图以宗教方式去求爱,但从后面的句子看来,他并未这样做,因为他不会像先知那样为某种高尚的坚持而丢掉脑袋,自然也不会为匆促的求婚决定使自己陷入窘境。这里隐含着一个故事,根据《圣经新约·马太福音》,希律王娶了自己弟弟的妻子希罗底,遭到施洗者约翰的多次谴责,希律王一直想杀他。在希律王的生日宴会上,希罗底的女儿萨罗米跳舞娱宾,希律王大悦,答应不管她要什么都给她,她因爱情屡遭约翰的拒绝,就说要约翰的头颅,于是希律王下令斩下约翰的头,放在盘子里送给萨罗米。诗中普鲁弗洛克自比施洗者约翰,却又庆幸自己成不了一心悟道的约翰,因为他不敢执着地做一件事,不敢冒险说破自己的心事。

29. I have seen the moment of my greatness flicker,/And I have seen the eternal Footman hold my coat, and

snicker， 我曾见我的伟大时刻/表现一闪即逝,/也曾见永恒的侍者(死神)为我执衣,笑我痴愚,

* flicker 和 hold my coat, and snicker 是动词不定式或动词不定式短语作宾语补足语。

And in short, I was afraid. 一句话,当时我害怕。

* 害怕说破求婚的目的,更害怕提出求婚后可能遭到的拒绝——他实在没有干"大事"的气魄和决心。

30. And would it have been worth it, after all,/After the cups, the marmalade, the tea,/Among the porcelain, among some talk of you and me， 那到底值不值得?/在咖啡、橘子酱和茶点之后,/在精瓷玉盏之间,在你我的交谈之中,

* 前面的 it 指的是眼前的庸俗氛围,也可看作形式主语,it = to be after the cups... and to be among the porcelain, among some talk of ...;后面的 it 代表前一节诗中所说的求婚。句子用的是对过去产生怀疑的虚拟语态。第三行的 you and I 指"我"的灵与肉。

31. Would it have been worth while,/To have bitten off the matter with a smile,/To have squeezed the universe into a ball/To roll it toward some overwhelming question,/To say:"I am Lazarus, come from the dead,/Come back to tell you all, I shall tell you all" — 这是不是就值得,/微笑着解决此事,/把整个宇宙挤成一个球/让它滚向某个迫在眉睫的问题,/还要说"我是拉撒路,从死人处回来,/回来告诉你一切,我把一切都告诉你"——

* 第一行的 it 是形式主语,真正的主语是后面连续几个不定式短语。另外,关于 Lazarus 拉撒路,还有一个典故:在《圣经新约·约翰福音》和《路加福音》中各有一个拉撒路,前者死后四天,由耶稣起死回生;后者是乞丐拉撒路,死后被耶稣超度,升入天国。诗中主人公普鲁弗洛克自比拉撒路,从死亡处归来,是想说他从那个死一般空虚沉寂的上流社会圈子里摆脱出来,把一切都告诉人们,但又担心未必有好结果,会被最终否定,请看——

32. If one, settling a pillow by her head,/Should say:"That is not what I meant at all./That is not it, at all." 如果那人,她在头边放好枕头,/却要说:"那并非我意,我全无此意。"

* one 即指他所暗恋的那个女人。看此人神态动作,淡如止水,对主人公的"告诉",连一点情感微澜都没有。Would it have been worth while if one should say...?条件句是对将来的虚拟,结果句是对过去的虚拟,可认为是交叉虚拟条件句,表明主人公从对未来表白的担心,转而怀疑自己过去对那个女人的爱恋是否值得。

33. And would it have been worth it , after all,/Would it have been worth while, 这到底值不值得,/这是不是就值得, = 到底值不值得在那个社会圈子里向女人求爱?那个女人是不是真的值得爱、值得表白?

* 第二句的 it 等于前一句中第二个 it。

34. After the sunsets and the dooryards and the sprinkled streets,/After the novels, after the teacups, after the skirts that trail along the floor —/And this, and so much more? —/It is impossible to say just what I mean! 在经过落日,走过庭院和洒水的街道之后,/在读小说、饮香茶和看长裙曳地之后——/这些,还有更多? /要说清我究竟什么意思,都不可能!

35. But as if a magic lantern threw the nerves in patterns on a screen:/Would it have been worth while/If one, settling a pillow or throwing off a shawl,/And turning toward the window, should say:/"That is not it at all,/That is not what I meant, at all." 但正如魔灯把神经图投射在屏幕上:/这到底值不值得? /如果有人,她放好枕头或脱掉披肩,/背过脸去对着窗,说什么:/"那并非我意,/我全无此意。"

* 这几句的总体意思是:在频遭所爱的女人反复无常的冷遇之后,过去的暗恋究竟还值不值得?

36. No, I am not Prince Hamlet, nor was meant to be;/(I) Am an attendant lord, one that will do/To swell a progress, start a scene or two, 不,我不是哈姆雷特王子,从来就不想做;/我只是个侍从爵士,一

个弄臣，/为皇家的巡行壮壮声势，逢场作戏，

　　＊ to swell a progress 为巡行、巡游壮大声威；to start a scene or two 捧捧场，弄一两个噱头

37. (I) Advise the prince; no doubt, an easy tool,/(I am) Deferential, glad to be of use,/Politic, cautious, and meticulous;　（我）给王子出出主意；无疑是一个称手的工具，/恭敬顺从，乐于为人所用，/精明，谨慎，而且小心翼翼；

38. (I am) Full of high sentence, but a bit obtuse;/At times, indeed, almost ridiculous —/Almost, at times, the Fool.　我高论滔滔，但不免迂腐；/其实有时可笑——/有时几乎是傻瓜。

　　＊ 文中提到的哈姆雷特王子虽经过犹豫、踌躇，而终于采取行动，直至牺牲自己的生命。另外还提到两个人物，施洗者约翰和拉撒路，他们都是行动的巨人，而普鲁弗洛克自己是成不了这样的人了，不过他也死不了人，尽管胆怯庸碌，却活得比他们都长久。还有诗中提到的弄臣，是在拿自己与《哈姆雷特》中的侍臣波洛涅斯比较。

39. I grow old . . . I grow old . . ./I shall wear the bottoms of my trousers rolled.　我老了……我老了……/我得把我的裤脚卷起。

40. Shall I part my hair behind? Do I dare to eat a peach? /I shall wear white flannel trousers, and walk upon the beach. /I have heard the mermaids singing, each to each.　我要在头后分梳长发吗？我敢吃个桃子吗？/我要穿白色法兰绒裤子，在海滩上漫步。/我听到了美人鱼的歌唱，此起彼落，一一对应。

　　＊ 普鲁弗洛克担心自己年老时，是否还能在头后分梳长发，头发稀疏，怕遮不住秃顶了。也担心老胃是否还能消化得了鲜桃。这都说明他生理未老，心态已老。

41. I do not think that they will sing to me.　我想，她们不会对我歌唱。

42. I have seen them riding seaward on the waves/Combing the white hair of the waves blown back/When the wind blows the water white and black.　我看到她们乘浪向海洋而去，/风吹海水，黑白相映，/迎风顶回的波涛，被她们梳理得白发飘飘。

43. We have lingered in the chambers of the sea/By sea-girls wreathed with seaweed red and brown/Till human voices wake us, and we drown.　我们徘徊在大海的重重幽室中，/周围有仙女用红褐色海草环绕，/直到人声惊醒我们，于是我们沉溺。

　　＊ 上述两条说明主人公害怕现实世界而进入神话世界，但美人鱼也要离他而去。当人声将他从幻象中唤回现实世界，他既不能得到现实中的那个女人，又不可能有幻境中的仙女相伴，于是逃避到孤零零的自我之中，"我们沉溺"。

参考译文——姚远

J. A. 普鲁弗洛克的情歌

那么，我们走吧，你和我，

此时，夜幕正向天空铺开，

像一个被乙醚麻醉躺在手术台上的病人；

我们走吧，穿过某些行人稀少的街道，

也穿过那些人声嘈嘈、一夜难眠的投宿处——

就在只住一宿的廉价旅店，

还有满地牡蛎壳和锯木屑的小饭馆：

街道蛛联网结,像用意险恶的冗长辩论,
把你引向一个压倒一切的问题……
啊,不要问,"问题是什么?"
我们走吧,做一次访问。

房间里的女人来来去去,
谈论的主题是米开朗琪罗。

黄雾在玻璃窗上蹭着脊背,
黄烟在玻璃窗上蹭着鼻子和嘴,
它用舌尖舐进黄昏的各个角落,
在排水沟的积水上犹豫徘徊,
听任烟囱里的煤灰落在它的背上,
它悄悄溜过阳台,突然纵身一跃,
发现金秋十月的夜晚夜色如此柔和,
于是在房子近旁蜷曲身子睡着了。

沿长街滑行的黄烟
的确还有时间
用它的脊背摩擦窗玻璃;
还有时间,还有时间
准备一张脸去会见你将遇的众多脸;
还有时间去谋杀和创造,
还有时间用双手去天天工作,
在你的盘子上把一个问题拿起又放下;
你还有时间,我也还有时间,
还有时间犹豫不决一百遍,
还可做一百次的想象和修改;
然后再去取一点烤面包和茶水。

房间里的女人们来来去去,
谈论的主题是米开朗琪罗。

的确还有时间
向自己发出疑问:"我可敢?""我可敢?"
还有时间转身走下楼梯,
露出我头发中心的那个秃顶——
(她们会说:"他的头发真是愈来愈稀了!")
我早晨的外套,硬领笔挺地顶住下巴,
我的领带富贵而不扎眼,用一根朴素的别针别住——
(她们会说:"他的胳膊腿可真细啊!")
啊,我可有勇气
搅动这宇宙?

一分钟之内还有时间
做出决定和修改,一分钟后也许会完全相反。

因为我已熟悉她们的一切,熟悉一切——
熟悉了那些黄昏,早晨,和下午,
我曾用咖啡勺衡量过我的生活;
听着远处房间飘来的乐声渐渐消失,
我也熟悉了渐渐消失的人声。
因此,我该怎样冒昧?

我已熟悉了那些眼睛,熟悉了它们的一切——
这些眼睛盯着你,用公式化了的词语把你评定,
而一旦我被公式化,趴伏在别针上,
就会被别针钉住,在墙上挣扎,
那我又该怎样开始
吐出我岁月和习惯的全部烟蒂?
那我又该怎样冒昧?

我已经熟悉这些胳膊,熟悉它们的一切——
戴手镯的,雪白裸露的胳膊,
(但是在灯光下,显出一层浅褐色的茸毛!)
是不是衣裙上的香味
使得我说偏了题?
手臂搁在桌上,或与披巾缠裹在一起。
那么,我该冒昧行动了吗?
我又该怎样开始?

  *   *   *   *   *   *   *   *   *

我是否该说,我黄昏时经过狭窄的街道,
看到男人们套着衬衫,探身窗外,
寂寞的烟斗在往上冒烟?

我应是一对形状粗陋的蟹螯,
急促地爬过沉寂的海底(赶快逃离)。

  *   *   *   *   *   *   *   *   *

这午后,傍晚,睡得多么安然!
被纤长的手指安抚过,
它困了……累了……或在装病,
躺在地板上,就在这儿——在你我身边。
我可否在饮过茶、吃过糕点和冰淇淋之后,
鼓起勇气把事情推向成败的关键?
我虽曾哭泣、斋戒和祈祷,
见过我(微秃)的头被放在盘里端进来,
但我不是先知——事情也并不伟大;

我见过我伟大的时刻一闪即逝，
也见过永恒的侍者为我执衣，笑我痴愚，
一句话，我不敢。

而且那（情景）到底值不值得（表白），
在茶杯、橘子酱和茶水之后，
在精瓷细盏之间，你我交谈之际；
这是不是值得，
用微笑来解决此事，
把宇宙挤压成一个球
让它滚向某个压倒一切的问题，
而且说"我是拉撒路，从死人处来，
回来告诉你们一切，告诉你们一切"——
如果有人在她头边放好枕头，
却还说："我不是那个意思。
不是，完全不是。"

而这到底是不是值得，
是不是值得，
在经过落日，庭院和洒过水的街道之后，
在边读小说边饮茶以及见过长裙曳地之后——
这，还有更多的别的？
不可能说清我的意思！
但正像一盏幻灯把神经网络图投射到屏幕上：
这是不是值得
假如有人放好枕头或甩掉披巾，
把头转向窗边，还要说：
"那并非我意，
我全无此意。"
＊　＊　＊　＊　＊　＊　＊　＊　＊　＊
不！我不是哈姆雷特王子，也从未想过要做他；
我只是个侍从爵士，一个弄臣，
为帝王巡行逢场作戏、壮壮声威，
给王子出出主意，无疑是个称手的工具，
恭敬顺从，甘心供人驱使，
精明，谨慎，而且小心翼翼；
我总有高见，但也有点迂腐；
其实常常有点儿可笑——
有时几乎是个傻瓜。

我见老了……我见老了……
我要把我的裤脚卷起了。

我还可把头发在后面分梳吗？还敢吃个桃子吗？
我要穿白色法兰绒裤子，在海滩上漫步。
我已听到美人鱼唱歌，互相呼应。

我想她们不会是对我歌唱。

我看见她们乘浪逐波向大海而去，
风吹海水，黑白相映，
她们把迎风的浪涛梳理得白发飘飞。

我们徘徊在大海的重重幽室，
周围有仙女们用红褐色海草环绕，
直到人声惊醒我们，于是我们沉溺。

＊ 这首诗属自由体诗，没有严格的格律和韵律。

主要内容归纳和总结

1. T. S. 艾略特出生在美国密苏里州的圣路易，先就读于家乡的史密斯学院，后在哈佛大学研读哲学和逻辑学，再后来在法国、德国和英国的牛津大学学习文学和哲学，对法国的象征主义诗歌尤其感兴趣。他 1915 年定居伦敦并结婚，1927 年加入英国籍，成为虔诚的英国国教信徒。1915 年他开始文学创作，并先后担任文学杂志《自我主义者》(The Egoist) 和《标准》(The Criterion) 的编辑和主编，他的名作《荒原》(The Waste Land) 就发表在《标准》创刊号上，他在 1948 年获得诺贝尔文学奖和功绩勋章 (the Order of Merit)。

他一生的世界观和政治观经历了巨大变化。他年轻时激进、悲愤，对各种社会问题进行尖锐讽刺，富有探索精神。他的《荒原》准确表达了一战之后青年一代恐怖、空虚和痛苦的思想情感。功成名就之后，他对社会主义的恐惧使他变成保守主义者，拥护等级制度，认为现代社会的弊病是每个社会成员灵魂深处弊病的总和，只有通过宗教救赎每个人的灵魂，才能救治整个社会。因此，他后期作品十分关注维持资本主义社会的现状。

在创作观念上，他主张"作品应保持非个性化"(his doctrine of impersonality)，诗人的头脑对创作题材应是惰性的 (inert)、中立的 (neutral)，诗人与他塑造的人之间应保持一条鸿沟。

2. T. S. 艾略特的主要作品：
a. 诗歌创作作可分两个阶段
第一阶段：1915～1925
《普鲁弗洛克与其他情况》Prufrock and Other Observations (1917)
《荒原》The Waste Land (1922)
《衰老》Gerontion
《空洞的人》The Hollow Man
《1915～1925 诗歌总结》Poems 1915～1925 (1925)
第二阶段：1927 年以后，主要有两部诗集
《星期三的烟灰》Ash Wednesday (1930)
《四个四重奏》Four Quartets (1944) 1948 年获诺贝尔文学奖

b. 5 部剧作

《教堂里的谋杀》*Murder in the Cathedral*（1935）

《家人团圆》*The Family Reunion*（1939）

《鸡尾酒会》*The Cocktail Party*（1950）

《机要人员》*The Confidential Clerk*（1954）

《年长的政客》*The Elder Statesman*（1959）

c. 散文

《传统与个人天才》*Tradition and Individual Talent* 最为著名,强调继承传统的重要性,主张非个性化,对于主题诗人的思想应当保持"惰性"（inert）和"中性"（neutral）。

重要信息句子

1. *Murder in the Cathedral* is the best of his plays in the sense that it contains the best poetry and the most coherent drama.

2. *The Waste Land*, Eliot's most important single poem, has been hailed as a landmark and a model of the 20th-century English poetry, comparable to Wordsworth's *Lyrical Ballads*.

3. *Four Quartets* is characterized by a philosophical and emotional calm quite in contrast to the despair and suffering of the early works, for which T. S. Eliot won the Nobel Prize in 1948.

V. 戴维·赫伯特·劳伦斯 David Herbert Lawrence（1885~1930）

词语解释和难句分析

1. to have married beneath her　嫁给地位、文化等某一个方面低于自己的人,下嫁

the conflict between the earthy, coarse, energetic but often drunken father and the refined, strong-willed and up-climbing mother　土气、粗鲁、精力旺盛然而经常喝醉酒的父亲与优雅、意志坚强和奋发向上的母亲之间的冲突

a talented young man, acutely observant of nature and delighting in story　一个敏锐观察大自然和乐于看小说的天才青年

the lack of warmth between people　人际关系缺少温情/冷漠

2. to have a deep and loving understanding of each other　具有深入周到、充满深情的相互理解

the utter foreignness between them　他们之间存在的完全的异国文化差别

to have physical passion for each other　相互的肉体吸引/情欲冲动

be fraught with conflicts　充满了/伴随着矛盾冲突

to fail to achieve the final fulfillment of the older generation　没有达到老一代(婚姻)的最后圆满

to carry the story on into the third generation　将故事继续进行下去直到第三代

to trace Ursula's life from childhood through adolescence up to adulthood　追寻着娥苏拉的人生轨迹,从童年、青少年直到成年

3. At the end of the novel, Ursula is left with much experience behind her, but still "uncreated" in face of the unknown future.　小说结尾,娥苏拉已经人生经历丰富,但面对未知的前途,依然是旧日模样,一片迷茫。

4. In Lawrence's opinion, the mechanical civilization is responsible for the unhealthy development of human personalities, the perversion of love and the failure of human fulfillment in marital relationships.　按劳伦斯的观点,机械文明乃人类个性病态发展、爱情扭曲变态和婚姻关系不得圆满的罪魁祸首。

5. In reading the novel, the reader often feels the threatening shadows of the disintegration and destructiveness of the whole civilized world which loom behind the emotional conflicts and psychological tensions of the characters.　读者在读这小说的时候,常常感觉到在人的情感冲突和心理压力背后隐现着整个文明世界瓦解和毁灭的可怕阴影。

　　＊ which 是关系代词,指代前面的 the disintegration and destructiveness,引导一个定语从句。

6. to strike an immediate kinship with each other　立刻相互吸引/擦出火花,一见钟情

　　be attracted by Gerald's physical energy　为杰拉德的体态健美、活力四射所吸引

7. The rest of the novel is a working out of the relationships of these four through interrelating events and conflicts of personalities.　另外,小说还通过相互关联的事件和人物的个性冲突展现了这四个人的关系。

8. ups and downs　坎坷浮沉

　　to reach a fruitful relationship by maintaining their integrity and independence as individuals　他们保持了作为个人的完整性(尊严)和独立性,关系达到了成熟的阶段

　　the passionate love between A and B　A 和 B 之间的情欲之恋/肉体吸引之爱

　　to experience a process of tension and deterioration　经历关系紧张、情感蜕变的过程

　　an efficient but ruthless coalmine owner　一个讲究高效但冷酷无情的煤矿主

　　to establish the inhuman mechanical system in his mining kingdom　在他的矿业王国里建立无人性的机械化管理体系

　　representing the whole set of bourgeois ethics　代表整个的资产阶级伦理学

　　a self-portrait of Lawrence　劳伦斯的自画像

　　to fight against the cramping pressures of mechanized industrialism and the domination of any kind of dead formulas　反对工业机械化(机械化的产业主义)带来的束缚和压力,以及各种形式的僵死教条的主宰和支配

　　be presented as a symbolic figure of human warmth, standing for the spontaneous Life Force　成为人类温情的象征性人物,代表着自发的生命力(冲动)

9. *Women in Love* is a remarkable novel in which the individual consciousness is subtly revealed and strands of themes are intricately wound up.　《恋爱中的女人》是一部出色的小说,它细致入微地揭示了个人的内心意识,事关主题的条条线索盘根错节地缠绕/糅合在一起。

10. the subordinate masculine relationship between Birkin and Gerald　附带的勃金与杰拉德两个男人之间的关系

　　be corresponding to and contrasting with the other　与另一个形成对应和比较

　　be regarded to be a more profoundly ordered novel than any other written by Lawrence　被认为是劳伦斯最有条理的小说

　　to deal more extensively with themes of power, dominance, and leadership　更广泛地涉足有关权力、主宰和领导的写作主题

　　to give symbolic fictional form to his preoccupation with the concept of "blood consciousness," a mythical religion of instinct　通过象征主义的虚构形式(小说手法)表现了他为之着迷的"血液固

有意识"的概念——一种崇拜天性本能的神秘宗教

to desert her half-man, half-machine husband 遗弃了她的半人半机器的丈夫

to condemn the civilized world of mechanism that distorts all natural relationships between men and women 谴责/抨击扭曲男女天性的机械文明社会

11. to turn his eyes outward to human society 他目光转向外面的人类社会

a proficient poet 一个技巧熟练的诗人

to <u>fall</u> roughly <u>into</u> three categories 概略地分成三类

not care much about the conventional <u>metrical rules</u> 不十分关注传统的格律规则

to catch the instant life of the immediate present 捕捉眼前生活的瞬间展现

to reveal the sheer unknowable otherness of the non-human life 揭示那种完全不可能知晓的非人类的另类生活

to try to find emotional fulfillment in her children 企图在她的孩子身上找到情感的满足/成就感,望子成龙

<u>in times of</u> crisis in their married life 在他们的婚姻经历危机的时刻

be presented with a higher degree of objectivity and detachment than the novels by Lawrence 比起劳伦斯的小说来,(他的剧本)表现出更高的客观性和不偏不倚的公正

to express a strong reaction against the mechanical civilization 表达了对机械文明的强烈反对

be brought up in hardship 在艰难困苦中长大

12. From his early time, Lawrence underwent a social dislocation which made him sensitive to the deadness of bourgeois civilization that caused the distortion of personality, the corruption of the will, and the dominance of sterile intellect over the authentic inward passions of man. 劳伦斯早年经历了("一战"时的)社会动荡,使他敏锐地感觉到造成人类个性扭曲的资产阶级文明的即将死亡,意志的腐化,以及空洞无聊的学问对真正的人类内心情感的威压。

13. <u>at the cost of</u> ravishing the land 以掠夺土地为代价

to start the catastrophic uprooting of man from nature 灾难性地使人类彻底脱离大自然

frenziedly worship the filthy materialism 狂热崇拜肮脏的物质主义/拜金主义

to make use of the <u>mechanisms of matter</u> to <u>inflict</u> their exploitative will <u>on</u> the workman, the society and the earth 利用物质的机械把他们的剥削意志强加给工人、社会和地球

be turned into inanimate matter 被转变为无生命的物质

be animated to destroy both man and earth 被赋予生命/被驱动去毁灭人类和大地

14. It is this agonized concern about the dehumanizing effect of mechanical civilization on the sensual tenderness of human nature that haunts Lawrence's writing. 机械文明对感官上的人类温情产生了灭绝人性的影响,而萦绕劳伦斯作品的正是对这种影响的极度痛苦的关切。

15. to introduce themes of psychology into his works 在他的著作中引进了心理学

to lie in the primacy of the life impulse, or in another term, the sexual impulse 就在于初始阶段的生命冲动,或者换句话说,即性冲动

to open up a wide new territory to the novel 为小说创作开辟了一方新土

16. But the writer's dilemma is that although those intimate feelings of love can be passionately experienced by individuals they can <u>hardly</u> articulate precisely in words <u>without</u> offending the authorities and middle-class readers who are narrow and bigoted in conventional moral ideas. 但是,作家的尴尬在于:虽然人们可以体验性爱的激情,但他们却几乎不能用文字精确地表达出来而不冒犯那些具有狭隘、偏执的传统道德观的所谓权威以及中产阶级读者/虽然人们可亲历性爱的激情,但他们一旦用文字生动地表达出来,就必定会招致那些具有狭隘偏执的传统道德观念的权威和中产阶级读者的

抨击。

17. to break the taboo　打破禁忌

to make deliberate use of those "four-letter" words　故意使用那些"四字母"的单词

any repression of the sexual impulse　对性冲动的任何压抑

to cause severe damages to the harmony of human relationships and the psychic health of the individual's personality　对人际关系的和谐和人的个性健康产生了严重的破坏

be accused of pornographic writer　被指控为淫秽作家

to combine dramatic scenes with an authoritative commentary　把戏剧场景与权威评论结合起来

be obviously seen in its detailed portraiture　在其细节描写中可明显地看出

to summon up all the physical attributes associated with the common daily objects　把一切生理属性与日常的普通物体联系起来

＊summon up　调动起,鼓起,摆出,浮现出,使得……显示出……

18. By using sets of natural images as poetic symbols to embody the emotional states of the characters and to illustrate human situations, Lawrence endows the traditional realism with a fresh psychological meaning.　把一系列的自然意象用作诗歌意象来体现人物的情感状态,说明人的处境,劳伦斯在传统的现实主义之中加入了新鲜的心理活动的内涵(描写)。

＊endow...with...　赋予……以……的内容

19. the innovating elements of symbolism and poetic imagination　改革中的象征主义元素和诗歌意象

to bring out the subtle ebb and flow of his character's subconscious life　展示他的人物内心潜在意识的微妙的跌宕起伏

＊bring out　显示,展示,激起,引起

to marry beneath her own class　下嫁给阶级地位低于自己的人

to estrange them from each other　使他们彼此疏远

to make her lavish all the affections upon her sons　使得她把全部的爱/感情都倾注到儿子身上

to come under the strong influence of the mother in affections, aspirations and mental habits　受到他母亲在情感、追求和心理习惯方面的强烈影响

to feel his exclusion　感到自己被排斥

20. Paul's psychological development is traced with great subtlety, especially his emotional conflicts in the course of his early love affairs with Miriam and Clara.　保罗的心理发展是觅迹寻踪、细致入微的,尤其是循着他早期与米莉安和克拉拉的情感纠葛展开的。

21. to make sense of the world around him　理解/认识他周围的世界

be incapable of escaping the overpowering emotional bond imposed by his mother's love　他无法逃脱母爱所施加给他的强大的情感束缚/枷锁

to end with Paul's rejection of despair and his determination to face the unknown future　(小说)结束的时候,保罗摆脱了绝望的情绪,决心面对未知的将来。

D. H. 劳伦斯作品选读

《儿子与情人》Sons and Lovers 第十章节选

词语解释和难句分析

1. to send in a landscape to the winter exhibition　给冬季画展送去一幅风景画

be washing in the scullery　正在炊具间洗碗碟

to fly to him, fling her arms round him for a moment　冲向他,张开双臂一下子抱住了他,半天不松手

suddenly bursting out in such frenzy　突然爆发,像疯了似的

tipped cap　尖顶帽

2. My word, that's something like!　哎呀,那真是太妙了! /我知道,早该这样了!

3. Paul was afraid lest she might have misread the letter, and might be disappointed after all.　保罗很担心,生怕她把信看错了,最后空欢喜一场。

4. to take the kettle off the fire and mash the tea　从火炉上取下壶,再弄碎茶

to recover her composure, apparently at least　她恢复了镇静,至少表面上是如此。

with his shirt turned back　他衬衫敞开

his hair sticking up wet　他的头发湿漉漉的,向上支棱着

5. That's just what you wanted to buy Arthur out.　这就够你赎出亚瑟了/这笔钱足够你为亚瑟担保了。

6. They caviled about sharing the twenty guineas.　如何分这20金币,他们争论了起来。

7. So they got over the stress of emotion by quarreling.　于是他们以争论克服了感情的过度兴奋。

8. I said I wor sure it wor a lie. But they said tha'd told Fred Hodgkisson.　我说这一定不是真的。但他们说是你告诉弗莱德·霍德金森的。

＊此句应为:I said I was sure it was a lie. But they said that you'd told Fred Hodgkisson.　矿工莫瑞尔句法、读音都不规范,这里有所显示。

9. "Has he, beguy!" he exclaimed. ＝"Has he got the first prize? Really wonderful (a good guy)!"　"得了一等奖? 好家伙(真棒)!"他喊了起来。

"Twenty guineas! Tha niver says (＝You've never said that)!" exclaimed Morel.　"20金币! 你从来没说过!"莫瑞尔吃了一惊。

＊不符合语法的话语旨在反衬莫瑞尔先生受教育程度不高。

10. I don't misdoubt it. But twenty guineas for a bit of a painting as he knocked off in an hour or two!　我不怀疑这点。但一两个小时就画完的一点小画,就能值20个金币!

11. He was silent with conceit of his son.　他沉默了,为儿子而骄傲。

12. His black arm, with the hand all gnarled with work, lay on the table.　他的黑手臂搁在桌上,只见他的手因长期劳作而扭曲,暴起许多节瘤。

13. to rub the back of his hand across his eyes　他用手背擦眼睛

the smear in the coal-dust on his black face　他黑脸上的煤灰污迹

14. "Yes, an' that other lad'ud 'a done as much if they hadna ha' killed'im," he said quietly. ＝"Yes, and that other lad (William) would have done as well if they hadn't killed him (if he were still alive)," he said quietly.　"是呀,那个小子(威廉)要是还活着,也一定会干得很出色。"他轻轻地说。

15. The thought of William went through Mrs. Morel like a cold blade.　一想到威廉,莫瑞尔夫人就感到像被刀子捅了一下似的,透心儿凉。

16. to smooth her hand over his shoulder/the silk collar　她用手抹抹他的肩/整整丝绸衣领

17. She passed her hand down his back to feel him.　她的手由上向下慢慢滑过他的背,抚摸着他。

18. be firm with pride and joy　肯定充满了自豪和快乐

(sb.) be started now　现在出人头地,崭露头角

shirt-front　衬衫的(硬)前胸/前襟,胸衣

dress shirt　配礼服穿的或上班系领带穿的白衬衫

elegant figure　优雅的体形

(sb.) looks likes quite a man　一副十足的男子气概/的确一表人才

19. He told her everything that took place, everything that was said.　他把发生的每一件事、说的每一句话都告诉了她。

20. be dying to introduce her to these new friends　极想/急于把她介绍给这些新朋友

　　to begin to spare her hands　开始怜惜她的双手

　　be work-gnarled　因过多劳作而变形

　　be shiny with so much hot water　因常泡在热水里而(皮肤)发亮

　　be careful to keep them out of soda　小心别让自己的手接触苏打水

　　to have more stylish blouses to suit her age　穿适合自己年龄的更时髦的衬衫

　　to go so far as to allow a black velvet bow to be placed on her hair　跑很远的路,买到一个黑天鹅绒发卡卡在自己的头发上

21. Then she sniffed in her sarcastic manner, and was sure she looked a sight.　她仍是一副讽刺别人的态度,傲气逼人,自信自己还引人注目。

22. The family was coming on. Only Morel remained unchanged, or rather, lapsed slowly.　整个家庭都在兴盛红火起来,唯有莫瑞尔一成不变,而且,还慢慢地越来越不起作用了。

23. be fading into the background　退居次要地位

24. He had shoveled away all the beliefs that would hamper him, had cleared the ground, and come more or less to the bedrock of belief that one should feel inside oneself for right and wrong, and should have the patience to gradually realize one's God.　他已经铲除了会妨碍他的一切信仰,扫清了道路,多少达到了基本的信仰准则,那就是一个人内心应当能辨别是非,应当有耐心逐渐认识自己的上帝。

25. the well-to-do middle class　富裕的中产阶级

　　in a tear　着急,难过

26. But in myself I am (equal to them).　但在我心中,我与他们(贵族)是平等的。

27. Only from the middle classes one gets ideas, and from the common people — (one gets) life itself, warmth. You feel their hates and loves.　只有从中产阶级那里,你才能获得思想,而从普通老百姓那里,你能得到生活本身和温暖。你能感受到他们的爱憎。

28. be snobbish about class　对阶级抱势利的态度

　　to combat him in his restless fretting　与一直六神无主、满心烦恼的他进行斗争

29. He still kept up his connection with Miriam, could neither break free nor go the whole length of engagement. 他依然与米莉安藕断丝连,既不能彻底摆脱,也不能下决心与她订婚。

30. And this indecision seemed to bleed him of his energy.　这种犹豫不决使得他筋疲力尽/耗尽了他的精力。

31. to suspect him of an unrecognized leaning towards Clara　怀疑他无意中倾心于克拉拉

　　to fall in love with one of the girls in a better station of life　爱上一个生活比较优越的女孩儿

　　be his social superior　社会地位优于他

　　to break away from old things　与旧东西决裂

　　to take the life in your own hands　把生活掌握在自己手中

32. and you began to think of settling your life — when you have the means — so that you could work without all this fretting　一旦你有了谋生的手段,你就开始考虑成家过日子,使自己不必带着许多烦恼工作。

33. to catch him on the raw of his wound of Miriam　触到他和米莉安(关系)伤口的痛处

　　to push the tumbled hair off his forehead　捋开额上蓬乱的头发

　　a woman's doctrine for life — ease of soul and physical comfort　一个女人的生活信条——灵魂安逸

和身体舒适

to call yours (= your doctrine of life) a divine discomfort　认为你的生活信条是天赐神授的不满足(吗?)

34. You never give it (= the happiness) a chance, but it does matter!　你从来就不给这幸福一个机会/你从来就不肯试试(这幸福),但它确实和重要!

35. Then suddenly all her passion of grief over him broke out.　突然,她为他牵肠挂肚/发愁烦恼的一切情感猛地爆发了出来。

36. And you ought to be happy, you ought to try to be happy, to live to be happy. How could I bear to think your life wouldn't be a happy one!　你应当幸福,你应当争取幸福,为幸福而活着。想到你的生活会不幸福,我又怎么受得了?

37. Your own's been (= Your own life has been) bad enough, mater, but it hasn't left you so much worse off than the folk who've been happier.　你的生活已经够糟糕的了,妈妈,但这并没使你比那些比较幸福的人差多少。

38. Struggles of this kind often took place between her and her son, when she seemed to fight for his very life against his own will to die.　当她似乎是在力图保全他这条性命而竭力打消他但求一死的念头(而搏斗)时,母子之间发生这样的争执是经常的。

39. So long as you don't feel life's (= life is) paltry and a miserable business, the rest doesn't matter, happiness or unhappiness.　只要你不认为人生是微不足道的悲惨事,其余的都不重要,幸福不幸福都另当别论。

40. say rather (= It would rather say) you want me to live　还不如说是你想要我活下去

41. to feel as if her heart would break for him　感到她的心为他操碎了

at this rate = if this state continues　如果这种情况继续下去

to have that poignant carelessness about himself, his own suffering, his own life　对他自己,自己的痛苦,自己的生命抱着那种令人痛心的满不在乎的态度

a form of slow suicide　一种变相的慢性自杀

to hate Miriam for having in this subtle way undermined his joy　憎恨米莉安这样不动声色地损毁了他的快乐

42. It did not matter to her that Miriam could not help it. Miriam did it, and she hated her.　米莉安并未故意损毁保罗的快乐,但这对莫瑞尔夫人无关紧要。反正米莉安起到了这个作用,所以她恨她。

＊句中第一个 it 是形式主语,代表 that 引导的真正主语(从句),后面的两个 it 都代表前面句子中的 undermine his joy,意为"逐渐地毁了保罗的快乐"。

主要内容归纳和总结

1. D. H. 劳伦斯出生在英国诺丁汉郡(Nottinghamshire)一个矿工家庭。父亲为文化很低的煤矿工人,母亲曾是教师,出身于中产阶级,算是"下嫁"了劳动人民。她望子成龙,把全部希望都寄托在子女的身上。粗俗的父亲和高雅的母亲之间的冲突,经常在他后来的小说和剧本中成为主题。

　　劳伦斯是 20 世纪最伟大的英语小说家之一。漫长的创作生涯使他完成了二十多部长篇小说,3 部戏剧,大量诗歌和一些短篇小说。他在作品中表达了对机器文明的深恶痛绝,揭示了资产阶级文明对人性的扭曲和摧残,人类关系的冷漠和疏远,劳动人民生活的艰辛和资产阶级的腐败。

　　他将心理分析引入创作,认为人类心理的健康(psychic health)主要在于生命的第一冲动,即性冲动(sexual impulse),性行为是生命活力的体现,社会或宗教对性冲动的压抑会导致人际关系和谐的破坏和人性的变态。因此,他的许多作品都直白地谈到性,他甚至被说成是黄色作家

(pornographic writer)。在艺术手法上,他常把传统的现实主义与诗化联想和象征主义(poetic imagination and symbolism)结合在一起,表现角色潜意识的跌宕起伏(the subtle ebb and flow of his characters' subconscious life)。

2. D. H. 劳伦斯的主要作品,带 * 的为其代表作:

a. 小说

《白孔雀》*The White Peacock*(1911)

《过客》或《逾矩的人》*The Trespasser*(1912)

*《虹》*The Rainbow*(1915)

*《恋爱中的女人》*Women in Love*(1920)

*《儿子与情人》*Sons and Lovers*(1913)

《亚伦神杖》*Aaron's Rod*(1922)

《袋鼠》*Kangaroo*(1923)

《带羽毛的蛇》*The Plumed Sergeant*(1926)

《查泰莱夫人的情人》*Lady Chatterley's Lover*(1928)

以下为短篇小说:

《圣摩尔》*St. Mawr*

《主角的女儿》*The Daughter of the Vicar*

《贩马的人》*The Horse Dealer's Daughter*

《船长的娃娃》*The Captain's Doll*

《普鲁士军官》*The Prussian Officer*

《贞女和吉普赛人》*The Virgin and the Gypsy*

b. 剧作三部曲

《矿工的周五夜晚》*A Collier's Friday Night*(1909)

《儿媳》*The Daughter in Law*(1912)

《守寡的霍尔罗伊夫人》*The Widowing Mrs. Holroyed*(1914)

c. 诗作,分为三类:

讽刺与幽默类的诗(satirical and comic poems);

关于人际关系与人类感情的诗(poems about human relationships and emotions);

关于大自然的诗(poems about nature)。

重要信息句子

1. Lawrence was recognized as a prominent novelist only after he published his third novel, *Sons and Lovers*.

2. *The Rainbow* (1915) and *Women in Love* (1920), are generally regarded as his masterpieces.

3. Lawrence was one of the first novelists to introduce themes of psychology into his works. He believed that the healthy way of the individual's psychological development lay in the primacy of the life impulse, or in another term, the sexual impulse. 劳伦斯是第一批把心理学主题引入创作的作家之一。他认为健康的个人心理发展方式在于初始阶段的生命冲动,或者换句话说,就是性欲冲动。

4. Lawrence's artistic tendency is mainly realism, which combines dramatic scenes with an authoritative commentary.

VI. 詹姆斯·乔伊斯 James Joyce（1882～1941）

词语解释和难句分析

1. to pass through a phase of religious enthusiasm　经历了宗教热情阶段

   to start a rebellion against the narrowness and bigotry of the bourgeois philistines in Dublin　开始叛逆都柏林盛行的资产阶级平庸之辈的狭隘和偏见

   to take the literary mission as his career　把文学创作作为他的职业选择／谋生手段

   except a few brief trips back to Ireland　除了几次回爱尔兰的简短旅程之外

   to regard exile as the only way to preserve his integrity and to enable him to recreate the life in Dublin truthfully, ...　（他）认为旅居国外是他保持诚实、能够在作品中忠实再现都柏林生活的唯一途径

2. be the first important work of Joyce's lifelong preoccupation with Dublin life　……是他毕生专注于都柏林生活的第一部重要著作

   to represent the entire course of moral deterioration in Dublin　表现了都柏林道德沦落的全过程

   to present death as an inscrutable fact in a small boy's existence　把死亡表现为小男孩的鲜活人生所不可理解的事情

   to end with a vision in which death is seen　（故事）以看见死亡的幻象作为结尾

   to evoke the national spirit of the Irish people　激发起／唤起爱尔兰人民的民族精神

   Joyce's theory of epiphany in fiction　乔伊斯小说中的突然顿悟理论

3. Each (story) is concerned with a sudden revelation of truth about life inspired by a seemingly trivial incident.　每一个故事都涉及对生活真谛的突然启示，而这都是由看似不起眼的小事引起的。

4. naturalistic account of the hero's bitter experiences and his artistic and spiritual liberation　对人物的痛苦经历以及他艺术和精神上的解放进行了自然主义的描写

   to become conscious of the oppressive pressure from the moral, political and spiritual environment　觉悟到来自道德、政治和精神环境的沉重／令人窒息的压力

   to rebel against　反对，反叛

   to turn to seek sensual pleasure as an outlet　转而寻找感官上的快乐作为一种发泄

   be tormented with his sense of moral sin and frightened by the terrors of the Last Judgment　受到道德上罪孽感的折磨，被最后审判的恐怖所吓倒

   the restless agony from his mind　思想上无休止的痛苦

   to devote himself to religion　献身于宗教

   be repelled by the chilly church life　为清苦的教会生活所排斥，受不了冷清的教会生活

   to reject the call to the priesthood　拒绝了让他做神职人员／牧师的要求

   artistic vocation　艺术行业／职业

   to cast off all those that try to tie him down　抛弃所有那些企图束缚他、牵制他的羁绊

5. (whether) be termed as a "novel" at all　究竟还能否称作为"小说"

   to lack almost all the essential qualities of the novel in a traditional sense　传统意义上小说的基本元素几乎全都没有

   (there is) little characterization in the usual sense　很少传统意义上的人物塑造

to give an account of man's life during one day in Dublin　描述了一个人在都柏林一天的生活

be divided into 18 episodes in correspondence with the 18 hours of the day　对应于一天 18 个小时,(小说)分成 18 个片段

to walk along the strand to town with random thoughts in mind　沿着海岸信步向城里走去,任大脑随意地胡思乱想

to go about Dublin on his day's routine activities　在都柏林市里随意漫步,照常进行每天的日常活动

to call in at the National Library　拜访了国家图书馆

to show up at the newspaper office where he sells advertising　在一家报社露面拍卖广告

to pursue persistently his own ruminations over his past　不停地追忆着过去

to cock an alert ear for what is going on around him　竖起警惕的耳朵注意着周围发生的情况

to roam along a beach at twilight　黄昏时沿着海滨漫步

to visit a maternity hospital to inquire about the birth of a friend's baby　去一家妇幼医院看望一个生孩子的朋友/询问一个朋友生孩子的情况

to propound his theory on Shakespeare's *Hamlet*　提出有关莎翁《哈姆雷特》的理论

to visit a brothel in the "Nighttown"　到"不夜城"/红灯区去逛妓院

be rescued in a drunken affray by Bloom　在醉酒闹市中被布鲁姆所救

be musing in a half-awake state over her past experiences as a woman　半梦半醒状态下,沉思着她过去作为女人的经历

the natural flow of mental reflections　思想意识的自然流动

the shifting moods and impulses in the characters' inner world　人物内心世界情绪和思想冲动的变化转移

be richly presented in an unprecedentedly frank and penetrating way　表达空前坦率,穿透力极强

6. to present a microcosm of the whole human life　展示了一幅整个人类生活的缩影图

be recapitulated in the happenings of one day　被概括/浓缩在一天所发生的事情中

to illustrate a symbolic picture of all human history　描绘一幅整个人类历史的象征性的图画

be portrayed as vulgar and trivial creatures with splitting personalities, disillusioned ideals, sordid minds and broken families　被描写为人格分裂、理想幻灭、思想肮脏、家庭破碎的平庸猥琐的人物/生灵

to search in vain for harmonious human relationships and spiritual sustenance in a decaying world　徒劳无益地在一个腐朽颓败的社会里寻找人类的和谐和精神的富有

7. to ambitiously attempted to pack the whole history of mankind into one night's dream　雄心勃勃地想把整个人类历史纳入一夜酣梦

no self-conscious logic, no orderly associations, no established values, no limits of time or space　没有自我意识的逻辑,没有有序的联系,没有既定的价值观,没有时间或空间的界限

be regarded as the most original experiment ever made in the novel form　被认为是小说形式上(曾经做过的)最富创意的试验

8. prominent literary figure　卓越的文学家

great artistic genius　伟大的艺术天才

to have created a body of work worthy of comparison with the other masterpieces of English literature　已经创作出一批堪与其他英语文学杰作媲美的作品

to gain the insight necessary for the creation of dramatic art　获得戏剧艺术创作所必需的洞察力

to rise to the position of a godlike objectivity　升华至上帝一般超然物外的客观地位

to depersonalize his own emotion in the artistic creation　在艺术创作中不受个人情感的影响

to appear as an omniscient author　以洞察一切的作者身份出现

to present unspoken materials directly from the psyche of the characters　表现出直接发自人物心灵的、没有用语言表达的心理活动

to <u>concentrate on</u> revealing the <u>psychic being</u> of the characters　笔墨着力于揭示人物的内心活动

9. But when he tries to render the so-called stream of consciousness, the style changes：incomplete, rapid, broken wording and fragmentary sentences are the typical features, which reflect the shifting, flirting, disorderly flow of thoughts in the major characters mind.　但是，当他采用所谓的意识流时，文体风格就会发生突变，其典型特点是叙述不完整，语气急促，措辞用句支离破碎，反映了主人公内心的游移、飘忽和思想混乱无序的流动。

10. mock-heroic style　讽刺英雄体的文风

to <u>elaborate</u> his style <u>into</u> parody, pastiche, symbolic fantasy, and narration by question and answer from an omniscient narrator　把他自己的文体精心地表现为拙劣的模仿、胡乱拼凑、象征性的幻想，以及无所不知的旁白/叙述者自问自答的讲述

a great master of innovation　一位创新大师

to <u>range from</u> "stream of consciousness" <u>to</u> his fantastic engagement with rhetoric, sentimental romance, historical stylistics, counterpoint and expressionist drama　（他激进的改革试验）范围很广，从"意识流"到涉及修辞、感伤主义浪漫传奇、历史文体学、对位法和印象主义戏剧的种种奇思怪想的综合运用

詹姆斯·乔伊斯作品选读

《都柏林人》中的"阿拉比" "Araby" from *Dubliners*

词语解释和难句分析

1. This tale of the frustrated <u>quest for</u> beauty in the midst of drabness is both meticulously realistic in its handling of details of Dublin life and the Dublin scene and highly symbolic in that almost every image and incident suggests some particular aspect of the theme.　这个在单调乏味的环境中追求美却招致失败的故事，既有细致入微的现实主义，又有高度概括的象征主义，现实主义在于它描绘了都柏林的生活细节和景象，象征主义在于它几乎每一个意象和事件都暗示着主题的某个特定方面。

2. to <u>draw on</u> his own childhood recollections　动用/利用他自己孩提时代的记忆

a reminiscence of Joyce's father　乔伊斯对父亲的往事回忆

a symbol of that isolation and lack of proper relation between "consubstantial" ("in the flesh") parents and children　象征着父母与子女这种固有的骨肉亲情关系的分离和缺失

3. (street) being blind　（街道）一端不通/没有出口

to set the boys free　让孩子们放学

uninhabited house of two storeys　无人居住的两层楼

to stand at the blind end　（房子）立在街道不通的一端

to <u>detach from</u> its neighbours in a square ground　与一片空地上的邻居分开着

(be) conscious of decent lives within them (= the houses)　有关起门来规规矩矩/正正经经过日子的意识

to <u>gaze at</u> one another with brown inperturbable faces　相互注视的神色倦怠而冷漠

4. to die in the back <u>drawing-room</u>　死在后面的起居室里

musty from having been long enclosed　因长时间关闭而发出霉味

the waste room behind the kitchen　厨房后弃置的房间

be littered with old useless papers　废旧/书本/纸张/报纸到处乱扔

a few paper-covered books　几本简装书

the wild garden behind the house　房子后面的野花园/荒凉花园

straggling bushes　四处蔓生的灌木丛

the late tenant's rusty bicycle-pump　已故房客生锈的自行车打气筒

charitable priest　慈爱的神父

to leave all his money to institutions and the furniture of his house to his sister　把他所有的钱都留给了慈善机构,房子里的家具留给他姐姐

5. to have grown somber　已渐入昏暗

the colour of ever-changing violet　变幻莫测的紫罗兰色

and towards it (= the violet space of sky) the lamps of the street lifted their feeble lanterns　在紫罗兰色的天空映衬下,街灯挺着头,发着微弱的光

to play till our bodies glowed　直玩到我们身体发热

to echo in the silent street　在寂静的街道上回荡

the career of our play　我们(奔跑追赶)的激烈游戏

the dark muddy lanes　黑暗泥泞的小巷/小路

to run the gantlet of the rough tribes from the cottages to the back doors of the dark dripping gardens　玩着闪躲野蛮部落鞭笞的游戏,从村舍小屋直跑到黑暗的湿淋淋的花园后门

＊ run the gantlet of　遭受……的攻击/批评等

to smooth and comb the horse or shake music from the buckled harness　为马梳好鬃毛,抖动着上了搭扣的缰绳/马具,发出好听的声音

to see him safely housed　看着他安全进屋

to peer up and down the street　上上下下仔细地打量着街道

to walk up to Mangan's steps resignedly　顺从地跟着曼根的脚步走,跟着曼根亦步亦趋

(her figure) defined by the light from the half-opened door　灯光从半开的门里泻出,映现/勾勒出她的身形

to tease her before he obeyed　在听从她之前,先逗逗她

to stand by the railings looking at her　站在栅栏旁注视着她

the soft rope of her hair　她头上柔软的发带

to toss from side to side　左右摆动

6. The blind was pulled down to within an inch of the sash so that I could not be seen.　窗帘被拉下来,拉到距窗框不到一英寸的地方,使我不会被发现。

7. to come near the point at which our ways diverged　走到我们快要分别的岔路口

except for a few casual words　除了几句无关痛痒/漫不经心的话以外

be like a summons to all my foolish blood　对我整个的傻脑袋来说,就像一声召唤

8. to have to go to carry some of the parcels　得去(替她)拿一些包包

to walk through the flaring streets　走过灯火闪烁的街道

be jostled by drunken men and bargaining women　被喝醉酒的醉汉和讨价还价的女人推推搡搡

the curses of labourers　出苦力的劳动者的诅咒

the shrill litanies of shop-boys who stood on guard by the barrels of pigs' cheeks　货桶旁店伙计的高声叫卖

* litany 枯燥冗长的讲述、介绍；on guard 值班，看守

the nasal chanting of street singers 街道歌唱家带鼻音的歌唱

to sing a come-all-you about O'Donovan Rosa 唱着关于奥多诺万·罗莎的流行小曲/街道民谣

to sing a ballad about the troubles in our native land 唱着讲述民族苦难/乡土苦情的民谣

to converge in a single sensation of life for me 对我来说，只是汇聚成一股生命的激情

to bear my chalice safely through a throng of foes 我端着圣杯，在一群敌人中平安穿过

9. Her name sprang to my lips at moments in strange prayers and praises which I myself did not understand. 在我念诵那些自己也不懂的奇怪的祈祷文和赞美诗的时候，她的名字时时会蹦到我的嘴边/常常会情不自禁念出她的名字。

10. at times a flood from my heart seemed to pour itself out into my bosom 不时从心底涌起一股热流，在我胸中奔腾起伏

11. to tell her of my confused adoration 对她表白我充满困惑的倾慕之情

12. But my body was like a harp and her words and features were like fingers running upon the wires. 但我的身体像一架竖琴，她的话语和身影就像手指在撩拨这琴弦。

13. Through one of the broken panes I heard the rain impinge upon the earth, the fine incessant needles of water playing in the sodden beds. 透过其中的一扇破玻璃窗，我听到雨点击打地面的声音，听到不绝如麻、绵密如针的细雨溅落在浸湿透了的花坛上，仿佛在嬉戏。

* incessant (a.) 不停的，不断的；从句法上可以把 heard 后面的部分看作两个带宾语补足语的复合结构，两个宾语分别是 the rain 和 the fine incessant needles of water，两个宾补分别是 impinge upon the earth 和 playing in the sodden beds，前者为不定式短语，后者为分词短语。

14. I was thankful that I could see so little. 我能看到的很少，对此我感到很欣慰。

15. All my senses seemed to desire to veil themselves and, feeling that I was about to slip from them, I pressed the palms of my hands together until they trembled, ... 我所有的感官似乎都想隐藏起来，在我感到即将脱离/失去它们时，就把手掌紧压在一起，直到两手颤抖……

* feeling that ... 是分词短语作状语，它的逻辑主语即主句主语"I"，that 引导的名词性从句是分词 feeling 的宾语，这是个带宾语从句的分词短语。

16. When she addressed the first words to me I was so confused that I did not know what to answer. 她说头两句时，我就感到茫然，不知道怎么回答。

17. to turn a silver bracelet round and round her wrist 一圈圈转着手腕上的银手链

a retreat in her convent 在她上学的女子修道院里的静修

be fighting for their caps 打闹着争抢他们的帽子

to hold one of the spikes, bowing her head towards me 一只手握住一个栏杆的刺尖，低着头朝向我

(light) to catch the white curve of her neck （灯光）照着她雪白的脖子，勾勒出它的曲线

to light up her hair that rest there, falling 照亮她披散在脖子上、垂落下来的头发上

(light) to fall over one side of her dress and catch the white border of a petticoat, just visible as she stands there at ease 灯光洒落在她衣裙的一侧，照见她衬裙的白滚边儿，这只有在她悠闲地站着时才看得见

18. What innumerable follies laid waste my waking and sleeping thoughts after that evening! 从那晚以后，不论是清醒时刻还是睡梦之中，有多少荒唐的念头充塞着/蹂躏着我的思想啊！

19. to wish to annihilate the tedious intervening days 真想毁了那段(介入其中的)令人生厌的日子

to chafe against the work of school 对学校的功课感到心烦

to come between me and the page I strive to read （她的形象）浮现在我的眼前，挡住了我努力阅读的书页/（她的形象）横亘在我与书页之间，使我读不下去

be called to me through the silence　通过这种沉静召唤我

(my soul) to luxuriate in the silence　（我的灵魂）沉浸在寂静之中

to cast an Eastern enchantment over me　（仿佛）对我施加了东方异国的迷幻魔法

to watch my master's face pass from amiability to sternness　看到我的老师的脸色从和蔼可亲变得严厉起来

to call my wandering thoughts together　从浮想联翩中集中起注意力

to have hardly any patience with the serious work of life　简直没有任何耐心去做生活中的正经事

ugly monotonous child's play　令人生厌的单调乏味的小孩儿把戏

be fussing at the hallstand 在衣帽架那里小题大做/故作烦恼地发脾气

front parlour　前厅

in bad humour　心情郁闷

20. The air was pitilessly raw and already my heart misgave me.　空气湿冷而无情,我的心已使我焦虑不安。

21. to sit staring at the clock for some time　坐着盯着闹钟看了一会儿

to mount the staircase and gain the upper part of the house　上楼梯到达楼上的房间

seeing nothing but the brown-clad figure cast by my imagination　别的什么也没看见,只看到想象中（她）身穿棕色衣衫的身影

＊brown-clad = brown-clothed 穿着棕色衣衫的;cast by my imagination 直译是:由我的想象所投射下来的。这是过去分词短语作 figure 的后置定语。

touched discreetly by the lamplight at the curved neck　灯光小心地轻抚着她脖子上的曲线

22. an old garrulous woman　饶舌的老太太

a pawnbroker's widow　当铺老板的遗孀

to have to endure the gossip of the tea-table　不得不忍受吃茶点时的闲聊

to begin to walk up and down the room, clenching my fists　开始在屋里走来走去,紧握着拳头

to put off your bazaar for this night of Our Lord　现在是主日的晚上,你要推迟去大巴扎/东方商贸市场了

to hear my uncle's latchkey in the hall-door　听到我舅舅在大厅门上插钥匙开锁的声音

to hear the hallstand rocking when it have received the weight of his overcoat　在他挂外套的时候,（我）听到衣帽架摇晃的声音

to have told him a second time　已经又给他讲了一次

be about to recite the opening lines of the piece to my aunt　正要把那首诗的开头几句背给舅妈听

23. You've kept him late enough as it is.　他被你拖到现在这么晚。

24. All work and no play makes Jack a dull boy.　整天工作不玩耍,杰克变成大傻瓜。

＊这里的 Jack 泛指任何人,类似于中国的"此地无银三百两,隔壁王二不曾偷"中的"王二",并非是某个具体人。

25. The sight of the streets thronged with buyers and glaring with gas recalled to me the purpose of my journey.　看到街市上购物者人头攒动,煤气灯耀眼夺目,使我想起了此行的目的。

＊thronged with 挤满……; glaring with gas 煤气灯闪烁,这两个分词短语都是 streets 的后置定语;recall to sb. 使某人想起……

26. to take my seat in a third-class carriage of a deserted train　在一列乘客稀少的火车三等车厢里找到一个座位

27. an intolerable delay　一段无法忍受的延搁

to creep onward among ruinous houses and over the twinkling river　在濒临倒塌的房屋之间和波光粼粼的河流之上缓慢行进

（people）to press to the carriage doors （人们）挤到车厢门口

a special train for the bazaar 开往大巴扎/东方大商贸市场的专车

to remain alone in the bare carriage 一人待在空荡荡的车厢里

to draw up beside an improvised wooden platform （火车）驶近/靠近临时搭建的木制月台

to pass in quickly through a turnstile 快速通过一个旋转栅门

a weary-looking man 一个看上去无精打采的人

to find oneself in a big hall girdled at half its height by a gallery 发现自己正置身于一个大厅之中，大厅的半高处有廊台环绕

to walk into the centre of the bazaar timidly 怯生生地走进大巴扎/东方大商贸市场的中心

be gathered about the stalls which were still open （人们）聚拢在一个还在营业的摊位前

28. I recognized a silence like that which pervades a church after a service. 我想起了礼拜式完毕后教堂里弥漫着的那种寂静。

29. Before a curtain, over which the words Café Chantant were written in coloured lamps, two men were counting money on a salver. 一块幕布上，彩灯拼凑出"歌唱咖啡屋"的字样，幕布前，有两个人正在一个托盘里数钱。

30. Remembering with difficulty why I had come I went over to one of the stalls and examined porcelain vases and flowered tea-sets. 好容易想起我来的目的，我走到一个摊位前，察看着瓷瓶和嵌花的茶具。

31. The tone of her voice was not encouraging; she seemed to have spoken to me out of a sense of duty. 她的声调没有想要人买的意思；她之所以跟我说话，似乎是出于一种义务。

32. to make my interest in her wares seem the more real 说是装出一副对她货品很感兴趣的样子似乎更确切/好像我真的对她的货品很感兴趣。

 * 此句是用不定式短语做主语。

33. I allowed the two pennies to fall against the sixpence in my pocket. 我任那两个一便士的硬币落进口袋击打在那个六便士的硬币上。

 * penny 便士，用于指硬币的个数；pence 便士，用于指币值。

34. Gazing up into the darkness I saw myself as a creature driven and derided by vanity. 凝望着黑暗深处，我感到自己是一个被虚荣所驱动、所嘲笑的生灵。

主要内容归纳和总结

1. 詹姆斯·乔伊斯出生在爱尔兰都柏林一个天主教家庭。他年轻时，家庭曾经很富有，后来逐渐变穷。他先在天主教学校接受宗教教育，后在都柏林大学学院接受大学教育。毕业后他离开爱尔兰，流连于欧洲大陆，主要待在法国、意大利和瑞士，除了短暂回爱尔兰旅行，他后半生大部分时间都生活在欧洲大陆，直到去世。

 乔伊斯不是商业作家，一生只写过三部长篇小说，一部短篇小说集，两部诗集和一部戏剧，故事的主题都是爱尔兰人民的生活，背景都是都柏林。他靠这点作品卖钱养活自己是有点困难的。然而，他却是 20 世纪文学最伟大的代表性作家，他的代表作《尤利西斯》是现代主义文学的首要典范（a prime example of modernism in literature），同时他又是最伟大的意识流小说家（stream-of-consciousness novelist）。

2. 乔伊斯作品的艺术特点

 a. 擅长用意识流的手法写出人物随机状态下的思想活动。

 b. 他本身的文风直白、清晰、富于逻辑，但一旦进入"意识流"，便急剧变化，变得支离破碎、杂乱无

章(broken wording and fragmentary sentences),显示出角色思想的无规则的自由流动(disorderly flow of thoughts)。

    c. 为塑造尤利西斯这一角色,他创造性地使用了所谓的讽刺英雄体(mock-heroic style),即用故意的拙劣模仿(parody)、拼凑(pastiche)和象征性的幻想(symbolic fantasy)等等不寻常的手法来表现人物。

    d. 在创作艺术手法上,他是文学革新第一人,不仅在意识流方面,而且还在修辞手法、历史性文体学以及表现主义戏剧等方面有激进的改革实验,是语言和文体的大师。

3. 詹姆斯·乔伊斯的主要作品:

    a. 三部长篇小说

《一个青年艺术家的肖像》*A Portrait of the Artist as a Young Man* (1916)

《尤利西斯》*Ulysses* (1922)

《菲尼根斯·伟克》*Finnegans Wake* (1939)

    b. 一部短篇小说集,包含 15 篇短篇小说

《都柏林人》*Dubliners* (1914)

    c. 两部诗集

    d. 一部戏剧

重要信息句子

1. Joyce is not a commercial writer. In his life time, he only wrote altogether three novels and a collection of short stories. But he is one of the most important literary figures of the first half of the 20th century.

2. Joyce spent 17 years working on his last important book, *Finnegans Wake* (1939). In this encyclopedic work, he ambitiously attempted to pack the whole history of mankind into one night's dream, which is regarded as the most original experiment ever made in the novel form.

3. To create his modern Odyssey — *Ulysses*, Joyce adopts a kind of mock-heroic style. The essence of the mock-heroic lies in the application of apparently inappropriate styles.

4. *Ulysses*, Joyce's masterpiece, has become a prime example of modernism in literature.

英国现代时期文学同步练习与答案

1. Modernism rose out of _____ and _____.

  a. skepticism/disillusion of capitalism   b. romanticism/imagination

  c. metaphysics/disillusion   d. realism/documentation

2. Which of the following is NOT the literary trend of modernism after the First World War? _____.

  a. Expressionism and surrealism   b. Futurism and symbolism

  c. Imagism and steam of consciousness   d. Romanticism and imagination

3. After the Second World War, a variety of modernism, or post-modernism, rose with the spur of the _____ idea that "the world was absurd, and the human life was an agony."

  a. modernist   b. existentialist

  c. disillusoioned   d. absurd

4. Modernism takes _____ and _____ as its theoretical base.

    a. Darwin's theory of evolution/social Darwinism

    b. the rational philosophy/the theory of psycho-analysis

    c. the irrational philosophy/the theory of psycho-analysis

    d. Marxism/scientific socialism

5. Modernism is a reaction against realism and _____ rationalism.

    a. agrees to   b. consistent with

    c. equal to   d. rejects

6. The first decades of the 20th century were golden years of _____. In stimulating the technical innovations of novel of creation, the theory of _____ played a particularly important role.

    a. the modernist novel/the Freudian and Jungian psycho-analysis

    b. the modernist novel/Marxism and Darwinism

    c. the realist novel/Marxist scientific socialism

    d. the realist novel/Darwin's theory of evolution

7. The 1930s witnessed _____ of modernist novels and the revival of _____.

    a. the rise/Ancient Greek culture   b. the decline/poetic drama

    c. the decline/dramatic monologue   d. the rise/romantic legend

8. Who wrote the play *Look Back in Anger* in 1956 and became known as the first "Angry Young Man"? _____.

    a. John Osborne   b. Samuel Beckett

    c. T. S. Eliot   d. Christopher Fry

9. Who wrote *Waiting for Godot* and is regarded as the most famous and influential play of the Theater of Absurd? _____.

    a. John Osborne   b. Synge

    c. Thomas Hardy   d. Samuel Beckett

10. G. B. Shaw's career as a dramatist began in 1892, when his first play _____ was put on by the Independent Theater Society.

    a. *Widower's Houses*   b. *Candida*

    c. *Man and Superman*   d. *St. Joan*

11. One of the most typical inversion is in _____, where the "deceived" husband is not outraged by his wife's extra-curricular friendship with a youthful poet, but is outraged instead by the poet's feigned indifference to the charms of his wife.

    a. *Widower's Houses*   b. *The Doctor's Dlemma*

    c. *Misalliance*   d. *How she Lied to Her Husband*

12. Which one of the following elements is the most important in Shaw's plays? _____.

    a. Plot of the story   b. Action

    c. Dialogue   d. characterization

13. Shaw's characterization has two features: one is to show up one character vividly at the expense of another; the other is that Shaw's characters are _____.

    a. people good at expressing themselves by talking

    b. the representatives of his ideas and points of view

    c. a group of conventional social animals

    d. persons with the gift of insight and freedom

14. According to Galsworthy, human life is just a struggle between _____.

a. the advance and the backward
b. the bourgeois and the proletariat
c. the landlord and the peasants
d. the rich and the poor

15. Galsworthy was a _____, even though he was influenced by the continental novelists.
   a. romantic poet
   b. modernist poet
   c. modernist novelist
   d. conventional writer

16. Technically, Galsworthy was _____, focusing on plot development and character portrayal.
   a. more modernist than realist
   b. more traditional than adventurous
   c. preferring exploration to inheritance
   d. fond of poetry more than novel

17. Yeats experienced a slow and painful change in his poetic creation, starting in _____ and finishing as a matured _____.
   a. realistic tradition/modernist poet
   b. romantic tradition/realist poet
   c. metaphysical tradition/symbolistic poet
   d. romantic tradition/modernist poet

18. During the last stage of his creation, Yeats came to realize that eternal beauty could only live in _____.
   a. the realm of art
   b. nature
   c. human nature
   d. religion

19. During his last stage of creation, Yeats' concern turned to the great subjects of _____.
   a. realism
   b. modernism
   c. dichotomy
   d. metaphysics

20. Yeats is also a dramatist, writing _____ in most of the cases.
   a. tragedy
   b. comedy
   c. farce
   d. verse plays

21. Even in his plays _____ has remained a lyrical poet. His plays are enjoyed more for the beauty of their language than for dramatic situations.
   a. Alfred Tennyson
   b. George Robert Browning
   c. William Butler Yeats
   d. Thomas Hardy

22. In his famous essay, "_____," T. S. Eliot put great emphasis on the importance of tradition both in creative writing and in criticism.
   a. Tradition and Individual Talent
   b. Book Reviews
   c. The Elder Statesman
   d. The Confidential Clerk

23. _____ by T. S. Eliot is the landmark of the 20th century English poetry, a poem concerned with the spiritual breakup of a modern civilization in which human life has lost its set of historical, cultural and religious themes.
   a. *Four Quartets*
   b. *The Waste Land*
   c. *Ash Wednesday*
   d. *Prufrock*

24. T. S. Eliot's most famous and representative poem is _____; he won the Novel Prize in 1948 for his volume of poetic works _____.
   a. *The Waste Land/ The Love Song of J. Alfred Prufrock*
   b. *The Waste Land/Ash Wednesday*
   c. *The Love Song of J. Alfred Prufrock/Four Quartets*
   d. *The Waste Land/Four Quartets*

25. _____, which bears a strong thematic resemblance to The Waste Land, is generally regarded as the darkest of Eliot's poem.

a. *The Hollow Men*   b. *Gerontion*

c. *Prufrock*   d. *Ash Wednesday*

26. T. S. Eliot, as an important verse dramatist, had written in his life time five full-length plays, which one of the following is NOT one of the five plays? _____.

a. *Murder in the Cathedral*   b. *The Family Reunion*

c. *The Countess Cathleen*   d. *The Cocktail Party*

27. D. H. Lawrence's first novel, _____, is a remarkable work of a talented young man, acutely observant of nature and delighting in story.

a. *The Trespasser*   b. *The White Peacock*

c. *Sons and Lovers*   d. *Kangaroo*

28. Lawrence was recognized as a prominent novelist only after he published his third novel, _____.

a. *The Rainbow*   b. *Women in Love*

c. *Sons and Lovers*   d. *Lady Chatterley's Lover*

29. The two novels, _____ and _____, are generally regarded as Lawrence's masterpieces.

a. *The White Peacock/Kangaroo*   b. *Aaron's Rod/The Plumed Serpent*

c. *The Daughter of the Vicar/St. Mawr*   d. *The Rainbow/Women in Love*

30. Lawrence was discovered to be an important playwright in 1968, his trilogy are *A Collier's Friday Night*, *The Daughter in Law*, and _____.

a. *The Widowing of Mrs. Holroyed*   b. *The Virgin and Gypsy*

c. *Lady Chatterley's Lover*   d. *The Prussian Officer*

31. Lawrence's trilogy in dramatic writing have in common _____ set in Nottinghamshire.

a. the middle-class environment   b. the typical working-class environment

c. the aristocratic family background   d. Christian background

32. Lawrence was one of the first novelists to introduce themes of _____ into his works.

a. humanism   b. psychology

c. mythology   d. the stream of consciousness

33. Lawrence's artistic tendency is mainly _____.

a. utopianism   b. materialism

c. Realism   d. romantism

34. All of James Joyce's novels and stories are regarded as his great works and have the same setting: _____, especially _____, and the same subject: _____ and their life.

a. America/Boston/the American people

b. England/London/the English people

c. Scotland/Edinburgh/the Scottish people

d. Ireland/Dublin/the Irish people

35. In 1916, Joyce published his first novel _____. Its title suggests a character study with strong autobiographical elements.

a. *Dubliners*   b. *Finnegan's Wake*

c. *A Portrait of the Artist as a Young Man*   d. *Ulysses*

36. The literary approach to the presentation psychological aspects of characters is usually termed as _____.

a. imagism   b. psychological description

c. characterization   d. stream of consciousness

37. To create his modern *Odyssey — Ulysses*, Joyce adopts a kind of _____.
   - a. mock-heroic style
   - b. sentimental romance
   - c. historical stylistics
   - d. counterpoint

38. Of the following writings by James Joyce, which is a prime example of modernism in literature? _____.
   - a. *Ulysses*
   - b. *A Portrait of the Artist as a Young Man*
   - c. *Dubliners*
   - d. *Finnegans Wake*

39. Which of the following is NOT true according to James Joyce? _____
   - a. *Ulysses* has become a prime example of modernism in literature.
   - b. Joyce is regarded as the most prominent stream-of-consciousness novelist.
   - c. Joyce is a realistic writer in English literature history.
   - d. His novel "A Portrait of the Artist as a Young Man" is a naturalistic account of the hero's bitter experiences and his final artistic and spiritual liberation.

40. The _____ can be regarded as one of the themes of Joyce's story "Araby".
   - a. loss of innocence
   - b. childish loves
   - c. awareness of harsh life
   - d. false sentimentality

41. After reading "Araby", one may feel the story has a _____ tone.
   - a. joyous
   - b. harsh
   - c. solemn
   - d. painful

42. In "Araby", Joyce's diction evokes a sort of _____ quality that characterizes the boy on this otherwise altogether ordinary shopping trip.
   - a. religious
   - b. moral
   - c. sentimental
   - d. vulgar

43. Among the great writers of the modern period, _____ might be the greatest in radical experimentation of technical innovations in novel writing.
   - a. Joseph Conrad
   - b. D. H. Lawrence
   - c. Virginia Woolf
   - d. James Joyce

44. As a literary figure, Stephen Dedalus appears in two novels written by _____.
   - a. E. M. Forster
   - b. Joseph Conrad
   - c. D. H. Lawrence
   - d. James Joyce

45. The mission of _____ drama was to reveal the moral political and economic truth from a radical reformist point of view.
   - a. T. S. Eliot's
   - b. J. Galsworthy's
   - c. G. B. Shaw's
   - d. W. B. Yeats'

46. Which of the following statements about D. H. Lawrence is NOT true? _____
   - a. His novel *Sons and Lovers* is largely autobiographical.
   - b. He was strongly against the dehumanizing effect of the mechanical civilization.
   - c. He believed that the primacy of life force was a guarantee in the healthy development of an individual's personality.
   - d. He was daringly innovative in the techniques of novel creation.

47. Eliot's "The Love Song of J. Alfred Prufrock" is presented as a(n) _____, suggesting an ironic contrast between a pretended "love song" and a confession of his incapability of facing up to love and to life in a sterile upper-class world.

a. interior monologue

b. authentic dialogue

c. lyric song

d. religious confession

48. Eliot's poem, *The Waste Land*, is mainly concerned with the _____ of a modern civilization.

a. social corruption

b. spiritual breakup

c. physical breakup

d. religious corruption

49. Thematically Yeats' poem, "The Lake Isle of Innisfree", _____.

a. celebrates the rich and colorful life of the modern people

b. criticizes the emptiness of the hermit's life in the remote country.

c. laments the loss of the Irish legendary tradition.

d. laments the emptiness of the urban life and advocates a return to the simple and serene life of nature

50. Which of the following statements about G. B. Shaw is NOT true? _____

a. He was one of the most influential members of the Fabian Society.

b. He was strongly against the credo of "art for art's sake".

c. He wrote plays to discuss social problems.

d. He vehemently rejected the traditions of realism in his dramatic creation.

51. According to the excerpt of *The Man of Property* in the textbook, the tense relationship between Soames, the husband, and Irene, the wife, is caused by _____.

a. Irene's free-minded way of thinking

b. Irene's love for Bosinney

c. Soame's love for Irene

d. Soame's strong desire to possess Irene

52. "Do you think I was brought up like you? Able to pick and choose my own way of life? Do you think I did what I did because I liked it, or thought it right . . . ?" According to the meaning of the above lines taken from Shaw's play, *Mrs. Warren's Profession*, which of the following statements is NOT true? _____

a. Mrs. Warren was brought up in a very poor situation.

b. Mrs. Warren's choice of her profession could be justified when she made the decision.

c. Although Mrs. Warren did not think what she did was right, yet she could not change her way of life even in her later years.

d. The words uttered by Mrs. Warren served only an excuse to cover her unwillingness to leave the profession in her later years.

53. Which of the following statements about John Galsworthy is NOT true? _____

a. He focused his attention primarily on the criticism of social injustice in his works.

b. He was mainly concerned with psychological development of characters in his novel.

c. Objective observation, naturalistic description and documentary precision are main features of his writing.

d. Technically, he was more traditional than innovative.

54. "And when I am pinned and wriggling on the wall,/Then how should I begin/To spit out all the butt-ends of my days and ways. " In these lines, the image of a life pinned on the wall is vividly presented to show Prufrock's current _____.

a. misery

b. laziness

c. predicament

d. struggle

Keys:adbcd/abada/dcbdd/bdacd/cabda/cbcda/bbcdc/daaca/daddc/dabdd/dcbc

第二部分
美国文学 AMERICAN LITERATURE

第一章 浪漫主义时期 The Romantic Period

词语解释和难句分析

1. to nurture the literature of a great nation 哺育了一个伟大国家的文学
   devoid of a heavy burden of the inherited past and history 毫无历史和过去遗留下来的沉重负担
   be flourishing into an independent country in politics, economy and culture 发展成为一个政治、经济、文化上独立的国家
   the time of westward expansion 西部开发的时代
   to affect rural as well as the urban life 既影响了乡村的生活也影响了城市的生活
   the sudden influx of immigration 移民的突然涌入
   to give a big push to the already booming industry 给已在蓬勃发展的工业一个巨大推动
   to feel an urge to have its own literary expression 迫切要求有自己的文学表达
   to make known its new experience that other nations did not have 展示/表达别的国家没有而自己特有的新鲜经验
   the early Puritan settlement 早期清教徒殖民者/移民定居者
   the frontiersmen's life, and the wild west 边疆开拓者的生活和西部荒原
   to bring about a spectacular outburst of romantic feeling 产生蓬勃的浪漫主义文学思潮/导致浪漫主义思潮蔚为壮观的大爆发

2. to exert a stimulating impact on the writers of the new world 对新大陆的作家产生了激励的作用/重大的影响
   a new emphasis upon the imaginative and emotional quality of literature 强调了文学的想象和情感描写
   to include a liking for the picturesque, the exotic, the sensuous, the sensational, and the supernatural 包括喜欢描写自然景物、异国情调、感官刺激、耸人听闻和超自然等形形色色的事物和人生百态
   to place an increasing emphasis on the free expression of emotions 越来越强调情感的自由表达
   to display an increasing attention to the psychic states of their characters 表现出作家日益关注他们的人物的心理状态
   to exhibit extremes of sensitivity and excitement （人物）显示出极端敏感和激动的个性

to exalt the individual and the common man　歌颂个人和普通人

Freneau's use of the "ruin of empire" theme　弗雷诺采用"帝国崩溃"的主题

Bryant's fascination by the Mound Builders　布莱恩特沉迷于那些在大河流域构筑墓冢和祭坛的印第安人

Irving's effort to exploit the legends of the Hudson River region　欧文努力开拓哈得孙河地区的传奇故事

3. native land　本乡本土，乡土

national experience of "pioneering into the west"　国家西部开发/"进军西部"的经验

a rich source of material for American writers to draw upon　为美国作家所利用的丰富的素材/创作源泉

virgin forests and endless prairies　原始森林和无边的草原

4. The wildness came to function almost as a dramatic character that symbolized moral law.　莽原几乎成了象征道德准则的一个戏剧人物。

5. the noble savages untainted by society　内心高尚的/还未受社会污染的野蛮人

cultural heritage/legacy　文化传统

to tend more to moralized than their English and European counterparts　比英国和欧洲的同行们更具有道德倾向

a preoccupation with the Calvinistic view of original sin and the mystery of evil　专注于研究加尔文主义的原罪思想和罪恶的神秘性

a host of lesser writers　一群较次要的小作家

6. a local phenomenon restricted only to those people living in New England　只局限于居住在新英格兰的作家群体中的一种现象

to carry out the movement as a reaction against the cold, rigid rationalism of Unitarianism in Boston　在波士顿开展的一项反对唯一神论的冷淡、古板的理性主义的运动

7. Transcendentalism has been defined philosophically as "the recognition in man of the capacity of knowing truth intuitively, or of attaining knowledge transcending the reach of the senses."　超验主义在哲学上被定义为"承认人凭直觉了解真理的能力，或超越感官范围获得知识的能力"。

8. comic fables, frontier adventures, narrative quests, Gothic tales and psychological romances　喜剧寓言体小说，边疆历险小说，长篇探险故事，哥特式小说以及心理传奇小说

be indispensable for the improvement of human nature　对于人性改善是不可缺少的

主要内容归纳和总结

1. 美国的文艺复兴——浪漫主义时期：从华盛顿·欧文《见闻札记》(The Sketch Book)的出版到沃尔特·惠特曼《草叶集》(Leaves of Grass)的问世，即从18世纪末到1861年内战爆发。

2. 美国浪漫主义文学的形成

随着美国独立政府的成立，美国人迫切要求有自己的文学，表达别国没有而自己独有的经历：早期清教徒的殖民，与印第安人的遭遇，边疆开拓者的生活，以及西部荒原的壮阔等。这为文学想象提供了广阔的空间。人口的剧增和报纸杂志的不断涌现，为文学的发展提供了读者市场和大量载体，整个国家洋溢着一派乐观主义情绪，因而在19世纪上半叶形成了蓬勃的浪漫主义思潮。

3. 美国浪漫主义主学的特点

a. 反对古典主义(classicism)时期的文学样式和思想，开创了较新的小说和诗歌形式。作品强调想象和情感描写，强调感官体验和超自然力的表现，特别注意人物的心理刻画，表现普通人、个人而不是要人、人的整体。

b. "西部开发"（pioneering into the west）成了作家取之不尽的创作素材,描写莽原、森林、大海、边民和开拓者的带着野性的作品扑面而来,开一时之风气,形成了美国文学中离开尘世、心向自然的传统。代表作品有库柏（Cooper）的《皮袜子的故事》（*Leather-Stocking Tales*）和梭罗（Thoreau）的《瓦尔登湖》（*Walden*）。

c. 由于清教徒首先到达美洲进行殖民,清教主义（Puritanism）思想成了美国的文化遗产（cultural heritage）,在文学上的表现就是道德倾向比欧洲文学浓厚得多,霍桑（Hawthorne）和麦尔韦尔（Melville）的作品中就都有加尔文主义的原罪思想（Calvinistic view of original sin）和罪恶神秘的观点显现。

d. 美国浪漫主义文学最具标志性的特征就是超验主义运动（transcendentalism movement）,代表人物是爱默生（Emerson）和梭罗（Henry David Thoreau）,主要观点是:"承认人凭直觉了解真理的能力,或者说超越感官范围获取知识的能力。"

＊ 美国文学中的诗歌,律诗极少,绝大多数都是自由体诗。本书所选用的美国诗歌中只有罗伯特·李·弗罗斯特的一首《雪夜林边停》是律诗,因此除这一首诗外不再进行格律与韵律分析。

重要信息句子

1. The Romantic period of American literature started with the publication of Washington Irving's *The Sketch Book* and ended with Whitman's *Leaves of Grass*. It is also called "the American Renaissance. "

2. The strong tendency to exalt the individual and the common man was almost a national religion in America.　歌颂个人和普通人的强烈倾向几乎成了美国的国家宗教。

3. In short, American Romanticism is, in a certain way, derivative.　简言之,美国的浪漫主义文学是以某种方式派生出来的（缺乏独创性）。

4. The desire for an escape from society and a return to nature became a permanent convention of American literature.　逃离社会、回归自然的愿望成了美国文学永久的传统。

5. The most clearly defined Romantic literary movement in this period is New England Transcendentalism. 这段时期最明确定义的浪漫主义文学运动是新英格兰超验主义运动。

I . 华盛顿·欧文 Washington Irving（1783～1859）

词语解释和难句分析

1. to earn an international reputation　赢得了国际声誉
   to write juvenile poems, essays and plays　写了许多幼稚的诗歌、散文和戏剧
   to conclude his education at private school　完成了他在私立学校的教育
   to enter a law office　进了一家律师事务所
   a series of youthful satires on New York society　一系列针对纽约社会的朝气蓬勃的讽刺文章
   to fashion a style which <u>reduces all to</u> foolishness, including the author's persona　想出/设计出一种把一切都归结为愚蠢的文风,包括作者自己。

2. to come to a crashing halt （希望、梦想）轰然一声破灭了/戛然而止

to find his refuge from the grief in the researches on... 在研究……之中找到了躲避悲伤的地方

a parody of the Dutch colony 对荷兰殖民地嘲弄性的模仿

to win a measure of international fame on both sides of the Atlantic 在大西洋两岸赢得了一定的国际声誉

Americanized versions of European folk tales 美国本土化了的欧洲民间故事

a carefully contrived persona 精心设计的人物形象

to juxtapose the Old World and the New 把新旧世界并置

manipulating his own antiquarian interest with artistic perspectives 从艺术的角度巧妙处理了他自己对古文物收藏的兴趣

3. to lack the creative energy and appeal of *The Sketch Book* 缺少《见闻札记》的活力和魅力

be sent to Spain as an Americ anattaché 被派遣到西班牙去任美国驻西公使馆随员

be secretary of the United States Legation in London 美国驻伦敦公使馆秘书

to make a adventurous trip to the Westward frontier on horseback 骑在马背上作了一次西部边疆的历险旅行

to spend the rest of his life in "Sunnyside" 他后半生的生活过得很阳光、很快乐

be away from home as Minister to Spain 离家赴西班牙出任公使

to acclaim the same admiration and recognition *The Sketches Book* did 得到与《见闻札记》相同的赞赏和承认

4. a patchwork of references, echoes, and burlesques. 由参考文献、重复仿效和滑稽模仿组成的大杂烩/拼盘

to have a strong flavor of Spanish culture 具有浓厚的西班牙文化的风味

Alhambra 爱尔汗布拉宫,13～14世纪西班牙南部格林纳达城(Granada)摩尔人的一座宫殿。欧文以此命名自己的著作,故被说成是"西班牙的见闻札记"。

be filled with English scenes and quotations from English authors and faithful to British orthography （作品里）充满了英国的风景和来自英国作家的引文,以及忠实于英国英语的拼写法

to make Washington Irving a household word and his fame enduring 使华盛顿·欧文成了家喻户晓的名字,他的声誉经久不衰

5. Washington Irving brought to the new nation what its people desired most in a man of letters——the respect of the Old World. 华盛顿·欧文给这个新国家带来了它的人民对文学家最期待的东西——对旧大陆的尊重。

   ＊ what...of letters 这个名词性从句是 brought 的宾语从句。

6. These two stories easily trigger off American imagination with their focus on American subjects, American landscape, and, in Irving's case, the legends of the Hudson River region of the fresh young land. 在他们关注美国主题、美国风景,就欧文来说,关注这新鲜年轻的国家哈得孙河流域的传奇故事时,这两部小说里的故事很容易触发美国人的想象。

7. social conservatism 社会保守主义

literary preference for the past 文学上对过去的偏好

to set against the background of the inevitably changing America 以不可避免地正在变化着的美国为创作背景

to present to us paralleled juxtapositions of two totally different worlds 向我们展示了平行并列的两个完全不同的世界

8. to charge his sentences with emotion so as to create a true and vivid character 给每一个句子都赋予情

感,以创作出真实生动的人物

be worth the honor of being "the American Goldsmith" for his literary craftsmanship.　凭他的文学艺术技艺,值得"美国金匠"美誉

9. The Gothic elements and the supernatural atmosphere are manipulated in such a way that we could <u>become so engaged and involved in</u> what is happening in a seemingly exotic place.　对小说中哥特式元素和超自然氛围驾驭自如,就仿佛我们深入其中,置身于似乎异国他乡发生的情境之中。

华盛顿·欧文作品选读

《瑞普·凡·温克尔》 *Rip Van Winkle* 节选

词语解释和难句分析

1. an indolent good-natured Dutch-American　一个懒散的、脾气温和的荷兰裔美国人

   his shrewish wife　他的强悍的/泼妇似的妻子

   a dwarflike stranger dressed in the ancient Dutch fashion　一个穿着古代荷兰人衣着的侏儒似的陌生人

   to play a game of ninepins　玩九柱戏

   to fall into a sleep　坠入梦乡

   <u>be</u> soon <u>befriended with</u> his generosity and cheerfulness　由于他的慷慨乐观,被当作朋友对待

2. his pervasive theme of nostalgia for the unrecoverable past　他的流行的怀旧主题,想念着一去不复返的过去/他的怀念过去的流行主题

3. happy mortals　乐天派,快乐的芸芸众生

   be of foolish, well-oiled disposition　糊里糊涂、醉醺醺的样子/脾性

   to take the world easy　随遇而安,得过且过,混天度日

   . . . can be got with least thought or trouble　不用太费艰辛就可得到,几乎不用费神或者费力就可得到……

   (sb.) <u>would rather</u> starve on a penny <u>than</u> work for a pound　宁可只剩一便士而挨饿,也不为挣一镑钱而工作

4. If (he had been) left to himself, he would have <u>whistled life away</u> in perfect contentment;　如果只剩下他一个人,他也会心满意足地吹着口哨度过一生

5. to keep continuously dinning in his ears about his idleness, . . .　总是要不停地在他耳边数叨他多么游手好闲

   <u>be sure to</u> produce a torrent of household eloquence　一定会引发一阵家长里短、雄辩滔滔的责难

   to <u>cast up</u> his eyes　向上翻白眼

   to provoke a fresh volley from his wife　激发起他老婆新一轮连续的责问

   be fain to <u>draw off his force</u>, and <u>take to</u> the outside of the house　不得不放弃抵抗/缴械投降,很习惯地跑到屋外去

   Rip's sole domestic adherent　他家里唯一的追随者/信徒

   be as much henpecked as his master　像它的主人一样非常怕老婆

6. to <u>look upon</u> Wolf with an evil eye, <u>as</u> the cause of his master's <u>going</u> so often <u>astray</u>　用恶毒的眼光看着"狼",把它看成是它主人经常走歪路的原因

in all <u>points of spirit</u> befitting an honorable dog　根据与一条忠诚体面的狗相宜的一切品质

be as courageous an animal as ever scoured the woods　与出没于<u>丛林</u>中的任何野兽同样的勇敢

to withstand the ever-during and all — besetting terrors of a woman's tongue　抵御/承受一个女人的舌头所产生的持久的不断袭来的恐惧

to droop to the ground, or curl between his legs　（狗尾巴）低垂在地上,或者蜷缩在两腿之间

to <u>sneak about</u> with a gallows air, casting <u>many a</u> sidelong glance at Dame Van Winkle　带着要受绞刑的神情,到处躲躲闪闪,还时常斜眼看看温克尔夫人

<u>at the least flourish</u> of a broomstick or ladle　扫帚柄或者长柄勺稍微一动

to fly to the door with yelping precipitation　吠叫着飞跑到门口

7. Time grew worse and worse with Rip Van Winkle as years of matrimony <u>rolled over</u>.　随着婚后的时光推移,瑞普·凡·温克尔的日子越来越难过。

8. tart temper　尖酸刻薄的脾气

to mellow with age　随年龄增长而变得成熟圆通

to console himself by frequenting a kind of perpetual club of the sages, philosophers, and other idle personages of the village　常去造访一个永久性的俱乐部以聊以自慰,村子里的智者、哲人和其他游手好闲的人是俱乐部的常客

9. that (= the club) <u>held its sessions</u> on a bench before a small inn, <u>designated by</u> a rubicund portrait of his majesty George the Third.　这个俱乐部经常聚谈于小酒馆前的一条长凳上,一幅乔治三世陛下脸色红润的肖像就是这家小酒馆的招牌

　＊(be) designated by　以……作招牌/标记

10. <u>talking</u> listlessly <u>over</u> village gossip　无精打采地谈论着村里的闲言碎语/小道消息

to tell endless sleepy stories about nothing　永无休止地讲着空洞无物、令人昏昏欲睡的故事

to <u>deliberate upon</u> public events some months after they had taken place　慎重考虑着几个月前发生的公众事件

11. How solemnly they would listen to the content, as <u>drawled out</u> by Derrick Van Bummel, the schoolmaster, a dapper learned little man, who was not to <u>be daunted by</u> the most gigantic word in the dictionary.　当德瑞克·凡·布梅尔慢条斯理读着旧报纸上的内容时,他们听得多么神情肃穆!这位学校教师是个机灵干练、有学问的小个子,字典中再难的字也唬不倒他。

　＊ as drawled out by . . . = as the newspaper was drawled out by . . .

12. the opinion of this junta　这群人的意见、看法

a patriarch of the village　本村德高望重的老人,族长

just moving sufficiently to avoid the sun, keep in the shade of a large tree　动一动也就刚好避过太阳,使自己待在树荫下也就可以了

to know how to gather his opinions　知道如何得到/猜测/推测他的意见

to <u>send forth</u> short, frequent, and angry puffs　气愤地喷出急促的烟雾

to inhale the smoke slowly and tranquilly, and emit it in light and placid clouds　缓慢而平静地吸进烟,然后再吐出轻盈平和的烟雾

to nod his head <u>in token of</u> perfect approbation　他点头表示认同/赞许

13. be <u>at length</u> routed by his termagant wife from even this <u>strong hold</u>　最终被她凶悍的老婆甚至从这个坚固的要塞里挖了出来

to <u>break in upon</u> the tranquility of the assemblage　突然打破这群人的平静

to <u>call</u> the members all <u>to naught</u>　把所有人都视若无物

nor was that august personage = that august personage was also called to naught　即使是那位威严的大

人物也同样被她所傲视

to scare from the daring tongue of this terrible virago　恐惧这可怕的悍妇那肆无忌惮的舌头

to charge him outright with encouraging her husband in habits of idleness　毫不隐讳地指责他怂恿她的丈夫游手好闲,积习不改

* outright　*ad.* 公然,无保留地,毫不隐讳地

14. his only alternative to escape from the labor of the farm and the clamor of his wife　他逃避农场劳动和老婆吵闹的唯一选择

to stroll away into the woods　进树林闲逛

sympathize with the dog as a fellow sufferer in persecution　同情和理解这条狗,把他看作同受迫害的难友

to look wistfully in his master's face　怅惘地看着他主人的脸

to reciprocate the sentiment with all his heart　竭诚地回报以同样的感慨

15. be hopping and twittering among the bushes　(鸟儿)在树丛间跳跃鸣叫

be wheeling aloft, and breasting the pure mountain breeze　(鹰)迎着山间纯净的轻风在高空盘旋

to recall the occurrences before he fell asleep　回忆他睡觉前发生的事情

the mountain ravine, the wild retreat among the rocks　山间沟壑,岩石间荒野的隐蔽处

the woebegone party at ninepins　那群愁眉苦脸玩九柱戏的人

16. the clean well-oiled fowling-piece　干干净净、油光锃亮的猎枪

to find an old firelock lying by him　看到身旁有一把旧枪

the barrel encrusted with rust, the lock falling off, and the stock worm-eaten　外面生锈的枪管,脱落的枪栓,以及被虫蛀坏了的枪托

the grave roysters of the mountain　山里疯狂闹酒的人／好酒滋事的人

to put a trick upon him　跟踪他

to dose him with liquor and rob him of his gun　给他灌了酒,下了他的枪

(dog) might have strayed away after a squirrel or partridge　(狗)也许追鹌鹑或灰山鹑已经迷了路

to whistle after him, shout his name　吹口哨唤他,大声喊他的名字

17. to revisit the scene of the last evening's gambol　再去昨晚游戏的地方看看

to find himself stiff in the joints, and wanting in his usual activity　发觉自己的关节僵硬,活动也不如平常灵便了

to lay me up with a fit of the rheumatism　使我得上风湿,卧床不起

to have a blessed time with Dame Van Winkle　可就交了大运,让温克尔太太没办法了

to get down into the glen with some difficulty　费劲地走下来进入山谷

to ascend up the gully　沿着这沟渠爬上去

to make shift to scramble up its sides　设法爬上岸

18. working his toilsome way through thickets of birch, sassafras, and witch hazel　在丛丛桦树、黄樟和金缕梅中吃力地穿过

(be) tripped up or entangled by the wild grape vines　被野葡萄藤绊倒和缠住

to twist their coils and tendrils from tree to tree　它们的藤蔓蜷曲在树间攀缘

to spread a kind of network in his path　在他所行的路上布下了网

19. to reach to where the ravine had opened through the cliffs, to the amphitheatre　到达沟壑,穿过重崖,走向山谷洞开的地方,那里就像半圆形的剧场

20. The rock presented a high impenetrable wall, over which the torrent came tumbling in a sheet of feathery foam, and fell into a broad deep basin, black from the shadows of the surrounding forest.　高崖巨石屹

立于前,形同一堵不可穿透的墙,石上湍流激荡,翻着泡沫,羽毛似的一片水流,注入宽阔的深潭,周围树林倒映,潭水幽暗。

21. be brought to a stand （某人）只好站住/不得已而站住

be only answered by the cawing of a flock of idle crows 回答他的只有群鸦懒散的聒噪

sporting high in air about a dry tree that overhung a sunny precipice 阳光下,枯树悬崖倒挂,乌鸦在上空嬉闹

to secure in their elevation 高高在上,逍遥自在,无忧无虑

to seem to look down and scoff at the poor man's perplexities 似乎在俯视、在嘲弄这个可怜虫的困惑与迷茫

to feel famished for his breakfast 感到饥饿,想吃早饭

to dread to meet his wife 害怕遇到他老婆

to shoulder the rusty firelock 扛着生锈的枪

22. turn his steps homeward 转身朝家走去

to have thought himself acquainted with everyone in the country round 认为自己熟悉村里的每一个人

to stare at him with equal marks of surprise 都以同样的惊奇盯着他

to cast their eyes upon him 把目光投向他

invariably strike their chins 无一例外地摸摸他们的胡子

to induce sb. involuntarily to do the same 诱导某人不由自主地做同样的动作

23. Their dress, too, was of different fashion from that to which he was accustomed. 他们的衣着也与他过去所习惯的款式不同。

＊ that＝that fashion, to which 引导定语从句修饰 that, was accustomed to 意为"习惯于"。

24. to enter the skirt of the village 走到村庄的边缘

to run at his heel, hooting after him, and pointing at his gray beard 跟在他后面,跑着叫着,指点着他的灰白胡须

those which had been his familiar haunts 那些曾经是他熟悉的、常来常往的地方

to misgive him that both he and the world around him were bewitched 使他思想上产生了疑虑:他本人和他周围的世界全都中了邪

25. There was every hill and dale precisely as it had always been. 每一座山、每一个山谷都还是原来的样子,分毫不差。

26. to approach his own house with silent awe 满怀敬畏,默默地走近自己的家

expecting every moment to hear the shrill voice of Dame Van Winkle 估计会随时听到凡·温克尔太太的尖叫

to find the house gone to decay — the roof fallen in, the windows shattered, and the doors off the hinges 发现房子已经破败——屋顶塌陷,窗户破烂,门枢脱落

＊ gone to decay, fallen in 和 shattered 三个分词短语以及 off the hinges 都是 find 的宾语补足语。

be skulking about it (＝the house) 绕着房子躲躲藏藏/鬼鬼祟祟

to call him by name 喊他的名字

an unkind cut 一个不小的(情感)伤害

be always kept in neat order （房子）总是被打扫得整洁有序

be empty, forlorn, and apparently abandoned （房子）空荡荡的,一片荒凉,明显早被弃置

(the desolateness) to overcome all his connubial fears （这荒凉孤独之感）压倒了他对婚姻/老婆的一切恐惧

to ring for a moment with his voice 一时间回荡着/响起了他的声音

27. to hasten to his old resort 急忙去他以前常去的地方

a large rickety wooden building 一座摇摇欲坠的大木楼

with great gaping windows, some of them broken, and <u>mended with</u> old hats and petticoats 张开大嘴的窗户,有的已经破了,用旧帽子和衬裙堵塞着

28. Instead of the great tree that used to shelter the quiet little Dutch inn of yore, there now was reared a tall naked pole (= now a tall naked pole was reared there). 昔日那棵为宁静的荷兰小酒馆遮阴蔽日的大树不见了,取而代之的是一根裸露的高杆竖立在那里。

29. be a singular assemblage of stars and stripes 是一种奇怪的星条组合

to have smoked so many a peaceful pipe 心平气和地抽了好多袋烟

be singularly metamorphosed 发生了古怪的变化/变形

be stuck in the hand instead of a scepter (某物)被拿在手里,取代了权杖

30. but none that Rip recollected = there is none that Rip recollected 一个人他也想不起来

a busy, bustling, disputatious tone about it (= character) 性格上带有一种毛毛躁躁、好争辩的情绪

instead of the accustomed phlegm and drowsy tranquility 不是惯常的懒散迟钝和昏昏欲睡的平静

uttering clouds of tobacco smoke instead of idle speeches 嘴里总是喷着烟而不是无聊的闲话

<u>doling forth</u> the contents of an ancient newspaper 一点点地读着旧报纸(上的内容)

<u>in place of these</u>, a lean bilious looking fellow 代替这些人的,是一个瘦瘦的脾气暴躁的家伙

be haranguing vehemently about rights of citizens 在热烈地慷慨陈词什么公民权利

be a perfect Babylonish jargon to the bewildered Van Winkle 对困惑不解的凡·温克尔来说,完全是一堆巴比伦式的胡言乱语

31. with his long grizzled beard, his rusty fowling piece, his uncouth dress, and the army of women and children that had gathered at his heels 他长着灰蓬蓬的长胡子,扛着生锈的猎枪,穿着古怪的衣裳,后面跟着一群女人和小孩儿

to attract the attention of the tavern politicians 吸引了这些小酒馆政客们的注意

eyeing him from head to foot, with great curiosity 怀着极大的好奇,从头到脚打量着他

to <u>bustle up</u> to him 匆忙走到他跟前

to draw him partly aside 稍微把他往旁边拉一拉

be equally <u>at a loss</u> to comprehend the question 对这个问题也同样是听不懂/一片茫然

putting them to the right and left with his elbows as he passed 他一边走一边用胳膊肘左推右搡

planting himself before Van Winkle, with one arm akimbo, the other resting on his cane 他昂然挺立在凡·温克尔的面前,一手叉腰,另一手放在手杖上

to demand <u>in an austere tone</u> 以一种傲慢的语调问道

to mean to <u>breed a riot</u> in the village 想要在村里制造骚乱

a poor <u>quiet man</u>, a native of the place, and a loyal subject of the King 一个可怜的不惹是非的/本分人,在这儿土生土长,是国王的忠实臣民

32. a <u>general shout</u> burst from the by-standers 人群中/旁观者中爆发出一片哗然

hustle him! away with him! 赶他走,叫他滚蛋

to assume a tenfold austerity of brow 摆/装出十倍傲慢的表情

to demand again the unknown culprit 再次盘问这不知名的罪犯

to mean no harm 没有恶意

used to <u>keep about</u> the tavern 过去常常待在这酒馆里

33. to bethink himself a moment 他想了一下

a thin piping voice　尖细的嗓音

a wooden tombstone in the church yard that used to tell all about him　墓地里有一块木制墓碑,上面有他一辈子的事儿

be rotted and gone　烂掉了

be drowned in a squall　在一场风暴中被淹死了

a great militia general　民兵团里的大将军

34. to die away　渐渐停止,逐渐消失/微弱下去

to find himself thus alone in the world　发现自己在这个世界上已孑然一身

by treating of such enormous lapses of time　对待倏忽流逝了这么多年的时光

to have no courage to <u>ask after</u> any more friends　没有勇气再探问别的朋友

to behold a precise counterpart of himself, as he went up the mountain　看见一个与自己上山时一模一样的人

to doubt his own identity　他怀疑自己的身份/不知自己是谁

at his wits end　他才穷智尽/江郎才尽

35. that's me yonder — no — that's somebody else, <u>got into my shoes</u>　远处那个人是我——不——那是另外一个人,顶替了我

　* yonder　*ad.* 远处

36. to wink significantly　(相互)交换着意味深长的眼色

to tap their fingers against their foreheads　他们用手轻拍着额头

a whisper about securing the gun　有轻声低语,叫人小心那枪

keeping the old fellow from doing mischief　别让这老头儿闯祸

to retire with some precipitation　急急忙忙地溜走了

a fresh likely woman　姣好可爱的少妇

to <u>press through the throng</u> to <u>get a peep at</u> the gray-bearded man　从人群中挤出来要看看/窥视这花白胡子的老人

to have a chubby child in her arms　她怀里抱着一个胖嘟嘟的孩子

to awaken <u>a train of</u> recollections in his mind　唤起了他脑海中一系列的回忆

37. to put it with a faltering voice　结结巴巴/犹犹豫豫地说出了另一个问题/一句话

to break a blood vessel in <u>a fit of passion</u> at a New-England peddler　在对一个新英格兰小贩发脾气

38. There was <u>a drop of comfort</u>, at least, <u>in this intelligence</u>. The honest man <u>could</u> contain himself no longer.　听了这消息,至少有一点儿安慰。这个老实人再也不能控制自己了。

39. tottering out from among the crowd　(某人)颤颤巍巍地从人群中走出来

to put her hand to her brow, and peeping under it in his face for a moment　她把手搭在眉头上,仔细端详他好一会儿

主要内容归纳和总结

1. 华盛顿·欧文出生在纽约城一个富商家庭,他是 11 个孩子中最小的一个,从小就博览群书,写诗写戏,中学毕业后,先在法律部门工作,但对文学创作的爱好,使他以乔纳森的笔名,屡屡向哥哥编辑的《晨报》(*The Morning Chronicle*)投稿,后来竟结集出版成《G. O. 乔纳森书信集》,后来就作品不断。他的代表作是 1819 年 ~ 1820 年出版的《见闻札记》(*The Sketch Book*),书中 33 篇文章大多描写英国的风光,但也有美国本土化了的像《瑞普·凡·温克尔》这样的欧洲传奇,在欧美两大洲

都为他赢得了声誉。

欧文的思想是保守的,他创造的人物常常对过去津津乐道,他是"完善了文学古典主义风格"的浪漫主义作家。他的作品行文优美流畅,犹如音乐,给人以轻松安逸之感,如入梦境。几乎看不到他进行道德说教(moral lesson),因为他就是要读者愉快和轻松。在创作艺术方面,他堪称" 美国的金匠"(American goldsmith)。他作品中的哥特式因素(Gothic elements)和超自然氛围(supernatural atmosphere)使人觉得置身在异国他乡(exotic places)。由于他的作品多为短篇小说,因此他被称为"美国短篇小说之父"(Father of the American short stories)。

2. 华盛顿·欧文的主要作品:

《G. O. 乔纳森书信集》*The Letters of Jonathan Oldstyle, Gent.* (1803)

《从开天辟地至荷兰人占领的纽约史》*A History of New York from the Beginning of the World to the End of the Dutch Dynasty* (1809)

《见闻札记》*The Sketch Book of Geoffrey Crayon, Gent.* (1819 ~ 1820)

《瑞普·凡·温克尔》*Rip Van Winkle*

《睡谷传奇》*The Legend of Sleepy Hollow*

《布莱斯桥大厦》*Bracebridge Hall* (1822)

《一位旅行家的故事》*Tales of a Traveler* (1824)

《爱尔汗布拉宫》*Alhambra* (1832)

重要信息句子

1. Washington Irving was regarded as an early Romantic writer in the American literary history and Father of the American short stories.

2. Washington Irving has always been regarded as a writer who "perfected the best classic style that American Literature ever produced." 华盛顿·欧文一直被认为是把美国文学产生的经典文风臻于完善的作家。

II. 拉尔夫·沃尔多·爱默生 Ralph Waldo Emerson (1803 ~ 1882)

词语解释和难句分析

1. be unanimously agreed to be the summit of the Romantic period 被毫无疑义地一致同意为浪漫主义时期的顶峰

a descendent of a long line of New England clergymen 新英格兰世代牧师的后裔

Unitarian minister 唯一神教牧师

be frugal, industrious, and undistinguished 为人节俭、勤奋,未显示出过人之处

to begin keeping journals 开始坚持记日记

to draw on the journals for materials for his essays and poetry 从日记里为他的散文和诗歌创作提取素材

to become a pastor in a church in Boston 变成了波士顿一个教堂的本堂牧师

be ardent in his service in religion　热衷于宗教仪式

to grow skeptical of the beliefs of the church　逐渐对基督教信仰产生了怀疑

feeling Unitarianism intolerable　感到唯一神教教义难以忍受

2. to embark on a leisurely European tour　开始悠闲的欧洲旅游

to become closely involved with German idealism and Transcendentalism　深入了解了德国唯心主义和超验主义

to pursue his new path of "self-reliance"　追求他"自力更生"的新路

the unofficial manifesto for the Club　该俱乐部非官方的宣言

to establish him ever since as the most eloquent spokesman of New England Transcendentalism　从此后他被确立为新英格兰超验主义最雄辩的代言人/代表

to live an intellectually active and significant life　学术活动非常活跃,非常有意义

be a slow anticlimax to his middle years　慢慢转入平庸,远不如中年时期

to honor him the most influential prophet and the intellectual liberator of their age　赞誉他为当时最有影响的预言家和思想解放者

3. and his reputation as a family man of conventional life and a decent, solid citizen has remained always.
他作为忠实于家庭生活的传统男人和正派可靠的公民,其声誉得以永远保持

＊has remained always = has always (_ad._) remained

4. to convey the best of his philosophical discussions and transcendental pursuits　表达了他的最佳哲学思想和超验主义精神追求

a reflection upon the aesthetic problems in terms of the present state of literature in America　美国文学现状方面美学问题的思考

5. philosophical school　哲学流派

to absorb some ideological concerns of American Puritanism and European Romanticism　吸收了美国清教主义和欧洲浪漫主义的某些唯心主义观念

with its focus on the intuitive knowledge of human beings to grasp the absolute in the universe and the divinity of man　重在人类掌握宇宙的绝对性和人的神性方面的直觉认识

to put forward his philosophy of the over-soul　推出他的超灵哲学

to reject the formal religion of the churches and the Deistic philosophy　反对传统/拘于形式的教堂宗教和自然神论哲学

to base his religion on an intuitive belief in an ultimate unity　他把自己的宗教建立在对高度统一的直觉的信仰之上

an all-pervading power from which all things come and of which all are a part　万物源于其中又由万物组成的无处不在的力量

6. Emerson's remarkable image of "a transparent eyeball" marks a paradoxical state of being, in which one is merged into nature, the over-soul, while at the same time retaining a unique perception of the experience.　爱默生著名的"透明眼球"意象标示了自相矛盾的存在状态,人融于自然,融于超灵,同时也获得了独特的经验感受。

＊retaining … experience = one is retaining … experience,现在分词短语与前面的过去分词短语merged into nature 是并列的谓语成分。

7. be affirmative about man's intuitive knowledge　肯定人直觉的认识

to decide what is right and to act accordingly　决定什么是正确,并采取相应的行动

be emblematic of the spiritual world, alive with God's overwhelming presence　象征/标志着与上帝同在的精神世界

＊ God's overwhelming presence　上帝威加宇内的存在/上帝无处不在

to sink yourself back into its influence　沉浸在大自然的影响中

to become spiritually whole again　重新获得精神的完整

8. By employing nature as a big symbol of the Spirit, or God, or the over-soul, Emerson has brought the Puritan legacy of symbolism to its perfection.　爱默生用大自然作为精神或上帝或超灵的象征,使清教的象征主义思想遗产臻于完善。

9. Emerson's junior by fourteen years, Thoreau embraced his master's ideas as a disciple.　梭罗比爱默生小14岁,作为弟子他秉承了大师的思想。

10. to give birth to a great transcendentalist work, *Walden*　产生/创作出一部伟大的超验主义作品——《瓦尔登湖》

be lost in spiritual communication with nature　陷入与大自然精神交流的沉思之中

to believe in self-culture/self-education　信仰自我教育

be eager to identify himself with the Transcendental image of the self-reliant man　渴望自己与作为自助者的超验意象统一起来/等同起来

to seek to reduce his physical needs and material comforts to a minimum to get spiritual richness 寻求把物质/生理需求和物质享受减少到最小程度,以达到精神上的富有

individual conscience　个人的良知

to consider the society fetters of the freedom of individuals　把社会当成是束缚个人自由的桎梏

his indebtedness to *Nature*　他从《论自然》这部著作得到的教益/蒙受的恩惠

11. to have a casual style　随意挥洒/行云流水的文风

be derived from his journals or lectures　取材于他的日记和讲演

a series of short, declarative sentences　用一系列短句,陈述如流

to flower out into illustrative statements of truth and thoughts　陈述似妙笔生花,内蕴思想的真理

to employ these literary sources to make and enrich his own points　利用这些文学源泉来形成和丰富自己的观点

to take the full rein of his discussion　完全控制他的思想讨论

爱默生作品选读

《论自然》*Nature* 前言和第一章

词语解释和难句分析

1. the idealist philosophy in relation to nature　与大自然有关的理性哲学

to believe in the mystical "Unity of Nature"　信仰神秘的"自然统一性"

to develop his concept of the "Over-Soul" or "Universal Mind"　孕育和发展了"超灵"或"宇宙思想"的概念

2. to build the sepulchers of fathers　建造父辈的坟墓

＊ sepulcher　尤指砖石砌的坟墓和凿石而建的崖墓。

3. The foregoing generations beheld God and nature face to face; we, through their eyes.　已逝的先辈们曾面对面见过上帝和自然,而我们则是通过他们的眼睛去看。

＊ we, through their eyes. ＝We behold God and nature through their eyes.

4. Why should not we also enjoy an original relation to the universe?　为什么我们不能也享有一种与宇宙独创的关系?

5. Why should not we have a poetry and philosophy of insight and not of tradition, and a religion by revelation to us, and not the history of theirs?　为什么我们不能拥有一种独具慧眼而不是囿于传统的诗歌和哲学? 为什么我们不能拥有一种通过我们自身得到的启示而形成的宗教,而不是他们得到启示的历史?

　　＊ and a religion ... theirs? ＝ Why should not we have a religion by revelation to us, and not the history of theirs? 这里 theirs ＝ their revelation。

6. Embosomed for a season in nature, whose floods of life stream around and through us, and invite us by the powers they supply, to action proportioned to nature, why should we grope among the dry bones of the past, or put the living generation into masquerade out of (＝from) its faded wardrobe?　当我们置身于自然的一个季节之中,它那生命的洪流在我们的周围和我们的身体之中奔涌,凭借着洪流的力量,吸引我们采取与自然和谐的行动,这时我们为什么还要在往昔的枯骨之间摸索,为什么要让生气勃勃的这一代人穿上往昔那褪色的服装去参加化装舞会?

　　＊ 整个句子是一个分词短语作时间状语加上 why 引导的反问句作主句。分词短语 embosomed for a season in nature ＝ when we are embosomed for a season in nature。nature 有定语从句 whose flood of life ... to nature, 从句有两个谓语动词 stream 和 invite, 从句主语 whose flood of life ＝ the flood of life of nature,意为大自然生命的洪流。

7. Let us demand our own works and laws and worship.　让我们呼唤我们自己的作品、自己的法律、自己的信仰。

　　＊ worship　n. 崇敬的对象,信仰

8. to have not questions to ask which are unanswerable　不会提出无法回答的问题

9. We must trust the perfection of the creation so far, as to believe that whatever curiosity the order of things has awakened in our minds, the order of things can satisfy.　我们必定相信迄今为止创造的完美,就如同相信无论事物的秩序在我们的脑海里引起怎样的好奇心,它都能满足。

10. Every man's condition is solution in hieroglyphic to those inquiries he would put.　每个人的状况就是他提出的询问的最形象的回答。

　　＊ hieroglyphic ＝ hieroglyph (n.) 象形文字,符号;in hieroglyphic 形象的,有寓意的;he would put 为修饰 inquiries 的定语从句。

11. He acts it as life, before he apprehends it as truth.　他把它作为生活来付诸实践,然后把它作为真理来领悟。

　　＊ 句中 it 指的是上句说的 solution,也即 condition。

12. In like manner, nature is already, in its forms and tendencies, describing its own design.　用同样的方式,自然已经在以自己的形式和倾向在描绘自己的设计。

　　＊ 注意句子是现在进行时态 is describing...; in its forms and tendencies 是方式状语短语。

13. Let us interrogate the great apparition, that shines so peacefully around us.　让我们质询那在我们周围如此平静地闪烁的伟大幻影。

14. We have theories of races and of functions, but scarcely yet a remote approximation to an idea of creation.　我们虽有关于民族和功能的理论,但几乎还没有一个哪怕远远接近于创造理念的理论(探索)。

15. and speculative men are esteemed unsound and frivolous　好思索的人被认为是不正常的和轻浮的

16. But to a sound judgment, the most abstract truth is the most practical.　对于一个正确/合理的判断,最抽象的真理就是最实际的。

17. Its test is, that it will explain all phenomena. 对它是否正确的检验方法是:它要能解释所有的现象。

18. Now many are thought not only unexplained but inexplicable; as (= such as) language, sleep, dreams, beasts, sex. 现在许多现象被认为不仅未得到解释,而且还无法说明,例如语言、睡眠、梦、野兽和性。

19. Strictly speaking, therefore, all that is separate from us, all which Philosophy distinguishes as the NOT ME, that is, both nature and art, all other men and my own body, must be ranked under this name, NATURE. 因此,严格地来说,一切与我们分离的东西,所有被哲学区别为"非我"的东西,即,自然和艺术,所有其他的人和我自己的身体,都必须列入"自然"这个名字之下。

   * 句子的主语是两个带定语从句的 all,谓语是 must be ranked under this name。the NOT ME 有同位语:both nature and art 和 all other men and my own body; that is 可认为是插入语,起解释作用。

20. In enumerating the values of nature and casting up their sum, I shall use the word in both senses: — in its common and in its philosophical import. 在列数自然的价值和累计其总和时,我要以双重的含义来使用这一词汇:其普通的含义和哲学的内涵。

   * cast up 把……加起来

21. In inquiries so general as our present one, the inaccuracy is not material; no confusion of thought will occur. 在像我们目前这样泛泛的询问中,不够精确不是实质问题/关系不大,不会发生思想混乱。

   * so general as our present one 是修饰 inquiries 的后置定语,one = inquire。

22. Nature, in its common sense, refers to essences unchanged by man; space, the air, the river, the leaf. "自然",按通常意义,指的是不会被人改变的本质,如空间、空气、河流和树叶。

23. Art is applied to the mixture of his will with the same things, as in a house, a canal, a statue, a picture. 艺术指的是意志与同样的这些东西的混合,如表现在一座房子、一条水渠、一座雕像和一幅画里的那样。

24. But his operations taken together are so insignificant, a little chipping, baking, patching, and washing, that in an impression so grand as that of the world on the human mind, they do not vary the result. 但他的一切行动加在一起却如此微不足道,以致一小点儿切削、烘烤、修补和清洗,在这个世界留在人脑海里的如此宏大的印象中,改变不了这结果。

   * 整个句子的句架就是 ... so... that ...,如此…… 以至于……; a little chipping, baking, patching, and washing 是主语 his operations 的同位语,是它的例释。they 指的是 his operations, 也包括 a little chipping, ... and washing, 即人的一切艺术行动;the result 指的是上句中所说的艺术的本质,即人的"意志与同样的这些东西的混合"。

25. To go into solitude, a man needs to retire as much from his chamber as from society. 要进入孤独状态,一个人不仅需要离开/退出社会,还要同样离开/退出他的房间。

26. The rays that come from those heavenly worlds, will separate between him and vulgar things. 那些天界射来的星光会把他和身外的俗事分离开来。

27. One might think the atmosphere was made transparent with this design, to give man, in the heavenly bodies, the perpetual presence of the sublime. 可以认为,由于这一安排,大气变得透明,以这些天体的形式,使人的崇高呈现永存。

28. Seen in the streets of cities, how great they are! 从城市的街道中可见,它们是多么伟大!

   * they 指的是那些天体星辰;过去分词短语 seen in ... cities 的逻辑主语就是后面的句子:how great they are. 此句可改写为:It is seen how great they are. it 是形式主语,how great they are 是真正的主语。

29. If the stars should appear one night in a thousand years, how would men believe and adore; and preserve

for many generations <u>the remembrance</u> of the city of God which had been shown! 如果这些星辰在一千年中只出现一个晚上,人们将怎样相信、崇拜并世世代代铭记曾经显示出来的上帝之城!

30. But every night come out these preachers of beauty, and light the universe with their admonishing smile. 但这些美的布道者每晚都出现,用它们那警戒的微笑照耀宇宙。

　　* 此句的主语为 these preachers of beauty,谓语有两个,一是 come out,一是 light the universe;with their admonishing smile 是 light 的状语短语。

31. to awaken a certain reverence 唤醒/激起一定的尊敬

　　be always inaccessible 永远遥不可及

　　never wear a mean appearance 永不会呈现卑琐的外表

32. but all natural objects <u>make a kindred impression</u>, when the mind <u>is open to</u> their influence 但是当人的大脑向它们敞开接受它们的影响时,一切自然的物体都会留下亲和的印象

33. Neither does the wisest man extort all her secret, and lose his curiosity by finding out all her perfection. 最聪明的人也不会硬逼出她(自然)的秘密,发现了她所有的完美,因而失去了好奇心。

　　* by finding out all her perfection 是原因状语,"由于发现了她的全部的完美"。

34. Nature never became a toy <u>to a wise spirit</u>. 对一个聪明的心灵,自然从不曾变成玩具。

35. The flowers, the animals, the mountains, reflected all the wisdom of his best hour, as much as they had delighted the simplicity of his childhood. 花、动物、山峦反映出他最佳时刻的全部智慧,正如它们曾给他童年的纯真带来欢乐一样。

36. When we <u>speak of</u> nature in this manner, we have a distinct but most <u>poetical sense</u> in the mind. We mean the integrity of impression made by manifold natural objects. 当我们以这种方式谈论自然时,我们脑海中就有一种清晰但非常诗意的感觉。我们指的是由多种多样的自然物体所形成的完整印象。

37. It is this which <u>distinguishes</u> the stick of timber of the woodcutter, <u>from</u> the tree of the poet. 正是这一点(诗意的感觉、自然物体的完整印象)将伐木者眼中的木头与诗人眼中的树区别开来。

38. be indubitably made up of some twenty or thirty farms 肯定无疑地由二三十个农场组成

　　the woodland beyond 林地深处

　　to own the landscape 拥有/独享这风景

39. There is a property in the horizon which <u>no man has but he</u> whose eye can integrate all the parts, that is, the poet. 地平线上有一笔财产,谁也不能拥有,只有一眼览尽天下万物/独具慧眼能将所有部分尽收眼底的人才能做到,那就是诗人。

40. This is the best part of these men's farms, <u>yet to this</u> their land-deeds give them no title. 这是这些人的农场的精华部分,但对此,他们在土地上的劳作却没有给他们带来任何权利。

41. At least they have a very a very superficial seeing. 至少,他们的所见也非常肤浅/表面。

42. The sun illuminates only the eye of the man, but shines into the eye and the heart of the child. 太阳只照进成人的眼睛,但照亮孩子的不仅是眼睛而且是心灵。

43. The lover of nature is he whose inward and outward senses <u>are</u> still truly <u>adjusted to</u> each other; who has <u>retained</u> the spirit of infancy even <u>into</u> the era of manhood. 热爱大自然的人是内心与外在的感受真正可以协调一致的人,是即使进入了成年时代还依然保留着孩童精神的人。

　　* 句子是主系表结构,表语是 he,带有两个定语从句,分别由关系代词 whose(所有格)和 who(主格)引导。

44. <u>In the presence of</u> nature, a wild delight <u>runs through</u> the man, <u>in spite of</u> real sorrows. 在大自然面前,即使真有痛苦,这个人也会感到一种狂喜在体内涌流。

45. Nature says, — he is my creature, and maugre (= despite) all his impertinent griefs, he shall be glad with me. 大自然说——他是我的生灵/创造的生物,尽管他有种种不协调的悲伤,但他应当为和我在一起感到高兴。

　　＊ shall 在句中是情态动词"应该"的意思,不是助动词"将要"的意思。

46. to yield its tribute of delight 产生它使人喜悦的东西

　　＊ its = of nature

47. for every hour and change corresponds to and authorizes a different state of the mind, from breathless noon to grimmest midnight. 因为每一个小时和变化都对应和认可一种不同的思想心态,从令人透不过气来的中午到幽暗的子夜。

48. Nature is a setting that fits equally well a comic or a mourning piece. 大自然是对喜剧或悲剧同样适应的大舞台背景。

49. a cordial of incredible virtue 由难以置信的美德酿造的美酒

　　crossing a bare common, in snow puddles 越过空地,来到雪坑里

50. . . . without having in my thoughts any occurrence of special good fortune, I have enjoyed a perfect exhilaration. 我心里(虽)未想过会有什么特殊的好运发生,但却享受了最完美的喜悦。

51. In the woods too, a man casts off his years, as the snake (casts off) his slough, and at what period soever of life, is always a child. In the woods, is perpetual youth. 在树林里也是如此,一个人摆脱他的年龄,就像蛇蜕去蛇蜕,无论在生命的哪个阶段,他总是一个小孩。在树林里,有永恒的青春。

　　＊ at what period soever of life = at whatsoever period of life; In the woods, is perpetual youth. = Perpetual youth is in the woods.

52. Within these plantations of God, a decorum and sanctity reign, a perennial festival is dressed, and the guest sees not how he should tire of them in a thousand years. 待在这些上帝的庄园里,在这端庄而圣洁的领域,永远穿着节日的盛装,这位客人感到即使在这里待一千年也不会厌倦。

　　＊ perennial festival 长年不断的、永久的节日;sees not 感觉不到,意识不到; tire of them 对它们感到厌倦,them 指的是"上帝的庄园"和"圣洁的领域"。

53. There I feel that nothing can befall me in life, — no disgrace, no calamity, (leaving me my eyes,) which nature cannot repair. 在那里我感到生活中什么也不会发生——不会有屈辱,不会有灾难,(勿伤我眼睛,我可亲见,)是大自然不能修复的。

　　＊ 关系代词 which 引导一个定语从句,修饰 disgrace 和 calamity。

54. Standing on the bare ground, — my head bathed by the blithe air, and uplifted into infinite space, — all mean egotism vanishes. I become a transparent eye-ball. 站在空旷的大地上——我的头沐浴在欢乐的空气中,被提升到无限的太空——一切卑琐的利己主义都消失了。我变成了一个透明的眼球。

　　＊ be bathed by 和 be uplifted into. . . 都是被动句式,省略了 be, 就变成了独立分词结构,作状语; standing on the bare ground 是分词短语作状语,但它的逻辑主语与主句主语 all mean egotism 并不一致,语法上不严谨,这可能与作者信笔写来、行云流水的文风有关。

55. The currents of the Universal Being circulate through me; I am part or particle of God. 宇宙生命的激流在我体内循环流动;我是上帝的一部分,上帝的一个微粒。

　　＊ Universal Being 在超验论里即指宇宙的灵魂,超灵,也即上帝本身。

56. The name of the nearest friend sounds then foreign and accidental. 那时连最亲近的朋友的名字听起来也很陌生和意外。

57. To be brothers, to be acquaintances, — master or servant, is then a trifle and disturbance. 要做兄弟,

做熟人——这时做主人还是做仆人,倒成了微不足道的小事和干扰和谐的障碍。

58. I am the lover of uncontained and immortal beauty.　我爱这自由奔放的美,不朽的美。

　　* uncontained　不受制约的,自由奔放的

59. I find something more dear and connate than in streets or village.　我(在树林里)发现了一些在街道和村庄里感受不到的更宝贵、更亲密的东西。

60. In the tranquil landscape, and especially in the distant line of the horizon, man beholds somewhat as beautiful as his own nature.　在宁静的风景里,尤其在遥远的地平线上,人看到了与他自己的本性同样美丽的东西。

61. The greatest delight which the fields and woods minister, is the suggestion of an occult relation between man and the vegetable.　田野和树林所带来的最大快乐是揭示了人与植物之间的神秘关系。

62. I am not alone and unacknowledged.　我并不孤独、无人知闻。

63. The waving of the boughs in the storm is new to me and old. It takes me by surprise, and yet is not unknown.　暴风雨中树枝摇摆对我是既新奇又古老。它使我吃惊,却也并不陌生。

　　* is new to me and old = is new and old to me　对我是既新奇又古老

64. Its effect is like that of a higher thought or a better emotion coming over me, when I deemed I was thinking justly or doing right.　它的效果就像当我认为自己所思、所为正当时,心头涌起的更崇高的思想,或更美好的感情。

65. Yet it is certain that the power to produce this delight, does not reside in nature, but in man, or in a harmony of both.　然而,可以肯定,产生这种快乐的力量,不在自然,而在人,或在两者的和谐。

66. It is necessary to use these pleasures with great temperance.　享受这些欢乐,必须有所节制。

67. For, nature is not always tricked in holiday attire, but the same scene which yesterday breathed perfume and glittered as for the frolic of the nymphs, is overspread with melancholy today.　因为,大自然并非总是打扮成节日的盛装,昨天芬芳扑鼻、光彩夺目像是仙女们欢乐聚会的景象,今日就会一片忧伤。

　　* be overspread with　满布/密布……

68. to wear the colors of the spirit　带有/呈现精神的色彩

69. To a man laboring under calamity, the heat of his own fire hath sadness in it.　对一个承受着灾难的人来说,他火热的激情之中包含着悲伤。

70. There is a kind of contempt of the landscape felt by him who has just lost by death a dear friend (= who has just lost a dear friend by death).　一个密友刚刚去世的人会感到周围的风景之中隐含着某种轻蔑。

71. The sky is less grand as it shuts down over less worth in the population.　当天空为众生中普通一员的离世垂首含悲的时候,它也就不如平时那么恢宏崇高了。

　　* less worth　价值不高的人,泛泛之辈,芸芸众生,普通人

主要内容归纳和总结

1. 拉尔夫·沃尔多·爱默生出生在美国新英格兰一个世代牧师家庭,父亲是唯一神教牧师(Unitarian minister)。他9岁入波士顿拉丁学校(Boston Public Latin School),14入哈佛大学神学院(Harvard Divinity School),一直坚持记日记,后来的写作多取材于此。

　　爱默生是公认的散文家,是《散文集》而不是《自然》奠定了他的文学地位。他的文句简短清新,如行云流水,比喻典故信手拈来,随意挥洒,深入浅出,妙语如珠,表现出明显的美国风格,故而

被称为"美国学者"(American scholar)。

2. 爱默生的超验主义是吸收了美国清教思想和法国浪漫主义形成的一个哲学流派,强调人类凭本能(instinct)即可掌握宇宙绝对真理,凭直觉(intuition)即可决定是非并采取行动。"超灵"是他超验主义思想的集中体现。他反对教堂的正式宗教,反对神学,提倡最终统一的直觉信仰(an intuitive belief in an ultimate unity)——超灵。他认为超灵是弥漫一切的力量(all-pervading power),一切事物皆源于它,又都是它的组成部分。他的著名比喻"透明眼球"(a transparent eyeball)的意象标志着一种似非而是的状态(paradoxical state of being),一方面人渐渐融入自然,融入超灵,另一方面,又获得了独特的经验感受。爱默生想要说服人们融入自然,与宇宙超灵进行精神交流,自立自助。他的这种想法实质上是上帝无处不在思想的另一种表达,他的自然,即超灵,即上帝。

3. 爱默生的主要作品:
《论自然》 *Nature* (1836)
《散文集》 *Essays* (1841),内含下列名篇:
＊《美国学者》 *The American Scholar*
＊《自助》 *Self-Reliance*
＊《超灵》 *The Over-Soul*
《散文集二》 *Essays: Second Series* (1944),内含下列名篇:
＊《论诗人》 *The Poet*
＊《论经验》 *Experience*

重要信息句子

1. Emerson is generally known as an essayist.
2. Emerson is the most representative of the philosophical and literary school which is American Transcendentalism.
3. Emersonian Transcendentalism is actually a philosophical school which absorbed some ideological concerns of American Puritanism and European Romanticism, with its focus on the intuitive knowledge of human beings to grasp the absolute in the universe and the divinity of man. 爱默生的超验主义实际上是吸收了美国清教主义和欧洲浪漫主义某些唯心主义观点的一个哲学流派,其核心在于掌握宇宙绝对真理和人的神性方面的直觉认识。
4. Emerson's essays often have a casual style, for most of them were derived from his journals or lectures.
5. The unofficial manifesto for the Transcendental Club was *Nature*.
6. *Nature* did not establish him as an important American writer. His lasting reputation began only with the publication of *Essays* (1841).

Ⅲ. 纳撒尼尔·霍桑 Nathaniel Hawthorne (1804～1864)

词语解释和难句分析

1. (be) imbued with an inquiring imagination, an intensely meditative mind, and unceasing interest in the

"interior of the heart" of man's being　满怀着/充满了探寻的想象,热烈的沉思冥想,以及对人的内在心灵的持久不断的兴趣

to remain one of the most interesting, yet most ambivalent writers　一直是最令人感兴趣、却又最情感矛盾的作家之一

to characterize the lives of so many American writers　成为那么多美国作家人生的特征

be born into a prominent Puritan family　出生在一个有声望的清教徒家庭

be active in 1650s in persecution of the Quakers　在 17 世纪 50 年代迫害贵格会教徒中表现很活跃

be a judge at the Salem witchcraft trials　在萨勒姆巫术审判案中担任法官

leaving at Salem a widow and three children in genteel poverty　在萨勒姆撇下了一个遗孀和三个孩子,过着上流社会的穷日子

with the financial support from his more prosperous maternal relations　由于得到他母亲娘家富裕亲戚的经济上的帮助

to pass a serene childhood　度过了宁静的童年时代

to spend his adolescence reading some books of those literary master minds　青年时期是在阅读那些文学巨匠/旗手的著作中度过的

2. The decision to devote himself to writing was gradually taking shape and finally put into practice during those years when he was living with his mother in Salem.　他献身于文学创作的抉择正逐步形成,并在他和母亲居住在萨勒姆的那几年里最终付诸实践。

3. to prove to be fruitful　证明是富于成果的

to attract critical attention　吸引了(文学)评论界的注意

4. A series of salient events of Hawthorne's life happened that mattered a lot to his literary imagination and creation.　霍桑生活中接连发生的一系列事件对他的文学想象和创作产生至关重要的影响。

* 句中 that 引导了一个主语的定语从句,是修饰 a series of salient events of Hawthorne's life 的,谓语是 happened;salient(*adj.*)喷涌而出的,接连发生的。

5. to strike up a very intimate relationship with Thoreau and Melville　开始了与梭罗和麦尔韦尔非常亲密的关系

to best demonstrate Hawthorne's early obsession with the moral and psychological consequences of pride, selfishness, and secret guilt that manifest themselves in human beings　最好地证明了霍桑早年一味追求表现人类经常显露出来的傲慢、自私和心灵罪恶所带来的道德和心理上的后果

* that 引导的是 pride, selfishness, and secret guilt 三个并列名词的定语从句。(be) obsessed with 沉湎于,专心致志于;to manifest oneself in. . .自身表现出来的。

be involved in and affected by the sin of adultery in different ways　以不同方式卷入一项通奸罪,并深受其影响

be based on the tradition of a curse pronounced on the author's family　创作的依据是对作者家族发出诅咒的传说

to work as American consul to Liverpool　在美国驻英国利物浦的领事馆做领事工作

a romance set in Italy　一个背景在意大利的传奇故事

be concerned about the dark aberrations of the human spirit　关于/涉及人的精神领域隐秘的心理失常/精神迷乱

6. to turn out to be a most disturbed, tormented and problematical one possible to imagine.　结果是可以想象的最烦恼不安、痛苦难熬和错综复杂(的一种文学境界)

to have much to do with his "black" vision of life and human beings　与他"黑色"的人生观和人类观有很大关系

to remain latent, perhaps, through the whole life　一直是隐伏的,也许贯穿一生

to rouse it to activity　唤起它的活性,激活它

7. A piece of literary work should "show how we are all wronged and wrongers, and avenge one another." 一部文学著作应当"显示出我们是如何都被冤枉、如何都冤枉别人,以及又是如何相互报复的"。

8. to discuss sin and evil　讨论罪孽和邪恶

to prove that everyone possesses some evil secret　证明每个人有一些邪恶的秘密

9. "The Minister's Black Veil" goes further to suggest that everyone tries to hold theevil secret from one another in the way the minister tries to convince his people with his black veil. 《牧师的黑面纱》进一步揭示:每一个人都试图互相包藏邪恶的秘密,采取的就是牧师用黑面纱说服别人的方法。

＊the minister tries to...veil 是 the way 的定语从句,介词短语 in the way 是 that 引导的宾语从句的状语。

10. "The Birthmark" drives home symbolically Hawthorne's point that evil is man's birthmark, something he is born with. 《胎记》从象征意义上透彻地讲述了霍桑的观点:邪恶诗人的胎记,是一种与生俱来的东西。

11. overreaching intellect　夸大其词、言过其实的伎俩,欺骗炫耀的才华

be too proud, too sure of himself　太过自负,太过自信

12. The tension between the head and the heart constitutes one of the dramatic moments when the evil of "overreaching intellect" would be fully revealed. 头脑和内心的紧张状况会形成一种戏剧性冲突的时刻,使得"言过其实、欺骗炫耀"的邪恶得以充分暴露。

＊关系副词 when 引导的是一个修饰 moments 的定语从句。

13. Hawthorne's intellectuals are usually villains, dreadful because they are devoid of warmth and feeling. 霍桑笔下的知识分子通常都是恶棍,因缺乏人情温暖而令人感到可怕。

14. What's more, they tend to go beyond and violate the natural order by doing something impossible and reaching the ultimate truth, without a sober mind about their own limitations as human beings. 更有甚者,他们往往超越和违背自然法则,而去做一些不可能完成的事情,想要达致不可逾越的真理,却没有关于自身人类局限的言出由衷的实事求是的思想。

＊doing 和 reaching 是作介词 by 宾语的两个并列动名词。

15. be but a few specimens of Hawthorne's chilling, cold-blooded human animals　仅仅是霍桑笔下那些令人寒心的人面冷血动物中的几个标本/样品罢了

to originate in Puritanism　源自清教教义

to live into the successive generations　遗传给后辈几代人

to often wonder if he might have inherited some of their guilt　常常想知道他是否已继承了祖先的某些罪过

to lead to his understanding of evil being at the very core of human life　使他懂得了就在人的生活的核心也存在着邪恶

be typical of the Calvinistic belief　恰好是加尔文主义的信仰

to atone for their sins　为他们的罪孽赎罪/做补偿

be shown in an almost totally negative light　暴露在几乎完全否定的光照下,几乎受到一片指责/批判

be attracted in every way to the Puritan world　各方面都受到清教徒社会的影响

to condemn its less humane manifestations　抨击/谴责清教徒不太人道的表现

16. his apparent preoccupation with the moral issues of sin and guilt　他对关于罪恶方面的道德话题,潜心研究/全神贯注

his keen psychological analysis of people　他对人深刻的心理分析

be brought to full display　得到充分的展现

to focus his attention on the moral, emotional, and psychological effects or consequences of the sin on the people in general　集中表现罪恶对一般人的道德、情感和心理方面产生的影响或后果

to prove fruitful to Hawthorne's imagination　证明对发挥霍桑的艺术想象力是卓有成效的

by relating his experience of discovering a small package　通过讲述他发现一个小包装盒的体验

to give his tale a sense of historical reality and an air of authenticity　赋予他创作的故事一种历史现实感和一丝真实性

to demonstrate fully his artistic pursuit and his theory about "Romance"　充分表现了他的艺术追求和他关于"浪漫传奇"这种文学体裁的看法

17. an extraordinary man of literary craftsmanship　一个杰出的文学艺术巨匠

to cater for the thematic concern　为主题服务/迎合主题的需要

be good at exploring the complexity of human psychology　善于探讨人物心理的复杂性

18. Thought propels action and grow organically out of the interaction of the characters, as we can find in *The Scarlet Letter*.　思想推动行动，并从人物的相互影响中有机地向前发展，正如我们在《红字》当中所看到的。

19. Whereas allegory is used to hold fast against the crushing blows of reality, the symbol serves as a weapon to attack and penetrate it.　鉴于寓言讽喻是用来紧扣抨击现实这个主题的，所以象征手法被作为批判现实、洞察现实的武器。

20. Hawthorne is a master of symbolism, which he took from the Puritan tradition and bequeathed to American literature in a revivified form.　霍桑是一个象征主义大师，他从清教传统中吸收了象征主义，并把它以新的形式移植到/遗传给美国文学。

　　＊关系代词 which 引导的是一个非限制性定语从句，修饰 symbolism。

21. to provide the most conclusive proof　提供最权威的/最具决定性的证据

the sin of adultery　通奸罪行

to prove himself to be one of the best symbolists　他证明自己是最优秀的象征主义者

to take on different layers of symbolic meanings as the plot develops　随着情节的发展，表现/呈现出不同层面的象征意义

to come up with different interpretations　得出不同的解释

霍桑作品选读

《好小伙布朗》*Young Goodman Brown* 节选

词语解释和难句分析

1. to plead him not to go to attend a witches' Sabbath in the woods　恳求他不要去出席森林里的信魔者夜半聚会

to find lots of prominent people of the village and the church　看到了村里和教堂里的许多重要人物

be about to be confirmed into the group　就要被批准/确认进入这个团体

" look up to the Heaven and resist the wicked one. "　"崇拜上帝，抵制恶徒。"

only to find he is alone in the forest　结果只看到自己孤独一人待在森林里

to live a dismal and gloomy life　过着沉闷、忧郁的生活

2. In the manner of its concern with guilt and evil, it exemplifies what Melville called the "power of blackness" in Hawthorne's work.　以关注罪与恶的方式,举例/具体说明了霍桑著作中存在的被麦尔韦尔称之为"黑暗力量"的东西。

3. to accept both society in general and his fellow men as individuals worth his regard　既接受作为整体的社会,也接受作为个人的值得他关心的伙伴

be confronted with the vision of human evil in one terrible night　亲眼看见那个可怕的黑夜里人类邪恶的幻象

to become thereafter distrustful and doubtful　从此就变得怀疑一切,不相信任何事情

(will) be aged in one night by an adventure that makes everyone in this world a fallen idol　经历了使世上众人个个都堕落成鬼影的历险,(他)将一夜老去

to pose the question of Good and Evil in man but withholds his answer　提出人心善恶的问题,却又不吐露/扣留了答案

be real or the mere figment of a dream　究竟是真的还仅仅是梦中虚幻

4. to come forth into the street at sunset　日落时分走上了大街

to put his head back to exchange a parting kiss with his young wife　转回头与他年轻的妻子吻别

be aptly named　起了个恰当的名字

to thrust her own pretty head into the street, letting the wind play with the pink ribbons of her cap 她把漂亮的脑袋伸到门外大街上,任风儿戏弄她帽子上粉红的缎带

put off your journey until sunrise　把你的行程推迟到日出以后吧

be trouble with such dreams and such thoughts that she's afeard of herself, sometimes　她会受到这样的梦魇和这样的想法的纠缠,有时连自己都会害怕

tarry with me this night of all nights in the years　一年三百六十五夜,只求你今夜和我待在一起

5. Of all nights in the year, this one night must I tarry away from thee.　一年三百六十五夜,就今夜我不能与你在一起/要离开你。

6. My journey, as thou callest it, forth and back again, must needs be done 'twixt (=betwixt=between) now and sunrise. = My journey, as you call it, forth and back again, must be done between now and sunrise.　我的这趟行程——你一再这样称呼它——必须从现在开始到日出之前结束。

7. say thy prayers = say your prayers　祈祷吧!

to pursue his way　匆匆前行/赶自己的路

be about to turn the corner by the meeting house　即将在礼拜堂那里拐弯

to see the head of Faith still peeping after him, with a melancholy air　看见菲丝依然在伸着头注视他,面带忧郁的神情

for his heart smote him　因为他的心在谴责自己/受着良心谴责

8. What a wretch am I, to leave her on such an errand!　我是怎样的一个无耻之徒,竟为了这样的一个小差事离开了她!

9. 't (=it) would kill her to think it　这样想会使她活不下去

10. After this one night, I'll cling to her skirts and follow her to Heaven.　今晚过后,我将依偎在她的裙下,伴随她直至天堂。

11. With this excellent resolve for the future, Goodman Brown felt himself justified in making more haste on his present evil purpose.　怀着对未来的美好决心,古德曼·布朗对赶去实现眼前的邪恶目的感到心安理得/理由充足。

12. to take a dreary road, darkened by all the gloomiest trees of the forest　选择了一条阴暗的道路,完全

为森林树木的浓荫所笼罩

13. The trees barely stood aside to let the narrow path creep through, and closed immediately behind. 树木勉强分开(几乎分不开)让狭窄的小道蜿蜒穿过,随后就立即闭合。

14. It was all as lonely as could be. = It was all as lonely as it could be. 周围的一切再孤寂不过了。

15. to know not who may be concealed by the innumerable trunks and the thick boughs overhead 不知道谁会隐藏在这无数的树干间和浓密的树枝下

16. With lonely footsteps, he may yet be passing through an unseen multitude. 伴随着孤独的脚步声,他也许正穿行在看不见的人群中。

17. to throw his companion the maple stick 他把橡木手杖这个老伙计也扔掉了

be as speedily out of sight, as if he had vanished into the deepening gloom 他很快就在视线中消失了,就像已消失在越发深沉的黑暗之中

thinking with how clear a conscience he should meet the minister, in his morning-walk 心里想着,在早晨散步的时候,他会以怎样坦然的心境与牧师相逢

18. And what calm sleep would be his, that very night, which was to have been spent so wickedly, but purely and sweetly now, in the arms of Faith! 那一夜,他会睡得多么安静!本来那一夜他会邪恶地度过,但现在却在菲丝的怀抱里睡得纯洁而甜蜜。

19. to hear the tramp of horses along the road 听见沿路传来的马蹄声

to deem it advisable to conceal himself within the verge of the forest 认识到躲进树林里是可取的/最好躲进森林里

* it 为形式宾语,等于不定式短语 to conceal ... of the forest,后者为真正宾语。

be conscious of the guilty purpose that had brought him thither 意识到把他带到那里去的目的令人内疚

20. On came the hoof-tramps and the voices of the riders, two grave old voices, conversing soberly as they drew near 马蹄声和骑马人的声音越来越近,当他们走近时可以听出,是两个庄重苍老的声音正在严肃地谈话

21. within a few yards of the young man's hiding-place 离那个小伙的藏身之处只几米之遥

owing, doubtless, to the depth of the gloom, at that particular spot 毫无疑问,由于那个地方特别幽暗/阴郁

22. Though their figures brushed the small boughs by the way-side, it could not be seen that they intercepted, even for a moment, the faint gleam from the strip of bright sky, athwart (= across) which they must have passed. 虽然他们的身体擦着了路边的树枝,他们也肯定曾穿过那条明亮的天空射下来的一线微光,但他却连一会儿也未看到那线微光被遮断过。

23. to alternatively crouch and stand on tip-toe 轮换着一会儿蹲下,一会儿踮脚尖儿站着

pushing aside the branches, and thrusting forth his head as far as he durst (= dared) 拔/分开树枝,尽可能大胆地伸出头来

without discerning so much as a shadow 除了阴影,什么也没看清(连阴影都没看清)

24. It vexed him the more, because he could have sworn, were such a thing possible, that he recognized the voices of the minister and deacon Gookin, jogging along quietly, as they were wont to do, when bound to some ordination or ecclesiastical council. 这更使他焦躁不安,因为他可以发誓,如果真会有那样的事,他肯定能听出牧师和执事古金的声音,他俩安静地缓缓前进,像他们惯常去参加圣职仪式或教会会议那样(慢条斯理)。

25. While yet within hearing, one of the riders stopped to pluck a switch. 这时他听到,有一个骑马人停下来折断了一根树枝。

26. had rather miss an ordination dinner than to-night's meeting 宁愿错过一次授任圣职的晚餐,也不愿错过今夜的集会

besides several of the Indian powwows 此外还有几个印第安的巫医

after their fashion 根据/看他们的样子

to know as much deviltry as the best of us （他们知道的魔术）与我们中最杰出的人物同样多

to be taken into communion 被带来参加教会活动

27. and the voices, talking so strangely in the empty air, passed on through the forest, where no church had ever been gathered 这些声音,交谈,如此怪异地在这虚无缥缈的空气中荡漾,穿越过森林,那里从无教堂有过集会

28. Whither (= where), then, could these holy men be journeying, so deep into the heathen wildness? 那么,这些圣洁的人,如此深入异教徒的荒野腹地,究竟往何处旅行呢?

29. to catch hold of a tree, for support , being ready to sink down on the ground, faint and overburdened with the heavy sickness of his heart （他）抱住一棵树,支撑住身体,以防跌倒在地,由于心脏病感到眩晕和心头沉重。

to stand firm against the devil 坚定地反抗魔鬼

to gaze upward, into the deep arch of the firmament 仰天凝视,直入深邃的天穹

(a cloud) to hurry across the zenith （一团云）匆匆掠过天顶

30. Once, the listener fancied that he could distinguish the accents of town's people of his own, men and women, both pious and ungodly, many of whom he had met at the communion-table, and had seen others rioting at the tavern. 一度这听者认为,他能够区别他小镇上的人的口音,无论男女,无论虔诚的和不虔诚的,其中许多人他在圣餐桌上曾经见过,也曾见过另一些人在酒馆里喧哗。

31. to have heard aught but the murmur of the old forest, whispering without a wind 除了原始森林的呢喃,无风时刻的细语,什么也没听到

a stronger swell of those familiar tones 那些熟悉的声音（变得）更加响亮

uttering lamentations, yet with an uncertain sorrow, and entreating for some favor, which, perhaps, it would grieve her to obtain 哭出悲痛,却又带有一种不可捉摸的忧伤,恳求某种恩惠,但得到这种恩惠会使她悲伤

32. As if bewildered wretches were seeking her, all through the wilderness. 仿佛许多困惑无措的人都正在寻找她,布满了荒野。

33. to hold his breath for a response 屏住呼吸,等待回答

(a scream) be drowned in immediately in a louder murmur of voices, fading into far-off laughter（尖叫声）立即淹没在更大的嘈杂声中,渐远渐弱变为远去的笑声

to flutter lightly down through the air, and caught on the branch of a tree 在空中轻轻地飘落,挂在一根树枝上

after one stupefied moment 呆了/愣了一会儿之后

34. be maddened with despair 绝望得发疯

to grasp his staff and set forth again 抓起他的家什（拐杖）,又开始前行

to fly along the forest-path, rather than to walk or run 仿佛沿着林间小路在飞,而不是在走或跑

to grow wilder and drearier, and more faintly traced, and vanish at length （路径）变得更加荒凉昏暗,更加模糊难辨,终于消失了

with the instinct that guides mortal man to evil 凭着诱人堕落的本能

be peopled with frightful sounds 充斥着可怕的声音

to toll like a distant church-bell （风）呼啸着像远处教堂的钟声

to give a <u>broad roar</u> around the traveler　（风）在这旅人周围发出雄浑的嚎叫

to laugh him to scorn　嘲笑他

to shrink not from its other horrors　在其他的恐怖面前也绝不退缩

＊ its = of the scen　这种场景里的

35. Think not to frighten me with your deviltry!　别想用你的魔法来威胁我!

36. all through the haunted forest　在整个鬼魂出没的森林中

to fly on, brandishing his staff with frenzied gestures　他以疯狂的姿势挥舞着拐杖不停地飞奔着

<u>now</u> <u>giving vent to</u> <u>an inspiration of</u> horrid blasphemy, and <u>now</u> shouting forth such laughter, as <u>set</u> all echoes of the forest <u>laughing</u> like demons around him　时而发泄一阵可怕的亵渎神灵的言辞,时而放声大笑,使得整个森林的回声就像他周围的魔鬼在大笑

37. The fiend in his own shape is less hideous, than when he rages in the breast of man.　连魔鬼的本形也不如怒火满腔的狂徒狰狞可怕。

38. Thus sped the demoniac <u>on his course</u>, until, quivering among the trees, he saw a red light before him, (=Thus the demoniac sped on his course, until he saw a red light before him, quivering among the trees,) as when the felled trunks and branches of a clearing have been <u>set on fire</u>, and <u>throw up</u> their lurid blaze against the sky, at the hour of midnight.　这样,这着了魔的人一路飞奔,直到他看到前面有一簇红光,在树林里闪烁,就像林中空地上被砍倒的树干和树枝着火燃烧,子夜时分,扬起炫耀的光焰,直冲天空。

39. to pause <u>in a lull of the tempest</u> that had driven him onward　驱使他前进的暴风雨般的心潮平静下来之后,（他）也暂时停止了前进

to hear the swell of what seemed a hymn, rolling solemnly from a distance, with the weight of many voices　听到了一首似乎是赞美诗的响亮唱颂,从远处传来,由许多人庄严合唱

a familiar one in the choir of the village meeting-house　这是一种在村里教堂唱诗班听过的熟悉的声调

40. The verse <u>died heavily away</u>, and was lengthened by a chorus, not of human voices, but of all the sounds of the benighted wilderness, pealing in awful harmony together.　唱诗声沉闷地低落下去,并以一种合唱的和鸣拖长下去,这不是人声的和鸣,而是幽暗的旷野万籁的和鸣,持久地鸣响在可怖的混合和声之中。

＊ a chorus of human voices 人声的合唱和鸣;a chorus of all sounds of benighted wilderness 幽暗的旷野万籁（各种声音）的和鸣;分词短语 pealing...together 是修饰 chorus 的定语成分。

41. His cry <u>was lost to his own ear</u>, by its unison with the cry of the desert.　他的叫声与这荒漠的呼应汇合在一起,连他自己都听不出自己的声音来了。

42. to <u>glare</u> full <u>upon</u> his eyes　闪光完全展现在他眼前

at one extremity of an open space　在一块空地的尽头

<u>be hemmed in</u> by the dark wall of the forest　被黑暗的森林之墙团团包围

bearing some rude, natural <u>resemblance</u> either <u>to</u> an altar or a pulpit　（岩石）有点粗糙,外形天然地像一个祭坛或布道的教坛

＊ bearing 意为"具有……的特点/性质"。

43. their tops aflame, their stems untouched = their tops were aflame, their stems were untouched　（松树）顶部在燃烧,树干毫无损伤

44. The mass of foliage, that had <u>overgrown the summit of the rock</u>, was all on fire, <u>blazing into</u> the night, and fitfully illuminating the whole field.　长得高出岩石顶部的一簇簇树叶都在燃烧,火焰冲入夜空,忽明忽暗地照亮了整个田野。

45. pendent twig and leafy festoon　下垂的树枝和串串的叶片

to alternately shine forth （火光中的人群）交替着显示出来

peopling the heart of the solitary woods at once 一下子在这孤寂的树林中心布满了人

46. quoth　*v.*　said 说(第一、三人称陈述语气过去式)

47. a grave and dark-clad company 一群庄重的穿黑衣服的人

＊ clad ［古］clothe 的过去式和过去分词

48. Among them, ... from the pulpits in the land. 这一长句总的句架是个倒装句,可概略如下:Among them, appeared faces that ... 其中 faces 是主语,that 引导的是主语的定语从句。可译为:在人影的前后晃动和火光明暗的交替中,一些脸呈现出来,其中一些将会在州议会上见到,另一些人每个安息日都会在圣洁的教坛上虔诚地仰望天空,仁慈地俯视教堂会众。

＊ 状语短语:quivering to-and-fro, between gloom and splendor 在人影前后的晃动之中,(火)光的明暗闪烁之间;that would be seen, next day, at the council-board of the province 第二天会在州议会上见到;and others which Sabbath after Sabbath, looked devoutly heavenward, and benignantly over the crowded pews, from the holiest pulpits in the land 而另外一些人,每个安息日都会从这里圣洁的教坛上仰望天空,仁慈地俯视熙熙攘攘的教堂会众。

＊ 这里关系代词 which 引导了一个定语从句修饰 others。

49. high dames well known to her (= the lady of the governor) 总督夫人非常熟悉的高贵夫人

widows, a great multitude, and ancient maidens, all of excellent repute 许多寡妇和享有极好声名的老处女

lest their mother should espy them 生怕/唯恐他们的母亲会发现她们

flashing over the obscure field 照亮阴暗的田野

to bedazzle goodman Brown （闪光)刺激得好小伙眼花

to recognize a score of the church-members of Salem village, famous for their especial sanctity 认出了20 个萨拉姆村以特别的圣洁闻名的教徒

to wait at the skirts of that venerable saint, his revered pastor 在他敬畏的牧师、令人崇敬的圣人身边伺候着

irreverently consorting with these chaste dames and dewy virgins 极不协调地与这些贞节高雅的夫人和纯真清新的处女混在一起

men of dissolute lives and women of spotted fame 生活放荡的男人和声名狼藉的女人

wretches given over to all mean and filthy vice, and suspected even of horrid crimes 劣迹斑斑、污秽不堪、甚至被怀疑犯下可怕罪行的恶棍

＊ be given over to 交托,具有,犯下(……罪孽); be suspected of 被怀疑(做了)……

50. It was strange to see, that the good shrank not from the wicked, nor were the sinners abashed by the saints. 很奇怪地看到好人并不退避坏人,罪人在圣人身边也不感到羞愧。

51. to scare their native forest with more hideous incantations than any known to English witchcraft 以比已知的英格兰巫术更加可怕的咒语使他们本土的森林变得更加可怕

52. Another verse of the hymn arose, a slow and solemn strain, such as the pious love, but joined to words which expressed all that our nature can conceive of sin, and darkly hinted at far more. 又一节圣诗唱起来了,曲调缓慢而庄严,像是虔诚的爱情诗,但配上词表达我们的本性对罪恶的一切可能的想象,隐晦暗示的就更多了。

＊ (be) jointed to 与……连接上,(给曲子)配上词;hinted at ... 是 which 引导的定语从句中与 expressed 并列的谓语动词。

53. Unfathomable to mere mortals is the lore of fiends. = The lore of fiends is unfathomable to mere mortals. 魔鬼的学识对凡人来说是深不可测的。

54. Verse after verse was sung, and still the chorus of the desert swelled between, like the deepest tone of a mighty organ.　圣诗唱了一节又一节,荒漠的和鸣在节与节之间响起,就像大风琴最深沉的曲调。

* between 在本句中是副词。

55. With the final peal of that dreadful anthem, there came a sound, as if...　随着这可怕的圣歌最后的奏鸣,传来一个声音,仿佛……

be mingling and according with the voice of guilty man, in homage to the prince of all　与负罪之人的声音混合在一起,和谐一致,向万物之主致敬

to throw up a loftier flame　扬起/升起更高的火焰

to obscurely discover shapes and visages of horror on the smoke-wreaths, above the impious assembly　在邪恶的集会上方,在换装的烟雾中,模糊地显现出恐怖的人形和面貌

to shoot redly forth, and form a glowing arch above its base　(岩石上的火焰)向前方射出一道红光,在基石的上方形成一道闪光的拱门

56. With reverence be it spoken, the apparition bore no slight similitude, both in garb and manner, to some grave divine of the New-England churches.　可以怀着敬畏地说,这幽灵无论在穿着还是举止上与英格兰教堂某个庄重的牧师无丝毫相似之处。

* with reverence be it spoken 可以倒过来看,等于 it can be spoken with reverence that . . .; to bear no slight similitude to. . . 意为与……无丝毫相同之处。

57. to bring forth the converts　把皈依本教者带上来

to echo through the field and roll into the forest　回声在旷野上回荡,向森林里滚滚而去

to step forth from the shadow of the trees, and approach the congregation　从阴影中走出来,走向集会大众

to feel a loathful brotherhood with sb.　感觉到与某人令人憎厌的兄弟情谊

to beckon him to advance　向他招手要他向前走

with dim features of despair　带有模糊的绝望神情

to warn him back　告诫他后退

to lead him to the blazing rock　把他领到冒着火焰的岩石跟前

the slender form of a veiled female　戴面纱女子的修长身材

the pious teacher of the catechism　虔诚地教义问答老师

to have received the devil's promise to be queen of hell　得到了魔鬼的承诺,让她做地狱的女王

a rampant hag　疯狂的女巫

58. There stood the proselytes, beneath the canopy of fire.　那里还有许多皈依者站在火焰的华盖下。

59. Welcome to the communion of your race! You have found, thus young, your nature and your destiny.　欢迎来参加你们同类的聚会! 你们这样年轻,就已发现了自己的本质和命运。

60. to look behind you　你请回头看

in a sheet of flame　一片火光/火焰

the fiend-worshippers　魔鬼崇拜者,魔鬼的信徒

61. The smile of welcome gleamed darkly on every visage.　每一长脸上都模糊地闪现出欢迎的微笑。

62. the sable form　黑暗的人形

to have reverenced sb. from youth　从小就一直尊重某人

to shrink from your own sin　对你们自己的罪孽退缩畏避

contrasting your sin with their lives of righteousness, and prayerful aspirations heavenward　把你们的罪孽与他们正直的生活和对上天虔诚地向往加以对比

worshipping assembly　敬神集会,礼拜集会

63. This night it will be granted (for) you to know their secret deeds.　今夜就允许你们知道他们的隐私。

64. hoary-bearded elders of the church　胡子花白的教堂长者

to whisper wanton words to the young maids of their house-holds　向家里的年轻侍女悄悄说下流话

be eager for widow's weeds　渴望寡妇的丧服/黑纱,想当寡妇

to give her husband a drink at bed-time　临睡前她给丈夫一杯毒酒

to make haste to inherit their fathers' wealth　急于继承他们父亲的财产

65. By the sympathy of your human hearts for sin, ye shall scent out all the places where crime has been committed, and shall exult to behold the whole earth one stain of guilt, one mighty blood-spot.　由于你们人类心灵对罪恶的同情,你们会发现一切发生过罪恶的地方,会很高兴地看到整个大地就是一块罪恶的污迹,一摊巨大的血迹。

66. It shall be your's (= yours = your job) to penetrate, in every bosom, the deep mystery of sin, the fountain of all wicked arts, and which, inexhaustibly supplies more evil impulses than human power — than my power, at its utmost! — can make manifest in deeds.　你们(的事)就是要看透每个人心中深藏的罪恶,这是所有邪恶伎俩的源头,它能无穷无尽地提供更多邪恶的动力,比人的力量——比我的最大力量——都还要大! ——并能在各种行为中显示出来。

　* mystery n. 隐私; the foundation of all wicked arts 是前面 the deep mystery of sin 的同位语,起解释作用;关系代词 which 指的是"心中深藏的隐私",即"邪恶伎俩的源头",有两个谓语动词:supplies 和 can make。

67. by the blaze of the hell-kindled torches　在地狱之火的光焰照耀下

trembling before that unhallowed altar　在那亵渎神圣的祭坛前颤抖

in a deep and solemn tone, almost sad, with its despairing awfulness　用低沉、庄严以及由于绝望的恐怖而几乎有些悲伤的语调(说)

once angelic nature　曾经有过的天使的本性

to mourn for our miserable race　哀悼我们悲惨的同类/为我们悲惨的同类而悲伤

68. be hesitating on the verge of wickedness, in this dark world　在这黑暗世界、罪恶的边缘犹豫不决

to contain water reddened by the lurid light　里面盛有被火红的光焰映红的水

the Shape of Evil　邪恶的化身

to dip his hand　把手伸在里面浸了一下

to prepare to lay the mark of baptism upon their foreheads　准备在他们的额上留下洗礼的印记

to be the partakers of the mystery of sin　分享罪恶的隐私

be more conscious of the secret guilt for others, both in deed and thought, than they could now be (conscious) of their own　无论在行为上还是思想上,更能够察觉的是别人的秘密罪行,而不是自己的

to cast one look at his pale wife　看了一眼他脸色苍白的妻子

69. What polluted wretches would the next glance shew (= show) them to each other, shuddering alike at what they disclosed and what they saw!　他们互相再看一眼,看到了多么肮脏卑鄙的罪行啊! 两人全都因所发现/所看到的东西而簌簌发抖。

　* the next glance shew them to each other = the next glance to each other show them. . .

70. to find himself amid calm night and solitude　他发现自己正处于宁静之夜,孤独一人

to die heavily away through the forest　(风)穿过森林沉重地消失

to stagger against the rock and feel it chill and damp　摇摇晃晃地靠在岩石上,感到石头凉冰冰的挺潮湿

to besprinkle his cheek with the coldest dew　在他的脸颊上洒下透凉的露水

staring around him like a bewildered man   瞪大眼睛四处张望

to bestow a blessing on goodman Brown   把祝福留给了好小伙布朗

to shrink from the venerable saint, as if to avoid an anathema   在可敬的生人面前退了回来,好像躲避一个令人讨厌的东西

at domestic worship   在家做礼拜/祈祷

the holy words of his prayer   他的神圣祈祷词

at her own lattice, catechizing a little girl   她在自家的格子门边,对一个小女孩儿讲解教义

to snatch away the child, as from the grasp of the fiend himself   一把拉开这孩子,仿佛是从魔鬼的手里把她抢过来似的

to turn the corner by the meeting house   在礼拜堂旁边拐过弯来

to burst into such joy at sight of him, that she skept (= skipped) along the street, ...   一看见他,突然变得很高兴,她蹦蹦跳跳地沿街跑过来了

to dream a wild dream of a witch-meeting   做了一个女巫聚会的荒诞梦

a dream of evil omen   一个不祥之兆的梦

71. A stern, a sad, a darkly meditative, a distrustful, if not a desperate man, did he become, from the night of that fearful dream. = He did become a stern, a sad, a darkly meditative, a distrustful, if not a desperate man from the night of that fearful dream.   从那夜可怕的梦魇之后,他确实变成了一个严厉、悲伤、喜欢阴郁地冥思苦想的人,如果说不是一个濒临绝望的人,那也一个的疑神疑鬼、怀疑一切的人。

72. to sing a holy psalm   高唱神圣的赞美诗

an anthem of sin   罪恶的颂歌

to rush loudly upon his ear and drown all the blessed strain   响亮地冲进他的耳朵,淹没了所有祝福的曲调

with power and fervid eloquence   以雄辩有力、热情洋溢的口才

to speak from the pulpit, of the sacred truths of our religion, and of saint-like lives and triumphant deaths and of future bliss or misery unutterable   在教坛上(雄辩滔滔地)宣讲我们宗教神圣的真理,圣徒般的生活和光荣的殉难,以及未来难以表达的福祉和苦难

to thunder down upon the gray blasphemer and his hearers   (屋顶)轰然塌下压在亵渎神圣的白发老人和他的听众头上

often awakening suddenly at midnight   常常半夜突然惊醒

to shrink from the bosom of Faith   推开菲丝的怀抱

to kneel down at prayer   跪下做祈祷

be borne to his grave   (尸体)被抬到坟墓

a hoary corpse   一具白发苍苍的老人尸体

a goodly procession   一列人数众多的队伍

to carve no hopeful verse upon his tomb-stone   他的墓碑上没有镌刻充满希望的诗句

主要内容归纳和总结

1. 霍桑于 1804 年出生在美国马萨诸塞州(Massachusetts)萨拉姆(Salem)一个有声望的清教徒家庭。他在美国的第一代祖先威廉·霍桑(William Hawthorne)是海湾殖民地(Bay Colony)的地方行政长官;第二代祖先约翰·霍桑(John Hawthorne)则是萨拉姆巫术审判案的法官。他的父亲是个船长,

1808 年死于黄热病(yellow fever)。他是在母亲娘家富亲戚的经济帮助下受到良好教育成长起来的。他在缅因州鲍登学院(Bowdoin College)就读期间就决心从文,并付诸实践。

2. 霍桑的世界观和作品的思想特点

霍桑的内心世界极度不安和痛苦,思想错综复杂,这与他黑暗的人生观有关。他认为人人内心都有罪恶,也许一生都潜藏着(to remain latent through the whole life),但在一定条件下就会活跃起来,文学作品就是要"表现我们是如何蒙冤和冤枉别人(be wronged and wrongers)的,又是如何相互报复的",所以他几乎在每部书中都讨论罪行和邪恶。他虽然不是清教徒(Puritan),但他这种对人性和人类历史的看法,却与他的先辈是清教徒、先辈的历史行为有密切的关系(如先祖约翰·霍桑是萨拉姆巫术案的审判官)。他认为"一代人的错误行为会遗传给下几代人",甚至怀疑自己遗传了他先辈的罪恶,因此他的作品随处可见对清教徒人生观念的批判,弥漫着道德说教的气息。

3. 霍桑艺术风格的两大特点

首先他是个象征主义的大师(master of symbolism),将象征手法运用得普遍而巧妙,代表作《红字》(The Scarlet Letter)中的红字 A 除了表示"通奸"(adultery),还有多种层面的象征意义;小女孩珠儿(Pearl)则是个主题性的象征——通奸给人们和社会带来的后果。为达到种种象征效果,作品的结构和形式都是经过精心设计的。霍桑作品的第二大特点就是特别注重人物的心理描写,把复杂的内心活动写得细致入微。

4. 霍桑的主要作品:

a. 短篇小说集

《尽人皆知的故事》*Twice Told Tales*(1837)

《古屋青苔》*Mosses from an Old Manse*(1846)

《雪的形象及其他尽人皆知的故事》*The Snow-Image and Other Twice-Told Tales*(1851)

b. 长篇小说

《红字》*The Scarlet Letter*(1850)

《七个尖角阁的房子》*The House of the Seven Gables*(1851)

《福谷传奇》*Blithedale Romance*(1852)

《玉石雕像》*The Marble Faun*(1860)

《好小伙布朗》*Young Goodman Brown*

《牧师的黑面纱》*The Minister's Black Veil*

《胎记》*The Birthmark*

重要信息句子

1. According to Hawthorne, "There is evil in every human heart, which may remain latent (隐伏), perhaps, through the whole life; but circumstances may rouse it to activity (唤醒,激活)."

2. Hawthorne's view of man and human history originates, to a great extent, in Puritanism.

3. One source of evil that Hawthorne is concerned most is overreaching intellect (言过其实,过分炫耀才华), which usually refers to someone who is too proud, too sure of himself.

4. Hawthorne is a master of symbolism, which he took from the Puritan tradition and bequeathed to (被遗传给,移植到) American literature in a revivified form.

Ⅳ. 沃尔特·惠特曼 Walt Whitman（1819~1892）

词语解释和难句分析

1. be considered a monumental work which commands great attention　得到极大关注的、被认为是里程碑式的作品

   its uniquely poetic embodiment of American democratic ideals as written in the founding documents of . . .　《草叶集》作为写在……的基本文件中的美国民主理想的独特诗歌体现

   ＊ its = of *Leaves of Grass*

2. to leave his schooling for food, and become an office boy　为温饱而辍学,当了个勤杂工

   in the <u>printing office</u> of a newspaper　为一家报纸做印刷工作

   to develop his potential for the writing career in the future　为将来的写作生涯开发自己的潜力/培养能力

   to formally <u>take up</u> journalism and <u>indulged himself in</u> the excitement of the <u>fast-growing</u> metropolis　正式从事新闻事业,沉浸在大都市迅速发展的兴奋中

   to begin to show his democratic partisanship　开始显示出他的民主的党派意识

   to take shape　成型

3. Feeling <u>compelled</u> to <u>speak up for</u> something new and vital he found in the air of the nation, Whitman turned to the manual work of carpentry around 1851~1852, as an experiment to <u>familiarized himself with</u> the reality and essence of the life of the nation.　由于感觉到必须为这个国家所发现的新生的和有生命力的事物呐喊欢呼,惠特曼于 1851 年~1852 年转而去干起了木匠的体力活,作为熟悉现实、熟悉这个国家生活本质的一种体验。

   ＊ to peak up for 支持,为……辩护; in the air of the nation 在这个国家的氛围内; he found in the air of the nation 是修饰 something 的定语从句。

4. to widen his reading to a new scale and make it more systematic　他的阅读量随之增加,并使之更加系统化

   to enrich himself simultaneously by these two very different approaches　同时以这两种不同的方式丰富自己

   to put forward his own <u>set of</u> aesthetic principles　提出他自己的一套美学原则

   be a poet with a strong <u>sense of mission</u>　是一位具有强烈使命感的诗人

   to <u>devote all his life to</u> the creation of the "single" poem, *Leaves of Grass*　倾毕生之努力,创作一部诗集:《草叶集》

   <u>be nothing less than</u> to express some new poetical feelings　完全是要表达一些新颖的诗歌情感

   to initiate a poetic tradition in which difference should be recognized　开创了一个承认差别性/独特性的诗歌传统

5. The genuine <u>participation</u> of a poet <u>in</u> a common cultural effort was, according to Whitman, to behave as a supreme individualist.　惠特曼认为,在真正参加共同的文化活动时,诗人要表现出充分的独特个性。

6. to identify his ego with the world, and more specifically with the democratic "en-masse" of America　把他的自我与世界统一起来，更具体地说，把自我与美国民主的整体统一起来

twain yet one　虽二而一

to achieve a kind of transcendent contact　取得一种超验的接触

to realize a community while remaining individuals　认识到保留个性基础上的整体性/同一性

7. He repeated his philosophy again and again to ensure his fellow citizens a full participation in a series of reciprocal relationships in the course of reading his poetry.　在阅读他的诗歌过程中，他一再强调他的观点，以确保他的同胞公民能充分参与一系列的相互接触和交流。

8. to define themselves in the new world of possibilities　在新生的无限机遇的国家里给自己定位

to voice freshness　表现了新鲜感

to show concern for the whole hard-working people and the burgeoning life of cities　关心艰苦工作的劳动人民和欣欣向荣的城市生活

to indicate a lively future　显示了生机勃勃的未来

squalid conditions and the slackness in morality　环境肮脏，道德低下

9. The realization of the individual value are also found a tough position in Whitman's poems in a particular way.　惠特曼个人价值观的实现在他的诗行里以一种独特的方式赢得了地位/惠特曼个人价值观在他的诗里以特殊方式得到了表现。

10. to sing of the "en-masse" and the self as well　既歌颂了美国整体也歌颂了自我

to give emphasis to the physical dimension of the self　强调了自我的生理存在

to openly and joyously celebrate sexuality　公开而快乐地歌颂性

be approved of repeated and affectionately in his lines　在他的诗行里得到了反复的、动情的赞美

11. Sexual love, a rather taboo topic of the time, is displayed candidly as something adorable.　性爱，当时一个非常禁忌的主题，被作为值得崇拜的事情，而直言不讳地展现出来。

12. What is to us what the rest do or think?　别人做什么、想什么于我们又有什么关系呢？

13. be politically committed　与政治密切相关，卷入政治

to stand firmly on the side of the North　坚定地站在北方一边/坚定地支持北方军

be gathered as a collection under the title of Drum Taps　（那些诗）被汇集成册，取名"鼓点"

to show a determination to carry on the fighting dauntlessly until the final victory　下定决心（对暴力和血腥）进行无畏的斗争，直到最后的胜利

to air his sorrow　公开表示他的悲痛

14. Mournful as these poems are, a reader can still detect in them a thin trace of ecstasy for the victory of progress.　虽然这些诗是表示哀悼的，但是读者依然可以从中察觉到一丝为进步力量取胜而表现出的狂喜。

15. To dramatized the nature of these new poetical feelings, Whitman employed brand-new means in his poetry, which would first be discerned in his style and language.　为了突出这些新诗的情感实质，惠特曼采用了崭新的诗歌表现手法，这种手法会首先从他的风格和语言上被识别出来。

16. be marked, first of all, by the use of the poetic "I"　惠特曼的诗风首先以用诗意的"我"为其特点，惠特曼诗歌的风格特点首先是语气上喜用第一人称单数——"我"

hence in a discovery of the self in the other with such an identification　因此以这样一个身份在其他人中发现了自我

17. Usually, the relationship Whitman is dramatizing is a triangular one.　通常，惠特曼突出表现的关系是一个三角关系。

＊ Whitman is dramatizing 是修饰 the relationship 的定语从句。

18. to <u>participate in</u> the process of sympathetic identification　加入同情者的队伍

    be radically innovative <u>in terms of</u> the form of his poetry　在诗歌的形式方面他是个激进的改革者

    poetry without a fixed beat or regular rhyme scheme　没有固定格律和押韵规则的诗歌

    a looser and more open-ended syntactical structure　更加松散、更加随意的句子结构

    be left lying side by side just as things are, undisturbed and separate　（不同长度的诗句）随意地并列排放，如物在原处，原封未动，松散自然

19. There are few compound sentences to draw objects and experiences into a system of hierarchy.　几乎不用复合句分级严谨的结构系统来表现客观事物和主观体验。

    ＊ to draw objects and experiences into a system of hierarchy　把客观事物和主观体验引入（复合句）严谨的结构系统

20. to turn the poem into an open field　把诗歌带入了随意的新天地

    to allow his own imagination to play　任凭他（读者）的想象自由驰骋

    parallelism and phonetic recurrence at the beginning of the lines　诗歌开头的排比结构和语音重复

    to <u>contribute to</u> the musicality of his poems　给他的诗歌增加了乐感

    contrary to the rhetoric of traditional poetry　与传统诗歌的修辞相反

21. Unifying images of the body, the crowd, the sexuality are pervasive in his poems.　他的诗歌里充满了表现人体、人群和性爱的统一意象。

22. to break down the social division based on religion, gender, class, and race　打破以宗教、性别、阶级和人种为基础的社会差别

    to make colors and images fleet past the mind's eye of the reader　让各种色彩和意象在读者面前一闪而过

23. This kaleidoscope was rather <u>laughed at</u> when it <u>made its first appearance</u>, but its effectiveness was acknowledged <u>before long</u>.　这种万花筒初次出现之时，曾受到攻击，但不久它的效果就得到了承认。

24. rarely-used words　罕用词语

    words of foreign origin　外来语词汇

    be attacked for his offensive subject matter of sexuality and for his unconventional style　因它令人不快的性爱主题和违反传统的诗风而遭到攻击

    his <u>influence over</u> the following generations　他对后代的影响

    be bound to increase to an unprecedented height　一定会增加到空前的高度

惠特曼作品选读

1. 有个孩子天天向前走 *There Was a Child Went Forth*

词语解释和难句分析

1. 这首诗描写了一个孩子成长的过程，所见所闻都变成了自己的营养，暗示了美国这个新生国家的成长历程。诗歌先写了身边的动物，再写常见的植物和邻家孩童和老人，父母之爱以及人生百态、万类霜天、沧海横流的浩大景象。There was a child went forth. ＝ There was a child who went forth every day. 从前有个孩子天天向前走。

2. be subsequently published under other titles until the present one was reached in the 1871 edition　后来

又接连用其他的名字出版,直到 1871 年版采用了现在的名字

be identified with the childhood of a young, growing America 与年轻的、正在成长的美国等同/统一起来

3. for the day or a certain part of the day, /or for many years or stretching cycles of years 在当天或当天的某个时候,/或者继续许多年或一个个世纪连绵不已

4. white and red morning-glories/white and red clover 白色红色的牵牛花和白色红色的三叶草

5. the song of the phoebe-bird/the Third-month lambs(= March lambs) 鹟鸟的歌声/三月的羊羔

6. the sow's pink-faint litter/the mare's foal/the cow's calf/the noisy brood of the barnyard 母猪的一窝粉红色小猪崽/母马的小驹/母牛的小犊子/谷仓场地上的一窝叽叽喳喳的雏鸡(雏鸟)

7. the water-plants with their graceful flat heads 头部扁平而好看的水生植物

8. the field-sprouts of Fourth-month and Fifth-month 四月和五月田野里新发的幼芽/幼苗

9. winter-grain sprouts 冬季谷类作物的幼苗

   the esculent (= eatable) roots of the garden 园子里可食用的植物/蔬菜的块根

10. the apple-trees cover'd with blossoms and the fruit afterward 缀满了花蕊的果树以及后来结的果子

    wood-berries 木本植物的浆果

    the old drunkard staggering home from the outhouse of the tavern 从小酒馆外的茅房跟跄回家的醉酒老汉

11. to father him = to be his father 作为父亲生养了他,做他的父亲,以父亲的身份抚育了他

    to conceive him in her womb, and birth him 在她的子宫里孕育了他,并生下了他

12. to give this child more of themselves than that 父母从自己身上给予这孩子的还不止于此;除了给孩子肉体以外,还给了他精神、思想的影响

13. a wholesome odor falling off her person and clothes as she walks by 她走过时会从身上和衣服上散发出有益健康的芳香

14. the blow, the quick loud word, the tight bargain, the crafty lure 吹牛自夸,急促的大声讲话,苛刻/斤斤计较的讨价还价,狡猾的引诱

    the family usage, the language, the company, . . . the yearning and swelling heart 家庭习惯,语言,交友,…… 渴望和膨胀的激情

15. affection that will not be gainsay'd (= gainsaid) 不可否认的慈爱

    the sense of what is real 真实感

    the thought if after all it should prove unreal 对究竟能否被证明属实的担心/生怕最终成为泡影的忧虑

16. The doubts of day-time and the doubts of night-time, /the curious whether and how 那些白天、黑夜的怀疑,奇怪的种种疑问/"是否"和"如何"

17. Whether that which appears so is so, or is it all flashes and specks? 似乎是那样的东西是不是就是那样,它会不会全是转瞬即逝的闪光或斑点呢?

    * 主语 that 带有一个定语从句,即 which appears so,"似乎是那样的"或"我们认为是那样的";谓语是系表结构 is so,即"(是否)真是那样呢"。

18. Men and women crowding fast in the streets, if they are not fleshes and specks what are they? 街道上熙熙攘攘的男女,若不是闪光和斑点,又是什么呢?

19. the facades of houses 房子临街的正面

    Vehicles, teams, the heavy-plank'd wharves, the huge crossing at the ferries 一队队车辆和拉车的牲口,厚木板铺的码头,跨越渡口的庞大工程

20. the village on the highland seen from afar at sunset, the river between 日落时,从远处可见高地上的

村庄和村庄之间的河流

＊ the village 和 the river between 以及后面几行诗中（直到24行）所表现的都是"看到"（seen）的景和物。

21. shadows, aureola and mist, the light falling on roofs and gables of white or brown <u>two miles off</u> 阴影,光晕和雾霭,落在两英里外房顶和白色、棕色山墙上的夕阳

22. the schooner <u>near by</u> sleepily <u>dropping down the tide</u>, the little boat <u>slack-tow'd astern</u>　近处可见懒洋洋顺波而下的红帆船,<u>缓缓拖在后面的小舟</u>

23. the hurrying tumbling waves, quick-broken crests, slapping　激流滚滚的浪涛,拍击中碎裂的浪峰

24. The strata of color'd clouds, the long bar of maroon-tint away solitary <u>by itself</u>　层层叠叠的彩云,孤独地待在天际的落日长霞

the spread of purity it lies motionless in　以及晚霞静卧的那片澄净的广漠天宇

25. The horizon's edge, the flying sea-crow, the fragrance of salt marsh and shore mud.　地平线上,飞翔的海鸥,盐沼和海岸泥土的香味。

26. These became part of that child who went forth every day, and who now goes, and will always go forth every day.　这些都变成那个孩子的一部分,那个天天向前走的孩子,他现在走,将永远天天向前走。

参考译文——姚远

有个孩子天天向前走

从前有个孩子天天向前走,
他看到的第一个东西,他就变成了那个东西,
当天或当天某个时候那个东西就成了他的一部分,
或持续许多年或许多世纪连绵不绝。

早开的丁香曾成为这个孩子的一部分,
青草和红色白色的牵牛花,红色白色的三叶草,鹟鸟的歌声,
三月的羔羊和母猪的一窝淡红色的小猪崽,母马的小驹,以及母牛的小犊,
还有仓前场地或池塘泥沼边的一窝叽叽喳喳的雏鸡,
还有在下面巧妙浮游着的鱼,和那美丽而奇妙的液体,
还有那优雅的头部扁平的水生植物,
所有这一切,都变成了他的组成部分。

四五月间田地里的幼苗变成了他的一部分,
冬季谷类作物和浅黄色玉米的幼苗儿,
以及园子里可食用的植物块根,
开满花朵的苹果树和后来的果实,木浆果,以及路边最普通的野草,
很晚才从小旅馆外面厕所里起来、踉跄而归的醉老汉,
到学校去而路过这里的女教师,
路过的要好的男孩和相互争吵的男孩,
干净整洁、脸蛋红红的小姑娘,赤脚的黑人娃娃,

以及他走过的城市和乡村的一切变化。

他自己的父母,那个做他父亲的男人和在子宫里孕育他并生出了
他的女人,
他们从自己身上给予这孩子的还不止此,
后来他们每天都给他,他们成了他的一部分。

母亲在家默默地把各种菜肴摆放到晚餐桌上,
母亲讲话温和,衣帽整洁,从身旁走过,她身体和衣服上会散发出
有益于身心健康的香味,
父亲强壮,傲慢,阳刚,果断,吝啬,爱发脾气,不讲道理,
自吹自擂,讲话急促,高声大嗓,做事斤斤计较,狡猾欺诈,
家庭习惯,语言,交友,家具,渴望和兴奋的情绪,
不可否认的慈爱感情,真实感,生怕最后成为泡影的忧虑,
对白天黑夜的怀疑,各种奇怪的问题,
那样出现的现象是否真是那样,是否全是些斑点和闪光,
大街上迅速聚集的男女,假如他们不是闪光和斑点,又是什么?
街道本身和房屋的临街门面,以及橱窗里的商品货样,
一队队车辆和拉车的牲口,铺着厚木板的码头,渡口规模宏大的跨越工程,
日落时从远处可见的高地村落,以及村落之间的河流,
阴影,光晕和雾霭,照在远处白色或棕色屋顶和山墙上的落日余晖,
近处懒洋洋地顺流而下的纵帆船,帆船后面是被拖着慢慢走的小船,
急流滚滚的波涛,在拍击中碎裂的浪峰,拍打着,
层层叠叠的彩云,长条状的紫色晚霞孤独地待在一边,静静地躺在澄净的广漠天宇之中,
地平线的边缘,飞翔的海鸥,盐沼和海岸泥土的香味,
这些都变成那个孩子的一部分,那个天天向前走的孩子,他现在走,而且将总是天天向前走。

2. 涉水的骑兵 *Cavalry Crossing a Ford*

词语解释和难句分析

1. be grouped under the *Drum Taps* section in the 1881 edition of *Leaves of Grass* 辑入 1881 年版《草叶集》的《鼓点辑》
2. to remind its readers of a scene of the American Civil War 使它的读者想起美国内战的景象
3. to come out of the watcher's imagination, rather than from the picture itself 是来自观察者的想象,而不是来自画面本身
4. a lime in long array 一支长长的年轻人的队伍
   to wind betwixt (= between) green islands 曲折蜿蜒行进在青翠的绿岛之间
   to take a serpentine course 采取蛇形路径/迂回蛇行
5. to flash in the sun 在阳光下闪耀
   to hark to the musical clank 听那悦耳的当啷撞击

  * hark to = listen to 听

6. in it the splashing horses loitering stop to drink = the splashing horses loitering in the river stop to drink
在河中蹚水的马匹,徘徊不前,停下来饮水
  * splashing 和 loitering 两个分词都是主语 horses 的定语,谓语是 stop to drink。

7. the negligent rest on the saddles 漫不经心/悠闲自得地在马鞍上休息
  to emerge on the opposite bank 在对岸出现
  be just entering the ford 刚刚走下河滩

8. while/Scarlet and blue and snowy white,/The guidon flags flutter gaily in the wind. = while the scarlet and blue and snowy white flags flutter gaily in the wind. 而那鲜红、深蓝和雪白的/骑兵的军旗在风中欢乐地飘动。

参考译文——姚远

涉水的骑兵

一支长长的年轻人的队伍曲折蜿蜒地行进在绿岛之间,

他们曲折蛇行,武器在阳光下闪亮

——听啊,那悦耳的当啷声,

你看那银色的河流上,蹚着水花悠闲前行的马匹停下来饮水,

你看那些紫红脸膛的骑兵,每一群、每一人,都是

一幅画,悠闲自得地歇在马鞍上,

有的已出现在对岸,还有的刚走下河滩

——而那鲜红、深蓝和雪白的

骑兵的军旗在欢快地迎风飘扬。

3. 自我之歌 *Song of Myself* 第一段

词语解释和难句分析

1. to set forth two principal beliefs: the universality and the singularity and equality of all beings in value
提出两个主要信仰:普遍性和价值观方面所有人的独特性和平等性

2. be illustrated by lengthy catalogues of people and things 通过对人和事物进行冗长啰唆的分类,对……加以说明

3. And what I assume you shall assume, = You shall assume what I assume, 我怎么想,你们也会怎么想,
  * 名词性从句 what I assume 是 You shall assume 的宾语从句,shall 是情态动词,意为"一定会""必定"。

4. as good 同样,也

5. I loafe (= loaf) and invite my soul,/I lean and loafe at my ease observing a spear of summer grass. 我闲游,邀我的灵魂同游,/我悠闲地俯身,观察一片夏天的青草。

6. form'd (= formed) from this soil, this air ……都是由这土壤、这空气构成/都生于斯,长于斯

7. born here of parents born here from parents the same　我在这里出生，我的父母也在这里出生
　 * born here from parents the same 是过去分词短语作定语修饰前一个 parents，此句直译就是"我是由同样在这里出生的父母生的"。

8. hoping to cease not till death = hoping not to cease till death（hoping to begin when I was young and in perfect health）　希望生命不息，歌唱不止（当我正年轻，身体健康时，立即开始）

9. Creeds and schools in abeyance,　教条和学派暂时搁开，

10. Retiring back a while（I）sufficed at what they are，but never forgotten,　稍作退却，（我）满足于它们的现状，但绝不把它们遗忘，
　　 * they 指的是 creeds and schools。

11. I harbor for good or bad, I permit to speak at every hazard,　我可包容善恶，我允许毫无顾忌地讲话
　　 * at every hazard　冒一切风险，毫无顾忌

12. Nature without check with original energy.　那无拘无束、带着原始活力的自然。

参考译文——姚远

自我之歌（节选）

我赞美我自己，歌唱我自己，
我怎么想，你们也定会怎么想，
因为我的每一个原子，也同样是你们的。

我闲游，还邀我的灵魂同游，
我边游边随意地俯身，观察一株夏天的青草。

我的舌，我血液中的每个原子，都由这泥土、
这空气构成，
我在这里出生，我的父母也在这里出生，我父母
的父母也同样在这里出生，
我，现在三十七岁，身体非常健康，立即开始歌唱，
希望永不停止，直到死亡。

教条和学派暂且搁开，
退后一步，满足于知晓它们的现状，但绝不能把它们忘记，
我可包容善与恶，允许毫无顾忌地讲话，
任大自然无拘无束，带着原始的活力。

主要内容归纳和总结

1. 沃尔特·惠特曼出生在纽约布鲁克林（Brooklyn）的一个工人阶级家庭，父亲是木匠。他 11 岁辍学，当过勤杂工，为报纸干过印刷，17 岁开始有诗作发表，正式从事文学创作是从他正式从事新闻

工作开始的。

2. 惠特曼的诗歌具有极其鲜明的特点

　　a. 他具有强烈的使命感(sense of mission)，毕生创作一部诗集《草叶集》。他创作这部诗集的目的就是要塑造一种新的民族精神，帮助美国人民脱离欧洲思想和殖民主义统治的影响，理解自己新的地位和在新的国家里给自己定位。诗集的绝大部分诗歌都是歌颂美国和自我的。他在歌颂自我的同时，强调自我的物理存在和性爱，洋溢着对爱情和幸福的热情追求；张扬开放性(openness)、自由性(freedom)和个性(idividualtion)，表达新的诗情，抒发独特的自我。在政治上，他站在内战中的北方一边，对林肯总统的被谋杀，用大量诗篇表达沉痛、愤慨和悲哀。

　　b. 他的诗总用第一人称，他利用"我"，诗的主题(the subject in the poem)和"你"即读者的三者关系，让读者也参与到诗情之中。

　　c. 他创造了新的"自由体诗"(free verse)，没有固定的节奏(fixed beat)和韵律(regular rhyme scheme)，语言结构松散自由，如行云流水(in the fluid)。他喜用口语，词汇涉及面非常广阔，有惊人的词汇量。

3. 惠特曼的主要作品：

《草叶集》*Leaves of Grass*，内含以下名诗：

《自我之歌》*Song of Myself*

《鼓点》*Drum Taps*

《有个孩子天天向前走》*There Was a Child Went Forth*

《涉水的骑兵》*Cavalry Crossing a Ford*

重要信息句子

1. Walt Whitman is a poet with a strong sense of mission, having devoted all his life to the creation of the "single" poem, *Leaves of Grass*, which has nine editions and the first edition was published in 1855.

2. Whitman's poetic style is marked, first of all, by the use of the poetic "I."

3. Usually, the relationship Whitman is dramatizing is a triangle one: "I" the poet, the subject in the poem, and "you" the reader.

4. What he prefers for his new subject and new poetic feelings is "free verse," that is, poetry without a fixed beat or regular rhyme scheme.

5. One of the most often-used methods in Whitman's poems is to make colors and images fleet past the mind's eye of the reader.

V. 赫尔曼·麦尔韦尔 Herman Melville (1819～1891)

词语解释和难句分析

1. to fail to offer him a decent livelihood　不能给他提供像样的生活

　　to gain the first-hand information about whaling　获得关于捕鲸方面的第一手资料

　　to serve on three different whalers, jumped ship　在三艘不同的捕鲸船、甚至遭抢劫的船上工作过

to take part in a mutiny　参加了一次船上哗变/叛乱

to live among the natives　与当地(土)人生活在一起

to have experienced the most brutalizing life in his time for a man　经历了当时一个人所能过的最野蛮的生活

to <u>furnish him with</u> abundant raw materials for most of his major fictions and his imaginative visions of life　为他后来大多数重要小说的创作以及对生活的独特想象都提供了丰富的原始素材

2. to have Nathaniel Hawthorne as his neighbor　与纳撒尼尔·霍桑做邻居

to exchange visits and write to each other　相互拜访,互通信件

Hawthorne's <u>black vision</u> regarding the evil of human beings　霍桑关于人类罪恶之论的"黑色"想象

to have changed Melville's outlook on life and the world　改变了麦尔韦尔的人生观和世界观

Hawthorne's allegorical way of exposition　霍桑寓言式的表述方法

to take a <u>full-time position</u> as Inspector of Customs at the Port of New York　在纽约口岸担任海关检查员的专职工作/全日制工作

3. to hold the position for the next nineteen years　后来在这个岗位上一直工作了 19 年

each <u>with something in common</u> <u>in the light of</u> the thematic concern and imaginative focus　就主题和想象的中心而论,每一类作品都有共同之处

be back from the sea　出海归来

(sb.) be considered to be at his best　(某人)被认为正处于创作的最佳时期

to <u>pour forth</u> like a torrent　(作品)如洪流般涌出

concerning the sufferings of a <u>genteel youth</u> among brutal sailors　关于一个温文尔雅的青年置身于粗鲁野蛮的海员之中的痛苦生活经历

to relate his life on a United States <u>man-of-war</u>　讲述他在美国军舰上的生活

＊ man-of-war＝man-o'-war　(旧时的)军舰

to reach the most flourishing stage of his literary creativity　达到他文学创作能力最强盛的阶段

4. a popular romance <u>intended for</u> the feminine market but provoking an outrageous repudiation　本意在打开女性文学市场却引发了猛烈谴责的通俗传奇小说

on the decline　下降了,降低了

to write a series of short stories or novellas　创作了一系列的中短篇小说

strikingly symbolizing the loneliness and anonymity and passivity of little men in big cities　象征性地表现了大城市里小人物的孤独、被动顺从和丧失个性

＊ strikingly　鲜明地,突出地

a novella about a ship whose black slave cargo mutiny holds their captain a terrorized hostage　一部描写商船上的黑奴叛乱、拘押船长为人质进行恐怖主义威胁的中篇小说

to use the Confidence-man in successive guises to explore the paradoxes of belief and the optimisms and hypocrisies of American life　塑造不断变换伪装的"骗子"来探索美国生活中信仰与乐观主义和伪善的自相矛盾

to deal with the theme of a conflict between innocence and corruption　表现了纯真与腐化矛盾冲突的主题

be more enthusiastic about setting out <u>on a quest for</u> the meaning of the universe　对(着手)探索宇宙的意义更有热情

be ardent and self-dramatizing "I," defying God　(人物)热情忠诚,对自"我"做戏剧化的角色处理,挑战上帝

to become more reconciled with the world of man　对人类社会表现得更为妥协退让

to penetrate as deeply as possible into the metaphysical, theological, moral, psychological, and social truths of human existence　对人的存在从玄学、神学、道德、心理学和社会学诸方面做了尽可能深刻的探讨

5. to well qualify for that distinction　对那殊荣当之无愧

with an overwhelming obsession to kill the whale which has crippled him　处心积虑要杀死这条使他瘸了腿的大鲸

in the chase of the big whale　追逐/追捕这大鲸

to build a literary monument to an era of whaling industry　建立了一个捕鲸时代的文学丰碑

to turn out to be a symbolic voyage of the mind in quest of the truth and knowledge of the universe(《白鲸》) 归根结底是一个探索宇宙真谛和宇宙知识的象征性的心理航程

a spiritual exploration into man's reality and psychology　深入人的真实生活和内在心理的精神探索

6. Instead of putting the battle between Ahab and the big whale into simple statements, he used symbols, that is, objects or persons who represent something else.　作者不是简单地描述阿哈布与大白鲸的搏斗,而是用了许多别有寓意的事物和人物作为象征来表现。

7. the microcosm of human society　人类社会的缩影

to join him in the pursuit of the big whale so as to pierce the wall, to root out the evil, but only to be destroyed by evil, his own consuming desire, his madness　与他一起去追捕那条大白鲸,从而刺穿那堵墙,根除这邪恶,但结果却是被邪恶所毁灭被他自己的强烈欲望,他的丧失理智的疯狂所毁灭

an ultimate mystery of the universe, inscrutable and ambivalent 宇宙的终极秘密,不可测知,模糊不清

8. The voyage of the mind will forever remain a search, not a discovery, of the truth.　探索真理的心路历程永远是探索,而不是发现。

9. to articulate, shape, and present the mighty theme of the book　明确有力地表达、塑造和呈现出这部书的宏大主题

10. Melville's great gifts of language, invention, psychological analysis, speculative agility, and narrative power are fused to make *Moby-Dick* a world classic.　麦尔韦尔在语言、创作、心理分析、思维敏锐以及叙述能力诸方面都有极高的天赋,这些才能融合在一起,就造就了《白鲸》这一世界文学经典。

11. to give the novel a moral magnitude　赋予这部小说以道德的分量

the manipulation of the whaling chapters for some philosophical speculation　用哲学思维来把握捕鲸的那些章节/对有关捕鲸的那些章节做某种哲理化的处理

to make the novel more than symbolic　使得这本小说超越了一般的象征

to turn the whole book into a symphony with all the musical instruments going on to form a melody　把整本书变成了由各种乐器演奏同一旋律的交响乐

to burn with a baleful fire, becoming evil himself in his thirst to destroy evil　胸中燃烧着邪恶之火,在渴望摧毁邪恶的同时,他自己也变得邪恶起来

麦尔韦尔作品选读

白鲸 *Moby-Dick* 最后一章节选

词语解释和难句分析

1. Chapter 135　*The Chase — Third Day*　第 135 章　追捕——第三天

2. the outcast youth Ishmael, feeling depressed　被抛弃的/落魄青年伊什梅尔,感到很沮丧

to sign for a voyage on the whaler Pequod　签署了一份在匹夸得号捕鲸船上航海捕鲸的合同

be a monomaniac　是个偏执狂/狂热者

to capture the fierce, cunning white whale　捕杀那凶猛、狡诈的白鲸

to have torn away his leg during their last encounter　在他们的上次遭遇中,(白鲸)撕掉了他的一条腿

to post a doubloon on the mast as a reward for the man who first sights the white whale　把达布隆金币放置在桅杆上,悬赏奖励第一个看到那条大白鲸的人

(sb.) be happy-go-lucky, and take perils as they come　(某人)是个无忧无虑、听天由命的乐天派,对于危险采取祸事临头再说的态度

be incapable of deep thought　不善于深入思考

the Negro cabin boy Pip　船舱服务员匹普

3. Intertwined with the plot of the Pequod voyage around the world, a comprehensive discussion is being carried on of the nature of the whale, the history of science and art relating to the animal, and the facts of the whaling industry.　围绕环球航行的计划,对鲸的本性,与鲸有关的科学、艺术史,以及捕鲸业的现状正经行一场全面的讨论。

4. but omens arise to indicate the disastrous end of Ahab　但有征兆出现,表明阿哈布会有灾难性的结果

the insanity of Ahab's favorite, Pip　阿哈布喜欢的匹普精神错乱了

to snap off the captain's ivory leg　夺去了船长的象牙腿

be sunk/swamped　(船)沉没了

be rescued by Queequeg's canoe-coffin　被(波利尼西亚王子)魁克的独木舟所搭救

5. On the third day the whale is harpooned, but the rope from Ahab's harpoon coils around his neck and snatches him from his boat.　第三天,那条大白鲸被捕鲸叉叉住了,但阿哈布捕鲸叉上的绳子绕住了他的脖子,把他拖下了海。

6. finding himself in a real world of hard work and danger and an unreal world of speculation and mystery　(伊什梅尔)发现自己既处在需艰苦劳动、还危险丛生的真实世界中,又处在要仔细思考的神秘莫测的虚幻世界中

a fabulous dramatization of Ahab's obsessed determination to revenge himself in the pursuit of one particular whale　(小说)对阿哈布一心痴迷于复仇、追捕那条特别的大白鲸的故事做了寓言式的戏剧化处理

to humiliate him by ripping off one of his legs　他一条腿被咬/撕掉/夺去,蒙受了奇耻大辱

7. Nevertheless, the book has been interpreted in so many things, allegorically and symbolically, that now we can safely conclude that *Moby-Dick* "means" almost as many things as it has readers who are deeply involved in the conflicts of life and sensitive enough to become involved in the spirit of conflict expressed in a work of art.　然而,这本书从寓言的意义上和象征主义的表现上已经有很多种诠释,我们现在可以很有把握地得出结论:《白鲸》有多少读者深深卷入生活冲突,又有多少读者多愁善感陷入艺术作品常表现的精神纠葛,那么,它就可解释出多少不同的含义。

8. be close to the conclusion of the book　接近这本书的结尾

to lower the boats in chase of the whale　把几条小船放下水,去追捕那条鲸

to have demolished two of the boats　毁掉了其中的两条船

all the human beings involved　所有涉及/相关的人

to remain moving but unmoved　(海水)依然像以往一样地波动着/依然亘古不变地波动着

9. Whether fagged by the three days' running chase, and the resistance to his swimming in the knotted hamper he bore; or whether it was some latent deceitfulness and malice in him; whichever was true, the

White Whale's way now began to abate, as it seemed, from the boat so rapidly nearing him once more; though indeed the whale's last start had not been so long a one as before. 不知是被连续追捕了三天累垮了,加上绳索缠绕阻碍了他的游速,还是他心里又起了什么欺诈歹毒的恶念,无论哪一种情况是真的,反正大白鲸与又一次飞速向他逼近的追捕船之间的距离似乎是越来越小了,尽管大白鲸最近的一次冲刺不如以前长久(也未能拉开距离)。

＊ whether fagged by... chase = whether he was fagged by... chase; the White Whale's way now began to abate, from the boat so rapidly nearing him once more = the White Whale's way from the boat so rapidly nearing him once more began to abate, 其中 way = distance; so rapidly nearing him 为分词短语,作 the boat 的定语。

10. to glide over the waves   飞掠过波涛

    to stick to the boat so pertinaciously   顽固地紧跟着小船

    to bite at the plying oars   咬嚼挥动的桨(叶)

    (blades) to become jagged and crunched   桨片变成锯齿状,被咬嚼成碎片

    to leave small splinters in the sea, at almost every dip   (桨叶)几乎每入水一次,就在海面上留下一些碎桨片

11. Heed him not (= Don't heed him)! those teeth but give new rowlocks to your oars.   别理他! 这些牙齿只能给你增添几个新桨架。

12. 'tis (= it is) the better rest, the shark's jaw than the yielding water. = The shark's jaw is the better rest than the yielding water.   比起柔软的海水,鲨鱼嘴是桨更好的支架。

13. to feast on the whale   饱尝鲸鱼盛宴,以鲸为食

    all alive = All are alive.   大家都振作起来/精神点儿

    to take the helm   掌好舵/把住舵

    to help him forward to the bows of the still flying boat   帮助他向前走到还在疾驶中的小舟的船头

    (the craft) be cast to one side   (小船)被抛到一边

    to run ranging along with the White Whale's flank   沿着白鲸的侧腹平行驶过

    to seem strangely oblivious of its advance   奇怪的是,(鲸)似乎没意识到小船的前行

    as the whale sometimes will   就像鲸类有时会表现的那样

14. Ahab was fairly within smoky mountain mist, which, thrown off from the whale's spout, curled round his great Monadnock hump.   阿哈布已完全驶进了像大山一样压来的朦胧烟雾之中,这烟雾由鲸鱼口里喷出,缭绕在他蒙纳得诺克山一样的巨大脊背周围。

15. with body arched back, and both arms lengthwise high-lifted to the poise   (阿哈布)背部拱起,双臂伸直,高高举起,蓄势待发

    to dart his fierce iron, and his far fiercer curse into the hated whale   把他凶狠的标枪/捕鲸叉和更凶狠得多的咒骂一起投入/插入那可恨的大鲸体内

    to sink to the socket, as if sucked into a morass   插入了眼窝,仿佛陷入泥沼

    to writhe sidewise   向一边扭动

    to roll his nigh flank against the bow   (鲸)向左侧腹滚动,撞击船头

    without saving a hole in it   未在船头留个洞/未在上面撞出个洞来

    to cant the boat over   使小船倾覆/翻了个跟头

16. had it not been for (= if it had not been for) the elevated part of the gunwale to which he then clung, Ahab would once more have been tossed into the sea   阿哈布要不是当时紧紧抓住翘起的船舷,他是会被再次抛进大海的

17. to foreknow not the precise instant of the dart 事先不知投掷鱼叉的准确时间

be unprepared for its effects 对它（标枪/捕鲸叉插入眼中）的后果未做好准备

be flung out 被抛了出去

18. but so fell, that, <u>in an instant</u> two of them clutched the gunwale again, and rising to its level on a combing wave, <u>hurled themselves</u> bodily <u>inboard</u> again 但就在（他们）那样落入海中的时候,有两个人刹那间又一次紧紧抓住了船舷,随着一股涌起的浪涛浮上了水面,整个身体猛扑进了船舱

* 此句的主语是 two of them,谓语动词有两个:clutched 和 hurled。

19. helplessly dropping astern, but still afloat and swimming 无望地在船尾落海,还依然在水中漂流

with a mighty volition of ungraduated, instantaneous swiftness 以难以衡量的、瞬间迅即下定的坚强意志

to dart through the weltering sea （鲸鱼）箭一般穿行于波涛滚滚的大海之中

to take new turns with the line, and hold it so 再转动几圈绳索,并固定这个位置不动

to command the crew to turn round on their seats 命令船员在各自的座位转动方向

to <u>tow</u> the boat <u>up to</u> the mark 把小船拉近目标

20. <u>The moment</u> the treacherous line felt that double strain and tug, it snapped in the empty air. 就在这不中用的绳子承受双倍的拉力的时刻,它在空中"砰"的一声绷断了。

21. What breaks in me? Some sinew cracks! — 'tis whole again; oars! Oars! <u>Burst in</u> upon him! 我身上什么东西断了? 有根筋断了! ——又得重来一遍;划桨啊! 划呀! 朝他冲过去!

22. hearing the tremendous rush of the sea-crashing boat 听到这劈波斩浪飞驰而来的小舟势不可当地冲来

to wheel round to <u>present</u> his blank forehead <u>at bay</u> （白鲸）转过身来,亮出他的大白额头迎去,欲作困兽之斗

but in that evolution, catching sight of the nearing black hull of the ship 但就在这次转身的时候,他看到了那只大船黑色的船体

seemingly seeing <u>in it</u> the source of all his persecutions 似乎从中发现了他遭受的一切迫害的根源

bethinking it a larger and nobler foe 认为它是更大更了不起的敌人

to <u>bear down upon</u> its advancing prow, smiting his jaws amid fiery showers of foam 气势汹汹地逼近/冲向它前面的船头,在漫天的水沫中用大嘴猛击（船头）

to smite his forehead 他拍打自己的额头

to grope my way 我摸索着走

23. Is't night? = Is it night? 现在是夜里吗?

the cringing oarsmen 畏缩不前的桨手

24. oars! oars! slope downwards to thy depths. 划桨啊! 快划呀! 桨（斜着）入水要深点儿呀!

* to thy depths 到你们的最大深度/尽可能深

25. O sea that <u>ere</u> it be <u>for ever</u> too late 啊呀! 万不可赶不上啊! /否则就太晚了呀!

26. Ahab may slide this last, last time upon his mark! 阿哈布可能是最后一次,最后一次驾船冲向目标了!

* this 指的是捕鲸小船。

27. to force their boat through the sledge-hammering seas 奋力驱动他们的小舟穿过急浪猛击的海涛

the before whale-smitten bow-ends of two planks 以前已经被鲸咬过的船头的两块厚木板

* before(*adv.*) 修饰过去分词 smitten。

to burst through 冲出,撞开,爆裂

in an instant almost 几乎在同一时刻

to lie nearly level with the waves 几乎与波浪同一水平,颠簸于波峰浪谷之间

its half-wading, splashing crew 船上半身浸在水里,浑身水淋淋的船员

to try hard to stop the gap and <u>bail out</u> the pouring water　奋力堵漏,把涌进的海水舀出去

28. for that one beholding instant　在那目睹壮观景象的时刻

master-head hammer　桅头锤

half-wrapping him as with a plaid　他半身被红旗裹住,像是披了件苏格兰彩格尼披风

＊plaid 为苏格兰彩格尼披风,美国的星条旗与其有些相似。

(the red flag) to stream itself <u>straight out</u> from him, as his own <u>forward-flowing</u> heart　(那面红旗)从他身上向外飘展出去,仿佛他自己向前飞扬的那颗心

standing upon the bowsprit beneath　正站在船首斜桅之下

to <u>catch sight of</u> the down-coming monster just as soon as he (does)　看到那个急冲下来的怪兽,同时那怪兽也看到了他们

up helm = up with the helm　转舵使船背风/向上推舵(使船头向下风)

Oh all ye sweet powers of air　你们天上所有可爱的天使啊

to hug me close　抱紧我

29. Let not Starbuck (the first mate) die, if die he must, in a woman's fainting fit. = Don't let Starbuck die in a woman's fainting fit, if he must die.　如果(大副)斯达伯克非得死,那么,也别让他在女人的晕厥中死去(死得像娘们一样)。

30. Is this the end of all my bursting prayers? All my life-long fidelities?　我所有满怀激情的祷告就是这样的结果吗? 我一生所有的忠诚就是这样的结果吗?

31. Ahab, lo, thy work!　阿哈布,瞧呀,干好你的工作!

32. Nay,Nay! Up helm again! He turns to meet us!　不,不! 再一次顺风上舵! 他向我们冲来了!

33. Oh, his unappeasable brow <u>drives on towards</u> one, whose duty tells him he cannot depart. My God, stand by me now!　啊,他愤怒难平的额头继续向一个人冲来,此人的职责告诉自己绝不能后退。上帝,现在帮帮我吧!

＊one = 后面的"I",即说话人自己。这里把第一人称的思想用第三人称的语气说出来,显得更客观、超然、大气。

34. <u>Stand not by me</u>, but <u>stand under</u> me now, whoever you are that will now help Stubb.　不要袖手旁观,而要支持我,不论你是谁,现在都要帮斯塔布(二副)。

＊whoever 是表语,that 引导的从句是表语的定语从句。

35. I <u>grin</u> at thee, thou grinning whale!　我嘲笑你,嘲笑你这龇牙咧嘴的大鲸!

36. Who ever helped Stubb, or kept Stubb awake, but Stubb's own unwinking eye?　谁曾帮助过斯塔布? 谁曾让斯塔布不得安眠,总睁着警觉的眼睛?

＊but Stubb's own unwinking eye = but kept Stubb's own unwinking eye

37. And now poor Stubb goes to bed upon a mattress that is all too soft; would it were <u>stuffed with</u> brushwood!　现在可怜的斯塔布躺在一张柔软之极的床垫上睡觉了,但愿这床垫里塞满了灌木枝!

＊would 是情态动词,"但愿"的意思,后面的句子应为虚拟,故 it is... 变成了 it were...。这句话的含义是斯塔布已葬身大海,"床垫"的确是柔软了,但叙述者宁愿他不死,"床垫"里满是扎人的树枝。

38. I call ye (= sun, moon, and stars) assassins of <u>as</u> good a fellow <u>as</u> ever <u>spouted up</u> his ghost.　我称你们为杀手,与那个曾喷射出鬼影的家伙同样好的杀手。

＊as...as... 结构中,第一个 as 为副词,修饰形容词 good,第二个 as 是关系代词,相当于 who,引导一个定语从句,修饰 a fellow。第一个 as 前的 of 也是可以不要的。

39. For all that, I would yet <u>ring glasses with</u> thee, would ye but (= if you would indeed) hand the cup!

因为这一切,如果你们真的举杯,我愿与你们碰杯!

40. Oh! thou grinning whale, but there'll be plenty of gulfing soon!　啊啊! 你这龇牙咧嘴的大鲸,你马上就有丰富的食物吞吃了!

41. Why fly ye not, O Ahab! For me, off shoes and jacket (fly) to it;　为什么不飞过去,啊,阿哈布! 若是我,我会脱光身子向那家伙扑过去;

42. let Stubb die in his drawers! A most moldy and over salted death, though.　让斯塔布死时身上有件囹圄衣裳(内裤)吧! 不过他死得太寒碜,都腌咸了。

43. Oh, Flask, for one red cherry ere we die!　唉,弗拉斯克(三副),乘我们还没死,先来一杯红樱桃酒!

44. I hope my poor mother's (= mother has) drawn my part-pay ere this.　我希望我可怜的母亲已经拿到了我这次出海的佣金。

45. From the ship's bows, nearly all the seamen now hung inactive.　从大船的船头开始,几乎所有的海员都一动不动地戳在船上。

46. Hammers, bits of plank, lances, and harpoons, mechanically retained in their hands, just as they had darted from their various employments.　他们机械地拿着锤子,许多小木块儿,长矛和捕鲸叉。

47. their enchanted eyes <u>intent upon</u> the whale　他们像着了魔似的紧盯着那大鲸的眼睛

   ＊intent upon the whale 是形容词短语,作 eyes 的后置定语。

   to vibrate his predestinating head　摇动着他决定命运的大头

   to send a broad band of overspreading semicircular foam before him　在他的前面,喷出一大片半圆形面积广阔的水沫

   retribution, swift vengeance, eternal malice　报复心,急切的复仇欲望,永远的敌意

   in his whole aspect　在他的全身

   the solid white buttress of his forehead　他前额坚硬的白色隆起部位

   to smite the ship's starboard bow　用嘴猛击大船的右舷船头

   to fall flat upon their faces　直挺挺地跌了个嘴啃泥

48. Like dislodged trucks, the heads of the harpooners aloft shook on their bull-like necks.　像被强行移动的桅顶,身在高处的叉鲸手在他们公牛般的脖子上晃动着头颅。

49. to pour the heard through the breach as mountain torrents down a flume　(海水)穿过裂口涌进舱底,仿佛山洪冲入山谷

   to divine beneath the settling ship　在沉船的下方潜游

   to run quivering along its keel　沿着船的龙骨颤巍巍地游动

   to swiftly shoot to the surface again　又像箭一般穿到了水面

   to lie quiescent for a time　静止不动地躺了一会儿

50. ye three unsurrendered spires of mine; thou uncracked keel; and only god-bullied hull　你们是我的三个永不屈服的尖兵,你们是打不断的龙骨,你们是震慑神鬼的船身

51. thou firm deck, and haughty helm, and Pole-pointed prow — death-glorious ship!　你们是坚固的甲板,骄傲的船舵和指向北极的船头——死亦光荣的巨舟!

52. Must ye then perish, and without me?　难道你们必得舍我而去吗?

53. Am I <u>cut off from</u> the last fond pride of meanest ship-wrecked captains?　难道我连船难中最体面丧尽的船长所珍视的最后一点尊严也被剥夺了吗?

54. Oh, lonely death on lonely life! Oh, now I feel my topmost greatness lies in my topmost grief.　啊,孤独的死亡源于孤独的生活! 啊,现在我感到我最崇高的伟大源于我最大的悲伤。

55. Ho, ho! From all your furthest hounds, pour ye now in, ye bold billows of my whole foregone life, and top this one piled comber of my death!　＝Ho, ho! Now ye <u>pour in</u> ye bold billows of my whole foregone

life from all your furthest hounds, and <u>top</u> this one piled comber of my death! 　你们,我往昔生命中的汹涌波涛,现在从最遥远的四面八方奔腾追逐、倾泻而来,而且超越了我死亡引起的这一层层叠加的巨浪。

56. Towards thee I roll, thou all-destroying but unconquering whale. 　我向你追逐而来,你这摧毁一切但却不能征服一切的大鲸。

57. to <u>grapple with</u> thee to the last 　与你搏斗到底

　　to <u>stab at</u> thee from hell's heart 　刺向你罪孽的要害

　　to <u>spit</u> my last breath <u>at</u> thee 　到死我都会蔑视你/与你斗争到最后一口气

　　to sink all coffins and hearses to one common pool 　所有的棺材和灵车都沉入一个共同的墓坑/水域

58. Let me then tow to pieces, while still chasing thee though tied to thee, thou damned whale! = Let me then <u>tow</u> thou damned whale <u>to</u> pieces, while still chasing thee though tied to thee! 　虽然跟你连在一起,却还在紧追不舍,我要把你这该死的大鲸撕成碎片!

　　* though tied to thee = though I am tied to thee

59. Thus, I give up the spear! 　看啊,我鱼叉出手了/我投鱼叉了!

60. the stricken whale 　被击伤的鲸鱼

　　to run through the grooves with igniting velocity 　像被烫着一样以闪电般的速度,迅速穿过海沟

　　to run foul 　弄乱/缠绕起来了

　　to stoop to clear it 　弯腰去解开绳结

　　the flying turn 　飞扬的绳圈

　　to catch him round the neck, and voicelessly as Turkish mutes bowstring their victim 　(绳索)缠绕住了他的脖子,毫无声息,就像土耳其哑巴用弓弦勒死受害者一样

　　be shot out of the boat 　像射箭一样被抛出了小船

61. Ere the crew knew he was gone. 　船员们还没来得及反应过来,他就消失了。

62. the heavy eye-splice in the rope's final end 　绳索末端沉重的索眼

　　to fly out of the stark-empty tub 　飞出那空空的索桶

　　to <u>knock down</u> an oarsman, and smiting the sea, disappear in its depths 　(索眼/绳套)击倒了一个桨手,又猛地击打水面,消失在大海深处

　　the tranced boat's crew 　神情恍惚/呆呆出神的小船上的船员

63. through dim, bewildering medium see her sidelong fading phantom, as in the gaseous <u>Fata Morgana</u>, only the uppermost masts out of water 　透过昏糊迷蒙的海面,看到了向侧面倾斜、渐渐消失的影子,像是空中的海市蜃楼,只剩下桅杆顶部还露在水面上

64. While <u>fixed</u> by infatuation, or fidelity, or fate, <u>to</u> their once lofty perches, the pagan harpooners still maintained their sinking look-outs on the sea. 　那些异教徒的叉鲸手,由于痴迷于工作或尽忠职守,抑或是听天由命的思想驱使而坚守在原本较高的位置,现在依然未离开正在下沉的瞭望台。

65. concentric circles 　许多的同心圆

　　to seize the lone boat itself, and all its crew 　把这孤独的小船和所有的船员全都包围起来

　　be spinning, animate and inanimate, all <u>round and round</u> in one vortex 　不管是有生命的还是无生命的东西,都在一个漩涡里一圈又一圈不停地旋转

66. But as the last whelmings intermixingly poured themselves over the sunken head of the Indian at the mainmast, leaving a few inches of erect spar yet visible, together with long streaming yards of the flag, which calmly <u>undulated</u>, with ironical coincidings, <u>over</u> the destroying billows they almost touched. 　但是当最后的漂浮物混杂着从已沉入水中的主桅杆上的印第安人头上涌流而过时,直直的桅杆已只能看见几英寸露在水面上了,与桅杆一起的还有展开几码长的旗,具有讽刺意味的巧合是,这

旗与桅杆就随着它们下方快要接触到的汹涌波涛一起平静地起伏波动。

67. At that moment, a red arm and a hammer hovered backwardly uplifted in the open air, <u>in the act of</u> <u>nailing</u> the flag faster and yet faster <u>to</u> the subsiding spar. 　就在这时,一条红色的手臂和一个跃跃欲试的锤子在空中向后挥起,原来这动作是在把旗更牢地钉在正在下沉的桅杆上。

68. to follow the main-truck downwards from its natural home among the stars 　从安筑在群星之中的大自然的老家跟着主桅杆而下

to <u>peck at</u> the flag, and incommode Tashtego there 　猛啄那旗子,还给塔西蒂哥捣乱

to chance to intercept its broad fluttering wing between the hammer and the wood 　碰巧在锤子和木杆之间卡住了它宽宽展开拍动的翅膀

69. Simultaneously feeling that ethereal thrill, the submerged savage beneath, in his death-gasp, kept his hammer frozen there. 　下面已经沉下去的野蛮人也同时感到了上天的激动,他手中的锤子静止不动,定格在他生命的最后一息。

70. archangelic shrieks 　天使(长)的尖叫声

his imperial beak 　他的威严的长喙

his whole captive form folded in the flag of Ahab 　他被阿哈布的旗卷住的整个被俘获的身子

71. His ship, like Satan, would not sink to hell till she had dragged a living part of heaven along with her, and <u>helmeted</u> herself <u>with</u> it. 　他的船,像魔鬼撒旦,不随身从天国卷走一部分生灵,作自己的保护工具(盔甲),就不会沉入地狱。

72. to fly screaming over the yet yawning gulf 　尖叫着飞过张开大口的海湾

a sullen white surf 　阴沉沉的白色浪涛

to beat against its steep sides 　击打着陡峭的海湾崖壁

the great shroud of the sea 　巨大的裹尸布一样的大海

主要内容归纳和总结

1. 赫尔曼·麦尔韦尔出生在纽约兰辛伯格(Lansingburgh)一个商人家庭,家里曾经很富有,后来父亲去世,家道中落。他15岁辍学,当过银行职员、推销员、农民和教师,都不成功。在20岁时,他开始航海,在南太平洋上捕鲸,经历了各种生活,积累了丰富的生活经验,使后来的文学创作有了厚实的基础。在《白鲸》(Moby-Dick)出版后,他又有很多小说作品,但均不成功,为经济考虑,他当了19年海关检验员,晚年写出了他的第二部名作《比利·伯德》(Billy Budd)。

麦尔韦尔与霍桑(Hawthorne)一样,是善用隐喻和象征(allegory and symbolism)艺术的大师,各种人物、事实被作为象征,成了各种思想、观念的代表,因而有普遍意义。他在《白鲸》中对捕鲸过程的哲理化处理(philosophical speculation)使小说超出了一般的象征,他对史诗和悲剧的了解以及杰出的语言才华使作品具有宏大的悲剧史诗氛围,各种层次语言的运用如同一部交响乐。

2. 麦尔韦尔的主要作品:

a. 早期作品(1846~1852),都是他出海归来后的写作,作品多取材于他在南太平洋岛屿上的历险,表现他追求对宇宙真谛的探索。

《泰比》Typee (1846)

《奥穆》Omoo (1847)

《玛地》Mardi (1849)

《雷德本》Redburn (1849)

《白外衣》White Jacket (1850)

《白鲸》*Moby-Dick*（1851）

b. 晚期作品,更多地主张与人类世界妥协调和,承认并服从规则。

《皮埃尔》*Pierre*（1852）

《抄写员,巴特尔比》*Bartleby, the Scrivener*（1850s）

《班尼托·撒瑞诺》*Benito Cereno*（1850s）

《骗子》*The Confidence-Man*（1857）

《比利·伯德》*Billy Budd*（1924 出版）

重要信息句子

1. *Moby-Dick* is regarded as the first American prose epic.

2. Like Hawthorne, Melville is a master of allegory and symbolism.

3. *Moby-Dick* is one of the few books in American literature that has produced an exciting effect upon readers, of which its author could not have dreamed.

美国浪漫主义时期文学同步练习与答案

1. Speaking of American Romanticism, _____ is unanimously agreed to be the summit of the Romantic period in the history of American literature.

    a. realism   b. modernism

    c. New England Transcendentalism   d. expressionism

2. _____ is the chief spokesman of the spiritual movement of New England Transcendentalism.

    a. Washington Irving   b. Ralph Waldo Emerson

    c. Nathaniel Hawthorne   d. Herman Melville

3. Emerson formed a club at Concord with people like Henry David Thoreau, Margaret Fuller, which was later known as _____.

    a. the Transcendental Club   b. Waldon Pond

    c. the Symbolistic Club   d. Puritan Church

4. The unofficial manifesto for the Transcendental Club is _____.

    a. Irving's *The Sketch Book*   b. Hawthorne's *The Scarlet letter*

    c. Whitman's *Leaves of Grass*   d. Emerson's *Nature*

5. Ralph Waldo Emerson also helped to found and edit for a time the Transcendental journal, _____.

    a. *Self-Reliance*   b. *The Over-Soul*

    c. *The Dial*   d. *The American Scholar*

6. Emerson's lasting reputation began only with the publication of _____.

    a. *Nature*   b. *Essays*

    c. *The Poet*   d. *Experience*

7. The _____ is one of the salient characteristics of Hawthorne's art.

    a. ambiguity   b. terseness

    c. concision   d. distinctive characterization

8. _____ drives home symbolically Hawthorne's point that evil is man's birthmark, something he is born with.

a. *Young Goodman Brown* b. *The Minister's Black Veil*

c. *The Birthmark* d. *The Scarlet Letter*

9. Hawthorne's view of man and human history originates, to a great extent, in _____.

a. idealism b. Puritanism

c. symbolism d. black vision of life

10. One source of evil that Hawthorne is concerned most is _____.

a. overreaching intellect b. greed

c. sexual desire d. hypocrisy

11. Hawthorne is a master of _____, which he took from the Puritan tradition and bequeathed to American literature in revivified form.

a. psychology b. Puritanism

c. symbolism d. magic realism

12. Whitman had devoted all his life into the creation of the "single" poem, _____.

a. *Song of Myself* b. *Drum Taps*

c. *Cavalry Crossing a Ford* d. *Leaves of Grass*

13. What Whitman prefers for his new subject and new poetic feeling is _____.

a. sonnet b. free verse

c. lyric poem d. narrative poem

14. In the early group of works, Melville is more enthusiastic on a quest for _____.

a. the meaning of the universe

b. the truth of human life

c. the theme of a conflict between innocence and corruption

d. an ordered society

15. In the late works, Melville become more reconciled with the world of man, in which, he admits, one must live _____.

a. on the vegetable food b. a more individualized life

c. by the rules d. what he likes to

16. _____ is regarded as the first American prose epic, which, in the form of a novel, seems like a prose poem.

a. *Nature* b. *The Scarlet Letter*

c. *Moby-Dick* d. *Rip Van Winkle*

17. The period before the American Civil War is generally referred to as _____.

a. the Naturalist Period b. the Modern Period

c. the Romantic Period d. the Realistic Period

18. In the following works, which signs the beginning of the American literature? _____.

a. *The Sketch Book* b. *Leaves of Grass*

c. *Leather Stocking Tales* d. *Adventures of Huckleberry Finn*

19. _____ is the author of the work *The Legend of Sleep Hollow*.

a. James Joyce b. Washington Irving

c. Walt Whitman d. Nathaniel Hawthorne

20. The phrase "a transparent eye-ball" compares philosophical mentation of Emerson's. It appears in _____.

a. *The American Scholar* b. *Nature*

c. *The Over-Soul*   d. *Essays: Second Series*

21. In 1837, Ralph Waldo Emerson made a speech entitled _____ at Harvard, which was hailed by Oliver Wendell Holmesas "Our Intellectual Declaration of Independence".

    a. *Self-Reliance*   b. *Divinity School Address*

    c. *The American Scholar*   d. *Nature*

22. _____ is the most ambivalent writers in the American literary history.

    a. Nathaniel Hawthorne   b. Walt Whitman

    c. Ralph Waldo Emerson   d. Mark Twain

23. In Hawthorne's novels and short stories, intellectuals usually appear as _____.

    a. saviors   b. villains

    c. commentators   d. observers

24. All the following are works by Nathaniel Hawthorne EXCEPT _____.

    a. *The House of the Seven Gables*   b. *White Jacket*

    c. *The Marble Faun*   d. *The Blithedale Romance*

25. Which of the following features CANNOT characterize poems by Walt Whitman? _____.

    a. Lyrical and well-structured   b. Free-flowing

    c. Simple and rather crude   d. Conversational and casual

26. The giant *Moby-Dick* may symbolize all EXCEPT _____.

    a. mystery of the universe   b. sin of the whale

    c. power of the great nature   d. evil of the world

27. Which of the following comments on the writings by Herman Melville is NOT true? _____

    a. *Barteby, the Scrivener* is a short story.

    b. *Benito Cereno* is a novella.

    c. *The Confidence-Man* has something to do with the sea and sailors.

    d. *Moby-Dick* is regarded as the first American prose epic.

28. *Cavalry Crossing a Ford* by Whitman reminds its readers of a picture, or a photo, of a scene of _____.

    a. the American War of Independence   b. the Westward Movement

    c. the American Renaissance   d. the American Civil War

29. Nathaniel Hawthorne held an unceasing interest in the "interior of the heart" of man's being, so in almost every book he wrote, Hawthorne discusses _____.

    a. love and hatred   b. sin and evil

    c. frustration and self-denial d. balance and self-discipline

30. In _____, Hawthorne discusses sin and evil and sets out to prove that everyone possesses some evil secret.

    a. *The Scarlet Letter*   b. *Young Goodman Brown*

    c. *The House of Seven Gables*   d. *The Marble Faun*

31. In *There Was a Child Went Forth*, Whitman's own early experience may well be identified with the childhood of a young, growing _____.

    a. America   b. England

    c. Greek   d. Roman

32. Of all the following issues, _____ is definitely not the focus of the Romantic writers in the American literary history.

a. Puritan morality   b. human bestiality

c. noble savages   d. divinity of man

33. Henry David Thoreau's work, _____, has always been regarded as a masterpiece of the New England Transcendental Movement.

     a. *The Pioneers*   b. *Nature*

     c. *Song of Myself*   d. *Walden*

34. "Nothing is at last sacred but the integrity of your own mind" is a famous quote from _____'s writings.

     a. Walt Whitman   b. Henry David Thoreau

     c. Herman Melville   d. Ralph Waldo Emerson

35. The famous 20-year sleep in "Rip Van Winkle" helps to construct the story in such a way that we are greatly affected by Irving's _____.

     a. involvement with the passage of time

     b. supernatural manipulation of man's life

     c. laziness and corruptibility of human beings

     d. transient beauty

36. According to Emerson, man's capacity is _____.

     a. ambiguous   b. limited

     c. infinite   d. subsidiary to God

37. *Moby-Dick*, the big white whale, is possibly read as symbolic of all the following EXCEPT _____.

     a. malignancy   b. beauty

     c. adultery   d. God

38. According to Nathaniel Hawthorne, romance should be _____.

     a. both imaginative and creative   b. full of adventures

     c. a true record of human life   d. a mixture of facts and fancy

39. Which of the following is NOT emphasized by the New Transcendentalism? _____

     a. Nature is not purely of matter, but alive with God's overwhelming presence.

     b. Individual human beings are depraved, hence they should be improved.

     c. Material economy is good for spiritual wealth.

     d. In every single human being there dwells the divine spirit.

40. *Leaves of Grass* commands great attention because of its unique poetic embodiment of _____, which are written in the founding documents of both the Revolutionary War and the American Civil War.

     a. the democratic ideals   b. the romantic ideals

     c. the self-reliance spirits   d. the religious ideals

41. According to Whitman, the genuine participation of a poet in a common cultural effort was to behave as a supreme _____.

     a. democrat   b. individualist

     c. romanticist   d. leader

42. Whitman is noted for his use of _____ language, which has a lot to do with his early career as a newspaperman.

     a. oral   b. poetic

     c. formal   d. archaic

43. In _____, Washington Irving agrees with the protagonist on the preferability of the past to the

present.

a. *Young Goodman Brown*　　　　b. *Rip Van Winkle*

c. *Daisy Miller*　　　　　　　　d. *The Confidence-Man*

Keys：cbadc/bacba/cdbac/ccabb/cabba/bcdbb/abdda/ccdba/bab

第二章 现实主义时期 The Realistic Period

词语解释和难句分析

1. be referred to as the Age of Realism 被称为现实主义时期

   be a reaction against Romanticism or a move from the bias towards romance and self-creating fictions 是对浪漫主义的反动，或者是背离了浪漫传奇和自创虚构的创作倾向
2. to provide rich soil for the rise and development of Realism 为现实主义文学的发展提供了肥沃的土壤

   the fifty years between the end of the Civil War to the outbreak of the First World War 从内战结束到第一次世界大战爆发之间的 50 年

   to characterize with changes 以变化为其特点

   to indicate a fundamental redirection in the nature and ideology of the American society 表明美国社会的性质和观念发生了根本的方向性改变

   to have transformed itself from a Jeffersonian agrarian community into an industrialized and commercialized society 已经从杰斐逊时期的农业社会转变为工业化和商业化的社会

   (wildness) to give way to civilization （荒野）让位于文明/得到了文明的开发

   to stimulate the technological development 刺激了技术的发展

   to complete the first transcontinental railway 建成了第一条横贯大陆的铁路

   to discover and extract various kinds of mineral wealth 发现和开采各种各样的矿藏

   capital invested in manufacturing industries 投入制造业中的资本

   to grow at a geometric rate 以几何级数增长

   the burgeoning economy and industry 迅速发展的经济和工业

   to step up urbanization 加速了城镇化
3. However, the change were not all for the better. 然而，这变化也并非总是向好的方面发展/转化。
4. be squeezed off the land to become city job-seekers, causing an oversupply of labor （农民）被挤出土地，成了城市中的求职者，从而引起劳动力供过于求

   to allow the industrialists to maintain working conditions of notorious danger and discomfort for men, women and children 使得实业家们给男女工人以及童工提供的工作条件非常危险恶劣，长期不予改善

   to start to show up the polarization of well-being, with the poor poorer and the rich richer 开始显示出财富的两极分化，穷的越穷，富的越富

   to give birth to buccaneers, tycoons and slums, and ghettos 产生出冒险家、巨头和贫民窟，以及贫民聚居区

   on a shaking ground 处于动摇状态

   to become dubious about the human nature and the benevolence of God 怀疑人的本性和上帝的仁慈
5. Gone was the frontier and the spirit of the frontiersman, which is the spirit of freedom and human connection. 边疆和边疆开拓者的精神不见了，而这种精神就是自由的精神，就是人类友爱的精神。

* 这是倒装句,gone 是表语,主语是 the frontier and the spirit of the frontiersman。which 引导的是非限制性定语从句, 修饰 the spirit。

6. Gone was the place to escape for the American dream.　　立即出走追寻美国梦的地方不见了。

7. In place of all this is what Mark Twain referred to as "The Gilded Age."　　代替这一切的是马克·吐温所称的"镀金时代"。

　　* 这是一个倒装句,what 引导的是主语从句,in place of 引导的介词短语是句子的表语。

8. The harsh realities of life as well as the disillusion of heroism resulting from the dark memories of the Civil War had set the nation against the romance.　　严酷的生活现实以及内战带来的悲惨记忆所产生的英雄主义的幻灭,使得整个国家都不再喜欢浪漫传奇。

9. be tired of the sentimental feelings of Romanticism　　对浪漫主义多愁善感的情调感到厌倦
be dissatisfied with the Romantic ideas in the old generation　　不满老一代的浪漫主义思想
to come up with the new inspiration　　产生了新的创作灵感
be characterized by a great interest in the realities of life　　其特点是对生活现实有极大兴趣/以……为其特点
to aim at the interpretation of the actualities of any aspect of life　　旨在诠释各方面生活的现实情况
to free from subjective prejudice, idealism, or romantic color　　摆脱主观偏见、唯心主义或者浪漫色彩

10. Instead of thinking about the mysteries of life and death and heroic individualism, people's attention was now directed to the interesting features of everyday existence, to what was brutal or sordid, and to the open portrayal of class struggle.　　人们的注意力不再集中在考虑生死的神秘和英雄的个人主义,而是指向日常现实中令人感兴趣的东西,指向野蛮或肮脏的现实,公开描写阶级斗争。

11. to describe the integrity of human character reacting under various circumstances　　描写了各种社会环境中反映出来的人性的正义
to picture the pioneers of the Far West　　描写向遥远的西部开发的开拓者们
to gain the favor of the reading public　　得到读者公众的支持
their emphasis on the dielelictic reflection of human reality　　他们强调忠实反映人类生活现实

12. I confess I do not care to judge any work of the imagination without first applying this to it.　　我坦言,未首先用这条标准对作品进行检验,我是不会对任何具有独创性/具有想象力的作品进行评判的
　　* this 指的是"这条标准",即"忠实反映人类生活现实"。

13. before anything else = first of all　　首先,最为重要的是
the motives, the impulses, the principles that shape the life of actual men and women　　反映男女实际生活的动机、动力和原则
the principles of adhering to the truthful treatment of life　　坚持真实对待生活的原则

14. In their works, instead of writing about the polite, well-dressed, grammatically correct middle-class young people who moved in exotic places and remote times, they introduced industrial workers and farmers, ambitious businessmen and vagrants, prostitutes and unheroic soldiers as major characters in fiction.　　在他们的作品中,不是描写那些彬彬有礼、衣冠楚楚、谈吐精确、经常游历异邦、徜徉历史的中产阶级青年,而是把工业工人、农民、雄心勃勃的商人和漂泊者、妓女以及胆怯的士兵作为小说的主要人物来描写。

15. a comprehensive picture of modern life in its various occupations, class stratifications and manners 对各种社会职业、社会阶层和各种方式的现代生活进行全面描写
a psychological exploration of man's subconsciousness　　对人的潜意识所做的心理探讨

16. to bring to fulfillment native trends in the realistic portrayal of the landscape and social surfaces　　实现了对风景地貌和社会大观的现实主义描写中的本土化倾向

* to bring sth. to fulfillment/perfection 使某事物得以实现/完成/臻于完善

to bring to perfection the vernacular style 使本土语言风格得到完美的表达

17. to explore and exploit the literary possibilities of the interior life 探讨和开拓了文学上表现人的心理活动的可能性

to make permanent the essential life of the eastern third of the continent as it was lived 忠实地记录/再现了东部三分之一大陆地区的真实生活

on the vanishing frontier, or the turbulent metropolis 在行将消失的边疆,或者骚动喧嚣的都市

to establish the literary identity of distinctively American protagonists 确立了独特风格的美国主人公的文学身份/文学作品中创作出了真正具有美国人独特风格的主人公

* 以前美国作家常常是用欧洲语言、风格进行创作和塑造人物,严格说来,那不是真正的美国文学。

the baffled and strained middle-class family 为生活所困、感到压力的中产阶级家庭

the psychologically complicated citizens of a new international culture 具有国际/多国文化背景的心理复杂的公民

* 注意美国是移民国家。

to set the example and chart the future course for... 为……树立了榜样和标示了未来的路线

to pay more attention to the "life" of the Americans 更注意美国人的"生活"

to lay a greater emphasis on the "inner world" of man 非常强调描写人物的"内心世界"

18. to hold a mirror to the surface of social life in particular times and places 拿一面镜子去照特定时间地点的社会生活表象

to probe the deepest reaches of the psychological and moral nature of human beings 对人的心理道德本质进行最深入的探索

to share the same concern in presenting the truth of the American society 在表现美国社会实际方面有共同的关注/(两位作家)都非常注意表现美国的社会实际

to prefer to have his own region and people at the forefront of his stories 喜欢以自己的家乡和家乡人作为自己小说创作的前沿/背景和人物

to come about as "local colorism," a unique variation of American realism 形成/产生了美国文学现实主义的一个独特变化——"地方色彩"

be characterized by local colors 以地方色彩为特点

be concerned with the life of a small, well-defined region or province 内容都是关于界限分明的狭小地区或地域的生活情状

the characteristic setting 独特的背景

be consciously nostalgic historians of a vanishing way of life 作为有怀旧情绪的作家,自觉而忠实地再现了正在消逝的旧生活方式

to dedicate themselves to minutely accurate descriptions of the life of their regions 一心一意、仔细准确地描写他们家乡的生活风貌

(the native life) be shaped by the curious conditions of the locale (本土生活方式)是由事发地点的奇特情况所形成的

to have certain common artistic concerns 有某一共同艺术追求/兴趣

to give rise to another school of realism: American naturalism 产生了又一个现实主义流派:美国自然主义

over the millennia 超越千年,千年以上

19. to evolve from lower forms of life 由一种低级生物进化而来

to have created men in his image　（上帝）按自己的形象创造了人类

to adapt to changing environment conditions　适应不断变化的环境条件

to have passed on their survival-making characteristics genetically　把他们适应生存的遗传特点传承下去

20. The American naturalists accepted the more negative implications of this theory and used it to account for the behavior of those characters in literary works who were conceived as more or less complex combinations of inherited attributes, their habits conditioned by social and economic forces.　美国自然主义者接受了这种理论比较消极的含义，并利用它解释文学作品中人物的行为，这些人物被认为是遗传特性的复杂结合体，他们的行为又受社会力量和经济力量的支配。

21. And consciously or unconsciously the American naturalists followed the French novelist and theorist Emile Zola's call that the literary artist "must operate with characters, passions, human and social data as the chemist and the physicist work on inert bodies, as the physiologist works on living bodies."　美国自然主义者自觉不自觉地追随法国小说家和思想家艾米尔·左拉的主张：文学艺术家"必须研究人物、情感、人和社会的各种信息，就像化学家和物理学家研究惰性物体、生理学家研究活的机体一样"。

22. to choose their subjects from the lower ranks of society　从社会的低层选取创作的主题

to portray misery and poverty of the "underdogs"　描写那些社会竞争的"失败者"的悲惨和贫穷

be compared to a draft-horse, a dog, a bear　被比喻为拉车的马、狗和狗熊

a superficially refined German-American girl　表面优雅的德裔美国姑娘

be drawn into an animalistic affection for her "bear" husband　被引入她"狗熊丈夫"的纵欲之爱

to draw heavily upon the naturalistic understanding of sexuality　对性关系的理解表现出浓重的自然主义倾向

be usually unpolished in language, lacking in academic skills and unwieldy in structure　通常语言粗糙，缺乏艺术技巧，结构笨拙

be always partially hidden from the eyes of the individual, or beyond his control　总是有部分隐藏是人所看不见的，或无法掌控的

23. Devoid of rationality and caught in a process in which he is but a part, man cannot fully understand, let alone control, the world he lives in.　由于缺乏理性和身在过程之中（的局限），人不能完全理解，更别说驾驭他所生活的世界。

　　＊in which he is but a part = He is only a part in the process. 这是修饰 a process 的定语从句。

24. (sb.) be left with no freedom of choice　没给某人留选择的自由

(naturalism) be no more than a different philosophical approach to reality, or to human existence　（自然主义）只是接近现实，或接近人的实际存在的另一种哲学途径

主要内容归纳和总结

1. 美国现实主义文学的成因

　　1865 年～1914 年，也就是美国内战结束到第一次世界大战前的 50 年，既是美国工农业和城市化成几何级数迅速发展的时期，又是权力和财富集中到少数冒险家（buccaneers）、巨头（tycoons）手中而劳动人民陷入无土地无工作的贫民窟中的时期，美国梦已不复存在，代之而来的是马克·吐温所说的"镀金时代"（The Gilded Age）。英雄形象的幻灭和现实生活的无情使主观的浪漫主义再无立足之地，注意现实生活的创作倾向受到了读者的欢迎，形成了美国的现实主义文学。

2. 美国现实主义文学的三个代表人物

威廉·迪恩·豪威尔斯（William Dean Howells）、马克·吐温（Mark Twain）和亨利·詹姆士（Henry James）是当时的现实主义"三杰"，但他们侧重点各有不同。前两位都注重描写美国的现实生活，但豪威尔斯重在表现上升中的中产阶级的生活方式，马克·吐温则喜欢把自己的家乡和家乡的人放在最前沿；而亨利·詹姆士则明显强调对人物内心世界（inner world）的揭示和描写。

3. 美国自然主义（naturalism）

美国的自然主义是现实主义的一个流派，它只是接近现实或接近人的现实存在的另一种哲学途径。它接受了达尔文进化论（Darwin's evolutionary theory）的负面意义（negative implications），认为人的特质是由遗传决定的，行为是受经济和社会支配的。同时它又受到法国小说家左拉（Emile Zola）的影响，认为文学家也要像化学家、物理学家研究惰性物体和生物学家研究活的机体一样，研究人、人的情感以及人和社会的各种因素，下层社会的人物经常成为自然主义作家们的研究标本。自然主义文学表现的最常见主题是人的"兽性"（bestiality），并用它来解释性欲（sexual desire）。弗兰克·诺里斯（Frank Norris）的小说《麦克提格》（*McTeague*）和德莱塞的《嘉莉妹妹》在性关系的处理上都有这种自然主义倾向。

重要信息句子

1. The three prominent writers differed in their understanding of the "truth." While Mark Twain and William Dean Howells seemed to have paid more attention to the "life" of the Americans, Henry James had apparently laid a greater emphasis on the "inner world" of man.

2. The <u>impact</u> of Darwin's evolutionary theory <u>on</u> the American thought and the influence of the 19th century French literature on the American men of letters <u>gave rise to</u> yet another school of realism: American naturalism.　达尔文的进化论对美国思想的冲击和法国文学对美国文学家的影响产生了一个新的现实主义的流派：美国的自然主义。

3. One of the most familiar themes in American naturalism is the theme of human "bestiality," especially as an explanation of sexual desire.　美国自然主义的一个最熟悉的主题就是人的"兽性"，尤其在说明人的性欲时，常用此说法。

4. In a word, naturalism is evolved from realism when the authur's tone in writing becomes less serious and less sympathetic but more ironic and more pessimistic.　简言之，当作者的笔调不太严肃、不太有同情而更多冷嘲和悲观主义的时候，现实主义就发展成自然主义。

I. 马克·吐温 Mark Twain（1835～1910）

词语解释和难句分析

1. to shape the world's view of America　形成了世界对美国的看法
an extensive combination of American folk humor and serious literature　把美国的民间幽默与严肃的文学广泛地结合起来

to seek his own fortune at the age of 12   在 12 岁时就出去寻求发迹之路

first eastward as a journeyman printer   首先向东发展,当了个熟练的印刷工

up and down the Mississippi as a steamboat pilot   在密西西比河上来来往往,当了轮船的领航员

to work as a newspaper columnist and as a deadpan lecturer   为一家报纸当过专栏作家,也曾是不带感情的演说家

during these formative western years   在西部经受锻炼/有助于成长的那些年

to take the form of humorous journalism of the time   以当时幽默的新闻报道的形式

to bring him recognition from the wider public   使他得到更广大的读者公众的承认

to poke fun at (= make fun of) the pretentious, decadent and undemocratic Old World in a satirical tone   以一种讽刺的笔调嘲弄了矫揉造作、颓废堕落和缺少民主的旧大陆/欧洲大陆

2. in the prime of his life   在他的壮年/盛年/人生的鼎盛时期

to draw upon the scenes and emotions of his boyhood and youth   采用/表现了他孩提时代和青少年时期的景象和情感

to work its way farther and farther west through Nevada to San Francisco and then to Hawaii   一路努力工作,向西远行,穿过内华达,来到旧金山,然后又到夏威夷

to describe a journey down the Mississippi undertaken by two fugitives, Huck and Jim   描写了两个逃亡者赫克和吉姆在密西西比河上进行的一次旅行

their episodic set of encounters   他们的由许多片段串联组成的种种遭遇

3. to present a sample of the small-town world of America   呈现出一幅美国小城镇社会的样板图景

to run through the heart of the country   贯穿了这个国家的心脏地区

4. A series of misfortunes happened to Twain's family that staggered him.   一连串的家庭不幸给了吐温沉重的打击/压得他摇摇晃晃承受不住。

5. to coexist with a caustic and increasingly bleak view of human nature   (马克·吐温的乐观主义精神)与一种讥讽的、日益冷酷的人性观相互并存

be traced long before in his social satire   ……可追溯到很久以前他的社会讽刺传统

to explore the scrupulous individualism in a world of fantastic speculation and unstable values   探讨了一个投机买卖层出不穷、价格变化难以捉摸的社会里有道德原则的个人主义/个人主义的道德原则

6. (*The Gilded Age*) to give its name to the get-rich-quick years of the post-Civil War era   (《镀金时代》)给后内战时代梦想一夜暴富的年月命了名

to follow the journey of a representative of modern technology and ideas into a historically backward, feudal society   紧随一个现代技术和思想的代表进入历史上落后的封建社会

7. Offering to develop the Arthurian world and rid it of superstition, Hank Morgan destroys it, instead of modernizing it.   汉克·摩根愿意为亚瑟王发展社会、祛除迷信,但他宁愿毁掉这个社会(重新建设),也不愿把它现代化。

　　* to rid it of = to rid the world of   为这个世界祛除……

8. to show the disastrous effects of slavery on the victimizer and the victim alike   显示出奴隶制对害人者和受害者都带来了灾难性的后果

be tormented by fear and remorse   受到了恐惧和悔恨的折磨

his cynicism and disillusionment with what Twain referred to regularly as the "damned human race"   他对经常被马克·吐温称之为"可恨的人类"的人感到悲观和绝望

　　* cynicism 犬儒主义,愤世嫉俗,怀疑一切,悲观绝望; disillusionment 理想破灭,幻灭

be a record of a vanished way of life in the pre-Civil War Mississippi valley   真实地再现了内战前密西西比河流域已经消逝了的生活方式

be noted for their unpretentious, colloquial yet poetic style and their universally shared dream of perfect innocence and freedom　（这两部书）之所以著称于世,就在于它们率真自然、口语化却又不失诗意的风格,以及它们所共有的天真无邪和自由奔放的梦想

9. as a sequel to *Tom Sawyer*　作为《汤姆·索亚历险记》的续篇

   to mark the climax of Twain's literary creativity　标志着马克·吐温文学创作的顶峰

10. Hemingway once described the novel (*Huckleberry Finn*) the one book from which "all modern American literature comes."　海明威曾把这部小说描述为"所有现代美国文学的源泉"。

    * from which... 引导了一个修饰 the one book 的定语从句。

11. be totally different from the rhetorical language used by Emerson, Poe, and Melville　完全不同于爱默生、爱伦·坡和麦尔韦尔所用的辞藻华丽的语言

    be not grand, pompous, but simple, direct, lucid, and faithful to the colloquial speech　（书中的语言）并不壮丽、浮华,而是简朴、直率、明晰,都是用口语

    the unpretentious style of colloquialism　毫不矫揉造作的口语风格

    running away from civilization for his freedom　他为了自由而逃脱文明

    be vividly brought to life　被描绘得栩栩如生/十分生动

    to come from the shape given to it by the course of the raft's journey down the Mississippi　（书的力量）来自乘木排在密西西比河上航行的旅程所给予的存在方式

12. The novel begins with a description of how Widow Douglas attempts to civilize Huck and ends with him deciding not to let it happen again at the hands of Aunt Sally.　小说从描写寡妇道格拉斯想对赫克进行文明教化开始,以赫克决定不让这样的事情再在萨利阿姨手中发生结束。

13. be polarized by the two opposing forces between his heart and his head, between his affection for Jim and the laws of the society against those who help slaves escape　被情感与理智、对吉姆的同情与反对帮助奴隶逃跑的社会法律之间完全对立的两股力量的冲突逼到了（非决断不可的）极点

    to follow his own good-hearted moral impulse rather than conventional village morality　遵循自己的内心的良知,而不是世俗的/传统的乡村道德准则

    to amount to vindication of what Mark Twain called "the damned human race," damned for its comfortable hypocrisies, its thoroughgoing dishonesties, and its pervasive cruelties.　等于证明马克·吐温所谓的"可恶的人类"、它该死的心安理得的伪善、十足的欺骗、劣迹斑斑的残酷都是正确的。

14. to shed light on the contemporary society　反映了当时的社会现实

    be his magic power with language, his use of vernacular　（吐温的又一独特之处）是他魔幻般的语言能力,他对本土方言的使用

    to skillfully use the colloquialism to cast his protagonists in their everyday life　熟练地运用口语化的语言,使他的人物更符合日常生活

    be confined to a particular region and to a particular historical moment　（使故事的背景）限于某一特定地区和某一特定历史时刻

    to make colloquial speech an accepted, respectable literary medium in the literary history of the country　使得口语化的本土方言成为美国文学史上被接受的、值得尊重的媒介

    to influence generations of letter　影响了几代文学家

15. practical jokes, comic details, witty remarks and actually tall tales　闹剧似的笑话,戏剧情节,以及吹牛夸张的故事

    to share the popular image of the American funny man　具有美国公众喜爱的幽默风趣人物的形象

16. Mark Twain's punning, facetious, irrelevant articles filled the newspapers.　马克·吐温语带双关、滑稽玩笑式、似乎无礼的文章充斥了各家报纸。

be characterized by puns, straight-faced exaggeration, repetition, and anti-climax, <u>let alone</u> tricks of travesty and invective 其(幽默的)特点是喜用双关语、喜欢词语重复、吹牛一本正经、故事讲到精彩处会突然降入平淡,不用说,滑稽模仿、挖苦骂人的技巧用得就更多了

witty remarks <u>mocking at</u> small things or farcical elements <u>making people laugh</u> 嘲笑细小滑稽之事,令人捧腹的机智语言

to criticize the social injustice and satirize the decayed romanticism 批判社会的不公,讽刺浪漫主义的沦落

马克·吐温作品选读

《哈克贝利·费恩历险记》Adventures of Huckleberry Finn
第三十一章节选

词语解释和难句分析

1. under the <u>motherly protection</u> of the Widow Douglas 受到寡妇道格拉斯的监护

   to come to demand the boy's fortune 来索要这个男孩儿的钱财

   to <u>transfer</u> the money <u>to</u> Judge Thatcher 把钱转交给了撒切尔法官

   to escape to Jackson's Island and meet Miss Watson's runaway slave 逃跑到杰克逊岛,遇到了沃特森小姐家逃亡的奴隶

   his <u>feud with</u> the Sheperdsons 他与谢波德逊家族的世仇

   to feud with... 与……结下世仇

   to cause bloodshed 造成流血冲突

   <u>giving refuge to</u> a gang of frauds: the "Duke" and the "King" 给"公爵"和"国王"这一帮骗子提供了避难所

   to culminate in the fraudulent exhibition of the "Royal Nonesuch" 在骗人的"王室珍奇"展览上,(他们的)表演达到了高潮

   to witness the lynching and murder of a harmless drunkard by an Arkansas aristocrat 目睹了一个阿肯色州的贵族用私刑害死了一个于他人无害的酒鬼

   to <u>intend</u> to claim legacies <u>as</u> Peter Wilke's brothers 假扮成彼得·威尔克兄弟索要遗产

   to interfere <u>on behalf of</u> the three daughters 代表三个女儿进行了干预

   be failed by the arrival of the real brothers 因真正的三兄弟来到而阴谋失败

   to try to rescue him 想要营救/搭救他

   to want the adventure of it 想拿它搞个冒险活动

2. to <u>describe</u> the typical American boy <u>as</u> a boy with "a sound heart and a deformed conscience" 把这个典型的美国男孩儿描写为一个"心理正常却良知畸形"的少年

   to use the raft's journey both realistically and symbolically to <u>shape</u> his book <u>into</u> an organic whole 把乘木排游大河的航程进行了既现实主义又象征主义的描写,使他的小说形成了一个有机的整体

   the innocent and reluctant rebel 天真的、不彻底的叛逆者

   <u>be deeply impressed by</u> Mark Twain's thematic contrasts between innocence and experience, nature and culture, wilderness and civilization 马克·吐温对天真与世故,自然与文化,野蛮与文明进行主题立意上的对比描写,给我们留下了深刻的印象

3. 由于《哈克贝利·费恩历险记》写的是没受过文化教育的孩子和黑奴,另外还有不少大河两岸下层的劳动人民,所以马克·吐温尽量用切合人物身份的语言,读错音、用错字、不符语法的地方俯拾皆是,但并不影响理解,却增添了乡土气息(vernacular style),读者阅读前先要有个思想准备。

4. (be) a mighty long ways (＞way) from home   离家已经很远了

   ＊ ＞表示"纠正",这里原文的"ways"应该改为"way",下同。

   to come to trees with Spanish moss on them, <u>hanging down from</u> the limbs like long gray beards   遇到一些长着西班牙青苔的树,青苔从树枝上倒垂下来,像灰色的长胡子

   to reckon they was (＞are) <u>out of danger</u>   他们以为自己脱离危险了

   to begin to work the villages again   又开始去(河岸的)村庄里活动(骗人)了

5. First they done (＞did) a lecture on temperance; but they didn't make enough for them both to <u>get drunk on</u>.   他们先做了一次宣传戒酒的演讲,但连喝醉酒的钱都没挣够。

   ＊ to make enough = to make enough money; to get drunken on = to get drunken on the money, 是修饰enough (money) 的定语。

6. to know no more how to dance than a kangaroo does   关于如何跳舞并不比袋鼠知道得多/也就和袋鼠知道的差不多

   ＊ 原文中they didn't know no more ... than... 应为they didn't know any more ... than... 或者they knew no more ... than..., 这是故意留下的错误。

   to make the first prance   刚跳了一下

   to prance them out of town   把他们赶得连蹦带跳地逃出了小镇

   to <u>try a go at</u> yellocution (＝elocution)   想尝试一下教教演讲

   ＊ go n. 尝试

   to get up and give them a solid good cussing and make them <u>skip out</u>   (人们)都站起来臭骂了他们一顿,骂得他们溜走了

   to have tackled missionarying, and mesmerizing, and doctoring, and telling fortunes, and a little of everything   (他们)曾搞过传教,搞过催眠术,搞过治病、算命,各种花样都耍过一点儿

   to get just about <u>dead broke</u>   简直已穷得身无分文

   to lay around the raft   懒洋洋地躺在木排上

   ＊ lay vi. 躺,斜倚

   never saying nothing (＞anything), by the half a day <u>at a time</u>, and <u>dreadful blue and desperate</u>   有时半天不说话,一副忧愁绝望到极点/ 走投无路的样子

7. to take a change   变了个花样,做了一个变化

   to <u>lay their heads together</u> in the wigwam and talk low and confidential   在窝棚里交头接耳,低声说着鬼话

   be studying up some kind of worse deviltry than ever   正在琢磨什么更坏的鬼花样

   to turn it over and over   把某事物颠来倒去,对某事物反复思考琢磨

   be going into the <u>counterfeit-money</u> business   去干制造假币的勾当

8. So then we was (＞were) pretty scared, and made up an agreement that we wouldn't <u>have nothing</u> (＞anything) in the world <u>to do with</u> such actions, and if we ever <u>got the least show</u> we would <u>give</u> them <u>the cold shake</u>, and <u>clear out</u> and leave them behind.   所以我们当时被吓坏了,两人商量好,我们绝不牵连到那些事情中去/绝不跟他们去干那些坏事儿,只要稍有机会,就把他们甩掉,溜之大吉,把他们丢在后面(随他们去)。

9. to hide the raft in a good safe place about two mile (＞miles) below a little bit of a shabby village, named Pikesville   把木排藏在一个安全妥当的地方,就在破破烂烂的派克斯维尔小镇下游一点儿,

离小镇大约两英里

to go up to town and smell around to see if anybody has got any wind to the Royal Nonesuch there 到镇上去打探消息，看是否有人听到过关于"王室珍奇"的风声

to wonder what's become of me and Jim and the raft 不知道我和吉姆，还有木排哪儿去了/成什么样子了

to take it out in wondering 感到震惊，抓瞎了

10. He said if he warn't (＞wasn't) back by midday, the duke and me would know it was all right, and we was (＞were) to come along. 他说假如到中午他不回来，公爵和我就该知道一切顺利，我们就要跟着也到镇上去。

11. So we staid where we was. ＝So we stayed where we were. 所以我们就待在原处。

12. to fret and sweat around 感到烦躁不安，走来走去地直冒汗

be in a mighty sour way 显得尖酸刻薄，脾气很大

to scold us for everything 每件事都骂人

to find fault with very little thing 很小的一件事儿都要挑毛病

13. Something was a-brewing, sure. ＞Something was brewing, sure. 肯定又在打什么鬼主意/有什么事在密谋策划。

14. We could have a change, anyway — and maybe a chance for the change, on top of it. 我们总算可以有点变化了(不用死待在那儿，可以活动活动了)——除了这个变化，说不定还能有机会做那个变化呢！

    ＊ it = 第一个 change；第二个 change 指的是上一段提到的"把他们甩掉"(give them the cold shake)。

15. to hunt around there for the king 在那儿到处找"国王"

by-and-by 不久，过一会儿

a lot of loafers bullyragging him for sport 许多游手好闲的二流子正在戏弄他/拿他消遣

and he a cussing and threatening with all his might ＝ and he gave them a cussing... 他也拼尽全力又骂又威胁

to abuse him for an old fool 骂他是个老糊涂蛋

to begin to sass back 开始还嘴(对骂)，顶嘴，反过来也粗鲁对待

be fairly at it (＝cussing) 骂得正起劲

to light out 迅速奔跑，突然离开，匆匆离去

to shake the reefs out 扬帆迎风以便航行得更快

    ＊ to shake the reefs out of my hind legs 我撒开大腿狂奔

to spin down the river road like a deer 像鹿一样沿着河边的路飞跑

to get down there all out of breath but load up with joy 跑到那里气都喘不过来了，但高兴得不得了

16. to set up a shout 大声喊叫

to set still long 长时间坐着不动

to run across a boy walking 偶然碰上一个小孩在走路

17. You bet I ain't. ＝You are sure I'm not looking for him. 你肯定知道我不是在找他。

18. to cut my livers out 挖出我的心肝

to tell me to lay down and stay where I was 叫我躺下，原地待着不动

19. He run off f'm down South, som'ers. ＝He ran off from the South, somewhere. 他是从南方的什么地方逃出来的。

20. It's a good job (＝luck) they got him. 他们抓住他了，真是交了好运。

＊ it 是形式主语,(that) they got him 是真正的主语。

21. It's like picking up money out'n (= out on) the road.   就像在路上白捡了一笔钱似的。

22. I could a had it if I'd been big enough. > I could have had it if I had been old enough.   要是我大一点,应该我得到这笔钱的。

23. and he sold out his chance in him for forty dollars.   他把捉拿他的奖额以 40 美元转卖给别人了。

24. You bet I'd wait (= I would wait), if it was seven year.   你知道,要是我,我是会等的,即使等七年。

25. That's me, every time, but maybe his chance ain't worth no more than that (> is not worth any more than that), if he'll sell it so cheap.   我也会等的,无论如何! 不过,他愿意卖得那么便宜,也许奖额就值那么多(40 美元)。

26. Maybe there's something ain't straight about it. = Maybe there's something which cannot be straight about.   也许其中有什么不便明言。

27. But it is straight as a string.   但事情再清楚不过了。

28. It (= the handbill) tells all about him, to a dot — paints him like a picture.   传单上把他什么都讲到了,分毫不差,像给他画了一幅画。

29. No-siree-bob, they ain't no trouble 'bout that speculation, you bet you. > Not at all, they are no trouble about that speculation,...   一点也不会错,这笔投机买卖准不会错,你就相信吧。

30. gimme a chaw tobacker, won't ye? > give me a chaw tobacco, won't you?   给我一口咀嚼的烟草,好吗?

31. to wear my head sore   头都(想)痛了
    to see no way out of trouble   找不到解决问题的办法/摆脱麻烦的法子

32. and after all we'd done for them scoundrels, here was it all come to nothing, everything all busted up and ruined, because they could have the heart to serve Jim such a trick as that, and make him a slave again all his life, and amongst strangers, too, for forty dirty dollars.   我们给这群王八蛋做了那么多,到了落了一场空,全都毁了,他们居然能有这么黑的心,耍这样的伎俩坑害吉姆,就为了 40 美元脏钱,让吉姆又一次当了奴隶,流落异乡,落到一帮生人手里。

    ＊ was it all come to nothing = was it that all come to nothing   画线部分是表语从句。

33. to give up that notion   放弃了那种想法
    be mad and disgusted at his rascality and ungratefulness for leaving her   对于逃离她的混蛋行径和忘恩负义感到愤怒异常、极为厌恶
    to make Jim feel their despisement all the time   使吉姆总是感到被他们蔑视
    to feel ornery and disgraced   (因此会)感到受不了和没脸见人/别扭和不光彩
    to get all around   (消息)到处传开
    be ready to get down and lick his boots for shame   因为丢了人,准备下跪向人家求饶
    to do low-down thing   做了卑鄙/不光彩的事情
    to take no consequences of it   不承担事情的后果

34. That was my fix (= difficult situation) exactly.   我的为难之处恰好就在这里。

35. to get to feel(ing) more wicked and low-down and ornery   更觉得自己坏、不光彩,更难受

36. it hit me all of a sudden that...   我猛然想起……

37. the plain hand of Providence   上帝圣洁的手
    be slapping me in the face   正打我的耳光
    be showing me there's One that's always on the lookout   向我显示老天爷时时刻刻都在监视着/睁着眼看着我呢
    be not going to allow such miserable doings to go(only just) so far and even further   不把那样的坏事

做到这个地步,不要走得更远

to drop in my tracks （几乎）当场吓趴下

38. And at last, when it hit me all of a sudden that was the plain hand of Providence slapping me in the face and letting me know my wickedness was being watched all the time from up there in heaven, whilst I was stealing a poor old woman's nigger that hadn't ever done no harm, and now was showing me there's One that's always on the lookout, and ain't agoing (> wasn't going) to allow no such miserable doings to go only just so fur and no further, I most dropped ... so scared. 最后我猛然想起,就在我把一个对我从无过错的老太太的黑奴偷走的时候,上帝圣洁的手却在打我的耳光,让我知道我的劣迹时刻都在上天的监视之中,现在正向我显示:有一个老天爷总在睁着眼看着我呢,不允许我把坏事做到那个地步,更不能走得再远,想到这里,我吓得要命,差点儿当场吓趴下。

＊ 句子的难点在于要看出 the plain hand of Providence 有四个谓语:was slapping me in the face; (was) letting me know... in heaven;now was showing me there's One ... on the lookout; ain't agoing to allow ... no further。另外整个句子中的语法错误是很多的,意在表现主人公没文化,要懂得正确的表达方法。

39. I tried the best I could to kinder soften it up (= soften it up to kinder) somehow for myself, by saying I was brung up (= brought up) wicked, and so I warn't (= wasn't) so much to blame. 我拼命想把自己的罪过减轻一点,心想自己就是干着坏事长大的,所以不能太怪我。

40. People that acts as I'd been acting about that nigger goes to everlasting fire. 干出像我那样帮助黑奴逃跑这种事情的人,会下到炼狱永受火刑。

41. to make up my mind to pray 定下心来做祈祷

to see if I couldn't try to quit being the kind of a boy I was > to see if I could quit being the kind boy I had been 看看我是否可以改邪归正/不做以前那样的坏孩子

42. It wasn't no use to try and hide it from Him. Nor from me, neither. > It was no use to try to hide it from Him, nor from me. 祷词想要隐瞒上帝是瞒不住的,连我也瞒不住。

43. to play double 要两面派/要滑头

be letting on to give up sin 假装改邪归正

be holding on the biggest one of all 还在紧抓着那件最大的坏事不肯松手/不肯改

be unable to pray a lie 祈祷不能撒谎

to find that out = to find out that 这一点我是弄清楚了

44. So I was full of trouble, (as) full as I could be. 所以我烦恼得不得了,不能再烦恼了。

45. to feel as light as a feather, right straight off 立即感到轻松得像一片鸿毛

to wash clean of sin for the first time I have ever felt in my life 我生平第一次感到洗清了一切罪过

to lay the paper down and set there thinking 放下那信纸,坐下来想想

46. and we a (= are > were) floating along, talking, and singing, and laughing 我们就这么顺着大河往下飘,一面谈话,一面唱歌,一面大笑

47. to strike no place to harden me against him, but only the other kind 没有找到他什么错处使我硬起心肠反对他,反倒是想起了他许多好处

to see him standing my watch on top of his'n (= his own = his own watch), stead of (= instead of) calling me 看到他除了值自己的班外,还替我值班,不叫醒我

to come to him again in the swamp, up there where the feud was; and such-like times; 在上游打冤架的那个地方,我又一次到泥塘里找他;一次次诸如此类的事情

48. and at last I struck the time I saved him by telling the men we had small-pox aboard 终于我想起有一次,我对那两些人说我们木排上有人得天花,结果救了吉姆

49. be a <u>close place</u> 左右为难

<u>sort of</u> holding my breath 有点儿喘不过气来

to let them stay said 说了就算数/说出的话要坚持到底

never thought no more about reforming > thought no more about reforming 再不想改邪归正了

to <u>shove</u> the whole thing <u>out of my head</u> 把所有这些事情都逐出脑海

be in my line = be in line with me 符合我的身份/思想,与我一致

be brung up (= brought up) to it 从小就是这样培养的

to steal Jim out of slavery again 偷出吉姆,让他再次摆脱奴隶境遇

as long as I was in, and in <u>for good (and all)</u>, I might as well <u>go the whole hog</u> 既然干了,就干到底/永久干下去,我倒不如干他个痛快淋漓/一不做,二不休,不如干他个天翻地覆

50. to set to thinking over how to get at it 开始动脑筋想怎么达到救他的目的

to turn over many ways in my mind 脑子里翻来覆去想了许多办法

to <u>fix up</u> a plan that suits me 确定了一个适合我办的计划

to <u>take the bearings of</u> a woody island that was down the river a piece 判明了河下游一点地方的一个长满树木的小岛的方位

to creep out with my raft and go for it 悄悄驾着木排溜出去,划向那个小岛

to turn in 上床睡觉

to sleep the night through, and get up before it is light 睡了一通宵,天亮前起身

to put on my store clothes 穿上备用/现成的衣服

to <u>tie up</u> some others and one thing or another in a bundle 把几件其他的衣服和一两件别的东西捆成了一个包

to take the canoe and clear for shore 驾了个小划子,划向河岸

to fill up the canoe with water, and load with rocks into her and sink her where I can find her again 在小划子里装满水,装上石头,沉没在我准备下次找它的地方

51. to strike <u>up the road</u> 顺着大路向上游突进/进军/走去

to come to the farmhouses two or three hundred yards <u>further along</u> 又往前走了二三百码,来到庄子跟前

to keep my eyes peeping 眼睛一直在悄悄观看

only want to get <u>the lay of the land</u> 只是想对这里的情况/地理形势有个大概了解

be going to turn <u>up there</u> from the village, not <u>from below</u> (装作)从上游的村庄走来,而不是从下游。

to just take a look, and shove along, straight for town 只看了一眼,就顺道直往小镇跑去

be <u>sticking up</u> a bill for the Royal Nonesuch — three — night performance – like that other time 正在为"王室珍奇"的演出贴海报——连演三天——像以前一样

to have the cheek 厚脸皮,不知廉耻

52. I was <u>right on</u> him, before I could shirk. 我还来不及躲开/溜掉,就与他撞了个面对面

53. Why, that's just what I was going to ask Your Grace. 嗨,我还要问你呢/这正是我要问你的问题,公爵大人。

What was <u>your idea for</u> asking me? 你怎么会想起问我呢?

54. to <u>go a loafing</u> around town to put in the time 在小镇上到处闲逛,消磨时间

to offer me ten cents to help him pull a skiff over the river and back to fetch a sheep 给我一毛钱,要我帮他把小划子划过河去,从那边装一头羊再划过来

to <u>leave</u> me <u>ahold of</u> the rope and go behind the sheep to shove him along (他)要我抓住绳子,自己跟

在羊后头,赶着羊走

to jerk loose and run　猛一下挣脱了绳子,跑掉了

to chase him all over the country till we tired him out　我们撵着它在乡下到处跑,直到累得它跑不动了

55. What did become of the raft then? ＝ What did the raft become of then?　木排怎么样了/到哪儿去了?

56. The loafers had matched half dollars with him and got every cent but what he'd spent for whisky. 那些游手好闲的二流子跟他抛硬币赌正反面,半美元一把,输得他付了酒钱,就什么也没有了。

57. to shake us and run off down the river　甩掉我们,往大河下头跑了

58. We are flat broke, there warn't (＞ wasn't) anything for it but to try the Royal Nonesuch another shake.　我们已一贫如洗,一点办法也没有/对此毫无办法,只好把"王室珍奇"再拿出来演演。

59. to have pegged along ever since　从那以后,就一直苦干受累,到处游荡

be dry as a powder horn　(一口酒没喝)嗓子眼儿干得快冒烟了(像个火药桶)

to whirl on me　突然转向我

to blow on us　泄漏我们的老底儿,使我们信誉扫地

60. We would skin him if he has done that.　如果他那么做了(泄漏我们的老底儿了),我们就剥了他的皮。

61. so dry up your blubbering　所以别哭了/擦干眼泪

to venture to blow on us　胆敢揭/泄我们的底,使我们信誉扫地

62. never see the duke look so ugly out of his eyes before　以前从未见过"公爵"的眼神那么难看,那么可怕

63. to go on whimpering　继续抽抽搭搭地哭

to have got to turn out and find my nigger　我得赶快出去找我的黑人

to look kinder (＞ kind of ＝ slightly) bothered, and stand there with his bills fluttering on his arm　他显得有点儿心烦,站在那儿,搭在胳膊上的传单/海报,被风刮得直啪嗒

wrinkling up his forehead　皱着眉头

64. He wanted to make sure of having me out of the way the whole three days.　他要确信/确保我在三天中不会碍事/捣乱/破坏。

65. I can walk it in three days.　有三天时间,这段距离我也能走下来了。

　＊walk　vt. 走完,走遍,走过,沿着……走

66. not to lose any time about it　走路别耽搁/浪费时间

nor do any gabbling by the way　路上也不要说废话

just keep a tight tongue in your head and move right along　闭紧嘴巴,一声不响地直往前走

67. don't get into trouble with us, d'ye (＝ do you) hear?　不要把我们搅进是非去/不要给我们带来麻烦,听到了没有?

68. That was the one I played for. I wanted to be left free to work my plans.　这正是我千方百计引出/想得到的一句话。我要的就是给我自由,好去实施我的计划。

69. to clear out　快走吧,赶走,离开;清空,消除

leastways ＝ at least　至少

70. don't work your jaw any between here and there　从这儿往那儿的路上,可不许乱说

　＊don't work your jaw ＝ don't talk anything ＝ don't open your mouth to say

71. And when you tell the handbill and the reward's bogus, maybe he'll believe you when you explain to him what the idea was for getting'em (＝ them) out.　你去跟他说,海报和奖金都是假的,再解释一下这么弄虚作假的人是怎么想的,也许他会相信你。

* getting them out 耍花招,公然弄虚作假; them 指的是前面的 the handbill 和 the rewards。

72. to strike for the back country 逃进/遁入镇背后的乡村

to tire him out at that (= watching) 让他看个够/看累了为止

to go straight out in the country as much as a mile, before I stopped 直接向镇外的乡下走去,走了一英里才停下

to double back through the woods towards Phelps's 折回原路,穿过树林,向菲尔普斯家走去

to start in on my plan straight off, without fooling around 不想东游西逛的耽误事,干脆立即进行我的计划

73. I didn't want no trouble with their kind. > I didn't want any trouble with their kind. 我实在不想跟他们那种人捣乱。

74. I'd seen all I wanted to (see) of them, and wanted to get entirely shut of them. 他们的那套玩意儿,我都看够了/想看的都看过了,现在就想彻底甩开/摆脱他们。

主要内容归纳和总结

1. 马克·吐温,门肯(Mencken)称之为"美国文学之父",海明威(Hemingway)说他的《哈克贝利·费恩历险记》是"一切美国文学的源泉"。马克·吐温原名塞缪尔·兰豪恩·克莱门斯(Samuel Langhorne Clemens),出生在密苏里州,在密西西比河边的汉尼巴尔(Hannibal)小镇长大。他家境贫寒,12岁出外谋生,当过印刷工、报纸专栏作家、轮船领航员,他对大河流域人情风貌的熟悉,使他后来成为真正使用美国本土语言、塑造出真具有美国本土特点人物的第一人。从这个意义上来讲,他确实是"美国文学之父"。

他的文学语言充满了地方色彩和浓郁的泥土芳香,穷尽密西西比河流域人们一切幽默滑稽的语言表达技巧:吹牛夸张的故事(tall tales),闹剧似的笑话(practical jokes),面无表情的神侃(straight-faced exaggeration),从高潮转入平淡的突降(anti-climax),以及双关语(punning)、风凉话(witty remarks)和滑稽模仿(tricks of travesty),等等,应有尽有。如果说以前的美国作家还在用欧洲这块旧大陆的语言、手法甚至思想写作的话,到了马克·吐温,才开始有了真正美国本土这块新大陆语言风格和真正美国人思维方式的美国文学。

2. 马克·吐温的主要作品:

《卡拉瓦拉县著名的跳蛙》*The Celebrated Jumping Frog of Calaveras County* (1865)

《傻瓜出国记》*Innocents Abroad* (1869)

《含辛茹苦》*Roughing It* (1872)

《密西西比河上的生活》*Life on the Mississippi*

《镀金时代》*The Gilded Age* (1873)

《汤姆·索亚历险记》*The Adventures of Tom Sawyer* (1876)

《哈克贝利·费恩历险记》*Adventures of Huckleberry Finn*

《亚瑟王宫廷中的美国佬》*A Connecticut Yankee in King Arthur's Court* (1889)

《蒲登海德·威尔森的悲剧》*The Tragedy of Pudd'nhead Wilson* (1894)

《败坏哈德莱堡的人》*The Man That Corrupted Hadleyburg* (1900)

《神秘的陌生人》*The Mysterious Stranger* (1916)

重要信息句子

1. H. L. Mencken considered Mark Twain "the true father of our national literature."
2. *The Adventures of Tom Sawyer* is usually regarded as a classic book written for boys about their particular horrors and joys.
3. *Adventures of Huckleberry Finn*, being a boy's book specially written for the adults, is Twain's most representative work.

II. 亨利·詹姆士 Henry James (1843～1916)

词语解释和难句分析

1. to conceive his career in international terms　按国际标准/条款考虑他的职业生涯
   be all the more conspicuous　更加引人注目
   be not obliged to work for a living　不会为谋生而被迫去工作
   to expose him early to an international society　他很早就接触国际社会
   the materialistic bent of American life and its lack of culture and sophistication　美国人生活的物质主义倾向,缺少文化和高层次的艺术产品
   to become a naturalized British citizen　归化为英国公民,加入英国籍
   largely in protest against America's failure to join England in the First World War　主要是为了抗议美国在第一次世界大战中没有站在英国一边
2. be bulky and voluminous, ranging from book reviews, travel accounts, autobiographies, novels, to literary criticism　（作品）总量庞大、卷帙浩繁,从书评、游记、自传、小说到文学批评,领域广阔
   to make him a fascinating case in the American literary history　使他成为美国文学史上一个很有魅力的作家
3. Nearly every work is important in its own way in terms of James' cultivation of the theme.　在主题耕耘方面,詹姆士几乎每一部作品都以自己的独特方式处理了重要的问题/显示了重要性。
4. to bring James international fame for the first time　第一次给詹姆士带来了国际声誉
   (the scene) be shifted back to America　（场景）又移回到美国
   be expatriated Americans　移居国外/被放逐国外的美国人
   to adapt oneself to the American life　使自己适应美国的生活
   to incarnate the clash between the Old World and the New　使新旧大陆的文化冲突具体化了/具体地表现了……
   to experiment with different themes and forms in his middle period　在他的中期创作中,试验了各种不同的主题和不同的形式
   to expose the anarchist conspiracy in the slum of London　发生在伦敦贫民窟里的无政府主义阴谋
   to make a hit 引起轰动
   be terrorized by "ghosts"　受到"鬼魂"的威胁恐吓,对"鬼魂"感到恐惧

5. *The Beast in the Jungle* focuses on the imaginative obsession of some haunted men and women with their personal disaster in future. 《丛林猛兽》集中描写了几个焦躁的男女关于自己未来会遭受灾难的胡思乱想的迷幻心理/强迫症。

6. be more at home in the craft of fiction 结构故事的技巧更加内行/纯熟

be set against a larger international background 设置了更大的国际背景

be centered on the confrontation of the two different cultures （内容）集中在两种不同文化的对抗/冲突

to affront his or her destiny 勇敢面对自己的命运

7. The unsophisticated boy or girl would be beguiled, betrayed, cruelly wronged at the hand of those who pretend to stand for the highest possible civilization. 那不通世故的男孩或女孩,会受到那些伪装代表最高文明的人的欺骗、抛弃和野蛮无礼的对待。

8. be used as the focal point of the confrontation between the two value systems 被用来作为两种价值体系对抗/冲突的焦点

9. to gain knowledge of good and evil from the conflict 从文化冲突中了解善与恶

to make an antithesis of American innocence versus European corruption 把美国人的天真与欧洲人的腐化拿来作对比

an indispensable part of his contribution to literature 他的文学贡献的一个不可分割的组成部分

be both concerned with form and devoted to human values 既关注形式,又注重人的价值

to find in his writings human experiences explored in every possible form 在他的作品中可以看到用各种形式探讨的人的不同经历

be concerned more with the inner life of human beings than with overt human actions 更关心人类的内心活动,而不是公开的人的行为

to render the drama of individual consciousness and convey the moment-to-moment sense of human experience as bewilderment and discovery 显示出个人意识的情景,把时时刻刻人体验到的感受表达为困惑和发现

10. And we as readers observe people and events filtering through the individual consciousness and participate in his experience. 作为读者,我们注意到书中的人物和事件都是经过作者个人意识过滤过的,我们也参加到他的这种体验之中。

11. be a big breakthrough in novel writing 是小说创作上的重大突破

be regarded as the forerunner of the 20th century "stream-of-consciousness" novels and the founder of psychological realism 被认为是20世纪意识流小说的先驱和心理现实主义的奠基人

12. one of James' literary techniques innovated to cater for this psychological emphasis 为突出心理分析而创造出来的文学技巧之一

* cater for 投合,满足需要

to avoid the authorial omniscience as much as possible 尽可能避免作者的无所不知

to make his characters reveal themselves with his minimal intervention 让他的人物自己暴露思想(尽可能少受外界干扰)

to learn the main story by reading through one or several minds and share their perspectives 通读一个或几个人的思想来理解主要故事情节,分享不同视角的观点

to prove to be successful in bringing out his themes 在突显主题方面证明是成功的

be always accurate in word selection 词语选择总是非常准确

to find the best expression for... 对……做出最佳的表达

be the most expert stylist of his time 是他那个时代最高超的文体大师

亨利·詹姆士作品选读

《黛西·米勒》*Daisy Miller* 第一部分

词语解释和难句分析

1. not to pay attention to the complex code that underlies behavior in European society　对作为欧洲社会行为基础的繁文缛节/复杂的道德准则，不予注意/理睬

   be shocked at Daisy's innocence and her mother's unconcern　对黛西的天真和她母亲的放纵感到震惊

   to have aroused suspicion by being seen constantly with Giovanelli, a third-rate Italian, without their being engaged　由于经常看到她和一个叫乔万尼的三流罗马人在一起，又没有订婚，因而引起怀疑

   be abandoned by her former friends　被她以前的朋友抛弃了

   be infected with Roman fever　染上罗马热

   to fall ill with malaria　染上疟疾病倒了

2. a celebrated cultural type who embodies the spirit of the New World　体现新大陆精神的著名文化典型

   innocence, the keynote of her character　天真纯洁，她品格的基调

   her defiance of social taboos in the Old World　她对旧大陆社会禁忌的蔑视

   to think of a tender flower crushed by the harsh winter in Rome　想起被罗马的严冬碾碎/摧残的一朵娇花

3. (the excursion with a young man) be soon in the air among the upper class in Rome　（与一个男青年一起远行的）风声很快就在罗马的上层社会流传

4. be seated upon the edge of a remarkably blue lake (= Lake Geneva)　坐落在蔚蓝色的湖边

   to behove every tourist to visit　每一个游客都应当/有必要去看看

   ＊behove　v. 对……来说是必要的，有必要……

   to present an unbroken array of establishment of this order, of every category　展现一连串整齐排列的这类旅馆，形式多种多样

   from the "grand hotel" of the newest fashion to the small Swiss pension of an elder day　从最时髦的"大宾馆"到旧式的瑞士家庭小旅店

   with a chalk-white front, a hundred balconies　房屋的正面为粉白色，阳台上百

   with its name inscribed in German-looking lettering upon a pink or yellow wall　用德文字样把它的名字镂刻在粉色或黄色的围墙上

   an awkward summer-house in the angle of the garden　花园一角有一座古拙的凉亭

   being distinguished from many of its upstart neighbors by an air both of luxury and of maturity　与许多新爆发起来的相邻旅店很不相同，具有一种既豪华又庄重的气质

   to assume some of the characteristics of an American watering-place　呈现出美国滨海地区的某些特点

   to evoke a vision, an echo, of Newport and Saratoga　使人联想起纽波特和萨拉托加的景色和声音

   a flitting of hither and thither of "stylish" young girls　到处都有年轻的时髦女郎/摩登少女在翩翩起舞

   a rustling of muslin flounces　薄纱衣裙花边摩擦的沙沙声

   a rattle of dance-music in the morning hours　叮叮咚咚的清晨舞乐

a sound of high-pitched voices at all times　随时(都听得见)尖声尖气的叫声

be transported in fancy to the Ocean House or to Congress Hall　在想象中仿佛住进了大洋宾馆或者国会大厅

5. But at the "Trois Couronnes (= Three Crowns)," it must be added, there are other features much at variance with these suggestions.　但在"三王冠"酒店里,必须补充说明的是,还有另外一些与前面提到的印象完全不同的特征。

6. secretaries of legation　公使馆秘书

held by the hand, with their governors　由他们的家庭教师牵着手一起走

a view of snowy crest of Dent Du Midi　米迪山的雪峰景色

the picturesque towers of the Castle Chillon　奇伦城堡如画的尖塔

looking about him rather idly at some of the graceful objects I have mentioned　悠闲地环顾四周,看着我提到过的一些美景佳人

and in whatever fashion the young American man looked at things　不管这个年轻的美国人看问题的方式如何

(Geneva) to have been for a long time his place of residence　他已在日内瓦居住很长时间了

be now shut up in her room smelling camphor so that he was at liberty to wander about　(米勒夫人)现在把她自己关在房间里,闻樟脑味,使得他可以随便地在这里闲逛

be extremely devoted to a lady　对一位女士极为倾心/一往情深

to have an old attachment for the little capital of Calvinism　对这小小的加尔文主义的首都怀有旧情

on trial of the gray old "Academy" on the steep and stony hillside　经受了这座位于陡峭的石头山坡上的灰色的古老"学府"的考验和磨练

7. to have finished that repast　已吃完了那顿美餐

to look like attaches　样子像公使馆随员

an urchin of nine or ten　一个九岁、十岁的淘气鬼/小顽童

be diminutive for his years　个头矮小,与年龄不相称

to have an aged expression of countenance, a pale complexion and sharp little features　面部表情有点老气,苍白脸色,生得小鼻子小眼

be dressed in knickerbockers and have red stockings that displays his poor little spindle-shanks　穿着灯笼裤和红色长筒袜,露出了他可怜的小细长腿

to wear a brilliant red cravat　带着一条很光鲜的红领带/领结

to carry in his hand a long alpenstock　手里拿着一根登山杖

to thrust the sharp point of the alpenstock into everything he approached　把登山杖的尖头戳进他走近的每一样东西

the flower-beds, the garden-benches, the trains of the ladies' dresses　花坛,花园长凳,女士服装的裙裾

8. to glance at the light table near him, on which his coffee-service rested　(温特伯恩)瞥了一眼身边的小桌,上面摆着令人的咖啡具

to carefully select three of the coveted fragments　仔细选了三块令人垂涎的糖果

to poke his alpenstock, lance-fashion, into Winterbourne's bench　他把登山杖像耍长矛似的戳进温特伯恩的长凳

to try to crack the lump of sugar with his teeth　他试着用牙齿嚼碎那糖块

9. He exclaimed, divesting vowel and consonant, pertinently enough, of any taint of softness.　他喊叫起来,使与这个形容词(hard)密切相关的元音和辅音失去了柔和的色彩。

10. to have immediately gathered that he might <u>have the honor of</u> <u>claiming</u> him <u>as</u> a countryman　他立即意识到可能有幸跟他认老乡/他可能是自己的美国同胞

on his friend's affirmative reply　得到了他朋友肯定的回答/点头肯定

to declare with assurance　肯定地说/宣布

to thank him for the compliment　感谢他的恭维

to <u>get astride of</u> his alpenstock　他跨在/骑在登山杖上

be always <u>blowing at</u> me　总是对我发脾气/训斥我

be <u>dressed in</u> white muslin, with a hundred frills and flounces and knots of pale-colored ribbon 穿着白色薄纱的衣裳,上面有许多褶和荷叶边,还有许多颜色淡雅的缎带

to <u>balance</u> in her hand a large parasol with a <u>deep border</u> of embroidery　撑起手中的大阳伞,阳伞上有宽宽的绣花伞沿

be strikingly, admirably pretty　(她)的美丽令人吃惊,值得欣赏

to straighten himself in his seat　他在座位上挺直身子

near the parapet of the garden, which overlooked the lake　(那地方)靠近花园低矮的护墙,护墙正对着湖面

to <u>convert</u> his alpenstock <u>into</u> a vaulting-pole　把他的登山杖变成撑竿跳高的杆子

be <u>springing about</u> in the gravel by the aid of the pole and <u>kicking it up</u> not a little　撑着手杖,在石子路上蹦蹦跳跳,踢起不少石子儿

to <u>give another extravagant jump</u>, scattering the pebbles about Winterbourne's ears　又放肆一跳,把碎石子儿都溅到温特伯恩的耳朵里

to <u>give no heed to</u> this circumstance, but look straight at her brother　一点儿也没注意周围的环境,而是直接盯着她弟弟

11. to have been <u>in a manner</u> presented　在某种意义上,就算是被引见了

to say <u>with great civility</u>　非常礼貌地说

12. In Geneva, as he had been perfectly aware, a young man wasn't <u>at liberty</u> to speak to a young unmarried lady <u>save</u> under certain <u>rarely-occurring</u> conditions.　在日内瓦,他完全知道,一个年轻男子是不能随便与一个未婚少女谈话的,除非是在难得一见的特定情况下。

13. to stand in front of you with all the confidence in life　(一个姑娘)充满自信站在你面前

whatever that might prove　不论后果,无论如何

to wonder whether he has gone too far　想知道/怀疑自己是不是走得太远/做得过分了

to have to gallantly advance rather retreat　必须勇敢向前,而不是退却

to <u>glance over</u> the front of her dress, and <u>smooth out</u> a knot or two of ribbon　看了看衣服的前襟,抚平/捋平一两个缎带的结

to <u>give her sweet eyes to</u> the prospect again　她再一次愉快地望着眼前的景物

to glance at him with lovely remoteness　看着他,温和而冷淡

14. to pursue with a slight drop of assurance　又追问了一句,稍微有点厚脸皮/带着过分自信

to feel vague emulations 隐隐有点妒意

to ask <u>of all the echoes</u>　大声地问

for ever so long　好久

to <u>risk an observation on</u> the beauty of the view　斗胆给她点评了一下眼前的美景

be ceasing to be <u>in doubt</u>　克服了犹疑不定

be not <u>in the least</u> embarrassed　(她)丝毫未感到窘迫

be cold, austere, and even be prim　冷淡,严峻,甚至拘谨古板

15. for that was apparently — he had already so generalized — what the most "distant" American girls did: they came and planted themselves straight in front of you to show how rigidly unapproachable they were 因为那就是明显的——他已做出总结——最"不友好的"美国女孩儿的表现：她们来了，直挺挺地戳在你面前，表现出她们是多么生硬、多么不可接近

16. not the slightest flush in her fresh fairness 她白皙新鲜的肤色绝不会有一点儿羞红

be clearly neither offended nor fluttered 很明显，她既不因受到冒犯而恼怒，也未感到激动不安

17. Only she was composed — he had seen before too — of charming little parts that didn't match and that made no ensemble. 她仅仅是由许多迷人的小部件——他以前也曾见过——组成的，这些部件并不相配，也组不成整体。

18. to look another way 向别处看

to seem not particularly to hear him 似乎并未特别听到他说什么

be simply her habit, her manner, the result of her having no idea whatever of "form" in any such connection 那只是她的习惯，她的风度，她不了解在这样的因果关系中究竟以什么"形式"存在的后果

with such a tell-tale appendage as Randolph 有兰道夫这样一个泄露机密的人跟随在身边

to point out some of the objects of interest in the view 指出景色中一些特别令人感兴趣的景物

none the less 还是，仍然

to give him more of the benefit of her attention 她恩赐给了他更多的注意

to see that act unqualified by the faintest shadow of reserve 看出其行为连最小的一点儿矜持都说不上

* that act 是 see 的宾语，unqualified by... 为宾补短语。

19. It wasn't however what would have been called a "bold" front that she presented, for her expression was as decently limpid as the very cleanest water. 然而那不是她表现出来的被说成是"放肆"的面貌，因为她的表情坦率透明如澄澈的清水。

20. be the very prettiest conceivable 那（眼睛）正是所能想象的最美丽的/非常美丽的

to haven't for a long time seen anything prettier than his fair country-woman's various features 已经很久没见过比他这位美丽的女同胞更漂亮的相貌特征了

to take a great interest generally in that range of effects 总的来说，对这方面的印象和感受有很大的兴趣

be addicted to noting and, as it were, recording them 可以说他有观察、分析女性面容五官的癖好

to make several observations in regard to the young lady's face 对这位年轻女郎的面容做了许多点评

21. It (= her face) wasn't at all insipid, yet at the same time wasn't pointedly — what point, on earth, could she ever make? — expressively. 她的脸绝非毫无生气，却也不善于表情——可这到底能说明什么呢？——意味深长。

22. and though it offered such a collection of small finenesses and neatnesses he mentally accused it — very forgivingly — of a want of finish 虽然五官是如此精美优雅的组合，但他心里依然很抱歉地认为她的面容并不是完美无缺的

23. He thought nothing more likely than that its wearer would have had her own experience of the action of her charms, as she would certainly have acquired a resulting confidence. 他认为这面容的拥有者很可能已有过自己发挥魅力的经验，她也肯定会从中产生自信。

* 言外之意黛西·米勒小姐是轻浮的。

24. but even should she (= even if she should) depend on this for her main amusement her bright sweet superficial little visage gave out neither mockery nor irony 但即使她依此作为她主要消遣的话，她的明亮、甜美、肤浅的小脸也不会表现出嘲弄、讥讽之类玩世不恭的神态来

25. be much disposed to conversation　非常喜欢与人交谈

26. this flower was gathered as from a large field of comparison　这朵花采自一块类似的大田(很难区别)

27. to have met Germans who speak like Americans, but not (= haven't met) any American with the resemblance she noted　曾经遇到过讲话像美国人的德国人,但从未遇到过她所说的那种相似的美国人(即讲话像德国人的美国人)

    be more at ease should she (= if she should) occupy the bench which he had just quitted　假如她坐在他刚腾出空儿的长凳上,就会更舒服些

    to quicken this current by catching hold of her small slippery brother　(温特伯恩)一把抓住了她的滑不溜秋的小弟弟,加速了这种趋势(了解情况的进程)

28. She answered that she liked hanging round, but she none the less resignedly, after a while, dropped to the bench.　她回答说她喜欢随便走走,但还是顺从了,过了一会儿,在长凳上坐了下来。

29. be unvarnished truth in response to this question　在回答这个问题的时候,显示出毫不掩饰的率真

    to level his alpenstock at his sister　把他的手杖对准/指着他姐姐

    to make free to reply　轻佻/挑逗/戏弄似地回答

    to seem perfectly indifferent to this point　对此似乎充耳不闻/麻木不仁

30. Winterbourne for a moment supposed this the manner in which the child had been taught to intimate that Mr. Miller had been removed to the sphere of celestial rewards.　一时,温特伯恩把这猜想成是教给小孩儿暗示米勒先生魂归天国的说话方式。

    ＊ suppose 的宾语是 this, 宾补是 the manner。

31. to ejaculate sb.　大声喝阻某人,突然喊叫制止某人继续说下去

    to lower her parasol and look at the embroidered border　她放下阳伞,看着那道绣花的镶边

    dragging his alpenstock along the path　沿路拖着他那根登山杖

    as with an artless instinct for historic truth　仿佛不具有历史方面的天赋

    to tap the spring of confidence at a touch　一碰就触发了自信的弹簧

    to hasten to reply　急忙回答

    to converse upon the affairs of her family and upon other topics　时而谈她的家事,时而又转到别的话题

    to sit there with her extremely pretty hands, ornamented by brilliant rings, folded in her lap　坐在那里,极为美丽的双手合抱于膝上,闪光的戒指更增添了光彩

    to address her new acquaintance as if she has known him a long time　与她的新朋友交谈的样子,就仿佛与他认识了好久

32. It might have been said of this wandering maiden who had come and sat down beside him upon a bench that she chattered.　可能会有人说起这位走来挨着他坐在长凳上的悠闲少女,聊起天来喋喋不休。

    ＊ 此句的真正主语是从句 that she chattered, it 只是形式主语,谓语是 might have been said of, 被动语态。this wandering maiden... upon a bench 可以认为是主语从句中 she 的同位语部分。

33. to sit in a charming tranquil attitude　坐着的神态很动人,很安静

    to have a soft slender agreeable voice　她的声音柔和又纤细,令人愉悦

    (her tone) be distinctly sociable　(她的声调)听来是特别善于与人交往的

    to give sb. a report of her movements and intentions　向某人报告了她的所到之处和意欲何往

    to enumerate in particular the various hotels at which they have stopped　特意列数了他们曾经停留的各家旅馆

    to make this remark with no querulous accent　说这番话,毫无抱怨的语气

    to appear to be in the best humor with everything　似乎对一切都很满意/心境极佳/没有意见

be perfectly entrancing 是完全令人着迷的

to say at once <u>without examining this analogy</u> 没有回味这个比喻的意思,就立即说

to resume in a moment 过了一会儿,又接着说/干

to pause again for an instant 又停顿了一会儿

be looking at Winterbourne with all her prettiness in her frank gray eyes and in her <u>clear rather uniform smile</u> 用她那美丽坦诚的灰色大眼睛看着温特伯恩,脸上始终如一地挂着明朗的笑容

34. He had never yet heard a young girl express herself <u>in just this fashion</u>; never at least save in cases where to say such things was to have at the same time some rather complicated consciousness about them. 他还从未听过一个年轻姑娘以这样的方式表白自己,至少从未有过,除非这样说的时候,对所说的事情有复杂的思想意识/思想意识不健康。

 * 言外之意就是他认为这女孩言行轻浮。

35. And yet was he to <u>accuse</u> Miss Daisy Miller <u>of</u> an actual or a potential arriere-pensee (= mental reservation 潜在的异见/异己/异类), as they said at Geneva? 然而,难道他要按日内瓦人的说法,指责黛西·米勒小姐是一个实际的或潜在的异类吗?

36. to have got morally <u>muddled</u> 道德是非上有点儿搞糊涂了

to <u>have lost the right sense for</u> the young American tone 对美国青年的说话腔调已经很不习惯/感到刺耳了

37. <u>Never</u> indeed since he had grown old enough to appreciate things <u>had he encountered</u> a young compatriot of so "strong" a type as this. 自从他长大能够识别世事以来,还从未碰到过一个如此典型的年轻的美国同胞。

38. Or was she a designing, an audacious, <u>in short</u> an expert young person? 或者说难道她是一个工于心计、胆大妄为,一句话,一个老练狡猾的年轻人吗?

39. (instinct) to have ceased to serve him for such a question （直觉)对这样一个问题,(直觉)已经不能帮他任何忙了/不起作用了

to <u>take</u> Miss Daisy Miller <u>for</u> a flirt <u>on the whole</u> 大体上是把黛西·米勒小姐当成一个轻佻女郎了

40. He had known here in Europe two or three women — persons older than Miss Daisy Miller and <u>provided</u>, for respectability's sake, <u>with</u> husbands — who were great coquettes. 他在欧洲这里也认识两三个女人——年龄都比黛西·米勒小姐大,而且为体面起见,都有丈夫相伴——她们都是毫不含糊卖弄风骚的女人。

41. One's light <u>commerce with</u> the dangerous terrible women might indeed <u>take a serious turn</u>. 一个人与这些危险、可怕的女人轻率交往确实可能会导致严重的后果。

42. But this charming apparition wasn't a coquette <u>in that sense</u>. 但是这位迷人的精灵可不是那种意义上的风情女郎/与那种风情女郎不可同日而语。

43. be almost <u>grateful for</u> having found the formula that <u>apples to</u> Miss Daisy Miller 几乎要感谢自己发现了适合黛西·米勒小姐的公式/符合黛西·米勒小姐风格的评语

to <u>lean back</u> in his seat 他把身子往座位的后背靠了靠

the regular conditions and limitations of one's <u>intercourse with</u> a pretty American flirt 与一个美丽、轻佻的美国姑娘交际需具备什么正规条件,接受什么约束/进行到什么程度就适可而<u>止</u>

to become apparent that he was <u>on the way</u> to learn 很明显,他已渐有所悟

to <u>point</u> with her parasol <u>to</u> the far-shining walls of the Chateau de Chillon 她用手中阳伞指着远处奇伦城堡发光的围墙

44. courier tour(ist) guide ,sight-seeing tour 导游,旅游服务员

to <u>suffer</u> dreadfully <u>from</u> dyspepsia 严重消化不良

to give out　宣布,发表,发出(光/热/声音/信号)

be not interested in <u>ancient monument</u>　对历史遗迹不感兴趣

45. But this sketch of Mrs. Miller's plea remained unfinished.　但是米勒夫人这种借口的说法还不是原因的全部。

46. be emboldened to reply　因受到鼓励而大胆地回答

with all serenity　非常平静地,若无其事地

to ask without a shadow of emotion　情绪微波不惊,没有情绪波动的痕迹,不动声色

be conscious that he had gone very far　他意识到自己已经走得太远了/太大胆冒昧了

to think it possible she has <u>drawn back</u>　心想她可能打退堂鼓了

47. But it seemed that both his audacity and his respect <u>were lost on</u> Miss Daisy Miller. 对他的大胆冒昧和恭敬有礼,黛西·米勒小姐似乎全无反应。

　　＊ be lost on sb.　对某人不起作用

48. <u>be not</u> much <u>bent on</u> going, anyway　反正(母亲)是不会很想去的

to like to ride round　喜欢出门走动/到处闲逛

the most fastidious man I ever saw　我以前见过的最爱挑剔的人

a splendid courier　一个光彩照人的旅游服务员

49. to reflect for an instant <u>as lucidly as possible</u>　思考了一会儿,尽量弄清(她)话中之意

with superb whiskers and wearing a velvet morning-coat and a voluminous watch-guard　留着漂亮的髭须,穿着天鹅绒晨燕尾服,胸前挂着闪闪发光的表链

looking sharply at her companion　目光犀利地看着她的同伴

50. He felt as if he ought to kiss the young lady's hand. Possibly he would have done so, — and quite spoiled his chance; but at this moment another person — presumably Eugenio — appeared.　他感到似乎应该亲吻一下这少女的纤手。也许真这么做了,可就毁了这次的机会了;但就在这时,另一个人——大概叫尤吉尼奥——出现了。

51. to <u>eye</u> Winterbourne <u>from</u> head <u>to</u> foot　把温特伯恩从头到脚打量了一遍

to <u>bow</u> gravely <u>to</u> Miss Miller　郑重其事地朝米勒小姐鞠躬

to <u>have the honor</u> to inform Mademoiselle that luncheon's on table　(我)荣幸地通知小姐,午餐开始了,请吧

to <u>strike</u> Winterbourne <u>as</u> impertinent　使温特伯恩感到很不礼貌

to <u>throw</u> a slightly ironical <u>light on</u> her position, event to Miss Miller's own apprehension　(语调中)把米勒小姐的身份显示了出来,其中的讽刺意味连小姐本人也感觉到了

　　＊ to throw light (up)on ...　把……阐述得很清楚,使某人了解……;前面的不定式短语也可译为:(语调中)捎带讽刺地显示出了米勒小姐的身份,连小姐本人都悟到了这种意味。

to back out　食言,撒手,退出

with an effect of offense for the young man　带着向这位年轻人挑衅的神色

so far as　以至于

to see <u>a tacit reflection on</u> Miss Miller's behavior and an insinuation that she "<u>picked up</u>" acquaintances　看出了对米勒小姐行为的含蓄批评,影射她随意结交异性

52. The courier still stood there with an effect of offense for the young man <u>so far as</u> the latter saw in it a tacit reflexion on Miss Miller's behavior and an insinuation that she "picked up" acquaintances.　这位旅游服务员依然站在那里,一副向年轻人挑衅的神色,使得这个年轻人也(从中)看出了他对米勒小姐随意交友的行为含蓄的批评。

　　＊ saw 有两个宾语,一个是 a tacit reflexion,另一个是 an insinuation,that 引导的从句是 insinuation

的同位语从句,即"影射"的内容。

53. to have the honor of presenting to you a person who'll tell you all about me　荣幸地向你介绍一个人, 她可以把我的一切都告诉你

to put up her parasol and walk back to the inn beside Eugenio　撑起她的阳伞,跟着尤吉尼奥向酒店走去

drawing her muslin furbelows over the walk　撩起拖在地上的薄纱裙褶

主要内容归纳和总结

1. 亨利·詹姆士出生在纽约城一个富裕家庭,父亲是神学作家,哥哥威廉·詹姆士是著名哲学家和心理学家,对"意识流"理论做过很大贡献。很小的时候,亨利·詹姆士就被家人带着几次横渡大西洋,接受欧洲教育,老早就面向国际社会。在哈佛大学读书时,他结识豪威尔斯(Howells),后又游历英、法、意等国,结识福楼拜(Flaubert)、莫泊桑(Maupassant)、左拉(Zola)和屠格涅夫(Turgenev)等欧洲文豪。他仰慕欧洲文明,鄙视美国的物质主义,于1915年加入英国籍。他在逝世前不久,因其功绩,获得了乔治五世国王颁发的功绩勋章(Order of Merit)。

亨利·詹姆士是一个以写国际主题著称的美国作家。他的创作生涯分三个阶段,第一、三两个阶段都是写国际主题,以欧美文化为背景,文化冲突是常见内容;第二阶段主要是对各种文学形式和主题的创作实验,写了不少中短篇小说,取得了成功。

亨利·詹姆士的现实主义关注人物内心活动,传达人的良知,较早使用心理分析的写作技巧,因而被普遍认为是20世纪意识流小说的先驱和心理现实主义的奠基人。他叙述故事的主张是:让人物自己表现自己,应该是多视觉的呈现,作者尽可能不要"无所不知"(avoid the omniscience as much as possible)。

2. 亨利·詹姆士的主要作品:

a. 第一阶段

《美国人》The American (1877)

《黛西·米勒》Daisy Miller (1878)

《欧洲人》The Europeans (1878)

《贵妇人的画像》The Portrait of A Lady (1881)

b. 第二阶段

《波士顿人》The Bostonians (1886)

《卡撒玛西玛公主》The Princess Casamassima (1886)

《私生活》The Private Life (1893)

《狮子之死》The Death of a Lion (1894)

《中年》The Middle Years (1897)

《螺丝在拧紧》The Turn of the Screw (1898)

《丛林猛兽》The Beast in the Jungle (1903)

c. 第三阶段

《梅西所知道的》What Maisie Knows (1897)

《鸽翼》The Wings of the Dove (1902)

《专使》The Ambassador (1903)

《金碗》The Golden Bowl (1904)

重要信息句子

1. Henry James was the first American writer to conceive his career in international terms.
2. *Daisy Miller* brought James international fame for the first time.
3. *The Portrait of a Lady* is generally considered to be his masterpiece.
4. James' fame generally rests upon his novels and stories with the international theme.
5. James' realism is characterized by his psychological approach to his subject matter.

Ⅲ. 艾米莉·狄金森 Emily Dickinson（1830～1886）

词语解释和难句分析

1. be strongly congregational　具有强烈的公理会气氛

   to suffer serious religious crisis　经历了严重的宗教危机

   affected by an unhappy love affair with. . .　受到与某人不幸爱情的影响

   to become a total recluse　成为完全的隐士/遁世者

   be pretty much in order　非常有序

   to keep the house　治家

   to draw commonly on. . . for allusion and references in her poetry　常常从……中吸收/汲取典故和参考资料，用于诗歌创作

2. Dickinson called this stream of tiny, aphoristic poems a continuous fragmented "letter to the world," a way to bridge her private world with the public.　狄金森把自己涓涓细流、格言警句式的小诗称作不断写给世界的片语式的书信，是她与外部世界沟通的一种方法。

3. to make Emily Dickinson, especially her withdrawn self, known to the outside world　使得艾米莉·狄金森，尤其是她离群索居的一面，为世人所知

   to continue to be issued after its first appearance　她的诗从第一次面世后，就不断地出版

   be recognized as a great poetess on her own right　被认为是拥有个人著作权的伟大的女诗人

4. her sorrows and joys　她的喜怒哀乐

   to address those issues that concern the whole human beings　处理了那些事关整个人类的话题

   to desire salvation and immortality　想要获得拯救和永生/不朽

   to deny the orthodox view of paradise　否定正统的天堂论

   to doubt His benevolence　怀疑上帝的仁慈

   ranging over the physical as well as the psychological and emotional aspects of death　（诗歌的主题）涉及人死亡时的生理、心理和情感等广泛的方面

   to imagine the journey of her soul to the unknown　想象她的灵魂去未知世界的旅程

   her greatest rendering of the moment of death　她最伟大的贡献是对死亡时刻的艺术处理

5. to dwell on the subject about love　总是写/强调关于爱情的主题

   striking and original depictions of the longing for shared moments, the pain of separation, and the futility of finding happiness   突出地、创造性地描写了她对与爱人共度美好时光的渴望,分离的痛苦,以及追求幸福的无望

to <u>focus on</u> the physical aspect of desire   集中描写了人生理欲望方面的事情

to deal with, allegorically, the influence of the male authorities over the female   以寓言式的方法,描写了男权地位对女性的影响

expressing a mixture of fear and fascination for the mysterious <u>magnetism between sexes</u>   表达了对神秘的异性相吸既迷恋又惊恐的复杂情感

to have aroused critical attention   引起了批评和关注

to show Dickinson's confusion and doubt about the role of women in the 19th century America   显示了狄金森对 19 世纪美国妇女作用的迷惘和怀疑

6. On the other hand, she <u>shared with</u> her romantic and transcendental predecessors who believed that a mythical bond between man and nature existed, <u>that</u> nature revealed to man things about mankind and universe.   另一方面, 她与认为人与自然存在着神秘联系的浪漫主义和超验主义的先辈们有一个共同的观点,就是大自然向人类揭示了人与宇宙之间的种种事情。

7. to feel strongly about nature's inscrutability and indifference to the life and interests of human beings   强烈地感觉到大自然的不可思议和对人类生活和利益的漠不关心

to write about nature <u>in affirmation of</u> the sheer joy and the appreciation   承认无条件的欢乐和感恩,以此态度描写自然

unaffected by philosophical speculations   没有受到哲学思考的影响

from keen perception to witty analysis   从敏锐的认识到巧妙的分析

8. be unique and unconventional in its own way   总是以自己的方式表现出独特的、不落俗套的风格

9. Her poems have no titles, hence are always quoted by their first lines.   她的诗无题,因此总是引用第一行作为诗题。

10. In her poetry there is a particular stress pattern, in which dashes are used as a musical device to create cadence and capital letters as a means of emphasis.   在她的诗里有独特的强调形式,破折号用作表达节奏的韵律手段,大写字母用作强调的方式。

11. be more or less like that (= the form) of the hymns in community churches   或多或少有点像社区教堂里唱的圣歌或赞美诗

(her idiom) <u>be noted for</u> its laconic brevity, directness and plainness   (她的习语/片语)以其简洁精炼、直率朴素著称

be centered on a single image or symbol and focused on one subject matter   集中表现单一意象和象征,聚焦单一主题

her deliberate seclusion   她故意/有意隐居独处

be very personal and meditative   多是表达个人情感和个人思考

to frequently use personae to <u>render</u> the tone more familiar <u>to</u> the reader   经常用第一人称,使读者感到语调亲切熟悉

to use personification to vivify some abstract ideas   用拟人化手法使抽象的思想栩栩如生

despite its ostensible formal simplicity   尽管表面上诗的形式简单

<u>be remarkable for</u> its variety, subtlety and richness   以其形式多样、描写细微和丰富多彩而著称

to have never confined the limitless power of her creativity and imagination   从未束缚她无限的创作力和想象力

狄金森作品选读

1. 这是我写给世界的信 *This is my letter to the World*

词语解释和难句分析

1. 这首诗表达了狄金森虽隐居独处,内心却激情澎湃,渴望与人交往的急切心情。

2. This is my letter to the World/That never wrote to Me — 这是我写给世界的信/世界却从不写信给我——

   * that 是关系代词,指代 the World,引导了一个修饰它的定语从句。

   The simple News that Nature told — = It is Nature that told the simple News — 是大自然透露了这简单信息——

   * 大自然以一片沉寂表达了外部世界没有回音,因为狄金森的信并未真正传达给外部世界,外界哪里来的回复呢?

   With tender Majesty 带着温柔的威严

3. Her Message is committed/To hands I can not see — (也许)她的信息交托给了/我看不见的手——

   * 这信息捎来时作者当然是毫不知晓,这是她虚幻的假想。

   For love of Her — Sweet — countrymen — 因为我对她的爱——我亲爱的同胞们啊——

   * 这里的"她",就是外部世界,此句话可以理解为:因为我对你们外部世界的同胞们的向往……

   Judge tenderly — of Me 评判我时,请温柔对待

参考译文——姚远

这是我写给世界的信

这是我写给世界的信
世界却从不给我写信——
是大自然透露这简单的信息——
带着温柔的威严

她的信息托付给了
我看不见的手——
因我对她的爱,亲爱的同胞们啊——
评判我时,请温柔对待

2. 我死时——听到一只苍蝇嗡嗡叫——
I hear a Fly buzz — when I died —

词语解释和难句分析

---

1. 这首诗描写的是死亡时刻的感受。

2. The Stillness in the Room/Was like the Stillness in the Air —/Between the Heaves of Storm — 房间里异常寂静/像暴风雨涌动之时/天空一片宁静——

3. to wring them（＝the eyes around）dry 挤干/拧干了至爱亲朋的眼泪

    the King＝the God of death 死神

4. The Eyes around — had wrung them dry — 周围的眼睛——都已哭干——

    And Breaths were gathering firm/For that last Onset — 人人都屏住呼吸/等待最后的一击——

    ＊ for that last onset＝waiting for that last attack 等待那最后的攻击（死亡的来临）

    When the King/Be witnessed — in the Room — 亲眼看到——/死神在房间里出现——

5. I willed my Keepsakes — Signed away/What portion of me be/Assignable — 我在遗嘱中言明遗赠——然后签字/凡我的拥有——可分配的一切/全都遗赠——

    ＊ what . . . assignable＝keepsakes，两者是同位语；signed away＝which was signed away，可以认为是 keepsakes 的定语。

    and then it was/There interposed a Fly — ＝and then it was there a Fly interposed 就在这时,/一只苍蝇飞进来打搅——

    ＊ interpose *vi.* 插入,干预

6. With Blue — uncertain stumbling Buzz —/Between the light — and me — 响着模模糊糊——断断续续的嗡嗡声——/飞在光明与我之间——

    ＊ blue 昏暗,微弱,模糊；stumbling 跌跌撞撞,结结巴巴

7. And then the Windows failed — and then/I could not see to see — 接着窗户看不清了——然后/我什么也看不见——

    ＊ to see 是不定式短语作 could not see 的宾语；could not see to see 意即看不见想要看见的东西。

参考译文——姚远

我死时——听到一只苍蝇嗡嗡叫——

我死时——听到一只苍蝇嗡嗡叫——
房间里异常寂静
像暴风雨涌动之时——
天空一片宁静——

周围人的眼睛——已经哭干——

人人都屏住呼吸

等待那最后的一击——亲眼看到——

死神在房间里出现——

我在遗嘱中言明遗赠——然后签字

凡我的拥有——可分配的一切——

全都遗赠——就在这时——

一只苍蝇飞进来干预——

响着模模糊糊——断断续续的嗡嗡声——

在光明——和我——之间——

接着——窗户看不清了——然后

我想见的,什么都看不见

3. 我喜欢看它—哩哩奔驰—— *I like to see it lap the Miles* —

词语解释和难句分析

1. 从这首诗可以看出狄金森如何采取动物化的手法,把火车变成了大自然的一部分。

2. I like to see it lap the Miles —/And lick the Valleys up — 我喜欢看它一哩哩/奔驰——/舔着一个个山谷而上——

   * lap the Miles 强调"蜿蜒驰过一哩又一哩的路程"这种意象,而不是"一掠而过数千里"的迅疾。

   And stop to feed itself at Tanks —/And then — prodigious step 停在水池旁喝足了水——/然后——迈开惊人的大步

3. Around a Pile of Mountains —/And supercilious peer/In Shanties — by the sides of Roads — 绕过层层的山峦——/目空一切的傲视/道路两旁的棚屋——

   * peer in 凝视/仔细地看

   And then a Quarry pare/To fit it's (> its) Ribs/And crawl between = And then crawl between a Quarry to pare to fit its ribs 然后是从中间爬过/为适应它的身材/凿山开拓的通道

   * 为使译文与原文更加对应,也可译为:然后是一个开凿的通道/以适合它的身材/好让它从中间爬过。

   * to pare to fit its ribs 是 quarry 的定语。

   Complaining all the while/In horrid — hooting stanza —/Then chase itself down Hill — 一直不停地抱怨着——/以可怕的——呼喊出的诗节——/赶着自己,冲下山去——

4. And neigh like Boanerges —/Then — prompter than a Star 像雷霆之子那样叫嚷——/然后——比星星更准时

   * Boanerges 雷神之子,耶稣的门徒约翰和雅各(John and James)传教非常狂热,大叫大嚷,耶稣称他们为(Sons of Thunder),后来被推而广之,所有的大叫大嚷的传教士和演说家都被叫作"雷神之子"。这里把嘶吼的火车也比喻为雷神之子。

   Stop — docile and omnipotent/At it's own stable door — 停下——驯服而有雄风/待在自家门前

* 注意整首诗就是一个完整的大句子,主干为 I like to see it lap the miles. 不定式短语 lap the miles 是宾补,后面一连串的动词 lick, stop to feed..., crawl, chase, neigh, stop at ... 都是与 lap 并列的 宾补不定式动词,表现着 it(火车)的动态。

参考译文——姚远

我喜欢看它一哩哩奔驰——

我喜欢看它一哩哩奔驰——
舔着一个个山谷而上——
停在水池旁喝足了水——
然后——迈开惊人的大步

绕过重重的山峦——
目空一切地傲视
道路两旁的棚屋——
然后从中间爬过

为适应它的身材
开凿的通道
一路总在抱怨
以可怕的——呼喊出的诗节——
驱赶着自己冲下山去

像雷霆之子那样叫嚷——
然后——比星星更准时
停下——驯服却有雄风
在它自己的家门口——

4. 因为我不能停下等候死神——
Because I could not stop for Death —

词语解释和难句分析

1. 狄金森在这首诗里把死亡和永生做了拟人化的处理,使人们能强烈感受到她的信仰。
2. The Carriage <u>held but</u> just Ourselves —/And Immortality. 车厢里只有我们俩(死神和我)——/外加上永生在座。
3. We slowly drove — He knew no haste 我们缓缓行驶——他知道不用匆忙

/447

And I had put away/My labor and my leisure too,/For His Civility — 我已经放弃了/一生的劳作和闲暇/当作他礼貌的回报——

4. We passed the School, where Children strove/At Recess — in the Ring — 我们经过学校,课间时——/操场上——孩子们斗志昂扬

We passed the Fields of Gazing Grain — /We passed the Setting Sun — 我们经过谷穗俯视的田野——/我们经过落日斜阳——

＊ 学校操场、庄稼成熟和落日斜阳比喻人生发展的三个阶段。

5. Or rather — He passed Us — 或者不如说——是他(死神)经过我们——

The Dews drew quivering and chill —/For only Gossamer, my Gown —/My Tippet — only Tulle — 露珠使我颤抖和寒冷——/因为我只穿着薄纱,长袍(寿衣)——/我的披肩——也只是薄网——

6. We paused before a House that seemed/A Swelling of the Ground — 我们停在一座房前/它像是一个地面的隆起——

＊ 这实际是在说灵车来到坟前,下面两句是讲坟的形状。

The Roof was scarcely visible —/The Cornice — in the Ground — 屋顶,几乎看不见——/屋檐——埋在土里面

＊ 前面5个诗节全都是说的过去,都是用的过去时态,最后一节说的是若干世纪之后今天的感受,用的是现在时态,认识到当时的走向坟墓,就是走向永生——当年拉灵车的马头朝向坟墓就是朝向永恒。

7. Since then —'tis centuries — and yet/Feels shorter than the Day = It's centuries since then — and yet/it feels shorter than the Day 从那时至今,已过去几个世纪——/却感到比一天还短暂

I first surmised the Horses' Heads/Were toward Eternity — 那时我就第一次猜出/马头朝向永恒——

＊ 注意 surmised 和 were 都是过去时态,说的是过去,要在翻译中体现出来。

参考译文——姚远

因为我不能停下等候死神——

因为我不能停下等候死神——
所以他好意停车等我——
车厢里只有我们自己——
外加上"永生"在座。

我们缓缓行驶,他知道不用着急
我已经抛弃了
劳作和闲暇,
作他礼貌的回报——

我们经过学校,课间时——
操场上——孩子们斗志昂扬——
我们经过谷穗俯视的田野——
我们经过落日斜阳——

或者不如说——是他(死神)经过我们——
露水引我颤抖和寒冷——
因为我只穿着薄纱,长袍(寿衣)——
我的披巾——也只是薄纱——

我们停在一座房前,
它就像隆起的地面——
房顶,勉强可看见——
房檐,埋在土里面——
从那时起——已过去几个世纪——
却感觉比一天还短
当初,我就首先猜出
那马头朝向永恒——

主要内容归纳和总结

1. 艾米莉·狄金森出生在马萨诸塞州艾默斯特小镇一个加尔文主义信徒的家庭,父亲是著名律师和国会议员,对她影响很大。1847 年她毕业于艾默斯特中等学校(Amherst Academy),进入蒙特霍利约克女子神学院(Mont Holyoke Female Seminary)学习,该院公理会(Congregational)气氛特别强烈,使她经受了宗教危机,不到一年就辍学回家,后又经受了与查尔斯·沃兹沃斯(Charles Wadsworth)的恋爱失败之痛,隐居在新英格兰乡村,开始了她的诗歌和书信写作。她常常以诗为心声,诗就是她写给世界的信,信即是诗。她留下了数量可观的文学遗产(1700 多首诗),是与惠特曼(Walt Whitman)一样对美国文学有重大影响的自由体诗人。

2. 狄金森诗歌的主题和特点

　　狄金森诗歌的主题主要围绕个人的喜怒哀乐和人生经验,尤其是她对宗教、死亡、永生(immortality)、爱情和自然的思考。对宗教,既有想获得拯救的渴望,也有对上帝漠视人间疾苦的不满;她对人死亡时的状态和灵魂何往(the journey of her soul to the unknown)有种种遐想和探索;爱情诗方面,她对异性相吸生理方面的欲望和心理方面的又惊又喜(the power of physical attraction of fear and fascination for the mysterious magnetism between sexes),以及对男权的不满(dissatisfied with the male authorities over the female)都有所表现。

　　她的诗歌的特点很鲜明:短小简练,超过20 行的诗不多;自由体,片语式(fragmented),不受严格的格律和韵律限制;单一意象、单一象征,多用第一人称;破折号被用作节奏(dashes are used as a musical device),大写字母被用作强调(capital letters as means of emphasis);所有的诗歌都无题,常用第一行诗句代之;拟人化的手法(personification,使得抽象的思维变得生动形象了(to vivify some abstract ideas),等等。

3. 艾米莉·狄金森的主要作品:

《我死时听到一只苍蝇嗡嗡叫》 *I heard a Fly buzz — when I died —*
《这是我写给世界的信》 *This is my letter to the World*
《我喜欢看它一哩哩奔驰》 *I like to see it lap the Miles —*
《因为我不能停下等候死神》 *Because I could not stop for Death —*
《如果郎君秋日来》 *If you were coming in the Fall*
《盛夏一日》 *There came a Day at Summer's full*

《不得与君同住》 *I cannot live with You* —
《我已退出，不再与他们为伍》 *I'm ceded — I've stopped being theirs*
《我是"妻"，那事已做完》 *I'm 'wife' — I've finished that* —

重要信息句子

1. Dickinson's poems are usually based on her own experiences, her sorrows and joys. Love is another subject Dickinson dwelt on.

2. More than five hundred poems Dickinson wrote are about nature, in which her general skepticism about the relationship between man and nature is well-expressed.

Ⅳ. 西奥多·德莱塞 Theodore Dreiser（1871~1945）

词语解释和难句分析

1. be generally acknowledged as one of America's literary naturalists　被普遍认为是美国自然主义的文学家

   to possess none of the usual aids to a writer's career　做一个作家/开始创作生涯，没有任何的背景/渊源/外来的帮助

   no formal education worthy of mention, no family tradition in letters　没有受过任何值得一提的正式教育，没有文学方面的家学渊源

   with every disadvantage piled upon him　堆在/压在他身上的每一个不利因素

   by his strong will and his dogged persistence　凭借他坚强的毅力和坚持不懈的精神

   to burst out and become one of the important American writers　出人头地/闯出来，成了美国重要作家之一

2. to read voraciously by himself　自己如饥似渴/贪婪地阅读

   to immerse himself in Dickens and Thackeray…　他埋头于/沉浸在阅读狄更斯、萨克雷……的作品中

   to work on his own, earning a meager support by doing some odd jobs　他开始自谋生路，打一些零工，勉强糊口

   to make a beginning by placing himself with one of Chicago's newspapers　在芝加哥的一家报馆谋到一个职位，开始了作家生涯

   to grope his way to authorship　摸索着走上作家之路

3. a prolific writer　一位多产的作家

   tracing the material rise of Carrie Meeber and the tragic decline of G. W. Hurstwood　描绘出一条嘉莉·梅伯物质享受得到满足和 G. W. 赫斯特伍德落得悲剧下场的发展线索

   a classic story of "misunderstood artist"　一个"被误解的艺术家"的经典故事

   be condemned for "obscenity and blasphemy"　被抨击为"淫秽和亵渎上帝"

   to lend their support　表示支持，伸出援手

to turn away from fiction and involved himself in political activities and debate writing　不再写小说,转而投身政治活动,写作辩论性的檄文

4. be launching himself upon a long career that would ultimately make him one of the most significant American writer of the school later known as literary naturalism　使他自己开始从事一项最终使他成为最重要的、后来被认为属于自然主义文学流派的美国作家

to emphasize heredity and environment as important deterministic forces shaping individualized characters　强调遗传和环境是形成个性化人物的重要决定性因素

5. Asked, during his middle years, about what he thought earthly existence was, Dreiser described it as "a welter of inscrutable forces," in which was trapped each individual human being.　在德莱塞进入中年,有人向他问到尘世生存究竟是什么的时候,他将它描写成一团"不可思议的力量的混乱纠缠",每个人都深陷其中。

6. be often subject to the control of the natural forces — especially those of environment and heredity　(书中人物)都受到自然力的控制,尤其是环境和遗传力量的控制

7. to find in Dreiser's fiction a world of jungle　在德莱塞的小说中看到了丛林世界

to shift from the pathos of the helpless protagonists at the bottom of the society to the power of the American financial tycoons　从描写社会底层无助的"主人公"的凄凉,转到描写美国金融寡头的巨大力量

to make Clyde's downfall inevitable　使得克莱德的破产不可避免

to encourage people to pursue the "dream of success" at all costs　鼓励人们不顾一切地追求"成功之梦"

8. to set himself to project the American values for what he have found them to be — materialistic to the core　他按自己所看到的样子来反映美国的价值观——彻底的物质主义

be obsessed with a never-ending, yet meaningless search for satisfaction of his desires　沉湎于无休止的、又毫无意义的满足欲望的追求之中

(money) be a motivating purpose of life　(金钱)是人生动机/激发人积极性的生活目的

to symbolize the acquisition of some social status of great magnitude　象征重要社会地位的获得

9. They are there like a powerful "magnetism" governing human existence and reducing human beings to nothing.　那些欲望就像一个强大的磁场,驾驭着人类的生存,并把人的存在变得毫无意义了。

　＊governing 和 reducing 引导的两个分词短语是 magnetism 的定语。

10. So like all naturalists he was restrained from finding a solution to the social problem that appeared in his novels and accordingly almost all his works have tragic endings.　所以,像所有自然主义作家一样,他的局限性使他不能对自己小说中出现的社会问题找到解决办法,因此他的所有著作都是悲剧性的结尾。

11. to appear more inclusive and less selective　似乎包容有余,选择不足

be burdened with massive detailed descriptions of characters and events　感到深为对人物和事件大量的细节描写所累,即对过于详细的描写感到累赘

be accused of being mixed and disorganized in voice and tone　语态和语气上组织不够严谨,受到指责

to break away from the genteel tradition of literature　打破文学上高雅的传统

be well calculated to achieve the thematic ends he sought　对达到他所追求的主题目标是很适合的

　＊calculated = suitable/possible　合适的

德莱塞作品选读

《嘉莉妹妹》Sister Carrie 最后一章

词语解释和难句分析

1. meager income and terrible work condition　勉强糊口的收入和可怕的工作条件

   to <u>fall in love with</u> Drouet's friend George Hurstwood　与德鲁埃的朋友乔治·赫斯特伍德相爱

   away from the atmosphere of success on which his life has been based　脱离了一直作为他生活基础的成功的氛围

   to think him too great a burden and leave him　认为他是个太大的负担,离开了他

   to sink lower and lower　越来越沉沦

2. Though received not favorably and <u>attacked</u> as immoral by the public in its time, *Sister Carrie* best embodies Dreiser's naturalistic belief that while men are controlled and conditioned (= adjusted) by heredity, instinct and chance, a few extraordinary and unsophisticated human beings refuse to accept their fate wordlessly and instead strive, unsuccessfully, to find meaning and purpose for their existence.　虽然《嘉莉妹妹》没有得到当时公众的高度赞扬,反而被抨击为有伤道德,但是它最好地体现了自然主义的信仰:当人们被遗传、本能和机遇所控制的时候,一些杰出的、不圆滑世故的人会拒绝默默接受这种控制,奋起抗争,发现他们生存的意义和目的,尽管不成功。

3. be merely a cipher in an uncaring world　仅仅是无情的世界上一个无足轻重的人

   to seek to grasp the mysteries of life　寻求掌握生活的奥秘

   to satisfy her desires for social status and material comfort　满足她寻求社会地位和物质享受的欲望

   to <u>turn on</u> the gas in a cheap lodging-house and end his life　在一个廉价的租住屋打开煤气,结束了他的生命

   be rocking comfortably in her luxuriant hotel room　在她豪华的旅馆房间里躺在摇椅上,舒适地摇晃着

4. The Way of the Beaten: A Harp in the Wind　穷途末路:寒风中的竖琴

5. to put his hands, red from cold, down in his pockets　把冻红了的手插在口袋里

   with death in his heart　心里怀有求死的念头

   a lodging-house　一家寄宿处

   with gas-jets in rooms　房间里装有煤气喷嘴

   to rent for fifteen cents　(房间)出租一天 15 美分

6. a comfortable-looking gentleman, coming, clean-shaven, out of a fine barber shop　一位神态悠闲的绅士,刚从高档理发店修了面出来

   ＊clean-shaven　修了面,胡子刮得很干净

   to <u>look him over</u> and <u>fish for</u> a dime　打量了他一下,伸手去摸一角硬币

   to be(well) rid of him　摆脱掉他,打发他走人,赶他走

   for the time being　暂时,目前

   the sharpest spell of the season　这个季节(冬季)最寒冷刺骨的一段时间

   to set in　到来,开始

   to <u>break gray and cold</u> in the first day　第一天天气突然变得阴冷

to have secured but ten cents by nightfall　到夜幕降临,只讨到/得到 10 美分

7. Especially fatigued because of the <u>wandering propensity</u> which seized him in the morning, he now half dragged his wet feet, shuffling the soles upon the sidewalk.　由于他上午满脑子都是想出去游荡,因而出去逛了一阵,感到特别累,所以现在他半拖着湿漉漉的脚,任鞋底在人行道上走过。

8. <u>be turned up about</u> his red ears　向上翻起,直拉到他冻红的耳朵边
   his cracked derby hat　他已破得裂开口子的圆顶帽
   be pulled down until it turned them (= ears) outward　(帽子)被拉下来(盖住了一切),只留下耳朵在外面听
   the <u>fire signs</u> were already <u>blazing brightly</u>　灯光闪亮的广告牌已经大放异彩
   gay companies　许多寻欢作乐的伴侣/男女/聚会
   (sb.) <u>be recalled</u> keenly <u>to</u> better things　某人被召唤到对往事的美好回忆中,使某人深深地回想起以前的好日子

9. be all up with me　我已经全完了
   his shambling figure　他落拓颓唐的形象
   to follow him with their eyes, to see that he did not beg of anybody　他们的目光紧追着他,务必使他不要/随时阻止他向任何人乞讨
   to pause in an aimless, incoherent sort of way　漫无目的、思绪茫然地停下来
   an imposing restaurant　一家气势恢宏的大饭店/餐厅

10. and through the large, plate windows of which (= the restaurant) could be seen the red and gold decorations, the palms, the white napery, and shining glassware, and, above all, the comfortable crowd.　透过宾馆的大平面玻璃窗,他可以看到红色和金色的装饰,棕榈树,白餐巾,闪光的玻璃餐具,尤其是那些悠闲自得的食客。

11. Weak <u>as</u> his mind had become, his hunger was sharp enough to show the importance of this (= eating).　尽管他的心神已十分虚弱,但极度的饥饿依然使他感到"吃"的重要性。

12. to stop stock still　(木头似的)呆呆地站住了
    his frayed trousers soaking in the slush　他磨损了的裤筒浸在雪水的泥浆里
    to peer foolishly in　向里面/窗内痴望着

13. That's right, eat. Nobody else wants any.　不错,要吃。别人都有得吃(= 别人都不存在吃的问题)。

14. At Broadway and Thirty-ninth Street was blazing, in incandescent fire, Carrie's name. = Carrie's name was blazing, in incandescent fire, at Broadway and Thirty-ninth Street.　百老汇和第三十九大街交汇处白炽灯闪耀着嘉莉的名字。

15. radiated fire　往周围辐射的灯光,光芒四射的灯光
    a large, gilt-framed poster-board　一面金边儿的广告牌
    a fine lithograph of Carrie, life-size　嘉莉的一张精美的平版印刷像,与真人一样大
    snuffling and hunching one shoulder　吸了吸鼻子,耸起一只肩膀
    be so <u>run down</u> that his mind was not exactly clear　如此衰弱不堪,连头脑也有些不太清楚了

16. He lingered, trying to think logically.　他磨蹭着,竭力想理出个头绪来。

17. "She's got it," he said, incoherently, thinking of money.　"她有钱了。"他前言不搭后语地说道,想起了钱。

18. to go over and shove him　走过来把他往外推
    almost tickled at the spectacle　看到这景象/样子几乎嗤笑起来
    be being hustled away　正在被人往外猛推/猛赶
    to slip and fall in the snow　滑倒在雪地里

some vague sense of shame　某种模糊的耻辱感

to well up　涌起,溢出

19. Now a fierce feeling against Carrie <u>welled up</u> — just one fierce angry thought before the whole thing <u>slipped out of</u> his mind.　这时,他对嘉莉涌起一股强烈的情感——也就是一股强烈的愤怒,过了一会儿,一切又风平浪静了。

20. to owe me something to eat　应该给(欠)我点儿东西吃

to <u>turn back into</u> Broadway again and slop onward and away　又转回到百老汇大街,畏畏缩缩地向前走去

losing track of his thoughts, one after another　迷失了思路,想起了这个,又忘却了那个

21. ... as a mind decayed and disjointed is wont to do.　就像大脑衰退、思想不连贯的人所惯常出现的那样。

　　* wont　*adj.* 惯常的,倾向于,易于……(后接不定式)

22. a wintry evening　一个寒冬的夜晚

the somber hue of night　昏暗阴沉的夜色

(be) <u>borne</u> forward by a swift wind <u>in</u> long, thin lines　被推压成/疾风吹成一条条长长的细线

be bedded with snow　被积雪覆盖,铺满/堆满了积雪

(be) churned to a dirty brown by the crush of teams and the feet of men　被车辗人踏搅成了黑褐色的脏东西

　　* teams　车队,车流

to pick their way in ulsters and umbrellas　穿着厚绒粗呢大衣、撑着雨伞小心翼翼地走着

to slouch through the Bowery with collars and hats pulled over their ears　低着头走过波威利街,竖起衣领,拉下帽子盖住耳朵

thoroughfare businessmen and travelers　繁华大街上的商旅

crowds on cold errands　在严寒中忙忙碌碌的人群

to shift pass dingy stores　慢慢走过肮脏幽暗的店铺

in the deep recesses of the stores　在店堂深处

be muffled by this fast-thickening mantle　被迅速堆积的雪所覆盖/包围

23. The usual clatter of the cable car was reduced by the mantle about the wheels.　车轮上的雪泥降低了缆车平常的嘎嘎声。

24. to catch nearly the full sympathetic significance of the story　几乎完全领会了故事令人感到痛快的意义

　　* sympathetic　意气相投的,感到痛快的

be borne in upon her　被她认识到

the old winding <u>procession of carriages</u> <u>rolling up</u> Fifth Avenue　蜿蜒不绝地在第五大道上驶过的车队

to go sleigh riding　去滑雪橇

25. (sth.) be keen with sb.　某事在某人脑子里还非常清晰,某人还想着某事

be sorry for sb.　同情某人

be <u>hard up</u>　穷困,艰难

to catch sight of some one falling down　看到有人跌倒了

to <u>shake</u> the snow <u>from</u> the handsome ulster　把雪花从漂亮的粗呢羊绒大衣上抖掉

to <u>stir his desire for</u> those pleasures which <u>shut out</u> the snow and gloom of life　激起了他寻欢作乐的欲望,把大雪和人生的愁苦统统关到门外

addressing a lounger in one of the comfortable lobby chairs　朝舒适地坐在客厅椅子里的一个游手好

闲的人说

26. about six and six = just so so　一般般,很一般,不怎么样
to introduce you to <u>something dead swell</u> (= absolutely fashionable people and things)　给你引见几个绝对的丽人

27. Wait'll (= wait until) I go upstairs and change my clothes　等一下,我上楼去换件衣服

28. be as light <u>on the wing</u> as ever　飞起来还像过去一样轻盈
on a incoming vestibuled Pullman　在正行驶而来的一列客车设有过廊的卧铺车厢里
first call for dinner in the dinning-car　餐车的第一次晚餐
to hasten through the aisle in snow-white apron and jacket　急急忙忙地穿过车厢的走廊,身上穿着雪白的围裙和上衣
to turn supercilious by fortune　由于幸运而变得非常傲慢
to <u>push</u> a euchre hand <u>away from</u> her　把一手纸牌摊开去
＊ a euchre hand = a hand of paper cards　一手纸牌

29. "…"inquired her husband, who was all that fine raiment can make.　"……"她丈夫问道,精美的衣服使得他风度翩翩。
＊ to make all　给了某人一切(风采)

30. She <u>was also a study in</u> what good clothing can do for age.　从她的身上可以看出服装会给上年纪的人带来多少美化作用。

31. Her husband studied her, for beauty, even cold, is fascinating <u>from one point of view</u>.　她丈夫欣赏着她,因为从某种观点看,尽管寒冷,美丽依然是迷人的。

32. We won't have much more of this weather.　这样的天气再受不了多久了(言外之意是要走了)。

33. one whose financial state had borne her personal inspection　一个经济上都得受她审查的人

34. This won't make any difference.　这没有什么关系/与此无干。

35. Passing down the aisle came a very fair-haired banker's son, also of Chicago. = A very fair-haired banker's son, also of Chicago, came passing down the aisle.　过廊里走来了一位头发浅黄的银行家的儿子,也是来自芝加哥。

36. to have long eyed this supercilious beauty　久久地注视着这个傲慢的美人
with a specially conjured show of indifference　故意摆出的一副迷人的不在乎的样子
wifely modesty　为人妇者的温驯,妇道人家的端庄

37. By so much was her pride satisfied. = Her pride was much satisfied by so.　这么做使她的傲慢心理得到了很大的满足。

38. His <u>one-time coat</u> of buff had been changed by soot and rain.　他以前曾是橘黄色的外套已被煤烟和雨水所改变。

39. He <u>mingled with</u> a crowd of men — a crowd which had been, and was still gathering <u>by degrees</u>.　他混在一群人中——已经是一群了,现在还在不断聚集。

40. to <u>hang about</u> the closed wooden doors and to <u>beat their feet</u> to keep them warm　在密闭的木门前徘徊,跺着脚取暖
to <u>have on</u> faded derby hats with dents in them　戴着褪色的圆顶帽,帽上满是凹痕
misfit coats　不合身的外衣
be heavy with melted snow　(衣服)被融雪浸湿,沉甸甸的
(be) frayed at the bottom and <u>wobbling over</u> big, soppy shoes　裤脚都磨损坏了,耷拉在泥浆湿透的大鞋上摆动着

41. (be) <u>worn</u> almost <u>to</u> shreds　几乎被磨成碎布条

to shift ruefully about　哀怨地踱步徘徊

to dig his hands into his pockets and leer at the crowd and the increased lamps　他把手深深地插进口袋,斜眼瞟着人群和一盏盏点亮的街灯

42. With the minutes, increased the number. = With the minutes, the number increased.　随着时间一分一秒地过去,人数不断地增加。

43. old men with grizzled beards and sunken eyes　灰白胡子、眼睛深陷的老人

shrunken by diseases　因疾病而形容枯槁/骨瘦如柴

in the thick of the collection　在密集的人群里

as white as drained veal　苍白得想失了血的小牛肉

(there were) still others with frames so lean that clothes only flapped about them　另外还有一些人,瘦得只剩下骨架,使衣服挂在上面,摆来摆去。

swollen noses, blood-shot eyes　肿起的鼻子,充血的眼睛

not a straight figure　没有一个挺直的身躯

not a straightforward, steady glance　没有一个坦然直视、坚定执着的目光

44. in the drive of the wind and sleet　在风雪肆虐中

to push in on one another　相互拥挤在一起

half covered by every conceivable semblance of a hat　各种各样算是帽子一样的东西并不能完全盖住的

＊semblance　外观,相似

to look stiff and bitten　看上去已冻僵冻肿了

to shift, now one foot, now another, almost rocking in unison　不住地换脚,几乎形成了统一的踩脚节奏

a running comment directed at any one in general　想到什么说什么的泛泛评论

oaths and slang phrases　咒骂和俚语黑话

45. a sharper lash of wind　一阵猛烈的、更加尖利的寒风(袭来)

to huddle closer　挤得更紧

an edging, shifting, pushing throng　朝向一边移动、挤压的人群

be all sullen endurance, unlightened by either wit or good fellowship　完全是愠怒的忍耐,无论是诙谐打趣还是友好交流都不能减轻

46. to go jingling by　(马车)叮叮当当地驶过

look at the bloke riding　瞧那个家伙在乘车兜风呢

the carriage having long since passed out of hearing　马车已过去好久,听不到声音了

to creep on　不知不觉中/悄悄来临

be bloomed ruddy with a steady flame　被持续的灯光照红

47. Still the crowd hung about the door, unwavering.　人群依然在门前徘徊,不想散去/毫不动摇。

48. to renew the general interest in the closed door　重新引起大家对那紧闭着的大门的兴趣,提醒大家注意那紧闭的大门

to gaze in that direction　注视着那个方向

to look at it as dumb brutes look, as dogs paw and whine and study the knob　眼盯着那扇大门,像哑巴野兽那样盯着它,琢磨着那球形把手

49. and still the snow whirled and cut them with biting flakes　雪花依然在盘旋飞舞,刺骨的雪片刮削着人们的脸

50. and water trickled off hat rims and down noses, which the owners could not reach to scratch.　雪水从帽

檐上滴下,沿着鼻子往下淌,人们却不能伸手去擦。

51. to stand with head lowered to the weather and bent his form　呆站在那里,向这鬼天气低头弯腰

to appear through the transom overhead　(灯光)从门顶的气窗透射出来

to send a thrill of possibility through the watchers　给了等待的人群希望,引起了他们的激动

a murmur of recognition　一阵喃喃的反应

to prick up its ears = to prick up the ears of the crowds　人群都竖起了耳朵

slow up there, now　喂,慢点儿,别挤

52. It was push and jam for a minute, with grim, beast silence to prove its quality, and then it melted inward, like logs floating, and disappeared.　人群向前拥挤,乱了一会儿,接着以阴森恐怖的野兽般的沉默证明自己的素质,然后向门里如浮木般散去,不见了踪影。

53. a cold, shrunken, disgruntled mass　一群冻得要命、形容枯槁、很不高兴的家伙

pouring in between bleak walls　从荒凉的墙壁间涌了进去

54. There was supper in every hurrying pedestrian's face.　从每一个匆忙的行人脸上都可以看出该吃晚饭了/已是晚饭的时间了。

55. to creep off with weary steps to his allotted room　拖着疲惫的脚步离开,爬进指定给他的房间

a dingy affair – wooden, dusty, hard　一个肮脏昏暗的东西(房间)——木板床,满是灰尘,坚硬得很

(gas-jet) to furnish sufficient light for so rueful a corner　(煤气喷嘴)给如此可悲的斗室提供了足够的光线

to stop first with his coat, and tuck it along the crack under the door　先用上衣堵住,把它塞在房门下面的那道缝里

＊stop 和 tuck 都是动词,"堵塞"的意思。

(be) hidden from view　无人看见

to turn the gas on/out　打开/关掉煤气

to apply no match　没用火柴点(煤气)

(be) hidden wholly in that kindness which is night (＝in that kind night)　完全隐藏在仁慈的夜色中

the uprising fumes　上升的煤气

to quit his attitude and fumble for the bed　放弃了他(站立)的姿态,摸索着上了床

to stretch himself to rest　摊开手脚躺下休息

56. And now Carrie had attained that which in the beginning seemed life's object, or, at least, (attain) such fraction of it (＝object) as human beings ever attain of their original desires.　现在嘉莉已经实现了她早先的人生目标,或者说,至少实现了人类满足基本物质欲望的部分目标。

＊as 是关系代词,指代 it (＝object),引导一个定语从句,在从句中作 attain 的宾语。

57. to look about on　打量,环顾

as the world takes it　如同社会的惯例,根据一般情况

to bow and smile in acknowledgement of her success　点头哈腰,满脸堆笑,肯定她的成功

to crave for　渴望,渴求,追求

58. Applause there was, and publicity — once far off, essential things, but now grown trivial and indifferent.　到处有掌声,有公众的关注——曾经是遥不可及的大理想,而现在已变成索然无味的琐细小事了。

59. In her rocking chair she sat, when not otherwise engaged (＝when she was not otherwise engaged)—singing and dreaming.　她在闲暇无事/没有其他的事情时,就会躺在摇椅上,浅吟低唱,梦里神游。

60. Thus in life there is ever the intellectual and the emotional nature — the mind that reasons, and the mind that feels.　因此生活中既有理性,也有感性。既有思辨的智士,也有善于感受的人。

61. **Of one come the men of action — generals and statesmen; of the other, the poets and dreamers — artists all.** 一种/前者造就了实干家——将军和政治家;另一种/后者,孕育出诗人和幻想家——都是艺术家。

　　*句子结构为倒装形式,也可按主谓的顺向形式大致写出:The men of action come of one; the poets and dreamers come of the other. 句中画线部分意为"出于,产生于,由……引起"。

62. **As harps in the wind, the latter respond to every breath of fancy voicing in their moods all the ebb and flow of the ideal.** 就像风中的风琴,后者(艺术家)对梦想的每一次呼吸都会做出反应,以他们自己的喜怒哀乐表达着理想的跌宕起伏。

　　*respond to 是句子的谓语动词,voicing 引导的分词短语作补充说明的状语。

63. **Man has not yet comprehended the dreamer any more than he has (not comprehended) the ideal.** 人们不懂得梦想家,就像他们不懂得梦想一样。

64. **be unduly severe** 过分的严厉

　　ever hearkening to the sound of beauty 曾经倾听过美妙的声音

　　straining for the flash of its distant wings 曾为振翅高飞、长风万里(的雄心)鼓足了劲

　　to watch to follow, wearing his feet in traveling 先是观望,然后效仿,使人旅程中的脚步疲惫不堪

65. **And it must be remembered that reason had little part in this.** 必须谨记,这里面理性几乎不占多大比重。

66. **Chicago dawning, she saw the city offering more of loveliness than she had ever known, and instinctively, by force of her moods alone, clung to it.** 她看到芝加哥的黎明显得比过去更加可爱,她本能地仅凭情绪的力量,依恋上了这座城市。

67. **Hence, she drew near these things.** 事实上,这些东西她差不多都有了。

68. **the world of fashion and the world of stage — these were but incidents** 时装界和演艺圈——这些只是人生的偶遇

69. **Not them, but that which they represented, she longed for. Time proved the representation false.** 她所渴望的不是这些,而是他们所代表的东西。时光证明他们代表不了什么(所代表的都不真实)。

70. **Oh, the tangle of human life! How dimly as yet we see.** 啊,人生是多么纷繁纠结啊!迄今我们看到的又是多么昏暗模糊啊!

71. **responding with desire to everything most lovely in life, yet finding herself turned as by a wall** 对生活中一切美好的东西都十分向往,但却发现自己处处碰壁

72. **Laws to say:"Be allured, if you will, by everything lovely, but draw not nigh (= near) unless by righteousness. (= If you will be allured by everything lovely, but draw not nigh unless by righteousness.)"** 法律对她说:"你可以被一切美好的东西吸引,却不能被俘虏/驱使,除非正义。"

73. **You shall not better your situation save by honest labor.** 除了诚实的劳动,你绝不可用其他的方式发财致富。

74. **If honest labor be unremunerative and difficult to endure;** 如果诚实的劳动无利可图,难以持久;

75. **if it be the long, long road which never reaches beauty, but wearies the feet and the heart;** 如果诚实的劳动道路太过漫长,永远不能实现美好的人生,反而使人身心交瘁;

76. **if the drag to follow beauty be such that one abandons the admired way, taking rather the despised path leading to her dreams quickly, who shall cast the first stone?** 如果追求美好生活的驱动力使得一个人放弃值得赞赏的(生活)方式,而选择一条通往梦想的不光彩的"捷径",谁第一个来惩罚她?

　　*who shall cast the first stone? 引自《圣经》,人们把一个犯了通奸罪的妇女带到耶稣面前,要耶稣判决。根据摩西律法,她应被石头砸死,但耶稣却弓腰用手指在地上写了一行字:Whichever one of you has committed no sin may throw the first stone at her. 意为:你们中未犯过罪的向她扔第一

块石头。人们看了,一个个走了,走得最早的是年纪最大的人。

77. Not evil, but longing for that which is better, more often <u>directs the steps of the erring</u>.　不是邪恶,而是对美好的渴望,更容易引导人步入迷途。

78. Not evil, but goodness more often allures the feeling mind unused to reason.　不是邪恶,而是美好的事物,更容易诱惑从不用理性思维的感性头脑。

79. to walk amid the <u>tinsel and shine</u> of her state, unhappy　她带着一身的浮华和光彩走来,心里并不快乐
    <u>be lifted into</u> that which is best　被提升进最美好的境界
    to offer her the best way　(似乎)给了她最好的生活

80. But since the world <u>goes its way past</u> all who will not <u>partake of</u> its folly, she now found herself alone.　但是(因为)这个世界的运行会抛弃/超越一切不加入其荒唐潮流的人,(所以)现在她又孤身一人了。
    ＊ partake of　共享,分享,参与

81. Her purse <u>was open to</u> him whose need was greatest.　她的钱包完全可以帮助极度贫困中的他。
    ＊ be open to　向……敞开/打开

82. Had they more of that peace and beauty which glimmered <u>afar off</u>, then were they to be envied.　如果他们再多一些从远处隐现的宁静与优美,就会被人羡慕了。

83. to abandon his claim　放弃他的权利/拥有权
    <u>setting out from</u> the pier at Twenty-seventh Street <u>to</u> the Potter's Field　从二十七大街码头出发,驶向帕特·菲尔德公墓
    upon its weekly <u>errand bore</u>　执行/完成它每周一次的使命/差事

84. Thus passed all that <u>was</u> of interest concerning these twain <u>in their relation to</u> her.　至此,涉及与她相关的那两个人的一切利益关系全都结束了。

85. Their influence upon her life is explicable alone by the nature of her longings.　仅凭她追求的性质,就可解释他们对她生活的影响。

86. <u>Time was when</u> both represented for her all that was most potent in earthly success.　曾几何时,这两个人对于她来说代表了一切最大的世俗成功。

87. the personal representatives of a state <u>most blessed to attain</u>　最想达到的理想境界的私人代表
    the titled ambassadors of comfort and peace, aglow with their credentials　冠有头衔、闪耀着文凭光辉的舒适和宁静的使者

88. It is but natural that when the world which they represented no longer allured her, its ambassadors should be discredited.　当他们所代表的世界不再使她迷惑的时候,它的使者就信誉扫地了,这只是自然的事情。

89. In his world, as in her own present state, was not happiness. = Happiness was not in his world, as in her own present state.　他的世界,跟她目前的状态一样,都不快乐。

90. Sitting alone, she was now an illustration of <u>devious ways</u> by which one who feels, rather than reasons, may be led <u>in the pursuit of</u> beauty.　她独自一人坐着,现在她就是走入歧途的一个实例。走入迷途,一个感性的人可能被引导去追求美好的事物,而不是追求理性。
    ＊ by which = by the ways; 短语 rather than reasons 常情况下放在句子最后。

91. Though often disillusioned, she was still waiting for that halcyon day <u>when she</u> <u>should be led forth among</u> <u>dreams</u> become real.　尽管常常幻想破灭,她依然等待在梦中被指引向前的幸福美好的日子变成现实。
    ＊ 画线部分为定语从句,修饰 halcyon day, when 为引导定语从句的关系副词。

92. Ames had <u>pointed out</u> a farther step, but <u>on and on</u> beyond that, if accomplished, would lie others for

her（＝others would lie for her）. 埃米斯曾为她指出向前的一步,但过了这一步,还要继续向前,走完了这一步,后面还有很多步在等她走。

93. It was forever to be the pursuit of that radiance of delight which tints the distant hilltops of the world. 将远方的山峰渲染得多彩多姿永远是对快乐的光辉的追求。

　　＊it 为形式主语,真正主语是 which 引导的主语从句。

94. Oh, blind strivings of the human heart! 呵,人的心灵在盲目地挣扎呀!

95. and where beauty leads, there it（＝human heart）follows 美在哪里指引,心就在那里跟随

96. the tingle of a lone sheep bell o'er（＝over）some quiet landscape 静谧的风景中,孤独的羊儿的铃声

the glimmer of beauty in <u>sylvan places</u> 茂密丛林里隐约闪现的美景

the show of soul in some passing eye 一闪而过的目光中灵魂的展示

97. It is when the feet weary and hope seems vain that the heartaches and the longings arise. 正是在身心疲惫、希望破灭的时候,人才会感到心痛不已,也才会激发起渴望和向往。

98. Know, then, that for you is neither surfeit nor content. 那么,要知道,对你来说,那既不过分,又不会满足。

主要内容归纳和总结

1. 西奥多·德莱塞(Theodore Dreiser)出生在美国印第安纳州泰勒·汉特(Terre Hante)一个德国移民家庭,他家里家境贫困,宗教气氛强烈。他童年时十分穷苦,先在当地天主教教会学校上学,后到沃沙(Warsaw)公学,受到一位老师的赏识和栽培,使他有幸能在印第安纳大学上了一年学。但他的成就更多是得益于他的广泛阅读和自己的大胆实践,他是摸索着走上专业作家道路的,最后成为一个多产的作家(prolific writer)。

　　自然主义是他一以贯之的创作风格,强调遗传因素和环境因素是形成典型环境中典型人物个性的决定性的力量。他作品中的人物都不能掌握自己的命运,几乎所有小说都是同一个悲剧的结尾。他的小说没有评论和判断,只有事实的陈述。对他来说,语言只是传达思想,而非艺术形式,故而作品的语言结构常显得烦琐、不简洁。他的作品包容有余,选择不足(more inclusive and less selective)。

2. 西奥多·德莱塞的主要作品:

《嘉莉妹妹》Sister Carrie（1900）

《黑人杰夫》Nigger Jeff

《老拉格姆和他的特里萨》Rogaum and His Theresa

《珍妮姑娘》Jennie Gerhardt（1911）

《欲望三部曲》Trilogy of Desire,包括:

＊《金融家》The Financier（1912）

＊《巨头》The Titan（1914）

＊《斯多葛》The Stoic（1947）

《天才》The Genius（完成于 1915,出版于 1923）

《美国的悲剧》An American Tragedy（1925）

《德莱塞眼中的俄国》Dreiser Looks at Russia（1928）

重要信息句子

1. His true literary influences were from Balzac, Charles Darwin and Herbert Spencer.
2. Theodore Dreiser is generally acknowledged as one of America's literary naturalists.
3. As a genre, naturalism emphasized heredity and environment as important deterministic forces shaping individualized characters.

美国现实主义时期文学同步练习与答案

1. The period ranging from 1865 to 1914 has been referred to as _____.
   a. the Period of Romanticism
   b. the Neoclassical Period
   c. the Modern Period
   d. the Age of Realism
2. The 50 years between the end of the Civil War to the outbreak of the First World War is a period in American history characterized with _____.
   a. stability
   b. changes
   c. technological innovation
   d. commercialization
3. The three dominant figures of the Age of Realism are _____, _____, and _____.
   a. William Dean Howells/Washington Irving/Ralph Waldo Emerson
   b. Mark Twain/Henry James/James Joyce
   c. Nathaniel Hawthorne/Walt Whitman/Herman Melville
   d. Mark Twain/William Dean Howells/Henry James
4. The three prominent writers in the Realistic Period differed in their understanding of the "truth." Mark Twain and Howells seemed to have paid more attention to _____, while _____ had apparently laid emphasis on the "inner world" of man.
   a. the American dream/Herman Melville
   b. the industrialization of America/Ernest Hemingway
   c. the "life" of the Americans/Henry James
   d. the Westward Expansion/Mark Twain
5. Who considered whom "the true father of our national literature" in America? _____.
   a. H. L. Mencken/Mark Twain
   b. Herman Melville/Washington Irving
   c. Ernest Hemingway/Mark Twain
   d. Henry James/Mark Twain
6. _____ is usually regarded as a classic book written for boys about their particular horrors and joys.
   a. *The Sketch Book*
   b. *The Adventures of Tom Sawyer*
   c. *Daisy Miller*
   d. *Adventures of Huckleberry Finn*
7. _____ is a boy's book specially written for the adults by Mark Twain.
   a. *Adventures of Huckleberry Finn*
   b. *The Gilded Age*
   c. *The Celebrated Jumping Frog of Calavera's County*
   d. *Innocent Abroad*
8. James' fame generally rests upon his novels and stories with the _____ theme.

a. international
b. psychological

c. realistic
d. vernacular

9. James' realism is characterized by his _____ to his subject matter.

a. philosophical exploration
b. psychological approach

c. individualism present
d. naturalistic representation

10. _____ is generally regarded as the forerunner of the 20th century "stream-of-consciousness" novels and the founder of psychological realism.

a. Mark Twain
b. Washington Irving

c. Henry James
d. Emily Dickinson

11. One of James' literary techniques innovated to cater for this psychological emphasis is his _____.

a. vernacular style
b. neoclassical style

c. European style
d. narrative point of view

12. _____ brought James international fame for the first time.

a. *The Europeans*
b. *The Turn of the Screw*

c. *Daisy Miller*
d. *The Portrait of a Lady*

13. _____ is generally considered to be Henry James' masterpiece.

a. *Daisy Miller*
b. *The Portrait of a Lady*

c. *The American*
d. *The Ambassadors*

14. _____, in Henry James' works, is regarded as a celebrated cultural type who embodies the spirit of the New World.

a. *Princess Casamassima*
b. *Daisy Miller*

c. *Maisie*
d. *Tom Sawyer*

15. Dickinson's poems are usually based on her own experiences, _____.

a. her religious belief
b. her sorrows and joys

c. her philosophical speculation
d. acute observation

16. Closely related to Dickinson's religious poetry are her poems concerning _____:

a. human beings and nature
b. the orthodox view of paradise

c. God's benevolence
d. death and immortality

17. Love is another subject of Dickinson dwelt on. One group of her love poems treats the suffering and frustration love can cause. The other group of love poems focuses on _____.

a. the physical aspect of desire
b. the influence of male authorities over the female

c. the female right
d. the equality of the male and the female

18. more than five hundred poems Dickinson wrote are about _____.

a. the living and the death
b. death and immortality

c. love and suffering
d. nature and man

19. Which of the following is generally considered as one of Dickinson's masterpieces? _____.

a. *This is my letter to the World*
b. *I cannot live with You*

c. *I heard a Fly buzz — when I died —*
d. *I'm "wife" — I've finished that —*

20. _____ proves to be Theodore Dreiser's greatest work.

a. *Sister Carrie*
b. *An American Tragedy*

c. *Jennie Gerhardt*
d. *The Titan*

21. In *Sister Carrie* Dreiser expressed _____ by expounding the purposeless of life and attacking the conventional moral standards.

a. his moral trends   b. his love and hatred

    c. his naturalistic pursuit   d. his sexual freedom

22. In *An American Tragedy*, Clyde's tragedy is a tragedy that depends upon the American social system which encouraged people to pursue _____ at all cost.

    a. material comfort   b. moral perfection

    c. personal individual liberation   d. the "dream of success"

23. From the first novel *Sister Carrie* on, Dreiser set himself to project the American values for what he had found them to be —_____ to the core.

    a. materialistic   b. sexual freedom

    c. created equal   d. individualized

24. _____ exerts the single most important influence on literary naturalism.

    a. Emerson   b. Jack London

    c. Theodore Dreiser   d. Darwin

25. One of the most familiar themes in American naturalism is the theme of human "_____".

    a. bestiality   b. goodness

    c. compassion   d. greed

26. Statement "_____" is not true in describing American naturalists.

    a. they were deeply influenced by Darwinism

    b. they were identified with French novelist and theorist Emile Zola

    c. they chose their subjects from the lower ranks or society

    d. they used more serious and more sympathetic tone in writing than realists

27. _____ is considered by H. L. Mencken as "the true father of our national literature".

    a. Hemingway   b. Poe

    c. Irving   d. Twain

28. Mark Twain shaped the world's view of America and made a combination of _____ and serious literature.

    a. English folk lore   b. funny jokes

    c. American folk humor   d. American traditional values

29. The book from which "all modern American literature comes" refers to _____.

    a. *The Great Gatsby*   b. *The Sun Also Rises*

    c. *The Adventures of Huckleberry Finn*   d. *Moby-Dick*

30. Henry James' fame generally rests upon his novels and stories with _____.

    a. international theme   b. national theme

    c. European theme   d. regional theme

31. In the following writers, _____ is generally regarded as the forerunner of the 20th-century "stream-of-consciousness" novels and the founder of psychological realism.

    a. Henry James   b. Mark Twain

    c. Emily Dickinson   d. Theodore Dreiser

32. In Henry James' *Daisy Miller*, the author tries to portray the young woman as an embodiment of _____.

    a. the corruption of the newly rich   b. the free spirit of the New World

    c. the decline of aristocracy   d. the force of convention

33. Daisy Miller's tragedy of indiscretion is intensified and enlarged by its narration from the point

of _____.

    a. the American youth Winterbourne   b. the author of Henry James

    c. her mother Mrs. Miller   d. the Italian youth Giovanelli

34. Which of the following is NOT a usual subject of poetic expression of Emily Dickinson's _____.

    a. War and peace   b. Love and marriage

    c. Life and death   d. Religion

35. The following titles are all related to the subject that escapes from the society and returns to nature EXCEPT _____.

    a. Dreiser's *Sister Carrie*   b. Copper's *Leather-Stocking Tales*

    c. Thoreau's *Walden*   d. Mark Twain's *The Adventure of Huckleberry Finn*

36. The greatest work written by Theodore Dreiser is _____.

    a. *Sister Carrie*   b. *An American Tragedy*

    c. *The Financier*   d. *The Titan*

37. More than five hundred poems that Dickinson wrote are about nature, in which her general _____ about the relationship between man and nature is well expressed.

    a. skepticism   b. realism

    c. determinism   d. humanism

38. "This is my letter to the World" is a poem expressing Emily Dickinson's _____ about her communication with the outside world.

    a. happiness   b. anger

    c. anxiety   d. sorrow

39. In her poems such as "I like to see it lap the Miles —", Dickinson describes a(n) _____, an embodiment of modern civilization.

    a. snake   b. animal

    c. the road   d. train

40. Theodore Dreiser always set himself to project the materialistic American values. For example, in *Sister Carrie*, there is not one character whose status is not determined _____.

    a. hereditarily   b. economically

    c. by his or her literalness   d. historically

41. Theodore Dreiser was influenced by many writers whose works he had read. But his true literary influences did not come from _____.

    a. Balzac   b. Charles Darwin

    c. Herbert Spencer   d. R. W. Emerson

42. After *The Adventure of Tom Sawyer*, Twain gives a literary independence to Tom's buddy Huck in a book called _____.

    a. *Life on the Mississippi River*   b. *The Gilded Age*

    c. *Adventures of Huckleberry Finn*   d. *A Connecticut Yankee in King Arthur's Court*

43. The novelistic technique of projecting the narrative through feelings and thoughts of the characters, reached a perfected form in the works of _____.

    a. Henry James   b. William Dean Howells

    c. Washington Irving   d. Emily Dickinson

44. Emily Dickinson's verse is most aptly characterized as _____.

    a. exposing the evils of the society

b. paving the way for the following generation of free verse poets

c. sharing the same poetic conventions as Walt Whitman

d. exhibiting a sensitiveness to the symbolic implications of experience, such as love, death, immortality and etc.

45. Of the following combinations of the works and their authors, the one which is incorrectly paired is _____.

a. *The Fall of the House of Usher*/Frank Norris

b. *Sister Carrie*/Theodore Dreiser

c. *The Red Badge of Courage*/Stephen Crane

d. *The Americans*/Henry James

46. The author of *The portrait of a Lady* is best at _____.

a. probing into the unsearched secret part of human life

b. a truthful delineation of the motives, the impulses, the principles that shape the lives of actual men and women

c. a dramatizing the collisions between two very different cultural systems on an international scene

d. disclosing the social injustices and evils of a civilized society after the Civil War

47. Generally speaking, all those writers with a naturalistic approach to human reality are _____.

a. transcendentalists   b. idealists

c. pessimists   d. impressionists

48. As a genre, naturalism emphasized _____ as important deterministic forces shaping individualized characters who were presented in special and detailed circumstances.

a. theological doctrines   b. heredity and environment

c. education and hard work   d. various opportunities and economic success

49. The childhood of Tom Sawyer and Huck Finn in the Mississippi is a record of a vanished way of life in the _____ Mississippi valley and it has moved millions of people of different ages and conditions all over the world.

a. early 16th century   b. late 16th century

c. post-Civil War   d. pre-Civil War

50. In 1915 _____ became a naturalized British citizen, largely in protest against American's failure to join England in the First World War.

a. T. S. Eliot   b. Henry James

c. W. D. Howells   d. George Eliot

51. American literature produced only one female poet during the 19th century. This was _____.

a. Anne Brontë   b. Jane Austen

c. Emily Dickinson   d. Harriet Beecher

52. While Mark Twain and William Dean Howells satirized European manners at times, _____ was an admirer of ancient European civilization.

a. O. Henry   b. Henry James

c. Walt Whitman   d. Harriet Beecher

53. "The Way of the Beaten: A Harp in the Wind" is the title of one chapter in Dreiser's novel _____.

a. *An American Tragedy*   b. *Sister Carrie*

c. *Dreiser Looks at Russia*   d. *Jennie Gerhardt*

54. The main theme of _____ *The Art of Fiction* clearly indicates that the aim of the novel is to present life.

a. Henry James'
b. Mark Twain's
c. Theodore Dreiser's
d. William Dean Howells'

55. Mark Twain's full literary career began to blossom in 1869 with a travel book _____, an account of American tourists in Europe.
    a. *Adventures of Huckleberry Finn*
    b. *The Gilded Age*
    c. *Innocents Abroad*
    d. *An American Tragedy*

56. In his realistic fiction, Henry Jame's primary concern is to present the _____.
    a. inner life of human beings
    b. American Civil War and its effects
    c. life on Mississippi River
    d. Calvinistic view of original sin

57. With the publication of _____, Henry James' reputation was firmly established on both sides of the Atlantic.
    a. *The Portrait of a Lady*
    b. *Sister Carrie*
    c. *Daisy Miller*
    d. *Jane Eyre*

58. _____ *The Art of Fiction* reveals his literary credo that representation of life should be the main object of novel.
    a. Henry James'
    b. Mark Twain's
    c. Theodore Dreiser's
    d. W. D. Howells'

59. Which of the following is NOT written by Henry James? _____.
    a. *The Ambassadors*
    b. *The Wings of the Dove*
    c. *The Bostonians*
    d. *The Mysterious Stranger*

60. One of the characteristics that have made Mark Twain one of the major literary figure in the 19th century American literature is the use of _____.
    a. vernacular
    b. interior monologue
    c. point of view
    d. photographic description

Keys: dbdca/baabc/dcbbb/dadcb/cdada/ddcca/abaaa/bacdb/dcada/ccbdb/cbbac/acada

第三章 现代时期 The Modern Period

词语解释和难句分析

1. to begin with a strong sense of social breakdown 以强烈的社会崩溃/危机意识开始
   a series of wars fought on the international scene 国际背景下发生的一系列战争
   to become the emblem of all wars 成了一切战争的象征

2. to mark a crucial stage in the nation's evolution to a world power 标志着美国发展成世界强国的关键阶段
   outstripping Britain and Germany in terms of industrial production 工业产量超过了英国和德国
   to have ceased to be curiosity but become a commonplace 不再是令人惊奇之物，而是常见的普通东西
   to begin imposing its own imagery on the nation at large 开始对国家施加全面的影响
   to have resulted in a mobility unimaginable to the previous generations 已经带来了以前人们所无法想象的机动性

3. booming industry and material prosperity 迅速发展的工业和迅速增加的物质财富
   a sense of unease and restlessness underneath 内心潜在的心神不宁和焦躁不安
   industrial depression and uneven distribution of wealth 工业萧条和财富分配不均
   the oversupply of goods 商品过剩
   be driven off their land 被迫背井离乡/离开土地
   to culminate in the collapse of the Stock Market 使股市出现了最大的崩盘
   the growth of radical labor force 基本劳动力的增加

4. the changes in the material landscape 物质方面的变化
   to make a big impact on 对……产生巨大的影响
   to become less certain about what might arise in this changing world 对动荡的社会究竟会发生什么事情感到没有把握
   to be more cynical about accepted standards of honesty and morality 对公认的诚实和道德的标准感到怀疑和悲观
   the idea of "size the day" or "enjoy the present" "抓住眼前""及时行乐"的思想
   as opposed to placing all hope in the future 与把一切寄托在将来刚好对立
   to have brief affairs with nurses and prostitutes 与护士和妓女做露水夫妻/寻觅短暂欢愉
   instead of thinking of sex as something obscene or wrong 不再把性行为当作淫秽或错误的事情
   to give loose to their sexual desire 放纵性欲

5. The censor of a great civilization being destroyed or destroying itself, social breakdown, and individual powerlessness and hopelessness became part of the American experience as a result of the First World War, with resulting feelings of fear, loss, disorientation and disillusionment. 由于第一次世界大战的影响，美国人在潜意识中体验到巨大的压抑，他们感到伟大文明正在被毁或自毁，社会崩溃，个人感到虚弱和无望，内心汇集了恐惧、迷茫、失去方向和幻想破灭等种种思想感情。

6. a big flush of new theories and new ideas in both social and natural sciences 社会科学和自然科学两方

面新理论和新思想的兴起

to play an indispensible role in... 在……方面发挥不可缺少的作用

7. The root cause of all behavior is economic. 一切行为的根本起因在经济。

the division of society into antagonistic classes based on a relation to the means of production 根据与生产资料的关系，社会化分成许多对立的阶级

to propound an idea of human beings themselves as grounded in the "unconscious" that controlled a great deal of overt behaviour 提出了人类的思想植根于控制大量外部行为的"无意识"之中

to make the practice of the psychoanalysis 创造了心理分析的方法

to emphasize the importance of the unconscious or the irrational in the human psyche 强调人的心理中无意识或非理性的重要性

be noted for his "collective unconscious" and "archetypal symbol" as part of modern mythology 他以现代神话中的"集体无意识"和"原型意象"而著名

interpretation of dreams 对梦境的解释，解梦

to infuse modern American literature 浸润美国现代文学

to probe into the inner world of human reality 深入探讨现实生活中人类的内心世界

8. the implications of modern European arts to modern American writings 现代欧洲艺术对现代美国艺术作品的介入/影响

the French Impressionist and the German Expressionist artists 法国印象派和德国表现主义艺术家们

to depict the human reality in a rather subjective point of view 以非常主观的视角描写人类世界

its (Cubism) emphasis on the multiple-perspective viewpoints （立体主义）强调多重视角

to engage the readers in creating order out of fragmentation 让读者自己参与创造——从支离破碎的形式中创造秩序

featuring dissonance and discontinuity rather than neat formal structure and appealing total harmonies 特点是把不和谐的、支离破碎的噪音带进了音乐，而不是追求匀称的结构形式、整体的统一和谐

9. a spiritual crisis but a full blossoming of literary writings 精神出现危机，但文学却很繁荣

the most recognizable literary movement 最被认可的文学运动

the expatriate movement 移居国外的运动

(be) disillusioned and disgusted by the frivolous, greedy, and heedless way of life in America 对轻浮、贪婪、事事无所谓的美国生活方式感到幻灭和绝望

to involve with other European novelists and poets in their experimentation on new modes of thought and expression 与欧洲的小说家和诗人一起，参与实验以新的思想方式和表达方式进行创作

10. Ezra Pound's one-image poem best demonstrates his principles of what a new poetry should be. 埃兹拉·庞德的单一意象诗最好地表达了他的所谓新诗应当遵循的原则。

＊ what a new poem should be 直译为"新诗应当成为的样子"，即"所谓新诗"。

11. to root his poetic imagination in American native tradition 他的诗歌想象植根于美国本土的文学传统

to refer to himself as a protest against self-importance 把自己称为一个反对自我托大的人

The Jazz Age of the 1920s characterized by frivolity and carelessness 以轻浮享乐为特点的 20 世纪 20 年代的"爵士时代"

be brought vividly to life 被表现得栩栩如生

be physically and psychologically scarred 在生理和心理上都留下了伤痕

to explore the motivation and frustration in his fictional characters 探讨了他小说中人物的思想动机和遭受的挫折

be depicted as socially alienated and emotionally suppressed 被描写为很少与人交往、情感压抑的

（一群人）

to present a documentary picture of the narrow and limited middle-class mind 对狭隘的、受到局限的中产阶级思想进行了纪实性的描写

the dispossessed and the wretched farmers during the Great Depression 经济大萧条时期流离失所/被剥夺得一无所有的可怜的农民

12. be remembered for his tragic view of life 因其悲剧性的人生观而被记住

be experimental with regard to dramatic structure and ways of theatrical production available through technology 在戏剧结构和利用技术手段进行舞台实践的方法方面做了试验性的探讨

to remind us of the stylized realism or German Expressionism 使我们想起程式化的现实主义或德国的表现主义

13. Though the scene of American drama was not so promising as fiction and poetry, Arthur Miller and Tennessee Williams were yet to acclaim the literary recognition and to hold the central position in American drama until the present times. 虽然美国戏剧的景况不像小说和诗歌那样大有可为,但亚瑟·米勒和田纳西·威廉姆斯却要为获得文学界的认同、成为当代美国戏剧核心人物而大声欢呼。

14. to exert a tremendous influence on the mentality of Americans 对美国人的思想和心理施加了巨大的影响

in the form of McCarthyism 以麦卡锡主义的形式(出现)

the resignation of Nixon because of the Water-Gate scandal 由于"水门"丑闻,尼克松总统辞职

to intensify the terror and toss the whole nation again into the grief and despair 使得恐惧的心里更加强烈,再次把全国投入悲伤和绝望之中

to reconsider the nature of man and man's capacity for evil 重新审视人的本性和作恶的能力

to think of life as a big joke or an absurdity 把生活当成玩笑,或是一个荒诞剧

be more estranged and despondent (人们)更加冷漠疏远,更加灰心失望

15. to compete with the works in the 1920s 可与20年代20年代的文学作品相媲美

to become noticeable due to their historical and literary significance 由于它们的历史意义和文学意义而值得注意

the postwar poets with Robert Lowell in the lead 以罗伯特·洛维尔为首的战后诗人

to express and classify their own feeling 表达和研究/分析/衡量他们自己的思想感情

showing a growing sense of resistance to the existing culture and at the same time an assertion of the self 显示出不断增长的对抗当时的现实文化,同时又肯定自我价值的情感

be grouped under different titles 根据题目的不同内涵加以分类

to liberate poetry from the academy and make it popular among the ordinary people 使诗歌摆脱学究气,力求通俗易懂,为普通大众所喜爱

to write about the traumatic experience within the military machine 描写了军事机器作用下的创伤经历

to become the manifesto of the Beat Movement (《嚎叫》Howl) 成了"垮掉的一代"文学运动的宣言

16. to follow Faulkner's footsteps in portraying the decadence and evil in the Southern society in a Gothic manner 追随福克纳的脚步,以哥特式的风格描写了南方社会的腐败和邪恶

drawing on the Jewish experience and tradition 汲取了犹太人的经验和传统

to examine subtly the dismantling of the self by an intolerable modern history 通过难以忍受的现代史,细致入微地探索和解剖了自我

be considered to be a spokesman for the alienated youth in the post-war era 被认为是战后感到孤独和被疏远的一代年轻人的代言人

Updike's Rabbit novels　厄普代克的"兔系列"小说

to examine the middle-class values and portray the troubled relationships in people's private life and their internal decay under the stress of the modern times　探索了中产阶级的价值观,描写了在当代压力下人们私生活里种种复杂烦恼的关系,以及他们内心世界的腐败

17. to be different from its predecessors　与(美国文学的)前辈们不同

... in that (= American fiction) the writers started to depart from the conventions of the novel writing and experimented with some new forms　美国文学中,许多作家开始脱离传统的小说创作方法,进行一些新形式的尝试

be referred to as "new fiction"　被称作"新小说"

with sb. at its forefront　以某人为先锋,某人走在……前列

be trapped in a meaningless world　陷入/沦落在一个毫无意义的世界中

to make sense of the human condition　理解/懂得人类的状况/处境

absurdist vision　荒诞的见解/看法

be integrated with an absurd form　与荒诞的形式结合在一起

be characterized by comic exaggerations, ironic uses of parodies, multiple realities, often two-dimensional characters and a combination of fantastic events with realistic presentations　其(荒诞)的特点是:戏剧性的夸张,各种讽刺的运用,如滑稽模仿、多重现实、常常是两维的平面人物的塑造,以及把幻想的事件与现实的存在结合在一起的手法,等等

be alive with a diversity of interests　(文学创作)思想活跃,各种倾向异彩纷呈

be beginning to make their voices heard　开始公开发表他们的声音/主张

to bring vitality to the American literary imagination　给美国的文学带来了生气勃勃的想象

18. in general terms　总而言之,总的来说

to convey a vision of social breakdown and moral decay　传达出一种关于社会崩溃和道德颓败的见解/看法

to develop techniques that could represent a break with the past　开发种种完全摒弃传统的新技巧

19. The defining formal characteristics of the modernistic works are discontinuity and fragmentation. 现代主义文学作品形式结构上的明显特点就是断断续续、支离破碎。

20. be notable for what they omit — the explanations, interpretations, connections, and summaries　值得注意的是他们放弃的东西——解释、说明、衔接和总结

to begin arbitrarily, to advance without explanation, and to end without resolution　开篇随心所欲,发展没有交代,结尾没有结果

be no longer a record of sequence and coherence but a juxtaposition of the past and the present,...　不再是按时间顺序、前后连贯的记录,而是过去和现在万事杂陈的拼贴

a book of fragments drawn from diverse areas of experience, including areas previously deemed inappropriate for literature　从各方面撷取经验、包括以前认为不适用于文学创作的许多方面的经验,由无数这些经验的片段组成一本书

21. There are shifts in perspective, voice, and tone, but the biggest shift is from the external to the internal, from the public to the private, from the chronological to the psychic, from the objective description to the subjective projection.　文学作品的视角、语气和风格方面都发生了变化,而最大的变化是描写的目标所向从外部世界转向了内心世界,从公众生活转向了私人生活,从按时间先后的顺序描写转向按人的心理感受和心路历程进行描写,从客观的描写转向主观的反映和想象。

22. The traditional educated literary voice, conveying truth and culture, has lost its authority to a more detached and ironic tone.　传统的熟练的传达真理和文化的文学风格已失去其影响力,为更为超

然的、讽刺的格调所取代。

23. to emphasize the concrete sensory images or details as the direct conveyer of experience　强调具体的、可以感觉到的形象或细节,直接表达人生的体验

24. They rely on the reference or allusions to literary, history, philosophical, or religious details of the past as a way of <u>reminding</u> readers <u>of</u> the old, lost coherence.　他们依赖过去的文学、历史、哲学掌故或宗教详情作为手段,提醒读者记住过去已经逝去的逻辑联系。

25. Myths from popular and folk cultures are exploited fully to construct stories out of vivid segments.　通俗民间文化中的神话被充分开掘,许多生动的片段成为故事。

26. Vignettes of contemporary life, dream imagery and symbolism <u>drawn from</u> the authors' <u>private repertory of life experiences</u> are also important.　源自作者私人生活积累的关于那个时代生活、梦境意象和象征主义的花边文字也是非常重要的。

27. Modernistic techniques and manifestos were initiated by poets first and later ended and transformed fiction in this period as well.　现代主义的技巧和现代主义的宣言发端于诗人,后来也进入这段时期的小说,并改变了小说。

28. to <u>spare of</u> words　节省文字

to <u>limit</u> the reader <u>to</u> the "central consciousness" or one character's point of view　把读者限制在"中心意识"或某一个人的观点上

to <u>accord with</u> the modernistic vision　与现代主义的看法一致

the product of a personal <u>interaction with</u> reality　人与现实相互作用的产物

主要内容归纳和总结

1. 对现代主义文学产生巨大影响的思想家首推达尔文以及他的达尔文主义。其次是卡尔·马克思(Karl Marx)和弗洛伊德(Freud)。另外还有美国的以意识流著称的心理学家威廉·詹姆斯(William James)和瑞士精神病学家荣格(Carl Jung),后者提出了现代神话中的"集体无意识"(collective unconscious)和"原型意象"(archetypal symbol)的观念。

   "迷惘的一代"(The Lost Generation)是一战以后,以美国旅居欧洲——主要是巴黎——的美国青年作家为主体,加上一部分欧洲国家的作家,形成的一派以悲观厌世为特点的作家群体。首次使用这个称谓的是同样在巴黎旅居的作家格特鲁德·斯泰因(Gertrude Stein)。代表作家有埃兹拉·庞德(Ezra Pound),威廉·卡洛斯·威廉姆斯(William Carlos Williams),罗伯特·弗罗斯特(Robert Frost)。庞德曾发起诗歌的单一意象运动(One-Imagist Movement)。

   "垮掉的一代"(Beat Generation)是二战后形成的反传统文化,充分肯定自己,废弃学究气,走通俗大众化道路的一代诗人群体,以罗伯特·洛维尔(Robert Lowell)为首,著名的诗人有嘉利·斯尼德(Gary Snyder),艾伦·金斯伯格(Allen Ginsberg)等。金斯伯格的诗集《嚎叫》(*Howl*, 1956)是"垮掉的一代文学运动"(Beat Movement)的宣言。

   "爵士时代"(The Jazz Age)出现在20世纪20年代,特点是轻浮草率,无忧无虑,尽情享乐,菲兹杰拉德的《伟大的盖茨比》(*The Great Gatsby*)是其代表作。

   菲兹杰拉德(F. Scott Fitzgerald),海明威(Ernest Hemingway)和福克纳(William Faulkner)是美国小说领域的大师。

   荒诞文学(Absurdist Literature)或"新小说"(New Fiction),产生于20世纪六七十年代,以库尔特·瓦尼格特(Kurt Vonnegut),约瑟夫·海勒(Joseph Heller),约翰·巴斯(John Bath)和托马斯·平肯(Thomas Pynchon)为先锋。其观点是:人类陷入了毫无意义的世界之中,上帝和人类本身都

理解不了人的处境。荒诞的思想带来的荒诞的文学形式是戏剧性的夸张,滑稽模仿,无立体感的平面人物,幻想的事件与现实主义存在相结合,等等。

2. 现代主义小说的特点是追求直接(directness)、紧缩(compression)和生动(vividness);偏爱用暗示(suggestiveness),多用第一人称或围绕一个人的观点讲述故事;多描写人的内心世界,而不是外部的客观世界;不是做时间顺序的连贯叙述,而侧重于人的心理感受和意识流动(the psychic and the stream of consciousness);认为真理不是客观存在,而是人与现实互相作用的产物。结果,美国现代小说的效果常常是令人震惊和不安的,同时也令人难懂。

3. 法国印象主义(Impressionism)和德国表现主义(Expressionism)的特点是不去表现外部现实,而以非常主观的角度描写人性的现实。

4. 立体主义(Cubism)是 20 世纪初期兴起的一个流行的绘画流派,着重强调艺术作品的形式结构,尤其强调从多视角的观点(multiple-perspective viewpoints)解释世界,让读者参与从支离破碎中创造秩序。

重要信息句子

1. We may say, the second American Renaissance, is the expatriate movement.

2. These expatriate American writers were later named by an American Writer, Gertrude Stein, also an expatriate, "The Lost Generation."

3. Ezra Pound's role as a leading spokesman of the famous Imagist Movement in the history of American literature can never be ignored.

4. The Jazz Age of the 1920s characterized by frivolity and carelessness is brought vividly to life in *The Great Gatsby* (1925) by F. S. Fitzgerald.

5. The leading playwright of the modern period in American literature is Eugene O'neill, who is remembered for his tragic view of life and followed by Arthur Miller and Tennessee Williams.

6. J. D. Salinger is considered to be a spokesman for the alienated youth in the post-war era and his *The Catcher in the Rye* is regarded as a students' classic.

7. If realistic fiction achieved its effects by accumulation and saturation, modern fiction preferred suggestiveness.

8. This limitation accorded with the modernistic vision that truth does not exist objectively but is the product of a personal interaction with reality.

I. 埃兹拉·庞德 Ezra Pound (1885~1972)

词语解释和难句分析

1. to launch modern literature   发起现代文学
decisively affected the course of the 20th-century American literature   决定性地影响了 20 世纪美国文学的进程

2. to make acquaintance with William Butler Yeats   熟悉了威廉·巴特勒·叶芝
be beneficial to both of them   对他们双方都有益

to lecture on Romance literature　讲授传奇文学

to span from 1917 to 1959　时间跨度从 1917 年到 1959 年

be collected in *The Cantos of Ezra Pound*　被收进《埃兹拉·庞德诗章》

to become involved in the experimentations on poetry　参与诗歌改革实验

to engage in some radio broadcasts of anti-Semitism and pro-Fascism　参加反闪米特主义和赞成法西斯主义的广播宣传

be brought back to the United States, accused of treason, but declared insane on examination　被遣返回美国,指控犯有叛国罪,但身体检查后又宣布有精神病

chiefly withdrawn from the public　大多数时间不在公众场合出现,深居简出

3. be politically controversial and notorious for what he did in the wartime　由于他战争期间的作为,政治上有争议,声名狼藉

4. His commitment to poetry was total: to poetry as a craft, as a moral and spiritual resource and eventually as means of salvaging culture, redeeming history.　他对诗歌的投入是全身心的, 他把诗歌当成技艺, 当成道德和精神源泉,并最终当成拯救文化、弥补历史的手段来献身。

　＊ commitment to　对……的投入/献身

5. be saturated with the familiar poetic subjects that characterize the 19th century Romanticism　充满了熟悉的具有 19 世纪浪漫主义特点的诗歌主题

the transience of beauty and the permanence of art　美的短暂和艺术的永恒

the delightful psychic experience　快乐的心理体验

the ecstatic moment　狂欢时刻

the possible sources of cultural renewal　文化更新的可能途径

6. From the perception of these things, stems the poet's search for order, which involves a search for the principles on which the poet's craft is based.　从对这些事物的感知中,诗人产生了寻求秩序的欲望,包括对艺术技巧基本原则的寻求。

　＊ stem from 源于……,由……造成/产生;第一个 which 代表 the poet's search, 第二个 which 代表 the principles, 两个 which 都是关系代词,都引导了定语从句;be based on 以……为根据/基础。

7. to best reflect Pound's appraisals of literary tradition and of modern writing　最好地反映了庞德对文学传统和现代文学作品的评价

to cast light on Pound's affinity to the Chinese and his strenuous effort in the study of Oriental literature　阐明了庞德对汉语的喜好以及他对东方文学研究方面艰苦奋发的努力

to offer us a clue to the understanding of his poetry and literary theory　向我们提供了理解他的诗歌和文学理论的线索/对我们理解……做了提示

8. From the analysis of the Chinese ideogram Pound learned to anchor his poetic language in concrete, perceptual reality, and to organize images into larger patterns through juxtaposition.　通过对表意汉字/汉语表意符号的分析,庞德学会了把诗歌语言扎根于具体可感的现实,通过多重组合的方法把各种意象进行组织和扩大。

9. be on full display in the history of the Imagist Movement　在单一意象运动的历史上得到了充分展示

to advance modernism in arts　在艺术上推进现代主义

to concentrate on reforming the medium of poetry as opposed to Romanticism　集中改革诗歌的媒介,反对浪漫主义

wordiness and high-flown language　啰唆冗长、夸夸其谈的语言

to endorse the group's three main principles　赞同这群意象主义诗人的三大原则

merely ornamental or superfluous words　仅仅是装饰性或者多余的词语

rhetorical composition in the sequence of the musical phrase rather than in the sequence of a metronome　诗歌节奏如同音乐,而不是机械的重复/节拍

* in the sequence of　以……的方式/顺序连贯起来

the word beyond formulated language　形式语言以外的语汇

to avoid rhetoric and moralizing　避免玩弄修辞和道德说教

to stick closely to the object being described　紧贴被描写的物体

to move from explicit generalization　避免明显/简单的一般化

to relate a delightful psychic experience by speaking out directly　通过直接地讲出,(把自己)与快乐的心理体验联系起来

10. He must "screen himself" and speak indirectly through an impersonal and objective story, which is usually a myth or a piece of the earlier literature, or "mask," that is, a persona.　他必须"屏蔽/隐藏自己",通过非人格化的、客观的故事间接地说话。故事通常也就是一个神话,或一段文学典故,或一个"面具,"也就是一个人物的表面形象。

11. As to his language, his lines are usually oblique yet marvelously compressed.　在语言方面,他的诗句往往拐弯抹角、婉转含蓄,但却非常凝练。

12. at the expense of syntax and summary statements　在句子结构和概括总结方面失于不够精益求精

庞德作品选读

1. 在一个地铁车站 In a Station of the Metro

词语解释和难句分析

1. The apparition of these faces in the crowd；　人群中这些脸庞幽灵般显现,
Petals on a wet, black bough.　湿漉漉的黑色枝条上的片片花瓣。

* 此诗是诗人对巴黎地铁站所见人脸真切的印象描绘,很像是日本俳句(Japanese haiku)的现代改编版。诗的形式由体验决定,体验赋予形式以灵感。无论这首诗是事实还是神话,都是单一意象运动史上著名的诗歌文献。

这首诗为典型的单一意象诗。上下两个诗句实际上只是两个名词性词组,前者的核心名词是apparition, 幻影、幽灵的意思;后者的核心词是 petals 花瓣,核心词后面的部分都是其定语。上下两句实际是相等的:地铁站里幽灵般显现的万千张面孔,就像是黑色树枝上的片片花瓣。

2. 河商妻子给丈夫的一封信 The River-Merchant's Wife: a Letter

词语解释和难句分析

1. to communicate indirectly the history of her feelings for her absent husband to whom she writes　间接地表达了她与正致函问候、久别在外的丈夫之间的感情史
by means of vivid images and shifting tones　通过栩栩如生的形象和变换的语调

2. While my hair was still cut straight across my forehead/I played about the front gate, pulling flowers. 　当我还是短发/(刘海覆额)的小女孩的时候,/常常在门前摘花玩耍。

3. You came on bamboo stilts, playing horse,/You walked about my seat, playing with blue plums. 你跨着竹竿而来,玩骑马的游戏,/绕着我的座位转来转去,手里玩着青色的梅子。

　　* bamboo stilts 直译为"竹竿做的高跷",但实际上即传统的"一根竹竿当马骑"的竹马。

4. And we went on living in the village of Chokan：/Two small people, without dislike or suspicion. 我们居住在同一个村子:长干里,/两个小孩儿一起玩耍,快快乐乐,毫无避讳和猜疑。

　　* Chokan 即长干里,属古金陵里巷,居民多经商,浓重的商业气氛使得封建礼教在这里相对较弱,男女孩童一起嬉戏,长大后又能直诉相思之苦,都是这种氛围影响的结果。

5. At fourteen I married My Lord you./I never laughed, being bashful. 　十四岁,我嫁给夫君你呀,/还羞怯得很,从不敢笑出声来。

　　* My Lord 用于称呼丈夫,既尊重又带亲昵、戏谑的意味。

6. Lowering my head, I looked at the wall./Called to, a thousand times, I never looked back. 　总是低头看着墙壁暗处,你喊我一千次,我也不肯转过身来。

　　* called to = being called to you

7. At fifteen I stopped scowling,/I desired my dust to be mingled with yours/Forever and forever and forever./Why should I climb the look out ? 　十五岁时,我不再紧张矜持(皱眉)(夫妻水乳交融)/愿与你生死与共,化为灰烬,也合在一起,/直至永远永远。/有此信念,哪里会想到有今日爬上望夫台等待丈夫归来的情景呢?

　　* 此节第三、四句李白的原诗"常存抱柱信,岂上望夫台"中有两个典故。其一出自《庄子·盗跖》:"尾生与女子期(约会)于梁(桥)下,女子不来,水至不去,抱梁柱而死。"其二是传说一女子日日爬上山顶望夫归来,最终化为石像。庞德英译这两句诗时,采用意译,未将典故本身说出来。the look out 　瞭望台,这里指望夫台。

8. At sixteen you departed,/You went into far Ku-to-yen, by the river of swirling eddies, 　十六岁时,你离我远行去经商,/在激流荡漾的大江边,你闯进了瞿塘滟滪堆的嶙峋礁石之中,

9. And you have been gone five months./The monkeys make sorrowful noise overhead. 　如今,你已离开我五个月了。/(你人在险途,)长江两岸猿猴啸叫之声却时常萦回在我耳边。

10. You dragged your feet when you went out./By the gate now, the moss is grown, the different mosses/Too deep to clear them away! The leaves fall early this autumn, in wind. 当初离家你依依不舍,欲行不行。/如今门边留下的脚印已长满青苔,/层层的青苔积淀太深,又为秋风落叶所盖,清扫不净!

　　* dragged your feet 　你拖着沉重的脚步,一副难分难离的样子。

11. The paired butterflies are already yellow with August,/Over the grass in the West garden;/They hurt me. I grow older. 　八月秋高,连蝴蝶都变黄了,/一对对飞行在西园衰草之上,/此情此景令人伤感,思念更增,我不知不觉地憔悴衰老了。

12. If you are coming down through the narrows of the river Kiang,/Please let me know beforehand, 在你穿过长江三峡回归之时,/请提前来封家书告诉我,

　　And I will come out to meet you/As far as Cho-fu-Sa. 　我会去迎候你/即使到七百里外的长风沙,也不嫌其远。

　　* 李白原诗《长干行·其一》

妾发初覆额,折花门前剧。

郎骑竹马来,绕床弄青梅。

同居长干里,两小无疑猜。

十四为君妇,羞颜未尝开。

低头向暗壁,千唤不一回。
十五始展眉,愿同尘与灰。
常存抱柱信,岂上望夫台。
十六君远行,瞿塘滟滪堆。
五月不可触,猿声天上哀。
门前迟行迹,一一生绿苔。
苔深不能扫,落叶秋风早。
八月胡蝶黄,双飞西园草。
感此伤妾心,坐愁红颜老。
早晚下三巴,预将书报家。
相迎不道远,直至长风沙。

3. 一个协议 *A Pact*

词语解释和难句分析

1. 惠特曼是美国新自由诗的先锋、开拓者和实践者,他的诗不注意形式工整,没有严谨的格律和韵律,曾受到年轻的庞德的批评和指责,后来庞德认识到惠特曼开一代新诗风的伟大功绩,主动示好输诚,有自我批评之意,这首诗就表达了这种情感。

2. to find some agreement between "Whitmanesque" free verse and the "verse libre" of the Imagists　在"惠特曼式"的自由诗与单一意象主义者的"自由诗"之间找到了某种一致性
to show more concern for formal values　更关注形式的价值

3. I make a pact with you, Walt Whitman —　惠特曼,我与你订个协议——
I have detested you long enough.　我一直厌恶你,够久了。

4. I come to you as a grown child　现在我走向你,已是一个长大的孩子
Who has had a pig-headed father;　曾有一个头脑顽固的父亲;
＊这里指作者自己以前曾有传统的思想观念,对惠特曼的认识有误,这是在表示歉意。who 引导一个定语从句,修饰 child。

5. I am old enough now to make friends.　我现在长大了,不再幼稚,已懂如何交友。

6. It was you that broke the new wood,　当初是你砍下的新木,
Now is a time for carving.　如今(我们)该将其雕琢。
＊注意上句与此句动词时态的变化。

7. We have one sap and one root —　我们有共同的树液、树根——
Let there be commerce between us.　让我们自由交流。

主要内容归纳和总结

1. 埃兹拉·庞德(Ezra Pound)出生在美国爱达荷州海莱(Hailey, Idaho),在宾夕法尼亚州(Pennsylvania)长大。学生时代他就掌握了九种语言,毕业后去威尼斯,认识了诗人叶芝(Yeats),获益良多,后在伦敦教授传奇文学,在巴黎加入格特鲁德·斯泰因(Gertrude Stein)主办的旅欧艺

术家沙龙,成为"迷惘的一代"(The Lost Generation)的成员,共同进行诗歌改革的实验,又在芝加哥重要杂志《诗刊》(Poetry)任外文编辑,并开始了他的伟大著作《诗章》(The Cantos)的创作,年限跨度从1917年到1959年。他也是诗歌单一意象运动(Imagist Movement)的主要代表人物。

庞德是一个政治上有争议的人,原因是"二战"爆发后,他帮助意大利政府进行反闪米特主义(anti-Semitism)和赞成法西斯主义(pro-Fascism)的宣传。战后,他被遣返回美国,受到指控,后以精神病禁闭在华盛顿刑事精神病院12年,在此期间,他从事中国文学的研究和翻译工作,他把李白的《长干行》译成英文,曾入选最佳英诗三百首。1958年获释后,他回到意大利,与妻女一起生活,深居简出,1972年逝世。

庞德主要的诗学主张集中体现在他领导的单一意象运动和对意象主义本质的解释中:"意象不是装饰,意象本身就是语言。"总之,他强调客观意境的创造,而不是浮华雕饰的词语。因此,含蓄、凝练甚至晦涩是他诗歌的特点。他的单一意象运动推动了现代主义诗歌艺术的发展。

2. 埃兹拉·庞德的主要作品:

a. 诗歌

《庞德早期诗集》*Collected Early Poems of Ezra Pound*

《埃兹拉·庞德诗章》*The Cantos of Ezra Pound* 包含116首诗

《人物》*Personae*(1909)

《休·塞尔温·莫伯利》*Hugh Selwyn Mauberley*(1920)

b. 文学评论

《更新》*Make It New*(1934)

《阅读入门》*The ABC of Reading*(1934)

《高雅散文》*Polite Essays*(1937)

《文学散文》Literary Essays(1954)

c. 译著

《埃兹拉庞德诗歌译文集》*The Translations of Ezra Pound*(1953)

《诗经》*Shih-Ching*(1954)

《孔子》Confucius(1969)

3. 单一意象运动(Imagist Movement)三大原则:

a. 直接处理诗歌主题;

b. 删去多余的装饰性词语;

c. 诗歌要有音乐语言的节奏。

重要信息句子

1. Ezra Pound is a leading spokesman of the "Imagist Movement."

2. Pound's earlier poetry is saturated with the familiar poetic subjects that characterize the 19th century Romanticism.

3. Pound's famous one-image poem "In a Station of the Metro" would serve as a typical example of the Imagist ideas.

II. 罗伯特·李·弗罗斯特 Robert Lee Frost (1874 ~ 1963)

词语解释和难句分析

1. to command a place　占有一定地位

   the Pulitzer Prize winner on four occasions　四次获得美国普利策文学奖

   to pass resolutions honoring his birthday　通过决议祝贺他的生日(向他致敬)

   to read his poetry at the inauguration of President John F. Kennedy　在约翰·肯尼迪总统的就职典礼上,朗诵自己的诗歌

   to graduate from high school as valedictorian and class poet　以在毕业典礼上发言的优秀学生代表和班级诗人的身份从中学毕业

   to work at odd jobs　打打零工,干些零活

   to support himself by various means　以各种手段谋生

   not to mention poetry writing　除了诗歌创作以外,更不必说诗歌写作

   to venture everything on a literary career　冒险闯荡文坛

   to sail for England　乘船去英格兰

   the appearance of a succession of books and papers　他的书和文章接连问世

2. to trace a boy's development from self-centered idealism to maturity　追寻一个男孩从自我中心的理想主义到成熟起来的发展进程

   the characteristic flavor of New England life　新英格兰地方生活的独特风情

   to show a brilliant insight into New England character and the background that formed it　对新英格兰人和他们成长的背景进行了深刻的探讨

   to see man as learning from nature the zones of his own limitations　认为人类应当向自然学习,弥补自己的不足和局限

   to probe the darker corners of individual lives in a situation when man cannot accept the facts of his condition　探讨了当个人不能接受自己实际环境的情况下生活中比较阴暗的角落

   the same expressive idiom and brilliant observation　同样有表现力的方言土语和才华横溢的评论

   to stem from the ambiguity of the speaker's choice between safety and the unknown　由于作者在安全和未知之间留下了模棱两可、含糊朦胧的意味

   to pose disturbing uncertainties about man's prowess and importance　对人类的才能和重要性的认识表现出令人不安的不确定性

   to translate modern upheaval into poetic material the poet could skillfully control　把现代社会的剧变动荡转化为诗人可以熟练驾驭的诗歌素材

3. At the age of seventy Frost took up, in different forms, a religious question he had explored before, most notably in "After Apple-Picking:" can a man's best efforts ever satisfy God?　在70岁时,弗罗斯特以不同的形式,重新着手研究以前曾经探讨过的一个宗教问题,在《摘苹果后》这首诗中,最引人注目的问题是:人类做出的最大努力能令上帝满意吗?

4. *A Masque of Reason* and *A Masque of Mercy* are comic-serious dramatic narratives, in both of which

biblical characters in modern settings discuss ethics and man's relations to God. 《理性的假面》和《仁慈的假面》都是严肃喜剧味的动人叙事诗,其中,圣经人物被置于现代环境中来探讨伦理学和人与上帝的关系。

5. be hardly classified with the old or the new 几乎不能用新老来进行划类

   to break with the poetic tradition 与诗歌的传统决裂

   to make experiment on form 对诗歌形式进行了改造试验

   to make the colloquial New England speech into a poetic expression 把新英格兰的方言口语用在诗歌创作中

6. A poem so conceived thus becomes a symbol or metaphor, a careful, loving exploration of reality, in Frost's version, "a momentary stay against confusion." 这样构思出来的诗歌即是一种象征,一种含蓄的比喻,一种对现实世界仔细、周到的探索,用弗罗斯特的说法,就是"一片混乱中的片刻安宁"。

7. be fragrant with natural quality 带有大自然的芬芳气息

   in the way that... 在……方面,从……角度来看

   on the informational level 在传达信息方面/层面

8. However, profound ideas are delivered under the disguise of the plain language and the simple form, for what Frost did is to take symbols from the limited human world and the pastoral landscape to refer to the great world beyond the rustic scene. 然而,在平实的语言和简单的形式背后表达了深邃的思想,因为弗罗斯特所表达的意象皆取自有限的人类社会和田园风光,寓意却在农村之外的广大世界。

9. be concerned with his love of life and belief in a serenity that only came from working usefully 他很注意表现自己对生活的热爱和有价值的劳动后才会有的宁静安详的神圣感

   to practice it himself throughout his life 一直如此,养成习惯

10. to achieve an effortless grace in his style 他的诗风高雅、自然、无雕饰

    rhyming couplets 双韵体

    idiosyncratic diction and syntax (某作者所)特有的措辞风格和句子结构

    the metrical forms and the free verse 格律诗和自由诗形式

    to bring the man and his rural world to life as vividly as if they were right in front of us 把农村的人和物表现得绘声绘色,如在眼前

罗伯特·李·弗罗斯特作品选读

1. 摘苹果后 After Apple-Picking

词语解释和难句分析

1. 这首诗回顾了在农场的经历,劳动结束之后,诗人有充实感、成就感,但在极度的疲倦之后,也产生了一种厌恶和随着冬季而来的一种莫名的消沉和空虚,并没有感受到成功的欢乐。

2. to leave the speaker with a sense of completion and fulfillment 给诗人留下了一种充实感和成就感

   to find him blocked from success by winter's approach and physical weariness 他发现由于冬天的临近和身体的疲劳,自己依然被拒于成功之外

3. My long two-pointed ladder's sticking through a tree/Toward heaven still,/And there's a barrel that I didn't fill/Beside it, and there may be two or three/Apples I didn't pick upon some bough. 我的双头长梯穿过一颗苹果树/伸向静静的天空,/梯边有一个桶我还未摘满,/也许有两三个苹果/没有摘,

还留在枝头。

4. But I am done with apple-picking now.　但现在我的采摘已完成。
Essence of winter sleep is on the night,/The scent of apples：I am drowsing off.　夜晚传出冬眠的气息,/苹果的香气啊,催我入眠。

5. I cannot rub the strangeness from my sight/I got from looking through a pane of glass/I skimmed this morning from the drinking trough/And held against the world of hoary grass.　今晨,我从饮水槽捞起一片冰,/透过冰,是一片枯白的草地,/"玻璃"后的陌生感/我实难从视线中抹去。
　*这是一个完整的主从复合句,定语从句里面套定语从句。I got from a pane of glass 是修饰主句里 strangeness 的定语从句,意为"我透过一片'窗玻璃'看到/感到的陌生";而 I skimmed ... and held... 又是 glass 的定语从句,说明这"玻璃"的出处原是一片冰,而且还被拿起来映照初冬的草地,这个定语从句中 I 有两个谓语动词 skimmed 和 held。上面的翻译是按意思进行的倒译。

6. It melted, and I let it fall and break.　冰化了,我听凭它落下,碎了。

7. But I was well/Upon my way to sleep before it fell,/And I could tell/What form my dreaming was about to take.　但它还未落地,/我就已悠然入梦,/我还可以告诉你——/我的梦境将如何呈现。

8. Magnified apples appear and disappear,/Stem end and blossom end,/And every fleck of russet showing clear.　苹果被放大,时隐又时现,/枝头花茎,每一个果皮斑点,/都清晰可见。

9. My instep arch not only keeps the ache,/It keeps the pressure of a ladder-round.　我的足背不仅一直疼痛,/它还承受着梯子横挡的压力。

10. I feel the ladder sway as the bough bend./And I keep hearing from the cellar bin/The rumbling sound/Of load on load of apples coming in.　树枝弯时,我感到梯子摇晃。/我还不断地听到——/地窖传来的隆隆声,/那是一堆堆苹果滚动进仓的声音。

11. For I have had too much,/Of apple-picking：I am overtired /Of the great harvest I myself desired. 采摘的工作,我已干得太多/对自己渴望的丰收,/也由劳累产生了厌恶。

12. There were ten thousand thousand fruit to touch,/Cherish in hand, lift down, and not let fall.　有千万只苹果经手触摸,/深情地拿在手里,轻轻地放下,不让它落地。

13. For all/That struck the earth,/No matter if not bruised or spiked with stubble,/Went surely to the cider-apple heap/As of no worth.　因为所有的苹果/一摔在地上,/不论是否擦伤或被树茬戳破,/都会被扔去做果酒,/似一堆无价值的废物。
　*这几句诗与上面的诗句互为因果关系。That struck the earth 是主语 all 的定语从句,即"所有摔在地上的苹果",谓语是 went surely to... heap; As of no worth＝as that （＝the heap） of no worth。

14. One can see what will trouble/This sleep of mine, whatever sleep it is.　你可以看出,什么会搅扰/我的睡眠,不管是怎样的睡眠。

15. Were he not gone, ＝If he were not gone,　如果土拨鼠还在,
The woodchuck could say whether it's like his/Long sleep, as I describe its coming on,/Or just some human sleep.　他会说这究竟是像他的/漫长休眠呢——如我所描述它正在来临,/还是人类的某种"睡眠"?
　*he＝the woodchuck; it's like...＝my sleep is like...; whether... or ... 引导了一个名词性从句,做 say 的宾语从句;土拨鼠的 long sleep 指的是它的"冬眠",而人类的长眠指的是"死亡"。

参考译文——姚远

摘苹果后

我的双尖长梯插进一颗苹果树，
静静地指向蓝天，
树边有个桶我还没装满，
可能还有两三个苹果
没有摘，留在枝头。
但此刻我的采摘已结束。
夜已深，散发出冬眠的气息，
苹果的香气呀，催我入眠。
今晨我从饮水槽撬起一块冰，
透过冰是一片枯白的草地，
这"玻璃"后的陌生感，
我实难从视线中抹去。
冰化了，我任它落下，打碎。
但它还未落地，
我就已悠然入睡，
我还可以告诉你，
我的梦境将如何呈现。
放大的苹果时隐时现，
枝头花茎，
每一个果皮斑点都清晰可见。
我的脚背不仅一直疼痛，
还一直承担长梯横挡的压力。
我还感到树枝压弯时长梯的摇晃。
耳里总听见地窖传来的
隆隆声——那是
一堆堆苹果滚动入仓的声音。
采摘的工作，我已干得太多：
曾经渴望的大丰收，
我已十分厌倦。
有千万个果子要用手去摸，
深情地拿在手里，轻轻放下，不让它们掉落。
因为一切
落地的苹果，
不论是擦伤还是被树茬戳破，
都会被扔去做果酒，
似一堆无用的废物。

你会看出

什么会打搅我的睡眠,无论什么睡眠。

如果土拨鼠还在,

就会告诉我们是像它的那种

休眠呢——如我所述它正在来临——

还只是人类的某种"睡眠"。

2. 未选择的路 *The Road Not Taken*

词语解释和难句分析

1. 这是一首沉思性质的诗,讲述了诗人在林间岔路口对人生道路的抉择。他选择了一条行人稀少的路,关键时刻的这一选择,使得人生发生了巨大的改变。但人生抉择是否正确要待生命结束时方可明确,诗人沉湎在一种人生不可测的多愁善感的情绪之中。

2. Two roads diverged in a yellow wood,　黄色的森林中路分两条,

    And sorry I could not travel both　可惜我不能够兼走两道。

    And be one traveler, long I stood　孤旅沉吟,我伫立良久,

    And looked down one as far as I could　顺着一条道极目远眺,

    To where it bent in the undergrowth;　直看到它拐弯隐入矮树丛。

3. Then took the other, as just as fair,　然后再走另一条,同样的适意、顺畅,

    And having perhaps the better claim,　也许它更应当被选上,

    Because it was grassy and wanted wear;　因为它野草丰茂,很少人踩踏;

    Though as for that the passing there　不过,今日走过那里

    Had worn them really about the same,　]两条路已踩成一样。

    * having the better claim　更有优先权/被选择权,更应当被选上

    * though as for that　尽管如此/有这个原因, 但……

    * the passing there/Had worn them (= the two roads) really about the same,　今日从此走过,两条路就都有人走过了。在这里动名词短语 the passing there 是句子主语。

4. And both that morning equally lay　那天早晨两条路一样清幽,

    In leaves no step had trodden black.　]路上的落叶还未被踏上泥污。

    Oh, I kept the first for another day!　呵,我把第一条路留待他日再走!

    Yet knowing how way leads on to way,　但我知道,脚下的道路路路相通,

    I doubted if I should ever come back.　我怀疑是否还要回来。

    * lie in 躺在/展现在……;no step had trodden black 是修饰 leaves 的定语从句。头两句的意思是"那天早晨,两条路都一样展现在还未被踩踏泥污的落叶之中";最后两句的意思是"因路路相通,怀疑是否还有必要原路回来"。

5. I shall be telling this with a sigh　许多年之后的某个地方

    Somewhere ages and ages hence:　我会叹息着讲起往事:

    Two roads diverged in a wood, and I —　林中本有岔路,而我——

    I took the one less traveled by,　选择了行人稀少的那一条

And that has <u>made all the difference</u>. 这使得一切都发生了改变。

* less traveled by 是过去分词短语作后置定语修饰 the one,"行人较少"的意思。
* 此诗韵律严谨,为 abaab 型。

参考译文——姚远

未选择的路

黄色的树林中路分两条,
可惜我不能够兼走两道
孤独的旅行者,我伫立良久
顺着一条道,我极目远眺
直看到路拐弯隐入矮林;

然后走上另一条,同样的合意,
也许,它更应当被选上,
因为它长满野草、无人践踏;
不过,今日从此过
两条路已踩成一样。

那天早晨,两条路同样盖满落叶,
无人行走,都还未被踏污。
哦,我留下第一条,改日再走!
但我知道,脚下的道路路路相通,
我怀疑,再回来是否必要。

许多年之后的某个地方,
我会叹息着这样讲:
树林中本岔开两条道,而我——
选择了行人稀少的那一条,
这造成了此后一切的不同。

3. 雪夜林边停 *Stopping by Woods on a Snowy Evening*

1. 本诗表面简单,只是说诗人雪夜在林边驻马,欣赏树林美景,令人不忍离去,但又因承诺在先,使命在身,路途正遥,不可逗留,于是继续前行,不知不觉间,某种哲理已隐含其中。

2. Whose woods these are I think I know. 我想这是谁的森林我知道,
   His house is in the village though; 他家就住在那村里;
   He will not see me stopping here 他不会看见我在他林边驻马
   To watch his woods <u>fill up with</u> snow. 正欣赏雪满林莽的美景。

3. My little horse must think it queer 我的小马一定感到奇怪，
   To stop without a farmhouse near 为何停在近无农舍的地方
   Between the woods and frozen lake 夹在树林和冰湖之间
   The darkest evening of the year. 又是一年中最黑暗的夜晚？

   ＊ 这四行诗是一个带复合宾语的完整的句子。其中 it 是形式宾语，形容词 queer 是宾补，真正的宾语是后面的三行诗：一个带地点状语和时间状语的不定式短语。停步在这样荒凉恶劣的环境和漆黑的夜晚，正是小马感到奇怪的原因。

4. He gives his harness bells a shake 他一甩脖子响起了铃铛
   To ask if there is some mistake. 问是否出了什么差错。
   The only other sound's the sweep 听不到其他的声音回答
   Of easy wind and downy flake. 只有轻风掠过，鹅毛雪飘。

   ＊ 头两行是一个完整句子，主句是双宾结构，a shake 为直接宾语，his harness bells 为间接宾语；不定式短语 to ask ... 是目的状语。

5. The woods are lovely, dark and deep, 树林如此的幽暗、深沉、可爱，
   But I have promises to keep, 但我有诺言要遵守，
   And miles to go before I sleep, 再走几哩，才能睡眠，
   And miles to go before I sleep. 再走几哩，才能睡眠。

   ＊ 此节中第一个 sleep 是真实的"睡眠"，林深夜静，旅途劳顿，想睡而又不能；第二个 sleep 意义似有延伸，带有"死亡"的意思，承诺在先，重任在肩，脚步不能停，到死方可休。

   ＊ 此诗韵律为 aaba/bbcb/ccdc/dddd。

参考译文——姚远

雪夜林边停

我想这是谁家的林子我知道，
他家就住在那边村子里；
他不会看见我在这里驻马
观赏他雪满林莽的美景。

我的小马一定感到惊奇，
为何停在这近无农舍的地方
在森林和冰封的湖泊之间
又是一年中最黑暗的夜晚？

他抖一抖脖子上的铃铛，
问是否出了什么差错。
没听到别的声音回答
唯有轻风掠过、鹅毛雪飘。

树林黑暗、深沉而又可爱，

但我还有诺言要遵守，

征程未尽，不可睡眠，

征程未尽，不可睡眠。

格律和韵律分析

罗伯特·弗罗斯特是一个半传统半现代的诗人，他的诗歌创作有时是现代主义的，不讲究格律和韵律，有时格律和韵律是比较严谨的。《雪夜林边停》即是后者。现以头两段为例进行格律分析：

·Whose woods/·these are/I ·think/I ·know.	a
His ·house/is ·in/the ·vil/lage ·though；	a
He ·will/not ·see/me ·stop/ping ·here	b
To ·watch/his ·woods/fill ·up/with ·snow.	a
My ·lit/tle ·horse/must ·think/it ·queer	b
To ·stop/with·out/a ·farm/house ·near	b
Be·tween/the ·woods/and ·fro/zen ·lake	c
The ·dar/kest ·e/vening of/the ·year.	b

两个诗节 8 行诗，共 32 个音步，每行 4 个音步。从重音标注可知，绝大多数音步都是抑扬格，后面两个诗节亦然，可得出结论：此诗格律为四步抑扬格。由韵律分析可知，前 3 个诗节押 aaba 型韵，第四节一韵到底，诗的总体韵律格式为 aaba。

主要内容归纳和总结

1. 弗罗斯特孩提时代在美国遥远的西部度过，7 岁时随家迁居新罕布什尔州。1892 年他进入达特茅斯（Dartmouth）学院，但很快辍学打工、写诗，1897 年又进哈佛大学，不料又因肺结核退学，在新罕布什尔州德里（Derry）的一个农场疗养，为谋生做了多种工作，直到 1912 年，他才决心闯荡自己的文学人生。

虽然总的来说他算是一位地方诗人（regional poet），他的诗主要写的是新英格兰的风光和人物，但他探讨了人类生活的基本问题，即个人对自己、对别人、对世界以及对上帝的关系。他的诗歌风格既继承传统，尤其是在自然诗（natural poetry）和田园诗（pastoral poetry）方面，又有他自己独特的新意，如以新英格兰口语入诗，节奏如谈家常。简朴的乡村生活、鸟兽虫鱼、风花雪月以及劳动后的安详和宁静皆可凝成诗中意象，十四行诗（sonnet）、双韵体（rhyming couplets）、无韵体（blank verse）与农民的方言习语交融在一起，形成其独特的诗体风格：既像律诗，又像自由诗，可算是半传统半自由诗体（semi-free and semi-conventional type）。

弗罗斯特是 20 世纪重要的诗人，曾四次获得美国普利策奖（Pulitzer Prize）：1923 年因诗集《新罕布什尔》"New Hampshire" 而获奖，1930 年为《诗集》"Collected Poems"，1935 年为《更远的境界》"Further Range"，1942 为《证人树》"A Witness Tree"。因他的贡献，美国参议院曾通过决议祝贺他的生日。1961 年，约翰·肯尼迪总统就职典礼时，87 岁高龄的诗人曾当场朗诵自己的诗歌。

2. 弗罗斯特的主要作品：

《一个男孩的愿望》*A Boy's Will*（1913）

《波士顿以北》*North of Boston*（1914）

《补墙》*Mending the Wall*

《家之埋葬》*Home Burial*

《山之间隔》*Mountain Interval*（1916），包括：

* 《未选择的路》*The Road Not Taken*

* 《白桦》*Birches*

《新罕布什尔》*New Hampshire*（1923），包括：

* 《雪夜林边停》*Stopping by Woods on a Snowy Evening*

《溪流之西》*West-Running Brook*（1928）

《诗集》*Collected Poems*（1930）

《更远的境界》*A Further Range*（1935）

《证人树》*A Witness Tree*（1942），包括：

* 《公开的礼物》*The Gift Outright*

《理性的假面》*A Masque of Reason*（1945）

《仁慈的假面》*A Masque of Mercy*（1947）

70 岁时弗罗斯特开始以各种形式探讨宗教问题，其中，最著名的一首诗是：

《摘苹果后》*After Apple-Picking*

Ⅲ. 尤金·奥尼尔 Eugene O'Neill（1888~1953）

词语解释和难句分析

1. be widely acclaimed "founder of the American drama"　得到广泛拥戴，被誉为美国喜剧的奠基人

2. to end up as a stereotyped mediocrity — playing his most successful part the Count in *The Count of Monte Cristo*　最终成了一个平庸的定型演员——总是扮演他最成功的角色：《基督山伯爵》里的伯爵

   to spend his early years with his parents on theatrical road tours　他小时候是与父母一起在戏剧演出的旅程中度过的

   a succession of religious boarding schools　接连几个教会学校

   be suspended a year after a drunken prank　一次酗酒闹事之后，被停学一年

   to drive him to sea　促使他走向航海的历程

   to stay at a sanitarium for several months recovering from tuberculosis　待在疗养院疗养了数月，好使自己的肺结核得到康复治疗

   to avidly read up on dramatic literature　热切地攻读戏剧文学

   drama workshop　戏剧工作室

   to have wholly dedicated to the mission as a dramatist　全身心投入到一个戏剧家的使命中去

3. one-act melodramatic plays　独幕传奇剧

   plays of various lengths　长短不一的戏剧作品

   full-length play　标准长度的戏剧作品

   be produced on Broadway　在百老汇的舞台上上演

   to make a great hit　大获成功，引起很大轰动

be dramatized more explicitly in *The Straw* 在《草》中得到了更明确细致的戏剧化表现

to deploy the developing complexity of O'Neill's personal vision 逐步展开了奥尼尔复杂的个人见解

a closed circle of possibilities from which it is impossible to escape 一个无法从中逃脱的、具备各种可能性的、封闭的圈子

4. his prominent achievements in symbolic expressionism 他在象征表现主义方面取得了突出的成就

be <u>daring forays into</u> race relations, class conflicts, sexual bondage... 都是对种族关系、阶级冲突、性禁锢等等主题的大胆突入和尝试

to highlight the theatrical effect of the rupture between the two sides of an individual human being, the private and the public 突出人类个体的两面,即私人自我和公开表现的自我相互割裂、冲突的戏剧效果

to <u>reach out</u> to extend his mastery of the stage and <u>work up to</u> the summit of his career 竭力扩展延伸他对舞台的把握,逐步达到戏剧生涯的顶峰

the affirmation of a pagan idealism 异教理想主义的证实

to deny the life-giving impulses and destroy the genuine artist 否定赋予生命的冲动和摧毁天才艺术家

Greek choruses, Elizabethan tirades, expressionist masks, populous crowd scenes, and orchestrated laughter 希腊歌剧中的唱词,伊丽莎白时代的长篇演说词,表现主义的面具,人群拥挤的场景,以及管弦乐奏出的笑声

to <u>bring together</u> <u>a multitude of</u> dramatic concerns 把许多戏剧方面的问题集中/聚集到一起

5. to keep working hard in isolation at his stately mansion 他将自己隔离在他的堂皇华屋里,一刻不停地埋头工作

6. *The Iceman Cometh* (1946) proves to be a masterpiece in the way it is a complex, ironic, deeply moving exploration of human existence, written out of a profound insight into human nature and constructed with tremendous skill and logic. 《冰人来了》具有复杂的情节,嘲讽的韵味,深刻动人地探讨了人类的生存,表现出对人性的深刻洞察力,结构情节的技巧和逻辑不同凡响,从各方面看,无疑是一部杰作。

7. to reach beyond its immediate subject 超出了它直接的主题

as a product of hard-won art 作为一部来之不易/难得的艺术作品

to mark the climax of O'Neill's literary career 标志着奥尼尔文学生涯的顶峰

8. to deal with the basic issues of human existence and predicament 处理基本的人类生存和艰难处境的问题

be constantly <u>wrestling with</u> these issues and <u>struggling with</u> the perplexity about the truth of life 不断思索这些问题,与对生活真谛的困惑做斗争

9. and his dramatic thought followed a tragic pattern <u>running through</u> all his plays, from a celebration and exaltation of "pipe dreams", the romantic dream <u>so to speak</u>, to the doubt about the reality of the dream or the inevitability of the defeat. 他的戏剧思想以悲剧的形式贯穿于他所有的戏剧作品中,从对"烟枪梦",也可以说对浪漫梦的歌颂和得意,到对梦境现实的怀疑或失败的不可避免性。

10. So his final dramas became "transcendental," <u>in the way that</u> the dramatization of man's effort in finding the secret of life <u>results in</u> reconciliation with the tragic impossibility. 所以,他人生最后阶段创作的戏剧成了"超验主义的,"表现在戏剧中,就是人物努力探求生活秘密的结果是:与悲剧的不可能性一致。

11. in full swing 处于鼎盛时期

abstract and symbolic <u>stage sets</u> 抽象的和象征性的舞台布景

to <u>set off against</u> the emotional inner selves and subjective states of mind 抵消内在的情感自我和主观

的思想状态

to write the lines in dialect　以方言土语写几行台词

spelled words in ways which indicate a particular accent or manner of speech　按特定口音和说话方式拼写的单词

be amplified by the accent　(含义)因口音而被放大/增强了

尤金·奥尼尔作品选读

《毛猿》*The Hairy Ape* 第八场节选

词语解释和难句分析

1. in the cramped forecastle of a transatlantic liner　在一艘横渡大西洋的客轮狭窄的前甲板上

   the recognized leader of the stokers　锅炉工中公认的头

   the ultimate products of a society subservient to machines　为机器所主宰/奴役的社会产生的终结产品

   ＊ subservient to　俯首贴耳,屈从/从属于……

   to make a slumming visit to the Stockholm　到斯德哥尔摩访问了一次贫民窟

   be shocked by the lurid atmosphere　为骇人听闻的可怕环境所震惊

   to faint at Yank's brutality　对杨克的粗暴野蛮感到晕厥

   to become sullen and morose　变得气愤难平、郁郁寡欢

   to swagger in dirty work clothes up the Fifth Avenue　穿着肮脏的工作服,大摇大摆地走在(纽约)第五大道上

   trying in vain to insult the aristocratic strollers　试图去侮辱散步的贵族,却徒劳无益

   a militant labor union　富于战斗精神/激进的劳工组织

   (be) thrown out of the hall　被扔出大厅

   the only creature with whom he can now feel kinship　他现在能感到(与之)有亲缘关系的唯一生灵

   to set the ape free　把老猿/大猩猩释放了

   to crush him to death　把他压死了

2. to concern the problem of modern man's identity　关于现代人身份的问题

   in his sympathy　出于同情

3. Yank's sense of belonging nowhere, hence homelessness and rootlessness, is typical of the mood of isolation and alienation in the early twentieth century in the United States and the whole world as well.

   杨克的无处归属,因而也就无家可归、无根可寻的感觉是20世纪初期美国乃至世界的与世隔绝、与人疏远的人之典型思想方式和心态。

4. be shrouded in shadow　被笼罩在阴影中

   to stand out　显示出,突显出

   be seen squatting on his haunches on a bench in much the same attitude as Rodin's "Thinker"　看到(大猩猩)正缩腰屈腿蹲伏在一张长凳上,神态非常像罗丹的雕塑"思想者"

   a chorus of angry chattering and screeching　一阵愤怒的吱吱声和尖叫声

   to turn his eyes and make no sound or move　转了转眼睛,一声不响,一动不动

with a hard, bitter laugh　带着一种苦笑

at the sound of　一听到……就

to die away into an attentive silence　（声音）逐渐平息下来,变成凝神倾听的沉寂

leaning over the railing　俯身在栅栏上

to stare in at its occupant　盯着（笼子）里面的猩猩（占有者）

a pause of dead stillness　短暂的/片刻的死寂

to talk in a friendly confidential tone, half-mockingly, but with a deep undercurrent of sympathy　以一种友好信任的语调说话,半带嘲笑却又深含同情

5. Say, yuh're hard-lookin' guy, ain't yuh? I seen lot's of tough nuts dat de gang called gorillas, but yuh're the foist real one I ever seen. = Say, you're hard-looking guy, aren't you? I've seen lots of tough nuts that the gang called gorillas, but you're the first real one I've ever seen.　喂,你看起来是个很壮实的家伙,是不是啊? 我见过许多被那帮家伙称作大猩猩的硬汉,但是你是我见到的第一个真猩猩。

6. Some chest yuh got, and shoulders, and dem arms and mits! I bet yuh got a punch in eider fist dat'd knock'em all silly! = Some (= wonderful/strong) chest and shoulders you've got, and them arms and mits! I bet (= dare say) you give a pouch with either fist that would knock them all silly!　多棒的胸脯,多棒的肩膀! 多棒的胳膊和手掌! 我敢说,你哪一只拳头打出去,都可以把他们这些蠢家伙打趴下!

7. This with genuine admiration. = He said this with genuine admiration.　他说这番话,是怀着真正赞赏的心情的。

8. to stand upright, swelling out his chest and pounding on it with his fist　直立起来,挺起胸膛,并用拳头猛打它

9. Sure, I get yuh (= you). Yuh (= You) challenge de whole woild (= the whole world), huh? Yuh (= You) got what I was sayin' (= saying) even if yuh (= you) muffed de woid (= the word). And why wouldn't yuh (= you) get me? Ain't we both members of de (= the) same club — de (= the) Hairy Apes?　真的,我懂得你的意思。你向全世界挑战,是吗? 就是你不懂语言,你也明白我说话的意思。你怎么会不懂我的意思? 我们不是同属一个俱乐部吗? ——毛猿俱乐部?

10. then bitterness creeping in　这时,话中渐带苦涩

　　* to creep in　渐渐进入

11. So yuh're (= you're) what she (had) seen when she looked at me, de (= the) white-faced tart! I was you to her, get me? On'y outa de (= Only out of the) cage — broke out — free to moider her (= free to murder her), see?　所以,你就是她朝我看时所看见的东西,那个白脸的婊子! 我就是你,懂我的意思吧? 只是我在笼子外边,突然发作,就可随意杀死她,懂吗?

　　* 这里所说的 she 就是横渡大西洋的客轮船主的女儿米尔德里德·道格拉斯(Mildred Douglas),她曾经到斯德哥尔摩访问了贫民窟,见到过杨克一类的锅炉工,为他们的粗暴和生存环境的野蛮所震惊。

12. Sure! Dat's (= That's) what she tought (= thought). She wasn't wise dat (= that) I was in a cage, too — worser'n (= worser than) yours — sure — a damn sight — 'cause (= because) you got some chance to bust loose — but me — (He grows confused.) Aw, It's all wrong, ain't it?　真的! 那就是她的想法。她不明白我也是在一个笼子里——比你的还糟——真的——难看死了——因为你还有机会打破牢笼冲出去——但我——(他糊涂了)哦,见鬼! 全都错了,是不是?

13. I s'pose yuh wanter (= suppose you want to) know what I'm doin' (= doing) here, huh? I (had) been warmin' (= warming) a bench down to de Battery — ever since last night.　我猜你想知道我来

这里是干什么的? 从昨晚开始,我就一直在巴特里公园焐板凳(在板凳上待着)。

14. and de (= the) ships comin' (= coming) in, sailin' (= sailing) out, all over de oith (= the earth) — and dey was (= they were) steel, too.   还有开进开出的船舶,航行全世界——它们也都是钢铁制造的。

15. De (= the) sun was warm, dey wasn't (= there were) no clouds, and dere (= there) was a breeze blowin' (= blowing). Sure, it was <u>great stuff</u>. I got it aw (= all) right — what Paddy said about dat bein' de (= that being the) right dope — on'y (= only) I couldn't <u>get in</u> it, see?   阳光温暖,万里无云,微风拂煦。感觉真是好极了/那可真是好东西。我全享受到了——就像派迪说的,那简直就是麻醉品——只是我不能获取/拥有。

   * what Paddy said about that being the right dope 应为 Just as what Paddy said, that was the right dope。未受过良好教育的杨克说话时常常会出语法错误,发音不准,他的原话会被人理解为:"派迪对此的讲话是很好的麻醉品"这显然不符合上下文的逻辑,所以翻译时做了些改动。

16. I couldn't belong in dat (= belong to that). It was over my head. And I kept tinkin' (= thinking) — and den (= then) I <u>beat it up</u> here to see what youse was (= you were) like.   我不可能属于那个地方,它高高地在我头顶上。我一直在想啊想啊——然后就胡打乱闹地跑到这儿来看看你是个什么样。

   * beat it up 寻欢作乐,胡闹

17. I waited till dey was (= they were) all gone to git yuh (= <u>get you</u>) alone. Say, how d'yuh (= do you) feel sittin' (= sitting) in dat (= that) pen all de (= the) time, havin' (= having) to stand for 'em comin' and starin' at yuh (= them coming and staring at you) — de (= the) white-faced, skinny tarts and de (= the) boobs what (= that) marry 'em (them) — makin' (<u>making</u>) fun of yuh (= you), laughin' (= <u>laughing</u>) at yuh (= you), gittin' (= <u>getting</u>) scared of yuh (= you) — damn 'em (= them)!   我等他们全走光了,只剩下你一个在这里才来。喂,你一直关在那牲口栏里,不得不站着让他们来瞪着个大眼看你——那些白脸的、皮包骨头的婊子,以及与她们结婚的蠢家伙们——拿你逗乐,大声嘲笑你,却又害怕你——他们这些该死的家伙! 你又做何感想?

18. to <u>pound on</u> the rail with his fists   拳头捶打栏杆

    to rattle the bars of his cage   摇晃撞击笼子的栅栏

    to set up an angry chattering in the darkness   在黑暗中发出一阵愤怒的吱吱声

19. Sure! Dat's de (= That's the) way it hits me, too. On'y yuh're (= Only you're) lucky, see? You don't <u>belong</u> wit'em (= <u>with them</u>) and yuh (= you) know it. But me, I belong wit'em (with them) — but I don't, see? Dey (= they) don't belong wit'me (= with me), dat's (= that's) what (= that's what the matter is). Get me? Thinkin' (= thinking) is hard – It's dis (= this) way, what (> that) I'<u>m driving at</u>.   确实,他们也是那样打击我的。只有你幸运,懂吗? 你与他们不是同类,而且你知道这一点。但是我,与他们是同类——但我却不知道,明白吧? 他们跟我却不同类,那就是问题的症结。懂我的意思吧? 思考真累——我要跟你说的正是这一点。

   * be driving at   意指,要说,要着力说明

20. Youse (= You) can sit and <u>dope dream in</u> de (= the) past, green woods, de (= the) jungle and de (= the) rest of it. Den yuh (= Then you) belong and dey (= they) don't. Den yuh kin (= Then you can) laugh at'em (= at them), see? Yuh're de (= You're the) champ of de woild (the world). But me — I <u>ain't got no</u> (got neither) past to tink (think) in, nor <u>nothin'</u> (> anythig) dat's commin' (that's coming)! on'y (only) what's now — and dat don't (= that dosen't) belong.   你可以坐在那

里做梦,梦想过去呀、绿树呀、丛林呀,一切的一切,都可以梦想。你原本就属于那里,而他们不是,你可以嘲笑他们,懂吗? 你是世界冠军。但我——既没有过去可想,也没有未来在前,只有现在——现在又不知归属何处。

21. Sure, you're de (= the) best off! You can't tink (= think), can yuh (= you)? Yuh (= You) can't talk neider (= neither). But I kin (= can) make a bluff at talkin' and tinkin' (= talking and thinking) — a'most git away wit' it (= almost get away with it) — a'most (= almost)! —and dat's (= that's) where de joker comes in (= the joke comes). (He laughs.) I ain't on oith (= earth) and I ain't in heaven, get me? I'm in de (= the) middle tryin' (= trying) to separate 'em (= them), takin' (= taking) all de woist (= the worst) punches from bot' of 'em (= both of them). 肯定的,你是最幸运的! 你没有思想,你没有吧? 你也不会说话。但是我可以装腔作势地说话、思想来吓唬人——几乎都能蒙混过去——几乎! ——笑话就出在这里。(他大笑起来)我不在地上,也不在天上,懂我吧? 我在天地中间想把它们分开,却受到它们两面最沉重的打击。

    * best off 是 well off 的最高级:最富裕,最幸运;make bluff at sth. 虚张声势地做某事; to get away with 做了错事而未被发觉,蒙混过去

22. Maybe dat's (= that's) what dey (= they) call hell, huh? But you, yuh're (= you're) at de (= the) bottom. You belong! Sure! Yuh're de on'y one in de woild dat does (= You're the only one in the world that does), yuh (= you) lucky stiff! And dat's (= that's) why dey gotter (= they go to) put yuh (= you) in a cage, see? 也许那就是他们所说的地狱吧? 可是你呢,就在最底层。你却适得其所,的确! 你是世界上唯一适得其所的,你这个幸运的家伙! 所以他们就把你关在笼子里,知道吧?

23. It beats it when you try to tink (= think) it or talk it — it's way down — deep — behind — you'n' (= you and) me we feel it. Sure! Bot' (= Both) members of dis (= this) club! (He laughs — then in a savage tone) What de (= the) hell! T' (= The) hell wit (= with) it! A little action, dat's (= that's) our meat! Dat (= That) belongs! 当你设法去想它或说它的时候,它就溜掉了——是往下跑——往深处——往后面——你和我,我们都感觉到了它。是的! 我们俩都是这个俱乐部的成员! (他大笑起来—然后用一种野蛮的语调) 去他妈的! 见鬼去吧! 采取点儿行动/动动拳脚,那是我们的拿手好戏! 那才管用!

24. Knock 'em (= them) down and keep bustin' 'em (= busting them) till dey (= they) croaks yuh (= you) with a gat — wit' (= with) steel! Sure! Are yuh (= you) game? Dey've (= They've) looked at youse (= you), ain't dey (= aren't they) — in a cage? Wanter (= Want to) get even? Wanter (= Want to) wind up like a sport 'stead (= instead) of croaking slow in dere (= there)? 打倒他们,不断地猛击他们,除非他们用手枪——用钢铁杀死了你! 的确! 你勇敢吗? 他们来看你了——看笼中的你,是不是? 想要报复吗? 想像赌博一样绷紧神经一下子痛快结束,而不要在那里被慢慢绞杀?

    * get even 扯平,算账,报复; wind up 结束,卷紧,绷紧

25. to roar an emphatic affirmative 吼叫声中,吼出了肯定和赞同
    to go on with a sort of furious exaltation 愤愤之中带着得意,继续说下去

26. Sure! Yuh're reg'lar (= regular)! Yuh'll (= You'll) stick to de (= the) finish! 的确,你真不错! 你要坚持到底!

27. We'll put up one last star bout dat'll (= that'll) knock 'em (= them) offen (> off) deir (= their) seats! Dey'll (= They'll) have to make de (= the) cages stronger after we're trou (> through)! 我们要进行一次最后的大较量,把他们从宝座上打下去! 打完后,他们会把笼子造的更坚固!

28. The gorilla is straining at his bars, growling, hopping from one foot to the other.　大猩猩用力推拉笼子的栅栏,咆哮着,双脚轮换着蹦跳。

29. to take a jimmy from under his coat　从外衣下面拿出一根撬棍

　　to force the lock on the cage door　强行撬笼子的门锁

　　to throw the door open　打开了门

　　pardon from de (= the) governor　州长赦免了你

　　to take you for a walk down Fifth Avenue　带你到第五大道上去散散步

30. We'll knock 'em (= them) offen de oith (= off the earth) and croak with de (= the) band playin' (= playing).　我们要把他们从地球上打掉,在乐队的伴奏中死去。

31. to scramble gingerly out of his cage　小心翼翼/轻手轻脚地从笼中爬出来

　　the secret grip of our order　我们这个阶层秘密的握法

　　the tone of mockery　嘲讽的语调

　　to enrage the animal　激怒了这动物

　　to wrap his huge arms around YANK in a murderous hug　以他巨大的手臂搂住了杨克,给了他致命的一抱

　　a cracking snap of crushed ribs — gasping cry　一阵压断肋骨的咔嚓声——上气不接下气的喊叫声

32. to let the crushed body slip to the floor　让那压断了的躯体滑到地板上

　　to stand over it uncertainly　犹疑不定地监视着它(瘫在地上的躯体)

　　to shuffle off menacingly into the darkness at left　拖着脚步,一副凶神恶煞的样子,走进左侧的黑暗之中

　　a great uproar of frightened chattering and whimpering from the other cages　从其他笼子里发出一阵惊恐的吱吱哇哇的乱叫

33. Say — dey oughter (= they ought to) match him — with Zybszko. He got me, aw (= all) right. I'm trou (= through). Even him (> he) didn't tink (= think) I belonged.　我说呀——他们应该让他——与西伯思科较量一下。他彻底打败了我。我完了。连他都认为我格格不入/不是同类。

　　* to match A with B　让 A 与 B 较量/比赛

34. Christ, where do I get off at (> get off)? Where do I fit in? (checking himself suddenly) Aw, what de (= the) hell! No squawkin' (= squawking) see! No quittin', get me! Croak wit (= with) your boots on!　上帝啊,我该从哪里出发?又到哪里才合适?(突然克制住自己)噢,见鬼去吧!莫抱怨,懂吧!莫放弃,懂得我的意思吧!要战斗到死!

　　* to die/croak with one's boots/shoes on　战死,死在工作岗位上,被绞死

35. to grab hold of = to catch hold of　紧紧握住

　　to haul himself painfully to his feet　他很痛苦地拖着身子立起来

　　to look around him bewilderedly　茫然/迷惘/困惑地打量四周

　　to force a mocking laugh　勉强发出/挤出嘲讽的笑声

　　in the strident tones of a circus barker　以马戏团招徕观众的人发出的刺耳的吆喝声

36. Ladies and gents, step forward and take a slant at de (= the) one and only — one and original — Hairy Ape from de (the) wilds of —　女士们,先生们,往前走一步,看一看这个独一无二的——独特原创的——来自荒野的毛猿——

37. to slip in a heap on the floor　在地板上瘫成一堆

　　to set up a chattering, whimpering wail　发出一阵吱吱哇哇的哀号

38. Perhaps, the Hairy Ape at last belongs.　也许,毛猿最终找到了归属。

主要内容归纳和总结

1. 尤金·奥尼尔出生在纽约一个艺术之家。其父詹姆斯·奥尼尔(James O'Neill),曾是演莎剧的著名演员,最终成了一个定型不变的平庸演员,总是扮演最成功的角色——《基督山伯爵》中伯爵。尤金·奥尼尔在康涅狄格州的新伦敦长大,1906年于普林斯顿大学中途停学。1909年一次失败的婚姻使他航行世界。后来,他又加入哈佛大学乔治·皮尔斯·贝克(George Pierce Baker)的戏剧工作室,开始了他作为戏剧家的创作生涯。他生平四次获得美国普利策文学奖,1936年获得诺贝尔奖,是至今以戏剧创作获得诺贝尔奖的第一人。

　　他一生写了49部剧,大多是悲剧,基本主题都是探讨人类的生存和困境,生与死,幻觉和幻灭,疏远和交流,梦境和现实,自我和社会,欲望和挫折,等等。他通过爱情、宗教、报复等不同方面,描写了剧中人物对人生归属、生活的含义和目的的追求,最终都归于失望和绝望。

　　敢于创新是他的一贯风格,20世纪20年代盛行的表现主义(Expressionism)也在他的多部作品中得到充分体现,他用抽象的象征的舞台背景(abstract and symbolic stage sets)来抵消(set off against)人物内心的情感和主观的想法,灯光和音乐都用来表现人物变化的心境。

2. 尤金·奥尼尔的主要作品:

《驶向东边的卡尔笛弗》*Bound East for Cardiff* (1916)

《天外边》*Beyond the Horizon* (1920)

《琼斯皇帝》*The Emperor Jones* (1920)

《草》*The Straw* (1921)

《安娜·克里斯蒂》*Anna Christie* (1921)

《毛猿》*The Hairy Ape* (1922)

《上帝的所有烟斗都有翅膀》*All God's Chillum Got Wings* (1924)

《榆树下的欲望》*Desire Under the Elms* (1924)

《伟大的布朗》*The Great God Brown* (1926)

《拉扎勒斯笑了》*Lazarus Laughed* (1927)

《奇怪的幕间戏》*Strange Interlude* (1928)

《冰人来了》*The Iceman Cometh* (1946)

《直到深夜的漫长一天》*Long Day's Journey into Night* (1956)

重要信息句子

1. Eugene O'Neill is unquestionably America's greatest playwright. He won the Pulitzer Prize four times and was the only dramatist ever to win a Nobel Prize (1936).

2. During his career as a dramatist, O'Neill wrote and published <u>forty-nine</u> plays altogether of various lengths.

3. His first full-length play, *Beyond the Horizon*, produced in 1920 on Broadway, made a great hit and won him the first Pulitzer Prize.

4. *Long Day's Journey into Night* has gained its status as a world classic and simultaneously marks the climax of O'Neill's literary career and the coming age of American drama.

Ⅳ. 斯科特·菲兹杰拉德 F. Scott Fitzgerald（1896～1940）

词语解释和难句分析

1. be mirror of the exciting age in almost every way　从各方面真实地反映那个亢奋的时代
   an active participant of his age　作为他那个时代的积极参加者
   never fail to remain detached and foresee the future and tragedy of the "Dollar Decade"　从来都能冷静超然地预见"十年金元时代"可悲的未来
   Be often acclaimed literary spokesman of the Jazz Age　常常被认为是爵士时代的文学代言人

2. to admire his gentlemanly father　欣赏他父亲彬彬有礼的绅士风度
   the poor Irish beginnings on his mother's side　他母亲贫穷的爱尔兰血统
   neglect of academic study　疏忽了学业/学术研究
   to accept an army commission　接受了一次军事派遣/委任/任务

3. to exploit his literary talent　开发/利用他的文学天才
   to win for him the expensive prize of Zelda Sayre, the beautiful, light-hearted daughter of a prominent judge
   为他赢得了宝贵的大奖,那就是一位著名律师的美丽的、无忧无虑的女儿塞尔达·塞拉
   So far as . . . is concerned　就……而论
   to figure so prominently in his fiction　在他的小说里频频出现的(人物)
   to drain his personal energies and corrodes his professional career　耗尽了他的精力,使他的创作事业也一蹶不振
   to bring relentless decline for Fitzgerald with a series of misfortunes　一系列的不幸,使菲兹杰拉德遭到无情的打击和事业衰退

4. beyond his reach　为他力所不及,他够不着
   The past is beyond his reach.　往事不可追。
   both an insider and outsider of the Jazz Age with a double vision　用内外两个不同的视角观察着爵士时代
   partaking of the wealth, frivolity, temptation of the time　分享那个时代的财富、轻浮和诱惑
   to reproduce the drama of the age by standing aloof and keeping a cold eye on the performance of his contemporaries　他置身事外,冷眼观察同时代人的种种行为,写出了那个时代的戏剧
   be infatuated with the vanity fair　迷恋着名利场
   the best embodiment of the spirit of the Jazz Age　爵士时代精神的最佳体现
   the upper-class society　上层阶级社会
   to have a sense of reckless confidence not only about money but about life in general　总的来说,对金钱对人生感到一种盲目的/不计后果的自信
   to feel excused from seeking the common good　因索取公共利益而感到歉疚

5. Plunging into their personal adventures, engaging themselves in casual sex and heavy drinking, they took risks that did not impress them as being risks, and they spent money extravagantly and enjoyed themselves

to their hearts' content.　他们悍然不顾地去进行个人冒险,性生活随意滥为,酗酒贪杯,冒险却不知在冒险,挥金如土,尽情享乐。

6. Beneath their masks of relaxation and joviality, there was sterility, meaningless and futility.　表面的轻松快活,掩盖着毫无生气、毫无意义和毫无成效的真实的精神世界。

7. ... amid the grandeur and extravagance (there was) a spiritual wasteland and a hint of decadence and moral decay.　在表面的豪华奢侈背后,是精神的荒原和道德颓败的迹象。

8. This undeniable juxtaposition of appearance with reality, of the pretense of gaiety with the tension underneath, is easily recognizable in Fitzgerald's novels and stories.　不可否认,在菲兹杰拉德的小说和故事中很容易看出表象与现实、虚假的快乐与背后的紧张并置。

9. never spared an intimate touch in his fiction to deal with the bankruptcy of the American dreams 他的小说从不回避描写美国梦的破产
   be highlighted by the disillusionment of the protagonists' personal dreams　借主人公个人梦想的破灭来突出(美国梦的破灭)
   the clashes between their romantic vision of life and the sordid reality　浪漫的人生幻想与肮脏现实之间的冲突

10. He is not seeking money so much as what money can bring to him.　与其说他追求金钱,还不如说他追求金钱能带给他的东西。
    ＊ what money can bring to him 是名词性从句,与 money 一样,都是 seeking 的宾语,两相比较。

11. Money is only a convenient and inadequate symbol for what he dreams of earning.　金钱只是便捷地但并不能充分地表明他梦想得到的东西。

12. to transport him to a magic world of eternal happiness　渡他到永久快乐的魔幻世界
    the dream of achieving a new status and a new essence, of rising to a loftier place in the mysterious hierarchy of human worth　梦想获得新的地位和新的生存方式,梦想在神秘的人类价值等级中晋升到更高的等级
    to direct his whole life to winning back her love　把赢回她的爱作为他毕生的目标
    to prove to be futile　证明是毫无希望的
    not to negate the affirmative role the "magic moments" play, which attend the hope and expectations of eternal happiness　不否认"魔幻时刻"剧所发挥的积极作用,它涉及永久快乐的希望和期待

13. be explicit and chilly　(文风)直言坦率,冷静从容
    his careful observation of mannerism, styles, models and attitudes　他对文体、形式、人物原型和人生态度的仔细观察
    to provide the reader with a vivid sense of reality　给读者提供了栩栩如生的现实感
    to follow the Jamesian tradition in using the scenic method　模仿詹姆士式的现场描写的传统
    sometimes with intervening passages of narration, leaving the tedious process of transition to the readers' imagination　有时还有叙述的段落介入,使单调乏味的过渡过程变成读者的想象空间

14. The bold impressionistic and colorful quality have all proved his consummate artistry.　大胆的印象主义的、绘声绘色的描写都证明了他完美的艺术技巧。

菲兹杰拉德作品选读

《了不起的盖茨比》*The Great Gatsby* 第三章节选

词语解释和难句分析

1. be set against the ending of the war　以战后为时代背景

   to sell bonds in New York　在纽约卖股票

   an oculist's faded billboard with a pair of great strange eyes behind yellow spectacles　一面眼科医生的褪了色的广告牌,黄色的眼镜背后有一双奇特的大眼睛

   his mansion and fabulous entertainments　他的豪宅和寓言/神话般的娱乐活动

   be financed by bootlegging and other criminal activities　以非法酿酒贩卖和其他不法活动之所得提供经济上的花销

   to try to win her back with his extravagant devotion　试图以极度的忠诚赢回她的芳心

   to have become reconciled to sb.　已经与某人和好/达成妥协

   to tell Mr. Wilson out of hatred of his rival that it was Gatsby who killed his wife　叫威尔森先生不要恨他的情敌,是盖茨比撞死了他的妻子

   to brood over Gatsby's dream　默默地沉思盖茨比的梦想

2. to evoke a haunting mood of a glamorous, wild time that seemingly will never come again　使人回想起那个似乎一去不返的时代——刺激,疯狂,难以忘怀

3. The loss of an ideal and the disillusionment that comes with the failure are exploited fully in the personal tragedy of a young man whose "incorruptible dream" is "smashed into pieces by the relentless reality."　理想的失败和随失败而来的幻灭感在一个青年的个人悲剧中得到了充分表现,他的"不可能破灭的梦想"被无情的现实打得粉碎。

4. to partake of a state of mind that embodies America itself　带有体现美国本身的思想

   his sense of commitment　他的负罪感

   to take him in search of his personal grail　带动他去追寻个人的长远目标

5. However, the affirmation of hope and expectation is self-asserted in Fitzgerald's artistic manipulation of the central symbol in the novel, the green light.　然而,菲兹杰拉德通过对小说中的主要象征——绿灯的艺术把握,肯定了(美国梦的)希望和期待,这是不言自明的。

6. to evoke both the romance and the sadness of that strange and fascinating era which we call the twenties　使人联想起我们称作 20 年代的那个奇特、迷人时代的浪漫和凄凉

7. to go like moths among the whisperings and the champagne and the stars　像飞蛾一样穿梭在低低絮语、香槟酒和点点繁星之间

   to watch his guests diving from the tower of his raft or taking the sun on the hot sand of his beach　观看他的宾客从筏船的塔台上跳水,或者躺在热烘烘的海滩沙子上晒太阳

   to slit the waters of the Sound　在桑德海湾劈波斩浪

   drawing aquaplanes over cataracts of foam　拖着滑水板滑行在瀑布似的白沫上

8. while his station wagon scampered like a brisk yellow bug to meet all trains　而他的货车则像一只敏捷的黄甲虫似的,匆匆忙忙地颠簸着去各火车站接客

9. to toil all day with mops and scrubbing-brushes and hammers and garden-shears, repairing the ravages of the night before　拿着拖把、板刷和园艺剪,忙碌辛劳了一整天,修理着前一天夜里造成的破坏

10. to leave his back door in a pyramid of pulpless halves　一半成了金字塔似的一堆果壳从后门运走

　　to extract the juice of two hundred oranges　榨出 200 个橘子的果汁

　　be pressed two hundred times by a butler's thumb　一个男管家的大拇指按 200 下按钮

　　once a fortnight　两周/14 天一次

11. a corps of caterers　一帮酒食承办人

　　on buffet tables, garnished with glistening hors-d'oeuvre　在自助餐桌上,摆放着/装点着五光十色的冷盘

　　spiced baked hams crowded against salads of harlequin designs　加香料烤的火腿,周围簇拥着图案五颜六色的沙拉

　　pastry pigs and turkey bewitched to a dark gold　裹面烤猪和烤得焦黄诱人的火鸡

12. In the main hall a bar with a real brass rail was set up, and stocked with gins and liquors and with cordials so long forgotten that most of his female guests were too young to know one from another.　大厅里,设有一个用真正的铜栏杆围起来的酒吧,备有杜松子酒、烈性白酒和久被遗忘的各色露酒,大多数的女宾客都太年轻,区分不出这些甜酒的种类。

　　＊ was set up 与 was stocked with 是并列的谓语。

13. No thin five-piece affair, but a whole pitiful of oboes and trombones and saxophones and viols and cornets and piccolos, and low and high drums.　不是快要垮掉的只有五件乐器的乐队,而是双簧管、拉管、萨克斯管、提琴、短号、短笛,以及低音鼓和高音鼓装了满满一乐池

　　(cars) be parked five deep in drive　私家道路上,车辆停了五排

　　be gaudy with primary colors　五彩缤纷,华丽而俗气

　　hair shorn in strange new ways, and shawls beyond the dream of Castile　头发剪成新奇的样式,方形披巾时髦得连浪漫的西班牙卡斯蒂利亚人做梦都想不到

　　in full swing　正充分/热烈地进行,酒兴正酣,正在全盛时期

　　floating rounds of cocktails permeate the garden outside　一巡巡鸡尾酒在漂浮流动中被送到外面的花园各处

　　＊ permeate　v. 遍布

　　(the air) be alive with chatter and laughter, and casual innuendo and introductions forgotten on the spot　空气中洋溢着欢声笑语,随意打趣和转身即忘的相互介绍

14. to lurch away from the sun　(地球)蹒跚而行,慢慢偏离开太阳

　　to pitch a key higher　提高一个音调

15. Laughter is easier minute by minute, spilled with prodigality, tipped out at a cheerful word.　后来,笑声变得越来越廉价,肆意漫溢,一句笑话,就能引起一片笑声。

　　＊ prodigality　n. 挥霍,浪费

16. to swell with new arrivals, dissolve and form in the same breath　随着新客的到来,人群涌大,消散和聚合,同时发生

　　to weave here and there among the stouter and more stable　在更加壮实稳固的人群中穿来穿去

　　to become for a sharp, joyous moment the center of a group　一段时间,成为人群的中心,快乐刺激一阵子

　　and then, excited with triumph, glide on through the seachange of faces and voices and color under the constantly changing light　然后,又带着胜利的激情,在变幻不定的灯光下,穿越在脸庞、嗓音和色彩形成的动荡的大海中

17. in trembling opal　头上戴的宝石摇曳颤抖

to seize a cocktail <u>out of the air</u>, and <u>dump it down</u> for courage　从空中抓过一杯鸡尾酒，一饮而尽，以壮胆气

moving her hands <u>like Frisco</u>　迅捷地挥舞胳膊，像旧金山人一样活力四射

to vary his rhythm obligingly for her　主动改变音乐的节奏，来配合她的舞蹈

18. and there is a burst of chatter as the erroneous news goes around that she is Gilda Gray's understudy from the *Follies*　周围爆发出一阵窃窃私语，传递着一个错误的信息，说她是《愚笨》一剧里明星演员姬尔达·格雷的 B 角

19. to <u>conduct themselves</u> according to the rules of behavior <u>associated with</u> an amusement park　根据娱乐场所的行为规则，就自行其是地来了

* associated with　与……相关的，它是引导过去分词短语修饰名词 behavior 的后置定语。

To come for the party <u>with a simplicity of heart</u> that is its own ticket of admission　就一门心思/一个心眼儿地来参加派对，这本身就是入场券

20. a chauffeur in a uniform of <u>robin's-egg blue</u>　一位穿着绿蓝色制服的司机

* robin's-egg blue = robin-egg 绿蓝色；chauffeur = driver 司机

to have intended to <u>call on</u> me <u>long before</u>　早就想登门拜访我

but a peculiar <u>combination of circumstances</u> had prevented it　但因种种特殊情况，未能做到/成行

in a majestic hand = in a bold handwriting　字体豪放/粗犷

21. to <u>wander around</u> rather <u>ill at ease</u> among swirls and eddies of people I didn't know　很不自在地在陌生人的旋涡中徘徊

a face I had noticed on the <u>commuting train</u>　一张我曾在月票火车上见过的脸

be immediately <u>struck by</u> the number of young Englishmen <u>dotted about</u>　立即注意到分散在四处的英国青年的人数之多

all <u>talking</u> in a low, earnest voice <u>to</u> solid and prosperous Americans　所有的人都在用低沉而诚挚的声音同壮实而富有的美国人交谈

22. They <u>were</u> at least agonizingly <u>aware of</u> the easy money <u>in the vicinity</u> and convinced that it was theirs for a few words <u>in the right key</u>.　他们至少痛苦地发现这里钱来得容易，几句话说得投机，钱就是他们的了。

* in the vicinity 附近，邻近地区，这里；in the right key = in a proper way 方式恰当，（讲话）得体/投机；it 指代的是前面说的 money。

23. to ask sb. his whereabouts　向某人打听他的行踪/下落

to <u>stare at</u> me in such an amazed way　竟然那样吃惊地瞪大眼睛看着我

to deny so vehemently any knowledge of his movements　矢口否认/口气强烈地否认知晓他的行踪

to <u>slink off</u> in the direction of the cocktail table　悄悄走开，走向鸡尾酒桌

to linger without looking purposeless and alone　孤独徘徊、盲目四顾

24. I was <u>on my way</u> to get <u>roaring drunk</u> from sheer embarrassment when …　我正想要喝得酩酊大醉，彻底摆脱尴尬，这时……

25. leaning a little backward　微微向后仰着

to find it necessary <u>to attach myself</u> to someone before I should …　认为有必要依附某人/拉个人搭伙，然后才好做……

to <u>address cordial remarks</u> to the passersby　向身旁走过的人亲切地打招呼

26. She held my hand impersonally, as a promise that she'd take care of me <u>in a minute</u>.　她不动感情地抓着我的手，算是兑现她"马上要照顾我"的承诺。

27. to give ear to two girls in twin yellow dresses 侧耳倾听两个穿同样黄色衣裙的女孩的谈话

golf tournament 高尔夫球比赛

28. ... but the girls had moved casually on and her remark was addressed to the premature moon, produced like the supper, no doubt, out of a caterer's basket. 但是,两个女孩已经漫不经心地往前走了,她(乔丹)的话就成了说给提前圆满的月亮听了,这月亮仿佛是端上来的晚餐,无疑出自酒食承办人的篮子。

29. to descend the steps and saunter about the garden 从台阶上走下,在花园里漫步

a tray of cocktails 一托盘鸡尾酒

to float at us through the twilight 穿过夜色飘到我们面前

to inquire sb. of sth. 向某人询问某事

to answer in a alert confident voice 警觉而自信地回答

to get a package from Croirier's with a new evening gown in it 收到一个克罗里尔服装店寄来的包裹,里面装着一件晚礼服

be too big in the bust (衣服)胸部太肥

be gas blue with lavender beads 瓦斯蓝色的衣服,配淡紫色的珠子

30. There's something funny about a fellow that'll do a thing like that. He doesn't want anything trouble with anybody. 这么做事的人有点儿意思啊,他不想给任何人添任何麻烦!

31. A thrill passed over all of us. 我们全都感到不寒而栗。

32. I don't think it's so much that, it's more that he was a German spy during the war. 我并不认为那有多么的了不得(那个),更不得了的是战争中他是德国间谍。

33. to lean together confidentially 相互信任地靠在一起

to nod in confirmation 点头表示确认,肯定地点点头

to assure us positively 向我们做了保证

to narrow her eyes 她眯起眼睛

34. It was testimony to the romantic speculation he inspired that there were whispers about him from those who had found little that it was necessary to whisper about in this world. 在这个世界上找不到什么值得窃窃私语的人们,现在却叽叽喳喳地议论起他(盖茨比)来了,这本身就证明他已激起了人们浪漫主义的想象。

* 开头的 it 是形式主语,真正的主语是第一个 that 引导的主语从句,直到最后。who 引导 those 的定语从句,其中 little 是宾语,后面 that 又引导一个 little 的定语从句,关系代词 that 在从句中作 whisper about 的宾语。另外在表语部分,he inspired 是省略了关系代词的定语从句,修饰 the romantic speculation。

35. There were three married couples and Jordan's escort, a persistent undergraduate given to violent innuendo, and obviously under the impression that sooner or later Jordan was going to yield him up her person to a greater or lesser degree. 那里有三对夫妻,外加乔丹相陪,还有一位执拗的大学生,他总是喜欢含沙射影地冷嘲热讽,显然认为乔丹迟早会委身于他,程度不同而已。

* (be) given to 沉湎于,热心于;(be) under the impression that... = have the impression that... 有个……的印象,抱着……的希望;前面的分词短语和后面的介词短语都是 a persistent undergraduate 的后置定语;to yield him up her person = to give up to him sexually(她)委曲求全,委身于他。

36. Instead of rambling, this party had preserved a dignified homogeneity, and assumed to itself the function of representing the staid nobility of the countryside — East Egg condescending to West Egg, and

carefully <u>on guard against</u> its spectroscopic gayety.　这群人并不四处走动,一直保持着道貌岸然、自成一体的样子,他们从东埃格村屈尊来到西埃格村,内心里却自担重责,以庄重的乡村贵族代表自居,小心地提防着这光怪陆离、灯红酒绿的享乐(尽量不失尊严)。

＊East Egg/West Egg　纽约的富人居住在东埃格村,作为暴发户的盖茨比则住在普通人居住的西埃格村。

37. after a somehow wasteful and inappropriate half-hour　在度过了无所事事、无所适从的半小时之后

to nod in a cynical, melancholy way　玩世不恭却又很忧郁地点点头

to try an <u>important-looking</u> door　试着打开一扇气派不凡的大门

(be) <u>paneled with</u> carved English oak, and probably transported complete from some ruin overseas　四壁镶嵌的是雕花的英国栎木,也许是整块的从某个海外废墟上搬来的

with enormous owl-eyed spectacles　戴着猫头鹰眼似的大眼镜

<u>staring</u> with unsteady concentration <u>at</u> the shelves of books　瞪大眼睛,犹疑不定地看着书架上的书

to <u>wheel</u> excitedly <u>around</u> and examine Jordan from head to foot　激动地转过身,从头到脚把乔丹打量了一遍

(needn't) bother to ascertain　(不必)费神作验证

a nice durable cardboard　漂亮耐用的硬纸壳

to cry triumphantly　得意(洋洋)地喊道

a bona-fide piece of printed matter　一件真正的印刷品

＊bona-fide = genuine　[拉丁语]真正的

to cut the pages　裁开书页

38. I thought it might <u>sober me up</u> to sit in a library.　我原以为坐在图书馆里也许能让我清醒/酒醒过来。

39. old men pushing young girls backward in eternal graceless circles, superior couples holding each other tortuously, fashionably, and keeping in the corners —　年老的男人拥着年轻的女郎无尽无休地转着圈子,边转边退,形态不雅;清高的男女则成双成对地拥抱着曲折回环,跳着时髦的舞步,守着舞场的边角——

40. and a great number of single girls dancing individualistically or <u>relieving</u> the orchestra for a moment <u>of</u> the burden of the banjo or the traps.　许多单身女孩跳起了独舞,或者为乐队弹起琴、打起鼓,让琴师和鼓手稍微歇一歇

41. celebrated tenor　著名男高音

notorious contralto　声名狼藉的女低音

a pair of stage twins　一对双胞胎演员

to do a baby act in costumes　穿上戏装,扮演儿童;粉墨登场,演儿童剧

be served in glasses bigger than finger-bowls　(酒)被盛在比洗指碗还大的酒杯里

42. and between the numbers people were doing "stunts" all over the garden, while happy, vacuous <u>bursts of</u> laughter rose toward the summer sky　在这些曲目之间,人们还在花园各处纷纷表演起自己的"拿手绝活",同时,阵阵快乐而又空洞的笑声时时在夏日的夜空下响起

43. and floating in the Sound was a triangle of silver scales, trembling a little to the stiff, tinny drip of the banjoes on the lawn　银色的三角形天秤星座浮现在桑德海湾的上空,随着草坪上铿锵的、细雨如珠似的琴声微微地颤动

44. a rowdy little girl　一个吵吵嚷嚷/爱闹腾的女孩

to <u>give way</u> upon the slightest provocation <u>to</u> uncontrollable laughter　一经小小的挑逗,就忍不住要大笑

be enjoying oneself　正在自得其乐

<u>at a lull</u> in the entertainment　在娱乐活动的短暂间隙中

45. and the scene had changed before my eyes into something significant, elemental, and profound　我眼前的景象已变得既质朴又深邃,意味深长

46. It was on the tip of my tongue to ask his name when Jordan looked around and smiled　我话到嘴边,想问他的名字,这时乔丹走来,环顾四周,微微一笑。

47. to <u>wave my hand at</u> the invisible hedge in the distance　对着远处看不见的篱笆摆了摆手

to send his chauffeur with an invitation　派他的司机送来一张邀请函

much more than understandingly　远远不止/只是理解

old sport　[美俚]老弟(对人的一种友好、随意的称呼,不分年龄)

48. It was one of those rare smiles with a quality of <u>eternal reassurance</u> in it, that you may <u>come across</u> four or five times in life.　这是难得一见的笑容,带有一种使人永远放心的感觉,一生中你也只可能遇到四五次。

49. to face the whole external world <u>for an instant</u>　一瞬间,(这笑容)朝向了整个外部世界

to <u>concentrate on</u> you with an irresistible prejudice <u>in your favor</u>　(然后)又带着不可抗拒的偏爱关注着你

＊ in your favor = in favor of you　支持/赞成你

an elegant young roughneck　一位儒雅却又带点鲁莽的男子

elaborate formality of speech　说话文绉绉的,有点拘谨

just miss being absurd　仅免于荒诞,几乎达到荒诞可笑的程度

be picking his words with care　字斟句酌,小心谨慎

50. and assured you that it had precisely the impression of you that, at your best, you hoped to convey.　(这笑容)让你相信他对你的印象,正是你希望表达的最佳时刻的印象

＊ it 指的是 the smile。

51. to identify himself　他自报身份

to call sb. on the wire　有电话找某人

to excuse himself with a small bow　微微一躬,请求原谅/表示抱歉

to constrain to assure her of my surprise　不得不向她表明我的惊讶

a florid and corpulent person in his middle years　一位面色红润、发了福的中年人

<u>be started on</u> the subject　开始琢磨起这个问题,对这个话题感兴趣

to answer with a wan smile　带着倦怠的微笑回答道

to <u>take shape</u> behind him　在他的身后形成/成形

to have the effect of stimulating my curiosity　产生的效果就是刺激了我的好奇心

to <u>spring from</u> the swamps of Louisiana or from the lower East Side of New York　从路易斯安那州的沼泽地或者纽约东城的贫民窟跳出来

in my provincial inexperience　根据我的狭隘经验

to drift coolly out of nowhere and buy a palace on Long Island Sound　(一个人)不知从什么地方不声不响地冒出来,在长岛的桑德湾买了一座宫殿

changing the subject with an urban distaste for the concrete　带着城市人对具体事物不感兴趣的情绪,改换了话题

the boom of a bass drum　低音鼓咚咚的响声

orchestra leader　乐队指挥

to ring out suddenly above the echolalia of the garden （乐队指挥）突然发出的声音盖过了花园里的嘈杂声

at the request of Mr. Gatsby 应盖茨比先生的邀请

to smile with jovial condescension 愉快地采取俯就的态度,微微一笑

52. The nature of Mr. Tostoff's composition <u>eluded me</u>, because just as it began my eyes fell on Gatsby, ... 陀斯托夫先生乐曲的精髓已不为我所记得,因为演奏一开始,我的眼睛就一直盯在盖茨比身上……

53. His tanned skin <u>was drawn</u> attractively <u>tight</u> on his face and his short hair looked as though it <u>were trimmed</u> every day. 晒得黑红的皮肤紧绷在他的脸上,颇有魅力,他的短发仿佛每天都经过修剪。

54. I wondered if the fact that he was not drinking helped <u>to set him off from</u> his guests, for it seemed to me that he grew more correct as the fraternal hilarity increased. 不知道是不是当时他不饮酒突显出了他的与众不同,因为对我来说,这种友好的狂欢越热烈,似乎就越显得他正统。

55. to see nothing sinister about him 看不出他有任何邪气

to set him off his guests 使他有别于众宾客,使他于众宾客中突显出不同

to put their heads on men's shoulders <u>in a puppyish, convivial way</u> 像尽情玩乐的哈巴狗似的,把头靠在男人的肩上

to <u>swoon backward</u> playfully <u>into</u> men's arms, even into groups 闹着玩似的假装晕倒在男人们的怀里,甚至往人堆里倒

knowing that someone would arrest their falls 知道后面会有人把她们托住

56. and no <u>French bob</u> touched Gatsby's shoulder, and no singing quarters were <u>formed with Gatsby's head for one link</u> 没有一个时髦的卷发女郎把头靠在盖茨比的肩上,也没有一个歌舞的人群是以盖茨比为中心形成的

57. <u>raising her eyebrows at me</u> in astonishment 她吃惊地向我高高扬起眉毛

to have jauntiness about her movements 她的一举一动都显出轻松活泼、无忧无虑

to walk upon <u>golf courses</u> on clean, crisp mornings 在清新凉爽的早晨漫步在高尔夫球场上

confused and intriguing sounds 乱哄哄的却又引人注意的声音

to <u>issue from</u> a long, many-windowed room which overhung the terrace （声音）从一个突出于平台之上的、长长的有很多窗户的房间里传出来

58. Eluding Jordan's undergraduate, who was now engaged in an obstetrical conversation with two chorus girls, and who implored me to join him, I went inside. 乔丹的那位大学生,正和合唱队的两个女孩谈堕胎的问题,他恳求我也参加,为了躲开他,我走进了房间。

59. to <u>engage in</u> song 正在唱歌

to fill it (= the pause in the song) with gasping, broken sobs 歌唱的停顿之处,总是喘气和断断续续的抽泣

to take up the lyric again in a quavering soprano （然后）以颤抖的女高音接着唱那抒情歌曲

to course <u>down her cheeks</u> 顺面颊流下

60. ..., for when they <u>came into contact with</u> her heavily beaded eyelashes they assumed an inky color, and pursued the rest of their way in slow black rivulets. 因为当眼泪触到涂多了眼睫膏而结团的睫毛时,泪珠就变成了墨水色,形成两道缓慢流动的黑色小溪,继续余下的行程。

61. ..., whereupon she <u>throw up</u> her hands, <u>sink into</u> a chair, and <u>go off into</u> a deep vinous sleep. 对此（建议）,她向空中挥了挥手,一屁股坐到了椅子上,酒醉如泥地沉沉入睡。

62. <u>be rent asunder</u> by dissension 由于意见分歧而分裂开来

be talking with curious intensity to a young actress　正带着强烈的好奇心与一位年轻的女演员交谈

to attempt to laugh at the situation in a dignified and indifferent way 对眼前的情况,试图保持尊严,装作若无其事,一笑置之

to resort to flank attacks　采取/诉诸旁敲侧击的方法

to hiss："You promised!" into his ear　对着她的耳朵,尖声嘘道:"你答应过的!"

be occupied by two deplorably sober men　（大厅里）只有两个可悲的清醒（没有酒醉）的男人

to sympathize with each other in slightly raised voices　提高了一点嗓门互相倾诉/互表同情

63. The reluctance to go home was not confined to wayward men.　不愿回家的情绪,并不限于任性妄为的男子。

64. Such malevolence was beyond credibility.　这样的恶劣居心令人难以置信。

65. . . . , but the eagerness in his manner tightened abruptly into formality as several people approached him to say good-bye.　当几个人走来与他告别时,他言谈举止中的急切之情,顿时收敛为拘谨守礼。

66. But I swore I wouldn't tell it and here I am tantalizing you.　但我发过誓不讲这件事,我这儿是跟你逗乐呢。

67. to yawn gracefully in my face　在我面前优雅地打了个哈欠

to wave a jaunty salute　轻松活泼地挥手致意

to melt into her party at the door　在门口融进她的伙伴之中

68. . . . , he rejoined me eagerly. "Don't give it another thought, old sport. "　他急切地嘱咐我:"老弟,别再想这件事了。"

69. The familiar expression held no more familiarity than the hand which reassuringly brushed my shoulder.　这一亲切的称呼(老弟)固然友好,但他用手抚慰我的肩膀则更加暖人心。

70. and suddenly there seemed to be a pleasant significance in having been among the last to go, as if he had desired it all the time　突然之间,感到待到最后一批走,似乎有了令人愉快的意义,仿佛他一直期待这一场景

71. The caterwauling horns had reached a crescendo and I turned away and cut down across the lawn toward home.　猫叫春似的汽车喇叭一声高过一声,我转身穿过草坪,回家了。

72. A wafer of a moon was . . . making the night fine as before, and surviving the laughter and the sound of his still glowing garden.　薄片似的一轮月亮……使夜色姣好如前,花园里灯火依旧,而人们的欢声笑语却消失了。

　＊ survive　vt. 活得/存在得比……长久;既然明月、夜色和灯光都比人声笑语存在得长久,那么,消失的就是欢声笑语了。

73. endowing the figure of the host with complete isolation　赋予主人的身影一种完全的孤独感

in a formal gesture of farewell　摆出一种正式的告别姿势

主要内容归纳和总结

1. 斯科特·菲兹杰拉德1896年出生在明尼苏达州圣·保罗(St. Paul),父亲经商,虽屡经失败,却依然保持上层阶级的风度,母亲有爱尔兰血统。祖父的遗产帮助他在普林斯顿(Priceton)的私立学校接受了良好的教育。后来由于疾病缠身,1917年他未毕业就提前离开大学,曾在亚拉巴马州(Alabama)从过军。他很早就进行文学创作,24岁就出版了他的第一本小说《天堂的这一边》(*This Side of Paradise*),一举成名。

菲兹杰拉德的小说最好地体现了爵士时代的精神,兴趣重点在描写上层社会,尤其是上层社会的年轻人。他们迷恋名利场(be infatuated with vanity),纵情声色(drown themselves in sex and pleasures),尽情享乐,不懂得社会责任,认为无须自己努力,社会自然会改善。作者虽也纵酒癫狂(drink much and do crazy things),但总能置身事外(standing aloof),冷眼观察同时代的众生百态(keeping an cold eye on the performance of his contemporaries),认识到当时纸醉金迷的社会状态(the corruptive nature of the society and the vanity fair)不会有光明的未来。

他的文风直言坦率,冷静从容(explicit and chilly),遵循詹姆士时代的文学传统,采用现场描写的方法(scenic method),常用反语冷嘲(ironic),以"集中意识"(central consciousness)观察各种事件。

2. 菲兹杰拉德的主要作品:

a. 长篇小说

《天堂的这一边》*This Side of Paradise*(1920)

《美丽而遭骂的人》*The Beautiful and Damned*(1922)

《了不起的盖茨比》*The Great Gatsby*(1925)

《夜色温柔》*Tender is the Night*(1934)

《最后的巨头》*The Last Tycoon* 未完成

b. 短篇小说

《吹捧者与哲学家》*Flappers and Philosophers*(1921)

《爵士时代的故事》*Tales of the Jazz Age*(1922)

《所有悲伤的小伙子》*All the Sad Young Men* 1926

《起床号》*Taps at Reveille*(1935)

《重访巴比伦》*Babylon Revisited*(1930)

重要信息句子

1. Francis Scott Fitzgerad was a most representative figure of the 1920s, who was a mirror of the exciting age in almost every way.

2. Fitzgerald's fictional world is the best embodiment of the spirit of the Jazz Age, in which he shows a particular interest in the upper-class society, especially the upper-class young people.

3. Fitzgerald is a great stylist in American literature. His styles, closely related to his themes, is explicit and chilly(直言坦率,冷静从容).

V. 欧内斯特·海明威 Ernest Hemingway(1899~1961)

词语解释和难句分析

1. be a good son in the sense that he complied with his parents' expectation 在顺从父母的意愿方面,他是个孝子

﹡ in the sense that ...　在……的意义上

to provide him with materials that he drew on for some of his best writing　为他的一些最佳作品提供了创作素材

　﹡ to draw on　利用,花费,凭借

be not comfortable with the polite, effete, but curiously materialistic culture of his time　他并不安心于那个时代高雅、柔弱却又过分讲究的物质主义文化

to serve as an honorable junior officer in the Red Cross Ambulance Corps　担任红十字会救护队一位颇有名气的下级官员

be awarded the Nobel Prize for literature　被授予诺贝尔文学奖

2. (be) exposed to and victimized by violence in various forms　经常耳闻目睹形形色色的暴力行为,并深受其害

with all the dignity and courage he could muster　怀着他所能激发起来的尊严和勇气

to confront situations which are not of his own choosing yet threaten his destruction　勇敢地面对他无法选择却预示着他的毁灭的种种局势

　﹡ threaten　预示,是……的征兆

to seek to endow prose with the density of poetry, making each image, each scene, and each rendered act serve several purposes　竭力给散文赋予诗歌的凝练,使每一个意象,每一个情景,每一个表演的动作具有多重的意义

3. to cast light on a whole generation after the First World War　清晰地表现了一战后的整个一代人

by way of a vivid portrait of "The Lost Generation"　通过"迷惘的一代"栩栩如生的形象……

to engage themselves in writing in a new way about their own experiences　他们自己投身写作,用新的方法写出了亲身经历

be caught in the war and removed from the path of ordinary life　(他们)陷入了战争,脱离了正常的生活轨道

4. to write the epitaph to a decade and to the whole generation in the 1920s　为 20 世纪 20 年代的 10 年和那个时期的整整一代人写了墓志铭

be disillusioned with the insanity and futility of the universe　对宇宙的非理性和无聊无效感到幻灭

to find some peace by disengaging themselves from society so as to concentrate on the intensity of their emotional life　通过脱离社会约束,找到和平宁静,以便全心全意享受他们热烈的爱情生活

the sense of doom　注定灭亡/世界末日的感觉

5. In this novel, Hemingway not only emphasizes his belief that man is trapped both physically and mentally, but goes to some lengths to refute the idea of nature as an expression of either God's design or his beneficence and to suggest that man is doomed to be entrapped.　在这部小说里,海明威不仅强调了他的关于人在肉体上和精神上都受到羁绊和困顿的信念,而且还花费一定力气驳斥了大自然就是上帝意图和仁慈的表现这种观念,暗示人类是笃定要被投入命运的陷阱的。

6. *The Old Man and the Sea* is a triumph, a tender fulfillment of the affirmative attitude that makes its first successful appearance in *For Whom the Bell Tolls*.　《老人与海》是积极乐观人生态度的一次胜利,一次可以感觉到的满足,这种情感曾在《丧钟为谁敲响》中第一次得到过成功的表现。

7. capping his career and leading to his receipt of the Nobel Prize　他的创作事业达到顶峰,使他获得了诺贝尔文学奖

(be) known for the Hemingway hero of athletic prowess and masculinity and unyielding heroism　以描写了具有运动员的勇猛、阳刚和不屈不挠精神的海明威式的英雄而著称

to present his philosophy about life and death through <u>the depiction</u> of the bullfight <u>as</u> a kind of microcosmic tragedy　通过把斗牛描写为一场微观宇宙的悲剧，展示了他的生死观

8. *The Green Hills of Africa* is about how the writer can survive against the threats to his talents of genteel traditions in America: success, money, and domestic entanglements.　《非洲的青山》讲的是作家怎样才能够顶住美国上流社会的传统——成功、金钱和家庭纠纷——对他们天才的威胁。

9. to attempt to <u>redeem</u> his imagination <u>from</u> the corrosions of wealth and domestic strife　力图从财富的腐蚀和家庭的纷争中找回他的想象力

to show Hemingway's characteristic pattern of a lonely individual struggling against nature and the environment　表现出海明威式的一个人孤独地与大自然和环境做斗争的人物类型

to measure them against an unvarying code　以不变的道德标准衡量他们

grace under pressure　压力下的风度/优雅

10. Those who survive <u>in the process of</u> seeking to master the code with the honesty, the discipline, and the restraint are Hemingway code heroes.　那些在生存斗争中一直在追求诚实、律己和克制的道德标准的人，就是海明威式的英雄。

11. However, though life is but a losing battle, it is a struggle man <u>can</u> dominate <u>in such a way that</u> loss becomes dignity.　然而虽然人生仅仅是失败的战斗，但它却是人可主宰的斗争——失败也保持尊严。

12. And this concern, closely connected with the code, even has the resonance that has <u>come to mark</u> his prose style.　这个主题与道德准则密切联系，甚至产生共鸣，这种共鸣最终成为他的文风特点。

13. Typical of this "iceberg" analogy is Hemingway's style, which he had been trying hard to get. = Hemingway's style is typical of this "iceberg" analogy, ...　这种"冰山"的类比是典型的海明威风格，他一直在努力表现这种风格。

14. to <u>set down exactly</u> every particular kind of feeling without any authorial comments, ... and with a bare minimum of adjectives and adverbs　精确地再现每一个特定情感，而不需任何作者的评论，……形容词和副词的使用也要最少

15. Seemingly simple and natural, Hemingway's style is actually polished and tightly controlled, but highly suggestive and connotative.　海明威的文风看似简单自然，实际上是经过精心修饰和严格掌控的，而且有深刻的暗示和含蓄的内涵。

16. While rendering vividly the <u>outward physical events and sensations</u> Hemingway expresses the meaning of the story and conveys the complex emotions of his characters with a considerable range and astonishing <u>intensity of feeling</u>.　在生动地表现外部事件和客观感受的同时，海明威以广阔的背景和令人惊讶的激情表达了故事的内涵和人物的复杂情怀。

17. (the characters) be <u>full of flesh and blood</u>　人物塑造得有血有肉/血肉丰满

to <u>have an effect of</u> clearness, terseness and great care　产生的效果是清晰、简练和严谨

be praised by the Nobel Prize Committee for "his powerful style-forming mastery of the art" of creating modern fiction　因为他在现代小说创作中"艺术精湛，形成独特风格（对形成风格的艺术技巧的有力把握）"而受到诺贝尔奖评定委员会的赞扬

18. This ruthless economy in his writing stands as a striking application of Mies van der Rohe's architectural maxim: "Less is more."　他写作中节约文字到了冷酷无情的程度，明显地利用了德裔美国建筑师密斯·范·德·罗厄的建筑学格言："简洁的更丰富。"

　　* stand as　表现为，突出地显示出

海明威作品选读

《印第安营地》*Indian Camp* 选自《在我们的时代》*In Our Time*

词语解释和难句分析

1. be representative of the early twentieth-century experience 代表了 20 世纪初的经历

   a reference to the well-known phrase from the Book of Common Prayer 参考/借鉴普通祷告者书上著名的警句……

   be devoted to a carefully planned account of Nick's character 重点对尼克的性格进行了仔细的描写

2. to deliver an Indian woman of a baby by Caesarian section, with a jack-knife and without anesthesia 用一把大折刀/折叠刀,未做麻醉,就给一个印第安妇女做剖腹产,接生孩子

   to bring the boy into contact with something that is perplexing and unpleasant 使这个男孩接触到了某种令人困惑和感到不安的事情

   Nick's initiation into the plain and violence of birth and death 尼克开始接触降生和死亡的痛苦和暴力

   an outward and visible sign of an inward and spiritual disgrace 内心精神世界失去尊严的外部表现

3. There was another rowboat drawn up. 还有一只划船停在那里。

   * drawn up 是过去分词短语,作 rowboat 的后置定语。

   to get in the stern of the boat 跨上船的尾部

   to shove the boat off 撑/推船离岸

   to hear the oarlocks of the other boat quite away ahead of them in the mist 雾中听到另一艘小船的桨架在领先我们很远的地方发出的声音

   to row with quick choppy strokes 频率很快地一下连着一下地划桨

   to pull the boat way up on the beach 把船拖上湖滩

4. through the meadow that was soaking wet with dew 走过被露水打湿的一片草地

   to follow a trail that leads to the logging road that runs back into the hills 沿着一条通向伐木滑道的小路走去,又折回到山里

   * that runs back into the hills 是 the logging road 的定语从句,路曲曲弯弯进了山,人自然也跟着进了山。

5. It was much lighter on the logging road as the timber was cut away on both sides. 伐木运输道/滑道要明亮得多,因为道两侧的树木都被砍掉了。

6. to come around a bend 绕了一个弯到了

   the lights of the shanties where the Indian barkpeelers lived 剥树皮的印第安人居住的小木屋里的灯光

   to lie inside on a wooden bunk 躺在屋里的一张木床上

   be going to have her baby 她就要生孩子了

   to have moved off up the road to sit in the dark and smoke out of range of the noise she made 走到屋外的路上,坐在黑暗里听不到她喊叫声的地方抽烟

7. What she is going through is called being in labor. 她正经历的是分娩/生孩子的过程。

8. to haven't any anesthetic　没有任何麻醉药

　　to <u>roll over against</u> the wall　翻过身背对着墙

　　to <u>motion to</u> the doctor that the water is hot.　向医生打了个手势,示意水已烧热了

　　be supposed to be born head first　希望孩子出生时头部先出来

　　to have to <u>operate on</u> this lady　得为这个妇女做手术

　　the young Indian who has <u>rowed</u> Uncle George <u>over</u>　那个划船送乔治叔叔来的印第安青年

9. There's some stitches to <u>put in</u>.　还要缝合几针。

10. I'm going to <u>sew up</u> the incision I made.　我要缝合手术的刀口。

11. to <u>put</u> the basin <u>out in</u> the kitchen　把脸盆拿出去放进厨房

　　to <u>smile reminiscently</u>　意味深长地笑着

　　to <u>put</u> some peroxide <u>on</u> that (= the incision)　在刀口/伤口上了一些过氧化物

　　be feeling exalted and talkative　感到得意,而且话多

　　doing a Caesarian with a jack-knife and sewing it up with nine-foot, <u>tapered gut leaders</u>　用一把折叠刀做剖腹产手术,用九英尺细羊肠线做缝合

　　the worst sufferers in these little affairs　在这些"小事"中,最受罪/折磨的人

12. I must say he took it all pretty quietly.　我敢说他非常镇定地承受了一切。

13. to <u>mount on the edge of</u> the lower bunk with the lamp in one hand and look in　他手里拿了盏灯,蹬着下床的边,爬了上去,朝里看

　　(blood) to have <u>flowed down into a pool</u> where his body sagged the bunk　他身体在床上压出了一个窝,血流了一摊

14. The open razor lay, edge up, in the blankets.　那把打开的剃刀,口朝上,摆在毯子上。

15. to <u>have a good view of</u> the upper bunk　把那个固定在墙上的上床看得一清二楚

　　to <u>tip</u> the Indian's head <u>back</u>　把那个印第安人的头扳了回来/扶正

　　all his post-operative exhilaration gone　手术后所有的兴奋都消失了

16. It was an awful mess to <u>put you through</u>.　让你经历了这样的事情,太可怕了。/让你看到了一件可怕的事情。

17. He'll <u>turn up</u> all right.　他就会好起来的。

　　＊ turn up = get better　康复

18. It all depends.　这要看情况。

19. to <u>trail</u> his hand in the water　他把一只手伸进水里,随船移动

主要内容归纳和总结

1. 海明威,美国最伟大的作家之一,1954 年因《老人与海》获得诺贝尔文学奖,达到他文学创作的最高峰。

　　他出生在伊利诺伊州奥克帕克(Oak Park),父亲是个很成功的外科医生。中学毕业后,他离家去堪萨斯城做记者工作。在第一次世界大战中,他是美国红十字会救护队的工作人员,双腿严重受伤,战后去巴黎,作为外国记者被《多伦多星报》(The Toronto Star)聘用。由于受到当时的名作家舍伍德·安德森(Sherwood Anderson)、斯蒂芬·克兰(Stephen Crane)和格特鲁德·斯泰因(Gertrude Stein)的影响,他开始文学创作,成为引人注意的作家。后来他积极投身西班牙内战和第二次世界大战,经历丰富,写下了大量作品。1961 年,他因不堪忍受病痛和精神抑郁,用猎枪自杀。

2. 海明威的主要作品：
   a. 短篇小说集
   《在我们的时代》*In Our Time*（1925）
   《没有女人的男人》*Men Without Women*（1927），包括：
   * 《未被击败的人》*The Undefeated*
   * 《杀人者》*The Killers*
   * 《五万元》*Fifty Grand*
   《午后之死》*Death in the Afternoon*（1932）
   《非洲的青山》*The Green Hills of Africa*（1935）
   《乞力马扎罗的雪》*The Snows of Kilimanjaro*（1936）
   《有与没有》*To Have and Have Not*（1937）
   b. 中长篇小说
   《春潮》*The Torrents of Spring*（1925）
   《太阳照样升起》*The Sun Also Rises*（1926）
   《永别了，武器》*A Farewell to Arms*（1929）
   《丧钟为谁敲响》*For Whom the Bell Tolls*（1940）
   《老人与海》*The Old Man and the Sea*（1952）
3. 海明威作品的主要风格特点
   a. 讲故事、写人物都如冰山一角，含蓄内敛，任由读者联想。
   b. 以同一道德标准塑造出同一环境背景下产生的海明威式的英雄：诚实、自律和克制，保持"压力下的风度"（grace under pressure）或曰"在生活的重压下保持自尊"。
   c. 人物语言口语化，笔墨经济、文字节约到冷酷无情的程度，"清晰，简练，严谨"（clearness, simple and great care）是其鲜明特点。他始终坚守建筑大师密斯·范·德·罗厄的建筑学格言："简洁的更丰富。"（Less is more.）

重要信息句子

1. Hemingway's world is limited. He deals with a limited range of characters in quite similar circumstances and measures them against an unvarying code, known as "grace under pressure."
2. In the general situation of his novels, life is full of tension and battles; the world is in chaos; man is always fighting desperately a losing battle.
3. Typical of this "iceberg" analogy is Hemingway's style, which he had been trying hard to get.

VI. 威廉·福克纳 William Faulkner（1897~1962）

词语解释和难句分析

1. simultaneously original and assimilative　既独创又兼收并蓄/吸收同化
   the most frequently and intensely interpreted writer of modern American literature　现代美国文学最经

常被热烈讨论的作家

to have been a local legend　已成为一个地方传奇人物

be the kind of <u>dynamic personality</u> around whom Faulkner's fiction develops　那种充满活力个性的名人,福克纳常围绕他构思小说

a reclusive man　一个不善交际的人

<u>be</u> increasingly <u>motivated to</u> become a writer　越来越有积极性当作家

to <u>enlist in</u> the British Royal Flying Corps　应征入伍,参加了英国皇家飞行队

2. In writing *Sartoris*, Faulkner began to see and feel the dignity and sorrow of what was to become his most frequently used subject matter.　在写《萨特瑞斯》时,福克纳看到并感受到了要成为他最常用主题对象的尊严和悲伤。

3. be thematically interwoven　主题相互交织

<u>not</u> to receive <u>a significant boost</u> <u>until</u> the publication of an anthology of his writings, *The Portable Faulkner*, edited by the critic Malcolm Cowley　直到批评家玛卡姆·卡莱编辑的福克纳代表作品集《袖珍福克纳》出版,才引起巨大的轰动

stratified society　等级社会

to have become an allegory or a parable of the Old South　已变成保守南方的一个象征或一个寓言

4. The Yoknapatawpha County series have an <u>overall pattern</u> in which the fate of a <u>ruined homeland</u> always <u>focuses on</u> the collision of Faulkner's intelligent, sensitive, and idealistic protagonist with the society of the twentieth century.　约克纳帕塔法系列小说有一个总体构架,作者总是借聪慧、敏感和理想主义的主人公与20世纪社会现实的碰撞反映失去家园的命运。

5. First of all, Faulkner exemplified T. S. Eliot's <u>concept</u> of modern society <u>as</u> a wasteland <u>in a dramatic way</u>.　首先,福克纳以激烈的文笔,用实例描写和解释了T. S. 艾略特现代社会即荒原的观念。

6. a kind of <u>cash register</u> like Jason Compson　一种像杰森·康普森一样的现金出纳机

to have lost his natural <u>response to</u> life, become <u>incapable of</u> love, mean, <u>money-minded</u>, and spiritually dead　他已经失去了对生活的自然反应,变成不会爱、吝啬小气、满脑子金钱、精神死亡的人

7. They are tragic because they are prisoners of the past, or of the society, or of some social and moral taboo, or of their own introspective personalities.　他们之所以有悲剧性命运,是因为他们为过去或社会的思想所禁锢,为某些社会道德禁忌所限制,或者为自己内在的人格个性所束缚。

8. By describing his protagonists the way he does, Faulkner suggests that society, which <u>conditions</u> man with its hierarchical stratification and with its laws and institutions, eliminates man's chance of <u>responding naturally to</u> the experiences of his existence.　福克纳以自己的方法描写主人公,暗示由于社会以不同等级的阶层和法律制度制约人,所以就剥夺了人自然反应自己人生经历的机会。

9. Against this imprisoned, confused, fragmented social being is the primitive man who, not conditioned by the civilization and social institutions, accepts the life-death pattern of human existence unquestionably, hence, attains an enviable strength and peace.　与这种受束缚、被困惑、四分五裂的社会存在相对应的是原始人类,由于他们不受社会文明和制度的制约,所以自然地(毫无疑问地)接受了人类生活的生死方式,因此,也就得到了令人称羡的力量和安宁。

10. Man, by <u>turning away from</u> reality, by <u>alienating</u> himself <u>from</u> truth with his attempts to explain the inexplicable, becomes weak and cowardly, confused and ineffectual.　人类,企图解释无法解释的东西,脱离了现实,远离了事实,因而变得弱小、胆怯、迷惘和无所作为。

11. be masterpieces by any standards　按任何标准都是杰作

to set off the present　通过对比衬托/突出现在

the immediate past — the world of childhood, innocent, and idealistic　最近的过去——天真、幻想的

童年世界

12. Faulkner once said that *The Sound and the Fury* is a story of "lost innocence," which proves itself to be an intensification of the theme of imprisonment in the past.　福克纳曾经说过,《喧嚣和骚动》写的是"失去天真"的故事,它强化了时事已变、思想还束缚在过去的时代主题。

13. to develop the theme of deterioration and loss by juxtaposing the childhood of the Compson brothers with their present experience　通过并列对比康普森兄弟的童年生活和今天的体验,表现出往事如烟、人生颓败的小说主题

with Caddy as the focal point of the juxtaposition to emphasize the theme of loss　以卡迪作为对比的焦点,突出了往事不可追的主题

Quentin's nostalgic feeling about past　昆丁对往事的怀旧情感

to remain <u>trapped within</u> its past　依然沉湎于往事之中

to convey a strong <u>sense of grief over</u> the deterioration of the South　传达出对南方日益衰败强烈的哀伤情怀

14. In *Light in August*, the mental landscape of the South is portioned into three separate fields on which operate <u>representatives of three</u> different attitudes toward life.　在《八月之光》中,南方人的精神世界分成三个独立的领域,这三个领域代表了三种人生态度。

　* 在 on which 引导的定语从句中,主语是 representatives of three different attitudes..., 谓语是 operate,"起作用,产生影响"的意思,on which = on the three fields 是状语。

15. be plainly obsessions, represented by the male characters as main protagonists　明显是沉湎,是男性主角所表现的沉湎

with Reverend Hightower <u>obsessed with</u> the past, the defeat of the South and Joe Christmas (obsessed) with blood or race　瑞弗伦·海塔沉湎于南方被打败的过去,乔·克瑞斯莫斯则沉湎于流血或种族冲突

to <u>contrast with</u> the other two in almost every aspect　与前两种在各方面有所不同

be concerned solely with <u>bringing forth</u> and preserving life　只关心创造新生活和维持新生活

16. *Absalom, Absalom*! is a novel entirely interpretation, the attempts of several characters — Miss Rosa, Mr. Compson, Quentin, and Shreve — to explain the past, <u>characterized by involutions of</u> narrative structure which express corresponding complexities of meaning.　《押沙龙,押沙龙!》完全是一部解释性小说,试图用露莎小姐、康普森先生、昆丁和施利夫几个人来解释过去,其特点是采用了可表达相应的复杂意义的叙述结构。

　*（be）characterized by 以……为特点;by involutions of 利/采用

17. a novel about history as an <u>epistemological problem</u>　一部把历史当作认识论问题的小说

to try to establish himself among the social elite of the South　试图跻身于南方的社会精英阶层/在南方的上流社会中确立自己的地位

with Quentin as the representing voice　以昆丁作为代言人

18. *Go Down, Moses* is in a sense a companion piece to *Absalom, Absalom*!, but at the same time another and very different attempt to handle the Southern reality of land, family and the plantation as a form of life.　《走下去,摩西》从某种意义上来说是《押沙龙,押沙龙!》的姐妹篇,但同时又是另一种非常不同的尝试,它反映了南方把土地、家庭和种植园当作一种生命形式的社会现实。

19. ..., in which (*The Besr*) family clans representing different social groups <u>are involved in</u> Faulkner's complex of themes about the South, ...　（在小说《熊》中,）代表不同社会集团的家族都进入了福克纳关于南方主题的作品的复杂情节之中。

20. to illuminate the problem of black and white in Southern society as a <u>close-knit</u> destiny of blood

brotherhood　反映了南方社会命运休戚相关的血亲兄弟——黑人和白人之间存在的问题

the moral abomination of slavery and the human entanglements which <u>result from</u> it　奴隶制的道德沦丧和由它而起的种种人间仇怨

to go beyond history, to the beginnings, to the mythic time　超越历史,追溯到历史的起源,追溯到神话的时代

skillfully <u>employ</u> an old crafty bear <u>as</u> a symbol of the timeless freedom of the wilderness　技巧娴熟地把一只狡猾的老熊作为大自然的荒野中永远自由的象征

21. to add to the theory of the novel as an art form and evolve his own literary strategies　为小说这种艺术形式丰富了理论,形成了他自己的创作技巧

to explore and represent the infinite possibilities inherent in human life　探索和表现人类生活所传承下来的无限可能性

to observe with no judgment whatsoever and reduce authorial intrusion <u>to the lowest minimum</u>　不带任何先入之见/偏见地去观察,尽量减少作者的介入

never step between the characters and the reader to explain　千万不要插入小说中的人物和读者之间,企图解释什么

to hinder <u>as little as possible</u> the reader's direct experience of the work of art　尽量不要妨碍读者对艺术作品的直接体验

to fragment the chronological time　打乱时间顺序

to deliberately <u>break up</u> the chronology of his narrative by juxtaposing the past with the present　故意打破按时间顺序进行的叙述,把过去和现在并列着推进

<u>in the way</u> the montage does in a movie　像电影中的蒙太奇手法一样

<u>be good at</u> presenting multiple <u>points of view</u>　擅长于表现多重视觉的观点

with various points of view <u>radiating from</u> it, or different people <u>responding to</u> the same story　各种观点从这个中心辐射出来,或各种不同的人对应着这同一个故事

22. to <u>have a part in</u> influencing Faulkner　对福克纳都有影响,在影响福克纳方面发挥了作用

(be) <u>marked by</u> long and embedded sentences, complex syntax, and vague reference pronouns on the one hand and a variety of "registers" of the English language　其语言特点是一方面多冗长的嵌进句、复杂的句子结构和指称模糊的代词,另一方面是英语语言的"使用域"令人眼花缭乱

23. It is not surprising to find in Faulkner's writings his syntactical structures and verbals paralleled, negatives <u>balanced against</u> positives, compounded adjectives swelling his sentences, complex modifying elements placed after the nouns, etc.　在福克纳的作品中看到排比的句子结构和动词短语,否定与肯定的相互平衡,复合形容词使句子臃肿,名词后跟着一堆修饰成分,等等,并不令人吃惊。

24. to sound very casual or informal sometimes　有时似乎是非常随意或者说不受拘束的

more refined and educated narrators like Quentin　像昆丁那样比较高雅、有教养的叙述者

be most of them <u>drawn from</u> nature　大多数象征和意象都源于大自然

福克纳作品选读

《给艾米莉的玫瑰》A Rose for Emily

词语解释和难句分析

1. Good as his short stories are, they seem always <u>at the threshold of</u> being absorbed into the Yaknapatawpha

saga — that legendary matrix which is Faulkner's real achievements. 尽管他的短篇小说很好，却似乎总是被堵在门口，不能归入约克纳帕塔法英雄传奇，那个传奇的发源地才是他真正的成就。

2. an eccentric spinster who refuses to accept the passage of time 拒绝接受时事变迁的有怪癖的老处女
   be pregnant with meaning 蕴含丰富的意义
   be the symbols of the Old South but the prisoners of the past 是思想束缚在过去的旧南方的象征
   to make best use of the Gothic devices in narration 最好地利用了哥特式的叙述方法

3. ..., the deformed personality and abnormality Emily demonstrates in her relationship with her sweetheart is dramatized in such a way that we feel shocked and thrilled as we read along. 艾米莉在与她心上人的关系上表现出来的畸形个性和心理变态都得到了生动的描写，我们读下去都会感到震惊和毛骨悚然。

4. the men through a sort of respectful affections for a fallen monument, the women mostly out of curiosity to see the inside of her house 男人出于对一座纪念碑倒下的敬慕之情，女人大多是出于好奇，都想看一看她屋子的里面
   no one save an old man-servant 除了一个年老的男仆，就再没有人

5. a big, squarish frame house 一座四方形构架的大房子
   to have been white, decorated with cupolas and spires and scrolled balconies in the heavily lightsome style of the seventies （房屋）带有浓重的 19 世纪 70 年代的轻盈风格：白色，装饰有圆形屋顶、尖塔和涡卷形阳台
   to set on what has once been our most select street 坐落在当年最考究的一条街上
   to have encroached and obliterated even the august names of that neighborhood 甚至已侵占和磨灭了那一带人家的赫赫威名
   lifting its stubborn and coquettish decay above the cotton wagons and the gasoline pumps — an eyesore among eyesores 依然突兀在棉花车和汽油泵中，显示着它的顽固不化和装腔作势却又十分破败的景象
   to have gone to join the representatives of those august names （如今她）已加入到那些显赫名字的代表人物中去了
   to lie in the cedar — bemused cemetery among the ranked and anonymous graves of Union and Confederate soldiers 他们静卧在雪松环绕、仿佛在默默沉思的墓地，周围是一排排北部联邦和南部邦联阵亡的无名将士们的坟墓

6. Alive, Miss Emily had been a tradition, a duty, and a care. 艾米莉小姐在世时，始终是一个传统的化身，义务的化身，也是人们关注的对象。
   * alive = being alive，是分词短语作状语，其逻辑主语就是主句主语 Miss Emily。

7. A sort of hereditary obligation upon the town, dating from that day in 1894 when Colonel Sartoris, the mayor — he who fathered the edict that no Negro woman should appear on the streets without an apron — remitted her taxes, the dispensation dating from the death of her father on into perpetuity. 镇上有一条沿袭下来的义务，就是免除她一切应缴纳的税款，这可追溯到 1894 年镇长萨特瑞斯上校首定法令：黑人妇女不穿围裙不准上街的那一天。免征税款从她父亲去世时开始，直到永远。

8. to invent an involved tale to the effect that ... 编造了一套复杂的故事，大意是……
   to loan money to the town 贷款给镇上
   as a matter of business 作为一种交易
   to prefer this way of repaying 选择了这种偿还的方法

9. Only a man of Colonel Sartoris generation and thought could have invented it. 只有萨特瑞斯上校时代和具有萨特瑞斯思想的人才可能杜撰出这样的方法。

10. to mail her a <u>tax notice</u>　邮给她一个纳税通知

　　to write her a <u>formal letter</u>　给她写了一个正式公函

　　to ask her to <u>call at</u> the sheriff's office <u>at her convenience</u>　请她在方便的时候给司法长官办公室打个电话

　　offering to call or to send his car for her　提出给她打电话和派车去接她

　　to receive in reply a note on paper of <u>an archaic shape</u>, in a thin, flowing calligraphy in faded ink 收到了一封写在古色古香信笺上的回函，字迹细小，书写流畅，墨水已不新鲜

11. The tax notice was also enclosed, without comment.　纳税通知也附在信封里，没表示意见。

12. to call a special meeting of the Board of Aldermen　召集/开一次参议员委员会特别会议

　　to wait upon sb.　侍候/恭候某人，拜访某人

　　to cease giving china-painting lessons years earlier　多年前就不再教瓷器彩绘课了

　　(a stairway) to <u>mount into</u> sill more shadow　（楼梯）向上通入一道更加黑暗的门槛

　　to smell of dust and disuse — a close, dank smell　闻到尘土和废弃物的气味——一股潮湿的久不透气的霉味儿

　　<u>be furnished in</u> heavy, leather-covered furniture　里面陈设着笨重的家具，全都包着皮革

　　to open the blinds of one window　打开一扇窗户的百叶窗

　　(a faint dust) to rise sluggishly about their thighs, spinning with slow motes in the single sun-ray（一阵细微的尘土）从他们的大腿周围慢慢浮动起来，许多尘粒在（透进来的）一缕阳光中缓缓旋转

　　on a tarnished gilt easel　在一个失去光泽的镀金画架上

　　a crayon portrait of Miss Emily's father　一幅艾米莉小姐父亲的炭笔画像

13. with a thin gold chain <u>descending to</u> her waist and <u>vanishing into</u> her belt　一根细金链，直挂到她腰间，进入腰带看不见了

　　<u>leaning on</u> an ebony cane with a tarnished gold head　挂着一根乌木拐杖，金杖头已经褪色

14. Her skeleton was small and spare; perhaps that was why what would have been merely plumpness in another was obesity in her.　她骨架瘦小，也许正应为这个缘故，在别人只是体态丰润，到了她就显得臃肿肥胖了。

15. to look bloated, like a body long <u>submerged in</u> motionless water, and of that pallid hue　样子肥胖臃肿，像泡在死水里很长时间的一具尸体，死白死白的

　　＊ of that pallid hue = like a body of that pallid hue　直译是：像一具非常/那样死白的尸体。

　　her eyes lost in the fatty ridges of her face　她的眼睛陷在脸上隆起的肥肉中，都快看不见了

　　to look like two small pieces of coal pressed into <u>a lump of</u> dough　看起来像两颗嵌在一块生面团里的小煤粒

　　to state their errand　表明了他们的来意/意图/任务

　　to come to a stumbling halt　终于结结巴巴地停下来/结束了讲话

　　to hear the invisible watch ticking at the end of the gold chain　听到那只看不见的表，在金链子那头滴滴答答地响着

　　to <u>gain access</u> to the city records and satisfy yourselves　查阅一下市镇档案，你们就什么都清楚了

　　＊ gain access to　进入

16. But there is nothing on the books to show that, you see. We must <u>go by the</u> —　但是纳税册上没有任何这方面的说明，你明白吧。我们必须根据……来判断。

17. to vanquish them, <u>horse and foot</u>　连人带马完全彻底地打败了他们

　　to have the temerity to call　冒冒失失地登门拜访

　　the only sign of life about the place　那个地方唯一的生命象征

going in and out with a market basket　挎着个赶集/购物的篮子进进出出

to keep a kitchen properly　把厨房收拾得井井有条、干干净净

be another link between the gross, teeming world and the high and mighty Griersons　是粗俗的、芸芸众生的世界与高贵的、有权有势的格里尔森家之间的另一联系

send her word to stop it (= the smell)　通知她清除异味

in diffident deprecation　非常客气地表示反对/抗议

18. I'd be the last one in the world to bother Miss Emily, but we've got to do something.　我是这个世界上最不愿意打搅艾米莉小姐的,但我们得做点儿什么。

19. Send her word to have her place cleaned up. Give her a certain time to do it in.　给她个通知,让她叫人给屋子好好地搞搞清洁,限期搞好。

20. to slink about the house like burglars, sniffing along the base of brickwork and at the cellar openings　像盗贼一样绕着屋子蹑足潜行,在砖墙的墙根和地窖的通风处使劲嗅

to perform a regular sowing motion with his hand out of a sack slung from his shoulder　他的手从挂在肩上的袋子里拿出什么东西来,不停地做着播种的动作

to break open the cellar door and sprinkle lime there, and in all the outbuildings　打开地窖的门,在里面以及所有的外屋里撒上石灰

her upright torso motionless as that of an idol　她笔直的躯干一动不动,像尊偶像

to creep quietly across the lawn and into the shadow of the locusts that line the street　蹑手蹑脚悄悄地穿过草坪,钻进街旁一排刺槐的树荫里

to hold themselves a little too high for what they really are　他们不切实际地高看了自己/自视甚高

to have long thought of them as a tableau　长期以来一直把他们看成一幅画

21. her father (is) a straddled silhouette in the foreground　她父亲叉开双腿的形象占据前面突出的位置

22. the two of them framed by the back flung front door　前门向后打开正好作他们两人的画像的相框/他们两人的画像正好嵌入向后打开的前门的门框

23. We were not pleased exactly, but vindicated; even with insanity in the family she wouldn't have turned down all of her chances if they had really materialized.　我们并没有为此感到真正的高兴,但是我们对这个家族的看法被证明是正确的;尽管这个家族出过神经病,但如果真有求婚的人来了,她也是不会放过一切机会的。

24. When her father died, it got about that the house was all that was left to her; and in a way, people were glad.　她父亲去世时,就有消息流传开来:房子就是留给她的全部遗产;从某一点看,人们还有点高兴。

25. Now she too would know the old thrill and the old despair of a penny more or less.　现在她也知道为一文钱的得失而激动万分和绝望至极。

26. to call at the house and offer condolence and aid, as is our custom　按我们的习惯,到她家拜望,吊唁/表达安慰和给予帮助

to persuade her to let them dispose of the body　劝说她让他们把尸体处理掉

be about to resort to law and force　正要诉诸法律和武力

to break down　垮下来,崩溃,攻克

27. and we know that with nothing left, she would have to cling to that which had robbed her, as people will.　我们知道她现在已一无所有,只好像人们常做的那样,紧紧抓住抢走了她一切的那个人不放

28. with a vague resemblance to those angels in colored church windows — sort of tragic and serene　与教堂彩色玻璃窗上的天使朦胧相似——带点儿悲哀,带点儿安详

to have just let the contracts for paving the sidewalks　刚跟人签了承包合同,铺设人行道

with a big voice and eyes lighter than his face　大嗓门,眼珠比他脸的肤色还浅

to follow in groups to hear him cuss the niggers　成群地跟在后面跑,听到他咒骂那些黑人

to see him and Miss Emily on Sunday afternoons driving in the yellow-wheeled buggy and the matched team of bays from the livery stable　看到他和艾米莉小姐在星期天下午驾车出游,车是黄轮的轻便马车,马是从代养马房挑来的一对枣红马

29. ..., who said that even grief could not cause a real lady to forget noblesse oblige — without calling it noblesse oblige　他们说,即使悲伤也不能使一个真正的贵夫人忘了"贵人举止"——尽管不那么称呼了

30. but years ago her father had fallen out with them over the estate of old lady Wyatt, the crazy woman　但是,多年前她父亲就为了那个疯姑奶奶怀亚特的房产与他们闹翻了

31. "Of course it is. What else could ..." This (was) behind their hands; rustling of craned silk and satin (was) behind jalousies closed upon the sun of Sunday afternoon as the thin, swift clop-clop-clop of the matched team passed: "Poor Emily."　"当然是啰,还能是别的什么?"这句话是捂着嘴轻声说的;当那对枣红马轻快地得得跑过时,尽管关起了百叶窗遮挡星期天午后的骄阳,也还是能听到车上人丝缎衣衫的窸窣声:"唉,可怜的艾米莉。"

　　* craned silk and satin　撑起/鼓起的丝缎衣衫

32. It was as if she demanded more than ever the recognition of her dignity as the last Grierson; as if it had wanted that touch of earthiness to reaffirm her imperviousness.　那高昂头颅的样子,就仿佛她比以往更需要人们承认她格里尔森家族末代子孙的尊严,仿佛这尊严要求世俗的接触重新肯定她不受外界任何影响/刀枪不入的顽固性格。

33. with cold, haughty black eyes in a face the flesh of which was strained across the temples and about the eyesockets as you imagine a lighthouse-keeper's face ought to look　一双黑眼冷酷高傲,面部肌肉绷得紧紧的,直达两边太阳穴和眼窝周围,就像你想象中的灯塔守望人所应有的样子

34. She looked back at him, erect, her face like a strained flag.　她直面回看着他,身板笔直,脸像一面绷紧的旗帜。

　　* erect = being erect = she was erect,可看作做分词短语的状语,也可看作主语补语。

35. ..., her head tilted back in order to look him eye for eye, until he look away and went and got the arsenic and wrapped it up.　她的头向后仰着,好与他双目对视,直到他目光旁顾,走了进去,取了砒霜包起来。

36. When she opened the package at home there was written on the box, under the skull and bones: "For rats."　她在家里打开药包,盒子上骷髅骨标记下有文字注明"毒鼠药"。

　　* 主句的主语是"For rats",其结构可改写得更明显一点: there was "For rats" written under the skull and bones on the box。

37. with his hat cocked and a cigar in his teeth, reins and whip in a yellow glove　他帽檐向上翘着,嘴里叼着雪茄,手戴着黄手套,抓着缰绳和鞭子

to force the Baptist minister to call upon her　强迫浸礼会牧师去拜访她

never divulge what happened during that interview　从不宣布/泄漏那次会晤发生的情况

to drive about the streets　驾着马车在街上兜风

to have blood-kin under her roof again　又有近亲来到她的家

to sit back to watch developments　坐观事态的发展

to have been the jeweler's and ordered a man's toilet set in silver, with the letters H. B. on each piece　曾光顾珠宝首饰店,也曾订购了一套男用盥洗用具,每件上都刻有"H. B."(Homer Barron 的首字母)

to have bought a complete outfit of men's clothing, including a nightshirt　已经买了全套的男子礼服，包括睡衣

be even more Grierson than Miss Emily had ever been　甚至表现得比艾米莉小姐更有格里尔森家族的气概

38. We were a little disappointed that there was not a public blowing-off, ...　我们有点儿失望，竟然没有一场轰动的情感表达，……

39. By that time it was a cabal, and we were all Miss Emily's allies to help circumvent the cousins.　这时，已形成一个阴谋小集团，我们全都是艾米莉的同盟军，帮助她设法击败堂姐妹。

40. Then we knew that this was to be expected too; as if that quality of her father which had thwarted her woman's life so many times had been too virulent and too furious to die.　我们明白那也都在预料之中，就像她父亲的性格——使女儿的人生屡遭挫折的性格——太凶狠、太狂暴，还不肯消逝似的。

41. to fit up a studio in one of the downstairs rooms　在楼下的众多房间里，安排了一间画室

be sent to her with the same regularity　（孩子们）被按时按点/按同样的规律送到她这里来学习

in the same spirit that they were sent to church on Sundays with a twenty-five-cent piece for the collection plate　其精神状态就像他们被送到教堂去做礼拜，还带着两毛五分硬币准备放在捐献盘里一样的神圣、认真

42. The front door closed upon the last one and remained closed for good.　直到最后一个学生都不来了，前门才关上，而且是永远地关上了。

43. to get free postal delivery　实施免费邮递制度

to refuse to let them fasten the metal numbers above her door and attach a mail box to it.　不让他们在她的门上钉金属门牌号和固定邮箱

44. The tax notice would be returned by the post office a week later, unclaimed.　一周后，纳税通知就会被邮局退回，无人认领。

45. like the carven torso of an idol in a niche, looking or not looking at us, we could never tell which（她）像神龛里的一个偶像雕塑的躯干，我们从来都看不出这偶像朝没朝我们看

＊句子的后半部改写如下，就更容易看清结构的意思：we could never tell which was looking or not looking at us. 关系代词 which 指的是 the carven torso of an idol in niche。

46. Thus she passed from generation to generation — dear, inescapable, impervious, tranquil, and perverse.　她就是这样度过了一代人又一代人的漫长时间——昂然突立，躲避不开，渗透不进，出奇的平静，存在有悖常理。

47. with only a doddering Negro man to wait on her　只有一个老态龙钟的黑人男子侍候她的饮食起居

48. for his voice had grown harsh and rusty, as if from disuse　因为他的嗓子已经嘶哑，仿佛是由于长久不用的缘故

＊as if from disuse = as if suffering from disuse

49. to prop on a pillow yellow and moldy with age and lack of sunlight　（头）搁在因长年不见阳光而发黄发霉的枕头上

50. He walked right through the house and out the back and was not seen again.　他直接穿过屋子，从后门走出去，从此不见踪影。

51. with the crayon face of her father musing profoundly above the bier and the ladies sibilant and macabre　在停尸架上方，挂着她父亲的炭笔画像，一脸深刻沉思的表情，另外还有女士们叽叽喳喳谈论死亡的声音

＊(with) the ladies sibilant and macabre = the ladies were sibilant and macabre

52. ..., confusing time with its mathematical progression, as the old do, to whom all the past is not a

diminishing road but, instead, a huge meadow which no winter ever quite touches, <u>divided from them</u> now by the narrow bottle-neck of the most recent decade of years. （老人们）以数学级数的速度很快把时间搞乱了，就像他们通常的那样。对他们来说，过去不是一条越来越窄的路，而是连冬天都不能对它有任何影响的广阔草地，只是最近10年才像狭窄的瓶颈，把他们与过去分隔开来。

* 注意句中 all the past is   divided from ... by ... 结构，相当于 A is divided from B by ... "A 被……把它与 B 分隔开了"。

53. A thin, acrid pall as of the tomb seemed to lie everywhere upon this room decked and furnished as for a bridal.   这装饰和布置得像新房的房间里，似乎处处都有一层薄薄的类似坟墓里尸衣样的东西覆盖着，气味刺鼻难闻。

54. the delicate array of crystal and the man's toilet things <u>backed with</u> tarnished silver   那一排精致的水晶质玻璃制品和失去光泽的银底男人盥洗用具

(be) so tarnished that the monogram was obscured   几乎完全失去了光泽，连上面的人名首字母都模糊不清了

55. Among them lay a collar and tie, as if they had just been removed, which, lifted, left upon the surface a pale crescent in the dust.   种种物件当中摆着一个硬领和一条领带，仿佛刚刚脱下，把它们拿起来，就会在台面的尘埃中留下淡淡的月牙痕。

56. beneath it（chair）the two mute shoes and the discarded socks   椅子下放着两只默默无言的鞋和脱掉不穿了的袜子

<u>looking down at</u> the profound and fleshless grin   俯视着那无肉的高深莫测、龇牙咧嘴的样子

to have apparently once lain <u>in the attitude of</u> an embrace   很明显曾经拥抱着躺在一起

* in the attitude of   以……的姿态

the long sleep that outlasts love, that conquers even the grimace of love   那比爱情更长久、甚至征服了爱情煎熬的长眠

to have <u>become inextricable from</u> the bed   已经与床无法分离了

even coating of the patient and biding dust   均匀的一层长年累月的积尘

the indentation of a head in the second pillow   头在第二个枕头上留下的凹痕

that faint and invisible dust dry and acrid in the nostrils   鼻子里嗅到那股淡淡的、无形的气味难闻的干尘土味儿

* dry and acrid，"干燥难闻"的意思，是 dust 的后置定语。

a long <u>strand of</u> iron-gray hair   一长绺铁灰色的长发

主要内容归纳和总结

1. 威廉·福克纳是一个既有独创性又对能外来文化兼收并蓄的美国作家。他1897年出生在密西西比州的新阿尔伯纳，长在牛津附近，并在那里待了一辈子。祖父福克纳上校参加过美国内战，是地方上的传奇人物，也是作家许多故事的源泉。母亲才思敏捷，有雄心壮志，对他的影响较大。他只在密西西比大学读了一年书就辍学了，却越来越想当作家。1918年他应征加入英国皇家飞行大队，被派到加拿大训练，在朋友菲尔·斯通(Phil Stone)和舍伍德·安德森(Sherwood Anderson)的帮助下，出版了第一卷诗歌《大理石农牧之神》(The Marble Faun)和第一部小说《士兵的薪酬》(Soldiers' Pay)。1926年的欧洲之旅使他了解了弗洛伊德的心理分析和乔伊斯(James Joyce)的意识流实验创作。另外，对他后来的创作产生巨大影响的还有埃德加·爱伦·坡的哥特式小说(Gothic novel)和纳撒尼尔·霍桑的象征主义(symbolism)写作手法。

福克纳的大多数作品都以美国南方为背景,以南方人的思想意识为重点。他把度过童年时代的牛津小镇作为小说中想象的背景之地——密西西比州北部的约克纳帕塔法县。

他的创作从不把自己的先入之见带给读者,而是让人物自己去表现,让读者去判断;他的叙述常不按时间顺序,过去和现在常并列交织;他娴熟地运用意识流手法(stream of consciousness)和内心独白(monologue)去表现和探索人类意识的本质;另外,他还善于从多重视角(multiple points of view)描述故事,往往以一个事件为中心,向多重视点辐射,达到高层次的表现真实性。

2. 威廉·福克纳的主要作品:

a. 1 卷诗歌

《大理石农牧之神》*The Marble Faun*(1924)

b. 19 篇长篇小说和75 篇短篇小说,包括:

《士兵的薪酬》*Soldiers' Pay*(1926)

《萨特瑞斯》*Sartoris*(1926)

《喧嚣与骚动》*The Sound and the Fury*(1929)

《我弥留之际》*As I Lay Dying*(1930)

《八月之光》*Light in August*(1932)

《押沙龙,押沙龙!》*Absalom, Absalom!*(1936)

《未被征服的》*Unvanquished*(1938)

《疯狂的手掌》*Wild Palms*(1939)

《小村庄》*The Hamlet*(1940)

《摩西,走下去》*Go Down, Moses*(1942)

《骚动中的侵入者》*Intruder in the Dust*(1948)

《寓言》*The Fable*(1954)

《小镇》*The Town*(1957)

《修女的挽歌》*Requiem for a Nun*(1959)

《大厦》*The Mansion*(1959)

重要信息句子

1. In 1950, Faulkner was awarded the Nobel Prize for the anti-racist *Intruder in the Dust* (1948).

2. Most of Faulkner's works are set in the American South, with his emphasis on the Southern subject and consciousness.

3. Of Faulkner's literary works, four novels are masterpieces by any standards: *The Sound and the Fury*, *Light in August*, *Absalom, Absalom!* and *Go Down, Moses*.

美国现代时期文学同步练习与答案

1. The Modern Period of American literature includes the following periods EXCEPT _____.

a. the first part of the 20th century

b. after the first and second World Wars

c. the period of the 1960s and 1970s

d. between the mid-19th century and the first decade of the 20th century

2. The expatriate American writers formed a community of writers and artists in Paris and were named by
_____, also an expatriate American writer, "The Lost Generation".
   a. Gertrude Stein
   b. Ezra Pound
   c. Robert Frost
   d. W. C. Williams

3. _____ is the leading spokesman of the famous Imagist Movement in the history of American literature _____.
   a. William James
   b. Ezra Pound
   c. Robert Frost
   d. William Faulkner

4. _____ of the 1920s characterized by frivolity and carelessness is brought vividly to life in *The Great Gatsby*.
   a. The period of the post-war
   b. The Gilded Age
   c. The Jazz Age
   d. The Beat Movement

5. The leading playwright of the modern period in American literature is _____.
   a. Arthur Miller
   b. Tennessee Williams
   c. Eugene O'Neill
   d. G. B. Shaw

6. _____ may be said the second American Renaissance.
   a. The Imagist Movement
   b. The Expatriate Movement
   c. The Beat Movement
   d. The Jazz Age

7. _____ is considered to be a spokesman for the alienated youth in the post-war era.
   a. J. D. Salinger
   b. F. Scott Fitzgerald
   c. Ernest Hemingway
   d. Arthur Miller

8. J. D. Salinger's _____ is regarded as a students' classic.
   a. *The Great Gatsby*
   b. *Rabbit*
   c. *The Grapes of Wrath*
   d. *The Catcher in the Rye*

9. Of all the following, only _____ is NOT among the greatest figures in the "The Lost Generation".
   a. Ezra Pound
   b. Robert Frost
   c. William Carlos Williams
   d. John Steinbeck

10. _____ is a representative of the 1930s, when "novels of social protest" became dominant on the American literary scene.
    a. Sherwood Anderson
    b. Sinclair Lewis
    c. John Steinbeck
    d. William Faulkner

11. Whose *The Grapes of Wrath* proves to be a symbolic journey of man on the way to finding some truth about life and himself during the Great Depression? _____.
    a. Arthur Miller's
    b. John Steinbeck's
    c. F. S. Fitzgerald's
    d. Sinclair Lewis'

12. Among the poems after the 2nd World War, _____ by Allen Ginsberg became the manifesto of the Beat Generation.
    a. *Howl*
    b. *Rabbit*
    c. *Leaves of Grass*
    d. *I heard a Fly buzz — when I died —*

13. Among the poets after the 2nd World War, _____ was in the lead, whose poems showed a growing sense of resistance to the existing culture and at the same time an assertion of the self.
    a. Gary Snyder
    b. Allen Ginsberg
    c. Robert Lowell
    d. Emily Dickinson

14. During the 1960s and 1970s, the "new fiction", i. e, absurdist literature, appeared, departing from the conventions of the novel writing, at the forefront were all of the following EXCEPT _____.
    a. Kurt Vonnegut   b. John Bath
    c. Robert Lowell   d. Joseph Heller

15. Which one of the following is Ezra Pound's life's work? _____.
    a. *Collected Early Poems of Ezra Pound*   b. *Personae*
    c. *Literary Essays*   d. *The Cantos of Ezra Pound*

16. Pound's famous one-image poem "_____" would serve as a typical example of the Imagist ideas.
    a. A Pact   b. In a Station of the Metro
    c. Personae   d. Confucius

17. _____ is up to now the only dramatist ever to win the Nobel Prize.
    a. George Bernard Shaw   b. William Shakespeare
    c. Authur Miller   d. Eugene O'Neill

18. _____ proves to be a masterpiece which is the best and greatest plays of the modern American theater late in Eugene O'Neill's life.
    a. *Beyond the Horizon*   b. *Strange Interlude*
    c. *The Iceman Cometh*   d. *The Hairy Ape*

19. _____ has gained its status as a world classic and simultaneously marks the climax of O'Neill's literary career.
    a. *The Emperor Jones*   b. *Long Day's Journey into Night*
    c. *Beyond the Horizon*   d. *The Iceman Cometh*

20. During all his career as a dramatist, O'Neill wrote and published about _____ plays altogether of various lengths.
    a. forty nine   b. thirty eight
    c. fifty two   d. twenty

21. Of all the plays O'Neill wrote, most of them are _____.
    a. tragedies   b. comedies
    c. tragicomedies   d. farce

22. Eugene O'Neill won Pulitzer Prize four times, the first of which was won because of his first full-length play _____.
    a. *The Straw*   b. *Beyond the Horizon*
    c. *Anna Christie*   d. *Strange Interlude*

23. O'Neill won the third Pulitzer Prize for _____, which also paved the way to the honor of the Nobel Prize in 1936.
    a. *The Great God Brown*   b. *The Iceman Cometh*
    c. *Strange Interlude*   d. *Long Day's Journey into Night*

24. Fitzgerald wrote one novel _____, in which he traces the decline of a young American psychiatrist whose marriage to a beautiful and wealthy patient drains his personal energies and corrodes his professional career.
    a. *Tender is the Night*   b. *The Great Gatsby*
    c. *This Side of Paradise*   d. *The Last Tycoon*

25. A masterpiece in American literature, _____ evoke a haunting mood of glamour, wild time that seemingly will never come again.

    a. *This Side of Paradise*   b. *Tender Is the Night*

    c. *The American Dream*   d. *The Great Gatsby*

26. Most critics have agreed that _____ is both an insider and an outsider of the Jazz Age with a double vision.

    a. Fitzgerald   b. Frost

    c. Cummings   d. Pound

27. Lots of people rushed to Gatsby's party at the weekend and they clustered around Gatsby's wealth like _____.

    a. gluttons   b. flies

    c. insects   d. moths

28. _____ is Hemingway's first true novel. It casts light on a whole generation after the First World War by way of a vivid portrait of "_____".

    a. *In Our Time*/The Angry Young Men

    b. *The Sun Also Rises*/The Lost Generation

    c. *A Farewell to Arms*/The Beat Generation

    d. *For Whom the Bell Tolls*/The Theatre of the Absurd

29. Hemingway's second success is _____, which wrote the epitaph to a decade and to the whole generation in the 1920s.

    a. *The Old Man and the Sea*   b. *A Farewell to Arms*

    c. *For Whom the Bell Tolls*   d. *The Snows of Kilimanjaro*

30. _____ capped Hemingway's career and led to his receipt of the Nobel Prize.

    a. *In Our Time*   b. *The Sun Also Riss*

    c. *The Old Man and the Sea*   d. *The Snows of Kilimanjaro*

31. According to Hemingway, good literature writing should be able to _____ without any authorial comments and conventionally emotive language.

    a. make readers feel the emotion of the characters directly

    b. make the story he writes very interesting

    c. be impressed very much by the readers

    d. be closely connected with the social and historical background

32. In 1950, Faulkner was awarded the Nobel Prize for the anti-racist _____.

    a. *The Sound and the Fury*   b. *Go Down, Moses*

    c. *Intruder in the Dust*   d. *Light in August*

33. In Faulkner's *The Sound and the Fury*, he used a technique called _____, in which the whole story was through the thoughts of one character.

    a. stream of consciousness   b. imagism

    c. symbolism   d. naturalism

34. William Faulkner makes use of the Gothic devices in narration in _____.

    a. *The Bear*   b. *The Sound and the Fury*

    c. *Light in August*   d. *A Rose for Emily*

35. Most of _____'s works are set in the American South, with the emphasis on the Southern subjects and consciousness.

    a. Faulkner   b. Fitzgerald

    c. Hemingway   d. Steinback

36. In Robert Frost's famous poem "Stopping by Woods on a Snowy Evening", there are four lines like these: "The woods are lovely, dark and deep,/But I have promises to keep,/And miles to go before I sleep,/And miles to go before I sleep". The second sleep refers to _____.

    a. die   b. calm down

    c. fall into sleep   d. stop walking

37. "For I have had too much/Of apple-picking: I am overtired/Of the great harvest I myself desired". From these lines we can conclude that the speaker _____.

    a. is happy about the harvest   b. is tired of the work of apple-picking

    c. is not tired when seeing the harvest   d. becomes indifferent of the job

38. In these lines "The apparition of these faces in the crowd;/Petals on a wet, black bough", Ezra Pound uses the figure of speech of _____.

    a. metaphor   b. simile

    c. hyperbole   d. contrast

39. Of the following American poets, _____ work was first recognized in England and then in America.

    a. Robert Frost's   b. Walt Whitman's

    c. Emily Dickinson's   d. Wallace Stevens'

40. Chinese poetry and philosophy had great influence on _____.

    a. Robert Frost   b. R. W. Emerson

    c. Ezra Pound   d. Emily Dickinson

41. The Hemingway code heroes are best remembered for their _____.

    a. indestructible spirit   b. pessimistic view of life

    c. war experiences   d. masculinity

42. "He got me, aw (> all) right. I'm trou (> true). Even him didn't tink (> think) I belonged." In these sentences taken from *The Hairy Ape*, the words "him" both refer to _____.

    a. Yank   b. God

    c. the ape in the zoo   d. a person unnamed

43. Nick's night trip to the Indian village and his experience inside the hut can be taken as _____.

    a. an initiation to pain and suffering

    b. a confrontation with evil and sin

    c. an essential lesson about Indian tribes

    d. a learning process of human connections

44. _____ is a school of modern painting, whose emphasis is on the formal structure of a work of art and especially on the multiple-perspective viewpoints.

    a. Expression   b. Impressionism

    c. Cubism   d. Imagism

45. In a class which discusses the Imagist Movement in the United States, we will definitely NOT include _____.

    a. William Carlos Williams   b. Ezra Pound

    c. Gary Snyder   d. Wallace Stevens

46. A typical modern work will NO longer have ONE of the following as its trademark, that is, a _____.

    a. record of sequence and coherence

    b. book of fragments drawn from diverse areas of experience

    c. juxtaposition of the past and present, of the history and memory

d. book that begins arbitrarily, advances without explanation, and end without solution

47. The American writer _____ was awarded the Nobel Prize for the anti-racist *Intruder in the Dust* in 1950.

    a. Ernest Hemingway   b. Gertrude Stein

    c. William Faulkner   d. T. S. Eliot

48. "The dignity of moveent of an iceberg is due to only one-eighth of it being above water." This "iceberg" analogy is put forward by _____.

    a. Mark Twain   b. Ezra Pound

    c. William Faulkner   d. Ernest Hemingway

49. "The apparition of these faces in the crowd; /Petals on a wet, black bough." comes from the poem _____ by the author _____, in which "petals" mean _____.

    a. *The Road Not Taken*/Robert Frost/steps

    b. *In a Station of the Metro*/Ezra Pound/human faces

    c. *After Apple-Picking*/Robert Frost/apples

    d. *Leaves of Grass*/Walt Whitman/leaves

Keys: dabcc/baddc/baccd/bdcba/abcad/adbbc/acada/abaac/abacc/acdb

翻译练习

Ⅰ. 诗歌部分

写出下列诗句的出处、作者、译文，并做必要的解释。

Part One: English Literature

1. (P16) A Gentle Knight was pricking on the plaine,
   Ycladd in mightie armes and silver shielde,
   Wherein old dints of deepe wounds did remaine,
   The cruell markes of many a bloudy fielde;

2. (P16) And ever as he rode, his hart did earne
   To prove his <u>puissance</u> in battell brave
   Upon his foe, and his new force to learne;

3. (P23) Faustus, begin thine incantations
   And try if devils will obey thy hest,
   Seeing thou has prayed and sacrificed to them.

4. (P38) Nor lose possession of that fair thou ow'st;
   Nor shall death brag thou wander'st in his shade,
   When in eternal lines to time thou grow'st:
   So long as men can breathe, or eyes can see,
   So long lives this, and this gives life to thee.

5. (P55) To be, or not to be — that is the question;
   Whether 'tis nobler in the mind to suffer
   The slings and arrows of outrageous fortune,
   Or to take arms against a sea of troubles,
   And by opposing end them?

6. (P55) To die, to sleep —
   No more; and by a sleep to say we end
   The heart-ache and the thousand natural shocks
   That flesh is heir to, 'tis a consummation
   Devoutly to be wish'd.

7. (P66) Busy old fool, unruly sun,

Why dost thou thus,

Through windows and through curtain call on us?

Must to thy motions lovers' seasons run?

8. (P68) One short sleep past, we wake eternally

And death shall be no more; Death, thou shalt die.

9. (P77) There rest, if any rest can harbor there;

And reassembling our afflicted powers,

Consult how we may henceforth most offend

Our enemy, our own loss how repair,

How overcome this dire calamity,

What reinforcement we may gain from hope,

If not, what resolution from despair.

10. (P93) Some to conceit alone their taste confine,

And glittering thoughts struck out at every line;

Pleased with a work where nothing's just or fit,

One glaring chaos and wild heap of wit.

11. (P94) True wit is Nature to advantage dressed,

What oft was thought, but ne'er so well expressed;

Something whose truth convinced at sight we find,

That gives us back the image of our mind.

12. (P153) The Curfew tolls the knell of parting day,

The lowing herd wind slowly o'er the lea,

The plowman homeward plods his weary way,

And leaves the world to darkness and to me.

13. (P154) The boast of heraldry, the pomp of power,

And all that beauty, all that wealth e'er gave,

Awaits alike the inevitable hour.

The paths of glory lead but to the grave.

14. (P171) When my mother died I was very young,

And my father sold me while yet my tongue

Could scarcely cry "weep! 'weep! 'weep!'weep!"

So your chimney I sweep, & in soot I sleep.

15. (P172) Because I was happy upon the heath,

And smil'd among the winter's snow;

They cloth'd me in the clothes of death,

And taught me to sing the notes of woe.

16. (P173) Tyger! Tyger! burning bright

In the forests of the night,

What immortal hand or eye

Could frame thy fearful symmetry?

17. (P180) For oft, when on my couch I lie

In vacant or in pensive mood,

They flash upon that inward eye

Which is the bliss of solitude；

And then my heart with pleasure fills,

And dances with the daffodils.

18.（P181）Earth has not anything to show more fair：

Dull would he be of soul who could pass by；

A sight so touching in its majesty；

19.（P182）She lived unknown, and few could know

When Lucy ceased to be；

But she is in her grave, and, oh,

The difference to me!

20.（P182）Behold her, single in the field,

Yon solitary Highland lass!

Reaping and singing by herself；

Stop here, or gently pass!

21.（P189）In Xanadu did Kubla Khan

A stately pleasure dome decree：

Where Alph, the sacred river, ran

Through caverns mesureless to man

Down to a sunless sea.

22.（P190）It was a miracle of rare device,

A sunny pleasure dome with caves of ice!

23.（P197）As the liberty lads o'er the sea

Bought their freedom, and cheeply, with blood,

So we, boys, we

Will die fighting, or live free,

And down with all kings but King Ludd!

24.（P199）Where burning Sappho loved and sung,

Where grew the arts of war and peace,

Where Delos rose, and Phoebus sprung!

Eternal summer gilds them yet,

But all, except their sun, is set.

25.（P209）Men of England, wherefore plough

For the lords who lay ye low?

Wherefore weave with toil and care

The rich robes your tyrants wear?

26.（P214）The trumpet of a prophecy! O, Wind,

If Winter comes, can spring be far behind?

27.（P220）Bold lover, never, never canst thou kiss,

Though winning near the goal — yet, do not grieve；

She cannot fade, though thou hast not thy bliss,

For ever wilt thou love, and she be fair!

28.（P221）When old age shall this generation waste,

Thou shalt remain, in midst of other woe

Than ours, a friend to man, to whom thou say'st,

"Beauty is truth, truth beauty," — that is all

Ye know on earth, and all ye need to know.

29. (P276) O, well for the fisherman's boy,

That he shouts with his sister at play!

O, well for the sailor lad,

That he sings in his boat on the bay!

30. (P277) Sunset and evening star,

And one clear call for me!

And may there be no moaning of the bar,

When I put out to sea,

31. (P278) It little profits that an idle king,

By this still hearth, among these barren crags,

Match'd with an aged wife, I mete and dole

Unequal laws unto a savage race,

That hoard, and sleep, and feed, and know not me.

32. (P279) As tho' to breathe were life. Life piled on life

Were all too little, and of one to me

Little remains: but every hour is saved

From that eternal silence, something more,

A bringer of new things;

33. (P280) 'Tis not too late to seek a newer world.

Push off, and sitting well in order smite

The sounding furrows; for my purpose holds

To sail beyond the sunset, and the baths

Of all the western stars, until I die.

34. (P287) ...; and I choose

Never to stoop. Oh sir, she smiled, no doubt,

Whene'er I passed her; but who passed without

Much the same smile? This grew; I gave commands;

Then all smiles stopped together. There she stands

As if alive.

35. (P289) A tap at the pane, the quick sharp scratch

And blue spurt of a lighted match,

And a voice less loud, through its joys and fears,

Than the two hearts beating each to each!

36. (P355) I will arise and go now, and go to Innisfree,

And a small cabin build there, of clay and wattles made:

Nine bean-rows will I have there, a hive for the honeybee,

And live alone in the bee-loud glade.

37. (P356) Down by the salley gardens my love and I did meet;

She passed the sallay gardens with little snow-white feet.

She bid me take life easy, as the leaves grows on the tree;

But I, being young and foolish, with her would not agree.

38. (P365) Do I dare

Disturb the universe?

In a minute there is time

For decisions and revisions which a minute will reverse.

39. (P365) And when I am formulated, sprawlng on a pin,

When I am pinned and wriggling on the wall,

Then how should I begin

To spit out all the butt-ends of my days and ways?

And how should I presume?

40. (P367) And would it have been worth it, after all,

Would it have been worth while,

After the sunsets and the dooryards and the sprinkled streets,

After the novels, after the teacups, after the skirts that trail along the floor —

And this, and so much more? —

It is impossible to say just what I mean!

Part Two: American Literature

41. (P452) There was a child went forth every day,

And the first object he look'd upon, that object he became,

And that object became part of him for the day or a certain part of the day,

Or for many years or stretching cycles of years.

42. (P456) A lime in long array they wind betwixt green islands,

They take a serpentine course, their arms flash in the sun — hark to the musical clank,

Behold the silvery river, in it the splashing horses loitering stop — to drink

Behold the brown-faced men, each group, each person, a picture, the negligent rest on the saddles,

43. (P457) I celebrate myself, and sing myself,

And what I assume you shall assume,

For every atom belonging to me as good belongs to you.

44. (P457) Creeds and schools in abeyance,

Retiring back a while sufficed at what they are, but never for Gotten,

I harbor for good or bad, I permit to speak at every hazard,

Nature without check with original energy.

45. (P520) This is my letter to the World

That never wrote to Me —

The simple News that Nature told —

With tender Majesty

46. (P 520) Her Message is committed

To hands I can not see —

For love of Her — Sweet — countrymen —

Judge tenderly — of Me

47. (P520) I heard a Fly buzz — when I died —

The Stillness in the Room
Was like the Stillness in the Air —
Between the Heaves of Storm —

48. (P521) With Blue — uncertain stumbling Buzz —
Between the light — and me —
And then the Windows failed — and then
I could not see to see —

49. (P521) I like it to see it lap the Miles —
And lick the Valleys up —
And stop to feed itself at Tanks —
And then — prodigious step

50. (P522) Because I could not stop for Death —
He kindly stopped for me —
The Carriage held but just Ourselves —
And Immortality.

51. (P523) We paused before a House that seemed
A Swelling of the Ground —
The Roof was scarcely visible —
The Cornice — in the Ground —

52. (P557) The apparition of these faces in the crowd;
Petals on a wet, black bough.

53. (P558) At fifteen I stopped scowling,
I desired my dust to be mingled with yours
Forever and forever and forever.
Why should I climb the look out?

54. (P560) I make a pact with you, Walt Witman —
I have detested you long enough.
I come to you as a grown child
Who has had a pig-headed father;

55. (P560) It was you that broke the new wood,
Now is a time for carving.
We have one sap and one root —
Let there be commerce between us.

56. (P565) And I keep hearing from the cellar bin
The rumbling sound
Of load on load of apples coming in.
For I have had too much
Of apple-picking: I am overtired
Of the great harvest I myself desired.

57. (P565) One can see what will trouble
This sleep of mine, whatever sleep it is.
Were he not gone,
The woodchuck could say whether it's like his

Long sleep, as I describe its coming on,

Or just some human sleep.

58. (P566) I shall be telling this with a sigh

Somewhere ages and ages hence:

Two roads diverged in a wood, and I —

I took the one less traveled by,

And that has made all the difference.

59. (P567) Whose woods these are I think I know.

His house is in the village though;

He will not see me stopping here

To watch his woods fill up with snow.

60. (P567) The woods are lovely, dark and deep,

But I have promises to keep,

And miles to go before I sleep,

And miles to go before I sleep.

Ⅱ. 散文和小说部分

写出下列引文的出处、作者、译文，并做必要的解释。

Part One: English Literature

1. (P61) They perfect nature, and are perfected by experience; for natural abilities are like natural plants, that need pruning by study; and studies themselves do give forth directions too much at large, except they be bounded in by experience.

2. (P62) If he be not apt to beat over matters and to call up one thing to prove and illustrate another, let him study the lawyer's cases. So every defect of the mind may have a special receipt.

3. (P109) My gentleness and good behaviour had gained so far on the Emperor and his court, and indeed upon the army and people in general, that I began to conceive hopes of getting my liberty in a short time. I took all possible methods to cultivate this favorable disposition.

4. (P134) Is not a patron, my Lord, one who looks with unconcern on a man struggling for life in the water, and when he has reached ground, encumbers him with help?

5. (P229) It is a truth universally acknowledged, that a single man in possession of a good fortune, must be in want of a wife.

However little known the feelings or views of such a man may be on his first entering a neighborhood, this truth is so well fixed in the minds of the surrounding families, that he is considered as the rightful property of some one or other of their daughters.

6. (P244) Let it not be supposed by the enemies of "the system," that, during the period of his solitary incarceration, Oliver was denied the benefit of exercise, the pleasure of society, or the advantages of religious consolation.

7. (P261) Do you think, because I am poor, obscure, plain, and little, I am soulless and heartless? —

You think wrong! — I have as much soul as you — and full as much heart!... I am not talking to you now through the medium of custom, conventionalities, or even of mortal flesh: — it is my spirit that addresses your spirit; just as if both had passed through the grave, and we stood at God's feet, equal — as we are!

8. (P270) He flung himself into the nearest seat, and on my approaching hurriedly to ascertain if she had fainted, he gnashed at me, and foamed like a mad dog, and gathered her to him with greedy jealousy. I did not feel as if I were in the company of a creature of my own species...

9. (P296) Marriage, which was to bring guidance into worthy and imperative occupation, had not yet freed her from the gentlewoman's oppressive liberty: it had not even filled her leisure with the ruminant joy of unchecked tenderness.

10. (P296) Her blooming full-pulsed youth stood there in a moral imprisonment which made itself one with the chill, colourless, narrowed landscape, with the shrunken furniture, the never-read books, and the ghostly stag in a pale fantastic world that seemed to be vanishing from the daylight.

11. (P305) But she soon found a curious correspondence between the ostensibly chance position of the cows and her wishes in this matter, till she felt that their order could not be the result of accident. The dairyman's pupil had lent a hand in getting the cows together of late, and at the fifth or the sixth time she turned her eyes, as she rested against the cow, full of sly inquiry upon him.

12. (P309) Tess, on her part, could not understand why a man of clerical family and good education, and above physical want, should look upon it as a mishap to be alive. For the unhappy pilgrim herself there was very good reason. But how could this admirable and poetic man ever have descended to the Valley of Humiliation, have felt with the man of Uz — as she herself had felt two or three years ago...

13. (P326) Then where are our relatives? My father? Our family friends? You claim the rights of a mother: the right to call me fool and child; to speak to me as no woman in authority over me at college dare speak to me; to dictate my way of life; and to force on me the acquaintance of a brute whom anyone can see to be the most vicious sort of London man about town. Before I give myself the trouble to resist such claims, I may as well find out whether they have any real existence.

14. (P334) The only way for a woman to provide for herself decently is for her to be good to some man that can afford to be good to her. If she's in his own station of life, let her make him marry her; but if she's far beneath him she cant expect it: why should she? It wouldn't be for her own happiness. Ask any lady in London society that has daughters; and she'll tell you the same, except that I tell you straight and she'll tell you crooked. That's all the difference.

15. (P347) Nothing in this world is more sure to upset a Forsyte than the discovery that something on which he has stipulated to spend a certain sum has cost more. And this is reasonable, for upon the accuracy of his estimates the whole policy of his life is ordered. If he cannot rely on definite values of property, his compass is amiss; he is adrift upon bitter waters without a helm.

16. (P349) He neither believed nor disbelieved her, but he knew that he had made a mistake in asking; he never had known, never would know, what she was thinking. The sight of her inscrutable face, the thought of all the hundreds of evenings he had seen her sitting there like that, soft and passive, but so unreadable, unknown, enraged him beyond measure.

17. (P377) Paul was afraid lest she might have misread the letter, and might be disappointed after all. He scrutinized it once, twice. Yes, he became convinced it was true. Then he sat down, his heart beating with joy.

"Mother!" he exclaimed.

"Didn't I say we should do it!" she said, pretending she was not crying.

18. (P380) He went out to dinner several times in his evening suit that had been William's. Each time his mother's heart was firm with pride and joy. He was started now. The studs she and the children had bought for William were in his shirt-front; he wore one of William's dress shirts. But he had an elegant figure. His face was rough, but warm-looking and rather pleasing. He did not look particularly a gentleman, but she thought he looked quite a man.

19. (P393) At last she spoke to me. When she addressed the first words to me I was so confused that I did not know what to answer. She asked me was I going to *Araby*. I forget whether I answered yes or no. It would be splendid bazaar, she said; she would love to go.

20. (P397) Then I turned away slowly and walked down the middle of the bazaar. I allowed the two pennies to fall against the sixpence in my pocket. I heard a voice call from one end of the gallery that the light was out. The upper part of the hall was now completely dark.

Gazing up into the darkness I saw myself as a creature driven and derided by vanity; and my eyes burned with anguish and anger.

Part Two: American Literature

21. (P408) Times grew worse and worse with Rip Van Winkle as years of matrimony rolled on; a tart temper never mellows with age, and a sharp tongue is the only edge tool that grows keener by constant use. For a long while he used to console himself, when driven from home, by frequenting a kind of perpetual club of the sages, philosophers, and other idle personages of the village...

22. (P413) There was, as usual, a crowd of folk about the door, but none that Rip recollected. The very character of the people seemed changed. There was a busy, bustling, disputatious tone about it, instead of the accustomed phlegm and drowsy tranquility. He looked in vain for the sage Nicholas Vedder, ...

23. (P427) Standing on the bare ground, — my head bathed by the blithe air, and uplifted into infinite space, — all mean egotism vanishes. I become a transparent eye-ball. I am nothing. I see all. The currents of the Universal Being circulate through me. I am part or particle of God.

24. (P446) On the Sabbath-day, when the congregation were singing a holy psalm, he could not listen, because an anthem of sin rushed loudly upon his ear, and drowned all the blessed strain. When the minister <u>spoke</u> from the pulpit, with power and fervid eloquence, and, with his hand on the open bible, <u>of</u> the sacred truths of our religion, and <u>of</u> saint-like lives and triumphant deaths, and <u>of</u> future bliss or misery unutterable, then did goodman Brown turn pale, dreading, lest the roof should <u>thunder down upon</u> the gray blasphemer and his hearers. Often, awakening suddenly at midnight, he shrank from the bosom of Faith, and at morning or eventide, when the family knelt down at prayer, he scowled, and muttered to himself, and gazed sternly at his wife, and turned away.

25. (P468) Oh, lonely death on lonely life! Oh, now I feel my topmost greatness lies in my topmost grief. Ho, ho! From all your furthest bounds, pour ye now in, ye bold billows of my whole foregone life, and top this one piled comber of my death! Toward thee I roll, thou all-destroying but unconquering whale; to the last I <u>grapple with</u> thee; from hell's heart I stab at thee; for hate's sake I <u>spit my last breath at</u> thee. Sink all coffins and all hearses to one common pool! and since neither can be mine, let me then tow to pieces, while still chasing thee though tied to thee, thou damned whale!

26. (P488) So I was full of trouble, full as I could be; and didn't know what to do. At last I had an idea; and I says, I'll go and write the letter — and *then* see if I can pray. Why, it was astonishing, the way

I felt as light as a feather, <u>right straight off</u>, and my troubles all gone. So I got a piece of paper and a pencil, all glad and excited, and set down and wrote:...

27. (P489) But somehow I couldn't seem to strike no places to harden me against him, but only the other kind. I'd see him standing my watch on top of his'n, stead of calling me, so I could go on sleeping; and see him how glad he was when I come back out of the fog; and when I come to him again in the swamp, up there where the feud was;... and at last I struck the time I saved him by telling the men we had small-pox aboard, and he was so grateful, and said I was the best friend old Jim ever had in the world,...

　　... I studied a minute, sort of holding my breath, and then says to myself:

　　"All right, then, I'll go to hell" — and tore it up.

28. (P511) Poor Winterbourne was amused, perplexed — above all he was charmed. He had never yet heard a young girl express herself in just this fashion; never at least save in cases where to say such things was to have at the same time some rather complicated consciousness about them. And yet was he to accuse Miss Daisy Miller of an actual or a potential *arriere-pensée*, as they said at Geneva? He felt he had lived at Geneva so long as to have morally muddled; he <u>had lost the right sense for</u> the young American tone.

29. (P539) And now Carrie had attained that which in the beginning seemed life's object, or, at least, such fraction of it as human beings ever attain of their original desires... For these she had once craved. Applause there was, and publicity — once far off, essential things, but now grown trivial and indifferent. Beauty also — her type of loveliness — and yet she was lonely. In her rocking-chair she sat, when not otherwise engaged — singing and dreaming.

30. (P573) And why wouldn't yuh get me? Ain't we both members of de same club — de Hairy Apes?

31. (P597) The caterwauling horns had reached a crescendo and I turned away and cut across the lawn toward home. I glanced back once. A wafer of a moon was shining over Gatsby's house, making the night fine as before, and surviving the laughter and the sound of his still glowing garden. A sudden emptiness seemed to flow now from the windows and the great doors, endowing with complete isolation the figure of the host, who stood on the porch, his hand up in a formal gesture of farewell.

32. (P608) He pulled back the blanket from the Indian's head. His hand came away wet. He mounted on the edge of the lower bunk with the lamp in one hand and looked in. The Indian lay with his face toward the wall. His throat had been cut from ear to ear. The blood had flowed down into a pool where his body sagged the bunk. His head rested on his left arm. The open razor lay, edge up, in the blankets.

33. (P609) "Do ladies always have such a hard time having babies?" Nick asked.

　　"No, that was very, very exceptional."

　　"Why did he kill himself, Daddy?"

　　"I don't know, Nick. He couldn't stand things, I guess."

34. (P629) For a long while we just stood there, looking down at the profound and fleshless grin. The body had apparently once lain <u>in the attitude of</u> an embrace, but now the long sleep that outlasts love, that conquers even the grimace of love, had cuckolded him. What was left of him, rotted beneath what was left of the nightshirt, had become inextricable from the bed in which he lay; and upon him and upon the pillow beside him lay that even coating of the <u>patient and biding</u> dust.

　　Then we noticed that in the second pillow was the indentation of a head. One of us lifted something from it, and leaning forward, that faint and invisible dust dry and acrid in the nostrils, we saw <u>a long strand of</u> iron-gray hair.

Ⅲ. 诗歌部分答案

1. 这 4 行诗选自文艺复兴时期著名诗人埃德蒙·斯宾塞(Edmund Spenser)的长诗《仙后》(*The Faerie Queene*)的第一册第一章,参考译文如下:

    一位高贵的骑士正策马驱驰在平原上,/他身披坚甲,手持银盾,/银盾上伤痕仍在,/那是多少次血腥战场的残酷标记。

    * Ycladd in mightie...shielde = (who was) clothed in mightie armes and silver shield,是过去分词短语作主语 a Gentle Knight 的定语;wherein (= in which) old dints...remaine 是关系副词引导的定语从句,修饰 silver shielde. The cruel markes ...fielde 是名词性短语作 old dints 的同位语。

2. 此 3 行诗选自斯宾塞《仙后》第一册第一章,参考译文如下:

    当他骑马前行,他的心时刻向往/在抗击敌人的无畏战斗中,/证明他的威力和学习的潜力。

    * hart = heart; earne = yearn; puissance = power prowess 威力,高潮的能力;in battell brave = in brave battle/fight against ...

3. 这 3 行诗引自文艺复兴时期英国剧作家克里斯托弗·马洛(Christopher Marlowe)的戏剧《浮士德博士》(*Dr. Faustus*)第一幕第三场,参考译文如下:

    浮士德,你开始作法吧,/看魔鬼们是否听从你的命令,/看到你已经祈祷、献过祭品了。

    * 注意这是浮士德的内心独白,他在自说自话,所谓 seeing,实际等于 I have seen...,I 就是他自己。

4. 此 5 行诗选自威廉·莎士比亚(William Shakespeare)的《十四行诗第十八首》(*Sonnet* 18),参考译文如下:

    不会失去你享有的美丽姿容;/死神不能吹嘘你落在他的阴影下——/在不朽的诗中你像时间无穷:/只要人还能呼吸,眼睛能看清,/我的诗就将流传并给你生命。

    * 诗歌的主题是在说"天地无常,唯诗歌艺术无限"的道理。

    * to brag thou wander'st in his shade (死神)吹嘘你会在他的阴影下徘徊

5. 这 4 行诗是莎士比亚悲剧《哈姆雷特》(*Hamlet*)第三幕第一场哈姆雷特王子的一段长篇内心独白的开头几句,可翻译如下:

    生存,还是毁灭,这是个问题;/怎样做才更高尚:是默默忍受/残暴命运的明枪暗箭,/还是拿起武器直面苦海,/用抗争结束苦难?

6. 诗句选自莎士比亚大悲剧《哈姆雷特》中哈姆雷特王子的长篇独白,参考译文如下:

    死去,长眠——/万事皆休,长眠中我们结束了/心灵的创伤,和凡人注定要承受的/千般苦难,这是衷心盼望的结局。

    * 这几行诗为一个完整的句子,it 为形式主语,三个不定式短语 to die, to sleep 和 by a sleep to say (that) ...为真正的主语。

7. 诗句选自文艺复兴时期玄学派诗人约翰·邓恩(John Donne)的《升起的太阳》(*The Sun Rising*)开头一段,参考译文如下:

    忙碌的老傻瓜,不安分的太阳,/为什么要这么干,/透过窗户和帘幕来探视我们? /难道情人的季节必得跟你转?

    * Must to thy motions lovers' seasons run? = Must lovers' seasons run to thy motions?

8. 诗句选自约翰·邓恩的《死神,你别得意》(*Death, Be Not Proud*),参考译文如下:

一次小睡过后,我们便永远醒来,/死亡将不会再有;/死亡,你将死亡。

9. 诗句选自文艺复兴时期伟大的反封建争自由的革命诗人约翰·弥尔顿(John Milton)的长篇史诗《失乐园》(*Paradise Lost*)第一卷,参考译文如下:

在那里休息一下,如果能在那里休息;/重新召集我们受重创的军队,/商讨如何最有效地打击/我们的敌人,如何弥补我们的损失,/如何克服这惨痛的灾难,/从希望中可获得怎样的鼓励,/反之,从绝望中下定怎样的决心?!

10. 诗句选自新古典主义时期作家亚历山大·蒲伯(Alexander Pope)代表作品《论批评》(*An Essay on Criticism*)第二部分,参考译文如下:

有些人只将自己的趣味局限于矫揉造作,/每一行中都编造出闪光的思索;/为一篇毫无可取的作品沾沾自喜,/作品中炫耀着混乱和胡乱堆砌的机智。

* 第一行可改写为 Some alone confine their taste to conceit;第三行完整的句子是 Some are pleased with a work where nothing's just or fit;第四行中的 one 是第三行中的 a work 的同位语。

11. 诗句选自蒲伯《论批评》的第二部分,可译为:

真正的机智是打扮得当的自然,/人们常想到,却从未表达得这么好;/我们一见就觉得其真实可信,/可以再现我们头脑中的思想。

* 第三行可改写为 Something whose truth we find convinced at sight,是主句的表语;第四行 that 引导的从句是修饰 something 的定语从句。

12. 诗句选自新古典主义时期墓园派诗人托马斯·格雷(Thomas Gray)的《写在乡村教堂墓园的挽诗》(*Elegy Written in a Country Churchyard*),参考译文如下:

晚钟为逝去的白昼敲起丧钟,/低鸣的牛群在草原上缓缓绕行,/犁地者慢吞吞踏上回家的疲惫之路,/把整个世界留给黑暗和我。

* 第三行可改写为 The plowman plods his weary way homeward.

13. 诗句选自托马斯·格雷《写在乡村教堂墓园的挽诗》,参考译文如下:

门第的炫耀,权势的显赫,/凡是美和财富所能赋予的一切,/都同样等待着那不可避免的时刻,/光荣的道路条条都通向坟墓。

* 第二行可改写为 And all that beauty and wealth ever gave,其中 that 引导的从句是 all 的定语从句。

14. 诗句选自英国浪漫主义时期诗人威廉·布莱克(William Blake)诗集《天真之歌》(*Songs of Innocence*)中的"扫烟囱的孩子"(*The Chimney Sweeper*),参考译文如下:

母亲死的时候,我还很小,/父亲卖我时,我还泥舌,/几乎喊不清"扫! 扫! 扫! 扫!"/就这样我为你们扫烟囱,睡觉睡在烟灰里。

15. 诗句选自布莱克诗集《经验之歌》(*Songs of Experience*)中的"扫烟囱的孩子"(*The Chimney Sweeper*),参考译文如下:

因为我原来在荒地里高高兴兴,/在冬天的雪地里也总是笑嘻嘻,/他们就给我穿上这件丧衣,/还教我唱这悲伤的曲。

* clothes of death 丧服,丧衣;the notes of woe 悲伤的歌/曲

16. 诗句为布莱克的名作《老虎》(*The Tyger*)的首节,参考译文如下:

虎! 虎! 光焰灼灼/燃烧在黑夜之林,/怎样的神手和神眼/构造你可畏的美健?

17. 诗句为浪漫主义时期著名诗人威廉·华兹华斯(William Wordsworth)名作《我如行云独自游》(*I Wondered Lonely as a Cloud*)的第四节,也即最后一节,诗名也叫《水仙》(*The Daffodils*),参考译文如下:

从此,每当我倚榻而卧,/或情怀抑郁,或心境茫然,/水仙呵,便在心目中闪烁——/那是我孤寂时分的乐园;/我的心灵便欢情洋溢,/和水仙一道舞蹈不息。

* the bliss of solitude　孤寂时分极大的快乐

18. 此 3 行诗选自华兹华斯的《在威斯敏特斯桥上》(*Composed upon Westminster Bridge*, September 3, 1802)，参考译文如下：

大地从未展示过比这更美的景象；/只有心灵麻木者才会漠然走过，/对如此动人的壮美熟视无睹；

* 第二、三两句可改写为 he would be dull of soul who could pass by/So touching a sight in its majesty；

19. 诗句为华兹华斯浪漫小诗《她住的地方人迹罕至》(*She Dwelt among the Untrodden Ways*)的第三节，参考译文如下：

露西活着无人知晓，/何时离世也少有人知道；/但是她正长眠在墓里，啊，/她与我现已是生死相隔！

20. 诗句选自华兹华斯诗作《孤独的收割者》(*The Solitary Reaper*)开头一节，参考译文如下：

看她，只身在田野上，/远处那孤独的高地姑娘！/独自收割，独自歌唱；/请驻足聆听，或静静走过！

21. 诗句选自浪漫主义时期诗人塞缪尔·泰勒·科勒律治(Samuel Taylor Coleridge)的名作《忽必烈汗》(*Kubla Khan*)，参考译文如下：

忽必烈汗建立上都，/修起富丽的逍遥宫，/那儿有神河阿尔夫/流经深不可测的洞穴，/注入不见太阳的海中。

22. 诗句选引自科勒律治的《忽必烈汗》，可译为：

这是个罕见的建筑奇迹，/一座阳光灿烂的欢乐冰宫！

23. 此 5 行诗引自乔治·戈登·拜伦(George Gordon Byron)的《卢德工人之歌》(*Song for Luddites*)，也译作《卢德派之歌》，参考译文如下：

海外的自由儿郎/直接用鲜血买到了自由；/年轻人，我们也要如此，/要么自由生活，要么战斗中死去，/打到一切国王，只要卢德王！

* cheaply 在这节诗里不是廉价、便宜的意思，而是直截了当、痛快淋漓、不拖泥带水的意思，意在歌颂美国的独立革命，他们就是英国的"海外儿郎"；King Ludd 指 Ned Ludd，砸毁机器、抗议解雇工人的斗士，后来的类似工人运动都称之为卢德派运动，Ned Ludd 被称之为 King Ludd 卢德王。

24. 诗句选引自拜伦的长诗《唐璜》(*Don Juan*)第三章的一段插曲《希腊诸岛》(*The Isles of Greece*)，参考译文如下：

你有过萨福如火的爱情和歌唱，/你上演过战争与和平的艺术，/提洛岛海中升起，太阳神由此诞生，/长夏的阳光为它们镀金——/除了太阳，一切都已沉沦！

25. 诗引自浪漫主义诗人雪莱(P. B. Shelley)的《致英格兰人》(*A Song：Men of England*)第一节，参考译文如下：

英格兰的人们，凭什么要给/蹂躏你们的老爷们耕田种地？/凭什么要辛勤劳动纺织不息，/用锦绣去装扮暴君们的身体？

* who lay ye low 把你们踩在脚下、蹂躏你们，是定语从句，修饰 the lords；weave rich robes your tyrants wear 织造暴君们穿的豪华衣袍，其中 your tyrants wear 为定语从句，修饰 robes。

26. 诗句引自雪莱的《西风颂》(*The West Wind*)的最后一节，可译为：

吹响预言的号角！哦，西风啊/冬天来了，春天还会远吗？

27. 诗句选自浪漫主义时期诗人约翰·济慈(John Keats)的名作《希腊古瓮颂》(*Ode on a Grecian Urn*)的第二节，参考译文如下：

大胆的情郎，你永远得不到一吻，/虽然接近了目标——你可别悲伤；/她永远不衰老，尽管摘不到幸福，/你永远在爱着，她永远美丽动人！

＊ never canst thou kiss = thou canst never kiss = You can never kiss,你永远得不到一吻;For ever wilt thou love, and she be fair! = You will love for ever, and she will be fair! 你永远爱着,她永远青春美丽!

28. 诗句引自济慈的《希腊古瓮颂》的最后一节,可译为:

等年老销蚀了我们这一代,那时,/你将仍是人类的朋友,并且/会遇到另一些哀愁,你会对人说/"美即是真,真即是美"——这就是/你们在世上所知道、该知道的一切。

＊ 第二行、第三行两句诗 Thou shalt remain, in midst of other woe/Than ours, a friend to man, to whom thou say'st, 可改写为 You will remain a friend to man and in midst of other woe than ours, and you will say to man: ... 句中画线部分意为"与我们不同的另一些哀愁",than 在这里是"除了……之外"的意思。

29. 诗句引自维多利亚时期诗人阿尔弗雷德·丁尼生(Alfred Tennyson)的《拍击,拍击,拍击》(Break, Break, Break)的第二节,参考译文如下:

啊,多快乐呀,那渔家童子,/他喊叫着与妹妹玩耍嬉戏! /啊,多快乐呀,那少年水手,/唱着歌在海湾里弄舟!

＊ 此节诗中两次使用了一个句型:(It would be) well for the fisherman's boy that he shouts with his sister at play! 只是诗中把括号部分省略罢了。其中 it 为形式主语,that 引导的是真正的主语从句。

30. 诗句引自丁尼生的诗作《越过沙洲》(Crossing the Bar)第一节,可译为:

夕阳西下,晚星闪烁,/一个清晰的声音对我呼唤! /愿沙洲无有哽咽声——/在我驾舟入海时。

31. 诗句引自丁尼生的诗作《尤利西斯》(Ulysses)的开头部分,参考译文如下:

那真是无益又无趣,一个百无聊赖的国王,/蜗居荒岛陡崖,傍着火炉,/伴着老妻,时而为个刁蛮的民族/办些立法、量刑的事情,而他们——贪财、贪吃、贪睡,全不知我的虎老雄心。

＊5 行诗句实为一个完整的句子,句型是 It little profits that...,it 为形式主语,that 引导的长句是真正的主语。to mete and dole unequal laws unto a savage race 对一个野蛮的民族颁布种种定罪量刑的法律;mete = measure;dole = give。

32. 诗句引自丁尼生的名诗《尤利西斯》,参考译文如下:

仿佛苟延残喘就算生命,/岁月重叠总觉得太少,/而我的余生已去日苦多:/每时每刻都是从永恒的沉寂中挣得,/重要的是,生命中还要有新的事物;

＊ and of one to me little remains = Little of one life remains to me.

33. 此5 行诗引自丁尼生的《尤利西斯》,可译为:

(来吧,我的朋友们) 前去寻找新世界还不太晚! /开船出发,各就各位坐好,/奋力击桨破浪,向着目标,/直挂云帆过夕阳,一直驶过/西方群星照耀的大海, 到死方休。

34. 诗句引自维多利亚时期诗人罗伯特·勃朗宁(Robert Browning)的《我的前公爵夫人》(My Last Duchess),参考译文如下:

于是我选择/绝不屈尊。哦,先生,她总是在微笑,/每逢我走过;但是谁人走过得不到/同样慷慨的微笑? 发展自此,/我下了令:于是一切微笑从此终止,/她站在那里,像活着一样。

35. 此4 行诗引自勃朗宁的《夜半相会》(Meeting at Night)一诗的第二节,参考译文如下:

轻扣窗户,一声嗦啦/蓝光一闪,火柴点亮,/惊喜交集,低声细语/还没有两颗紧贴着的心跳得响!

36. 此4 行诗为威廉·巴特勒·叶芝(William Butler Yeats)的名诗《茵尼斯弗利岛》(The Lake Isle of Innisfree)开头一节,参考译文如下:

我要起身走了,去茵尼斯弗利岛,/用泥土和枝条,建造起一座小屋;/我要有九排芸豆架,一个蜜蜂巢,/在林间听群峰歌唱,独居于幽处。

37. 诗句选自叶芝的优美小诗《走过黄柳园》(*Down by the Salley Gardens*)的第一节,参考译文如下:

　　黄柳园畔,我和爱人相遇;/她纤足雪白,走过柳园。/她劝我从容相爱,如叶生树梢;/可我年轻糊涂,未听她劝告。

38. 此4行诗引自托马斯·斯特恩·艾略特(Thomas Stearns Eliot)的《J. A. 普鲁弗洛克的情歌》(*The Love Song of J. Alfred Prufrock*)一诗,参考译文如下:

　　我敢不敢/把宇宙的宁静搅乱?/一分钟后还有时间/有决断或转念的时间,一分钟后也可全改变。

39. 此5行诗引自英国现代时期著名诗人T. S. 艾略特的诗作《J. A. 普鲁弗洛克的情歌》,参考译文如下:

　　等我被公式化表达,趴伏着被扎在针上,/等我被钉在墙上,扭动,挣扎,/那么我将如何开始/吐出我生活和习惯的烟蒂?/我怎敢不自量力(大胆妄为)?

40. 此7行诗引自T. S. 艾略特的《J. A. 普鲁弗洛克的情歌》,参考译文如下:

　　这究竟值不值得,/值不值得,/在落日、庭院与洒过水的街道之后,/在小说之后,在茶杯之后,曳地的长裙之后——/这些,还有更多?/要表达我的意思,实在太难!

41. 诗句选自美国浪漫主义时期诗人沃尔特·惠特曼(Walt Whitman)诗集《草叶集》(*Leaves of Grass*)中的名诗"有个孩子天天向前走"(*There Was a Child Went Forth*),参考译文如下:

　　有一个孩子天天往前走,/他看见的第一件东西,他就成了那件东西,/而那件东西就在当天或当天的某个时候成了他的一部分,/或者持续许多年和绵延许多世纪。

　　＊这个孩子指的是当时新生的美国。

42. 诗句选自惠特曼《草叶集》中的诗歌"涉水的骑兵"(*Cavalry Crossing a Ford*),参考译文如下:

　　一支长长的队伍在青葱的岛屿间蜿蜒行进,/他们采取迂回的路线,他们的武器在太阳下闪/耀,——你听那铿锵悦耳的声音,/你看那亮晶晶的河流上,蹚水的马匹在踟蹰不前,饮着河水,/你看那些脸色黧黑的骑兵,每一群、每个人都是/一幅图画,歇在马鞍上随意消停。

43. 引诗出自惠特曼《草叶集》中的诗歌"自我之歌"(*Song of Myself*),参考译文如下:

　　我赞美我自己,歌颂我自己,/我所承当的一切,你也必定承当,/因为属于我的每一个原子,也同样属于你。

　　＊And what I assume you shall assume, = And you shall assume what I assume.

44. 引诗出自惠特曼《草叶集》中的诗歌"自我之歌"(*Song of Myself*)第一节,参考译文如下:

　　信条和学派暂时不论,/且退后一步,满足现状,但绝不会被遗忘,/不论我包容善与恶,都容许表达思想,/不避风险,/不受约束的自然,保持原始的活力。

　　＊sufficed at what they are = Creeds and schools sufficed at what they are;第三、四两句多家译本有不同见解,这里是本书作者的理解;at every hazard = at all hazards 冒一切风险;without check 不受约束;这里的 nature 与其说是"自然"不如说是"自由"。此节诗的含义就是:打破一切清规戒律,自由表达思想。

45. 引诗出自美国文学现实主义时期女诗人艾米莉·狄金森(Emily Dickinson)的诗作《这是我写给世界的信》(*This is my letter to the World*)第一节,参考译文如下:

　　这是我写给世界的信/它不曾给过我一个字——/是自然告诉我的简单消息——/以温柔而庄严的方式

46. 诗句引自艾米莉·狄金森的诗作《这是我写给世界的信》第二节,参考译文如下:

　　(也许)她的信息是交给了/我看不见的手——/凭我对她的爱,亲爱的,同胞们啊——/评判我时——请温柔些

　　＊这首诗里的"世界"指外部世界。狄金森长期不与外界交往,所谓给世界的信,不过是心灵的

向往，"世界"当然也就无信息给她，只能寄意沉寂的大自然作为信使。对外虽少交往，"爱"却是存在的。

47. 诗句引自艾米莉·狄金森的诗作《我死时——听见一只苍蝇嗡嗡叫——》(I heard a Fly buzz — when I died —)第一节，可译为：

当我死时，听见一只苍蝇嗡嗡嗡——/房间里一片寂静/就像是天空中的沉寂/出现在风暴的涌动之间——

48. 诗句引自艾米莉·狄金森的诗作《我死时——听见一只苍蝇嗡嗡叫——》第四节，可译为：

带着蓝色的——断断续续的嗡嗡声——/在光明与我——之间/然后窗户暗淡了——接着/原本看见的，我再无法看见——

49. 诗句引自艾米莉·狄金森的诗作《我喜欢看它一哩哩奔驰——》(I like to see it lap the Miles —)第一节，可译为：

我喜欢看它一哩哩爬过——/爬过一条条山谷而上——/有时停在水塔下牛饮——/然后，迈开惊人的大步

50. 诗句引自艾米莉·狄金森的诗作《因为我不能停下等候死神——》(Because I could not stop for Death)第一节，可译为：

因为我不能停步等候死神——/他殷勤停车接我——/车厢里只有我们俩——/还有永生相伴。

51. 诗引自艾米莉·狄金森的诗作《因为我不能停下等候死神——》第五节，可翻译如下：

我们停在一栋屋前，这屋子/仿佛隆起的地面——/屋顶，勉强可见——/屋檐，低于地面——

52. 引诗是美国著名现代主义诗人埃兹拉·庞德(Ezra Pound)最有代表性的单一意象诗《在一个地铁车站》(In a Station of the Metro)，参考译文如下：

人群中这些脸庞幽灵般显现，/湿漉漉的黑色枝条上的片片花瓣。

53. 诗句选自埃兹拉·庞德的《河商妻子给丈夫的一封信》(The River-Merchant's Wife：a Letter)，此诗翻译自我国大诗人李白的《长干行》，本选段为英文译诗的第二节，可直译成中文如下：

十五岁时，才不再羞怯拘谨，欢颜相对，/愿与你白头偕老，死后同穴(骨灰都合在一起)，/生死同心，爱情永久。/怎会有登上高台盼望丈夫归来的忧愁呢？

* 李白原诗：十五始展眉，愿同尘与灰，常存抱柱信，岂上望夫台。

54. 诗句选自埃兹拉·庞德的诗作《一个协议》(A Pact)，可译为：

惠特曼，我和你订个协议——/我不喜欢你已经够久了。/现在我走向你，像个长大的孩子，/有个头脑顽固的父亲。

55. 诗句选自埃兹拉·庞德的诗作《一个协议》，可译为：

当时是你砍伐新木，/现在是该雕刻了。/我们有共同的树液和树根——/让我们好好交流。

56. 诗引自罗伯特·李·弗罗斯特(Robert Lee Frost)的诗作《摘苹果后》(After Apple-Picking)参考译文如下：

我耳朵里总是听见地窖里/一堆一堆苹果/滚动入仓的声音。/因为我摘苹果/已经摘得我够受。我已经过分/厌倦于我自己/曾经期望的大丰收。

57. 诗句引自弗罗斯特的诗作《摘苹果后》，参考译文如下：

你可以明白，什么样的事情会打搅/我睡的这一觉，不论觉是怎样的，/如果土拨鼠还没离去，/就能告诉我们，是像他的那种，/我说正在到来的——长眠，/抑或只是人类的某种"睡眠"。

58. 诗句引自弗罗斯特的诗作《未选择的路》(The Road Not Taken)最后一节，参考译文如下：

在很久以后的某处，/我会一声叹息，重把往事提起。/树林中曾经有两条歧路，当初，/我选择了人迹罕至的一途，/这就造成了此后的全部差异。

59. 诗句引自弗罗斯特的诗作《雪夜林边停》(Stopping by Woods on a Snowy Evening)的第一节，参考译

文如下：

这是谁的树林我想我清楚，/他家就住在那边林子里；/他不会看见我停在树林边，/正观赏他茫茫大雪盖莽林。

60. 诗句引自弗罗斯特的诗作《雪夜林边停》第四节，即最后一节，参考译文如下：

这树林可爱，阴暗，幽深，/但是我还有许诺的事要完成，/临睡前还要再赶几哩路程，/临睡前还要再赶几哩路程。

Ⅳ．散文和小说部分答案

1. 此段选自英国文艺复兴时期著名思想家和散文作家弗朗西斯·培根（Francis Bacon）的《论学习》（*On Study*），参考译文如下：

读书学习可以弥补天性之不足，经验又可弥补读书之不足；因为天赋才能犹如自然草木，需要读书学习来修剪；学问虽可给人指导，但过多过滥，会流于空泛，必得依靠实践经验才能扎下根基。

2. 引文出自弗朗西斯·培根的《论学习》，参考译文如下：

如果不善于全面考察事物，不会举一反三、从一件事来论证、推理另一件事，就让他去学习律师的案例。这样每个人头脑中的思想缺陷，都会找到针对性的治疗良方。

* be apt to do sth. 善于做某事，易于做某事；to call up 提出……来考虑；to beat over 全面考察

3. 引文出自英国新古典主义时期作家乔纳森·斯威夫特（Jonathan Swift）著名小说《格列佛游记》（*Gulliver's Travels*），参考译文如下：

我的和蔼和善良的行为博得了皇帝和朝臣的欢心，军队和人民也普遍喜欢我，所以我就抱着在短期内可以获得自由的希望。我想尽一切办法来讨好他们。

* to gain on/upon sb. 博得某人的好感，巴结上某人；to conceive hopes of getting my liberty 意识到/感到有希望获得自由

4. 引文出自新古典主义时期学者塞缪尔·约翰逊（Samuel Johnson）的《致尊敬的切斯特菲尔德伯爵》（*To the Right Honorable the Earl of Chestrtfield*），参考译文如下：

阁下，难道所谓赞助人不就是这样的一个人——当别人在水中为求生而苦苦挣扎的时候他冷眼旁观，而当这人爬上岸时却要给予帮助、让他受蒙恩之累——吗？

* to encumber sb. with help　以给予帮助使某人挑上受人恩惠的思想负担

5. 引文出自英国浪漫主义时期女作家简·奥斯汀（Jane Austen）的长篇小说《傲慢与偏见》（*Pride and Prejudice*）第一章，参考译文如下：

凡是有钱的单身汉，总想娶位太太，这已经成一条举世公认的真理。

这样的单身汉，每逢新搬到一个地方，四邻八舍虽然不了解他的性情如何，见解如何，可是，既然这样的一条真理早已在人们心目中根深蒂固，因此人们总是把他看作自己某一个女儿理所应得的一笔财产。

* in possession of 拥有，占有；in want of 缺少，没有；some or other 这个或那个

6. 引文出自英国维多利亚时期伟大的小说家查尔斯·狄更斯（Charles Dickens）的小说《雾都孤儿》（*Oliver Twist*）第三章，参考译文如下：

反对这套"体制"的人可不要以为，在这段单独禁闭的时间里，奥利弗被剥夺了有益的身体锻炼，愉悦的社会交往，或是神圣的宗教慰藉。

* 句中 it 为形式宾语，真正的宾语是 that 引导的从句。

* solitary incarceration 单独关押/禁闭；the advantages of religious consolation 宗教慰藉的好处

7. 引文出自维多利亚时期女作家夏洛特·勃朗特(Charlotte Brontë)的著名小说《简·爱》(*Jane Eyre*)第二十三章,参考译文如下:

　　难道你认为,因为我穷,默默无闻,不漂亮,个子瘦小,我就没有灵魂了吗? ——你想错了! ——我的心灵跟你一样丰富,我的心胸跟你一样充实! …… 我不是用习俗、常规,甚至不是用血肉之躯跟你说话,而是我的灵魂同你的灵魂对话,就像两个灵魂一起穿过坟墓,我们同时站在上帝脚下,彼此平等——本来就是如此!

　　* to gift sb. with beauty 赋予某人美貌; to address your spirit 与你的灵魂对话

8. 引文出自维多利亚时期女作家艾米莉·勃朗特(Emily Brontë)的著名小说《呼啸山庄》(*Wuthering Heights*)第十五章,译文如下:

　　他猛地一下坐进最近的一张椅中,当我急急地走过去看她是不是晕过去时,他对我咬牙切齿,口吐白沫,像条疯狗,还带着贪婪的嫉妒神色把她抱得紧紧的。我觉得仿佛不是和自己的一个同类在一起……

　　* to fling oneself into 猛地一下扑进/坐进; in the company of 与……相伴/在一起

9. 引文出自英国维多利亚时期女作家乔治·艾略特(George Eliot)的代表性小说《米德尔玛琪镇》(*Middlemarch*)第二十八章,参考译文如下:

　　婚姻本应引导她进入有益的、必要的工作,然而并没有使她从名门淑女无所事事的压抑中解脱出来:甚至太多的闲暇时间,没能使她陶醉在柔情款款心猿意马的快乐之中。

　　* to bring guidance into 指引,引导进入/走向……; to fill her leisure with the ruminant joy of unchecked tenderness 她在闲暇时间,思绪绵绵,柔情款款

10. 引文出自乔治·艾略特的《米德尔玛琪镇》第二十八章,参考译文如下:

　　她那充满活力、跃跃欲试的青春,遭到了精神上的禁锢,这与那阴冷、单调、狭隘的冬日景色,那蜷缩的家具,从未打开过的书,那仿佛见不得阳光的、苍白虚幻的世界中那头幽灵似的公鹿,是完全一致的。

　　* to make itself one with 使本身与……一致起来;be vanishing from the daylight 从日光中消失/绝迹

11. 引文出自英国维多利亚时期作家托马斯·哈代(Thomas Hardy)的名著《德伯家的苔丝》(*Tess of the D' Urbervilles*)第三部分第十九章,参考译文如下:

　　但是她不久就发现奶牛出现的顺序虽然似乎完全偶然,却总和她对此的愿望完全一致。她终于意识到它们的顺序并非出自偶然了。奶场老板那位学徒近来在帮忙赶牛,这样的事发生到第五六次的时候,苔丝便转过脸去望着他,头靠在牛身上,眼里满是隐藏的疑问。

　　* the ostensibly chance position 表面上看似偶然的位置;to lend a hand in getting the cows together 帮忙把牛赶在一起;full of sly inquiry upon him 满眼隐藏着对他的疑问

12. 引文出自托马斯·哈代的名著《德伯家的苔丝》第三部分第十九章,参考译文如下:

　　而在苔丝这方面,她也不明白,为什么一个出身牧师家庭,受过良好教育的男人,并无物质上的匮乏,却把生命当作苦难? 对她这位不幸的朝圣者来说,是有充分的理由。但是这位令人钦佩、富有诗意的男人为什么也会堕入耻辱谷呢?

　　* above physical want 没有不能满足物质需求的情况;to look upon it as a mishap to be alive 把活着看成不幸/受罪

13. 引文出自英国现代时期伟大剧作家乔治·萧伯纳(George Bernard Shaw)的名作《华伦夫人的职业》(*Mrs. Warren's Profession*)第二幕,参考译文如下:

　　那么,我们的亲戚在哪儿? 我的父亲? 我们家庭的朋友? 你声称有做母亲的种种权利:把我叫作傻瓜、孩子的权利;用学校里有权威的女人都不敢用的语气对我讲话,主宰我的生活方式;强迫我认识一个粗俗的家伙,任何人都看得出他是伦敦城里最邪恶的那种人。在我费心费神地来对抗你这些要求的权利之前,我不妨先弄明白,这些权利是否真的存在?

＊ in authority over me 有权（威）管我；to dictate my way of life 发号施令干预我的生活方式；to force on me the acquaintance of sb. ＝to force the acquaintance of sb. on me 强迫我与某人相识

14. 引文出自萧伯纳的名剧《华伦夫人的职业》第二幕，译文如下：

　　　对于一个女人来说，能给她提供一个体面生活的唯一途径就是：对一个有经济能力对她好的男人好。如果她处于和他一样的社会地位，她就该让他娶她，但如果她的地位比他低得多，她就别做这个指望，她怎么能指望呢？这不会给她带来幸福。问问在伦敦社会中的、有女儿的任何一个女士，她会告诉你这同样的答案，只是我直截了当地告诉你，而她则是转弯抹角地告诉你。这就是唯一的差别。

15. 引文出自维多利亚时期作家约翰·高尔斯华绥（John Galsworthy）的小说《财主》（*The Man of Property*）第十三章，参考译文如下：

　　　世界上肯定没有一件事会比福尔赛家的人发现某件事的实际花费超过预先规定更使他恼火的了。这也是人之常情，因为他生活上的大政方针都是根据精密计划来安排的。如果他不能依赖固定的财产价值计划安排，他的方向盘就不准了；他就像似在茫茫苦海上随波逐流的一只无舵的船。

　　＊ be ordered upon the accuracy of his estimates　是根据准确的预算/计划作安排的

16. 引文出自约翰·高尔斯华绥的小说《财主》第十三章，参考译文如下：

　　　她的话他既相信又不相信，但是他知道自己这话是问错的；她的心思他从来就不知道，而且永远不会知道。看着她这付心意难测的脸，想到无数夜晚她总是这付柔顺的样子坐在那里，然而是那样的不可理解，无法知晓，使他怒不可遏！

　　＊ the sight of ＝seeing. . . 看见……；the thought of ＝thinking . . . 想到……；to enrage him beyond measure 使他怒不可遏/极端愤怒

17. 引文出自英国现代时期作家戴维·赫伯特·劳伦斯（David Herbert Lawrence）的小说《儿子与情人》（*Sons and Lovers*）第十章，参考译文如下：

　　　保罗担心她误读了信的意思，最终会大失所望。他将信件仔细查阅了一遍、两遍，不错，确信这是真的。于是也坐了下来，他的心也因极度兴奋而扑通直跳。

　　"妈!"他大叫起来。

　　"我不是说过我们应该试一试嘛!"她说道，她在哭，却试图掩饰。

　　＊ be afraid lest. . . ＝be afraid that . . . 这里 lest 用于表示恐惧、担心、危险等的词的后面，起连接从句的作用，相当于 that。

18. 引文出自 D. H. 劳伦斯的小说《儿子与情人》第十章，参考译文如下：

　　　他曾穿着威廉原来的晚礼服出去吃过几顿饭。每次他的母亲都很得意，很欢喜。他现在是出人头地了。她和她的孩子们替威廉买的饰钉都钉在他的衬衫前襟；他穿着威廉配礼服穿的一件白衬衣，但他体态更优雅。他的脸虽显得粗犷些，却充满热情，讨人喜欢。他看上去虽不见得特别像绅士，然而在她看来，他的确是一表人才的男子汉。

　　＊ be firm with pride and joy　（内心）肯定是充满了自豪和快乐

19. 引文出自英国现代时期伟大作家詹姆斯·乔伊斯（James Joyce）短篇小说集《都柏林人》（*Dubliners*）中的第三篇"阿拉比"（*Araby*），参考译文如下：

　　　她终于和我说话了。当她说头两句时，我茫然无措，不知如何作答。她问我去不去阿拉比，我忘了答的是去还是不去。她说那将是个绝好的东方贸易市场，她非常希望她能够去。

20. 引文出自詹姆斯·乔伊斯短篇小说集《都柏林人》第三篇"阿拉比"结尾几行，参考译文如下：

　　　然后我慢慢地转过身走进市场中间，任那两个一便士的硬币落进口袋击在那个六便士的硬币上。我听见一个声音从廊台的尽头传来——灯熄灭了，会厅的上部全部陷入了黑暗。

　　凝望着黑暗的深处，我感到自己是一个被虚荣所驱使、所嘲笑的人，痛苦与愤怒在我眼中燃烧。

* penny 用以表示单个硬币数,如 two pennies 两个一便士的硬币;pence 用以表示面值,如 a sixpence,一枚六便士的硬币。

21. 引文出自美国浪漫主义时期作家华盛顿·欧文(Washington Erving)的小说《瑞普·凡·温克尔》(*Rip Van Winkle*)第一部分,参考译文如下:

随着婚后时光的推移,瑞普·凡·温克尔的日子越来越难过。尖酸的个性永不会随着年龄变得圆润温软,刻薄的舌头是唯一在反复使用下会日益锋利的带刃的工具。曾经在很长一段时间里,他常常在被赶出家门后造访一个永久性的俱乐部,以聊以自慰。其中都是村子里的智者、哲人和其他一些游手好闲的人物。

22. 引文出自华盛顿·欧文的小说《瑞普·凡·温克尔》第二部分,参考译文如下:

门口像往常一样聚集着一群人,可瑞普回想不起见过其中的任何一个,人们的性情也似乎变了,带有一种忙碌、焦躁、好争辩的神气,一改往日安于自守的平和与昏昏然的沉静。他张望着却没见到睿智的尼古拉斯·维德……

* a busy, bustling, disputatious tone about it (= the door)周围一派忙碌、吵闹、好争辩得气氛;the accustomed phlegm and drowsy tranquility 习惯性的懒散迟钝和昏昏欲睡的平静

23. 引文出自美国浪漫主义时期著名散文作家拉尔夫·沃尔多·爱默生(Ralph Waldo Emerson)的《论自然》(*On Nature*)第一章,参考译文如下:

站在空旷的大地上——我的头沐浴在欢乐的空气中,被提升到无限的空间——一切卑鄙的利己主义都消失了。我变成了一颗透明的眼球。我什么都不是。我看到了一切。宇宙万物的流动通过我而循环。我是上帝的一部分和一个颗粒。

24. 引文出自美国浪漫主义时期象征主义作家纳撒尼尔·霍桑(Nathaniel Hawthorne)的小说《好小伙布朗》(*Yong Goodman Brown*),参考译文如下:

在安息日,当会众们唱起神圣的赞美诗时,他听不得,因为罪恶的颂歌大声地冲进他的耳朵里,并且把所有祝福的语调都淹没了。当牧师把手放在翻开的《圣经》上,有力度而又激昂、滔滔不绝地向教徒宣扬我们宗教的神圣真理,宣扬圣人般的生活和光荣的殉难,宣扬未来的幸福,或难以表达的苦难时,好小伙布朗的脸色变得苍白,生怕屋顶会轰的一声坍塌在这亵渎神灵的白发老人和他的听众头上。他常常会半夜惊醒,推开菲丝的怀抱。早晨或黄昏当全家都跪下做祈祷时,他满面怒容,喃喃地自言自语,严厉地盯着他的妻子,然后转身离去。

* to speak from the pulpit of 在教坛上宣扬……;to thunder down upon 轰然塌下压在……上

25. 引文出自美国浪漫主义时期作家赫尔曼·麦尔韦尔(Herman Melville)的代表作《白鲸》(*Moby-Dick*)第一百三十五章,参考译文如下:

哦,孤独地活着,孤独地死去!啊,我感到我最崇高的伟大就源于这最大的悲伤。嘀嘀!从你最远的跳跃中,涌进来吧,我全部昔日生命中你勇敢的波涛,超越我的死亡这一层层涌起的浪潮!我朝你卷来了,你这能摧毁一切却征服不了一切的白鲸;我会与你搏斗到底。即使到了地狱中心,我也要捅你一刀,我最后一口气也要吐向你。把所有的棺材和灵车都沉到一个共同的水域深渊!既然哪一个都不可能是我的,那就与你绑在一起,穷追不舍,直到把你这该死的大鲸撕成碎片!

* to grapple with 与……搏斗到底;let me then tow to pieces,... thou damned whale! = let me then tow thou damned whale to pieces! 那么,让我把这该死的大鲸撕成碎片!

26. 引文出自美国文学现实主义时期著名作家马克·吐温(Mark Twain)的代表作品《哈克贝利·费恩历险记》(*Adventures of Huckleberry Finn*)第三十一章,参考译文如下:

所以我心里非常苦恼,简直不能再苦恼了,不知怎么才好。最终我想出了个主意;我就说,我去写信吧——然后再看我能不能祷告得成。哈,奇怪得很,我马上就觉得轻松得像根鸡毛似的,

什么苦恼也没有了。于是我就拿起一张纸和一支铅笔,兴致十足地坐下来写。

　　* the way I felt as light as a feather = I felt as light as a feather in this way 这么一想,我感到轻松得像一个鸡毛似的;right straight off 立即,马上

27. 引文出自马克·吐温的《哈克贝利·费恩历险记》,参考译文如下:

　　　　可是不知怎么的,我好像找不出那一点来,可以叫我狠起心来对他,反倒老是想起他的好处。我老是看见他自己轮完了班,接着又替我轮班,并不把我叫醒,为的是让我依旧睡下去;又看见他在我从大雾里回来的时候,那副高兴的样子;还有在上游那回打冤家的地方,我上那泥塘里再去找他的时候,他又是多么欢喜…… 后来我又想起那一回,我告诉那两个人说我们木排上有人害天花,结果就救了吉姆,他感激得什么似的,说我是老吉姆在世界上最好的朋友……

　　　　我琢磨了一会儿,好像连气都不敢出似的,随后才对自己说:

　　　　"好吧,那么,下地狱就下地狱吧。"——接着我就一下子把它(信)扯掉了。

　　* to strike no place to harden me against him 没有找到/发现/想起什么差错叫我硬起心肠对付他;to stand my watch on top of his'n 除了值自己的班以外,又替我值班(his'n 为 his 的绝对形式)

28. 引文出自美国文学现实主义时期作家亨利·詹姆士(Henry James)的中篇小说《黛西·米勒》(*Daisy Miller*)第一部分,参考译文如下:

　　　　可怜的温特伯恩感到有趣、迷惑,首先是着迷了。他还从来没听见过一个年轻姑娘如此表白她自己——除非是在类似时间怀着复杂的思想意识说这些事情的场合,从来没有过这样。但是否要按照日内瓦的规矩指责黛西·米勒小姐实际行为上或潜在思想上非常异类呢?他觉得自己在日内瓦待得太久,道德是非上有点糊涂了,他对美国年轻人的说话腔调没有好感了。

　　* to lose the right sense for 对……失去了好感

29. 引文出自西奥多·德莱塞(Theodore Dreiser)的《嘉莉妹妹》(*Sister Carrie*),参考译文如下:

　　　　现在,嘉莉已经实现了她以前所追求的人生目标,或者说,至少实现了能用来满足人的基本物质欲望的那一部分…… 这些都曾是她梦寐以求的。她被掌声包围着,成了公众注意的焦点,而这些以前看来遥不可及的东西,现在却显得如此的索然无味。美貌是她的另一可爱之处,然而却依然掩饰不住她的孤独。在她闲暇无事的时候,她就躺在摇椅上浅吟低唱,神游梦里。

　　* when not otherwise engaged (她)什么别的事也不干,什么事也不想的时候/无事可干,闲暇无事的时候

30. 引文出自美国文学现代时期著名剧作家、唯一一位以剧作获得诺贝尔文学奖的人尤金·奥尼尔(Eugene O'Neill)的作品《毛猿》(*The Hair Ape*)第八场,参考译文如下:

　　　　你怎么会不懂得我的意思呢?难道我们不是同一个俱乐部,毛猿俱乐部的会员吗?

31. 引文出自美国文学现代时期"爵士时代"文学代言人斯科特·菲兹杰拉德(Scott Fitzgerald)的代表作《伟大的盖茨比》(*The Great Gatsby*)第三章,参考译文如下:

　　　　汽车喇叭的鸣叫声像猫叫,越来越响,我转身离开,穿过草坪向家中走去。我回头向后看了一眼。一轮薄薄的圆月照在盖茨比的房屋之上,使夜色和原来一样美好,明月依旧,而欢声笑语已经从依然光辉灿烂的花园里消失了。一阵突然的空虚此刻似乎正从窗口和一扇扇大门之中涌流而出,使主人的身影陷于完全的孤独,他正站在门廊处,举着一只手,摆着一种正式的告别姿势。

　　* endowing with complete isolation the figure of the host = endowing the figure of the host with complete isolation 给主人带来了孤独,使主人陷于完全的孤独之中

32. 引文出自美国文学现代时期著名作家欧内斯特·海明威(Ernest Hemingway)的短篇小说《印第安人营地》(*Indian Camp*),参考译文如下:

　　　　他拉开盖在印第安人头上的毯子。他的手缩回来,湿漉漉的。他拿着灯,踏着下层木床的边,向上层床里看去。那印第安人脸朝墙躺着。他的喉咙从耳朵到耳朵被割开了。鲜血流到他

的身体在床上压出的凹坑处,形成一汪血泊。他的头枕在他的左臂上。那打开的剃刀刀口朝上放在毯子上。

 ＊ to mount on the edge of the bunk 踩在/踏上床的边沿;to sag the bunk 使床下陷成凹坑

33. 引文出自海明威的短篇小说《印第安人营地》,参考译文如下:

　　"女士们生孩子总是这么痛苦吗?"尼克问。

　　"不,这是非常、非常少的例外。"

　　"他为什么要自杀,爸爸?"

　　"我不知道,尼克,我想,他受不了这些。"

34. 引文出自威廉·福克纳(William Faulkner)的短篇小说《给艾米莉的玫瑰》(*A Rose for Emily*),参考译文如下:

　　我们在那里站了很久,俯视着那没有肉的脸上令人莫测的龇牙咧嘴的样子。那尸体躺在那里,显出一度是拥抱的姿势,但那比爱更持久、甚至战胜了爱之百态的永恒长眠使他再不能向情人施爱了。他所遗留下来的肉体已在破烂的睡衣下腐烂,跟他躺着的木床连在一起,难分难解了。在他身上和他身旁的枕上,均匀地覆盖着一层长年累聚的积尘。

　　后来我们才注意到旁边那个枕头上有人头压过的痕迹。我们当中有一个人从那上面拿起了什么东西,大家凑近一看——这时一股淡淡的干燥发臭的气味钻进了鼻孔——原来是一绺长长的铁灰色头发。

 ＊ in the attitude of an embrace 以相互搂抱的姿态;the grimace of love 表达爱的种种方式/形态;to cuckold sb. 给某人戴了绿帽子;(转意为)使某人不能再为人夫/向情人施爱了;to become inextricable from 与……不可分离,难以摆脱……;the patient and biding dust 长期积累的尘土

第四部分

英诗格律和韵律分析练习

Ⅰ．诗句格律分析

对下列诗句划分音步,用"ˈ"符号标注重音(未标者为轻音),并判断其格律。例如,I ˈwon/dered ˈlone/ly ˈas/a ˈcloud, 此句的格律为四步抑扬格。

1. Art is long and time is fleeting.
2. merrily merrily shall I live.
3. Like a child from the womb, like a ghost from the tomb.
4. I shot an arrow into the air,/It fell to earth, I know not where;
5. I breathed a song into the air
6. (P16) A Gentle Knight was pricking on the plaine,
7. (P16) But on his brest a bloudie Crosse he bore,
8. (P23) Now that the gloomy shadow of the night,
8. (P27) And we will sit upon the rocks,/Seeing the shepherds feed their flocks,
10. (P28) The shepherds' swains shall dance and sing/For thy delight each May morning;
11. (P38) So long as men can breathe, or eyes can see,/So long lives this, and this gives life to thee.
12. (P68) Death, be not proud, though some have called thee
13. (P68) One short sleep past, we wake eternally
14. (P95) Be not the first by whom the new are tried,/Nor yet the last to lay the old aside.
15. (P153) The curfew tolls the knell of parting day,/The lowing herd wind slowly o'er the lea,
16. (P180) And then my heart with pleasure fills,/And dances with the daffodils.
17. (P182) She lived unknown, and few could know/When Lucy ceased to be;
18. (P219) Thou still unravish'd bride of quietness,/Thou foster-child of silence and slow time,
19. (P277) Twilight and evening bell,/And after that the dark!
20. (P567) My little horse must think it queer/To stop without a farmhouse near
21. (P567) He gives his harness bells a shake/To ask is there is some mistake.
22. (P567) The woods are lovely, dark, and deep,
23. (P567) And miles to go before I sleep.

Ⅱ．诗节格律和韵律分析

对下列诗节划分音步、标注重音、判断其格律，并判断诗节的韵律。

24.（P37）Shall I compare thee to a summer's day?
　　　Thou art more lovely and more temperate：
　　　Rough winds do shake the darling buds of May,
　　　And summer's lease hath all too short a date：
　　　Sometime too hot the eye of heaven shines
　　　And often is his gold complexion dimmed；
　　　And every fair from fair sometimes declines,
　　　By chance or nature's changing course untrimmed；
　　　But thy eternal summer shall not fade,
　　　Nor lose possession of that fair thou ow'st；
　　　Nor shall death brag thou wander'st in his shade,
　　　When in eternal lines to time thou grow'st：
　　　So long as men can breathe, or eyes can see,
　　　So long lives this, and this gives life to thee.

25.（P93）Some to conceit alone their taste confine,
　　　And glittering thoughts struck out at every line；
　　　Pleased with a work where nothing's just or fit,
　　　One glaring chaos and wild heap of wit.

26.（P171）When my mother died I was young,
　　　And my father sold me while yet my tongue
　　　Could scarcely cry "'weep! 'weep! 'weep! 'weep!"
　　　So your chimney I sweep, & in soot I sleep.

27.（P179）I wandered lonely as a cloud
　　　That floats on high o'er vales and hills,
　　　When all at once I saw a crowd,
　　　A host, of golden daffodils；
　　　Beside the lake, beneath the trees,
　　　Fluttering and dancing in the breeze.

28.（P182）She dwelt among the untrodden ways
　　　Beside the springs of Dove,
　　　A Maid whom there were none to praise
　　　And very few to love；

29.（P199）The isles of Greece, the isles of Greece!
　　　Where burning Sappho loved and sung,
　　　Where grew the arts of war and peace,
　　　Where Delos rose, and Phoebus sprung!
　　　Eternal summer gilds them yet,

But all, except their sun, is set.

30. （P211）O wild West Wind, thou breath of Autumn's being,

Thou, from whose unseen presence the leaves dead

Are driven, like ghosts from an enchanter fleeting,

Yellow, and black, and pale, and hectic red,

Pestilence-stricken multitudes: O Thou,

Who chariotest to their dark wintry bed

31. （P289）Round the cape of a sudden came the sea,

And the sun looked over the mountain's rim:

And straight was a path of gold for him,

And the need of a world of men for me.

32. O, my Luve's like a red, red rose,

That's newly sprung in June;

O, my Luve's like the melodie

That's sweetly play'd in tune.

Ⅲ. 格律和韵律分析答案

1. 'Art is/ 'long and/ 'time is/ 'fleeting.　诗句格律为四步扬抑格。

2. 'merrily/ 'merrily/ 'shall I live.　诗句格律为三步扬抑抑格。

3. Like a 'child/ from the 'womb,/ like a 'ghost/ from the 'tomb.　诗句格律为四步抑抑扬格。

4. I 'shot/ an 'ar/ row 'in/ to the 'air,// It 'fell/ to 'earth,/ I 'know/ not 'where；　两个诗句格律均为四步抑扬格。

5. I 'breathed/ a 'song/ into/ the 'air　诗句格律为四步抑扬格。

6. A 'Gen/ tle 'knight/ was 'pri/ cking 'on/ the 'plaine,　诗句格律为五步抑扬格。

7. But 'on/ his 'brest/ a 'blou/ die 'Crosse/ he 'bore,　诗句格律为五步抑扬格,第一音步为扬抑格。

8. Now 'that/ the 'gloo/ my 'sha/ dow 'of/ the 'night,　诗句格律为五步抑扬格,第四音步为抑扬格。

9. And 'we/ will 'sit/ u 'pon/ the 'rocks,// 'Seeing/ the 'she/ pherds 'feed/ their 'flocks,　两个诗句基调格为四步抑扬格,只有 seeing 是扬抑格。

10. The 'she/ pherds' 'swains/ shall 'dance/ and 'sing// For 'thy/ de 'light/ each 'May/ 'morning；　两个诗句均为四步抑扬格。

11. So 'long/ as 'men/ can breathe,/ or 'eyes/ can 'see,// So 'long/ lives 'this,/ and 'this/ gives 'life/ to 'thee.　两个诗句均为五步抑扬格。

12. Death, * / be 'not/ proud, 'though/ some 'have/ called 'thee　尽管第一音步缺一个音节,用 * 号表示,但其余四个音步都是抑扬格,故诗句为五步抑扬格。

13. One 'short/ sleep 'past,/ we 'wake/ e'ter/ nally　诗句格律为五步抑扬格,最后一个音步为抑抑格。

14. Be 'not/ the 'first/ by 'whom/ the 'new/ are 'tried,// Nor 'yet/ the 'last/ to 'lay/ the 'old/ a'side.　两个诗句均为五步抑扬格。

15. The 'cur/ few 'tolls/ the 'knell/ of 'par/ ting 'day,// The 'low/ ing 'herd/ 'wind 'slow/ ly 'o' er/ the 'lea,　两个诗句格律为五步抑扬格。

16. And ·then/my ·heart/with ·plea/sure ·fills,//And ·dan/ces ·with/the ·da/ffo·dils.　两个诗句均为四步抑扬格。

17. She ·lived/un·known,/ and ·few/could ·know//When ·Lu/cy ·ceased/to ·be;　两行诗句的格律分别为四步抑扬格和三步抑扬格,总体上可说是四三音步抑扬格。

18. Thou ·still/un·ra/vish'd ·bride/of ·qui/etness,//Thou ·fos/ter-·child/of ·si/lence and/slow ·time.　两行诗句 10 个音步绝大多数为抑扬格,故诗句格律均为五步抑扬格。

19. Twi·light/and ·eve/ning ·bell,//And ·a/fter ·that/the ·dark!　两个诗句均为三步抑扬格。

20. My ·lit/tle ·horse/must ·think/it ·queer//To ·stop/wi·thout/a ·farm/house ·near　两个诗句都是四步抑扬格。

21. He ·gives/his ·har/ness ·bells/a ·shake//To ·ask/if ·there/is ·some/mis·take.　两个诗句都是四步抑扬格。

22. The ·woods/are ·love/ly, ·dark,/ and ·deep　诗句格律为四步抑扬格。

23. And ·miles/to ·go/be·fore/I ·sleep.　诗句格律为四步抑扬格。

24. Shall ·I/com·pare/thee ·to/a ·sum/mer's ·day?　　　a
Thou ·art/more ·love/ly and/more ·tem/perate:　　　b
Rough ·winds/do ·shake/the ·dar/ling ·buds/of ·May,　　a
And ·sum/mer's ·lease/hath ·all/too ·short/a ·date:　　b
Some ·time/too ·hot/the ·eye/of ·hea/ven ·shines　　c
And ·o/ften ·is/his ·gold/com·ple/xion ·dimmed;　　d
And ·e/very ·fair/from ·fair/some·times/dec·lines,　　c
By ·chance/or ·na/ture's ·chan/ging ·course/un·trimmed;　　d
But ·thy/e·ter/nal ·sum/mer ·shall/not ·fade,　　e
Nor ·lose/po·sse/ssion of/that ·fair/thou ·ow'st;　　f
Nor ·shall/death ·brag/thou ·wan/der'st in/his ·shade,　　e
When in/e·ter/nal ·lines/to ·time/thou ·grow'st:　　f
So ·long/as ·men/can ·breathe,/ or ·eyes/can ·see,　　g
So ·long/lives ·this,/ and ·this/gives ·life/to ·thee.　　g
莎士比亚这首十四行诗格律为五步抑扬格,韵律为 ababcdcdefefgg。

25. ·Some to/con·ceit/a·lone/their ·taste/con·fine,　　a
And ·glit/tering ·thoughts/struck ·out/at ·e/very ·line;　　a
·Pleased with/a ·work/where ·no/thing's ·just/or ·fit,　　b
One ·gla/ring ·cha/os and/wild ·heap/of ·wit.　　b
这一节诗每句都是 5 个音步,除了第二句第二音步有 3 个音节,为抑抑扬格以外,所有音步都是两个音节,绝大多数是抑扬格,所以诗的格律为五步抑扬格,韵律为 aabb。

26. ·When my/·mother/died ·I/was ·ve/ry ·young,　　a
And ·my/·father/·sold me/while ·yet/my ·tongue　　a
Could ·scarce/ly ·cry/"·weep! ·weep! /·weep! ·weep!"　　b
So ·your/·chimney/I ·sweep/, & in ·soot/I ·sleep.　　b
除第三行诗是 4 个音步外,其他每行诗都是 5 个音步,大多数音步都是抑扬格,故此诗的格律为五步抑扬格,韵律为 aabb。

27. I ·wan/dered ·lone/ly ·as/a ·cloud　　a
That ·floats/on ·high/o' er ·vales/and ·hills,　　b
When ·all/at ·once/I ·saw/a ·crowd,　　a

A ˈhost,/ of ˈgol/den ˈda/ffoˈdils；　　　　　　　　　b

Beˈside/the ˈlake,/ beˈneath/the ˈtrees,　　　　　　c

ˈFlutter/ing ˈand/ˈdancing/in the ˈbreeze.　　　　　c

此节诗除第六句第一和第三音步为扬抑格,第四音步为抑抑扬格,其余均为抑扬格,因此格律为四步抑扬格,韵律为 ababcc。

28. She ˈdwelt/aˈmong/the ˈun/trodden ˈways　　　a

Beˈside/the ˈsprings/of ˈDove,　　　　　　　　　b

A ˈMaid/whom ˈthere/were ˈnone/to ˈpraise　　　a

And ˈve/ry ˈfew/to ˈlove;　　　　　　　　　　　b

一、三行诗为四步抑扬格,二、四行诗为三步抑扬格,此节诗可以说是四三音步抑扬格,韵律为 abab。

29. The ˈIsles/of ˈGreece,/ the ˈisles/of ˈGreece!　a

Where ˈbur/ning ˈSa/ppho ˈloved/and ˈsung,　　　b

Where ˈgrew/the ˈarts/of ˈwar/and ˈpeace,　　　a

Where ˈDe/los ˈrose,/ and ˈPhoe/bus ˈsprung!　　b

Eˈter/nal ˈsum/mer ˈgilds/them ˈyet,　　　　　　c

But ˈall,/ exˈcept/their ˈsun,/ is ˈset.　　　　　　c

诗节格律为四步抑扬格,韵律为 ababcc。

30. O ˈwild/West ˈWind,/ thou ˈbreath/of ˈAu/tumn's ˈbeing,　　a

ˈThou, from/whose ˈun/seen ˈpre/sence the/leaves ˈdead　　　b

Are ˈdri/ven, ˈlike/ˈghosts from/an enˈchanter/ˈfleeting,　　　a

ˈYellow,/ and ˈblack,/ and ˈpale,/ and ˈhec/tic ˈred,　　　　　b

ˈPesti/lence-ˈstri/cken ˈmul/ti ˈtudes:/ O ˈThou,　　　　　　b

ˈWho ˈcha/rioˈtest/to ˈtheir/ˈdark ˈwin/try ˈbed　　　　　　b

每行诗都为 5 音步,绝大多数音步是抑扬格,故这两节诗格律为五步抑扬格,韵律为 aba/bcb。

31. Round the ˈcape/of a ˈsud/den ˈcame/the ˈsea,　　　a

And the ˈsun/ˈlooked ˈover/the ˈmoun/tain's ˈrim:　　b

And ˈstraight/was a ˈpath/of ˈgold/for ˈhim,　　　　　b

And the ˈneed/of a ˈworld/of ˈmen/for ˈme.　　　　　b

每行诗都为 4 音步,除了 1 个扬抑抑格(looked over),6 个抑抑扬格(阴影部分)外,其余 9 个音步为抑扬格,故此诗为四步抑扬格,韵律为 abba。

32. O, ˈmy/ˈLuve's like/a red,/ red ˈrose,　　　　a

That's ˈnew/ly ˈsprung/in ˈJune;　　　　　　　b

O, ˈmy/ˈLuve's like/the ˈme/loˈdie　　　　　　c

That's ˈsweet/ly ˈplay'/d/in ˈtune.　　　　　　b

一、三行诗为 4 个音步,二、四行诗为 3 个音步,除了 3 个扬扬格(阴影部分),其余大多数音步为抑扬格,故这节诗格律为四三音步抑扬格,韵律为 abcb。

附　　录

I.《英美文学选读》全国统一命题自学考试
优化标准预测试卷

PART ONE(40 POINTS)

I. Single Choice（40 points in all, 1 for each）

1. （P7）In Renaissance, the European humanist thinkers and scholars made attempts to do the following EXCEPT _____.
   a. getting rid of those old feudalist ideas
   b. getting control of the parliament and government
   c. introducing new ideas that expressed the interests of the rising bourgeoisie
   d. recovering the purity of the early church from the corruption of the Roman Catholic Church

2. （P10）_____ was the first person who introduced printing into England.
   a. William Caxton
   b. Florio
   c. Homer
   d. Plutarch

3. （P30）_____ is not a comedy.
   a. *A Midsummer Night's Dream*
   b. *The Twelfth Night*
   c. *As You Like It*
   d. *Romeo and Juliet*

4. （P33）Which of the following sentences about Shakespeare's greatest tragedies is NOT true？_____
   a. Hamlet, the melancholic scholar-prince, faces the dilemma between action and mind.
   b. Othello's inner weakness is made use of by the outside evil force.
   c. The old king Lear who is willing to totally give up his power makes himself suffer from treachery and infidelity.
   d. Macbeth's lust for power stirs up his ambition and leads him to incessant crimes.

5. （P37）"So long as men can breathe, or eyes can see,/So long lives this, and this gives life to thee."（Shakespeare, *Sonnet* 18）What does "this" refer to？_____.
   a. Lover
   b. Time
   c. Summer
   d. Poetry

6. （P55）"The slings and arrows of outrageous fortune" is an example of _____.

a. allegory   b. simile

c. metaphor   d. irony

7. (P71) Among the works by John Milton, which is indeed the only generally acknowledged epic in English literature since *Beowulf*? _____.

a. *Paradise Regained*   b. *Samson Agonistes*

c. *Areopagitica*   d. *Paradise Lost*

8. (P80) The eighteenth century England is also known as the Age of Enlightenment or the Age of _____.

a. Intellect   b. Reason

c. Rationality   d. Science

9. (P81) Among the following writers, _____ is not an enlightener.

a. John Bunyan   b. John Dryden

c. Alexander Pope   d. Joseph Addison

10. (P98) All of the following novels by Daniel Defoe are the first literary works devoted to the study of problems of the lower-class people EXCEPT _____.

a. *Robinson Crusoe*   b. *Captain Singleton*

c. *Moll Flanders*   d. *Goldsmith*

11. (P106) Drapier is the pseudonym of _____.

a. Swift   b. Defoe

c. Fielding   d. Goldsmith

12. (P161) _____ defines the poet as a "man speaking to men", and poetry as "the spontaneous overflow of powerful feelings, which originates in emotion recollected in tranquility."

a. William Blake   b. William Wordsworth

c. Samuel Taylor Coleridge   d. John Keats

13. (P166) Which of the following is the Gothic novel? _____.

a. P. B. Shelley's *Prometheus Unbound*   b. John Keats' *Lamia*

c. Mary Shelley's *Frankenstein*   d. Jane Austen's *Pride and Prejudice*

14. (P176) All of the following poems by William Wordsworth are masterpieces on nature EXCEPT _____.

a. "I Wandered Lonely as a Cloud"   b. "An Evening Walk"

c. "Tintern Abbey"   d. "The Solitary Reaper"

15. (P207) Which of the following comments on the poem "Ode to the West Wind" is NOT true? _____

a. It is written in the terza rima form.

b. In the poem, the author expresses his eagerness to enjoy the boundless freedom from the reality.

c. The author gathers a wealth of symbolism in this poem.

d. The author of the poem is F. Scott Fitzgerald.

16. (P222) Jane Austen's first novel is _____.

a. *Pride and Prejudice*   b. *Sense and Sensibility*

c. *Emma*   d. *Plan of a Novel*

17. (P236) "The Vanity Fair" is a well-known part in *The Pilgrim's Progress*, which of the following writers later adopted it as the title of a novel? _____.

a. Dickens   b. Thackeray

c. Fielding   d. Hardy

18. （P200）Among the works by Charles Dickens _____ presents his criticism of the Utilitarian principle that rules over the English education system and destroys young hearts and minds.

    a. *Bleak House*   b. *The Pickwick Paper*

    c. *Great Expectation*   d. *Hard Times*

19. （P257）The success of *Jane Eyre* is not only because of its sharp criticism of the existing society, but also due to its introduction to the English novel the first _____ heroine.

    a. explorer   b. peasant

    c. worker   d. governess

20. （P301）_____ believes that man's fate is predeterminedly tragic, driven by a combined force of "nature", both inside and outside.

    a. Charles Dickens   b. Thomas Hardy

    c. Bernard Shaw   d. T. S. Eliot

21. （P313）Modernism is, in many aspects, a reaction against _____. It rejects rationalism which is the theoretical base of realism.

    a. Romanticism   b. humanism

    c. symbolism   d. realism

22. （P316）All of the following are stream-of-consciousness novels EXCEPT _____.

    a. *Pilgrimage*   b. *Ulysses*

    c. *Mrs. Daloway*   d. *Tess of D' Urbervilles*

23. （P321）George Bernard Shaw's play _____ established his position as the leading playwright of his time.

    a. *Widower's Houses*   b. *Too True to Be Good*

    c. *Mrs. Warren's Profession*   d. *Candida*

24. （P360）_____ is a poem concerned with the spiritual breakup of a modern civilization in which human life has lost its meaning, significance and purpose.

    a. *Ulysses*   b. *The Waste Land*

    c. *The Confidential Clerk*   d. *Dubliners*

25. （P372）Which of the following is considered to be a better-structured novel? _____.

    a. *Women in Love*   b. *Sons and Lovers*

    c. *The Rainbow*   d. *Lady Chatterley's Lover*

26. （P401）Henry David Thoreau's work, _____, has always been regarded as a masterpiece of New England Transcendentalism.

    a. *Walden*   b. *The pioneers*

    c. *Nature*   d. *Song of Myself*

27. （P429）_____ is one of the most ambivalent writers in the American literary history.

    a. Hawthorne   b. Whitman

    c. Emerson   d. Thoreau

28. （P433）In many of Hawthorne's stories and novels, the Puritan concept of life is condemned, or the Puritan past is shown in an almost totally negative light, especially in his _____.

    a. *The Scarlet Letter*   b. *The Blithedale Romance*

    c. *The Marble Faun*   d. *Twice-Told Tales*

29. （P450）Whitman's poems are characterized by all the following features EXCEPT _____.

    a. the strict poetic form   b. the free and natural rhythm

c. the easy flow of feelings

d. the simple and conversational language

30. (P458) Melville is best-known as the author of one book named _____ which is one of the world's greatest masterpieces.

    a. *Return*

    b. *Moby-Dick*

    c. *Pierre*

    d. *White Jacket*

31. (P434) _____ is not a fictional character in *The Scarlet Letter*.

    a. Hester

    b. Arthur Dimmersdale

    c. Pierre

    d. White Jacket

32. (P479) Hemingway once described Mark Twain's novel _____ the one book from which "all modern American literature comes."

    a. *Adventures of Huckleberry Finn*

    b. *The Adventures of Tom Sawyer*

    c. *The Gilded Age*

    d. *Roughing It*

33. (P495) While Mark Twain and William Dean Howells satirized European manners at times, _____ was an admirer of ancient European civilization.

    a. O. Henry

    b. Henry James

    c. Walt Whitman

    d. Jack London

34. (P499) Daisy Miller's tragedy of indiscretion is intensified and enlarged by its narration from the point of view of _____.

    a. the author of Henry James

    b. the Italian youth Giovanelli

    c. the American youth Winterbourne

    d. her mother Mrs. Miller

35. (P520) "This is my letter to the world" is a poetic expression of Emily Dickinson's _____ about her communication with the outside world.

    a. indifference

    b. anger

    c. anxiety

    d. sorrow

36. (P525) With the publication of _____, Dreiser was launching himself upon a long career that would ultimately make him one of the most significant American writers of the school later known as literary naturalism.

    a. *Sister Carrie*

    b. *The Titan*

    c. *The Genius*

    d. *The Stoic*

37. (P551) _____ is considered to be a spokesman for the alienated youth in the post-war era and his *The Catcher in the Rye* is regarded as a students' classic.

    a. J. D. Salinger

    b. John Updike

    c. Norman Mailer

    d. Herman Wouk

38. (P578) Fitzgerald wrote the following EXCEPT _____.

    a. *The Great Gatsby*

    b. *In Our Time*

    c. *Tender Is the Night*

    d. *This Side of Paradise*

39. (P601) _____ is Hemingway's masterpiece.

    a. *A Farewell to Arms*

    b. *For Whom the Bell Tolls*

    c. *The Sun Also Rises*

    d. *The Old Man and the Sea*

40. (P616) In Faulkner's *The Sound and the Fury*, he used a technique called _____, in which the whole story was told through the thoughts of one character.

    a. stream-of-consciousness

    b. imagism

    c. symbolism

    d. naturalism

PART TWO (60 POINTS)

II. Reading Comprehension (16 points in all, 4 for each)

41. (P38) "Nor lose possession of that fair thou ow'st;/Nor shall death brag thou wander'st in his shade,/ When in eternal lines to time thou grow'st:/So long as men can breathe, or eyes can see,/So long lives this, and this gives life to thee."

    Questions:

    a. Where does the poem come from? Who wrote it?

    b. What does "lines" mean?

    c. What does the word "this" in the last line refer to?

42. (P181) "Never did sun more beautifully steep/In his first splendor, valley, rock, or hill;/Ne'er saw I, never felt, a calm so deep! /The river glideth at his own will:/Dear God! the very houses seem asleep;/And all that mighty heart is lying still!" (William Wordsworth's sonnet "Composed upon Westminster Bridge, September 3, 1802")

    Questions:

    a. What does the word "glideth" in the fourth line mean?

    b. What kind of figure of speech is used by Wordsworth to describe the "river"?

    c. What idea does the fourth line express?

43. (P457) "My tongue, every atom of my blood, form'd from this soil, this air,/Born here of parents born here from parents the same, and their parents the same,/I, now thirty-seven years old in perfect health begin,/Hoping to cease not till death."

    Questions:

    a. Identify the poet and the title of the poem.

    b. What do "soil" and "air" represent in the first line?

    c. What does the poet try to say in the above four lines?

44. (P522) "Because I could not stop for Death —

    He kindly stopped for me —

    The Carriage held but just Ourselves —

    And Immortality."

    Questions:

    a. Who is the author of the poem?

    b. What does "He" refer to?

    c. What does "Carriage" refer to?

III. Questions and Answers (24 points in all, 6 for each)

45. (P73) Why is John Milton the greatest writer of his time?

46. (P225) *Pride and Prejudice* is Jane Austen's masterpiece. What does *Pride and Prejudice* concern about?

47. (P383) "You never give it a chance," she said. Then suddenly all her passion of grief over him broke out. "But it does matter!" she cried. "And you ought to be happy, you ought to try to be happy, to live

to be happy. How could I bear to think your life wouldn't be a happy one!" (D. H. Lawrence, *Sons and Lovers*)

Explain why Mrs. Morel couldn't bear to think Paul's life wouldn't be a happy one.

48. (P476) What is the difference between realism and naturalism?

IV. Topic Discussion (20 points in all, 10 for each)

Write no less than 150 words on each of the following topics in English in the corresponding space on the answer sheet.

49. (P34) *Hamlet* is one of Shakespeare's great tragedies. Try to discuss the social significances of Hamlet and analyze the character *Hamlet*.

50. (P375) Discuss the striking feature of Paul, the main character in *Sons and Lovers*.

KEYS:

I. Single Choice

badcd/cdbaa/abcdd/bbddb/dddba/aaaab/dabcc/aabda

II. Reading Comprehension

41. a. The poem is "Sonnet 18" by Shakespeare.

b. "Lines" means lines of the poem and other sonnets.

c. A nice summer's day is usually transient, but the beauty in poetry can last forever.

42. a. To move smoothly and quietly, as if no effort was being made.

b. Personification. Here the river is personified so that it has its own will.

c. Wordsworth emphasizes that the river runs freely in the early morning because there is no barges or streams or other kind of man-made burdens imposed on it to hinder its running.

43. a. Walt Whitman, "Song of Myself".

b. America, his country, his native land.

c. I was born and nurtured by this land and shall from now on devote my whole life to the country.

44. a. Emily Dickinson.

b. Death.

c. Hearse or carriage for carrying a coffin at a funeral.

III. Questions and Answers

45. In his life, Milton shows himself a real revolutionary, a master poet and a great prose writer. He fought for freedom in all aspects as a Christian humanist, while his achievements in literature make him tower over all the other English writers of his time and exert a great influence over later ones.

46. It mainly tells of the love story between a rich, proud young man Darcy and the beautiful and intelligent Elizabeth Bennet. The title tells of a major concern of the novel: *Pride and Prejudice*. If to form good relationships is our main task in life, we must first have good judgment. Our first impressions, according

to Jane Austen, are usually wrong, as is shown by those of Elizabeth. In the process of judging others, Elizabeth finds out something about herself. She discovers her own shortcomings. On the other hand, Darcy too learns about other people and himself. In the end false pride is humbled and prejudice dissolved.

47. a. Because Mrs. Morel was born in a middle-class family.

b. Mrs. Morel is a strong-willed, intelligent and ambitious woman and she couldn't bear to think his son, Paul, had an unhappy life.

48. a. Naturalism: evolved from realism/an extreme from realism/no more than a different philosophical approach to reality or human existence.

b. Realism: concerned with what is absorbed by the senses;/Naturalism: application of scientific theories of art.

c. Naturalism: human subject to heredity and environment/the real and true always beyond control.

d. the tone of Naturalism writings more ironic and pessimistic and less sympathetic and serious than realistic writings.

Ⅳ. Topic Discussion

49. The social significance of *Hamlet*: The play is Shakespeare's most detailed expose of a corrupted court — "an unweeded garden" in which there is nothing but "a foul and pestilent congregation of vapours". By revealing the power seeking, the jostling for place, the hidden motives, the courteous superficialities that veil lust and guilt, Shakespeare condemns the hypocrisy and treachery and general corruption at the royal court.

The character of Hamlet: Hamlet is neither a frail and weak minded youth nor a thoughtsick dreamer. He has none of the single minded blood lust of the earlier revengers. It is not because he is incapable of action, but because the cast of his mind is so speculative, so questioning and so contemplative that action, when it finally comes, seems almost like defeat. Trapped in a nightmare world of spying, testing and plotting, and apparently bearing the intolerable burden of the duty to revenge his father's death, Hamlet is obliged to inhabit a shadow world, to live suspended between fact and fiction, language and action only to deny its possibility, for he is too sophisticated to degrade his nature to the conventional role of a stage revenger. By characterizing Hamlet, Shakespeare successfully makes a philosophical exploration of life and death. Hamlet is also a humanist, a man who is free from medieval prejudices and superstitions. He has an unbounded love for the world rather than heaven. He cherishes a profound reverence for man and a firm belief in man's power over destiny.

50. a. He gradually comes under the strong influence of the mother in affections, aspiration and mental habits, and sees his father with his mother's eyes;

b. Paul depends heavily on his mother's love and help to make sense of the world around him;

c. In order to become an independent man and a true artist he has to make his own decisions about his life and work, and has to struggle to become free from his mother's influence;

d. Paul is proved to be incapable of escaping the overpowering emotional bond imposed by his mother's love, so he fails to achieve a fulfilling relationship with either girl;

e. Finally, Paul determined to face the unknown future.

II.《英美文学选读》全国统一命题自学考试优化考前冲刺试卷

PART ONE (40 POINTS)

I. Single Choice (40 points in all, 1 for each)

1. (P7) Which of the following is NOT regarded as one of the characteristics of the Renaissance? _____
   a. Rediscovery of ancient Greece and Roman culture.
   b. Attempt to remove the old feudalist ideas in medieval Europe.
   c. Introducing new ideas that expressed the interests of the rising bourgeoisie.
   d. Praise of man's efforts in soul delivery and personal salvation.

2. (P9) Which of the following is NOT true about Renaissance? _____
   a. Humanism is the essence of the Renaissance.
   b. Attitudes and feelings which had been characteristics of the 14th and 15th centuries persisted well down into the era of Humanism and Reformation.
   c. It was Chaucer who initiated the Reformation.
   d. The Elizabethan drama, in its totality, is the real main stream of the English Renaissance.

3. (P31) Shakespeare's _____ are mainly written under the principle that national unity under a mighty and just sovereign is a necessity.
   a. history
   b. tragedies
   c. comedies
   d. plays

4. (P37) "Shall I compare thee to a summer's day? /Thou art more lovely and more temperate:/Rough winds do shake the darling buds of May,/And summer's lease' hath all too short a date", the above beautiful sonnet was written by _____.
   a. John Donne
   b. John Milton
   c. William Shakespeare
   d. Francis Bacon

5. (P80) The British bourgeois or middle class believed in the following notions EXCEPT _____.
   a. self-esteem
   b. self-reliance
   c. self-restraint
   d. hard work

6. (P99) In this part the hero of the story, *Robinson Crusoe*, narrates in _____ how he goes to sea, gets shipwrecked and marooned on a lonely ioland, struggles to live for twenty-four years there and finally gets relieved and returns to England.
   a. the second person
   b. the first person
   c. the third person
   d. Defoe's mouth

7. (P107) The best fictional work of Jonathan Swift is _____.
   a. *A Tale of a Tub*
   b. *The Battle of the Books*
   c. *A Modest Proposal*
   d. *Gulliver's Travels*

8. （P119）The play of *The Tragedy of Tragedies* is written by _____.
   - a. Marlowe
   - b. Fielding
   - c. Shakespeare
   - d. Sheridan

9. （P162）_____, defined by Coleridge, is the vital faculty that creates new wholes out of disparate elements.
   - a. Exaggeration
   - b. Imagination
   - c. Rhetoric
   - d. Soliloquy

10. （P168）Literarily _____ was the first important Romantic poet, showing a contempt for the rule of reason, opposing the classical tradition of the 18th century, and treasuring the individual's imagination.
    - a. William Wordsworth
    - b. William Blake
    - c. Robert Burns
    - d. Samuel Taylor Coleridge

11. （P169）In the *Songs of Innocence* and *Songs of Experience*, by William Blake, what is central to Blake's concern? _____.
    - a. *Youthhood*
    - b. *Childhood*
    - c. *Aged*
    - d. All the above are not

12. （P176）In 1805, Wordsworth completed a long autobiographical poem entitled "_____".
    - a. The Excursion
    - b. The Prelude
    - c. Lucy Poems
    - d. The Lyrical Ballad

13. （P179）William Wordsworth assets that poetry originates from _____.
    - a. form
    - b. thoughts
    - c. artistic devices
    - d. emotion

14. （P208）Which is Shelley's masterpiece? _____.
    - a. *Queen Mab*
    - b. *Prometheus Unbound*
    - c. *Prometheus Bound*
    - d. *The Revolt of Islam*

15. （P236）The Victorian Age was largely an age of _____, eminently represented by Dickens and Thackeray.
    - a. poetry
    - b. drama
    - c. novel
    - d. epic prose

16. （P259）The success of the novel _____ is due to its introduction to the English novel of the first governess heroine.
    - a. *Wuthering Heights*
    - b. *Pride and Prejudice*
    - c. *Jane Eyre*
    - d. *Sister Carrie*

17. （P300）Which of the following descriptions of Thomas Hardy is WRONG? _____
    - a. Most of his novels are set in Wessex.
    - b. *Tess of the D'Urbervilles* is one of the most representatives of him as both a naturalistic and a critical realist writer.
    - c. Among Hardy's major works, *Under the Greenwood Tree* is the most cheerful and idyllic.
    - d. From *The Mayor of Casterbridge* on, the tragic sense becomes the keynote of his novels.

18. （P311）In the mid-19th century, Karl Marx and Friedrich Engels put forward the theory of _____.
    - a. ideal socialism
    - b. materialism
    - c. scientific socialism
    - d. analytical psychology

19. （P313）Modernism is, in many aspects, a reaction against _____. It rejects rationalism which is the theoretical base of realism.

a. Romantism
b. humanism
c. symbolism
d. realism

20. (P316) The following are English stream-of-consciousness novels EXCEPT _____.
    a. *Pilgrimage*
    b. *Ulysses*
    c. *Mrs. Dalloway*
    d. *A Passage to India*

21. (P324) *Mrs. Warren's Profession* is one of George Bernard Shaw's plays. What is Mrs. Warren's profession then? _____.
    a. Real estate
    b. Prostitution
    c. Houses keeping
    d. Farming

22. (P362~363) "The Love Song of J. Alfred Prufrock", in a form of dramatic monologue, presents the meditation of an aging _____ man over the business of proposing marriage.
    a. grown
    b. lunatic
    c. old
    d. young

23. (P369) Which of the following writings is NOT the novel of D. H. Lawrence's? _____.
    a. *Sons and Lovers*
    b. *A Portrait of the Artist as a Young Man*
    c. *The White Peacock*
    d. *The Rainbow*

24. (P399) The development of the American society nurtured "the _____ of a great nation".
    a. literature
    b. painting
    c. music
    d. art

25. (P431) Of the following works by Hawthorne, which one was a romance set in Italy? _____.
    a. *The House of the Seven Gables*
    b. *The Blithedale Romance*
    c. *The Marble Faun*
    d. *Twice-Told Tales*

26. (P433) Which of the following works best illustrates the Calvinistic view of original sin? _____.
    a. Mrs. Stowe's *Uncle Tom's Cabin*
    b. James' *The portrait of a Lady*
    c. Hemingway's *A Farewell to Arms*
    d. Hawthorne's *The Scarlet Letter*

27. (P450) Whitman's poems are characterized by all the following features EXCEPT _____.
    a. the strict poetic form
    b. the free and natural rhythm
    c. the easy flow of feelings
    d. the simple and conversational language

28. (P459) Herman Melville wrote his semi-autobiographical novel _____ concerning the sufferings a genteel youth among brutal sailors.
    a. *Typee*
    b. *Redburn*
    c. *Moby-Dick*
    d. *Mardi*

29. After the American Civil War, the literary interest in the so-called "reality" of life started a new period in the American literary writings known as the Age of _____.
    a. Realism
    b. Reason and Revolution
    c. Romanticism
    d. Modernism

30. (P476) Generally speaking, all those writers with a naturalistic approach to human reality tend to be _____.
    a. transcendentalists
    b. optimists
    c. pessimists
    d. idealists

31. (P479) As an equal to *The Adventures of Tom Sawyer*, _____ marks the climax of Mark Twain's literary activity.
    a. *Adventures of Huckleberry Finn*
    b. *Life on the Mississippi*

    c. *The Gilded Age*   d. *Roughing It*

32. （P498）Linguistically, compared with the writings of Mark Twain, Henry James' fiction is noted for his _____.

    a. frontier vernacular   b. rich colloquialism

    c. vulgarly descriptive   d. refined elegant language

33. （P518）Which of the following works does NOT show Dickinson's confusion and doubt about the role of women in the 19th century America? _____.

    a. *I'm "wife" — I've finished that*   b. *If you were coming in the Fall*

    c. *I cannot live with You —*   d. *I'm ceded — I've stopped being theirs*

34. （P525）*The Financier*, *The Titan* and *The Stoic* written by _____ are called his "Trilogy of Desire".

    a. Henry James   b. Theodore Dreiser

    c. Mark Twain   d. Herman Melville

35. （P550）Which terms can best describe the modernists' concern of the human situation in their fiction? _____.

    a. Fragmentation and alienation   b. Courage and honor

    c. Tradition and faith   d. Poverty and desperation

36. （P561）The first book Robert Frost wrote was _____.

    a. *Mountain Interval*   b. *New Hampshire*

    c. *A Further Range*   d. *A Boy's Wit*

37. （P565）In _____, Robert Frost compares life to a journey, and he is doubtful whether he will regret his choice or not when he is old, because the choice has made all the difference.

    a. *After Apple-Picking*   b. *The Road Not Taken*

    c. *Stopping by Woods on a Snowy Evening*   d. *Fire and Ice*

38. （P583）In the beginning paragraph of Chapter 3, *The Great Gatsby*, Fitzgerald describes a big party by saying that "men and girls came and went like moths". The author most likely indicates that _____.

    a. there was a crowd of party goers   b. such life does not have real meaning

    c. these people were light-hearted   d. these were crazy and ignorant characters

39. （P604）In Hemingway's *Indian Camp*, Nick's night trip to the Indian village and his experience inside the hut can be taken as _____.

    a. an essential lesson about Indian tribes   b. a confrontation with evil and sin

    c. an initiation to the harshness of life   d. a learning process in human relationship

40. （P612）The American writer _____ was awarded the Nobel Prize for the anti-racist *Intruder in the Dust* in 1950.

    a. Ernest Hemingway   b. Gertrude Stein

    c. William Faulkner   d. T. S. Eliot

PART TWO (60 POINTS)

II. Reading Comprehension (16 points in all, 4 for each)

41. （P56）" And thus the native hue of resolution/Is sicklied o'er with the pale cast of thought. " (Shakespeare, *Hamlet*)

    Questions:

a. What does the "native hue of resolution" mean?

b. What does "the pale cast of thought" stand for?

c. What idea do the two lines express?

42. (P452) "The early lilacs became part of this child,/And grass and white and red morning-glories, and white and red clover, and the song of the phoebe-bird,/And the third-month lambs and the sow's pink-faint litter, and the mare's foal and the cow's calf,/And The noisy — brood of the barnyard or by the mire of the pond-side,/And the fish suspending themselves so curiously below there, and the beautiful curious liquid,/And the water-plants with their graceful flat heads, all became part of him."

Questions:

a. Name the author of the poem.

b. What is the poetic style called?

c. What does the passage describe?

43. (P457) "I celebrate myself, and sing myself,/And what I assume you shall assume,/For every atom belonging to me as good belongs to you./I loafe and invite my soul,/I lean and loafe at my ease observing a spear of summer grass." (from Walt Whitman's "Song of Myself")

Questions:

a. Whom does "myself" refer to?

b. how do you understand the line "I loafe and invite my soul"?

c. What does "a spear of summer grass" indicate?

44. (P627) "And so she died. Fell ill in the house filled with dust and shadows, with only a doddering Negro man to wait on her, we did not even know she was sick; we had long since given up trying to get any information from the Negro. He talked to no one, probably not even to her, for his voice had grown harsh and rusty, as if from disuse."

Questions:

a. Identify the author and the title of the work which the passage is taken.

b. Who dies?

c. How do you describe the relationship between her and her neighbors?

III. Questions and Answers (24 points in all, 6 for each)

45. (P33) What are the common features in Shakespeare's characterization of the four greatest tragedy heroes?

46. (P121) What is the position of Henry Fielding in the history of English literature?

47. (P450) Whitman has made radical changes in the form of poetry by choosing free verse as his medium of experience. What are the characteristics of Whitman's free verse?

48. (P527) Give the brief analysis of Carrie Meeber in Theodore Dreiser's *Sister Carrie*?

IV. Topic Discussion (20 points in all, 10 for each)

49. (P316) Discuss what is "stream-of-consciousness" in novel writing.

50. (P51,P161) Under the influence of the leading romantic thinkers like Kant and the Post-Kantians, Romanticists demonstrated a strong reaction against the dominant modes of thinking of the 18th-century's Neoclassicists. Discuss the relation to the works you know, the difference between Romanticism and

Neoclassicism.

KEYS

I. Single Choice

dcaca/bdbbb/bbdbc/cdcdd/bdbac/dabac/adcba/dbbcc

II. Reading Comprehension

41. a. The true qualities of Hamlet's determination (determinedness, action, activity...).

　　b. "The paleness of thought" stands for too much consideration and hesitation.

　　c. Too much thinking made action/activity impossible.

42. a. Walt Whitman.

　　b. Free verse.

　　c. The passage describes the growth of a child who is wandering and admiring the scene around him. In the poem, the early experience of the poet may well be identified with the early days of a young and growing America.

43. a. The poet himself and the American people.

　　b. This line indicates a separation of the body and the novel.

　　c. The phrase indicates Whitman's optimism and experience.

44. a. William Faulkner's *A Rose for Emily*.

　　b. Emily dies.

　　c. She is secluded from her neighbors.

III. Questions and Answers

45. a. Each portrays some noble hero, who faces the injustice of human life and is caught in a difficult situation.

　　b. Heroes' fate is closely connected with the fate of the whole nation.

　　c. Each hero has his weakness of nature.

46. Henry Fielding was the first of all the 18th century English novelists to write the "comic epic in prose", and the first to give the modern novel its structure and style. Before him, the narration of the novel was either in the epistolary form or through the mouth of the hero. Fielding used "the third-person narration" in which the author remains the omniscient God. Thus, "He" can not only represent the behaviours of the characters, but also the internal workings of their mind. In form, Fielding retains a grand epic style and keeps to a realistic representation of common life as it is. So, he has been regarded as "Father of the English novel".

47. What he prefers for his new subject and new poetic feelings is "free verse", that is, poetry without a fixed beat or regular rhyme. A looser and more open-ended syntactical structure is frequently favored. Lines and sentences of different lengths are left lying side by side just as things are, undisturbed and separate. There are few compound sentences to draw objects and experiences into a system of hierarchy.

48. Carrie Meeber is the protagonist of *Sister Carrie*. Penniless and "full of the illusions of ignorance and

youth", she leaves her rural home to seek work in Chicago. She got to know Charles Drout, a salesman and she became his mistress. During his absence, she falls in love with Drout's friend George Hurstwood, a middle-aged, married, comparatively intelligent and cultured saloon manager. They finally elope and live together for more than three years. Carrie becomes mature in intellect and emotion, while Hurstwood, away from the atmosphere of success on which his life has been based, steadily declines. At last she thinks him too great a burden and leaves him. She finally succeeded in her career but feels lonely.

Sister Carrie best embodies Dreiser's naturalistic belief that while men are controlled and conditioned by heredity, instinct and chance, a few unsophisticated human beings refuse to accept their fate and try to find meaning and purpose for their existence. Carrie, as one of such, senses that she is merely a cipher in an uncaring world yet seeks to grasp the mysteries of life and thereby satisfies her desires for social status and material comfort.

Ⅳ. Topic Discussion

49. Stream-of-consciousness is a literary trend of modernism with the notion that multiple levels of consciousness existed simultaneously in human mind, that one's present was the sum of his past, present and future, and that the whole truth about human beings existed in the unique, isolated and private world of each individual. Writers like Dorothy Richardson, Jamce Joyce and Virginia Woolf concentrated all their efforts on digging into human consciousness. In their writings, the past, the present and the future are mingled together and exist at the same time in the consciousness of an individual.

50. a. Neoclassicists upheld that artistic ideals should be order, logic, restrained emotion and accuracy, and that literature should be judged in terms of its service to humanity, and thus, literary expressions should be of proportion, unity, harmony and grace. Pope's *An Essay on Criticism* advocates grace, wit (usually through satire/humour), and simplicity in language (and the poem itself is a demonstration of those ideals, too); Fielding's *Tom Jones* helped establish the form of novel; Gray's "Elegy Written in Country Churchyard" displays elegant in style, unified structure, serious tone and moral instruction.

b. Romanticists tended to see the individual as the very center of all experience, including art, and thus, literary work should be "spontaneous overflow of strong feelings", and no matter how fragmentary those experiences were (Wordsworth's "I Wandered Lonely as a Cloud," or "The Solitary Reaper," or Coleridge's "Kubla Khan"), the value of the work lied in the accuracy of presenting those unique feelings and particular attitudes.

c. In a word, Neoclassicism emphasized rationality and form but Romanticism attached great importance to the individual's mind (mention, imagination, temporary experience...).

Ⅲ. 文学术语简释

1. Alexandrine verse　亚历山大格式的诗行,15 世纪时采用的六步抑扬格(iambic hexameter)诗行,3 音步后一停顿。下面的诗句引自济慈的《圣爱格尼斯节前夜》(*The Eve of St. Agnes*),正是亚历山大格式:

　　She 'sighed/for 'Ag/nes' 'dreams,/ the 'swee/test 'of/the 'year.

2. **allegory** 寓言,讽喻,用具体的故事情节表达抽象的思想和道德准则,一般都有两个意思,一是文学意义,一是象征意义。班扬(John Bunyan)的《天路历程》(*The Pilgrim's Process*)就是英语文学中最著名的寓言。

3. **alliteration** 头韵,通常是诗句中词语开头相同辅音的重复,这样使用主要有两个目的:悦耳和对头韵词语的强调。头韵首先为盎格鲁—撒克逊人的吟游诗人(scop)所用,第一部英语史诗《贝奥武夫》(*Beowulf*)中就有很多运用头韵的诗句,例如:And the heathen's only hope, Hell. 后来的诗人也有应用,英国浪漫主义诗人科勒律治(S. T. Coleridge)的名诗《忽必烈汗》(*Kubla Khan*)中就有运用头韵的名句:Five miles meandering with a mazy motion. 曲曲折折地闲逛了五英里。

4. **allusion** 典故

5. **American Naturalism** 美国自然主义,美国的自然主义来源于欧洲。自然主义是现实主义过度发展的结果,是19世纪后期工业发展、科学、心理学、人的行为和社会思想潮流的理论反映。当时,以法国左拉(Emile Zola)为代表的一些思想家和作家感到了人类社会的冷漠和无助,认为人生的命运完全受遗传和环境两种力量的控制,这是自然主义的核心观念。而美国自然主义则是由于战争、社会剧变以及达尔文主义(Darwinism)对传统信仰的颠覆性影响所形成。

   美国文学界的自然主义者采取极端客观和坦率的手法,表现遗传和环境决定了命运的社会下层人物,偏好早期浪漫主义的感觉主义(sensationalism),但又不同于浪漫主义,他们强调世界是无道德是非的(amoral),人无自由意志,人生为遗传和环境所控制,生而悲惨,死后即被遗忘。自然主义作家的作品中充斥着悲观主义和决定论的思想(pessimism and deterministic ideas),代表作家有史蒂芬·克兰(Stephen Crane),弗兰克·诺里斯(Frank Norris),克杰·伦敦(Jack London)和西奥多·德莱塞(Theodore Dreiser)等。

   克兰·玛吉(Crane Maggie)的《街道女孩》(*A Girl of the Streets*)是第一部美国自然主义小说。

   弗兰克·诺里斯(Frank Norris)的《麦克蒂格》(*McTeague*)是美国自然主义的宣言。

   西奥多·德莱塞(Theodore Dreiser)的《嘉莉妹妹》(*Sister Carrie*)是美国自然主义文学达到成熟的标志。

   虽然美国的自然主义文学描写世界表现出野蛮现实主义(brutal realism)倾向,但是依然有通过社会变革使世界变得更好的美好愿望。

6. **American Puritanism** 美国的清教主义,即美国清教徒的宗教信仰和宗教活动。清教徒是新教教会(Protestant Church)的一个派别的成员,产生于英国伊丽莎白一世和詹姆斯一世统治时期,也是最早移民美洲的成员。他们主张更加严格的、宗教化的道德原则,想使宗教信仰和宗教仪式更加净化,反对英格兰教会在组织上和教义上过于接近罗马教廷,是一批主张恢复到早期完全"纯洁"状态的宗教理想主义者(religious idealists)。他们相信命运前定(predestination)、原罪(original sin)和人性本恶(depravity)、由上帝教化仁善以赎前罪的教义,但是在严酷的生存斗争(the grim struggle of survival)中变得越来越实际。清教徒生活严格自律、非常清苦,排斥住地以外一切他们认为危险的思想观念,因而经受着周围环境的迫害。作为一种文化遗产,清教主义对美国的文学产生了深远的影响。在某种程度上,它成了国家的一种文化形态,而不是一套教义。

7. **American Transcendentalism** 美国超验主义,又叫"新英格兰超验主义"或"美国文艺复兴"。与其说这是美国超验主义者的哲学,不如说是他们的倾向和态度。所谓"超越"就是要超越某种限制。超验论者从欧洲的浪漫主义文学、新柏拉图主义(Platonism),德国的唯心主义哲学(idealistic philosophy)和东方神秘主义的文化启示(the revelations of Oriental-mysticism)中汲取思想,鼓吹文化更新,反对美国社会的物质主义。其特点如下:

   a. 超验主义者认为宇宙中最重要的东西是精神和超灵(over-soul);

   b. 个人是最重要的社会元素;

   c. 大自然是精神和上帝的象征;其信仰基础是超越感觉世界可以通达最基本的生死真谛;

d. 作为哲学和文学的运动,超验主义兴盛的时间、地点是 19 世纪 30 年代至南北战争开始时期,美国新英格兰地区。

爱默生的《自然》(*Nature*)被称作"美国超验主义的宣言"(manifesto),《美国学者》(*The American Scholar*)被认为是"智识独立的宣言"(Declaration of Intellectual Independence)。

梭罗(Thoreau)在瓦尔登湖(Walden Pond)边筑茅屋而居两年,写出了超验主义名著《瓦尔登湖》(*Walden*)。

对于经历了内战恐怖的后代人来说,超验主义的劝化(transcendental persuasion)——人就像神,邪恶并不存在——似乎是一种乐观主义的傻话(folly)。

作为哲学,超验主义既不合逻辑,也不系统。情感高于理智,个人表现高于法律和习俗的制约。它对从霍桑(Hawthorne)到惠特曼(Whitman)等许多伟大的美国作家都产生了巨大影响。

8. antagonist　对手,反面人物

9. antithesis　对偶

10. aphorism　格言,警句

11. apostrophe　省略

12. aside　旁白

13. assonance　半韵,半谐音,即相同元音(vowel sound)的重复,尤其是在诗歌中。例如济慈的《希腊古瓮颂》(*Ode on a Grecian Urn*)中的诗句:Thou foster child of silence and slow time.

14. ballad　民谣,又叫民间民谣(folk ballad),是用诗歌讲故事,在民间传唱的最早的文学形式,不知作者,传唱了几个世纪都不曾形诸文字。民谣形式产生于普通人的日常生活,主题常为悲剧——情场失意、嫉妒、复仇、祸从天降和冒险的经历,等等。艺术手法多为叠句,递增的重复和密码式语言。后来发展起来的文学民谣(literary ballad)就是模仿民间民谣的风格。最著名的文学民谣是科勒律治(S. T. Coleridge)的《古舟子咏》(*The Rime of Ancient Mariner*)。

15. blank verse　无韵诗,素体诗,用无韵的五步抑扬格(unrhymed iambic pentameter)写成的诗。大诗人莎士比亚和弥尔顿都经常使用这样的诗歌形式。

16. Bohemianism　放荡不羁的生活方式,主要指一战后两部分美国青年的生活方式:一是经常出入于纽约廉租屋——格林尼治村(Greenwich Village)的作家、艺术家;二是旅居欧洲——主要是巴黎文学沙龙(literary salon),被女作家格特鲁德·斯泰因(Gertrude Stein)称为"迷惘的一代"(The Lost Generation)的美国青年作家。他们许多人一开始怀着当英雄的思想投身一战,企图"以战争结束战争",但现代战争的残酷、恐怖和对文明的疯狂摧毁震慑了他们的灵魂,粉碎了他们的爱国主义雄心,觉得整个世界都发疯了,毫无意义(crazy and meaningless),这使他们抛弃了传统的宗教观、价值观,采取轻浮(frivolous)、贪婪(greedy)、无所用心(heedless)的生活态度,漫无目的地游荡,焦躁不安(wandering pointlessly and restlessly),尽情享受。但因此也出现了一批用特殊风格写作的艺术家群体,海明威(Hemingway),庞德(Pound),卡明斯(Cummings),菲兹杰拉德(Fitzgerald)就是"迷惘的一代"作家中的佼佼者。

17. Calvinism　加尔文主义,欧洲宗教改革时期在日内瓦(Geneva)的法国神学家加尔文(Calvin)创立的教义。其内容包括命运前定(predestination)、原罪论(original sin)、人性本恶(total depravity)、通过上帝仁慈教化、选择性地救赎虔诚的信徒(limited atonement)等教义。

18. canto　诗章,长诗的各个章节或部分。如但丁的《神曲》(*Devine Comedy*),亚历山大·蒲伯的《夺发记》(*The Rape of the Lock*)和《乔治·高登》(*George Gordon*),拜伦的《唐璜》(*Don Juan*),都包含许多诗章。

19. caricature　夸张模仿,用夸张或扭曲(exaggeration and distortion)使人物具有喜剧味儿(comedy)或变得可笑(ridiculous)。

20. Carpe Diem Tradition　及时行乐,Carpe Diem 在文学上就是"抓住当前,过好今天"(seize the day,

live for today)的意思。罗伯特·赫里克(Robert Herrick)的诗作《多花时间去泡处女》(*To the Virgins, to Make Much of Time*)中的诗句"Gather ye rosebuds while ye may"(采摘玫瑰花蕾更待何时)充分体现了这种及时行乐的思想。

21. characterization　人物塑造

22. classicism　古典主义,强调一切艺术创作都需遵循古希腊、古罗马的原则,重视传统和普遍,强调理性、清晰、平衡和有序,与浪漫主义强调情感和个人想象完全对立。

23. climax　高潮

24. conceit　奇喻,别出心裁、牵强附会的比喻、想法,一种违反常理把两种不可类比的东西进行勉强比较的比喻手法,产生令人吃惊的效果。文艺复兴时期玄学派诗人(metaphysical poet)约翰·邓恩(John Donne)经常使用这种异乎寻常、甚至带有学识炫耀的晦涩的比喻。下面的诗句中,邓恩把一对情人的灵魂比作罗盘固定的脚,不动则已,一动俱动,非常同步。真是奇特的比喻!

If they be two, they are two so	就还算两个吧,两个却这样
As stiff twin compasses are two;	和一副两脚规情况相同;
Thy soul, the fix'd foot, makes no show	你的灵魂是定脚,并不会移动
To move, but doth, if th' other do.	另一脚一动,它也动。

25. conflict　冲突,如文学作品中的情节冲突、人物内心的思想冲突、任务之间的矛盾冲突等。

26. connotation　蕴涵、延伸的意义,含义,内涵,与表示字面意义或者字典意义(literal or "dictionary" meaning)的 denotation 相对。如 springtime,字面为春天时光,但蕴涵着青春、新生和浪漫的意思;shroud,字面意义是寿衣、裹尸布,但暗含着死亡、黑暗、忧郁、神秘等含义。

27. consonance　辅音韵,诗行中词尾或重读音节中辅音的重复。如 litter/letter;green/groan。

28. couplet　对句,偶句,两行尾韵相谐的诗句。如莎士比亚《麦克白》(*Macbeth*)中的对句:

Hear it not, Duncan; for it is a knell	别听到这钟声,邓肯,这可是召唤你
That summons thee to heaven or to hell.	前去天堂或地狱的丧钟声。

29. denotation　本意,字面意义和字典意义,与 connotation(内涵)意义相对。

30. denouement　结局,故事、戏剧等的情节发展到高潮之后,矛盾冲突得到解决,与情节有关的秘密都得到解释而大白于天下,最后的结局就来了。

31. dictionary　措辞

32. dissonance　不谐和音

33. dramatic monologue　戏剧独白

34. dramatic irony　戏剧反语,戏剧人物说的话与观众听懂的意思相反。当作品给我们机会扮演上帝、知道了人物本身都没理解到的东西时,那就是戏剧反语起作用了。

35. elegy　哀歌,挽歌

36. emblematic image　寓言意象,与传统的道德意义和宗教意义联系在一起的词语画面想象。

37. The English Renaissance　英国文艺复兴,由于岛国与欧洲大陆的疏离,英国的文艺复兴迟来一步,首先是模仿(imitation)和同化(assimilation),最杰出的文学形式是诗歌和诗剧(poetic drama)。伊丽莎白时代的戏剧是文艺复兴的主流(mainstream),古希腊、古罗马时期的文学经典与英国本土的内容相结合,使因果戏剧臻于成熟和完美。马洛(Christopher Marlowe),莎士比亚(William Shakespeare)和本·琼森(Ben Jonson)是这个时期最伟大的剧作家。

38. epic　史诗

39. epigram　警句,警句短诗

40. epigraph　(卷首和章节前的)引语,格言

41. epilogue　尾声,后记

42. epiphany　顿悟

43. epitaph 墓志铭,纪念死者的诗文。

44. essay 随笔,一篇短小的文字,针对一个主题表达一个特定的观点,往往结构紧凑,幽默风趣。

45. exemplum 布道比方,插进布道文中的劝谕性的故事,说明某种道德原则。乔叟的《坎特伯雷故事集》(*The Canterbury Tales*)中有一篇"宽恕者的故事"(*The Pardoner's Tale*)就是一篇布道比方,说明的道德原则是"贪婪是邪恶的根源"(Greed is the root of all evil.)。

46. exposition 叙述或戏剧的提示部分,主要揭示重要的背景信息。

47. The Father of English Poetry 英国诗歌之父,指乔叟(Geoffrey Chaucer)。他把各种形式的韵诗尤其是五步抑扬格的对句韵诗(the rhymed couplet of iambic pentameter,后来称之为英雄偶句 heroic couplet)引进英语诗歌,取代了古老的盎格鲁—撒克逊头韵诗(alliterative verse)。他是第一个用现代英语写诗的人,他的《坎特伯雷故事集》是英国文学史上的第一部史诗,具有极其重要的地位。

48. fable 寓言

49. farce 滑稽剧,一种以逗笑场景为基础的喜剧,表现的多为类型化人物(stereotyped characters)。滑稽剧的幽默大多是打闹(slapstick),包括粗陋的形体动作(crude physical action),剧中人物常常就是笑柄,如一块奶酪饼飞贴到他们的脸上,床塌下来压在他们身上。

50. fiction 小说

51. figurative language 修辞语言,不是想要解释字面意义(literal sense),而是常常意在言外。莎士比亚的大悲剧《麦克白》(*Macbeth*)结尾时,麦克白的著名独白(soliloquy/monologue)就用了修辞语言:

> Out, out, brief candle! 灭了了,灭了了,短命的蜡烛!
> Life's but a walking shadow, a poor player 生命不过是个可怜演员走动的影子,
> That struts and frets his hour upon the stage 在舞台上,他趾高气扬,磨尽时光,
> And then is heard no more. 而后——再也无人知晓。

作者并非说生命真的是摇曳的蜡烛(flickering candle)、影子,或在台上走来走去的神经质的演员,而是把生命与这些不同类的东西进行对比,指出其相似之处。修辞语言借助想象提供了一种新的看待世界的方法,包括夸张(hyperbole),隐喻(metaphor),换喻(metonymy),逆喻或矛盾形容法(oxymoron),拟人化(personification),明喻(simile)以及举隅法或提喻法(synecdoche)。

52. figure of speech 修辞或修辞格,著名的比喻修辞例句如下:

> It's raining cats and dogs. 大雨滂沱。
> Tou're the apple of my eye. 你是我的掌上明珠/心肝宝贝。

53. flashback 倒叙

54. foreshadowing 预示,用暗示或线索(hints or clues)表示后来会发生的事情,引起读者的兴趣,制造悬念(to build suspense)。

55. free verse 自由诗,没有固定格律和韵律的诗,早期曾用于圣经的赞美诗(psalms),但更多地用于19世纪和20世纪的诗歌中,美国大诗人惠特曼的《草叶集》(*Leaves of Grass*)中的诗歌就是自由诗。

56. Hemingway Heroes 海明威式主人公,指的是海明威作品中的主人公,他们往往是普通人(average man),毫无疑问具有男子汉气概(masculine tastes),敏感而聪明,是少言寡语的行动派(a man of action and of few words),喜欢独处,乐做旁观者,善于控制感情,清心寡欲(stoic),在恶劣环境下能够自律(self-disciplined)。海明威式的主人公代表着整整一代人,在一个实际上混乱嘈杂、毫无意义的世界上,他们与一种甚至都不理解的力量进行着孤独的斗争,明知最终会失败,却也显示出"绝望的勇气"(despairing courage,伯特兰·罗素 Bertran Russel 语),正是这勇气使他们像男子汉一样行动,面对逆境(adversity)表现出尊严,这就是海明威式主人公的荣誉和气节所标志的本质。

57. **heroic couplet** 英雄偶句体,英雄双行诗,对句,指一对押韵的五步抑扬格诗行。这种形式由乔叟引入英语诗歌,后被广泛运用。由于17世纪的英雄诗(史诗)和英雄剧、描述古代英雄事迹的翻译作品(如查普曼所译的《奥德赛》*Odyssey* by George Chapman)中都用这种形式的押韵双行诗,故而被称作"英雄偶句体"。

58. **hyperbole = exaggeration** 夸张

59. **humanism** 人文主义,文艺复兴的主要原则(key-note),反映了新兴资产阶级的世界观。人文主义者认为:外部障碍妨碍了人和世界的不断更新;人可以根据自己的愿望塑造世界,在运用智慧祛除外部障碍的过程中获得快乐。他们强调人的尊严和现世生活的重要;人不仅有权享受生活之美,而且有能力完善自己,创造奇迹(to perform wonders)。

60. **imagism** 意象主义,一战以后20世纪20年代在美国出现的一股文学潮流,强烈反对维多利亚时代道德化倾向(moralizing tendency)严重的诗歌,反对它们装进了过多的诗歌以外的东西(extra-poetic matter),反对传统的五步抑扬格,强调语言使用要节约简练,要运用主要意象,这就是文学史上的意象运动。最重要的代表诗人物是庞德(Pound),另外还有威廉·卡洛斯·威廉姆斯(William Carlos Williams)、华莱士·史蒂文斯(Wallace Stevens)、E. E. 卡明斯(E. E. Cummings)、卡尔·斯坦伯格(Carl Standburg)、T. S. 艾略特(T. S. Eliot)等。

意象主义者主张对事物进行直接表达,节奏像音乐语言(musical phrase),不需要诗人告诉读者感觉到了什么,意象本身就可产生激情,为自己说话。

意象主义的诗歌通常是没有固定节奏的自由诗,十分短小,用稍纵即逝的意象捕捉人的情感,凝固瞬息的时间。他们还从规则严苛的日本俳句吸取灵感,俳句第一行5个音节,第二行7个,第三行5个。

纯意象主义诗歌在20世纪20年代以后就难得一见了,但它的思想对现代诗和读诗的方法产生了很大的影响。

61. **incremental repetition** 渐进重复,即对前一诗行或前几行的重复,但每一次重复都有少许变化,叙述就这样一个诗节一个诗节地往前推进、发展,多见于民谣(folk ballad)。

62. **In Medias Res** 直入本题,拉丁文,相当于英文 in middle of things,即直接进入故事中心,然后通过一个倒叙(flashback)再补述前面发生的事情的技巧。

63. **inversion** 倒装,颠倒正常词序的技巧。

64. **invocation** 祷文,史诗的开头常有恳求缪斯(Muse)、神仙或精灵(Spirit)赐给灵感(inspiration)的文字。例如《失乐园》(*Paradise Lost*)的开头,弥尔顿用祷文恳请司天女神乌拉尼亚(Urania)、诗歌女神缪斯恩赐给他创作灵感。

65. **irony** 反语,反讽,冷嘲,陈述的内容与真正表达的意思之间、预计发生的事情与实际发生的事情之间出现对立和不一致就叫反讽。反讽有三种:

a. 词语反讽(verbal irony),讲话人说的是一件事,意指的却是另一件事。例如莎翁大悲剧《麦克白》(*Macbeth*)中苏格兰贵族莱恩诺克斯(*Lennox*)告知另一贵族的话,背景是阴谋篡位的大臣麦克白杀了国王邓肯(*Duncan*)后又杀了两个侍卫当替罪羊,听听他的话中之话、言外之意,是怎样反讽的:

How it did grieve Macbeth! Did he not straight	麦克白为了这件事多么痛心!
In pious rage the two delinquents tear,	他不是乘着一时的忠愤,杀了
That were the slaves of drink and thralls of sleep?	两个酗酒贪睡的渎职卫士吗?
Was not that nobly done?	那件事不是干得很忠勇吗?

b. 戏剧反讽(dramatic irony),读者或观众察觉或意识到的事情,小说或戏剧中的人物却浑然不知。例如《麦克白》第一幕第六场中,一面是麦克白和他的妻子正阴谋杀害邓肯王(观众都知道了),另一面却是邓肯王与班柯(Banquo)高兴地谈论着眼前安详宁静的美好环境(the serenity and loveliness of the setting),全然不知死亡在逼近。

c. 情境、形势反讽(irony of situation),作者对某项行动或情势的预期结果不同于实际结果。例如托马斯·哈代(Thomas Hardy)的小说《三个陌生人》(*The Three Strangers*)中,两个待在烟囱角落的陌生人原来竟一个是执行绞刑的刽子手(hangman),另一个是被预谋要绞死的受害人(intended victim),真没想到他们会在一起。

66. The Jazz Age　爵士时代,对许多人来说,一战是旧价值观、旧政治学和旧思想观念的可悲的失败,社会气氛是混乱与绝望的混合。但表面上,美国在20世纪20年代似乎并不绝望,进入了繁荣和表现狂的10年。对酒精饮料的法律禁止与其说达到抑制效果,不如说起到鼓舞作用,奢侈即时尚,道路挤满了汽车,到处是广告,查尔斯顿(Charleston)黑人舞蹈风靡一时,人们甚至坐到了旗杆顶上。新奥尔良的音乐沿大河而上传到芝加哥,纽约哈莱姆(Harlem)黑人区剧院里演奏着象征那个时代的音乐,这就是喧嚣的20年代(Roaring Twenties),这就是爵士时代。它以表面的浮华掩盖了安静中的痛苦,掩盖了格特鲁德·斯泰因(Gertrude Stein)在巴黎就注意到的失落感(the sense of loss),菲兹杰拉德(F. S. Fitzgerald)把爵士时代的人描写为沉迷在享乐中的"美丽而该死的"一代人。

67. kenning　隐喻语(用于古代诗歌中),如盎格鲁—撒克逊诗歌《航海者》(*The Seafarer*)中用鲸鱼(whales)和家乡(home)隐喻大海。

68. local colorism　地方色彩

69. Lost Generation　迷惘的一代,用于描述一战后的一代美国人,其中有寓居欧洲特别是巴黎的作家、艺术家,著名的有贫困中的海明威,还有回到故国却感到沧桑巨变、陌生迷茫的那些美国人。

70. lyric　抒情诗

71. masque　假面剧,假面舞会,16世纪晚期到17世纪初期在英国贵族中流行的一种精致而独特的戏剧娱乐活动,多为诗剧,利用唱歌、舞蹈、五彩缤纷的服装,产生令人吃惊的舞台效果。

72. melodrama　传奇剧,情节剧,该剧人物类型化(stereotyped character),激情夸张,矛盾冲突都是让各方面都好的男女角色与无处不坏的反派角色(all-evil villain)展开斗争。melos在希腊文中是song的意思,所以该剧不仅有动作,还有"歌唱",每个角色都有歌唱的主题,故而不分男女,每次都得上台。

73. metaphor　隐喻,暗喻

74. metaphysical poetry　玄学派诗歌,以约翰·邓恩为首的17世纪的一派诗人用相同风格写的诗,特点是词语睿智而过滥,结构精巧(ingenious structure),格律不规则(irregular meter),口语入诗,意象精致,把不同思想熔于一炉,但也有比喻怪诞、晦涩难懂之不足。

75. meter　音步,格律

76. metonymy　换喻,转喻,用与一样东西密切相关的某种东西来代替或暗示这样东西,这种修辞方法叫换喻。例如用帆(sails)代替船(ships),用王冠(crown)代替国王(king),用安全帽(hardhat)代替工人(worker),用白宫(White House)比喻美国总统(President of the United States)。

77. miracle play　奇迹剧,中世纪流行于英国的宗教剧,是以圣徒故事(stories of saints)和宗教历史(sacred history)为主要情节的戏剧。

78. mock epic　讽刺喜剧史诗,故意以史诗般的宏大和英雄体式的风格来处理细小的主题,也被称作讽刺英雄体诗(mock-heroic poem)。蒲伯(Alexander Pope)的《夺发记》(*The Rape of the Lock*)是英国最伟大的讽刺喜剧史诗。

79. moral　寓意

80. morality play　道德剧,奇迹剧的过度发展,流行于15、16世纪,美德和罪恶在剧中都拟人化了。

81. motif　文学作品中反复出现的主题、故事、人物、事件、思想、情景,如名称、形象或短语等的重复。这种重复有助于突出短篇故事、小说、诗歌、戏剧的主题。劳伦斯(D. H. Lawrence)在《弹簧马优胜者》(*The Rocking-Horse Winner*)中所用的主题词是 luck,故事的主人公男孩保罗(Paul)发现自己有预测赛马胜负的能力,然而,由于他越来越迷信这种能力,这具有讽刺意味的 luck 结果把他毁了。

主题重复指的是一些普遍使用的情节或人物类型。"丑小鸭主题重复"(ugly duckling motif)指的是"相貌平常的人转变为美人"这样的情节。另外两个老套主题是"罗密欧与朱丽叶"(Romeo and Juliet)主题和"霍雷肖·阿尔杰"(Horatio Alger)主题,前者表示两个有情人注定失败;后者是美国少年文学作家阿尔杰(Alger)笔下常见的励志故事:普通职员奋斗成了公司总裁。

82. motivation 动机

83. myth = mythology 神话

84. narrative poem 叙事诗

85. narrator 叙述者

86. naturalism 自然主义,现实主义的极端形式或过度发展(overgrowth),是悲观的现实主义(pessimistic realism)。自然主义者描写生活的阴暗面(sordid side),笔下的人物严肃而无望,为遗传(heredity)和环境所限制。

87. Neoclassicism 新古典主义,17、18 世纪有序、平衡、和谐的古典主义标准在文学界的复兴,约翰·德莱顿(John Drydon)和亚历山大·蒲伯(Alexander Popes)为新古典主义派的代表作家。

88. novel 长篇小说

89. octave 八行诗体,意大利十四行诗的前 8 行,后 6 行叫六行诗体(sestet)。

90. ode 颂诗,一种复杂而漫长的抒情诗,以庄严堂皇的形式表达某些崇高而严肃的主题。颂诗常描写一个特定情境,歌颂一个人、一个季节或纪念一个事件。雪莱的《西风颂》(*Ode to the West Wind*)和济慈的《希腊古瓮颂》(*Ode on Grecian Urn*)是最为著名的颂诗。

91. onomatopoeia 拟声(词),其发音在某种程度上模仿或暗示了它的意义。鸟类名称尤其多用拟声词,如布谷鸟(cuckoo),北美夜莺(whippoorwill),猫头鹰(owl),乌鸦(crow),红眼雀(towhee),山齿鹑(bobwhite)。科勒律治的《古舟子咏》(*The Rime of the Ancient Mariner*)中的诗句再现了冰冻地带可怕的声音:It cracked and growled, and roared and howled/Like noises in a swound! 冰雪在怒吼,冰雪在咆哮,/像人昏厥时听到隆隆巨响!

92. ottava rima 八行体诗,八行诗节,其韵律(rhyme scheme)为 abababcc。

93. oxymoron 矛盾修辞,把相互对立、矛盾的思想或术语结合在一起的修辞方法。它表达一种悖论,往往只用一两个单词。如活地狱(living death),可爱的敌人(dear enemy),甜蜜的悲哀(sweet sorrow),聪明的傻瓜(wise fool)等。

94. paradox 自相矛盾、似是而非的隽语,悖论,一段揭示了真理但刚开始似乎自相矛盾和不正确的陈述。英国 17 世纪保皇党诗人理查德·勒夫里斯(Richard Lovelace)的诗《从监狱致阿尔西亚》(*To Althea, from Prison*)中就含有著名的悖论:

Stone walls do not a prison make,　　　　　石墙未必形成监狱,

Nor iron bars a cage;　　　　　　　　　　铁栅未必造就牢笼;

Minds innocent and quiet take　　　　　　清白求静的智者

That for a hermitage...　　　　　　　　　　把监狱当隐居之地……

95. parallelism 排比

96. parody 滑稽模仿,文学、艺术、音乐作品中通过夸张或拙劣可笑的模仿达到幽默的效果,可用于情节描写与人物塑造,形成写作风格、艺术情趣和思想主题。

97. pastoral 牧歌式、田园式文艺作品,如田园诗。最典型的田园诗就是马洛(Christopher Marlow)的《深情的牧羊人致恋人》(*The Passionate Shepherd to His Love*)。

98. pathos 文艺作品中哀婉动人的因素,常会唤起读者、观众对人物命运的同情。通常指清白无辜

的人蒙受不白之冤而遭受苦难。如莎翁大悲剧《麦克白》(*Macbeth*)第四幕第二场中麦克德夫(Macduff)夫人和他的儿子被麦克白的杀手所谋杀。

99. protagonist　主人公,主角

100. psalm　赞美诗,圣歌,歌颂上帝的歌或抒情诗,通常指《圣经》圣歌篇中的150首宗教抒情诗。

101. pun　双关,用一个单词或一个短语同时表达两个或两个以上的意义,通常是幽默的。莎翁《麦克白》第二幕第三场中,看门人用了双关语:Come in tailor, here you may roast your goose. 其中的goose有两个意思,一指真鹅,一指裁缝的熨斗。

102. quatrain　四行诗节,四行一节的诗,其韵律(rhyme scheme)通常是abab或abcb。

103. realism　现实主义,文学艺术中如实地表现生活,既不带感伤主义情绪,也不把生活理想化。现实主义作品常常描写日常生活,运用普通人的口语,有时会详细地描写生活的阴暗面。

104. refrain　叠句,叠歌,诗歌中单词、词语、诗句或一组诗句有规则地一再重复叫叠句,通常出现在每个诗节的末尾。叠句主要用在民谣(ballad)和叙事诗(narrative poetry)中,旨在创造一种如歌的节奏(rhythm),有助于产生悬念(suspense),也能强调某种特定思想。

105. The Reformation　16世纪发生在欧洲的宗教改革运动,由德国新教徒马丁·路德(Martin Luther)发起,旨在清除中世纪罗马教廷的腐败和迷信(corruption and superstition),恢复早期宗教的纯洁性。在英国,宗教改革从亨利八世开始,他宣布与罗马教廷决裂,对寺院(monasteries)进行大规模的镇压(wholesale suppression),没收(confiscated)教会的财产,充实新兴资产阶级贵族。新兴的宗教教条(dogma)叫新教(Protestantism)主义,赢得了广大的信徒。宗教改革实际上是新兴资产阶级反抗封建阶级及其思想观念的一场阶级斗争。

106. rhyme　押韵,诗歌中相互接近的两个或两个以上的单词或短语的发音重复。如river/shiver, song/long, leap/deep。最常见的是韵出现在诗行的尾部,叫尾韵(end rhyme);出现在诗行中间的叫内韵(internal rhyme),如科勒律治《古舟子咏》中的诗句 The Wedding — Guest he heat his breast 就含有内韵;单词最后的元音和辅音都押韵的叫精确韵(exact rhyme),如(cook/look);只有最后的辅音押韵的叫近似韵(approximate rhyme),如cook/lack;上一诗节中一个不押韵的诗行与下一诗节中的一个诗行押韵,叫连锁韵(interlocking rhyme),连锁韵经常出现在三行诗节、隔句押韵(terza rima)的意大利诗歌形式中。

107. rhymed scheme/pattern　韵律,诗歌押韵的规律。如威廉·布莱克(William Blake)的名诗《老虎》(*Tyger*)中的一个诗节,韵律明显是aabb:

In what distant deeps or skies	a
Burnt the fire of thine eyes?	a
On what wings dare he aspire?	b
What the hand, dare seize the fire?	b

108. rhythm　节奏,各种轻、重读音节按一定格式的排列。节奏赋予诗歌一种独特的音乐性,产生美感。诗歌也可用节奏表达意义,在丁尼生(A. L. Tennyson)的诗歌《拍击,拍击,拍击》(*Break, Break, Break*)中,锤击式的节拍(pounding rhythm)强化了波涛冲击陆地的形象:

　　　　'Break,/ 'break,/ 'break,//On thy 'cold/'gray 'stones,/ O 'Sea

两行诗都是3个音步,虽然第一行是3个单音节词构成3个音步,但读音却都有3个音步足够的持续时间。第二行3音步分别为抑抑扬格、扬扬格和抑扬格。

109. Romance　骑士传奇,浪漫传奇,早先是指中世纪国王、王后、骑士和贵妇人爱情和历险的故事以及种种不可能的超自然的事情,现在泛指以理想化世界为背景或描写英雄历险、善恶之战和人妖之战(battles between good characters and villains or monsters)的想象性文学作品。《高文爵士和绿衣骑士》(*Sir Gawain and the Green Knight*)是中世纪最优秀的骑士传奇,济慈(John Keats)的《圣爱格尼斯节前夜》(*The Eve of St. Agnes*)是最伟大的浪漫传奇律诗之一。

110. **Romanticism** 浪漫主义,从反叛古典主义开始,在 19 世纪大部分时间都非常兴盛繁荣的一场文学、哲学、音乐和艺术运动。其主要观点由湖滨派诗人华兹华斯(William Wordsworth)和科勒律治(S. T. Coleridge)首先表达出来:反对一切遵循古希腊、古罗马经典规则的教条,主张个人主观想象,反对纯客观的外观描写,重视人的内心世界和大自然的描写和赞美,等等。不同的时代、地域产生多种多样的浪漫主义。

111. **scansion** 格律分析,音步划分,根据格律分析诗歌的方法。格律是以音步(feet)来划分的。一个音步通常由一个重读音节(stressed syllable)和一个或两个非重读音节(unstressed syllable)组成。标准的诗歌音步有:

   a. 抑扬格(iamb),一个非重读音节后跟着一个重读音节;

   b. 扬抑格(trochee),一个重读音节后跟着一个非重读音节;

   c. 扬抑抑格(dactyl),一个重读音节后跟着两个非重读音节;

   d. 抑抑扬格(anapest),两个非重读音节后跟着一个重读音节。

   诗的格律是以音步的格式和数量命名的,如五步抑扬格(iambic pentameter),四步扬抑格(trochaic tetrameter),六步扬抑抑格(dactylic hexameter),三步抑抑扬格(anapestic trimeter),等等。

112. **sestet** 六行诗体,六行诗或六行诗节,通常指的是意大利十四行诗(sonnet)的最后六行。前 8 行叫八行诗体(octave)。

113. **soliloquy/monologue** 戏剧独白

114. **sonnet** 十四行诗,通常是以五步抑扬格写成的十四行抒情韵诗,表达一个主题或一个思想,结构和韵律(rhyme scheme)会有变化,但总的可分为两类:

   a. 彼特拉克或意大利十四行诗(Petrarchan or Italian sonnet),起源于 13 世纪,由两部分组成,前 8 行叫八行诗体(octave),后 6 行叫六行诗体(sestet),韵律为 abbaabba/cdecde。两部分在内容表达上时有不同,有时前 8 行提出问题,后 6 行回答;有时后 6 行反对或扩展前 8 行的意见。大诗人彼特拉克(Francesco Petrarch)曾用这种格式给自己倾慕的劳拉(Laura)女士写了 300 多首十四行诗,故意大利十四行诗也叫彼特拉克十四行诗。

   b. 伊丽莎白或莎士比亚十四行诗,彼特拉克鼓舞了十四行诗在英国伊丽莎白时代的风行,诗人们都按彼特拉克的模式给情人写十四行诗,只有莎士比亚颠覆了这种状况,写出了自己独特的十四行诗。它包括 3 个四行诗和一个对句,其韵律为 abab/cdcd/efef/gg。另外还有斯宾塞十四行诗(Spenserian sonnet),韵律格式为 ababbcbccdcdee。

115. **Spenserian stanza** 斯宾塞九行诗诗节,一个诗节 9 行,韵律为 ababbcbcc,前 8 行为五步抑扬格,第九行为六步抑扬格(*iambic hexameter*),也叫亚历山大体诗行(Alexandrine,三音步后一停顿)。该诗体由斯宾塞(Edmund Spenser)在创作《仙后》(*The Faerie Queene*)时首创,也曾被罗伯特·彭斯(Robert Burns)、济慈(John Keats)和雪莱(P. B. Shelley)所采用。

116. **Sprung Rhythm** 弹跳节奏,跳跃韵,诗人霍普金斯(Gerard Manley Hopkins)创造出来的术语,用以为一个重音节可与不同数量非重读音节结合的可变型诗歌格律命名。弹跳节奏的诗歌格律不规则,发音像自然说话。

117. **stereotype** 套式人物,类型化人物,文学作品中老生常谈的人物类型,一出场就立即为读者所熟悉。套式人物又叫保留人物,相貌和举止相同,表现出相同的人物特性。例如性格影星,健谈的出租车司机,精神失常的科学家,唇髭打蜡的反派人物,说话俏皮、不懂感情的私家侦探等。

118. **stream of consciousness** 意识流,模仿人物所经历的思想、感情、反应、记忆和心理意象(mental images)的自然流动的写作风格。

119. **style** 风格,文风,一个作家独特的写作方法,由选词、连词成句的安排、句子与句子的联系所决定。有的作家喜欢短小简练,有的喜欢带学者味儿的长句,有的极少用形容词,有的则用很多。文风指的是一个作家运用意象(imagery)、修辞(figurative language)、节奏(rhythm)的特定方法,是一个作家区别于其他作家的总体素质和特征之和。

120. suspense　悬念,故事、小说和戏剧使读者或观众对事件的结果感到悬疑不定、感到紧张的素质或效果。悬念使读者要问"下面会发生什么?"或"怎么会这样的?"因而吸引读者读下去。当悬念集中到一个读者非常关切、非常同情的人物(sympathetic character)身上时,这是最伟大的悬念。悬念也会产生好奇(curiosity),尤其是在人物必须做出决定或找出某件事的答案时。

121. symbol　象征,一个物体、人、地方或行为除了本身的意义之外还代表着超出本身的某种东西,譬如一种品质、态度、信仰或价值观。例如玫瑰花象征爱情和美丽,骨架象征死亡,春天和冬天常象征青春和老迈。

122. symbolism　象征主义,19世纪后期产生于法国的一种文学运动,对20世纪的英国作家尤其是诗人产生了巨大影响。对象征主义诗人来说,情感是模糊不清的(indefinite),难以交流,他们往往避免意义的直接表达,而是通过情感上的强烈象征标志来暗示这种意义和情绪。

123. synecdoche　举隅法,提喻,用部分代替整体的修辞方法。例如,艾略特(T. S. Eliot)在诗歌《序曲》(Preludes)中用脚(feet)和手(hand)代替人(people)。

124. terza rima　三行诗节隔句押韵法,由许多三行诗节组成的一种意大利诗歌,每诗节的第一、三行押韵,第二行与下一诗节的一、三行押韵,依此类推,韵律格式为aba/bcb/cdc ...。雪莱(P. B. Shelley)的《西风颂》(Ode to the West Wind)就是用的这种押韵法,下面是该诗的头两节:

O wild West Wind, thou breath of Autumn's <u>being</u>,	a
Thou, from whose unseen presence the leaves <u>dead</u>,	b
Are driven, like ghosts from an enchanter <u>fleeting</u>,	a
Yellow, and black, and pale, and hectic <u>red</u>,	b
Pestilence-stricken multitudes：O Thou,	c
Who chariotest to their dark wintry <u>bed</u>	b

125. theme　主题

126. tone　语气,作者对其作品的主题、人物或观众所采取的态度。如代兰·托马斯(Dylan Thomas)在写童年时代的诗歌《弗恩·希尔》(Fern Hill)中的语气是怀旧(nostalgic),塞缪尔·约翰逊(Samuel Johnson)在《为莎士比亚作序》(Preface to Shakespeare)中表达出来的语气是严肃和欣赏(serious and admiring)。每部作品都表现出作者的态度和语气,语气是通过词语和细节的选择表达出来的。

127. tragedy　悲剧

128. Tragicomedy　悲喜剧,悲剧、喜剧情景混合在一起的剧作。这种剧通常既有人物冲突,又有光明结局(hopeful end)。

129. Transcendentalist Club　超验主义俱乐部,美国一些新英格兰地方人士反对当时的物质主义倾向(materialistic-oriented life),组成一个思想交流俱乐部,即超验主义俱乐部,讨论美国人整体的价值取向问题,并出版自己的刊物《日晷》(The Dial),宣传自己的声音。俱乐部有30多个男会员和两个女会员。著名的代表人物有爱默生(Emerson),梭罗(Thoreau),布朗森·阿尔卡特(Bronson Alcott)和玛格丽特·富勒(Margaret Fuller)。大多数成员是教师或神职人员,都是反对波士顿唯利是图的商人信仰、反对唯一神论(Unitarianism)的冷酷顽固的持有理性主义思想的激进分子。

130. The Tudors (1485～1603)　都铎王朝,亨利七世(1485～1509)在玫瑰战争中击败了篡位的理查三世(Richard III),建立了都铎王朝(The Tudor Dynasty),一个全新的中央集权的君主制(centralized monarchy)王朝,满足了新兴资产阶级的需要,赢得了他们的支持。

131. Unitarianism　唯一神论,上帝一位论,与其他更为偏颇的宗教信仰(more partial religious belief)不

同,上帝一位论更加理性,符合逻辑,不走极端,更为中庸一点。它的原则为大多数人赞同,包括上帝的圣父地位,人类的兄弟之情,耶稣的领导身份(但无视耶稣的神性 divinity),人类灵魂的得救(salvation of soul),人类不断的自我完善。这是对加尔文主义(Calvinism)的明显的改进,加尔文主义是不接受人类可以达到完美的前景的。上帝一位论或唯一神论对美国作家特别是爱默生和梭罗有明显的影响。

132. University Wits 大学才子,指伊丽莎白一世女王时代的剧作家(playwright)和编写小册子的作家(pamphleteer)。其时,最具天才(most gifted)的"大学才子"是克里斯托弗·马洛(Christopher Marlowe)。

133. verse 韵文,分行写出的作品形式,每一行都有重读音节和非重读音节组成的格式,几行文字形成押韵的一节,这就是韵文。诗可以用韵文写出,但不能指望任何是韵文的文字就是诗。

134. The Wars of the Roses 玫瑰战争(1455~1483),指英国历史上两大王室家族争夺王位继承权而进行的战争,持续了约 30 年。约克家族(House of York)族徽(badge of clan)为白玫瑰,兰开斯特家族(House of Lancaster)族徽为红玫瑰,故而叫玫瑰战争。最后兰开斯特家族的亨利·都铎胜利登上王位,建立了都铎王朝。他娶了前国王约克家族的爱德华四世的女儿为王后,达到两个家族的平衡,才结束了玫瑰战争。

135. wit 机智,颖悟力,风趣,卓越敏锐的洞察力(perception)加上聪慧的表达。在 18 世纪,机智和天性是提供宇宙规则的相互有密切联系的禀赋(related-nature)。机智和理解力可以解释和表达这些规则。

参 考 文 献

[1] 拜伦.唐璜[M].查良铮,译.北京:人民文学出版社,1995.

[2] 济慈.济慈诗选[M].屠岸,译.北京:人民文学出版社,1997.

[3] 约翰·但恩.艳情诗与神学诗[M].傅浩,译.北京:中国对外翻译出版公司,1997.

[4] 雪莱.雪莱诗选[M].杨熙龄,译.济南:山东大学出版社,1998.

[5] 布莱克.布莱克诗集[M].张炽恒,译.上海:上海三联书店,1999.

[6] 全国高等教育自学考试指导委员会.英美文学选读自学考试大纲,1999.

[7] 陈新.英汉问题翻译教程[M].北京:北京大学出版社,2000.

[8] 华兹华斯.华兹华斯抒情诗选[M].黄杲炘,译.上海:上海译文出版社,2000.

[9] 张伯香.英美文学选读自学辅导[M].北京:外语教学与研究出版社,2001.

[10] 胡家峦.英国名诗详注[M].北京:外语教学与研究出版社,2003.

[11] 卞之琳.英国诗选[M].北京:商务印书馆,2005.

[12] 拜伦.拜伦诗选[M].杨德豫,译.北京:外语教学与研究出版社,2011.

[13] 布莱克.布莱克诗选[M].袁可嘉,查良铮,译.北京:外语教学与研究出版社,2011.

[14] 济慈.济慈诗选[M].屠岸,译.北京:外语教学与研究出版社,2011.

[15] 刘坤尊.英诗的音韵格律[M].桂林:广西师范大学出版社,2011.

[16] 雪莱.雪莱诗选[M].江枫,译.北京:外语教学与研究出版社,2011.

[17] 狄金森.狄金森诗选[M].江枫,译.北京:外语教学与研究出版社,2012.

[18] 弗罗斯特.弗罗斯特诗选[M].江枫,译.北京:外语教学与研究出版社,2012.

[19] 华兹华斯.华兹华斯诗选[M].杨德豫,译.北京:外语教学与研究出版社,2012.

[20] 莎士比亚.莎士比亚十四行诗[M].屠岸,译.北京:外语教学与研究出版社,2012.

[21] 叶芝.叶芝诗选[M].袁可嘉,译.北京:外语教学与研究出版社,2012.

[22] 勃朗宁.勃朗宁诗选[M].飞白,汪晴,译,北京:外语教学与研究出版社,2013.

[23] 惠特曼.惠特曼诗选[M].赵梦蕤,译.北京:外语教学与研究出版社,2013.